THE VICTORIA HISTORY OF THE COUNTIES
OF ENGLAND

A HISTORY OF MIDDLESEX
VOLUME XIII
CITY OF WESTMINSTER, PART 1

INSCRIBED TO THE MEMORY OF HER LATE MAJESTY

QUEEN VICTORIA

WHO GRACIOUSLY GAVE THE TITLE TO AND

ACCEPTED THE DEDICATION OF THIS HISTORY

THE VICTORIA HISTORY OF THE COUNTIES OF ENGLAND

JOHN BECKETT DIRECTOR AND GENERAL EDITOR

ALAN THACKER EXECUTIVE EDITOR

ELIZABETH WILLIAMSON ARCHITECTURAL EDITOR

THE UNIVERSITY OF LONDON

INSTITUTE OF HISTORICAL RESEARCH

A HISTORY OF
THE COUNTY OF
MIDDLESEX

EDITED BY PATRICIA E.C. CROOT with
ALAN THACKER AND ELIZABETH WILLIAMSON

VOLUME XIII

CITY OF WESTMINSTER
PART 1

PUBLISHED FOR THE

INSTITUTE OF HISTORICAL RESEARCH

BY BOYDELL & BREWER · 2009

First published 2009

A Victoria County History publication
in association with The Boydell Press
an imprint of Boydell & Brewer Ltd
PO Box 9   Woodbridge   Suffolk IP12 3DF   UK
and of Boydell & Brewer Inc.
668 Mt Hope Avenue   Rochester   NY 14620   USA
website: www.boydellandbrewer.com
and with the
University of London Institute of Historical Research

ISBN 978–1–90435–622–6
ISSN 1477–0709

A CiP catalogue record for this book is available
from the British Library

Typeset by Pru Harrison, Hacheston, Suffolk
Printed in Great Britain by
CPI Antony Rowe, Chippenham and Eastbourne

CONTENTS OF VOLUME THIRTEEN

LIST OF ILLUSTRATIONS

LIST OF MAPS

All maps were drawn by Cath D'Alton from drafts prepared by Patricia E.C. Croot. © University of London. For historic maps *see* above.

MIDDLESEX VICTORIA COUNTY HISTORY COMMITTEE

As at 1 March 2008

Acting Chairman ALAN THACKER
Honorary Secretary R.J. SARGENT
Honorary Treasurer R. HARRISON

Representatives of the following London Boroughs

Camden

Kensington and Chelsea

Hackney

Tower Hamlets

Hammersmith and Fulham   Westminster

Islington

Representatives of

London Metropolitan Archives
The London and Middlesex Archaeological Society
The Institute of Historical Research

Co-opted Members
ANDREW SAINT, Survey of London, English Heritage
MATTHEW DAVIES, Centre for Metropolitan History, Institute of Historical Research

FOREWORD AND ACKNOWLEDGEMENTS

THE PRESENT volume is the sixth to have been compiled for the Middlesex VCH Committee formed in 1979 to complete the Middlesex History. The University of London gratefully acknowledges the help of the Committee, and in particular the assistance of Mr Roy Harrison as Treasurer and Mr John Sargent as Secretary, who have continued to keep the Committee functioning in difficult circumstances. Work on the enormous task of researching and writing the history of the City of Westminster started in 1994, when the Committee's work was supported by the City of Westminster and the London Boroughs of Kensington and Chelsea, Islington, and Hackney. The University of London is grateful for their support over many years. Due to pressures on local government funding, by 2004 all four boroughs had ceased their contributions. The completion of the work for the present volume was only made possible by the very generous contributions received from the Aurelius Charitable Trust, Camden History Society, Grosvenor, the Manifold Trust, the Marc Fitch Fund, Mercers' Company of London, County History Trust, and contributors to the Middlesex Appeal, all of whom are thanked warmly for their support. The work to enable this volume to proceed to publication has been made possible by a substantial donation from the estate of the late Sydney Stedman (1920–2008) and an additional grant from the City of Westminster in 2008 for which the University is very grateful.

Since permanent funding for the Middlesex VCH ceased, the remaining member of Staff, the County Editor, Dr P.E.C. Croot, had to take early retirement in September 2004, and has subsequently completed the work necessary for the present volume on a consultancy basis. The Committee are currently seeking ways forward for carrying on the work for the Middlesex VCH, in order to complete the Westminster history and the remaining Middlesex parishes in inner London.

Those who have provided information are named in the footnotes, and they are sincerely thanked for their help. We are especially grateful to Richard Mortimer, Tony Trowles, and Christine Reynolds of Westminster Abbey Library, for their assistance over several years, and to the staff at the National Archives, Westminster City Archives, the London Metropolitan Archives, and the Guildhall Library for their help in various ways. We would also like to record our thanks to past and present staff of the Survey of London for their kind assistance, including the use of their notes from the Burghley MSS. Much additional help has been provided by Professor Derek Keene, of the Centre of Metropolitan History at the IHR, Dr Simon Bradley, of the Buildings of England, Dr R. Darwall-Smith, archivist of Magdalen College, Oxford, Dr J.M. Kaye, keeper of the archives at the Queen's College, Oxford, and the staff of the Department of Manuscripts at Nottingham University Library. We are also grateful to Professor Martin Biddle of Hertford College, Oxford, and the staff of the Museum of London Archaeological Service, especially Robert Cowie, for providing much archaeological material on Westminster.

SCHEME FOR THE HISTORY OF WESTMINSTER

THE STRUCTURE and aims of the Victoria County History as a whole are set out in the *General Introduction* (1970) and its *Supplement* (1990). The contents of the first seven volumes of the Middlesex History are listed and indexed in outline in a booklet, *The Middlesex Victoria History Council*, which also describes the work of the precursor of the present Middlesex Victoria County History Committee. Further information about the history and present work of the Middlesex VCH and about the contents of the volumes is available on the county website, .

The VCH's history of Westminster was planned as four volumes, each with two sections, which would together cover the usual aspects of the VCH, plus the unique feature of Westminster, the presence of royal and national government: Introduction and infrastructure, Settlement and growth, Landownership, Royal court and national government, Economic history, Social and cultural history including education and charities, Religious history, and Local government including public services. By the time funding ceased for Middlesex, about a third of the research had been carried out, and enough material gathered and written for two sections, producing one volume. Most of the research and writing was done prior to 2001, with only brief updating on some current buildings. As this first volume is being published in advance of any further planned publication, it seemed advisable to include in this volume a general introduction to the city and its history, raising a number of aspects which will be treated in more detail in subsequent volumes: the history and impact on Westminster of the royal palaces, chapels and parks, including Somerset House and the Savoy, economic history including markets and exchanges, details of the growth and character of the individual areas within Westminster, and the extent and character of *Lundenwic*, amongst other topics.

NOTE ON SOURCES

WESTMINSTER is fortunate that the muniments of Westminster Abbey (WA) and its successors, the dean and chapter, from the Middle Ages onwards have remained largely intact, and are the chief source of material both for medieval Westminster and local government in St Margaret's up to the end of the 19th century. Charters up to 1215 have been calendared and commented on in *Westm. Charters*. This material is supplemented by the British Library's collections of charters and rolls and other documents, and medieval and later material in the Guildhall Library (GL), including the Christ's Hospital estate records. The London Metropolitan Archives (LMA) holds the Bedford Estate records covering Covent Garden, but is also the principal source of much official material, such as the sewer commissions, quarter sessions records, district surveyors returns, MBW records, most of which are listed in a separate Westminster series, corresponding to the general LCC series for the rest of inner London. The Westminster City Archives is the principal source of much local Westminster material, including vestry records and the Grosvenor Estate records. Church records are divided between the diocesan collection in GL, some diocesan material in LMA, parish records in the WCA, and records and wills for St Margaret and St John in WA.

There is no comprehensive history of the City of Westminster: the size of the city, the complexity of the parish structure, and the volume of material, make even a small survey a daunting task. This volume is the start of the VCH's attempt to produce such a comprehensive history, and will require four volumes just to cover the topics treated by the VCH. Two recent secondary works of great value which focus on aspects of the community and settlement are Rosser on medieval Westminster, mainly St Margaret's, and Merritt on early modern Westminster, mainly St Margaret's and St Martin's. For the 16th century onwards there are many monographs and articles on various aspects of Westminster's history: indeed, the range of secondary material on Westminster is daunting in itself, and can be explored in the excellent *Bibliography of Printed Works on London History to 1939*, ed. H. Creaton (1994), which is regularly updated on London's Past online, included in the Royal Historical Society's (RHS) online bibliography (www.rhs.ac.uk). Westminster's built environment is well served by the Survey of London's volumes: those for St Margaret and St Martin were published early in the 20th century and are brief and incomplete, but since the Second World War the Survey has produced several volumes on parts of Westminster which not only describe the buildings, old and new, but give much institutional history as well: St James (4 volumes), St Anne, St Paul, Knightsbridge, and the Grosvenor's Mayfair estate in St George (2 volumes), have all made a major contribution to Westminster's history and made the VCH's task immeasurably easier. In addition, the recent update of Pevsner by Bradley, on the City of Westminster, covers building history into the 21st century: the earlier edition of the 1950s is also of value for buildings which have disappeared. All the above works, and others found useful for this volume's subject matter, are detailed in the Abbreviations and Commonly Cited Works. Except where stated otherwise all website URLs were correct to the end of 2008.

ABBREVIATIONS AND COMMONLY CITED WORKS

Archit. Hist.	*Architectural History* (journal)
BL	British Library
Beauchamp Charters	*The Beauchamp cartulary charters, 1100–1268*, ed. E. Mason (Pipe Roll Soc. 81, 1980)
Beeman, 'French Chs in London'	G.B. Beeman, 'Notes on Site and Hist. of the French Chs in London', *Procs Hug. Soc. London*, VIII, 1905–8)
Birch, *Cart. Saxon.*	W. de G. Birch, *Cartularium Saxonicum*, 3 vols (1885–93)
Bodl.	The Bodleian Library, Oxford
CJ	*Commons Journals*
Calamy Revised	*Calamy Revised*, ed. A.G. Matthews (1934)
Cameron, *Scots Kirk*	G.G. Cameron, *The Scots Kirk in London* (1979)
Chantry Cert.	*London and Middlesex Chantry Certificate, 1548*, ed. C.J. Kitching (London Record Society, XVI, 1980)
Ch in London, 1375–92	*The Church in London, 1375–1392*, ed. A.K. McHardy (London Record Society XIII, 1977)

Chrimes, *Admin. Hist.*	S.B. Chrimes, *An Introduction to the Administrative History of Mediaeval England* (1966)
Clarke, *London Chs*	B.F.L. Clarke, *Parish Churches of London* (1966)
Clinch, *Mayfair*	G. Clinch, *Mayfair and Belgravia: being an historical account of the Parish of St George, Hanover Square* (1892)
Colby, *Mayfair*	R. Colby, *Mayfair. A Town within London* (1966)
Colvin, *Brit. Architects*	H.M. Colvin, *A Biographical Dictionary of British Architects, 1600–1840* (4th edn, 2008)
Craven Papers	MSS in Bodleian Library
Crouch, *Beaumont Twins*	D. Crouch, *The Beaumont Twins: the roots and branches of power in the twelfth century* (1986)
DNB	*Dictionary of National Biography*
EH	English Heritage
Eastlake, *Gothic Revival*	C.H. Eastlake, *History of the Gothic Revival* (1970 edn)
Ebury map, 1614	Map of the manor of Ebury, 1614, reproduced in Gatty, *Mary Davies*, vol. I, Plate 31.
Ebury plan c.1663	*A Plan of the Manor of Ebury c.1663–1670* (London Topographical Society, publication no. 39, 1915) (plan and text from BL, Add. MS 38104).
Endowed Chars London, II	*Endowed Charities (County of London)*, II (Parl. Papers, 1899 (93), LXIX)
Endowed Chars London, V	*Endowed Charities (County of London)*, V (Parl. Papers, 1903 (181), XLIX)
Endowed Chars London, VI	*Endowed Charities (County of London)*, VI (Parl. Papers, 1904 (334), LXXI)
Evinson, *Cath. Chs of London*	D. Evinson, *Catholic Churches of London* (1998)
Fifty New Chs	*The Commission for Building Fifty New Churches*, ed. M.H. Port (London Record Society XXIII, 1986)
Friedman, *Georgian Chs*	T. Friedman, *The Georgian Parish Church: 'Monuments to Posterity'* (2004)
Gatty, *Mary Davies*	C.T. Gatty, *Mary Davies and the Manor of Ebury* (2 vols, 1921)
Green, *Who Owns London?*	S. Green, *Who Owns London?* (1986)
Guildhall MSS	City of London, Guildhall Library. Contains London diocesan records including registers of wills of the commissary court of London (London Division) (MS 9171), bishops' registers (MS 9531), diocesan administrative records (MSS 9532–9560), and registers of nonconformist meeting houses (MS 9580)
Harris and Bryant, *Chs and London*	H.W. Harris and M. Bryant, *Churches and London* [1914]
Harvey, *Westm. Abbey Ests*	B. Harvey, *Westminster Abbey and its Estates in the Middle Ages* (1977)
Hennessy, *Novum Rep.*	G. Hennessy, *Novum Repertorium Ecclesiasticum Parochiale Londinense* (1894)
Hervey, *Life of Thos Howard*	M.F.S. Hervey, *The Life, Correspondence and Collections of Thomas Howard, Earl of Arundel* (1921)
Hist. King's Works, I	*History of the King's Works*, vol. I, *The Middle Ages*, ed. R.A. Brown, H.M. Colvin, A.J. Taylor (1963)
Hist. King's Works, III	*History of the King's Works*, vol. III, *1485–1660 (Part I)*, ed. H.M. Colvin, D.R. Ransome, J. Summerson (1975)
Hist. King's Works, IV	*History of the King's Works*, vol. IV, *1485–1660 (Part II)*, ed. H.M. Colvin, J. Summerson *et al.* (1982)
Hist. King's Works, V	*History of the King's Works*, vol. V, *1660–1782*, H.M. Colvin *et al.* (1976)
Hobhouse, *Cubitt*	H. Hobhouse, *Thomas Cubitt* (1973 edn)
Hollar's London	*Hollar's London: 37 etchings of London views (1636–1667)*. Life of Wenceslaus Hollar and Survey of the London views, by Paul Hulton and John Fisher. (Gloucestershire 1980)
Howarth, *Lord Arundel*	D. Howarth, *Lord Arundel and his Circle* (1985)
Hug. Soc.	Huguenot Society of London
Johnson, *Berkeley Sq.*	B.H. Johnson, *From Berkeley Square to Bond Street* (1952)
LCC	London County Council
LCC, *Burial Grounds*	LCC, *Return of Burial Grounds in the County of London* (1895)
LMA	London Metropolitan Archives. Formerly the Greater London Record Office (GLRO)
LMA, E/BER	Bedford Estate Records in LMA
MBW	Metropolitan Board of Works

Mackeson's Guide	C. Mackeson, *A Guide to the Churches of London and Its Suburbs* (1866 and later edns)
Macray's Cal. Temple Bar	Magdalen College Oxford, Macray's Calendar of Deeds, Temple Bar estate
McKisack, *Fourteenth Cent.*	M. McKisack, *The Fourteenth Century* (1959)
McMaster, *St Martin-in-the-Fields*	J. McMaster, *A Short History of St Martin-in-the-Fields* (1916)
Merritt, *Early Modern Westm.*	J.F. Merritt, *The Social World of Early Modern Westminster: Abbey, court and community, 1525–1640* (2005)
Middx County Rec.	*Middlesex County Records* [1550–1688], ed. J.C. Jeaffreson (4 vols. 1886–92)
Middx County Rec. Sess. Bks 1689–1709	*Middlesex County Records, Calendar of the Sessions Books 1689–1709*, ed. W.J. Hardy (1905)
Morgan, *Map of London* (1682)	William Morgan, *Survey of London and the surrounding area* (Westminster and Southwark) (1682)
Mudie-Smith, *Rel. Life*	R. Mudie-Smith, *The Religious Life of London* (1904)
NMR	English Heritage (formerly Royal Commission on Historical Monuments of England), National Monuments Record
NRA	National Register of Archives
Needham and Webster, *Somerset Ho.*	R. Needham and A. Webster, *Somerset House Past and Present* (1905)
Newcastle MSS	Nottingham University Library, Newcastle MSS
Newcourt, *Rep.*	R. Newcourt, *Repertorium Ecclesiasticum Parochiale Londinense* (2 vols. 1708–10)
Old OS Map	*Old Ordnance Survey Maps*: edition published by Alan Godfrey, Gateshead, from 1983 (reduced facsimile reproductions of 1:2,500 maps c.1865–1914). Westminster is covered by London sheets 61 (1870, 1894, 1914), 62 (1873, 1914), 74 (1871, 1894, 1914), 75 (1869, 1894), 76 (1872, 1914), 88 (1869, 1894)
ONS	Office for National Statistics, Birkdale. Formerly the General Register Office (GRO)
PO Dir.	*Post Office Directory*
Paterson, *Pietas Lond.*	James Paterson, *Pietas Londinensis* (1714)
Pevsner, *London I* (1973 edn)	N. Pevsner, *The Buildings of England: London I, Cities of London and Westminster*, revised B. Cherry (1973 edn)
Pevsner, *London II*	N. Pevsner, *The Buildings of England: London except the Cities of London and Westminster* (1952)
Pevsner, *London 3: NW*	B. Cherry and N. Pevsner, *The Buildings of England. London 3: North West* (1991)
Pevsner, *London 6: Westm.*	S. Bradley and N. Pevsner, *The Buildings of England. London 6: Westminster* (2003)
Port, *Six Hundred Chs*	M.H. Port, *Six Hundred New Churches* (1961)
PN Middx (EPNS)	*Place-Names of Middlesex* (English Place-Name Society, vol. XVIII, 1942)
Queen's Coll. Archives	Archives at The Queen's College, Oxford
RIBA	Royal Institute of British Architects
Rec. Templars	*Records of the Templars in England in the 12th Century*, ed. B.A. Lees (British Academy 1935)
Regency A to Z	*The A to Z of Regency London*, intro. P. Laxton (Lympne Castle, Kent, 1985). Reproduction of R. Horwood's *Plan of the Cities of London and Westminster* (1813 edn)
Robinson, *Gilbert Crispin*	J.A. Robinson, *Gilbert Crispin. Abbot of Westminster* (1911)
Rocque, *Map of London* (1741–5)	J. Rocque, *Exact survey of the cities of London, Westminster, and the borough of Southwark, and the country near ten miles around* (1746, facsimile edn 1971)
Rosser, *Medieval Westm.*	G. Rosser, *Medieval Westminster 1200–1540* (1989)
Rottmann, *London Cath. Chs*	A. Rottmann, *London Catholic Churches* (1926)
Rutton, 'Manor of Eia'	W.L. Rutton, 'The Manor of Eia, or Eye next Westminster', *Archaeologia*, LXII (1910)
Sawyer, *A.-S. Charters*	P.H. Sawyer, *Guide to Anglo-Saxon Charters* (1968)
Smith, *St John Evangelist*	J.E. Smith, *St John the Evangelist, Westminster: Parochial Memorials* (1892)
Smyth, *Church and Par.*	C. Smyth, *Church and Parish: Studies in Church Problems, illustrated from the Parochial History of St Margaret's, Westminster* (1965)
Somerville, *Savoy*	R. Somerville, *The Savoy* (1960)

Stone, *Crisis of the Aristocracy*	L. Stone, *Crisis of the Aristocracy* (1979 edn)
Strype, *Survey*	J. Strype, *Survey of the Cities of London and Westminster* (continuing the Survey by John Stow), 2 vols (1720)
Summerson *Archit. in Britain*	J. Summerson, *Architecture in Britain 1530–1830* (9ᵗʰ edn, 1993)
Survey of London	London County Council, later Greater London Council, later Royal Commission on Historical Monuments, now English Heritage, *Survey of London*
Survey of London, X	LCC, *Survey of London*, vol. X, *Parish of St Margaret, Westminster* (Part I) (1926)
Survey of London, XVIII	LCC, *Survey of London*, vol. XVIII, *Parish of St Martin-in-the-Fields* (Part II, Strand) (1937)
Survey of London, XX	LCC, *Survey of London*, vol. XX, *Parish of St Martin-in-the-Fields* (Part III, Trafalgar Square) (1940)
Survey of London, XXIX–XXX	LCC, *Survey of London*, vols. XXIX–XXX, *Parish of St James, Westminster* (Part 1, North of Piccadilly) (1960, 2 vols)
Survey of London, XXXI–XXXII	LCC, *Survey of London*, vols. XXXI–XXXII, *Parish of St James, Westminster* (Part 2, South of Piccadilly) (1963, 2 vols)
Survey of London, XXXIII–XXXIV	GLC, *Survey of London*, vols. XXXIII—XXXIV, *Parish of St Anne, Soho* (1966, 2 vols)
Survey of London, XXXVI	GLC, *Survey of London*, vol. XXXVI, *Parish of St Paul, Covent Garden* (1970)
Survey of London, XXXVIII	GLC, *Survey of London*, vol. XXXVIII, *The Museums Area of South Kensington and Westminster* (1975)
Survey of London, XXXIX	GLC, *Survey of London*, vol. XXXIX, *The Grosvenor Estate in Mayfair*, Part 1 (General History) (1977)
Survey of London, XL	GLC, *Survey of London*, vol. XL, *The Grosvenor Estate in Mayfair*, Part 2 (Buildings) (1980)
Survey of London, XLI	GLC, *Survey of London*, vol. XLI, *Southern Kensington: Brompton* (1983)
Survey of London, XLV	EH, *Survey of London*, vol. XLV, *Knightsbridge* (2001)
TLMAS	*Transactions of the London and Middlesex Archaeological Society* (1856 to date). Consecutive numbers are used for the whole series, although vols VII–XVII (1905–54) appeared as NS I–XI.
Tout, *Chapters*	T.F. Tout, *Chapters in the Administrative History of Mediaeval England* (6 vols, 1920–33)
Tout, 'Modern Capital'	T.F. Tout, 'Beginnings of a Modern Capital: London and Westminster in the 14ᵗʰ Century' (1923), in Collected Papers, III (1934), 249–75
VCH Berks. IV	*Victoria History of the County of Berkshire*, vol. IV (1924)
VCH London, I	*Victoria History of the County of London*, vol. I (1909)
VCH Middx, I	*Victoria County History of Middlesex*, vol. I, General (1969)
VCH Middx, VII	*Victoria County History of Middlesex*, vol. VII, *Acton, Chiswick, Ealing, Willesden* (1982)
VCH Middx, VIII	*Victoria County History of Middlesex*, vol. VIII, *Islington and Stoke Newington* (1985)
VCH Middx, IX	*Victoria County History of Middlesex*, vol. IX, *Hampstead and Paddington* (1989)
VCH Middx, XII	*Victoria County History of Middlesex*, vol. XII, *Chelsea* (2004)
VCH Warws. II	*Victoria History of the County of Warwickshire*, vol. II (1908)
WA	Westminster Abbey, Library and Muniment Room
WAD	Westminster Domesday, in the Library
WAM	Westminster Abbey Muniments, in Library
WCA	Westminster City Archives, St Ann's Street
Walker Revised	*Walker Revised*, ed. A.G. Matthews (1948)
Westm.	Westminster
Westm. Charters	*Westminster Abbey Charters 1066–c.1214*, ed. E. Mason (London Record Society XXV, 1988)
Wheatley, 'Durham Ho.'	H.B. Wheatley, 'Original Plan of Durham House and Grounds, 1626', *London Topographical Record*, X (1916), pp. 150–61.
Williams, *Early Holborn*	E. Williams, *Early Holborn and the Legal Quarter of London* (2 vols, 1927)
Wilson, *Dissenting Chs*	W. Wilson, *History and Antiquities of Dissenting Churches*, III (1810), IV (1814)
Wyngaerde, *View*	Anton van den Wyngaerde, *The Panorama of London circa 1544* (London Topographical Society, publication no. 151, 1996).

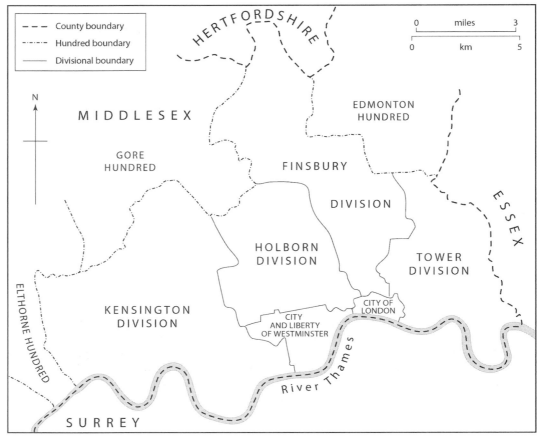

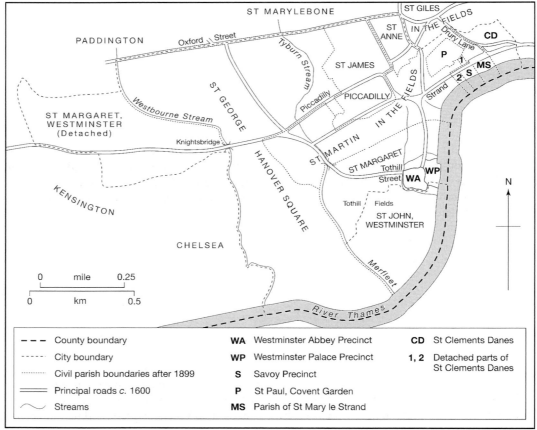

1. *Map of Ossulstone Hundred* (above); *City of Westminster and its Parishes,* c. *1730* (below)

CITY OF WESTMINSTER

WESTMINSTER is known throughout the world as Britain's seat of government, and in the United Kingdom the word Westminster is used colloquially to refer both to the Houses of Parliament and their members. This has been true since the Middle Ages, when 'going to Westminster' meant going to the palace there to attend the king, the courts of law, or meetings of Parliament. This role goes back almost to Westminster's origins, in particular to Edward the Confessor's re-foundation of the Anglo-Saxon church of St Peter in the mid 11th century as a great Benedictine abbey accompanied by a royal palace. The abbey was definitively established as England's coronation church in 1066, and later on the palace became a primary royal residence and seat of government. This volume will focus in particular upon the ways in which Westminster's unique role affected two crucial aspects of its history, the pattern of landownership and religious life. The following introduction is intended to give an overview of Westminster's emergence as the capital of England, and of some of the aspects of its history which will be treated in depth in future volumes.

Despite its importance, Westminster was in most respects overshadowed by its powerful neighbour, the City of London. Although after the mid 11th century the City contained neither the seat of government nor the monarch's preferred residence, it was London which, because of its economic pre-eminence, gave its name to the capital of the kingdom. Moreover, medieval Westminster as a place had little identity outside palace and abbey, and tended to be seen by outsiders merely as an appendage of London; orders for its administration frequently listed it among the liberties, suburbs, or adjoining parts of London. Yet many of London's most important features were located in Westminster; in addition to Parliament, the major departments of state, and the main residence of the monarchy, Westminster also contained the 'West End', effectively the centre of the capital's entertainment and cultural life and its retail trade, setting the fashions for the whole of the United Kingdom.

TOPOGRAPHY AND GOVERNMENT

The city of Westminster, which from 1965 formed part of the eponymous London borough with Paddington and Marylebone, covered an area of 1,141 hectares in 2001, and is bounded on the south by the river Thames, on the west by the parishes of Chelsea and Kensington, on the north by the parishes of Paddington, Marylebone, and St Pancras, and on the north-east and east by the parishes of St Giles-in-the-Fields and St Andrew, Holborn, and the liberties of the City of London. It encompasses the ancient parishes of St Margaret, St Martin-in-the-Fields, and St Clement Danes, the later civil parishes of St Paul, Covent Garden, St Anne, Soho, St James, Piccadilly, St John the Evangelist, St Mary le Strand, and St George, Hanover Square, and the extra-parochial precincts of Westminster Abbey and the Savoy. In the Middle Ages, except for some properties along the Strand, it was divided between two great vills or manors, those of Westminster and Eye or Ebury (below).

GEOLOGY AND WATERCOURSES

The city of Westminster is situated on the north or west bank of the river Thames as it meanders to the sea. The solid geology is London Clay over which a variety of river terrace gravels were deposited. Alluvium, consisting of sandy silt and clay with some organic (peat) layers, was deposited over the gravel in a wide band along the Thames in the southern parts of Westminster and Ebury, and in narrow strips along the lines of the Tyburn and Westbourne rivers. At the Strand, on the north bank of the Thames, the river current has left very little alluvium over the gravel. The alluvium was once thought to be a uniform layer over the whole area roughly south of St James's Park, but more recent surveying has refined this to show three main areas of gravel over which no alluvium was deposited, and which therefore presumably formed prehistoric 'aits' (or islands) in the (then wider) river Thames. These lie between Lupus Street and the Thames in southern Ebury, at the western end of Victoria Street between Stag Place and Westminster Cathedral, and under Westminster Abbey, the area traditionally known as Thorney Island.[1] Historical evidence shows that there were other areas where the gravel was either never covered, or was very near the surface, principally the area of Tothill fields from Broadway to Vincent Square, and that the gravel of Stag

---

1 Geol. Surv. map., 1:10 000 series, solid and drift (1995 edn) (sheets TQ 27 NE, TQ 28 SE, TQ 38 SW, TQ 37 NW).

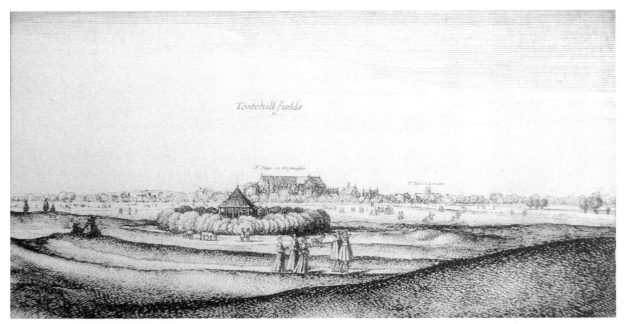

2. *A view across Tothill fields northwards c.1650, with Westminster Abbey in the distance, and old St Paul's, London, to its right.*

Place may have extended a little further north-eastwards to Buckingham Gate: both areas were being dug for gravel and sand by the 16th century.[1] It seems most likely that the 'tothill' itself was, like Thorney Island, a gravel outcrop at the north end of Tothill fields, and in the early Middle Ages a more distinct feature than it afterwards became. From St James's Park and from the site of Ebury farm (near the present-day Ebury Square) northwards to the city's northern boundary at Oxford Street and Bayswater Road the drift is all of gravels, cut by the alluvium valleys of the Westbourne and Tyburn; over the gravel around Covent Garden and west and east of Buckingham Palace are deposits of Langley Silt or brick earth.

Two streams run through Westminster to the Thames. The Westbourne, which forms the western boundary of the city of Westminster and of the vill of Eye, was apparently so-named only in the 19th century. In medieval documents it is referred to as the stream belonging to Knightsbridge; Kerswell is associated with it.[2]

The Tyburn (*Teoburn*), whose name means boundary stream, rose in Hampstead and from the point at which it crossed Oxford Street to its junction with the Thames at Merfleet (*Merfleote*), marked the western limit of the vill or manor of Westminster, dividing it from Eye. First mentioned in a charter generally dated to 959, the southern part of its course, downstream from Cowford

(in the modern Green Park) is somewhat problematic; apparently it took the form of a watercourse called the old ditch until it ran into *Bulinga* fen (presumably the western limit of Tothill fields) and thence to the Thames. This part of the stream seems later to have been known as the Eye or Tyburn brook.[3] In the mid 13th century, and occasionally later, the part between the later Piccadilly and Cowford was called the watercourse of St Edward the King.

This southern section of the Tyburn has been the subject of speculation. A late 19th-century map of the stream, partly based on John Norden's map of Westminster published in 1593, added an unsubstantiated watercourse from the abbey to the Tyburn near Eybridge (near the later Buckingham Palace). Both the compiler of this map and a later writer on London's rivers concluded, for some unknown reason, that the Tyburn did not run to its outfall at Vauxhall Bridge Road until the 17th century,[4] despite good medieval evidence that the stream did indeed follow that course. Unfortunately, because the 19th-century map was used to indicate watercourses on published geological survey maps in the mid 20th century,[5] its charting of the route of the Tyburn has been taken as proven. There is, however, no evidence to substantiate that route – there is, for instance, no alluvial band indicating a watercourse running from the Tyburn at Buckingham Palace to the Thames near the abbey – and there is no evidence that

1 e.g. WAM 17949.
2 *PN Middx* (EPNS), 8.
3 Ibid., 6–7; Sawyer, *A.-S. Charters*, nos 670, 903; Robinson, *Gilbert Crispin*, 167–8, 170; Rutton, 'Manor of Eia', 32–3.
4 J.G. Waller, 'The Tybourne and the Westbourne', *TLMAS*,

VI, map opp. p. 272 and text; N. Barton, *Lost Rivers*, 30–6. The former also mis-locates Cowford.
5 i.e., Geol. Surv. map, drift (1936 edn). Geol. survey does not investigate surface features, hence use of Waller's plan. Current (1995) edn of geol. survey does not show streams.

3. *Westminster Bridge from the north c.1750. On the north bank Westminster Abbey and, nearer the river, Westminster Hall stand on the distinct elevation of Thorney Island. Towards the centre of the view the four towers of the 18th-century church of St John the Evangelist, Westminster, can be seen amidst the new houses it served south of the abbey close.*

the medieval watercourses around the abbey site were linked to the Tyburn. Furthermore, in 1222 the western boundary of the parish of St Margaret was said to follow the Tyburn to the point where it disgorges into the Thames. As there has never been any suggestion that the meadows and fields which the stream borders to the south of the abbey were not in St Margaret's, the document must be indicating that the medieval Tyburn did indeed run to its present junction with the Thames near Vauxhall bridge.

The geological survey also shows two streams running into the Thames near Charing Cross, one arising in two branches near Haymarket, the other just south of St Martin's church; the actual courses of those have no documentary support, but parts of their lines are mentioned in charters. The latter may be the stream (*rivulus*), known in the 13th century as Ivybridge or *Ulebrigg*, which crossed the Strand at Ivy Lane, and was possibly the one that ran from St Martin's well to the Thames in the 13th century.[1] The eastern part of Westminster had a number of other natural springs and streams arising in the gravel: these had largely disappeared by the 16th century, the water having been diverted into domestic use, so their whereabouts is only approximately known, from early charters and topographical evidence. One was a well-known place of resort in the 12th century called St Clement's well, a few

yards north-west of Temple Bar. In the 16th century there was also a stream which started in the parish of St Giles-in-the-Fields, and ran southwards close to St Clement's well; it was apparently the source of the water supply to Arundel House in the late 16th century, with a bridge by the east end of the church of St Clement Danes. Another stream crossed the Strand at Strand Bridge, at or near the junction with Duchy Lane.

Medieval evidence also mentions 'ditches', which may have been natural watercourses or springs. The most significant of those was later called Longditch. It arose either in Spring Gardens or on the northern side of Pall Mall and ran southwards, forming a major boundary between properties in King Street and the meadows belonging to St James's Hospital, and after crossing Tothill Street near the abbey it ran around south of the abbey precinct to join the Thames: from the Middle Ages it was used as part of a network of streams which served the abbey's tidal mill. North of the abbey and the palace precinct another stream ran into the Thames; it is not clear if this ran from Longditch. In the Middle Ages it was called the Clowson and was culverted under King Street. Part was still in existence in the 17th century when it was known as the king's ditch. Properties in Longditch were affected by tides from the Thames as late as the early 16th century.[2] Other streams arose within the area of the later St James's Park at its south-west quarter.

1 WAM 17144; 17146.
2 Below, Landownership: Secular Inns and Ests, Mauduit.

BOUNDARIES AND LOCAL GOVERNMENT

MANOR AND LIBERTY OF WESTMINSTER

The abbot's secular authority derived from the manor or vill of Westminster within which the abbey itself stood. The earliest charter of St Peter's minster to have a genuine basis, that of Edgar *c.*959, defined its estate as extending from a line in the west marked by the Merfleet and the Tyburn, thence along 'the wide army street' (later Oxford Street and High Holborn), which formed its northern boundary, to the church of St Andrew Holborn in the east. At St Andrew's the estate's eastern boundary ran southwards from the army street through the fen outside the city walls to midstream in the Thames, which formed the limit back to Merfleet.[1] These bounds remained roughly the same in 1002, when the minster estate acquired an outlier or berewick on the north side of the army street, except that the land and river south of the Strand were excluded.[2] At some later date, probably before 1200, the City liberty was extended westwards along Fleet Street to Temple Bar; pensions payable from churches in Fleet Street in the 1180s suggest, however, that the area was then still part of the abbey's lordship.[3]

Thereafter, throughout the Middle Ages the abbey's manor, usually referred to as the vill of Westminster, consisted of almost all the territory between the Tyburn and Temple Bar, except for a small area which lay within the honor of Leicester and later the liberty of the Savoy. The latter comprised the land south of the Strand between Temple Bar and Ivybridge stream (which crossed the Strand about two-thirds of the way from Temple to Charing Cross), together with that part of the parish of St Clement Danes extending north from the Strand to Hollowell Lane and Butcher Row (Wych Street).[4] The berewick lying north of Oxford Street had been granted out by the abbey in 1066, and seems to have become entirely alienated from the monks' possession.[5] Land nearby was granted to the hospital of St Giles at its foundation *c.*1100, and later formed the parish of St Giles-in-the-Fields; it was occasionally said to be in the vill of Westminster, which may account for indications in grants that property there was located in

Westminster or that Westminster retained residual rights over it.

The origins of what by the 13th century was termed the liberty of Westminster lay in Edward the Confessor's grant to the abbot of exclusive judicial rights over his lands and his men, as the king himself had possessed them.[6] In 1235, Henry III made a fresh grant of an extensive secular jurisdiction, including the Crown pleas and almost all the pleas normally held before the local sheriff. In effect, royal officials, except the occasional judge on a special commission, were almost entirely excluded from all the abbot's lands. Their authority was vested in the abbot's own officials, in particular, his seneschal or steward, who had ultimate responsibility for the abbey's lands as a whole, and – more locally – the bailiff of the liberty of Westminster.[7] In the reign of Edward I (1272–1307), basing himself upon the charter of 1235, the abbot of Westminster claimed that in Middlesex his privileged jurisdiction was based upon two main estates, the vill of Westminster and the manor of Staines. Along with several other estates, the vill of Eye and the adjacent manors of Knightsbridge and Westbourne were said to be members of the vill of Westminster and so presumably formed part of the liberty administered by its bailiff.[8] This extensive secular jurisdiction should not be confused with the ecclesiastical exemption from the authority of the bishop of London, which the abbey had claimed since the 12th century and which it was finally awarded in 1222; that was based upon the much more restricted area of the parish of St Margaret.[9]

Vill of Eye

Like Westminster, the vill of Eye represents the area of a Domesday manor, and the name continued in use late in the 15th century to denote location of property or place of residence. It was bounded on the east by the Tyburn and on the west by the Westbourne, and stretched from the Roman road on the north to the Thames. At its northern end, south of the army street and on the eastern side of the road to Tyburn, lay the Ossulstone, the stone which presumably marked the meeting place of the hundred of that name.[10] Originally in secular

1 Sawyer, *A.-S. Charters*, no. 670; Robinson, Gilbert Crispin, 170; S. Keynes, 'The Dunstan-B Charters', Anglo-Saxon England 23 (1994), 177.

2 Sawyer, *A.-S. Charters*, no. 903; M. Gelling, 'Boundaries of the Westminster Charters', *TLMAS*, new ser. XI (1954), 101–4; below, Landownership: Manorial Ests, Westminster.

3 Below; Landownership: Intro.; Religious Life: Intro.

4 Extent of vill mainly ascertained from charters and deeds; below.

5 Below, Landownership: Manor of Westm.

6 F. Harmer, *Anglo-Saxon Writs* (1952), no. 83, pp. 319, 349–50.

7 Sawyer, *A.-S. Charters*, no. 1127; *Cal. Chart R. 1226–57*, 208–9; *1257–1300*, 238–9; Rosser, *Medieval Westm.* 230–1; F.M. Powicke, *King Henry III and the Lord Edward* (1947), I. 330.

8 *Placita de Quo Warranto* (Rec. Com. 1818), 479–80. Cf. murder case of 1344: Rutton, 'Manor of Eia', 40.

9 Below, Parishes; Religious Hist.: Intro. For such confusion between boundary of abbot's secular authority and that of his spiritual authority in parish of St Margaret see G. Saunders, 'Situation and extent of Westminster', *Archaeologia*, XXVI (1836), 223–41.

10 Rutton, 'Manor of Eia', 39; *PN Middx* (EPNS), 81.

hands, Eye was acquired by the abbey in 1097 and by the late 13th century was considered a member of the liberty of Westminster. Although Eye had few inhabitants it had its own manorial court.[1] Ebury (*Eyebury*), the manorial farm, stood in what is now Pimlico on the higher gravel ground at the edge of the alluvial marsh, and the abbot also had an important country house at Neat, originally on a slight island in the marsh nearer the river. The vill was said to be part of the parish of St Martin-in-the-Fields in the later 13th century (below).

Vill in Medieval Usage

By the middle of the 15th century the use of vill as a location for property in land grants was being dropped in favour of a parish designation, or used in ways that suggested that contemporaries were not sure what the vill was. The word increasingly came to denote the settlement or 'town' of Westminster, and was therefore most commonly used as the place of residence of parties in contemporary documents. It is fairly clear, however, that in the 14th century 'town' did not mean the same to Westminster residents as it did later, since they also referred to Eye, which had little settlement, as a 'vill'.

CITY OF WESTMINSTER

After the dissolution of Westminster Abbey, the secular rights and liberties exercised by the abbot passed to his successors, the dean and chapter of Westminster, while spiritual jurisdiction passed to the new bishopric of Westminster, created in December 1540, when Westminster became officially known as a city.[2] Thereafter Westminster was designated a 'city' rather than a 'vill' in common usage. The term 'city', however, referred only to the parish of St Margaret (as instituted by Henry VIII: below), while the other members of the vill, namely the parish of St Martin-in-the-Fields, which included the vill of Eye, the parts of St Clement Danes and St Mary of Strand north of the Strand, and some residual interests in St Giles-in-the-Fields, were officially known as the liberties of the city of Westminster. Collectively the two former vills were covered by the phrase 'the city and liberties of Westminster'.[3] The area south of the Strand remained separate, in the duchy of Lancaster. Whether this arrangement was ever the result of direct definition or just emerged is unknown. However, occasionally locations in St Martin's would be said to be in the city: for example Charing Cross Street (the western end of the Strand) in 1546, and land between the Strand and Covent Garden in 1547.[4] The bishopric of Westminster was abolished in 1550 and its jurisdiction was amalgamated with the diocese of London, but Westminster continued thereafter to be called a city. In 1585 city government was formally instituted by an Act, which inaugurated a court of burgesses, with a high steward and deputy, 12 burgesses and 12 assistants, whose function was similar to a court leet.[5] The appellation of city was confirmed by letters patent in 1900 to apply to the newly-created metropolitan borough, and continued after the creation of the London boroughs in 1965.[6]

DUCHY OF LANCASTER'S LIBERTY

The liberty of the Savoy belonging to the Duchy of Lancaster as mapped in the 18th century seems to be the same as that set out in 1602: it covered all the land south of the Strand between the Temple and Ivybridge, together with a small area on the north side between Catherine and Burleigh streets, which was the site of Burghley House in the late 16th century.[7] The liberty derived from an amalgamation of the soke of Leicester and the Savoy estate.[8] At first only on the south side of the Strand, the estate was extended to include four tenements on the north side, acquired by the earls of Lancaster in the 14th century. At some point after 1399, and probably for administrative convenience, the Crown's other rights in the area – in particular those over the band of land in the highway on which the church of St Clement Danes and many houses stood – passed to the duchy, which collected quitrents and administered local government functions there by the 16th century, similar to the Westminster court of burgesses. This separate civil jurisdiction continued until 1901, but its functions were gradually eroded in the 19th century by other bodies.[9]

The soke of Leicester was associated with a prominent feature in the Strand, the stone cross, to be distinguished from Edward I's memorial to Queen Eleanor at Charing. Allegedly set up by William II (1089–1100), it is first recorded in 1242 as the place at which the pleas of the county of Middlesex were held. The cross probably lay in the highway very near the point where it was joined by Little Drury Lane, possibly marking the boundary of St Clement Danes; Hollar's mid-17th century view shows a feature at this site, perhaps the remains of the cross.[10] By the early 14th century the soke of Leicester's court was held there and by 1313 the monument had apparently given its name to the manor. It was also used as a distinguishing address for nearby properties in the Strand. It was evidently in decay by 1333 when the earl of Leicester's court was said to be at 'the broken cross', but was still in existence in 1598.[11]

1 WAM 27000–27009.

2 *L&P Hen. VIII*, XVI, p. 174 (no. 379/30).

3 e.g. St Margt in city of Westm; St CD in liberty of Westm.: TNA, E 179/141/127 (1541 tax assessments).

4 *Cal. Pat. 1547–8*, 199.

5 W.H. Manchée, *The Westminster City Fathers (The Burgess Court of Westminster), 1585–1901* (1924), 5.

6 J. Beckett, *City Status in the British Isles, 1830–2002* (2005), 14, 63.

7 Somerville, *Savoy*, 152–3, and endpaper.

8 Below, Landownership: Manorial, Soke of Leic.

9 Somerville, *Savoy*, Chaps 14 and 15, passim.

10 *Hollar's London*, Plate 5.

11 *Cal. Pat. 1232–47*, 291; J. Stow, *Survey of London*, II. 91;

PARISHES

Both St Margaret's and St Martin's parishes had strong lay vestries active in parish life by the 16th century, and during that century the vestries took an increasing role in local government. In addition to the two main parishes, there were also three small parishes along the Strand: St Clement Danes, which had a complex role in local government because it straddled the vill of Westminster and the duchy of Lancaster's liberty; St Mary of Strand; and the short-lived Holy Innocents. Although a city government was introduced in the 1580s, its inability to raise revenue meant its role was limited, and in Westminster, as elsewhere in Greater London, the parish became the main instrument of local government, responsible for improving the increasingly urban environment as well as implementing orders from the justices of the peace. When the new parishes of St Paul, St Anne, St James, and St George, were created out of St Martin to serve newly-built areas and an increasing population, they also became civil authorities as well as ecclesiastical, taking over local government functions from their parent parish. The pre-eminent role of the parishes continued until some functions were taken over by various local boards which were created in the 19th century.[1]

St Margaret's and St Martin's

The parish of St Margaret (of Antioch), Westminster, in existence by the early 12th century, represented the extent of the abbot's spiritual jurisdiction, within which he had full authority directly under the pope, and into which he could invite whomsoever he wished in episcopal orders to perform the functions reserved to bishops. As defined in 1222 the bounds of the parish extended eastwards from the Tyburn which formed its western limit. In the north the boundary was formed by Oxford Street from the point at which it was crossed by the Tyburn to the hospital and parish of St Giles; it then turned southwards along the line of Drury Lane to the Strand, returning west along the Strand to the point at which it was crossed by the Ivybridge stream and thence south to the Thames and back along the river to the mouth of the Tyburn. Within the area thus enclosed lay the unspecified territory of the church and cemetery of St Martin at Charing, significantly expressly excluded from abbot's liberty. Outside, to the north and west, Knightsbridge, Westbourne and the chapelry of Paddington, all described in the late 13th century as members of the vill of Westminster, were said to pertain

to St Margaret and hence by implication were included in its ecclesiastical liberty.[2]

The relation of the parish of St Margaret to that of St Martin is highly problematic. It has generally been assumed that the latter was created *c.*1250,[3] but there was certainly a parish in existence by *c.*1200 which included territory at Charing[4] and the vill of Eye (like the church and cemetery outside the abbot's ecclesiastical exemption).[5] There is also evidence to suggest that there may have been a church on the site much earlier in the Anglo-Saxon period.[6] The extent of the parish within the vill of Westminster during the Middle Ages is, however, uncertain. The failure to define boundaries for St Martin's in 1222, and the seeming lack of clear distinction between it and St Margaret's until 1534, may reflect the fact that the two parishes were originally one. In any case, in medieval Westminster manorial and administrative boundaries were always more significant than parochial ones, particularly in land-holding. Since all the tithes in Westminster went to the abbey, whether to the abbot, prior or sacrist, depending on which church and on whether they were great or small tithes, it may not have seemed necessary to define in full a parish for St Martin's.

In 1534 all this was changed when Henry VIII instructed the abbot to arrange with the vicar of St Martin-in-the-Fields for all the inhabitants of St Margaret's dwelling within precincts of St Martin north and east of the king's Palace of Whitehall and Westminster, to be removed from the former parish. Henceforth they were to be parishioners of St Martin's, paying their tithes and receiving sacraments and burial there; the abbot's jurisdiction over the parish of St Margaret and his community's appropriation of St Martin's made this possible, and the king required it because of the danger to his household of infection from corpses, and from the clothes of their bearers, as they passed along King Street to St Margaret's for burial. Shortly afterwards Henry wrote to the vicar and churchwardens of St Martin's, directing them to notify the inhabitants within the precincts, bounds, and limits of their parish that every one dwelling north of the new gate of the recently enlarged palace precinct, even if hitherto a parishioner of St Margaret's, was thereafter a parishioner of St Martin's.[7] The wording of the letters implies a lack of clear juridical distinction between St Margaret and St Martin; though the latter had a defined area or 'precincts', yet inhabitants there could still be parishioners of St Margaret's, a confusion evident in property conveyances, where the parish of St Margaret existed on

---

Hollar's London, Plate 5; below, Landownership: Manorial (Soke of Leic., Soke of Mohun); Episcopal Inns (Chester; Worcester); Other Eccles. (Abbey of Combe); Secular Inns and Ests (Convers).

1 Reserved for treatment under Local Govt in a later vol.
2 *Acta Stephani Langton* (Cant. & York Soc. vol. L), 69–73;

below, Religious Hist.: Intro.
3 E.g. Rosser, *Medieval Westm.* 230, 253.
4 WAM 17141–2.
5 WAM 17160; WAD, ff. 334–v. (deeds of later 13th cent.).
6 Below: Early Settlement; Religious Hist.: Parishes, St Martin.
7 TNA, SP 1/87, pp. 27–8; SP 1/90, pp. 140–1.

north side of Strand, cut off from the remainder of St Margaret's by land in St Martin's.[1] Covent Garden was said to be in St Margaret's as late as 1536, and later in the 16th century lengthy law-suits turned on which parish certain land was said to be in. Whereas formerly land was simply described as in the vill of Westminster, with the increasing importance of the parish, it was essential to give the correct parish designation.[2]

St Margaret's bounds thereafter remained the same until the creation of the parish of St John the Evangelist in 1728, which took the area south of the abbey precinct and Rochester Row.[3] However, the steps necessary to separate the two parishes were never carried out, so the vestries of the two parishes had to co-operate over rating for the church, poor, and other purposes; over the ensuing 170 years various Acts created bodies to make this possible, the last being the creation of the united vestry of St Margaret and St John in 1888.[4]

St Martin's and the Later Civil Parishes

After the establishment of the boundary at Whitehall in 1534, St Martin's parish consisted of all the land in the vill of Westminster north of a line running roughly east–west from the Thames through Horse Guards to the Tyburn, as well as the whole vill of Eye. As earlier, it excluded the land south of the Strand and east of Ivy Lane, and the small areas on the north side of Strand that lay in St Clement Danes detached and St Mary of Strand. As building expanded, St Martin's was reduced by the creation of new parishes. St Paul, Covent Garden, became a chapelry, and then a separate parish in 1646; the parish of St Anne, Soho, followed in 1678, St James, Piccadilly, in 1685, and finally in 1724 St George, Hanover Square, took in not only Mayfair but the whole of Eye as well, leaving St Martin's as a truncated and ill-shaped remnant.[5]

The Strand Parishes

The parishes along the Strand lay within or near the area of the *wic* or trading settlement, established to the west of the walled city in the 7th century and forming London's principal centre of population until the Viking attacks of the 9th. That and the fact that that settlement was associated with several cemeteries suggest that one or more of the Strand churches may have pre-Viking origins.[6] Nevertheless, it must be borne at mind that the parishes were small and only emerge in the record late, in

the 11th or 12th century. Furthest east, just west of Temple Bar and adjoining the liberty of the City of London lay St Clement Danes, whose church was built on royal land taken out of the highway of the Strand. Its name suggests a connection with Danish settlers of the early 11th century, who are known to have had a cemetery in London. First recorded in the late 12th century, it was by then parochial.[7] The parish lay either side of the Strand, and included nearly all of the band of land in the Strand on which the church stood, which ran from the modern church of St Mary le Strand to just short of Temple Bar. The part of the parish north from the Strand up to Hollowell Street and Butcher's Row (Wych Street, the extension of Drury Lane towards Temple Bar) lay within the vill of Westminster, while that to the south lay originally in the soke of Leicester, later the duchy of Lancaster. The parish's eastern boundary was marked by Shire Lane to the north of Temple Bar and to the south by the Temple itself, the westward extent of which (and with it the city's boundary), may have varied in the Middle Ages, as it did in the 16th century.[8] The western limit of the parish was a line formed by Aldwych Street (Drury Lane) and Little Drury Lane, and continued south to the Thames.[9] On the north and north-east the parish adjoined St Giles and Lincoln's Inn. By the 19th century the parish also included two detached areas:[10] the first lay on the north side of the Strand between Burleigh and Wellington streets, and was probably the site of the early 16th-century rectory house;[11] the second lay on the south side of the Strand between Cecil Street and the Savoy, possibly connected with Holy Innocents.[12]

Adjoining the western boundary of St Clement's lay the medieval parish of St Mary of Strand. The church itself, of uncertain origin, was demolished in 1548. It lay south of the Strand, but its parish, the boundaries of which are not fully known, also extended to a few houses north of the highway, on the east and west sides of Little Drury Lane. In the 12th century St Mary's was closely associated with the soke of Leicester, but the site of the Savoy palace, which was united with the soke in the late 13th century, seems always to have been technically extra-parochial, although from the mid 16th century it was closely linked with the Strand parish.

When a new church was built in the Strand by the commissioners for building fifty new churches, consecrated in 1723 as St Mary le Strand, the commissioners

---

1 Poss. an enclave formed by the former Holy Innocents' par.: below, Strand Pars.

2 TNA, C 1/736/47; E 178/1391.

3 See map, city of Westminster.

4 Smith, *St John Evangelist*, 194–206.

5 See map, City of Westm. below, Religious Hist., Parish Chs.

6 G. Malcolm, D. Bowsher, R. Cowie, *Middle Saxon London: Excavations at the Royal Opera House, 1989–99* (MoLAS Monograph 15, 2003), 2.

7 Below, Religious Hist.: Parish Churches, St Clement Danes.

8 Below, Landownership: Episcopal Inns (Exeter).

9 Drury Lane was the name given to the upper part of Aldwych Street; the lower section running south-eastwards into the Strand at Temple Bar, survived as Wych Street until destroyed to make way for the Aldwych: *PN Middx*, 185.

10 *Old OS Maps*, sheet 62 (1873).

11 Below, Landownership: Later Creations (Burghley Ho.).

12 Below.

added to the old Strand parish parts of St Clement Danes and St Martin-in-the-Fields on the north side of the highway, and two houses from St Paul Covent Garden.

A third and even smaller parish along the Strand was attached to the church of the Holy Innocents, which had originated as a chapel on a small estate, given by Gilbert of Ghent to the abbot of Abingdon in 1086.[1] The exact position of the chapel, which stood on the north side of the Strand opposite the gate of the abbot's mansion, is unknown, but in 1235 it lay opposite land which was later part of the Savoy,[2] and that part of the Strand was sometimes called *vicus Innocentium*. Its parish, first recorded in 1219, included at least eight properties opposite the Savoy, close to the likely site of the church, and land in the parish stretched from the Strand to the wall of Covent Garden *c.*1220.[3] Many references to property in the parish of the Holy Innocents occur in the first three decades of the 13th century,[4] and grants made later suggest that the parish included the Pied Friars' garden.[5] The parish seems to have ceased to exist in the mid 13th century, after the abbot of Westminster successfully claimed jurisdiction over the church and its houses on the north side of the Strand and they were incorporated into the parish of St Margaret.[6]

Although it is possible that the parish lay only on the north side of the Strand, in the later 13th century it was said to have included the site of the Savoy palace.[7] It also seems likely that it included Carlisle Inn, which lay in a part of the Strand called *vicus Dacorum* (street of the Danes) in 1259, and after the parish had disappeared was in a detached portion of St Clement Danes. This otherwise inexplicable detachment is best explained as deriving from an earlier history as part of Holy Innocents' parish. The abbot did not lay claim to the land south of the Strand, which was outside his vill, but, once he had taken over the church and houses to the north, the remainder had little viability. If the Templars were still connected with both churches, as they had been in the late 12th century, uniting the area with St Clement Danes may have seemed the simplest solution.

SETTLEMENT

ROADS

The main Roman road from London to the west, the 'wide army road', left the City at Newgate and formed the northern boundary of the later vills of Westminster and Eye. It seems possible that a road also ran west from the Roman Ludgate along the line of Fleet Street. A street within the Roman walls led to this road, which the charter of *c.*1002 (extant only in a 14th-century copy) was described as Akeman Street (*Akemannestraet*), the name given to the Roman road to Bath much further west.[8]

Whether Roman or not, in the Middle Ages the road from Ludgate following the line of the river to the palace and abbey of Westminster was the principal route through the area. It linked the City of London with the centre of government. Known after leaving Temple Bar as the Strand, it followed the top edge of a steep bank rising from the Thames, before becoming Charing (later

Charing Cross) Street at its western end, up to the bend at Charing, and then finally King Street, south to the palace. At Charing another branch continued westward to the hospital of St James and thence to Knightsbridge via a ford across the Tyburn at Cowford, already in existence in the 10th century.

Two routes of some antiquity led into Westminster from the Roman road in the north at High Holborn or St Giles High Street; one, Aldwych Street (later Drury Lane), ran south-eastwards to St Clement Danes and Temple Bar, while the other, near St Giles's Hospital, ran south-westwards towards the later Piccadilly, and may be the road referred to in the early 13th century as Old Street (*Eldestrat*). In the south, Tothill Street led westwards from the abbey precinct, with branches south-west to the abbot's manor house at Neat, and north-west across Eybridge towards Knightsbridge; another road ran from mid-way along Tothill Street north through fields to St James's Hospital.

1 Below, Religious Hist.: Par. Chs (Holy Innocents).
2 TNA, CP 25/1/146/9, no. 117.
3 TNA, CP 25/1/146/5, nos 4–6; 282/6, no. 19; *Westm. Charters*, 165; WAM 17136.
4 TNA, CP 25/1/146/5, nos 4–6; 146/6, no. 50; 282/6, no. 19; BL, Harl. MS 1708, f. 111v; printed in *Reading Abbey Cartularies*, ed. B.R. Kemp, I (Camden Soc. 4th ser., vols 31, 1986), nos 472–4.
5 Below, Landownership: Later Creations (Bedford).
6 Below, Religious Hist.: Par. Chs (Holy Innocents); Landownership: Other Eccles. (Pied Friars).
7 TNA, DL 25/2344; /2342.
8 *PN Middx* (EPNS), 9.

EARLY SETTLEMENT

BEFORE 959

There is little evidence of Roman activity in Westminster. The most intriguing site is the cemetery at St Martin's, burials from which were first discovered in 1725 and again in excavations associated with the redevelopment of the crypt in 2005–7.[1] Otherwise there are only artefacts found out of context. The Roman bath in Strand Lane is of Italian origin and was probably one of the antiquities brought to Arundel House by the 2nd earl of Arundel in the 17th century.[2]

For the early Anglo-Saxon period, the evidence is much more abundant. The crucial area is the extensive settlement of *Lundenwic* which flourished from the 7th to the 9th century. This open site outside the walls of the Roman city was probably the largest of the English trading and manufacturing centres known as *wics* which constitute such a distinctive feature of the pre-Viking period. The original nucleus probably lay north of the Strand and around Aldwych Street, whose name, meaning 'old *wic*', preserves a memory of the settlement; excavations in Keeley Street (St Giles's parish) show that settlement extended east of Drury Lane.[3] By the late 7th century *Lundenwic* had started to expand and eventually, before its contraction in the 9th century it extended westwards to Trafalgar Square.[4] Associated with the early *wic* were two cemeteries, which then lay on its periphery, one at Covent Garden near the Royal Opera House, the other at St Martin's-in-the-Fields. That at Covent Garden was later built over,[5] but that at St Martin's, seems to have remained open land, perhaps because it was associated with a church.[6]

Further south, not far from what was to become the core area of abbey and palace, important finds have been made at the site now occupied by the Treasury on the east side of the highway later known as King Street. They include a substantial hall, grand enough to have been of royal status, and likely to date from the 8th century. This and its associated structures perhaps provide a context for a number of high status objects of similar date found nearby.[7] Finds on Thorney Island itself, of a similar pattern to those from the Treasury site, suggest that

there was also activity there in the 8th and 9th century. That lends some slight credence to the late Westminster tradition that there was a church on the island before the establishment there of St Peter's minster, *c.*959.[8]

The Viking attacks in the 9th century and the ensuing replanning of the walled city in the 880s mark a major change in the pattern of London's settlement, but whether the *wic* was totally abandoned or simply contracted is unclear. Certainly settlement in the area around Covent Garden and on the Treasury site appears to have ended in the mid 9th century.[9] The fate of the church on Thorney Island, if such there was, is unknown.

ABBEY, PALACE AND SETTLEMENT, *c.*959–1200

Westminster's settlement and growth were influenced by two very different factors: one was the development of agriculture, with settlement by landholders near their land; the other was the creation and growth of the abbey and the palace by the river. The two factors hardly impinged on each other: agriculture was concentrated in the north and west of the area, on the higher and dryer gravels, while the abbey and the accompanying palace of Edward the Confessor were situated on a gravel island in the riverside marsh created by the Thames and streams that flowed into it, still called Thorney ('thorn island') in 969 in a grant to St Peter's minster.[10] The earliest occurrence of the name Westminster in a contemporary document is in 993; other early occurrences are from post-conquest copies of charters, many of which were forgeries.[11]

In 1086, the vill of Westminster had 19 villeins and 42 cottars holding land and presumably living in the vill. There were also 25 houses belonging to the abbot's knights and other men,[12] the locations of which are unknown, but which almost certainly, as later, lay mainly near the abbey and palace, at Charing, and in St Clement Danes.

Settlement around the core area of abbey and palace seems to have extended along King Street to the north and Tothill Street to the west. Despite the establishment

1 Below, Religious Hist.: Parish Churches, St Martin.

2 Below, Landownership: Episcopal Inns (Bath).

3 MOLAS excavation report, 2000 (LAARC online catalogue, under KEL00)

4 A. Vince, *Saxon London: An Archaeological Investigation* (1990), 13–25, 118; Malcolm, Bowsher, Cowie, *Middle Saxon London*, 1–4, 17–19, 32–4, 54–8, 109–11; D. Keene, 'London from the Post-Roman Period to 1300', in *Cambridge Urban Hist. of Britain* I (2000), 188–9; below.

5 Malcolm, Bowsher, Cowie, *Middle Saxon London*, 17–19, 26–32.   6 Below, Religious Hist.: St Martin's.

7 R. Cowie and L. Blackmore, *Early and Middle Saxon Rural Settlement in the London Region* (MoLAS Monograph 41, 2008), 91–100.

8 C. Thomas, R. Cowie, J. Sidell, *The Royal Palace, Abbey and Town of Westminster on Thorney Island* (MoLAS Monograph 22, 2006), 45–6.

9 Malcolm, Bowssher, Cowie, *Middle Saxon London*, 128–34; Cowie and Blackmore, *Rural Settlement*, 100.

10 Sawyer, *A.-S. Charters*, no. 774.

11 *PN Middx* (EPNS), 165.

12 *VCH Middx*, I. 122.

4. *New Palace Yard looking west in 1647, with Westminster Hall on the south side, and the Clock House marking the way into the Woolstaple and Canon Row north of the Yard. The main gate into King Street is just visible in the background.*

there of St Peter's church *c.*959, Thorney Island has yielded very little archaeological evidence, except for an interesting indication that there may have been late 10th-century activity on the palace site.[1] Further north on the east side of King Street and beside the Thames, lay Endehithe (*terra de Anedeheða* or 'wharf frequented by ducks'), where a house had been established by the later 12th century and where there may well have been earlier commercial buildings.[2]

Further north still, settlement probably continued at Charing after the contraction of the *wic*. Its place name, first mentioned in a 14th-century copy of Æthelred's charter of 1002 (the earliest contemporary record is in 1198), almost certainly derives from the Old English word for 'turning', a reference to its location at the distinctive right-angled bend of the river, where the current has scoured the channel back to the gravel bank. Not only did it lie on the Thames at a convenient landing-place, it was a focus of early land communications in the area, at the junction of roadways from the City in the east, Knightsbridge in the west, the army road in the north, and the abbey in the south.[3]

There was also settlement along the Strand. The name of the church of St Clement Danes suggests the presence of Danish traders probably established there in the early 11th century.[4] By the 12th century, however, it seems likely that the influence of London had made itself felt in a greater density of occupation than elsewhere in the vill and in the preponderance of gardens, perhaps already producing food for the city (below). The existence of road names using *vicus* or 'street', such as Aldwych

Street, Westminster Street and South Street (both now part of the Strand) suggests that the area was well settled.[5]

Despite such evidence, only one residence is recorded along the Strand before the 12th century: the substantial private inn granted by Gilbert of Ghent to the abbots of Abingdon in 1086 together with the chapel of the Holy Innocents opposite. The inn lay between the highway and the river, with the chapel before its gates on the north side of the Strand, approximately opposite the later Savoy. The latter, originally three separate holdings, may have included the site of Abingdon's inn, but no link can be established.

In the west, in the vill of Eye, some manorial buildings presumably existed on the site of Ebury farm by 1065. In 1086 the manor had 24 customary tenants farming half of its arable land.[6] As later, settlement in the area was probably mainly along the highway to Knightsbridge, with other clusters possibly on or around the islands of Ebury and Neat.

THE MEDIEVAL FIELDS

Westminster and Eye both had open arable fields, meadow, and some pasture. In 1086 the manor of Westminster was said to have arable for 11 ploughs, with enough meadow to support the animals, enough pasture for the cattle of the vill, and also had woodland for 100 pigs.[7] Those totals, however, probably included Paddington, Westbourne and Knightsbridge,[8] where most of the woodland may have lain. The manor of Eye had arable for 8 ploughs, enough meadow both to

1 Thomas, Cowie, Sidell, *Royal Palace, Abbey and Town*, 40–6.   2 Rosser, *Medieval Westm.* 18–20.
3 Robinson, *Gilbert Crispin*, 169; *PN Middx* (EPNS), 167.
4 Vince, *Saxon London*, 44.

5 Above, Roads.
6 *VCH Middx*, I. 125.
7 *VCH Middx*, I. 122.
8 Harvey, *Westm. Abbey Ests*, 353n.

support the animals and render 60*s.* from the hay, and pasture rendering 7*s.*[1] The location of arable and meadow in the two vills probably already followed the pattern recorded in the late 13th century.[2] The arable lay on the gravel soils which covered most of Westminster with a spur into Tothill fields and the northern half of Eye, while the meadow lay on the alluvial land in bands along the Thames and the Tyburn and Westbourne valleys, stretching inland in the southern part of Eye. There were a few smaller areas of meadow within the arable fields along smaller streams, such as Lousmede near Longditch, and the meadow by the Tyburn near Rosamund. There are no indications of large areas of waste apart from the common pasture of Tothill, later known as Tothill fields, but waste along the highways was gradually granted away. The land in Knightsbridge manor at Kensington Gore (*Gara*), which in the 1130s the abbot of Westminster granted to the nuns of Kilburn for assarting, was probably of that kind,[3] although most recorded grants of waste were for building or enclosure into curtilages.

The arable fields were large and open, divided by highways, with a few out-takes for springs south-east of St James's Hospital. In the early 13th century the fields of Charing contained strips of arable, and land near Covent Garden was also used for arable or gardens.[4] Along highways near medieval settlements – for example, east of St Martin's church, along the Strand and along King Street – were closes, some attached to tenements and many used as gardens. The large area of Covent Garden was also open, but held in severalty and apparently without common rights. South of Tothill Street was an arable field with strips adjoining the common pasture, and nearby to the east the abbey's precinct included a large orchard and great meadow.

Much, if not all, the arable was in strips in named furlongs in the open fields, some of which are known to have had common grazing rights. By the late 15th century all the arable fields had Lammas grazing rights and so lay open between 1 August and 2 February, but by the mid 16th century those rights were being eroded by enclosure.[5] The arable of Tothill field, however, was being held in severalty in the Middle Ages, and in fact may never have had grazing rights; it lay towards the road, and some plots in it had buildings along the highway. The area later known as Tothill fields was presumably the vill's common pasture, which continued to be pastured by commoners at the end of the 15th century.

THE CREATION OF WESTMINSTER

Westminster's early history is not significantly different from other areas around the City of London; the crucial factor determining its unique character was its emergence as a centre of government. An important element here was the establishment of the abbey as England's coronation church in 1066. This was by no means inevitable; it was political chance – the rivalry for the succession to Edward the Confessor and the need to acquire legitimacy through association with the dead king – which promoted Westminster Abbey to this importance, retained under later monarchs. Coronation in the abbey became essential to confirm royal authority. Nevertheless, apart from the special case of the burial there of the English queen Edith/Matilda in 1118, it was not really a focus of royal interest from the later 11th century until the reign of Henry III (1216–72). Although a remarkable great hall was built at Westminster at the end of the 11th century to accommodate large royal assemblies, under the Normans and Angevins the palace itself was simply one of many royal residences, occupied only episodically by peripatetic kings. It was Henry III's intervention, inspired by devotion to Edward the Confessor, and its continuation by his son Edward I (1272–1307), which ensured that the abbey not only became rich and important, but acquired such strong royal associations, and so many royal burials, that its buildings, monuments and archives survived the Dissolution when most other great religious houses were destroyed.[6]

Westminster and London

Westminster's developing role as the seat of government, discussed below, cannot be divorced from its proximity to London, the commercial capital and, since the time of William I, site of that major expression of royal power, the Tower. While from the time of Henry II (1154–89) Westminster became more and more the seat of justice and finance, London was principal home to the royal treasure. Under Edward I, London and its environs, of which the most notable, of course, was Westminster, became firmly established as a capital in the modern sense. Edward developed the practice of summoning Parliament to meet at Westminster, established as the norm after 1330, except for a period in the mid 15th century. Yet while much administrative activity became thus more or less permanently fixed, the kings' presence, when they were not away on campaign, was less constant. Although they resided more and more

1 *VCH Middx*, I. 122, 125.
2 Acct below based largely on deeds in WA.
3 *Westm. Charters*, p. 119.
4 WAM 17539, 17548.

5 Reserved for treatment under Economic Hist., in a later vol.
6 P. Binski, *Westm. Abbey and the Plantagenets* (Yale, 1995), esp. 3–5, 90–120.

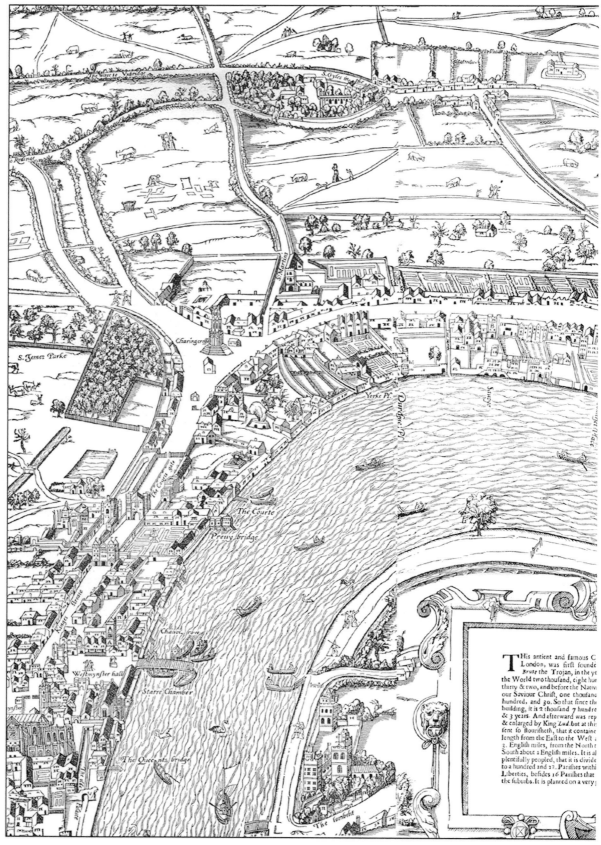

5. *Westminster depicted on the Wood-cut Map, showing the limited extent of its built-up area c.1550. Prominent in the view, from east to west are Temple Bar (the Strand boundary with City), the Savoy hospital, Charing Cross, and in the far south-west, Westminster Abbey and Hall*

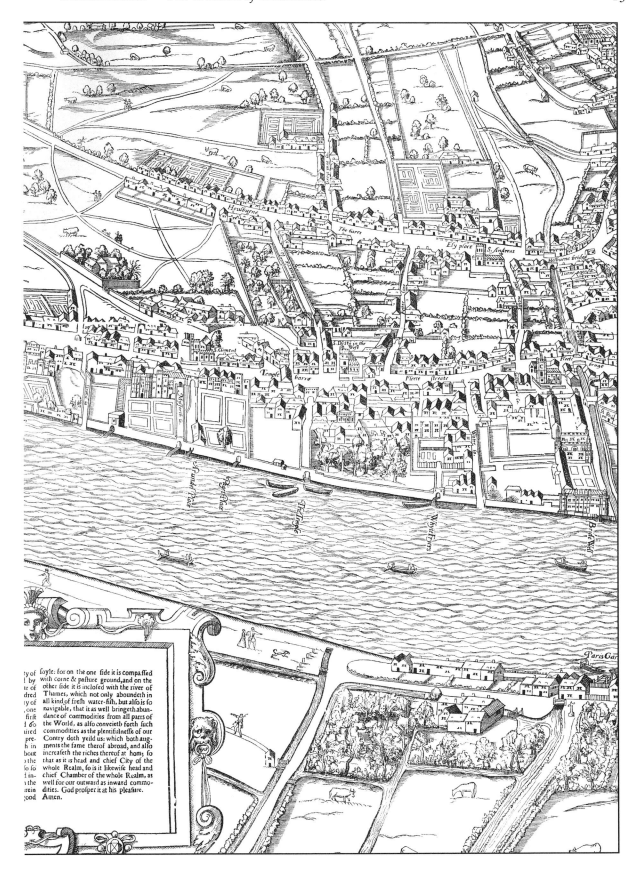

soyle: for on the one fide it is compaffed
with corne & pafture ground, and on the
other fide it is inclofed with the river of
Thames, which not only aboundeth in
all kind of frefh water-fifh, but alfo is fo
navigable, that it as well bringeth abun-
dance of commodities from all parts of
the World, as alfo convieth forth fuch
commodities as the plentifulneffe of our
Contry doth yeild us: which both aug-
ments the fame therof abroad, and alfo
increafeth the riches thereof at hom; fo
that as it is head and chief City of the
whole Realm, fo is it likewife head and
chief Chamber of the whole Realm, as
well for our outward as inward commodities. God profper it at his pleafure.
Amen.

frequently near London, they did not necessarily live either in Westminster or the City.[1]

The king's involvement in London and its environs was paralleled by his great magnates. The archbishops of Canterbury provide perhaps the most notable instance. They had had a presence in the City since the late 9th century and finally definitively established themselves opposite Westminster, on the other side of the Thames at Lambeth, in the 1190s.[2]

GROWTH OF GOVERNMENT BUREAUCRACY

Under the Normans, the king's officials travelled with him in England or Normandy, leaving a permanent treasury with its records in England based at Winchester. The records and money were carried from Winchester to the Exchequer court, which met twice at year at Easter and Michaelmas to settle the king's accounts and collect his revenues. From 1172, however, the Exchequer court most often met at Westminster, which no doubt influenced the decision to move the main Treasury store to London, a move completed by 1189.[3] The reasons for the choice of Westminster for meetings of the court were probably London's good communications by land and water, as well as the palace with its magnificent hall ideal for large gatherings and the existence of the Exchequer's own two-storeyed building beside the hall by 1156.[4]

The placing of the Exchequer records in one fixed place was of great importance in creating a capital, and therefore in ensuring Westminster's crucial role as that capital. Although the Exchequer court met only twice a year, before each court the clerks had to examine the records and send writs to each sheriff and other accountant around the country summoning them and detailing everything they owed. As the amount of revenue required increased under King John (1199–1216), the Exchequer's sessions lengthened considerably until it extended over most of the year.[5] With the audits and records mainly settled at Westminster, the lesser officers of the Exchequer became a more or less permanent staff who seem to have taken up residence in the vicinity of Westminster hall before the end of the 12th century.

The introduction of the writ system under Henry II (1154–89) led to an expansion of royal justice, opened up to a wider public and at first handled by the Exchequer court. As the court of common pleas it later became a separate court with its own records and staff, but fixing it in one known place, unlike the king's court which travelled around with the monarch, was important in making royal justice accessible and pre-eminent, and it

usually met at Westminster.[6] Later other administrative departments also went 'out of court'; their records and the majority of their clerks became fixed at Westminster rather than travelling around the country with the king, the most important of these being Chancery in the later 13th century.

Although fixing the administration in one place became necessary because of the increase in its work and functions, there was nothing inevitable about its location in Westminster, and when necessary it did move; under Edward I it migrated to Shrewsbury when the king was fighting in Wales and to York when he was fighting in Scotland; in the 1330s, when Edward III was fighting the Scots, it again moved to York for five years, to the impoverishment of Westminster.[7] War with France, however, led to the main departments being sent back to Westminster in 1338, and thereafter there was no reason for the courts, their clerks and records to leave the south.[8]

EFFECTS OF GOVERNMENT

Twice a year every sheriff was summoned to account at the Exchequer, as were bailiffs and stewards of honors, reeves of towns, custodians of vacant bishoprics and abbacies and of escheated baronies, together with many other Crown debtors. The holding of the Exchequer audits thus produced a large and regular influx of visitors, quite apart from the occasional visits of the king and his household.[9] With the great growth in the judicial business of the king's court, this influx was reinforced by a steady stream throughout the year during the periods when the court of common pleas sat. The king's council, his leading officers, also frequently met in Westminster, sometimes in the king's absence, and from 1330 Parliament usually met there.[10] During the 14th century the growing importance of the royal council and of Parliament meant not only that leading lay magnates now visited Westminster more often, bringing with them large retinues, but also many knights of the shires and burgesses visited Westminster more frequently. Later administrative changes served to enhance Westminster's dominant position. As more functions of the king's court were institutionalised and officers of the royal household developed their own bureaucracies,[11] Westminster became an ever greater centre of political power and patronage, to which men seeking advancement were increasingly attracted in the 16th and 17th centuries.

All those visitors presented the inhabitants of Westminster with economic opportunities in providing

1 Keene, 'London to 1300', 211–16 (1975), 157–8, 363–4; C. Barron, London, '1300–1540', in Cambridge Urban Hist. of Britain, I, 438–40.

2 C.N.L. Brooke and G. Keir. *London 800–1216*, 157–8, 363–4.

3 R.A. Brown, ' "The Treasury" of the later Twelfth Century', *Studies Presented to Sir Hilary Jenkinson*, ed. J.C. Davies (1957), 35–49.

4 Tout, *Chapters*, I. 178; *King's Works*, I. 538–9.

5 R.V. Turner, *Men Raised from the Dust* (1988), 47.

6 Chrimes, *Admin. Hist.* 48–9; Tout, *Chapters*, I. 178; W. Holdsworth, *Hist. of Eng. Law*, I (7th edn, 1956), 195–6.

7 Rosser, *Medieval Westm.* 169.

8 Tout, 'Modern Capital', 249–75; Chrimes, *Admin. Hist.* 190.

9 Chrimes, *Admin. Hist.* 57–8; Tout, 'Modern Capital'; Tout, *Chapters*, I. 97–8, 101.

10 Tout, 'Modern Capital', 264–5.

11 Chrimes, *Admin. Hist.* 266.

victualling inns and taverns, stabling, and lodgings. The growth in public accommodation, initially quite slow, became noticeable by 1400.[1] The presence of royal government also, however, created problems. The palace's lack of accommodation for the royal household led to widespread billeting by the king's steward and exemptions from this unpopular practice were regularly granted by the king by the mid 13th century.[2] It remained a problem, however; in 1331, for example, the inhabitants of Westminster complained to the king and council about oppressive billeting, noting a steep increase in the number of people and horses lodged meant that they and their families were often expelled from their own houses.[3]

The settlement of a permanent administration in Westminster had more profound effects than increasing the number of visitors. As offices went out of court and more functions were carried out solely at Westminster, the king's leading ministers obtained premises near the palace, providing accommodation for their growing number of clerks as part of their own households within which much day to day work was carried out.[4] To provide for their clerks, whether in the form of lodging or just meals, as well as for their household servants, leading ministers required substantial residences, generally known as inns, in the vicinity of Westminster; the staff of the Chancery in the 14th century, for example, numbered 48 clerks of different grades.[5] The characteristic form of private inn, the residence of officials and ministers, usually comprised a hall and suitable private rooms for its proprietor, with lodgings for his household and visitors, stabling and, usually, gardens. Most inns and houses of any size in Westminster, whether in the hands of ecclesiastical or lay owners, can be related to service with the king. From the mid-14th century public inns, offering accommodation similar to private ones, started to appear, catering for those who did not have a town house of their own or lacked access to a private inn. Such commercial enterprises became increasingly ubiquitous and by the 15th century were even being used by grand families.[6]

Acquisitions by royal officials are well documented from the later 12th century.[7] Many royal servants, high and low, had property near the palace along King Street and Tothill Street, as well as in the palace precinct itself, before 1300.[8] The Mauduit family,

hereditary chamberlains of the king and therefore barons of the Exchequer, had a house in Winchester, but in the 1180s began building up an estate in Tothill, which included a residence and chapel at the north end, in Longditch (in the south-east corner of the later St James's Park). The estate filled the north side of Tothill Street, and many lesser officials of the Exchequer were tenants of the Mauduits there.[9] Richard of Ely, treasurer to Henry II, had a residence at Endith ('Enedehithe'), by the river to the south of York Place, before he became bishop of London in 1189, and surrendered it to his kinsman, William of Ely, who succeeded him as treasurer.[10] The fixing of functions in Westminster also brought the justiciars and other soldier-administrators to Westminster on a regular basis; William the Marshal, earl of Pembroke, had an inn at Charing before 1199, as did William Briwere, baron of the Exchequer and justice,[11] and c.1224 the justiciar Hubert de Burgh acquired William of Ely's house at Endith.[12] Possibly as early as 1205 Brian de Lisle (d. by 1234), soldier-administrator, acquired the core of the property which later became the Savoy.[13]

Episcopal Inns

At first the concentration of those residences was as close to the palace as could be arranged, but as lesser officials and members of the king's household were crammed in, the higher ranks seem to have preferred to settle further away, where there was more room. That seems to have been the origin of the well-known episcopal inns which lined the south side of the Strand by the late Middle Ages. All those inns that can be traced back to the 12th century or first decade of 13th were the creation of royal ministers. The earliest recorded, later the inn of the bishops of Worcester, was built towards the end of the 12th century by Godfrey de Lucy, a royal clerk and justice, and sold by his son John to Mauger bishop of Worcester at the beginning of the 13th century. Early in the 14th century the bishop of Worcester resumed some of the tenanted plots on the site, probably to enlarge or rebuild the inn for his own use when he was chancellor from 1310.[14]

Bath Inn had a similar history, being built up from plots acquired by Eustace de Fauconberg when a royal justice; he was later treasurer before becoming bishop of London in 1221. By 1230 the inn had passed to another

1 Rosser, *Medieval Westm.* 122.

2 e.g. *Cal. Chart. R.* 1226–57, 190, 404, 469; *Cal. Pat.* 1247–58, 482, 607, 632 (and later vols); WAM 17356; Rosser, *Medieval Westm.* 31–2.

3 TNA, SC 8/200; /263; *Cal. Pat.* 1330–4, 219.

4 Chrimes, *Admin. Hist.* 116, 209–10; A.L. Brown, 'The Privy Seal Clerks in early 15th cent.', *The Study of Medieval Records: Essays in Hon. of Kathleen Major*, ed. D.A. Bullough and R.L. Storey (1971), 265; J.A. Burrow, *Thomas Hoccleve* (Authors of the Middle Ages 4, c.1994), 6–8.

5 Chrimes, *Admin. Hist.* 209–10.

6 Barron, 'London 1300–1540', 439–40.

7 Gerin, minister of the king, obtained property at Endith 1138x57, but possibly because of a connection with abt of Westm.: *Westm. Charters*, p. 126.

8 Rosser, *Medieval Westm.* 18–32.

9 Below, Landownership: Secular Inns and Ests (Mauduit).

10 Ibid.: Episcopal Inns (York).

11 D. Crouch, *William Marshal* (1990), 146; *Westm. Charters*, p. 106; *Cal. Chart. R.* 1226–57, 167–8.

12 Below, Landownership: Episcopal Inns (York).

13 Ibid.: Manorial Ests (Soke of Leic.).

14 Ibid.: Episcopal Inns (Worcester).

former royal official and sub-chancellor, Jocelin of Wells, bishop of Bath, who granted it to his bishopric.[1] Three other inns are first referred to during or after the episcopate of a bishop who had been or was continuing to be a king's minister. Norwich was in being by the death of Bishop Thomas de Blundeville, a king's clerk, in 1236,[2] and Durham at the death in 1237 of Bishop Richard Poore, baron of the Exchequer and son of Richard of Ilchester, though the inn may also have belonged to his predecessor Bishop Richard Marsh (1217–26), chancellor from 1214.[3] Walter Mauclerc, bishop of Carlisle 1223–46, treasurer 1228–33, and royal envoy both before and after he became bishop, was said to have an inn in 1238,[4] but it only became the property of that bishopric when it was granted to the see by his successor, Silvester de Everdon, keeper of the Great Seal 1242–3, chancellor 1244–6, and bishop of Carlisle 1246–54.[5]

When a bishop was appointed who was not involved in the royal administration, his inn in the Strand was generally occupied by a royal minister and his household and clerks, often at the direction of the king. The bishop of Exeter, for example, was asked by the king to hire his inn out to the keeper of the privy seal in 1417, and was thereby excused from attending Parliament as he would have nowhere to stay.[6] The keeper had previously used the bishop of Coventry's inn (Chester Inn) in 1411–12, when Thomas Hoccleve wrote *The Regiment of Princes* there. Three lay chancellors in the 1340s also hired episcopal inns, including Chester Inn and Worcester Inn.[7]

Lay Ministers and Lesser Officials

By the middle of the 14th century, as building increased in Westminster, lesser royal officials were acquiring houses of their own, mainly in St Clement Danes and on the north side of the Strand, and some may have housed their own clerks. Clement's Inn, north of the church, was held and occupied by one of the auditors of the Exchequer in 1404, and his will was written there and witnessed by four clerks lodged or working there.[8] A property at the corner of the Strand and Little Drury Lane called the Fleur de Lys, with houses, shops, and garden, was leased in 1440 to a Master of Chancery, who was living there in the 1450s.[9] The establishment in Westminster of households of clerks involved in the judicial processes of the administration also led eventually to the growth of teaching in legal processes and ultimately to the emergence of the chancery inns for common lawyers.[10]

Not all important offices were held by churchmen in the 14th and 15th century, but until the mid 15th lay ministers, like the royal clerks, owed their positions to royal service and had little power or influence of their own. They had neither means nor need to acquire an inn at Westminster; when they needed space for a large household they rented one of the episcopal inns. As more important offices passed to laymen, so there was an impetus for men such as the lawyer Sir John Fortescue, who acquired Bosham's Inn in the 1440s, to acquire a place of their own. An early harbinger of this movement, however, was a lay official who is also known to have built a house in Westminster rather than just acquiring one. Sir Walter Hungerford, steward of the household to Henry V and an executor of Henry's will, acquired a freehold messuage at Charing Cross in 1425 and a 90-year lease of the adjoining property from Westminster Abbey, and built a new house there by 1426 which stretched from the highway to the Thames. As Baron Hungerford he was treasurer of England 1426–32, a leading member of the Council, as well as chief steward of the Duchy of Lancaster, and his house, known as Hungerford's Inn, continued in that family until the 1680s.[11]

The fact that Hungerford had to build for himself, however, suggests that lay officials who rose from county gentry families would find it increasingly hard to acquire a substantial house when lay magnates became interested in living in Westminster. From the 16th century the administration had to compete for accommodation with the political world, as men seeking power and fortune through office were attracted to the royal court at Westminster.

LATE MEDIEVAL BUILT AREAS

Westminster in the later Middle Ages developed from two main directions, under quite different influences. Around Westminster Abbey and the palace the principal roads were King Street, which ran north to Charing, approximately along the line of the later Whitehall, and Tothill Street which ran westwards. Both streets were lined with a variety of tenements, some agricultural properties, some private inns, some public inns, and various trades and crafts. The second centre was in the parish of St Clement Danes, especially along the Strand and Aldwych Street, which formed continuations of the residential and commercial property lining Fleet Street. Together with the adjoining area around Chancery Lane, St Clement Danes was beginning to have the

1 Ibid.: Episcopal Inns (Bath).
2 Ibid.: Episcopal Inns (Norwich).
3 Ibid.: Episcopal Inns (Durham); *Handbk of British Chronology*.
4 M. Paris, *Chronica Majora*, III (Rolls Ser.), p. 485.
5 *Handbk of British Chronology*; below, Landownership: Episcopal Inns (Durham).
6 Brown, 'Privy Seal Clerks', 265.
7 T.F. Tout, 'The Household of the Chancery and its

Disintegration' (1927), *Collected Papers of T.F. Tout* (1934), II. 151.   8 Guildhall MS 9171/2, f. 46v.
9 *Cal. Close*, 1447–54, 238–9; TNA, C 54/3–2, m. 27d.; PROB 11/4, f. 144v.
10 To be treated under Lawyers' Inns and Law Cts, in a later vol.
11 J.S. Roskell, 'Three Wiltshire Speakers', *Wilts. Arch. Mag.* 56, 301–41; below, Landownership: Secular Inns and Ests (Hungerford).

preponderance of lawyers which marked it out in later centuries. From the 12ᵗʰ century onwards St Clement's had numerous tenements, some of agricultural origin, but many held by crafts and tradesmen. Some were later amalgamated to form larger public and private inns, including the emerging chancery inns. Beyond St Clement Danes, the Strand, running westwards to Charing Cross, was also built up with tenements, those on the south side, backing onto the Thames, being amalgamated to form the episcopal inns that existed there, often fronted by small tenements or rents. On the north side of the Strand, and also along Aldwych Street, there were a number of gardens, commercial property influenced by the London market. In the middle of these two centres stood the settlement by the river at Charing, where the existence of the nearby St Martin's church by the mid 12ᵗʰ century suggests an established community.

THE SPREAD OF THE BUILT AREA

THE IMPACT OF THE MONARCHY

The second defining moment in the creation of Westminster came with the establishment of a new relationship between the monarchy and the aristocracy at the Tudor court. The wars of the 15ᵗʰ century, the change of regime, and the elimination of possible claimants to the throne had greatly reduced the old noble families and left many of the most important estates and affinities in the hands of the king. As a result, from Henry VII's reign onwards any worthwhile advancement for the ambitious was through service to the monarch. The Court became the centre of political power and advancement, and its hold over nobles and gentry was maintained by the lure of offices and lands. Retaining political power and influence required proximity to the monarch, and anyone seeking the help of courtiers to get a post, grant, or pardon increasingly found it advantageous to be in Westminster. Westminster became a fixed centre for a new kind of royal government, and a house in Westminster became essential for political leaders. Thereafter, although the role of the monarchy changed over the centuries, Westminster remained the centre of power and political life.

Henry VII's contribution to the imagery of Westminster had been the addition of a magnificent chapel to Westminster Abbey, but it was his son Henry VIII, who as a Renaissance prince, appropriated that chapel to dynastic ends.[1] He also made Westminster an important element in the landscape of royal residences in and around London, by establishing permanent and architecturally ambitious royal lodgings at the former York Place (Whitehall) and on the site of St James's Hospital (St James's Palace). Yet under Henry, Elizabeth and the Stuart monarchs, the palaces at Westminster were by no means the only or even the most favoured royal residences, and much time and many resources were spent at established palaces in the Thames Valley, such as Greenwich and Eltham (Kent) as well as acquisitions such as Hampton Court, Nonsuch and Oatlands in Surrey.[2]

Nevertheless, Henry made a crucial contribution to the development of Westminster. At Westminster, he extended the precinct of the existing palace to include a new palace at Whitehall. New men – friends and jousting partners of the king, able ministers, men loyal to the Tudor dynasty – were ennobled, appointed to royal posts, and required housing near the Court. Many were given the inns belonging to various bishoprics, whose London houses were redundant as the king ceased to use clerics as ministers. Men who were not housed at court or helped to an inn in the vicinity of Whitehall had to rent privately in the area, and the demand for housing and for commercial inns grew. Additionally, the settlement near the old palace and abbey filled with inhabitants offering services and provisions for the Court and its visitors, and when Henry VIII took several dwellings in King Street to create his new palace, the inhabitants began filling the area around Charing Cross and the Strand as well. The continuing concentration of the political and fashionable upper class in Westminster had a crucial effect upon its later development.

The enhanced royal presence had a great impact on the topography and landscape of Westminster from the 16ᵗʰ century. Henry VIII, in particular, had a lasting influence through his creation of St James's and Hyde parks, both opened to the public in the 17ᵗʰ century; the former was enlarged by the addition of Green Park. The royal parks provided central London with one of its most attractive features, at different periods becoming centres for fashionable gatherings, public meetings, and general recreation, and a welcome relief from pavements and buildings in the city as well as, especially in more recent decades, from the incessant road traffic.[3] St James's Park in particular, however, did have a significant effect on the development of Westminster, since it formed a physical break between the older settlement around Tothill Street and the abbey from the areas in northern Westminster, which saw new and more fashionable building from the 17ᵗʰ century onwards. Although there were some attractive pockets of modern houses south of the park, such as Queen Anne's Gate and some streets south

---

1 Binski, *Westm. Abbey*, 206.
2 S. Thurley, *Royal Palaces of Tudor England* (1993), esp. 39–63, fig. 92.

3 Reserved for treatment under Royal Ct & Govt, in a later vol.

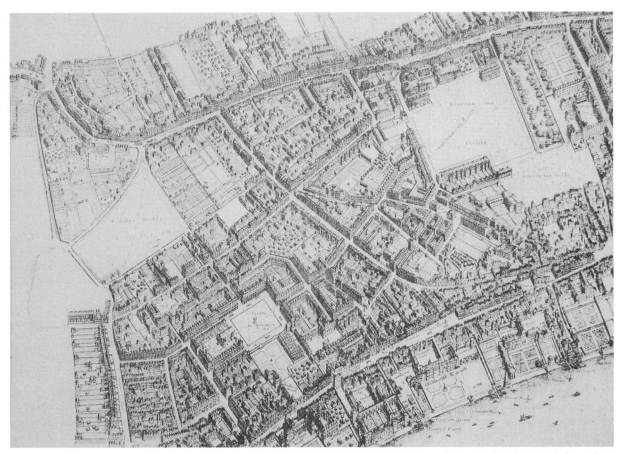

6. *Bird's eye plan by Wenceslaus Hollar, c.1660 of the west central district of London looking north from the Thames. The area depicted extends from St Martin's Lane (extreme left) almost to Temple Bar (just beyond right margin). The Strand follows the line of the Thames; it is lined with houses, shops and taverns, with behind them aristocratic mansions with gardens. Drury Lane runs from Temple Bar, past the north side of St Clement Danes, and north to High Holborn, the Roman road to Newgate. A new piazza covers the site of Covent Garden, with St Paul's church on the west side and Bedford House and grounds between the piazza and the Strand. This whole area of Westminster by then was built up as far as the boundary with St Giles; although there is still open ground, almost all the streets are lined with buildings.*

of the abbey, as time went on most of the Tothill area degenerated into some of the city's worst slums, as upper and middle class residents preferred the spacious and modern streets in northern Westminster.

Other urban schemes and buildings associated with the monarchy gave Westminster some of its most outstanding features and major attractions. Though Whitehall Palace was largely destroyed by fire in January 1697/8, Westminster Palace, St James's Palace, Somerset House (which had passed to the Crown in 1552), and Buckingham Palace (the former Buckingham House acquired in 1762) continued to grace the scene. In the early 19th century, the Prince Regent's desire for a grand route from his palace of Carlton House to Regent's Park was realized in Regent Street and its associated buildings, designed by John Nash, which had a major impact on the West End. The demolition of the royal mews at Charing made way for Trafalgar Square, London's grandest

public space, which had been proposed by Nash but was not fully realised as a national focus until the mid 19th century after two key elements, the National Gallery and Nelson's column, had been built. In the early 20th century, Admiralty Arch and the Mall were created to provide a ceremonial thoroughfare to Buckingham Palace.

The late 17th century saw the establishment of the Crown's first standing army, housed in Westminster. The advantages that a standing army had given Oliver Cromwell were not lost on Charles II, and soon after the Restoration a regiment of Foot Guards and two troops of Horse Guards were created for the king's protection, and known as the Life Guards. Horse Guards was built in Whitehall in 1663–4 to accommodate the Guards and their horses, replaced 1750–9 with a greatly enlarged building.[1] Additional barracks were provided later on the south side of Knightsbridge road in the 1760s, and in

1 *Hist. King's Works*, V. 433, 439–40.

7. *The Palace of Whitehall c.1650, from King Street looking south towards the early 16th-century Holbein Gate, with Inigo Jones's Banqueting House of 1619–22 on the east, adjoining older parts of the palace.*

Hyde Park in the 1790s;[1] by 1810 barracks on the south side of St James's Park later known as Wellington Barracks, were also occupied by the Guards.[2]

THE IMPACT OF SOCIETY

The presence of the government in Westminster and the regular meetings of Parliament, held from the revolution of 1688, meant a large and regular influx of leading aristocrats and their families, with whom a social life grew up and became formalized into the London Season. The presence of the monarchy and leading aristocrats and gentry meant that Westminster developed trades and services to meet their needs.

Westminster had a local market in King Street, which moved into the Woolstaple, on the north side of New Palace Yard, in the 16th century.[3] From the mid 17th century, new building laid out on former fields was accompanied by the introduction of retail markets created under the royal prerogative by letters patent; the most significant of these had permanent market houses or covered stalls, and were usually held three times a week. They included Clare market in St Clement Danes from *c.*1648 (confirmed in 1662), Covent Garden market by 1654 (confirmed 1670), St James's market, close to the west side of the Haymarket, licensed in 1663, Hungerford, on part of Hungerford Inn at Charing Cross, in 1678, Newport, near Leicester House, in 1686, and Lowndes, later Carnaby, on the east side of Carnaby Street, Soho, in 1720. The market-houses, most of which

had upper storeys, served as quasi-public buildings, often housing religious meetings of nonconformists, foreign churches, or parish charity schools.

Retail markets dwindled in the early 19th century as a wide range of provision shops appeared. In London, unlike other major English cities, the covered retail markets disappeared, and by the mid 19th century there remained only unofficial street markets, such as that in Berwick Street, used by the poor, catering for local needs, and eventually regulated. Only Covent Garden survived the trend, becoming a wholesale market, largely because of the size of the area in its charter and the continuous ownership of the freehold and franchise by a very wealthy family, which in the 19th century could improve its buildings and extend its area. By the time such private ownership became a drawback, Covent Garden had already achieved its unique position as a national wholesale market which set the fruit, vegetable and flower prices for the whole country.[4]

The collection of so many of the richest, most powerful and most fashionable people in England in Westminster for part of the year led to its taking a leading role in the development of a variety of social and cultural activities. Opera, theatre, and concerts were centred on the area, and it also became the focus of gentleman's clubs. Beyond the upper class, however, the people who lived and worked in the expanding Westminster of the 18th and 19th centuries gave it especial vibrancy. They created a vigorous intellectual life in a

1 *Survey of London*, XLV. 23–4, 64.
2 Pevsner, *London 6: Westm.* 690.
3 For the Woolstaple, below, Landownership: Other Eccles.

Ests (Coll. of St Mary and St Stephen).
4 *Survey of London*, XXXVI. 130.

8. *Weekday shoppers at Berwick Street market, July 2009.*

wide variety of spheres, not available at the universities at that time, and apparent in the numerous and diverse learned societies which from the mid 18th century were either set up in Westminster or moved there. These included the Royal Society (1666), the Royal Society of Arts (1754), the Royal Academy (1769), the Society of Antiquaries (1780), and the Royal Watercolour Society (1804). Ultimately, the importance of the connections available in the area, led many major companies in Great Britain to set up their headquarters in Westminster, even when most of their business took place elsewhere.

The opportunities that Westminster presented also attracted immigrants from overseas from the later 17th century. Huguenots moved out from their original centres in the City of London and Stepney to the West End. Later on, French émigrés came to Soho in the 1790s to escape persecution in the French Revolution. Jewish immigrants also moved westward from their settlements in the City and east of London. These groups particularly affected the tenor of religious life in Westminster.

THE DEVELOPMENT OF THE CITY

Much of the so-called westward expansion of London was actually the growth of Westminster northwards. Starting with St Clement Danes and Covent Garden in the mid 17th century, streets of houses were built over former fields and gardens, initially occupied by servants and tradesmen. Westminster had a number of crafts and trades, as did all the parishes surrounding the City of London, but its unique character meant it had special concentrations.

The increasing richness and vibrancy of Westminster

life meant a steady spread of building from the old centres of settlement. The influx of both the nobility and gentry, and the tradesmen and others serving them, put continual pressure on housing and inevitably led to new building on Westminster's fields and gardens. While in earlier centuries the leading politicians were contented with older houses as they became available, by the later 17th century ministers' growing importance led to the building of new and imposing mansions on former open fields. Meanwhile, more modest housing was being built for tradesmen and the new middle classes, beginning with the large-scale development of Covent Garden in the mid 17th century, which accelerated after the Restoration and, in particular, after the Great Fire of 1666 which destroyed so many homes in the City of London.

By the late 17th century the whole of St Clement Danes parish and the area of Covent Garden from the Strand to the boundary with St Giles was largely built up, the only remaining open ground being behind the buildings lining the streets. Several major houses such as Essex, Arundel, and Durham had been demolished to be replaced by streets, and those that still survived, such as Drury House, had lost their gardens to building. Development had extended westward from Covent Garden to line St Martin's Lane and Haymarket, and to fill the area between Piccadilly and St James's Park as far west as St James's Street. A great deal of building had been carried out around Soho Square and on the north side of Piccadilly at its eastern end, but open ground still remained in those areas, as did the gardens of mansions such as Leicester House, Newport House and Burlington

9. *Royal Opera House, Bow Street, established here in 1731–2 and rebuilt in 1857–8 to designs of E.M. Barry, with to its south Covent Garden market's Floral Hall, also designed by Barry and built in 1858–9.*

House. West of St James's Street was still largely fields or park, with an occasional major house or farm. By the road at the west end of St James's Park stood Arlington House and Tart Hall, with a few smaller houses lining the road and fields behind them. South of the park Petty France had been built up and a few other houses stood near the New Chapel and the north end of Tothill fields, while streets were being laid out south of the abbey precinct on the former orchard and fields near the tidal mill and down the Thames bank to the horse ferry.[1] The growth of housing was such that new civil parishes were created, accompanied by elegant and striking parish churches, many provided by the commission for building fifty new churches, creating a framework which remained the basis for local government in the city of Westminster until the end of the 19th century (above).

By the mid 18th century the eastern side of Westminster from its boundary with the liberties of the City of London as far west as New Bond Street comprised a mass of generally irregular streets and courts occasionally interspersed with an open square. Most of Mayfair was also built over up to Park Lane with a more regular grid of streets radiating from Grosvenor Square and Berkeley Square, though some streets on the west side of Berkeley Square were laid out but not yet built up. At Westminster, several streets and alleys full of houses were swept away for Westminster's first permanent link with the Surrey side of the Thames, Westminster bridge, built 1738–50, which was accompanied by the creation of some new streets to form the bridge approaches, including Parliament Street (later the southern end of Whitehall).[2] South of St James's Park was also densely built over as far west as the Broadway and south to the road to the horse ferry, but Tothill fields remained open land surrounded by cultivated fields and market gardens. The former vill of Eye remained unbuilt, with Hyde Park taking up a swathe in the north, and agricultural land south of the road to Knightsbridge. In the extreme south near the Thames, the Chelsea waterworks were laid out, with the remaining area, around the Neat House, cultivated as market and nursery gardens.[3]

By the second decade of the 19th century, the remaining open land in Mayfair had been built over, and building had begun to fill the main roads around Buckingham Palace. Some terraces of houses were beginning to appear along the road to Chelsea near the parish boundary. New streets had been laid out south of Horseferry Road, where the New Penitentiary was planned, and across the former Tothill fields area, where occasional building was starting to appear. The Chelsea waterworks now had several wharves close to the King's Road. Most of the area south of the waterworks was still market and nursery gardens, with some industrial buildings on the Thames bank. Building in Westminster south of St James's Park had extended westwards to Buckingham Palace and was starting to fill in the area southwards towards the former Tothill fields. The new Vauxhall Bridge Road was laid out to connect with Vauxhall bridge, opened in 1816.[4]

By 1835 the streets of Belgravia with Belgrave and Eaton squares had been laid out and much of the area was already built up southwards to the later Buckingham Palace Road. South of the latter the Grosvenor canal was opened in 1825[5] along the line of the old

1 Morgan, *Map of London* (1682).
2 Pevsner, *London 6: Westm.* 246, 273.
3 Rocque, *Map of London* (1741–5).
4 *Regency A to Z.*
5 Pevsner, *London 6: Westm.* 777.

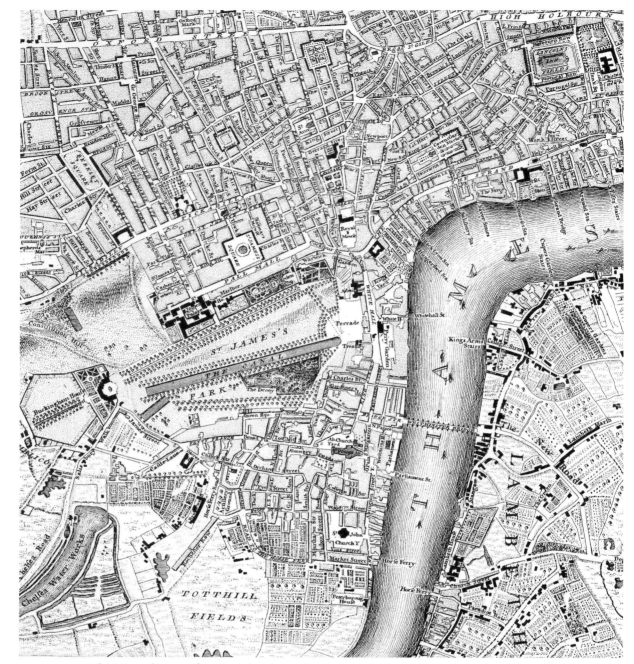

10. *John Rocque's map of 1741–5, detail showing the spread of building by the mid 18th century. The whole area between Soho Square in the north and Green Park to the west has been laid out with streets, and most of them are already built up.*

Chelsea waterworks from the Thames to the Grosvenor Basin, which with its wharves lay just south-west of Buckingham Palace in the area then known as Pimlico. Some market gardens still remained, though new roads had been laid out across the area, with some houses built near Vauxhall Bridge Road. In St Margaret's most of the former Tothill fields had been laid out with roads, and building was proceeding, including the prison and house of correction and a small area preserved for playing fields for Westminster School. In the detached part of St Margaret's, along the later Kensington Gore, some houses were being built by the highway.[1] Over the next 25 years all the remaining unbuilt land was laid out with streets and houses. The Grosvenor Basin was replaced with Victoria station, and railway lines ran south-west to the river alongside the remnant of the Grosvenor canal.

SINCE THE MID 19TH CENTURY

The population of the city of Westminster, which had

1 Plan of Westminster, 1835, *Archaeologia*, XXVI (1836), plate 27.

11. *Millbank Housing Estate, built, like the Tate Gallery, on the site of the former penitentiary, with all the blocks named after British artists. An impressive and costly scheme by the LCC to rehouse former slum dwellers displaced by various street improvement schemes, and completed in 1902, this photograph of 1963 shows Rossetti and Ruskin buildings.*

been 222,053 in 1841, reached its peak of just over a quarter of a million *c.*1861; thereafter it experienced a steady fall, from 254,533 in 1861, to 229,238 in 1881, 182,759 in 1901, 129,579 in 1931, 99,048 in 1951, and 61,022 in 2001.[1] Many factors contributed to this decline, which started even before the area of the City had been entirely built up. A factor peculiar to Westminster was the expansion of the government bureaucracy, which by the mid 19th century was being blamed for driving away families in the Whitehall area and turning residential accommodation into offices. The increase both in the number of government departments and in the size of existing departments led to a continual increase in the space occupied by the Civil Service, and although towards the end of the 20th century there was some impulse to move departments to provincial centres, aided by the development of internet connections and online government services, ministerial offices still needed to remain within physical reach of Parliament and cabinet meetings.

Westminster also suffered from the decline usual in inner London. As new suburban parishes around London north and south of the Thames were developed for residential housing, and transport links with the centre of London improved, many middle and lower-middle class residents moved away from the centre to the newer, attractive and healthier suburbs, a flight which is reflected in changes in religious activity and the closure of many churches in Westminster.

By the mid 19th century many of the areas in Westminster developed in the 18th century or earlier had degenerated into over-crowded slums occupied by the poor, and the Thames was heavily polluted, culminating in the infamous Great Stink of 1858. Population decline in those areas was firstly due to improvement schemes

12. *Leicester Square, an important venue for West End entertainment in the late 20th century, with the striking Odeon Cinema of 1937 on the east side.*

for new roads, which were deliberately run through slum areas in order to sweep away poor housing as well as to

1 ONS, *Census tables.*

13. *Aerial view of the west side of Whitehall, 2002, showing the New Government Offices, built 1899–1915, overlooking Parliament Square and Great George Street (top), and the Foreign and Commonwealth Office, built 1862–75, large complexes which dwarf Downing Street and the Treasury at the bottom of the picture.*

create more convenient road connections across Westminster: Victoria Street through the slums of Tothill, for example, or Shaftesbury Avenue through the southern part of Soho. Congestion along the Strand was ameliorated by the creation of the Victoria Embankment designed in 1858–9, with a road cutting through the former sites of Strand mansions and a sewer to help cleanse the Thames. Later on poor housing was also replaced under the Working Class Housing Acts, which again reduced the population in the affected localities, and from 1889 the London County Council (LCC) continued improvement schemes and built working-class housing itself, as it had difficulty in finding companies willing to provide dwellings. The scheme of 1895–9 to widen the Strand and to form Kingsway and the Aldwych displaced 3,700 people and radically altered the orientation of streets in the northern part of St Clement Danes, while the Westminster improvement scheme of 1900, involving the widening of Millbank, extension of Victoria Tower Gardens, and the embankment to Lambeth Bridge and street improvements near Smith Square, displaced 2,242 people; the LCC provided several housing estates, at Drury Lane and Millbank, to house some of those displaced. Despite such schemes, however, in 1902 35 per cent of Westminster's

population were considered to be living in poverty, and 13 per cent to be over-crowded; as a result efforts to house working-class residents continued into the later 20th century, by which time the Second World War had also helped to reduce the population.[1]

By the late 20th century rebuilding was endemic in much of Westminster as in other parts of central London. That was partly because the introduction of new technologies required different building specifications to house them satisfactorily, so that office buildings of the 1960s were replaced only 30 or 40 years later, but also because a rampant market for residential housing developed at the turn of the 21st century making it profitable to replace or convert offices, hospitals, and other large buildings with high-priced residential apartments. This trend may halt or reverse population decline, though it is unlikely to have much effect in the foreseeable future, as the high cost of private housing and the decline in social housing has put home-buying in the city of Westminster beyond the reach of most of the population.

Although many aspects of Westminster have changed over the centuries, at the start of the 21st century it remains the political centre for the United Kingdom, and the leading attraction for tourists and visitors to the

1 S. Durgan, ' "Profit with Benevolence"? Victorian Philanthropic Housing in Westm.', *Westm. Hist. Rev.* 2 (1998), 28–32; ead., 'Leading the Way: Council Housing in Westm.', *Westm. Hist. Rev.* 3 (1999), 25–32.

14. *Admiralty Arch in 1924. It was built 1908–11 as part of the national monument to Queen Victoria, with the Mall beyond and provided the imperial capital with an impressive processional route from Buckingham Palace, just visible in the background.*

British Isles, where Britain's royal and imperial past can be sampled. It also remains the national centre for fashion retailing and for selling products to the very rich, as well as to anyone else interested in the latest and most novel goods. Although local trades and manufacturing have largely disappeared, showrooms for fashion and other crafts still exist and some new specialisms have arisen. Soho, for example, became the centre for the film industry in the later 20th century, and remains an area with services for film and video as well as the newer digital industries. Traditionally an area housing immigrants from Europe, it still retains some of those aspects, together with a large Chinese community which has become a tourist attraction, and with some other parts of Westminster also attracts visitors to a wide range of restaurants, clubs, and other entertainments. Westminster shares in the economic polarization of residential central London, with some public housing but a great deal more very expensive private housing, while the presence of many overseas residents studying or working in London, has given new life to many churches in the city.

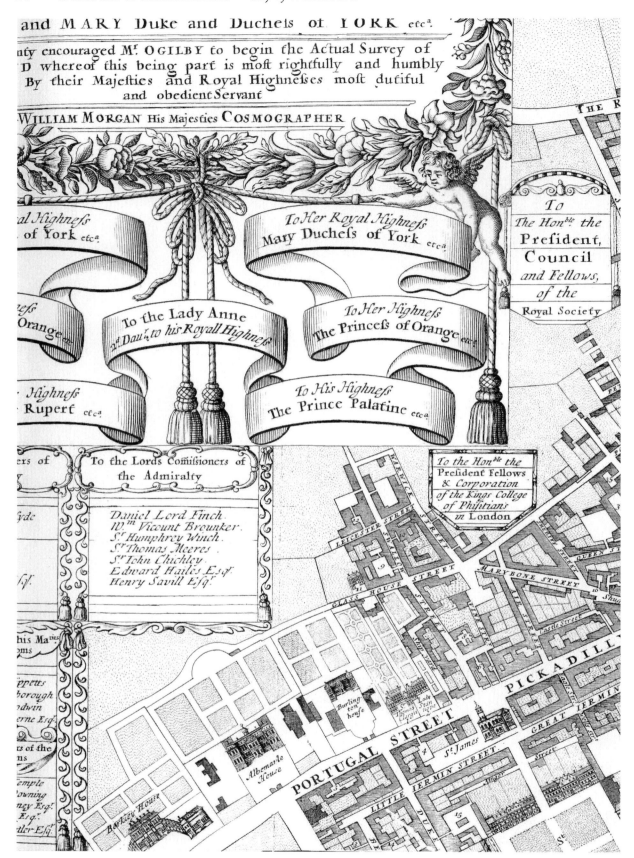

15. *William Morgan's map of 1682, section showing the newly-built streets north of St James's Park and west including Berkeley, Burlington and Albemarle houses in Piccadilly,*

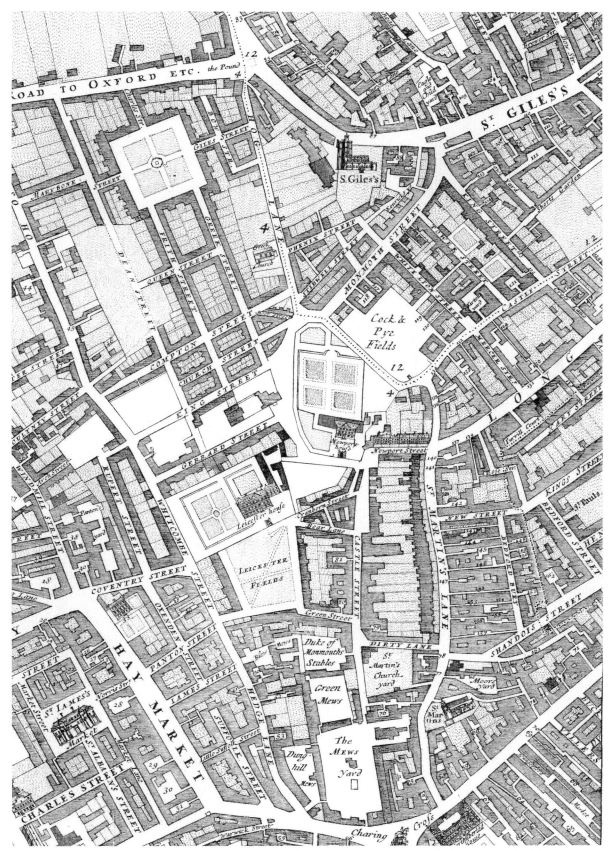

of St Martin's Lane. Many of the aristocratic mansions of the late 17th century were built on estates in this area, and Leicester and Newport houses near Soho.

LANDOWNERSHIP

THE CITY of Westminster was covered by two principal manors in 1086, the abbey's manor (Westminster) stretching from the boundary of the liberties of the City of London on the east to the Tyburn, and the vill of Eye from the Tyburn to the Westbourne; the latter, which was in secular hands until given to Westminster Abbey by 1097, was very different in landholding structure and customs from Westminster.

Those two manors covered all the area of the city of Westminster except for the band of land between the Strand and the river Thames from the Temple westwards to at least Charing Cross, and possibly all the way up to and including the palace precinct. The only property bordering the river in this band which was held of the abbey c.1196 was the messuage which became part of the Archbishop of York's inn, and it is not clear whether that had been part of Westminster manor or was a later acquisition by the abbey. The rest of the property by the river was either in the king's hands or held of him by tenants in chief other than the abbey; the eastern end from the Temple nearly to the Savoy was held of the honor of Leicester, and its tenants included the bishops of Llandaff and Bath and Wells, and the prior of St Sepulchre, Warwick. Other estates in this band of land were held by the archbishop of York and the bishops of Carlisle, Coventry, Durham, Norwich, and Worcester; the remainder comprised Almayne, Ronceval, Savoy and the Templars, as well as property later belonging to the college of St Stephen in the Palace of Westminster. The soke of Mohun was presumably also held of the king, and this intriguing estate, not well documented, could have included the advowson of St Martin-in-the-Fields.

By the high Middle Ages there were several free holdings in the manor of Westminster whose origin is unclear. They could have been descended from the villein holdings of 1086, or possibly the holdings of the abbot's knights, although where the service they were held for is known, it is almost entirely a money service and not a military one.

THE CROWN AND ESTATE FORMATION

Until the reign of Henry VIII the Crown had little direct land holding in Westminster apart from the precinct of the Palace of Westminster, which included some land by the Thames to the north of the palace. To this was added in 1399 property belonging to the duchy of Lancaster, which in Westminster consisted of the Savoy palace and quitrents and other dues from the land south of the Strand and in the southern half of St Clement Danes. From the 1530s, however, Henry VIII's desire for a new palace led to the enlargement of the palace precinct between the river Thames and King Street, and the addition of land on the west side of King Street for further royal building. Most of this was acquired from Westminster Abbey and St James's Hospital by exchange. The dissolution of religious houses from the late 1530s, and the subsequent suppression of chantries and religious guilds added more land to the Crown's holding in Westminster, and by 1540 Henry had acquired nearly all the unbuilt land in Westminster and Eye. Large tracts were emparked to form St James's Park, land largely acquired from the hospital of St James, and Hyde Park, which included the former manor of Hyde.

Whatever Henry's aim in acquiring the land – he may have wanted a demesne surrounding his new Palace of Whitehall, for example – the necessity of rewarding courtiers, and other financial needs, meant that much of his acquisition had to be granted away, quite a lot of it in fee. Further alienations were made under Edward VI, and although Elizabeth I's grants were mainly of 21-year leases, many more grants were made in the early 17th century, often for feefarm rents, themselves later granted away. Most of the estates covered below of 'modern' origin – that is formed in the 16th century or later – were the result of those grants by Henry VIII and his successors, and were mainly of agricultural land which was built on from the later 17th century, when restrictions on the growth of building in and around London were relaxed. A large block of land, mainly the former estate of St James's Hospital was retained by the Crown and used as dower for several queen consorts in the 17th century, though often let on long leases. Most of Henry's acquisitions which were not emparked or granted away were gathered into bailiwicks for management; in Westminster these were St James, which included more than just the former hospital land, Westminster, and Ebury/Neat.

The accounts below are arranged in three groups: the main manorial estates; other freehold estates, both lay and ecclesiastical, whose history is recorded in the medieval period; and later estates created from Crown grants, mainly of monastic and chantry property. They exclude the royal palaces and parks, and the Crown's own property in Westminster and elsewhere, now owned by the Crown Estate.[1] They deal chiefly with landownership up to the period of substantial urban development, a detailed account of which will be given in a subsequent volume. In general the buildings described are the principal houses of each estate; those built by tenants and lessees are mostly excluded.

---

1 To be treated under Royal Court and Govt in a later vol.

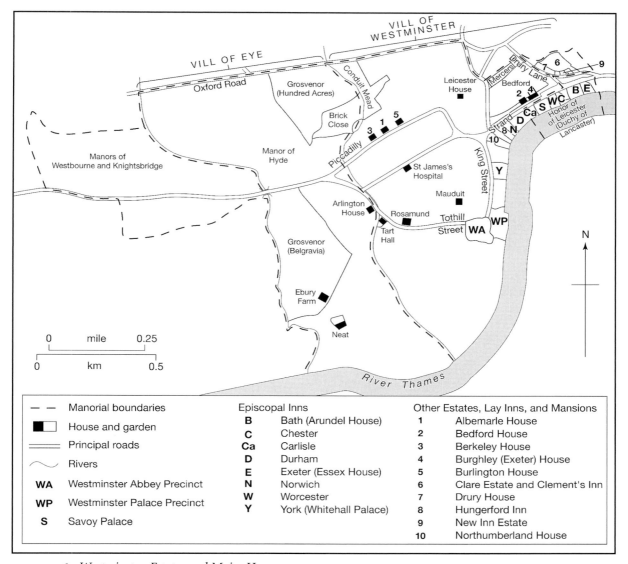

16. Westminster: Estates and Major Houses.

MANORIAL ESTATES

MANOR OF WESTMINSTER

The manor of Westminster was part of the foundation grant of Westminster Abbey. King Edgar permitted Archbishop Dunstan to buy 5 *mansiunculas* ('hides') *c*.959 from the royal demesne to endow the church and monks at the place called Westminster, part of the land which it was claimed had formerly been given to the monks by King Offa; the bounds given were the Tyburn on the west, the old wooden church of St Andrew (St Andrew, Holborn) and London fen on the east, the main highway (later Oxford Street) on the north and the middle of the Thames on the south.[1] The boundaries of the earlier estate seem to have remained roughly the same in 1002 when King Æthelred II granted additional land at *Berewican*, near Tyburn.[2] The main change seems to be the exclusion of land between the river and the highway later called the Strand and there referred to as Akeman Street, although the bounds as described are very imprecise in this area. The extension of the City's

---

1 Birch, *Cart. Saxon.* no. 1048, vol. III, p. 260; Sawyer, *A.-S. Charters*, no. 670; Harvey, *Westm. Abbey Ests*, 354–5.

2 Sawyer, *A.-S. Charters*, no. 903; Gelling, 'Boundaries', 101–4.

liberty to Temple Bar is almost certainly later. The use of the alderman's mark to define the eastern boundary apparently refers to a marker in front of the wall (as in Winchester), presumably on about the line of the Fleet. The extension of the City liberty westwards to Temple Bar accompanied the expansion of the suburb along the line of Fleet Street, perhaps in the 12th century; there are indications that 'beyond the Fleet' was not recognized as a ward in the 1120s and that the abbot was still claiming lordship of churches in Fleet Street in the 1180s.[1] At some date, possibly after 1185, the manor also lost a wedge-shaped piece of land along Chancery Lane, which was later in the liberty of the Rolls.[2]

Berewican was probably the berewick (*berwicum*, outlier) of the vill of Westminster called *Totenhala* granted *c.*1086 by Abbot Gilbert to Baynard to hold for life, for service of a knight,[3] and can be identified with the 3 hides held in 1086 by the abbot's only tenant in chief in the vill, Bainiard, and valued at £6 in 1065, £1 when he received it (*c.*1086), and £3 in 1086.[4] A 13th-century copy of the so-called '*Telligraphus* of Blessed King Edward' names the 3 hides as *Totenheale*.[5] The estate was held by a descendant of Baynard in 1166, who was listed among the abbot's enfeoffed knights, and passed with the holders of Baynard's Castle in London.[6] Most historians of Westminster, following Robinson, have identified *Totenhala* with Tothill,[7] while overlooking the obvious link with *Totenhale* (Tottenhall in Blooms-bury), which later belonged to the dean and chapter of St Paul's. Tothill is a very unlikely identification since lists of the abbey's lands put *Totenheale* outside the vill of Westminster but among its nearby manors such as Knightsbridge and Paddington. The subinfeudated berewick was never recovered by the abbey, while Tothill, on the abbey's doorstep, was part of its medieval demesne.

In 1086 the abbey's Westminster manor consisted of 13½ hides in the (unnamed) vill in which the abbey stood, with 19 villeins and 42 cottars; it had always belonged to the demesne of St Peter's Church, Westminster.[8] It may also have included the abbey's manors of Chelsea, Knightsbridge, and Paddington,[9] which were not separately mentioned in the Domesday Book. Said to have been worth £10 when the abbot received it (in 1049), it was valued at £12 in 1065, and £10 again in 1086.

By 1065, land near the abbey had been taken for the palace and its precinct, and by *c.*1100 land by the northern boundary was taken out of the manor to found the hospital of St Giles and its parish, though the manor of Westminster still had residual links with the parish of St Giles-in-the-Fields at the Dissolution.[10] The hidage of Middlesex *c.*1125 gives the same assessment as Domesday, namely 16½ hides including *Totenhale*,[11] but soon afterwards King Stephen acquitted the monks of geld on 6½ hides in the manor because the court and palace and the infirmary of St Giles were situated there.[12]

Although the manor as a whole was held by the abbey in demesne at all times, from Henry II's reign the abbey resumed by gift or purchase many parcels of land held in fee within the manorial boundaries.[13] That suggests that much land within the manor had been subinfeudated by the abbey after 1086, though some of the land perhaps originated as the villein holdings of 1086. Confirmations by the abbey indicate a lot of land was granted in fee for a small money service, particularly property held by royal officials. Holdings in the manor were assigned among various offices within the abbey, and income was divided between the prior's office, cellarer, sacrist, chamber, infirmarer, refectory, almoner, keeper of the chapel of St Mary, and new (building) work of the abbey.[14] Most received both fixed rents from property granted in fee and rents from leased land from the demesne under the economic control of the abbey.

In 1535 the abbey's gross income from its property in the vill of Westminster was about £400.[15] Although large, it had once been larger, for by then it no longer held the property in Westminster which Henry had forced it to exchange in 1531 to found Whitehall Palace. That exchange comprised all the abbey's property on the west side of King Street from the Axe brewhouse in the south to Charing Cross in the north; its holdings on the east side of King Street between St Mary Ronceval at the north end and the palace in the south; and all its land from St James's Hospital south to Tothill Street between Longditch on the east and Eybridge on the west, including Rosamund and Petty Caleys (the area which became St James's Park).[16] In 1536 the abbot also had to exchange with the king his manor of Neat and several other properties including most of the abbot's portion in Westminster.[17] The remainder of the abbey's rights and property were surrendered to the king in January 1540 when the convent was dissolved.[18]

1 D. Keene, 'London from the Post-Roman Period to 1300', in *The Cambridge Urban History of Britain* I: 600–1540 (Cambridge, 2000), 192; Gelling, 'Boundaries'. *TLMAS* n. s. 11 (1953), 101–4; below, Religious Life: Intro.

2 *Rec. Templars* (1185) still included Chancery Lane in vill of Westm.

3 Robinson, *Gilbert Crispin*, 38.

4 *VCH Middx*, I. 122.

5 Robinson, *Gilbert Crispin*, 40; *Manuscripts of Westminster Abbey* (1909), 24; BL, Cotton Faust. A. III, f. 47.

6 Robinson, *Gilbert Crispin*, 38.

7 Robinson, *Gilbert Crispin*, 40–1.

8 *VCH Middx*, I. 122.

9 Harvey, *Westm. Abbey Ests*, 354.

10 Croft called Lyndrapers in St Giles: TNA, SC 12/3/13.

11 *VCH Middx*, I. 137.

12 *Westm. Charters*, p. 67 (no. 118).

13 Rosser, *Medieval Westm.* 45–50. Recorded in WAD, and orig. deeds in WAM.

14 Harvey, *Westm. Abbey Ests*, 354.

15 *Valor Eccl.* I. 410–23.

16 TNA, E 211/72.

17 TNA, E 305/3/B44; *L&P Hen VIII*, XI, pp. 84–5.

18 *VCH London*, I. 447.

DEAN AND CHAPTER'S ESTATE

At the end of 1540 the bishopric of Westminster was created, and the former monastery was reconstituted as a cathedral church. In addition to the bishop, the cathedral establishment included a chapter comprising a dean and 12 prebendaries or canons, the last abbot of Westminster, William Boston (also Benson), becoming the first dean.[1] In 1542 the king granted estates to the new dean and chapter to fulfil various obligations in addition to maintaining the abbey church and its functions; property granted then included rents of assize, quitrents, and leaseholds in the city of Westminster, St Martin-in-the-Fields, St Mary of Strand, and St Clement Danes, a field in St Giles-in-the-Field, and the rectories of St Margaret's and St Martin-in-the-Fields, to a total value of £402.[2] The chapter incurred many costs before receiving their estates, including building a school house and chambers by command of the king, and charges in the suit to establish the cathedral church, towards which the king allowed £200 to be written off in 1544 against the amount they owed him.[3] Another of the chapter's obligations was to support 20 students in the universities of Oxford and Cambridge; to be relieved of this, the dean and chapter granted back to the king in 1545 manors in Essex and 3 messuages and two gardens in Longditch,[4] and in 1546 several more properties in Westminster, including the watermill, meadows, and gardens on the south side of the abbey close, and buildings in the sanctuary.[5]

In 1550 the bishopric of Westminster was abolished and its diocese was united with the bishopric of London. At the same time the institution of the dean and chapter of Westminster was confirmed.[6] In 1556 the chapter's Westminster estate was surrendered to the re-instituted abbey,[7] but returned to the restored dean and chapter in 1560.[8] When the property was confirmed to the dean and chapter by James I in 1604, it was referred to as 'that manor of Westminster in Westminster';[9] the earlier grants do not mention a manor of Westminster nor any particular liberties and franchises in the grants.

The dean and chapter's Westminster estate consisted of the cathedral church and precinct; the rectory and church of St Margaret's; the manor of Knightsbridge; messuages within the close; buildings and land outside the close, in Tothill Street, the Almonry, and Longditch, within the precinct of the sanctuary, in King Street and Thieving Lane, and within the cemetery of St Margaret; yearly tithes of the rectory of St Martin-in-the-Fields; messuages, rents and service in Charing Cross Street (the

western end of the Strand), in the parishes of St Martin-in-the-Fields and St Mary of Strand, and outside the bars of Temple Bar; a yearly rent of 6s. 8d. and service from a croft of land called Lyndrapers in St Giles-in-the-Fields; 12d. from a tenement formerly held by Elizabeth Stockwood in St Martin-in-the-Fields; a yearly pension of 66s. 8d. from lands formerly of the college of St Stephen Westminster; the advowson of the vicarage and free chapel of St Mary Magdalen, Tothill Street; the head and spring of the canal or aqueduct in Crossleys Field in Hyde Park, and the aqueduct thence to the abbey, with rights of entry to inspect and repair.[10]

In 1645 a new dean was appointed but not installed, and a special committee was established by the House of Commons to oversee the collegiate church and its income.[11] When in 1649 all deans and chapters were abolished and their lands made available for sale,[12] an Act for the continuance of the school and almshouses of Westminster transferred the chapter's Westminster estate and other lands to some 56 named governors, to manage and fulfil obligations of the former chapter costing in all £1,930.[13] Much of the estate's management therefore carried on as before. In 1660 the manor was restored to the chapter.

The dean and chapter continued to hold the Westminster estate, consisting of rents and quitrents mainly in St Margaret's parish and a few in the Strand, until 1869. The estate was reduced in the 18th and 19th centuries by small sales for public works, such as Westminster Bridge, new streets, and improvement schemes. Westminster School, supported from the income of the dean and chapter, had been so neglected by them that under the Public Schools Act, 1868, an independent governing body was set up to manage the school. Some property in the abbey precinct, mainly in Little Dean's Yard, was transferred to the governing body, to include three of the chapter's houses when each became vacant. The latter included the distinguished Ashburnham House, which despite efforts by the dean and chapter to transfer another in its place, was lost to the chapter in 1881 on the death of its occupant.[14]

In 1869, after long pressure by the Ecclesiastical Commissioners and strong resistance by the chapter, the Scheme for the commutation of the chapter's estates was established by Order in Council, under which most of the estates of the dean and chapter (excluding the abbey precinct) were transferred to the Ecclesiastical Commissioners.[15] The chapter retained ownership of, and received additions to, some lands in western counties (mainly Herefs. and Worcs.), together with Belsize

1 *L&P Hen VIII*, XVI, pp. 154, 174.
2 TNA, E 315/426, ff. 33–5.
3 TNA, E 315/104, f. 77v.
4 TNA, E 305/7/D42.
5 TNA, E 305/10/E76.
6 Act 5 & 6 Edward VI, c. 10 (Private).
7 *Cal. Pat.* 1555–7, 348–50.
8 Ibid. 1558–60, 397–403.

8 TNA, C 66/1639, m. 17.
10 *Cal. Pat.* 1558–60, 397–403.
11 *VCH London*, I. 453; WAM 18179, 18186, 18192.
12 *Acts and Ordinances of the Interregnum, 1642–60*, II. 81–104.
13 Ibid., II. 256–77.
14 *A House of Kings*, ed. E. Carpenter (1966), 290–1, 324–6.
15 *London Gaz.* 13 Aug. 1869, 4524–47.

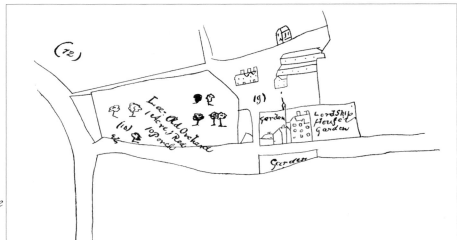

17. *The buildings of Ebury Farm in 1675, when its house was known as Lordship House.*

House (Hampstead) and property in Broad Sanctuary and Abingdon Street, Westminster, to provide them with an income of £20,000 considered sufficient to pay all salaries and wages and maintain church services and the fabric of the church and collegiate buildings.[1] Some alteration to this was made in 1888.[2]

MANOR OF EYE (EBURY)

In 1066 the manor of Eia or Eye was held by Harold, son of Earl Ralf, then under the guardianship of Queen Edith, widow of King Edward the Confessor. Subsequently William the chamberlain held it of the queen in feefarm for £3 a year, and after her death he continued to hold it of the king until losing it in 1082. In 1086 it was held by Geoffrey de Mandeville, earl of Essex, and the £3 had not been paid for four years.[3] Describing it as his 'little manor near the church', Geoffrey granted Eye to Westminster Abbey in perpetuity for the souls of himself, his children, and his first wife Athelais, who was buried in the abbey cloister.[4] The grant was confirmed by William II by 1097, and subsequently by Henry I.[5] The abbey held the manor until 1536, apart from a period following a vacancy of the abbacy, presumably on the death of Abbot Richard de Kedyngton in 1315, when Edward II retained the manor, called then Eyebury and Neat (*La Neyte*), holding it until his death.[6] On his accession in 1327 Edward III ordered Eyebury and Neat to be delivered to the abbot.[7]

Eye covered the whole area between two rivers, the Tyburn on the east, marking the boundary with the vill of Westminster, and the Westbourne on the west, and stretched from the Roman road (Bayswater Road) on the north to the Thames. Confusion over the nomenclature and number of manors in Eye[8] seems to stem from contemporary use of 'manor' to indicate a residence and the fact that the abbot, the lord of the manor, occupied a house at Neat rather than at the nearby demesne farm, which was eventually called Eybury or Ebury. Neat was thus part of the manor of Eye, while Hyde (below), also linked with Eye, was a sub-manor held by a freeholder and later acquired by the abbey. Courts are only found for Eye, or Ebury as it was later called, and Neat was part of that manor. As Eye was a Domesday manor, land within its bounds was also referred to in the Middle Ages as being in the vill of Eye. Villeins and others were listed in 1086, and their holdings may be the forerunners of the freeholders' estates. These were quite extensive in the 13th century, but the abbey gradually resumed possession of much by gift and purchase.

In 1536 the manor of Ebury with Neat and Hyde were among the lands which the abbot granted to Henry VIII in an exchange,[9] and the king also acquired, by purchase and exchange, most of the smaller parcels of Eye still held by freeholders. In 1536 Sir Anthony Browne was appointed bailiff of Ebury, Neat, and Hyde, and keeper of Neat (house) and the garden there, with fees of 2*d.* a day as bailiff, 2*d.* as keeper of Neat, and 2*d.* as keeper of the garden.[10] Under the Crown the house at Neat and the rents from Ebury and other land in Eye and Westminster acquired by Henry VIII were accounted for as the bailiwick of Neat.

The freehold of the manor was disposed of by the

1 *House of Kings*, 320. Manorial rights will be treated under Local Govt in a later vol.   2 *VCH Middx*, IX. 96.

3 *VCH Middx*, I. 125.

4 Robinson, *Gilbert Crispin*, 139. As extent of manor was 10 hides, its 'littleness' presumably referred either to manor bldgs, or to its role in his ests.

5 *Reg. Regum Anglo-Norm.* I. 102; ibid. II. 57.

6 *Cal. Close*, 1327–30, 4; *Cal. Pat.* 1324–7, 121; 1348–50, 141. Accts by king's bailiff survive from 1316: TNA, SC 6/919/14.

7 *Cal. Close*, 1327–30, 4.

8 E.g. manor of la Neyte cum Eyebury, 1318: TNA, E 210/6937.

9 TNA, E 305/3/B44.

10 TNA, E 315/232, f. 58.

Crown in the same divisions in which the abbot of West-minster had leased the lands. Most of the land remained in the manor called Ebury, but included in it were some Crown acquisitions in Westminster; the lease of this land until the sale of the freehold in 1623 is described below. The origin and later descent of Neat, which from 1536 passed separately with some adjoining land, is also described below. The later history of the bulk of the estate, after 1623, is dealt with under Later Estates (Grosvenor). Some small parcels in the manor, sold in 1564, are dealt with under Later Estates (Jennings). A few others were incorporated into Hyde Park, which is reserved for treatment in a separate volume dealing with the Royal Court and National Government and including the royal parks.

The Lease of Ebury

In 1519 the abbot let the manorial site, Ebury farm, with all its demesne and grazing, amounting to approxi-mately 478 acres, and 2 closes in Longmore in the vill of Westminster, to Richard Whashe, together its rents and juridical rights, for 32 years at £21 a year and 6 loads of hay cut in Neat. The lease specifically excluded Neat house and its garden, and other associated property, all occupied by the abbot (below, Neat). At least three other demesne parcels, Priors croft, Priors Hope, and Brick close, let in 1520 to Elizabeth Vincent for 39 years at 33s. 4d.,[1] must also have been excluded from Whashe's possession. Whashe had a house near Thamesmead, possibly Ebury farm,[2] and other land in Westminster, and was one of four wealthy Westminster residents contributing to the loan of 1522.[3] By 1536 the lease had passed to William Whashe of Ebury, probably Richard's son, but in 1544 William's children, William and Joan, were taxed on land or orphan's goods in Westminster, and the lease and interest were in the possession of John Wevant and his wife Isabel, perhaps William's widow; in 1544 they surrendered it to the Crown for another lease for 41 years.[4] A lease in reversion for 31 years from 1584 was granted to William Gibbes, gentleman pensioner, in 1567,[5] and a few days later he assigned his interest to William Whashe. Whashe by his will of 1569 left the lease and reversion to his son Francis, with his widow Margery having the profits for life on payment of lega-cies to the children. She married Christopher Lacon and the lease was assigned in trust. After Lacon's death Margery asked the trustees to assign it to John Southcott for her and her children. She then married Edmund Yorke and with her husband and Southcott assigned the lease to William Worley; in view of later possession of

the lease, this may have been a sale rather than in trust. Worley left it to his son who assigned it to Cuthbert Lynde.[6] In 1591 Francis Whashe sought possession under Gibbes' lease against Lynde, presumably unsuc-cessfully since in 1595 and 1597 he sought to have an adverse chancery decree overturned.[7] However, in 1596 a tenant of some fields under lease from the Yorkes claimed against Francis Whashe who had taken posses-sion as administrator of his father's goods.[8]

In 1584 the Crown granted a lease in reversion to Thomas Knyvett, gentleman of the bedchamber, later created Baron Knyvett of Escrick, for 60 years from 1615,[9] and in 1591 Knyvett assigned a moiety each to Cuthbert Lynde or Lyne and Edmund Doubleday. In 1611 the holders implied that they had possession under Gibbes's lease as well as the lease in reversion, when they sold back to King James their leasehold interest in three pieces of land by St James's Park, totalling 4½ acres, used for the Mulberry Garden.[10] Lynde's moiety passed to his son Humphrey Lynde (knighted 1613)[11] and in 1614 Lynde and Doubleday made a partition of the manor, each paying their part of the rent to the Crown. Lynde's portion was assigned to William Hay or Hayes in 1614, and after the latter's death was sold for £4,670 in 1618 to trustees for Sir Lionel Cranfield, later earl of Middlesex, who bought the freehold of the whole manor in 1623.[12] Edmund Doubleday died c.1620 and his portion, which included Ebury farm, passed to his executor, William Man. Man assigned a third in 1623 to trustees for Doubleday's widow Margaret, her husband John Duncombe, gentleman sewer to Prince Charles, and their issue for the remainder of the term;[13] in 1646 Frances, widow of Thomas Doubleday, Francis Doubleday, and John Duncombe all held shares in Ebury farm.[14] The family's interest may have continued until the Crown lease expired in 1675. Possession of this farm then passed to the owner of the freehold, the guard-ians of Alexander Davies's heir, Mary, and subsequently to her husband and heirs, the Grosvenor family.[15]

Ebury farm and its outbuildings lay on the north side what is now Buckingham Palace Road near the junction with Pimlico Road. In a plan of 1675 it is called Lordship House and is shown as a three-story building of 17th-century appearance.[16]

NEAT

At the beginning of the 13th century the site that was later known as Neat was called in Latin *insula*, the island; in English this was rendered as the 'Eyte' (ait),[17] of which 'Neyte' or 'Neat' was a corruption. This 'island' was

1 WAM 4823.
2 TNA, SC 12/11/42.
3 TNA, SP 1/25, frame 205.
4 TNA, E 315/216, f. 147v.
5 *Cal. Pat.* 1566–9, 41.
6 TNA, SP 12/173, no. 42.
7 TNA, C 2/Eliz/W23/48; W8/56; W6/59.
8 TNA, C 2/Eliz/F9/47.
9 TNA, C 66/1259, m. 16.
10 TNA, E 214/1154; below, Later Creations (Buckingham Ho.).

11 Shaw, *Kts of Eng.* II. 153.
12 Below, Later Creations: Grosvenor.
13 TNA, C 8/636/9.
14 *Cal. Cttee Comp.* II. 1340, 1521, 1592.
15 Below, Later Creations (Grosvenor).
16 Rutton, 'Manor of Eia', 50–1.
17 Earliest known use of Eyte is Rob. del Eyte in mid 13th cent.: WAD, f. 334. 1st ref. to site 1283x1307: f. 333.

probably the freehold in the vill or manor of Eye which Arnald of Harlow held of Westminster Abbey, and which passed to William of Harlow. In 1206 William granted to William le Petit (*parvus*), of Eye 3 acres of land, an acre of meadow and two messuages in Eye for a service of 5*s*.[1] Between 1217 and 1221 he also granted to Petit all the land he held of Westminster Abbey in the vill of Eye, described as a hide and half a virgate, with appurtenances which included water and mills, stew-ponds and fisheries. For this Petit was to pay William and his heirs 100*s*. a year and the 6*s*. annual service to the abbey.[2]

Petit's property apparently passed to his son Laurence, a clerk, who granted to Westminster Abbey for the souls of himself and his parents all his land in the island formerly held by Arnald of Harlow, then described as the whole enclosure and everything in it and around the island with the mill and appurtenances. In return the abbey was to pay the 100*s*. due to William of Harlow. Thereafter, the abbey granted to Laurence half a virgate which his father had held of the abbey, another half virgate which his father had held of William of Harlow, and all the liberties that Harlow had held except the close of the island. By a fine in 1236 Laurence warranted to the abbey a carucate in the island of Eye in return for 11 marks a year for life. William of Harlow confirmed Laurence's grant, and also granted to the abbey, in exchange for land elsewhere, the fee, homage and service of 100*s*. that Laurence rendered to him both for the whole close of the island as well as for the half virgate outside the close.[3]

Neat was thereafter held in demesne by Westminster Abbey with Eye as part of the abbot's portion of the estates,[4] and the abbot had a residence there soon after its acquisition. At a date after 1238 the abbot, probably Richard of Berking (d. 1246), ordained a chaplain to say masses to St Mary in the chapel of the island,[5] which later provided reeds for strewing in the abbey church on Richard's anniversary.[6] In 1271 the abbot granted the convent the right to order his steward to use his goods from the island and Eye to repair the Thames walls in his absence should it be necessary.[7] Successive abbots continued to keep Neat and its close in hand as a residence, but temporarily lost possession to Edward II with the manor of Eye from 1315 to 1327.[8] Edward used it as a residence and so later did other members of the royal house; the Black Prince stayed there in 1360 and 1361.[9] In 1389 its accommodation was sufficiently desirable for John of Gaunt to ask for temporary use of it for himself

and his household during a session of Parliament, possibly 1384.[10] The buildings included a great chamber, the chapel with an image of St Mary, a lower chamber next to the gate, a bakehouse and a kitchen,[11] and the site, of about 2 acres, had productive gardens from which not only a wide range of herbs and vegetables were obtained but also hemp, flax, and willows in the 14th century.[12] By the end of the 15th century the gardens also produced medicinal herbs for the abbey, prepared in a distillery in the abbot's garden.[13]

The abbot still occupied Neat in 1535, and received the rents from its lands and tenants.[14] Described in 1536 as a moated manor house, its associated amenities which included buildings, gardens, orchards, and fishing suggest that it was indeed a place of recreational resort for the abbot. In that year, it formed part of his forced exchange of property with Henry VIII which also included the land excepted out of the lease of Ebury in 1519, namely a close lying opposite the site on the south side called Twenty Acres, a meadow called Abbotsmead, later said to be 14 acres, and a piece of land on the east side called Calsehawe or Cawsey wall.[15] These lands were presumably those valued separately in 1535 as occupied by the abbot. The king appointed Sir Anthony Browne as keeper of the manor house at Neat and bailiff for life in 1536,[16] and he received a lease for 21 years of Abbotsmead and the close of 14 acres at Neat, as well as most of the small parcels bought by Henry VIII and included in the bailiwick of Neat, amounting to about 96 acres. All the land except Neat and its gardens were in the hands of tenants.[17]

In 1537 the king allowed Thomas Cromwell to use Neat as a residence when his house at the Rolls became plague-stricken.[18] In 1545 Sir Anthony Browne, by then the king's master of the horse, requested the purchase of Neat house and its site and gardens, and this was granted in 1547 after the king's death, to be held by knight service and 9*s*. 8¾*d*. a year.[19] No land was specified but later descriptions of the site seem to indicate that the Twenty Acres, stretching from the house site to the Thames, was included. He died in 1548 and was succeeded by his son, also Sir Anthony. In 1549 the 'farm place' called the Neat was held by Browne, who kept a man there but let the 73 acres of arable, 22 of meadow, and 14 of pasture which he leased from the king.[20]

In 1551 Sir Arthur Darcy was granted the freehold of a close of 14 acres by Neat and Abbotsmead, described as

1 TNA, CP 25/1/146/3, no. 40.
2 WAD, f. 100.
3 WAD, ff. 100v.–101v.; TNA, CP 25/1/146/10, no. 144.
4 Harvey, *Westm. Abbey Ests*, 428.
5 Ibid., 166, 361; WAD, f. 638.
6 WAD, f. 378.
7 WAD, f. 94.
8 Above, Manor of Eye.
9 *Black Prince's Reg*. IV. 351, 371–2, 378.
10 WAM 4761*.   11 TNA, E 210/6937.

12 M. Thick, *The Neat House Gardens* (1998), 80–1.
13 B. F. Harvey, *Living and Dying in England: 1100–1540* (1993), 84.   14 *Valor Eccl*. I. 410.
15 Above, Manor of Westm.
16 TNA, E 315/232, f. 58.
17 TNA, E 315/209, f. 36v.
18 *L&P Hen. VIII*, XII (2), p. 491 (App. 44).
19 TNA, E 318/6/184; *Cal. Pat*. 1547–48, 241.
20 J.V. Kitto, *St Martin-in-the-Fields, Churchwardens' Accts 1525–1603* (1901), 579–80.

being in the parish of St Margaret's,[1] to hold by 1/40th of a knight's fee and annual payments of 9s. 10d. as tenths and 25s. 1d. as feefarm rent.[2] Though there was confusion here and in other references to the location and acreage, the grant seems to be of the close lying on the east side of Neat. In 1557 Browne, created Viscount Montague in 1554, conveyed the capital messuage and house called the Neat together with 2 tofts, a dovecot, garden, and orchard, and 10 acres of land, 10 of meadow, 12 of pasture, 3 of wood, and 12 of waste, all in the parish of St Martin-in-the-Fields, to Darcy and his heirs. It presumably included the Twenty Acres, and possibly his leasehold interest in Calseyhawe and Abbotsmead:[3] by 1560 Darcy held a Crown lease of the other parcels of land which Browne had held in 1537.[4] In 1560 Darcy conveyed Neat with Abbotsmead and Twenty Acres to Sir William Cecil (later Lord Burghley), the queen's principal secretary.[5] The tenths and feefarm rent reserved on Neat were conveyed by the Crown to John Conyers and William Haber in 1564; they are not recorded thereafter, so were probably also conveyed to Cecil. In 1579 Cecil granted Abbotsmead back to the Crown as part of an exchange, with a proviso for its grant to Thomas Vincent.[6] Thereafter it passed separately from the rest of Neat (below).

Neat House and the Twenty Acres

After Burghley's death in 1598 Neat House and the remaining Twenty Acres passed to his heir Thomas, Lord Burghley, later earl of Exeter, and was settled by him as the Neat farm near Tothill fields with other estates in 1611.[7] The Cecil family seem to have disposed of the property thereafter, as in 1675 it was in the possession of Edward Peck,[8] and in 1685 William Peck and his wife Gertrude conveyed the manor of Neat with a messuage, 6 cottages, 10 gardens, 20 acres of land, and 3 of meadow in the parishes of St Martin-in-the-Fields and Colebrooke (Stanwell), with other manors to Paul Bowes and Philip Weston for 100 years at 1s. a year, possibly a mortgage or settlement.[9] In 1723 the estate was said to belong to Mr Stanley, and seems to have descended in the Sloane Stanley family of Paultons (Hants.), as it was the property of Cyril Sloane Stanley in the 1920s.[10]

The abbatial house itself survived at least until 1685. The earliest representations of it were made in 1614, when it was moated and had three ranges round a courtyard open to the road, and in 1675, when it is shown more sketchily as incorporating a tower. The site lay

across the west end of the modern Warwick Way where it meets Ebury Bridge.[11]

Abbotsmead

The freehold of Abbotsmead was sold by James I to William Whitmore and James Verdun, from whom it was bought in 1616 by William Man and John Burgess in trust for Edward Doubleday. Man then bought it from Doubleday, who with Burgess released it to him in 1618.[12] Man held it at his death in 1635 as 14 acres of meadow, with tenements, stables and other buildings on it, and with his other property it passed to John and Dorothy Ingham.[13] By 1650 it was in the possession of Roger Price and his wife Ann, and was settled on them and their children in 1658. The property was used to secure a loan in 1679, with a 500-year lease, and with Price's consent this term was assigned in 1688 to Thomas Price, whose relationship (if any) to Roger is not known. In 1709 Roger's children sold their interest to Thomas Price's son and heir Pendock Price, who held the 500-year term. In 1713 Pendock sold it to Henry Wise, who held it in 1730.[14] In the 1920s part belonged to Sir Watham Waller, Bt, to whom it had passed from the Wise family by marriage.[15]

HYDE

Hyde is recorded in the late 13th century as an estate held of the abbey by the Kendale family. Before 1283, Abbot Richard de Ware of Westminster granted two *culturas* of land in Cressewellfield and Ossuleston, together with pasture and meadow and 2 acres of land beside the Westbourne river and another 2 acres near the highway, to Sir Hugh of Kendale for life. In 1285, Hugh and John of Kendale brought a suit against Abbot Walter and the monks for warranty in 90 acres land in Eye which they claimed to hold by charter, and the abbey confirmed all the land to Hugh and John and their heirs for suit of court and 4d. a year.[16] In 1291 Sir Hugh and John acquired the freehold of 5 acres, 'next to the Hyde' and adjoining their land, from William son of John of Paddington in 1291.[17] John of Kendale later demised all his lands and tenements at the Hyde next to Knightsbridge in the parish of St Martin-in-the-Fields to Sir Walter de Beauchamp, steward of the royal household, and his wife Alice; they remitted the property back to him for 2 marks a year during their lives.[18] John was in possession again in 1315, when he exchanged his land with John of Pelham, clerk and citizen of London, for the latter's land at Pinner and 30 marks, also granting to

1 Perhaps because tithes (tenths) had been paid to the abbot.
2 *Cal. Pat.* 1550–53, 150–1.
3 TNA, CP 25/2/74/630/3&4P&MEASTER; *Cal. Pat.* 1555–7, 336.   4 *Cal. Pat.* 1563–6, 470–1.
5 Ibid., 1558–60, 336; TNA, CP 40/1183.
6 TNA, E 210/10357.
7 Cal. of Burghley Ho. MSS, NRA 6666, 32/2 & 3.
8 Gatty, *Mary Davies*, 40.
9 TNA, CP 25/2/806/1Jas2/Mich.

10 Gatty, *Mary Davies*, 40.
11 Rutton, 'Manor of Eia', 36–9, 41.
12 WCA, Ac. 181/1.
13 TNA, C 142/544, no. 50.
14 WCA, Ac. 181/1.
15 Gatty, *Mary Davies*, 40.
16 WAM 4875; TNA, CP 40/60, rot. 6.
17 WAM 4874, 4882; TNA, CP 40/64, rot. 8.
18 WAM 4879.

Pelham and his wife Denise of Wedeshale all crops on the land and goods and chattels at the Hyde. This suggests there was a house there, and indeed later deeds indicate that it was the residence of Denise.[1]

Pelham also acquired an acre in Eye called Ossuleston, lying amongst Kendale's land, from Adam of Haliwell in 1316.[2] After Pelham's death, his widow Denise leased the lands to John Eustace for 7 years, and then for her lifetime, confirmed by Pelham's heir Nicholas in 1329.[3] Denise married John Convers in 1347 and Nicholas quitclaimed his right in his father's lands to them both in 1348; Convers also acquired Eustace's lease.[4] John and Denise died of the plague and all Convers's land passed to his sister Christian or Christine and her husband Peter of Alnmouth. In 1350 they conveyed the (sub)manor of Hyde, described as a messuage and 100 acres in Eye and held of the abbey for 18d. service and fealty, to agents acting for Prior

Nicholas of Litlington for his anniversary in Westminster Abbey, paying 6s. 8d. to the poor and 3s. 4d. to the Boy Bishop;[5] the feoffees transferred it to the abbey in 1354.[6] Early in 1353 an inquiry was ordered after armed men had broken into the buildings of the manor, taking goods from chests and assaulting the servants there,[7] possibly connected with the claims of Convers's first wife Amy and their daughter.[8] The manor was first assigned to the cellarer, but later to the new work in the abbey. In 1535 the new work paid 7s. quitrent for the Hyde to the manor of Ebury.[9] In 1513 a freehold tenement in Knightsbridge was said to be held of the abbot of his manor of Hyde, perhaps for convenience rather than as a tenant of land in the Hyde;[10] a rental of the manor of Hyde of 1417 lists rents in Knightsbridge and Westbourne as well as farms of the lands of Hyde itself, suggesting that the abbey administered all its lands in the Knightsbridge area together.[11]

MANOR OF KNIGHTSBRIDGE

The manor of Knightsbridge was included in lands confirmed to Westminster Abbey by King Edward the Confessor, and held in demesne at all times. Its name, not expressly mentioned in Domesday, possibly because the manor was included in the abbey's Westminster estate, it is first named in recorded in the 12th century or early 13th century; the bridge in question was that over the Westbourne while the 'knights' may well have been the *cnihtas* of the well-known London guild, in existence by the time of the Confessor, and clearly an association of prominent citizens.[12] The manor's lands lay in the detached part of St Margaret's parish, and extended into the vills of Littleton, Paddington, and Westbourne.[13] The 13th-century copy of the '*Telligraphus* of King Edward' describes Knightsbridge as 4 hides.[14] The weekly farm of the Westminster monks of food and rents c.1120 included 7s. from Knightsbridge,[15] and in an agreement of 1225 between Abbot Richard of Berking and the monks, Knightsbridge was assigned to the convent for the sustenance of the monks.[16] In 1291 the convent's receipts from Knightsbridge including rents and forfeited animals was valued at £11 3s. 8d.[17]

After the acquisition of the manor of Hyde in 1350 the abbey seems to have administered Knightsbridge with

Hyde: in 1414 the new work of the abbey received £13 6s. 8d. from the farm of Hyde and Knightsbridge,[18] though often the name 'Knightsbridge' was omitted from the accounts' headings. In 1442 the manor was farmed to William, bishop of Salisbury, for 40 years at the rent of £13 6s. 8d., with payment of the chief rent of 7s. 8d. to the manor of Eye and the 15ths for the manor of Hyde.[19] The abbey leased the site of the manor with 4 gardens and a close adjoining it and other land in 1474 for 38 years, for 23s. 4d. paid to new work,[20] and the farm of the manor in 1488 for 30 years at £14.[21]

In 1542 the grant of lands to the newly-founded dean and chapter of Westminster included the manor of Knightsbridge in the parish of St Margaret with its appurtenances in Knightsbridge, Kensington, Westbourne, and Paddington.[22] In 1597 the dean and chapter received rents of £6 13s. 4d. from nine tenants holding a variety of free and copyholds and parcels at will in Knightsbridge and Westbourne, and common fines of 3s. 10d. from Knightsbridge and 21d. from Westbourne paid annually at the manorial court.[23] Approximately the same rental was received in 1636 with the addition of 4d. each for licences for three signposts (shop signs) erected on the waste by the highway,[24] and the same was

1   WAM 4871, 4872.

2   WAM 4776; 4829.

3   WAM 4770. Deeds dated at La Hyde, presumably her residence.

4   WAM 4827; 4767; below, Secular Inns and Ests (Convers).

5   WAM 5406.

6   WAM 4780; 4882; 5406; TNA, CP 25/1/150/63/274; C 143/311, no. 15; Harvey, *Westm. Abbey Ests*, 353, 418.

7   *Cal. Pat.* 1350–4, 395.

8   Below, Secular Inns and Ests (Convers).

9   *Valor Eccl.* I. 413, 421.

10   TNA, C 142/28, no. 52.

11   WAM 16334.

12   *P.N. Middx*, 169; F. Harmer, *A.-S. Writs* (1952), 231–5; D. Keene, 'Text, Visualisation and Politics: London, 1150–1250', *TRHS*, 6th ser. XVIII (2008), 89; inf. from D. Keene.

13   Harvey, *Westm. Abbey Ests*, 353.

14   Robinson, *Gilbert Crispin*, 40.

15   *Westm. Charters*, pp. 185–6.

16   BL, Cotton Faust. A. III, f. 225; WAD, f. 629v.

17   *Tax. Eccl.* (Rec. Com.), 13.   18   WAM 23479.

19   WAM 16268.   20   WAM 16179.

21   WAM 23577.

22   TNA, C 66/714, m. 5.

23   WAM 40627.

24   WAM 16329.

received in 1649 by the successors of the dean and chapter.[1]

The manor was restored to the dean and chapter in 1660, and remained in their ownership until it was transferred to the Ecclesiastical Commissioners with the chapter's other estates in 1869.[2] A court was held annually, in January in 1754, and the copyhold tenure was Borough English with an arbitrary fine.[3] Land formerly in the manor of Hyde, consisting of waste along the highway near Hyde Park, continued to be administered as part of Knightsbridge manor.[4]

SOKE OF LEICESTER AND THE SAVOY

The honor or estate attached to the earldom of Leicester, created between 1101 and 1107 and held of the king in chief by the earl for his service as Steward of England, included an area between the Strand and the river Thames. By the late 12th century, a number of properties, held there of the earl or of his chief barons, formed the Westminster soke of Leicester.[5]

Created from the lands of the Beaumont and Grandmesnil families, the honor may have had an antecedent in the Strand in the property of Gilbert of Ghent, one of William the Conqueror's leading supporters. In 1086 Gilbert granted to the abbot of Abingdon a messuage which lay between the Thames and the highway from London to Westminster (i.e. the Strand). As Ivo de Grandmesnil married one of Gilbert's daughters, it is possible that his rights in the land by the Strand passed to Grandmesnil, particularly as Abingdon's possession of a messuage there cannot be traced after 1152. The Abingdon messuage has not been certainly identified later, but was most likely one of the holdings that later made up the Savoy, or the bishop of Carlisle's inn next to it.[6]

On the death of the first earl of Leicester, Robert de Beaumont, count of Meulan, in 1118, the earldom of Leicester passed successively to the younger of his twin sons, Robert II (d. 1168), to the latter's son Robert III, styled Blanchemains (d. 1190), and to his son Robert IV. The last died in 1204 without issue, and in 1207 the Leicester estates were partitioned between his sisters Amice, widow of Simon de Montfort II, and Margaret, wife of Saer de Quincy, earl of Winchester; Amice (d. 1215), whose share included the honor and the London property, was styled countess of Leicester. Her son, Simon de Montfort III (d. 1218) was unable to obtain possession of his mother's share because he was a vassal of the French king; the lands were granted to a series of keepers, and in 1227 Ranulph, earl of Chester, keeper since 1215, received a life grant. In 1231 de Montfort's youngest son, the famous Simon de Montfort, to whom his elder brother had relinquished his English claim,

came to England and was successful in obtaining the reversion of the lands from Henry III, whereupon Earl Ranulph relinquished possession to him. In 1239 de Montfort received a formal grant of the earldom of Leicester.[7]

On his death at the battle of Evesham in 1265, de Montfort's lands were forfeited to the Crown, and Henry III granted them together with the earldom and honor to his younger son Prince Edmund.[8] Edmund also acquired the Savoy, and became earl of Lancaster in 1267: the London property of the honor was combined soon after with the nearby Savoy estate and administered as part of the Lancaster estates, later the duchy of Lancaster.[9]

Robert Beaumont IV, earl of Leicester, had evidently held his lands with extensive liberties and franchises.[10] In 1265 the king granted to Edmund and his heirs as earl of Leicester the right to hold his lands and fees with all liberties and free customs, quit of suits of shires and hundreds and sheriff's aid, and with many other judicial and fiscal franchises. Those rights also applied to the land when it became part of the duchy of Lancaster; the area was the only part of Westminster that lay outside the liberty of the abbots of Westminster and their successors, and it had a separate civil authority on a par with that of the abbot.[11]

The inclusion of the honor's lands with the Savoy estate in the duchy of Lancaster has obscured its extent in the Strand area, but from evidence for various landholdings it appears to cover the area between the Strand and the Thames extending from the New Temple westward as far as the church of St Mary of Strand. The earl of Leicester had several tenants in the Strand by the late twelfth century, though some plots of land by the river were at the disposal of the earls in the fourteenth century, possibly either held in demesne as the site of a former dwelling, or as escheats. Robert III, earl of Leicester, may have had a residence by the Strand: William de Turville attested a charter at St Mary of Strand *c.*1180 confirming a grant by Earl Robert, an indication that the earl was holding a court there.[12] By

1 *Acts and Ordinances of the Interregnum, 1642–60*, II. 262–71.   2 *London Gaz.* 13 Aug. 1869, 4524–47.

3 WAM 48054; 63834.

4 WAM 17285.

5 L. Fox, 'The Honor and earldom of Leicester: Origin and Descent, 1066–1399', *EHR*, LIV (1939), 385–6; D. Crouch, *The Beaumont Twins* (1986).

6 BL, Cotton Claud. C.IX, f. 138; below, Episcopal Inns, Carlisle.

7 J.R. Maddicott, *Simon de Montfort* (1994), 3–4, 7–9, 15; GEC, *Complete Peerage*, IV. 523.

8 R. Somerville, *Hist. of the Duchy of Lancaster* (1953), I. 2.

9 Below.

10 *Rot. Chart.* 124.

11 *Cal. Chart. R.* II. 67.

12 BL, MS Cotton Tib. D. VI, f. 111; Crouch, *Beaumont Twins*, 179n.

1313 there is evidence that the earl's court was held at the stone cross in the Strand, which seems to have been sited near the junction with Little Drury Lane.[1] If this does mean literally at the cross, it may indicate that the earl no longer had a suitable building available in which his tenants could meet.

In 1327 the earl was said to have had a dwelling on a plot of land, not precisely located, by the banks of the Thames.[2] Simon de Montfort, however, was using the bishop of Durham's house in 1258,[3] and there is no evidence he had an inn of his own in Westminster. Edmund, earl of Lancaster and of Leicester, was occupying the Savoy by 1278,[4] as did his successors, and would have little use for another inn by the Thames. It is possible, therefore, that the property described as the 'hospital of St Clement', which Edmund had granted into the keeping of the priory of St Sepulchre, Warwick, by 1278, was the earl's former residence,[5] although it is perhaps more likely that the residence had been on the plot with a gateway and chamber granted in 1356 to the rector of St Mary of Strand (below).

Some of the earl's chief barons held land in the honor, including William de Turville, who granted 3 *mansuras* of land at London (presumably within the soke in Westminster) to the abbey of Reading between 1124 and 1150, a grant confirmed by the earl,[6] and Robert de Harcourt, whose tenant, Henry son of Reiner, granted land *c.*1200 in the parish of St Clement Danes to the bishop of London, which later formed part of the bishop of Bath's inn in the Strand. The bishop of Bath owed suit at the earl of Leicester's court at the 'broken cross' in 1333,[7] and part of his property emanated from Richard son of Edward of St Mary of Strand, one of Earl Robert IV's men and reeve of his soke *c.*1200,[8] to whom King John in 1204 granted freedom from tallages, suits and customary dues in London and outside, and the same liberties as the Earl and his other men had.[9] The New Temple, which lay within the liberties of the City of London, was also held of the honor,[10] and some of the Templars' rents in 1185 both within the Bars of the liberties and without came from tenants in the Leicester fee, including 5 *s*. from the croft of Amicius granted by Robert de Watenville,[11] and a pound of cumin from land between Amicius's croft and the Thames held by William son of Isabel, sheriff of

London. About eight other rents of the fee of Leicester probably lay within the Bars.[12] Other landholdings connected with the honor included a garden and rents in the parish of St Clement Danes held of the earl by Peter son of Meilania before 1188;[13] five messuages held by the priory of St Sepulchre, Warwick, for suit and 3 *s*. 10 *d*., later the inn of the bishop of Exeter;[14] and the two messuages which the abbey of Combe acquired in 1293, one in St Mary of Strand, the other close by in St Clement Danes, held of the earl for 11 *s*. 10 *d*.[15] By 1287, the bishop of Llandaff had built an inn on land granted to him by Edmund, earl of Leicester, on the west side of which Edmund's son Thomas granted another plot in 1311. All this probably lay east and south of St Mary of Strand.[16] The church of St Mary itself may stand on the honor's land: Henry, earl of Lancaster, gave land to extend the churchyard, and a plot by the Thames with a gate and chamber for a house for the parson.[17]

Edmund died in 1296 succeeded by his son Thomas of Lancaster, who as one of the richest and most powerful men in the kingdom was able to take advantage of political successes to increase his estate. In 1314 at the York Parliament Aymer de Valence, earl of Pembroke, yielded to him the manor of the New Temple and former Templars' lands in the suburbs, held of the honor of Leicester.[18] However Thomas was executed for treason in 1322, and though his heir, his brother Henry of Lancaster, was given possession of the earldom of Leicester in 1324, most of its lands went to the Despensers. Henry succeeded in getting the sentence on Thomas reversed in 1327, and was reinstated in most of the Lancastrian inheritance with the title of earl of Lancaster.[19]

In 1313–14, before Thomas acquired the Templars' lands, the earl's income from the Strand manor, called the Stone Cross, and the Savoy totalled £6 0 *s*. 11 *d*. It included £2 11 *s*. 4 *d*. in rents of assize at the Strand, plus 6 *d*. rent for a messuage there, less 14 *s*. rent owed by the bishop of Llandaff for his houses at the Strand, which was remitted for an obit. Other sums received were 6 *d*. rent for a plot within the garden at the Strand, 5 *s*. for fruit of the garden, and 3 *s*. 6 *d*. for a plot there let for repairing boats, with 'use of the lord's houses' there; 19 *s*. 3 *d*. for perquisites of two views of frankpledge at the Strand, and 40 *s*. 10 *d*. in perquisites of court. From the

1 Above, Gen. Intro.: Duchy of Lancaster's Liberty.

2 TNA, C 135/6.

3 *Matthaei Parisiensis, Monarchi Sancti Albani, Chronica Majora*, ed. H.R. Luard, V (Rolls Ser. 57, 1880), 706; below, Episcopal Inns (Durham).   4 TNA, DL 25/149.

5 TNA, DL 42/2, f. 217, no. 3; below, Other Eccles. Ests (Priory of St Sepulchre).

6 BL, MS Eg. 3031, f. 40. Identified as prob. in Westm. from later docs.: i.e. BL, Harl. MS 1708, ff. 111v.–112; TNA, CP 25/1/146/6, no. 50; CP 25/1/146/5, no. 6. Printed in *Reading Abbey Cartularies*, ed. B.R. Kemp, I (Camden Soc. 4th ser., vol. 31, 1986), no. 460–1.

7 TNA, E 40/1665; below, Episcopal Inns (Bath).

8 TNA, E 40/1665.

9 *Cartae Antiquae*, II, p. 113; *Rot. Chart.* 124.

10 TNA, C 135/6 (1327).

11 Probably Vatteville, a castle on Beaumont's Normandy fief: Crouch, *Beaumont Twins*, 4, 72, 190, 193.

12 *Rec. Templars*, 13–15.

13 BL, Harl. MS 4015, f. 135.

14 TNA, CP 40/43, rot. 123; C 143/167, no. 4; below, Episcopal Inns (Exeter); Other Eccles. (Priory of St Sepulchre).

15 TNA, C 143/19, no. 16.

16 TNA, DL 42/2, f. 217, no. 11; C 143/72, no. 3. Llandaff's gdn was on boundary of St Mary of Strand and St Clement Danes: below, Episcopal Inns (Llandaff).

17 TNA, C 143/138. no. 27; *Cal. Pat.* 1354–8, 488; below, Religious Hist.: Par. Chs (St Mary of Strand).

18 McKisack, *Fourteenth Cent.* 67; *Cal. Pat.* 1313–17, 184–5.

19 McKisack, *Fourteenth Cent.* 75, 96.

account 24*s.* was paid in rent to the bishop of Worcester for houses in the Savoy.[1] The rents of assize were similar in 1322–3, with a bailiff and collector receiving 6*s.* 8*d.*[2] By the time the late earl's estates in the Strand were valued, in 1327, the New Temple was in the king's hands, and a plot of land about 140 ft by 120 ft by the river had been taken into the inn of the bishop of Exeter. The former Templars' estate which the earl had held comprised £4 9*s.* in rents of assize within and without the Bars and 15 acres called Ficketsfield, valued at 15*s.*[3]

In 1361 the earl of Lancaster was said to receive only 16*s.* 6*d.* in rent from free tenants as of the honor of Leicester, parcel of the Savoy, but by this time the honor's land by the Strand had little separate identity.[4] Quitrents in St Clement Danes and St Mary formerly belonging to the honor were collected as part of the duchy of Lancaster, and the land was administered as duchy land. The duchy's estate there included the Savoy and covered the whole area between the Strand and the Thames west of Temple Bar up to the boundary with the parish of St Martin-in-the-Fields. It also included the large 'island' of land in St Clement Danes parish between the Strand and Holywell Lane, on which St Clement Danes church and other buildings stood, which seems to have been taken out of the king's highway for building by the 12th century and paid quitrents collected by the sheriff of London for the Crown, later paid to the duchy.[5] The duchy continued to administer the area as a separate local government jurisdiction until the area became part of the new borough of Westminster following the Local Government Act, 1899.[6]

THE SAVOY ESTATE

Brian *de Insula* (de Lisle), an Anglo-Norman soldier-administrator in the service of King John, was granted property in the Strand by the Thames sometime before his death (by 1234).[7] In 1235 Brian's heirs, Thomas Brito, his wife Alice, and William of Glamorgan, granted and quitclaimed to the king's chancellor, Ralph, bishop of Chichester, two thirds of a messuage opposite the church of the Holy Innocents, probably their conveyance to the king of Brian's property.[8] In 1246 the king granted it to his wife's uncle, Peter of Savoy,[9] who also received the right to grant it to anyone he wished in 1254.[10] Peter also acquired a plot and garden from Thomas son of

Bartholomew de Venyt (Veniz?), which lay between Brian's former messuage and land of the bishops of Carlisle on the west, and stretched from the highway to the Thames; St James's Hospital granted to Peter rent of 16*d.* they received from land opposite the church of Holy Innocents, either this or Brian's messuage.[11] Before his death in 1268, Peter granted his house in the Strand to the hospital of Mont Joux, Savoy.[12] In 1270 Queen Eleanor bought back the property, described as buildings, gardens, plots, and rents in the parish of the Holy Innocents, from the hospital for 100 marks, giving it to her younger son Prince Edmund, earl of Leicester and of Lancaster, confirming the grant in 1284.[13]

Edmund added to the estate in 1278 by acquiring from Roger de Meuland, bishop of Coventry and Lichfield, a plot of land in the parish of St Mary of Strand lying on the east side of the Savoy estate, and stretching from the Strand to the Thames, which the bishop had purchased from Roger the *aumerer* (almoner) in 1257, who in turn had acquired it in 1253 from William son of Bartholomew.[14] Edward I confirmed the whole estate to his brother in 1285[15] and in 1293 Edmund received a licence to crenellate his house called Savoy.[16] In 1294 he also acquired a messuage from Richard the brewer which lay between the east side of the Savoy estate and the bishop of Worcester's property,[17] but this remained a separate holding and was granted to the bishop of Worcester in 1316 for anniversaries in Worcester cathedral.[18] Edmund, died in 1296 and was succeeded by his son Thomas of Lancaster, executed for treason in 1322.[19] Thomas's heir, his brother Henry of Lancaster, although given possession of the earldom of Leicester in 1324, lost most of its lands,[20] and the king granted the Savoy to his son Prince Edward, earl of Chester (later Edward III), to hold and keep in repair.[21]

In 1327 Henry of Lancaster was reinstated in most of the Lancastrian inheritance with the title of earl of Lancaster.[22] It is not clear, however, whether he had regained possession of the Savoy. A reference to his garden, where in 1335 it was said that treasure trove was dug up at night under a pear tree and carried off, may well be to the palace precincts.[23] Edward III apparently made grants of the manor of the Savoy to his mother's butler for life in 1347–8 and 1352;[24] nevertheless, after Henry's death in 1345, charters of local landowners to

1 TNA, DL 29/1/3, m. 13d.

2 TNA, SC 6/1146/20.

3 TNA, C 135/6. Part inc. Ficketsfield passed to Knights Hospitaller (below, Other Eccles. Ests).

4 TNA, C 135/160, no. 5.

5 *Chanc. R.* 1196 (PRS), NS. VII, 208; *Rot. Canc. 3 John*, 103; *Mem. R.* 1231–2, 219.

6 To be treated under Local Govt in a later vol.

7 Farrer, *Honors and Kts' Fees*, II. 151–3; *Cal. Chart. R.* 1226–57, 292.

8 TNA, CP 25/1/146/9, no. 117; W. Page, *London. its Origins and Early Development* (1923), 157.

9 *Cal. Chart. R.* 1226–57, 292.

10 *Cal. Pat.* 1247–58, 337.   11 TNA, C 47/9/1, mm. 4, 6.

12 *Cal. Pat.* 1266–72, 242.

13 TNA, DL 25/2344; DL 25/2342. Elsewhere 300 marks: DL 42/1, f. 12v.

14 TNA, DL 25/149; DL 27/67; CP 25/1/147/18, no. 336; Strype, *Survey*, I, bk iv. 105.   15 *Cal. Pat.* 1281–92, 189–90.

16 Ibid., 1292–1301, 30.

17 TNA, DL 42/11, f. 23d; CP 25/1/148/35, no. 249.

18 *Cal. Pat.* 1313–17, 441.

19 Above.

20 McKisack, *Fourteenth Cent.* 75.

21 *Cal. Pat.* 1324–7, 4.

22 McKisack, *Fourteenth Cent.* 96.

23 *Cal. Pat.* 1334–38, 206.

24 Ibid., 1348–50, 210; 1350–4, 196.

18. *View of the Savoy
from the Thames in
1808, showing the early
16th-century hospital
built within the site of
the Savoy Palace and
incorporating some of
the medieval riverside
range. The main dormi-
tory, north, was cruci-
form and a west range
had at its northern end
the hospital chapel,
later used as a parish
church. Other parts of
the complex were used
as nonconformist and
foreign chapels from the
mid 17th century.*

his successor, his son Henry of Grosmont, were dated at
the Savoy and in 1349 a charter of the earl himself was
dated in his manor of Savoy and confirmed by the king.[1]

Grosmont, created duke of Lancaster in 1351, was a
friend of Edward III and a successful soldier in France
with several brilliant victories. He was granted the castle
and town of Bergerac which he had captured, and from
the profits he built a great house at the Savoy, by then
clearly firmly in his possession.[2] In 1348 and 1350 he
also bought four tenements opposite the Savoy, which
were thereafter let as two inns;[3] they may be the three
tenements said to have been appropriated by the duke
on which the cellarer of Westminster Abbey lost 9s. 8d.
in rent.[4] Lancaster died in 1361, holding the Savoy
palace (described as a messuage in St Clement Danes),
with 7 shops annexed to it, and the lands of the honor of
Leicester, and leaving as his heirs his two daughters,
Maud wife of William duke of Bavaria, and Blanche wife
of Edward III's son John of Gaunt, earl of Richmond.
John became earl of Lancaster, and when in the
following year Maud, then a widow, also died, he
obtained the whole property in right of his wife and was
elevated to the dukedom.[5]

Gaunt was widely blamed for the unpopular government of Richard II's minority and in 1381 a London
mob attacked the Savoy; a fire, started probably by the
explosion of gunpowder stored in the buildings,
destroyed most of its contents and shops and houses
around the site. Gaunt did not bother to rebuild, prefer-
ring to lodge in the royal household or in episcopal
houses when visiting Westminster. Some 17 shops
belonging to the Savoy were still not rebuilt in 1420, a

loss of £4 13s. 4d. a year.[6] At about the same time vacancies in the four messuages opposite the Savoy reduced
rental income there from 53s. 4d. to 31s. 4d. One garden
belonging to the messuages was let for 20d., which had
formerly brought in 2s. in fruit and herbage; another
garden was in hand and brought in 17d. in fruit and
herbage, and 13s. 4d. was received for the garden in the
Savoy itself. In the 1390s some rebuilding took place,
with new timber for the great gates and lime, timber,
lead and ironmongery for work on the Symeon tower,
and stone and a mason for the watergate. A new length of
mud wall was made on the west side, and old wall there
tiled. New stone walling was built east of the gates.[7]

At his death in 1399 Gaunt was succeeded by his son
Henry Bolingbroke, who later that year seized the throne
and was crowned Henry IV; thereafter the lands of the
duchy of Lancaster including the Savoy passed with the
Crown of England. A separate administration was maintained for all the duchy estates, however, and grants of
property at the Savoy were made under the duchy seal.
Repairs were made to the Savoy, parts were let, and part
used for the administration of the Savoy manor, but it
was not used as a royal residence.

In 1510 Henry VIII conveyed the Savoy to the executors of the will of Henry VII for the establishment of a
hospital there.[8] In 1553 the hospital and its lands were
surrendered to Edward VI, and under an agreement with
the mayor and corporation of London, the Bridewell
and all the possessions of the hospital, except its site and
buildings and the nearby Savoy Rents, were conveyed to
the mayor and citizens of London, in return for which
they were to maintain the Bridewell to accommodate

1 *Cal. Pat.*, 1348–50, 469; TNA, DL 42/11, f. 24.
2 McKisack, *Fourteenth Cent.* 254.
3 TNA, DL 42/11, ff. 23d.–24d.
4 Rosser, *Medieval Westm.* 67n.

5 TNA, C 135/160, no. 5 [4th from end]; C 136/169, no. 3.
6 TNA, DL 41/437.
7 TNA, DL 29/287/4706.
8 TNA, DL 42/22, f. 16d.

poor men formerly lodged in the Savoy and pay the hospital's debts. In 1556 the Savoy hospital was refounded with the whole site, its gatehouse, houses, garden within the site, and its lands. The lands, however, remained with the corporation of London, and the hospital was endowed with certain concealed estates of dissolved monasteries. Ralph Jackson, chaplain to the king and queen, was appointed as master for life, and four chaplains were instituted.[1]

When the hospital was finally dissolved in 1702, the Savoy precinct was subject to treasury control until the duchy of Lancaster laid claim to the hospital site and Savoy precinct in 1717. Officials of the Exchequer and the duchy then fought over who should have ownership until an Act in 1772 laid out a compromise: the interior part with the hospital buildings, including the barracks, the two German churches, and the prison, but excluding the chapel, were deemed the property of the Crown and administered by the Exchequer, and the outer part and chapel belonged to the duchy. To facilitate development, however, the Act provided for either party to transfer its part to the other, and this took place in 1811 under letters patent when the Exchequer's part was transferred to the duchy. The site was redeveloped 1817–23, and included the approach road to Waterloo bridge.[2] The property was still part of the duchy of Lancaster estates in 2008.

SAVOY PALACE AND THE HOSPITAL OF ST JOHN

The 14th-century palace was built in a single programme to replace any previous property on the site, and was probably influenced by the character of buildings Henry, earl of Lancaster, had encountered in Aquitaine. Accounts at the time of its destruction indicate it was arranged round two courtyards, the one towards the Strand with an imposing gatehouse, the other with a water gate, and that it included hall, chapel, and private apartments facing inwards away from the river. The complex, which also incorporated extensive service accommodation, a garden and a fishpond, was enclosed by a wall.[3] Much was built of stone, and some buildings had thatched roofs. Some alterations were carried out in 1375–7 by Henry Yevele and William Wintringham for John of Gaunt, who intentionally left the palace a ruin after 1381. The water gate and Symeon's tower were repaired in 1400 by Stephen Lote, Yevele's successor as master mason to the Crown, and seem to have been the only roofed buildings for over a century, one them being used as a prison.[4] Between 1404 and 1405 the Strand wall was rebuilt, but in 1442–3 Kentish Rag was being sent from the ruins to Eton College which had been given the Savoy by the king. Any part which had survived must have been almost completely subsumed in the extensive and irregular buildings of the hospital constructed between 1510 and *c.*1517.[5] From later depictions it seems likely that the whole river range, including the water gate were adapted for use by the hospital, whose main buildings, decorated with chequered flint and stone, were a long and cruciform dormitory and a west range, with at its northern end the hospital chapel, later used as a parish church. Other parts of the complex were used as foreign chapels.[6]

SOKE OF MOHUN

The soke of William IV de Mohun (d. 1193) in London and Middlesex paid 13s. 4d. to the sheriff in 1197–8 and 1198–9.[7] William's son Reynold de Mohun came of age in 1206, but died in 1213 leaving a son Reynold II (d. 1258), who held the soke after he came of age in 1227. Reynold may also have inherited Briwere land in Westminster through his mother after 1233.[8] Reynold granted the soke of Mohun with all its appurtenances and liberties and advowsons of churches, within and without the City of London between the Fleet bridge and Charing, with his daughter Alice in marriage to Robert de Beauchamp of Hatch (Som.) and their issue *c.*1245.[9] In 1252 Robert and Alice granted the soke with its homages, rents, reliefs, escheats, suits, pleas, liberties, and advowsons to Westminster Abbey, to hold of Alice and her heirs; for this the abbot paid 85 marks and quitclaimed to Robert and his heirs the half mark annual service that Robert paid to the abbey for the manor of Shepperton.[10] Thereafter the soke became part of the abbey's manor of Westminster, but the abbot may have continued to hold a separate court for the soke or to account separately for its fixed rents, as it continued to be mentioned in accounts, as for example in 1327.[11]

By the early 13th century, when a local man, Bartholomew son of Robert, was bailiff of the soke,[12] its land in Westminster was held by tenants. The soke included land in the parish of St Martin at Charing near land of William the Marshal, earl of Pembroke, and held in the 1190s by Richard son of William Noloth for 20d.;[13] a holding at Charing near the Thames which

1 Somerville, *Savoy*, 38–41; *Cal. Pat.* 1555–7, 543.

2 Somerville, *Savoy*, 87–8, 98–103, 109, 113.

3 The acct follows A. Emery, *Greater Medieval Houses of England and Wales 1300–1500*, 3 (Cambridge, 2006), 240–1.

4 *Hist. King's Works*, I. 213, 281.

5 Acct of the hosp. will be included in a subsequent volume.

6 Ibid., V, Plate 49 (from *Vetusta Monumenta*, 11, 14); Somerville, *Savoy*, 233–4. Below, Religious Hist., for royal chapel of St Mary of the Savoy and foreign chapels.

7 *Rot. Canc.* 3 John, 103.

8 I.J. Sanders, *English Baronies* (1960), 114; WAM 17161.

9 *Two Beauchamp Registers*, ed. H.C. Maxwell-Lyte (Som. Rec. Soc. XXXV, 1920), 61.

10 TNA, CP 25/1/147/17/318.

11 TNA, SC 6/1109/4.

12 WAM 17148A.   13 WAM 17141; 17142; 17445.

Stephen of Berking received in marriage with his wife Idonia in the early 13th century, held for 10½*d.*, and which had three subtenants;[1] and a messuage with a garden and meadow which Geoffrey son of Bernard of Hyde held of William son of Robert of Rockingham.[2] A

messuage lying between Aldwych Street (later Drury Lane) and the Strand at the stone cross, bounded on the west by the later Little Drury Lane, was still described as lying in Mohun soke in 1391.[3]

ESTATES OF MEDIEVAL ORIGIN

EPISCOPAL INNS AND THEIR SUCCESSORS

The episcopal inns, whose history is described below, all lay close together, strung out along the shoreline of the Thames, on the south side of the Strand or just around the river bend at the northern end of King Street.[4] Except for Llandaff's inn, which had already been secularized by the early 16th century, they were all granted to Henry VIII or to courtiers close to him in the 1530s and became the sites of secular mansions. York Place alone remained permanently in royal hands, forming the core of the new Palace of Whitehall. By the late 17th century many sites were being redeveloped to accommodate shops and houses, a change which was reinforced by the destruction of the Palace of Whitehall in 1698.

BATH INN AND ARUNDEL HOUSE

Bath Inn, which in the Middle Ages belonged to the bishops of bath and Wells and thereafter became Arundel House, stood on the south side of the Strand just south-west of St Clement Danes church. The estate derived from the considerable property belonging to the Reiner family, first documented in 1203 when Stephen the tailor quitclaimed to Henry son of Reiner, Henry's brother Richard, and William the carpenter, a curtilage and 5 messuages.[5] In the early 13th century Henry son of Reiner granted to Eustace de Fauconberg (presumably before he became bishop of London in 1221) all the land he held of Robert de Harcourt, one of the earl of Leicester's principal tenants, and also the land formerly belonging to Richard the fruiterer, with the exception of three messuages held by William the carpenter; all the land seems to have lain between the highway and the Thames.[6] In 1204 Alexander the chaplain of Waltham quitclaimed to Eustace the clerk and his heirs in perpetuity 7*s.* out of 19*s.* rent which Eustace paid him from a messuage in the parish of St Clement's; Eustace paid 56*s.* 8*d.* for this.[7] The fine in 1205 recorded that Alexander

the chaplain conveyed two messuages and their curtilages, which stretched from the highway to the Thames, to Eustace son of William and to the heirs of Eustace de Fauconberg for the service of 12*s.* and half a pound of cumin, perhaps on behalf of Fauconberg. By the same fine Fauconberg assigned the 12*s.* service to Eustace who was to pay the service of 10*s.* due to the hospital of St Bartholomew as lord of the fee, which in turn held it of Richard son of Edward, the reeve of the earl of Leicester.[8]

By 1230 all this property was referred to as the place in the street (*vicus*) of St Clement formerly belonging to Eustace de Fauconberg, bishop of London (d. 1228), and was in the possession of Jocelin, bishop of Bath and Wells;[9] in 1232 the king confirmed Jocelin's grant of the property with its houses and buildings to his diocese and his successors as bishops to hold in frankalmoign.[10] Between 1231 and 1233 the hospital of St Bartholomew sold to the bishop the quitrent of 10*s.*, and in 1233 Richard son of Edward granted to the bishop the rent of a pound of pepper which the bishop paid him on behalf of St Bartholomew's, together with a plot of land lying between those of John parson of St Clement's and Richard son of Edward towards the Thames, and the plot of Walter the Marshal towards the street, reserving to Richard the suit owed by the bishop's men and their successors.[11] The bishop's representative did suit for the property in the 14th century at the court of the earl of Leicester.[12]

The Medieval Inn

The date the bishop first took up residence is not known, although possibly Bishop Jocelin built on the property and had an inn there. In 1238 the bishop appointed his servant Geoffrey as keeper of his property in St Clement's for life, to collect rents and repair the buildings, for a fee of 3*d.* a day,[13] which suggests that it may all have

1 WAM 17148 A and B; 17161.   2 WAM 17420.
3 *Cal. Close*, 1392–6, 107.
4 Above, Gen. Intro.: Creation of Westm. (Effects of Govt), for discussion on origins and function of Episcopal Inns.
5 TNA, CP 25/1/146/2/22.
6 TNA, E 40/1665.
7 *Cur. Reg. R.* III. 191.
8 TNA, CP 25/1/146/3, no. 44; below.

9 Ibid., 146/7, no. 73.
10 *Cal. Chart. R.* 1226–57, 168–9.
11 HMC, *Cal. of MSS of D & C of Wells*, I (1907), 474–5; TNA, CP 25/1/146/9, no. 103.
12 *Reg. of Ralph of Shrewsbury Bp of Bath & Wells, 1329–63*, I (Som. Rec. Soc. 9, 1896), 157.
13 *Cal. Chart. R.* 1226–57, 235; *Cal. Lib. R.* 1240–5, 168; 1245–51, 173.

been let, but by 1291, when there was no record of any rents received from St Clement's,[1] it is more likely that the bishops occupied the whole site themselves. The inn had some substantial building by 1312, when counterfeit keys were used to enter the bishop's cellar and steal wine and goods,[2] and a wall divided the property from that of the bishop of Exeter on the east in 1338.[3]

Many of those who became bishops of Bath were, or had recently been, royal ministers, and some continued in those posts: Robert Burnell (bishop 1275–92) was chancellor 1274–92, William de Marchia (1293–1302) was treasurer 1290–5; John Stafford (1424–43) was keeper of privy seal 1421–2 and chancellor 1432–50; Thomas Beckington (1443–65) was secretary to Henry VI; Robert Stillington (1466–91) was chancellor 1467–73. For some there is no evidence they ever set foot in their diocese,[4] so one may assume that their inn in St Clement Danes was heavily used. Bishops who did not often visit London let their inn to royal ministers: Walter Skirlawe, keeper of the privy seal, occupied the inn in 1383–4, when a large amount of his silver plate was stolen, and he probably housed the clerks of the privy seal there as well.[5] In the early 16th century the inn, like others, was also used for lodging official visitors: Lorenzo Campeggio, the pope's legate, stayed there in 1518, and again in 1528 during negotiations over Henry VIII's divorce.[6]

In addition to the main residence 20 small tenements, some with gardens, worth £6 13s. 4d. a year had been built in the inn by 1424, fronting the Strand and lying either side of the gatehouse.[7] In 1509 the keeper, William Clarvys, received a tenement at the front of the inn and the use and profits of the orchards and gardens; he was also appointed receiver of rents, for which he received a fee of 2½d. a day, a robe of the livery of the bishop's gentlemen when distributed, and food and drink when the bishop was in residence. If his fee was in arrears, he had the right to distrain in two of the tenements, the Cardinal's Hat and the Tabard. In 1513 the keepership and house were granted on the same terms to Jerome Vergil, brother of Polydore Vergil, archdeacon of Wells, for his good service to the bishop.[8] In 1534 Bishop John Clerk granted to his mother Alice, widow of John Bromwich, the keepership and the house and garden by the inner gate.[9] In 1535 the bishop's rents in London were valued at £32 16s. 4d., after payment of

33s. 4d. service to St John of Jerusalem as lord of the fee,[10] and the keeper's fee.[11]

Later Ownership of the Property

In 1539 Henry VIII forced the bishop to exchange his inn in St Clement Danes for the property of the Minoresses, east of the City of London, and an Act was passed assuring Bath Place to the lord admiral, William Fitzwilliam, earl of Southampton, and his issue; Southampton had taken possession by August that year, and the inn was then sometimes known as Hampton Place.[12] When he died in 1542 without issue, Southampton's property in St Clement Danes consisted of the mansion or capital messuage, 8 messuages with gardens, including one called the keeper's house, and 10 others including one called the Cardinal's Hat, all occupied by tenants; the value excluding the mansion house was £36 13s. 4d. net.[13] Within a fortnight of his death, another nobleman in need of a mansion was begging for the property, but in 1545 it was granted to Sir Thomas Seymour, an admiral of the fleet and brother-in-law of Henry VIII, in fee for payment of £700, as a reward for his naval service;[14] he renamed it Seymour Place. He was created Baron Seymour of Sudeley and lord admiral in 1547. The inn returned to the Crown on Seymour's attainder and execution in March 1549, and was granted that year to Henry Fitzalan, 12th earl of Arundel, in free socage, together with all Seymour's goods, chattels and household implements in the inn, which was thereafter known as Arundel House. The grant was confirmed in 1554, shortly after which a settlement was made on the earl and countess, their son Lord Maltravers, and their two daughters, Mary wife of Thomas Howard, earl of Surrey (later 4th duke of Norfolk), and Jane wife of Sir John Lumley, Lord Lumley.[15] Maltravers died in 1556 without issue, Mary in 1557 leaving one child, Philip, and Jane without issue in 1576. When Lord Arundel died in 1580, he was succeeded under another settlement of 1570 in the honor of Arundel by his grandson Philip Howard, who thereby became earl of Arundel; Lord Lumley conveyed his life interest in Arundel House, from a settlement of 1566,[16] to Philip. Another life interest in Arundel House had been settled on Philip's father, Thomas Howard, duke of Norfolk, but on the duke's attainder and execution in 1572 his residual rights passed to the Crown; the queen granted

1 *Tax. Eccl.* 13.

2 *Cal. Pat.* 1307–13, 530.

3 *Cal. Pat.* 1338–40, 127.

4 *Cal. Close,* 1429–35, 181; 1461–8, 457. John Barnet (1363–6) and Walter Skirlawe (1386–8) never visited; Rob. Stillington only once: *Christianity in Somerset,* ed. R.W. Dunning (1976), 8.

5 *Cal. Pat.* 1381–5, 285, 495; Tout, *Chapters,* V. 71.

6 *Brit. Libr, Harl. MS 433,* ed. Horrox & Hammond, III. 166; *L&P Hen. VIII,* IV(2), p. 2099 (no. 4857).

7 TNA, E 153/1019, [m. 1]; C 1/187/65; C 1/214/86.

8 HMC, *Cal. of MSS of D & C Wells,* II (1914), 215, 232–3.

9 TNA, E 164/45, f. 10.

10 Above, Manorial, Soke of Leic.

11 *Valor Eccl.* I. 122.

12 *L&P Hen. VIII,* XIV(1), p. 405 (no. 868); XIV(2), p. 15 (no. 48).

13 TNA, E 150/497/3.

14 *L&P Hen. VIII,* XVII, p. 555 (no. 997); XX (2), p. 453 (no. 910/77).

15 *Cal. Pat.* 1548–49, 245; 1553–4, 234, 315.

16 TNA, CP 25/2/259/8Eliz/East.

those rights to Philip in 1581 in exchange for lands of similar value.[1] Philip himself was attainted and imprisoned in 1590, and the freehold of Arundel House again escheated to the Crown, and was granted to the lord chamberlain[2] to hold for a rent of £30.[3] Philip's wife had a life interest in the property which began on her husband's death in the Tower in 1595, but as there is no trace of her involvement with the house after 1590, she may have already surrendered her interest to the Crown.

In 1603 James I granted Arundel House with its associated messuages to Charles Howard, earl of Nottingham, and his heirs, but on payment to Nottingham of £4,000 by Philip's son and heir, Thomas Howard, earl of Arundel and Surrey, they were surrendered in 1607, enabling the king to grant them to Arundel in fee simple.[4] Lord Arundel died abroad in 1646, leaving Arundel House to his wife Alatheia (d. 1654) for life, but as she was a reputed Catholic living abroad in 1650, Arundel House and the rents of what were described as 100 tenements nearby passed to Parliament. Arundel's son and heir Henry Frederick was also a recusant and royalist who compounded for his estates,[5] but in 1651 his father's executors requested discharge of the house which had been left to them to pay debts, and pictures, statues, and other goods in the house were sold for that purpose.[6] Henry, Lord Arundel, died in 1652 at Arundel House, succeeded by his eldest son Thomas. The latter had become mentally impaired after an illness, but in 1660 at the petition of his male relatives the title of duke of Norfolk was revived for him and, failing any male issue, for the male descendants of the 4th duke. Thomas died in 1677, succeeded as 6th duke by his brother Henry Howard, Lord Howard of Castle Rising, earl of Norwich, and Earl Marshal, and Arundel House and its site thereafter remained as part of the estates of, and descended with, the dukedom of Norfolk. It was in the ownership of the trustees of the settled estates of the duke in the 1970s, but had been sold to a property company by 1997.[7]

Arundel House

The bishop of Bath's medieval inn was said to have been rebuilt by Sir Thomas Seymour,[8] but a mid-17th century illustration and other evidence suggests rather that he

added to the medieval buildings. It seems certain that Seymour acquired part of the garden of Strand Inn to the west side of Bath Place,[9] and he created a new lane from the Strand down to the Thames, presumably Strand Bridge Lane, by taking a tenement and part of two gardens west of Bath Place to give access to the Strand: after the property returned to the Crown in 1549 on his attainder, the farms of two of the Bath inn tenements, the Cardinal's Hat and the Axe, were offered to Nicholas Gravenor as part of an exchange between him and the king for the property taken for the lane.[10] Either Seymour or Henry, earl of Arundel, added the tall range with polygonal bays and tower, which must have been a rebuilding of the private accommodation at the high, west end of the hall and is shown on the so-called Agas copper plate map of c.1558. That map also shows the line of a building stretching southward to the Thames from the western end of that range. Norden shows it as a long wing, two-storeyed at least at the river end, on his map of c.1593, and in Hollar's plan of the west central district, made between c.1658 and 1666, it is flat-roofed and for most of its length has a series of square bays to east and west overlooking the gardens, which were terraced because of the steep slope of the site. The wing was presumably built by Philip Howard, earl of Arundel, and contained a gallery or galleries.[11]

A survey made of Arundel House in 1590 describes a courtyard inside the first (street) entrance, two gardens, an orchard, several walks, a bowling alley, with 'divers beautiful buildings' and barns and stables. It only detailed the buildings in need of repair, many of which are identifiable in their original timber-framed form, or as they had been remodelled early in the 17th century.[12] The accuracy of those depictions by Hollar can probably be relied on, as he was brought to England by Lord Arundel in 1636 and lodged at Arundel House.[13] The buildings mentioned were, in the great court, a storehouse, lodgings next to the barn, new barns and stables, bakehouse and coalhouse; the bowling alley 138 feet long by 18; lantern on top of the hall; buildings in kitchen court east of the hall; common bridge (landing-stage), slaughterhouse, privy bridge. The great brick house and galleries, presumably the two western ranges, required only £30 of work by plumbers, plasterers, tilers,

1 GEC, *Complete Peerage*, I. 250–3; *Cal. Pat.* 1580–2, 61 (no. 352).

2 Either queen's cousin Hen. Carey, Lord Hunsdon, or poss. Chas Howard, Lord Effingham, later earl of Nottingham, who entertained the queen at Arundel Ho. 1602: *DNB.*

3 TNA, E 164/45, ff. 1–14v.; BL, Lansd. MS 68, no. 75, f. 169; Lansd. 45, no. 85, ff. 219–21.

4 *Cal. SP Dom.* 1603–10, 31, 390; TNA, E 214/1333; Hervey, *Life of Thos Howard*, 41.

5 *Cal. Cttee Money*, III. 1256; *Cal. Cttee Comp.* IV. 2463, 2477, 2479.   6 *Cal. Cttee Comp.* IV. 2465–6.

7 *TLMAS*, XXVI. 250; Moorfield Group plc (www.moorfield.com, 20 May 2005).

8 *Survey of London by John Stow*, ed. C.L. Kingsford, II. 91.

9 15th-cent abutments indicate some land S. of hos along Strand, later in Arundel est., was not in Bath's inn: above, Episcopal Inns, Chester.

10 TNA, E 318/29/1645. An 'Axe' was still part of Bath Place 1590 but may be a different tenement: TNA, E 164/45, f. 9. View of 1543 shows a lane leading to a bridge about on the line of the later gallery, i.e. very close to W end of existing ho., and probably used by his tenants and others along Strand: poss. Seymour wished to move this further away to west side of his new gardens to build new wing and give privacy to gardens.

11 *Hollar's London*, Plate 5.

12 *Hollar's London*, Plates 21–2.

13 *Oxford DNB* (viewed online at www.oxforddnb.com/view/article/13943, 7 Nov 2008).

19. *Arundel House, the outer courtyard in 1646: above, a view south towards the medieval hall and service buildings, with a block of lodgings on the east side; below, a view north, with St Clement Danes's tower just visible over the gatehouse.*

and carpenters. There was a vault in the cellar under a paved court 25 feet by 20, perhaps the little court between the hall and the brick house.[1]

Lady Arundel (d. 1630) requested the use of certain rooms and gardens in 1590, when her husband was imprisoned: the accommodation she asked for included many of the buildings round the great court and the lodgings she occupied west of the great hall, on all three floors of the 16th-century chamber block. She required a little room over the hall porch used to house the evidences for Arundel Rape (Sussex), the chamber adjoining it and another with a garret over them both, the decayed storehouse for a kitchen and other offices on the western side of the court, a chamber over the middle gate reached by stairs from the eastern end of the storehouse, and buildings stretching to the barn on the eastern side. She also asked for the sole use of the garden with the bowling alley, lying on the west side of her lodgings, free passage to the common watergate, and access to all the buildings listed and to the house of office. A small water pipe from the main supply was to serve the countess's kitchen. The lord chamberlain, the Crown's tenant, agreed to her requests, but thought that the garden and bowling alley should be held in common, with the countess having a key to use them for her and her children's recreation as she wished, as well as any other gardens of the house.[2] It is not clear how long Lady Arundel or the lord chamberlain resided in the house: Charles Howard, earl of Nottingham, was apparently

living there in 1602. In 1603 the duc de Sully, French ambassador at the coronation of James I, stayed at Arundel House, which had been specially prepared to receive him, and gave it fulsome praise.[3]

Thomas Howard, earl of Arundel, and his wife, Alatheia Talbot, who owned the house from 1607, were renowned as collectors of works of art and patrons of architecture. In 1613–14 they toured Italy, accompanied by Inigo Jones, who became a friend and close associate. Impressed by Italian town-planning, in 1615 Arundel persuaded James I to create the commission for new buildings in London, in which he, Inigo Jones and others could try to influence the appearance of the rapidly expanding city and suburbs. The Arundels also brought back from Rome the beginning of a collection that eventually amounted to hundreds of ancient Greek and Roman sculptures and inscriptions, most of which were arranged in the library, sculpture and painting galleries and in the garden, as well as paintings, drawings and manuscripts, used by Arundel to educate both the aristocracy and artisans. Other aristocrats had collected before, but none with such breadth of taste. He collected every form of art with superb examples of each: Hellenistic Greek bronzes, Hellenistic marble figures, notebooks of Leonardo, Raphael altarpieces, the earliest accounts of Greek history, a superb library of medieval manuscripts.[4] A whole gallery was devoted to Holbein's paintings, in addition to many complete sketch-books by the artist.[5] Arundel valued the works

1 TNA, E 164/45, ff. 1–14v.
2 BL, Lansd. MS 45, no. 85, ff. 219–21.
3 Hervey, *Life of Thos Howard*, 119n.

4 Howarth, *Lord Arundel*, 2.
5 Hervey, *Life of Thos Howard*, 255–6.

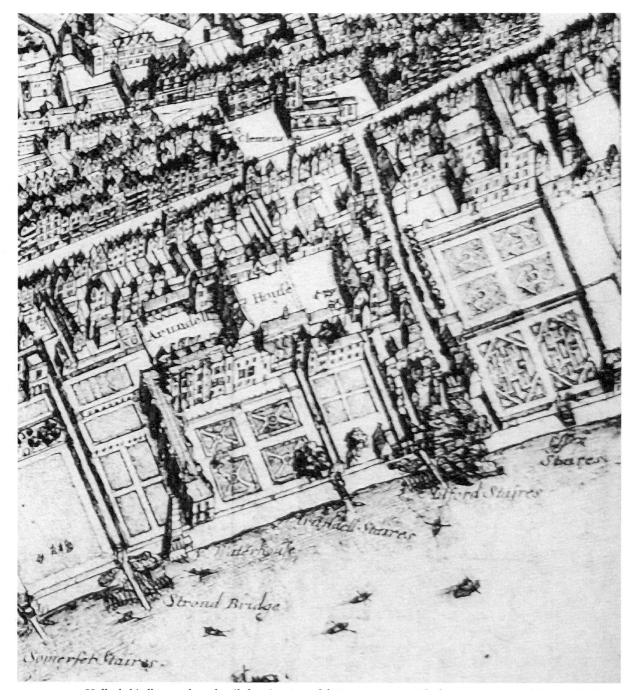

20. *Hollar's bird's-eye plan, detail showing Arundel House c.1660, with the outer courtyard (shown in the same artist's two perspectives, below) lying towards the Strand and later residential ranges west and south-west of it closer to the river.*

not just for their beauty but for what they revealed about ancient cultures which could benefit the present. Although not a scholar himself he valued scholarship and made his collections available to others, using them to educate both the aristocracy and artisans and employing a full-time keeper.[1]

In 1616–17 the Arundels supervised the lay-out of galleries and gardens at Arundel House. Perhaps because

of chronic financial problems Arundel did not completely rebuild the house, but Inigo Jones designed for him some minor but influential alterations, including changes to the long western wing, which probably contained the sculpture and picture galleries. Daniel Mytens's companion portraits of the Earl and Countess, painted *c.*1618, appear to show idealized representations of them,[2] and Joachim Sandrart seems to

1 Howarth, *Lord Arundel*, 87, 96, 122, 187.

2 Ibid., 59, 63.

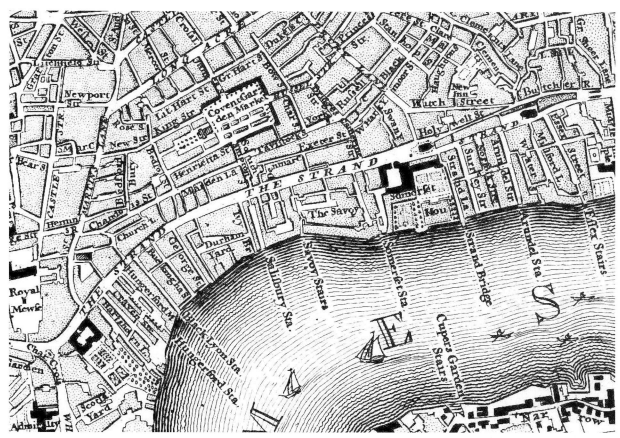

21. *John Rocque's map of 1741–5, detail showing how the mansions and gardens along the Strand had given way to streets lined with buildings by the mid 18th century. Ivy Bridge still marks the eastern limit of the medieval parish of St Martin-in-the-Fields. Both St Martin's church and that of St Clement Danes had been rebuilt, and the church of St Mary le Strand had been moved to a new site.*

confirm that the picture gallery was '… the long gallery … where the works of Hans Holbein held the master place' and that this was entered from the garden.[1] Jones certainly remodelled in Italianate style the windows of a 16th-century gallery and installed some chimneypieces. The block shown at the southern end of the western wing on Hollar's plan of the west central district, and also as an Italianate building in his view of the house from the Thames, was no doubt the result of Inigo Jones's alterations to that wing, perhaps the 'rooms towards the water' on the which he was working in 1618–19.[2] Jones also designed two classical gateways for the gardens,[3] and, later, a 'room for designs'.[4]

Lord Arundel accompanied Princess Mary to the Netherlands in 1642 and never returned to England. His heir returned in 1646 and was living at Arundel House at his death in 1652,[5] but the house was also used as a garrison in 1650.[6] The collections that remained,

especially in the garden, were greatly neglected, and the marbles (all those with inscriptions in Latin or Greek) were rescued by John Evelyn in 1667, who was permitted by Henry Howard to take them to Oxford University, where they formed the basis of the collection in the Ashmolean Museum.[7] Many pieces remained, however, to be damaged in later building work,[8] or sold off piecemeal. The Royal Society met at Arundel House in 1668.[9]

Rebuilding on the Site In 1671 the guardians of the 5th duke of Norfolk obtained a Private Act giving them power to make leases for years of the house and tenements for rebuilding,[10] and in 1672 they leased it all to Henry Howard, then Lord Howard, for 60 years, except for a plot staked out for a new mansion and garden.[11] Howard began redeveloping the site of Arundel House in 1676–7, and commissioners including William Winde, appointed under the Act to lay out the site,

1 Recited in Hervey, *Life of Thos Howard*, 255–6.
2 Ibid., 142; *Hollar's London*, Plates 1, 5; Howarth, *Lord Arundel*, Fig. 84.
3 Howarth, *Lord Arundel*, 57; Colvin, *British Architects*, 590.
4 Howarth, *Lord Arundel*, 102.
5 *Oxford DNB*, s.vv. Howard, Thos.; Howard, Hen. Fred.
6 *Cal. SP Dom.* 1650, 405.

7 *Diary of John Evelyn*, ed. W. Bray & H.B. Wheatley (1906), II. 225.
8 E.g. in 1680: *Middx County Rec.* IV. 143–4.
9 *Cal. SP Dom.* 1668–9, 79.
10 HMC, *9th Rep.* App. II, 2 (22–23 Car. II, c. 19, Private Act).
11 TNA, C 54/4525, no. 12.

formed Arundel, Surrey, and Norfolk streets, and regulated the architecture. Winde may have had some involvement in the design of the new house, begun in 1677 and subsequently abandoned.[1] Some agreements for building leases were made by the commissioners in 1676–7.[2] In 1677 Howard obtained from the king a grant in fee simple of the ground 40 feet wide between the wall of Arundel House and the river, stretching the whole way between Strand Bridge and Milford Stairs, to even up the river frontage.[3] The old house was demolished 1680–2, and a new mansion built near the river, itself demolished in the 1720s.[4]

CARLISLE INN, WORCESTER HOUSE AND SALISBURY HOUSE

The bishops of Carlisle had an inn east of the bishop of Durham's inn by 1238.[5] In 1259 the nephew and heir of Silvester of Everdon, bishop of Carlisle 1246–54, quitclaimed all right in two messuages in the *vicus Dacorum* (Street of the Danes) in Westminster to Bishop Robert of Carlisle in right of his church.[6] This seems to refer to Carlisle Inn: the stretch of the Strand outside the inn and a neighbouring property to the east was always called the *vicus Dacorum*, and later the inn lay in a detached part of St Clement Danes parish. The inn stretched from Durham Place on the west to the Savoy on the east; a mud wall was built between the latter and Carlisle Inn in 1395.[7] The whole property remained the freehold of the bishops of Carlisle until 1539, but by then building on the estate had led to a division into two parts.

In 1402 the bishop let the east end of the Strand frontage, stretching from the Savoy to the inn's gatehouse and stables, to John Boteler, citizen, his wife Julian, and William their son for 40 years,[8] on which they were to build shops fronting the highway, and to enclose the plot with a mud wall on the south and west to divide it from the bishop's garden. A second lease to them the following year granted to them the equivalent frontage on the west side of the gatehouse up to Ivy Lane, which ran from Ivybridge in the Strand to the Thames and marked the parish boundary as well as the boundary with the bishop of Durham's inn; they were also granted a frontage down to the stone wall along the Thames, presumably along Ivy Lane. Again they had to enclose the plot with a mud wall along the bishop's garden and the lane, and to make within the garden a stew-pond for fish and a suitable latrine on the stone wall.[9]

In 1438 Marmaduke Lumley, bishop of Carlisle, let to Thomas Hay of London, fruiterer, a garden with a little lodge for 40 years at 13*s.* 4*d.* a year. In 1463 Hay sold his term to William Fowler of London and his wife Joan, when the property was said to be have been late in the tenure of John Mersh, fruiterer.[10] Bishop Marmaduke also let a place belonging to his bishopric called the Vernacle in the parish of St Clement Danes, presumably part of Carlisle Inn; it was granted to William Lomley (perhaps a relative) for a term of years, and Lomley subsequently built a small house on waste by the highway, 6 feet wide by 16 feet long, adjoining the Vernacle, for which the king pardoned him in 1449, allowing him to keep the house during the term.[11]

Use of the inn by the bishops themselves was probably intermittent, especially for prelates who did not play a part in national government, and others also used the inn. Edward Story, bishop of Carlisle 1468–78, continued after translation to the see of Chichester to use Carlisle Place as his London residence until *c.*1486.[12]

Roger Layburn, bishop 1503–8, held in right of his bishopric 25 messuages in the parish of St Clement Danes, valued at £8 a year,[13] presumably consisting of the bishop's house, which with its garden formed the eastern part of the property, shops along the Strand frontage, and messuages in the western part of the inn called Carlisle Rents (below). The Rents were valued at £16 4*s.* a year in 1535.[14] In 1537 Bishop Robert was approached by a servant of Thomas Cromwell about a lease of his inn, but stated that his predecessor had already leased everything for some years to come.[15] Soon afterwards, however, and presumably on the king's instruction, the bishop was involved in a tripartite exchange, whereby he granted the freehold of Carlisle Place to John, Lord Russell, who was to pay him £16 a year, while the bishop was to have the bishop of Rochester's house in Lambeth, and Rochester was to have Russell's mansion place in Chiswick. All this was confirmed by Act of Parliament in 1539.[16]

Russell Place or Bedford House

The inn was granted to Russell and his issue to hold in chief for a fifth of a knight's fee, with reversion to the Crown.[17] The bishop's house and garden became known as Russell Place or (after 1550) Bedford House. The 1st earl of Bedford died there in 1555, as did Francis, 2nd earl, in 1585,[18] and the inn then passed to Anne and Elizabeth, the daughters and coheiresses of the latter's

1 Colvin, *British Architects*, 1134.
2 Cal. of Arundel Castle MSS.
3 *Cal. SP Dom.* 1676–7, 226, 236; 1677–8, 153–4.
4 *TLMAS*, XXVI. 210.
5 *Matthaei Parisiensis. Chronica Majora*, ed. H.R. Luard, III (Rolls Ser. 57, 1876), 485.
6 TNA, CP 25/1/147/21, no. 409.
7 TNA, DL 29/287/4707.
8 Assuming same location as in 1682: Morgan, *Map of London* (1682).

9 *Cal. Pat.* 1401–5, 344. Cf. Carlisle Rents and Dacre Ho.
10 *Cal. Close*, 1461–8, 192.
11 *Cal. Pat.* 1446–52, 296.
12 *Rec. of Hon. Soc. of Lincoln's Inn: Black Bks*, IV. 283–4.
13 TNA, E 150/468/8.
14 *Valor Eccl.* V. 273.
15 *L&P Hen. VIII*, XII(2), p. 299 (no. 848).
16 *L&P Hen. VIII*, XIV(1), p. 403 (no. 867).
17 TNA, C 66/1550, m. 8.
18 *Survey of London*, XXXVI. 23.

22. *Some of the Strand's aristocratic mansions, looking north from the Thames, c.1640: the hall of Durham House is on the water's edge; east of it (centre) but set back stands Little Salisbury House adjoining Salisbury House, and nearby (right) is Worcester House.*

eldest son John, Lord Russell (d. 1584). In 1600 Anne married Henry Somerset, Lord Herbert, eldest son of Edward, 4th earl of Worcester, while Elizabeth died unmarried a few weeks later.[1] The queen confirmed the mansion to Lord Herbert and his heirs in 1601 together with the reversion of the remaining property of the inn and a moiety of Ivy Lane, forming the inn's boundary, holding in chief for a fifth of a knight's fee.[2] Later that year Lord Herbert and his wife sold to Sir Robert Cecil, later earl of Salisbury, for £1,000 the freehold of the former Carlisle Rents, which then comprised Dacre House and all the Carlisle property between Russell House and Ivy Lane, for a rent-charge of 20s. towards the £16 a year still paid to the bishops of Carlisle.[3]

Worcester House

Edward Somerset, earl of Worcester, apparently took up residence in Russell Place, which became known as Worcester House, and this was probably the house of the earl that was burgled in 1608.[7] He died there in 1628, having shortly before his death settled Worcester House with its gardens, orchards and yards on Henry, Lord Herbert, and the latter's son Edward.[8] In 1629 Henry as 5th earl and his wife resettled Worcester House, described as 16 messuages in St Clement Danes, on the marriage of their eldest son Edward to Elizabeth Dormer.[9]

Henry, who was created marquess of Worcester in 1643, fought for the king in the civil war and lost his estates; he died in 1646, to be succeeded by his son Edward, then living abroad.[10] In 1648 Worcester House was excluded from the sale of delinquents' estates,

presumably because it was being used by the government;[11] although later in 1648 the house was ordered to be surveyed before sale to the earl of Salisbury,[12] the sale did not go through. Throughout the Interregnum the county committee for Middlesex and Westminster met at Worcester House,[13] as did the trustees and officers under the Act for sale of the king's lands from 1649, and various other parliamentary committees; inquisitions into charities were also held there in 1655.[14] The survey of 1648 described the house as having 60 rooms, mostly ancient, a stable for eight horses, and two coach-houses. Seen in maps and views, the house in the 17th century looked far from ancient: it appears to be a compact two-storeyed block with six regular bays, divided by pilasters, and six gables over them towards the Thames.[15] The main garden adjoined the Thames, stretching 238 feet from Salisbury House garden on the west to a passage to the waterside belonging to the Strand tenements; it was 107 feet wide on the west, and 137 on the east. Another garden, lying between the main garden and the tenements, measured 90 feet by 82, and an 'ancient' house next to the street also belonged to Worcester House.[16] Two tenements fronting the Strand were discharged from sequestration in 1652 having been bought from the Treason Trustees by the tenants.[17]

In 1652 Edward returned to England, submitted to Parliament, and was imprisoned in the Tower until 1654.[18] In 1659 Parliament ordered £6 a week be paid to Margaret, countess of Worcester, as long as the government was using Worcester House, but by May 1660 records concerning the late king's lands were being moved out.[19] Lord Worcester's estates were restored

4 GEC, *Complete Peerage*, II. 77; XII(2), 858.

5 TNA, C 66/1550, m. 8.

6 TNA, C 54/1713 (unnum.). Below, Salisbury Ho. for later hist. Cecil moved Ivy Lane westward, so Ivy Bridge Lane shown on Morgan (1682) and later maps is not on same line.

7 *Middx County Rec.* II. 42.

8 TNA, C 142/442, no. 26.

9 TNA, DL 41/314.

10 GEC, *Complete Peerage*, XII(2), 858.

11 *Acts and Ordinances of the Interregnum, 1642–60*, I. 1056–7.

12 HMC, *7th Rep.*, App., p. 17a.

13 *Cal. SP Dom.*, passim.

14 *Cal. Cttee Comp.* I–V, passim; IV. 2465–6; *Acts and Ordinances of the Interregnum, 1642–60*, II. 188, 538; *Cal. SP Dom.* 1653–4, 205; TNA, C 93/23/11, 12.

15 Drawing by W. Hollar, engraved 1808, pub. by W. Herbert and R. Wilkinson (Guildhall Libr., Main Print Colln, Pr.W2/STR).

16 *Cal. Cttee Comp.* I. 119.

17 *Cal. Cttee Comp.* III. 1714.

18 *Complete Peerage*, XII(2), 861.

19 *Cal. SP Dom.* 1659–60, 130, 200, 600.

1660–1, and he settled Worcester House and its tenements on himself for life and his male heirs.[1] He let Worcester House to Edward Hyde, the chancellor (Lord Clarendon from 1661), for £500 a year, and Hyde occupied the house until his own house in Piccadilly was ready *c.*1665. Hyde's eldest daughter Anne was secretly married at Worcester House in 1660 to James, duke of York, and their first child was baptized there in 1661.[2]

Lord and Lady Worcester lived in Spring Gardens on the south bank of the Thames while Worcester House was let, returning in 1665. Edward died suddenly at Worcester House in 1667; his property in St Clement Danes consisted of the capital messuage formerly occupied by Lord Clarendon, valued at £200 a year net, and 21 messuages in the hands of individual tenants, valued at between £15 and £40 each, with a total net value of £373 a year.[3] His son Henry succeeded him as 3rd marquess, and was created duke of Beaufort in 1682. Worcester House continued to be used as the family's London residence until Henry bought the duke of Buckingham's former house at Chelsea in 1681.[4] Worcester House was then demolished and Beaufort Buildings built on the site 1682–3, together with Herberts Passage and Fountain Court. The whole property was sold *c.*1763 by the trustees of the 5th duke of Beaufort.[5] The Buildings were in turn demolished in the 1880s to make way for the Savoy Hotel; Savoy Court marks their former entrance.

Carlisle Rents and Salisbury House

Thomas Dacre (d. 1525), Lord Dacre of Gilsland and Lord Greystoke, built a residence in Carlisle Rents, of which his son William, Lord Dacre (d. 1563), obtained a lease from the bishop in 1527,[6] and was living there in 1534.[7] It passed to his son Thomas, Lord Dacre (d. 1566), and then to the latter's son George, who died as a minor in 1569 leaving three sisters as coheiresses.[8] The Dacre leasehold in Carlisle Rents passed to the youngest sister, Elizabeth, and her husband, Lord William Howard, who rebuilt the house and used it as his London residence. In 1598 it was occupied by Sir Thomas Cecil, 2nd Lord Burghley, who afterwards leased it to Thomas Sackville, Lord Buckhurst (later earl of Dorset). These leasehold interests were acquired by Sir Robert Cecil, later earl of Salisbury, who in 1600 bought from Lord Herbert and his wife the freehold of Dacre House at Ivy Bridge (the parish boundary) and its outbuildings and garden along the east side of Ivy Lane,

together with a little messuage adjoining the north end of the lane and other shops and buildings by the Strand, all of which Cecil had recently demolished, giving him ownership of all the part of the former Carlisle inn between Russell Place and Ivy Lane. The grant also included the use of the eastern half of Ivy Lane belonging to the former inn. In 1601 the Herberts confirmed to Cecil all the property and new buildings, walls and chimneys he had erected on the site since the previous deed.[9]

The Dacre House site was apparently only about 75 feet wide: the later Carting Lane seems to have marked the division from Worcester House. Cecil therefore added to the site on the west side of Ivy Lane, buying the five easternmost houses in Durham Rents, fronting the Strand, from William Fortescue in 1601 and 1602, which had a total frontage to the Strand of about 65 feet.[10] He also obtained a feefarm grant of a piece of Durham House garden south of the Durham Rents houses giving him the whole strip from the Strand to the Thames and rights over the whole of Ivy Lane.[11] Ivy Lane, 10 feet wide at the Strand end and 13 by Durham garden, was incorporated into the site of Salisbury House and garden, and about 10 feet on the western side of Cecil's acquisitions was used for a new lane to the Thames, also known as Ivy or Ivy Bridge Lane.[12] Stow reported in 1603 that Robert Cecil had recently built there 'a large and stately house of brick and timber' and had also levelled and paved the highway adjoining, presumably the Strand.[13] A survey of the manor of the Savoy in the liberty of the duchy of Lancaster made in 1602 bears this out. It found that Cecil, like other residents along the Strand, had incorporated 1½ feet of the public highway within the pale of his new house, running for some 70 feet along the Strand.[14] Salisbury House, begun by Simon Basil, later Surveyor to the King's Works, in 1600 was complete enough to entertain Queen Elizabeth in December 1602. In the 1630s, when Hollar drew it, the mansion appeared to have three ranges round a forecourt with wall and gate to the Strand. The three wings had battlemented parapets and ogee cupolas to corner towers no higher than the three-storeyed main ranges. Building continued on the west side of the site, but still to the east of the new Ivy Bridge Lane, where Little Salisbury House, itself a large but less architecturally pretentious and according to Hollar perhaps not completely independent house, was not finished until 1610.[15]

After Salisbury's death in 1612 the estate passed with

1 TNA, DL 41/314.
2 *Cal. SP Dom.* 1660–1, 466, 506; below, Later Creations, Clarendon.   3 TNA, DL 41/314.
4 M. McClain, *Beaufort: the Duke and his Duchess 1657–1714* (2001), 103; *VCH Middx*, XII. 126.
5 Glos. RO, D2700, Cal. to Badminton Muniments, vol. II.
6 *Survey of London*, XVIII. 120.
7 *L&P Hen. VIII*, VII, p. 117 (no. 281).
8 GEC, *Complete Peerage*, IV. 18.
9 TNA, C 54/1713 (unnum.).

10 TNA, C 54/1713 (unnum.); C 54/1746 (unnum.).
11 *Survey of London*, XVIII. 121.
12 TNA, C54/1713 (unnum.).
13 John Stow, *A Survey of London*, reprinted from 1603 text (1908), 91–7.   14 TNA, DL 44/635.
15 Colvin, *British Architects*, 105; A.P. Baggs, 'Two designs by Simon Basil', *Archit.History*, 27 (1984), 104–10; Strype, *Survey*, I, bk 4, chap. 7, 120; drawing by W. Hollar, engraved 1808, pub. by W. Herbert and R. Wilkinson (Guildhall Libr., Main Print Colln, Pr.W2/STR).

the earldom to his son William (d. 1668), and then to his grandson James (d. 1683), 3rd earl, and the latter rebuilt part of the estate. The part of Little Salisbury House immediately adjoining Salisbury House and over the long gallery, was by 1671 converted into an exchange, called Middle Exchange, popularly known as Salisbury Change, and this was extended to the Thames by a long room with shops on each side, with stairs to the water-side. The 3rd earl received a royal licence in 1673 to build new houses on the ground west of Great Salisbury House; the rest of Little Salisbury House was demolished and Salisbury Street laid across the site from the Strand to the Thames. In 1690 James, 4th earl of Salisbury, decided to demolish Great Salisbury House and replace it with shops and houses, for which an Act was obtained in 1694 after his death. His son's guardians carried out the plans, laying out Cecil Street and building houses there. Salisbury Street was rebuilt in 1765–73, with a comprehensive street façade designed by the architect James Paine. The whole Salisbury estate in the Strand was sold in 1888.[1] No. 80 Strand, built as Shell-Mex House in 1931–3, occupied most of the site in 2008.[2]

CHESTER INN

The priory of Coventry, one of the seats of the bishop of Coventry and Lichfield, also known as the bishop of Chester,[3] had property in the Strand by 1218–36, when the bishop of Worcester acquired land on its east side.[4] Roger de Meuland, bishop of Coventry and Lichfield (1257–95), also acquired a nearby plot of land in St Mary of Strand in 1257, but granted it away in 1278 to Prince Edmund, younger son of Henry III, to become part of the Savoy.[5] The priory's property seems to have been assigned to the bishop by the later 13th century, as in 1291 the bishop of Chester held rents to the value of 24s. in St Mary of Strand.[6] The first indication of an epis-copal residence there was, however, under Walter Langton, treasurer of England (1295–1307) and bishop of Coventry from 1296 until his death in 1321.[7] He acquired a plot of land with buildings next to the church of St Mary from John de Moeles by 1300,[8] and in 1305 Thomas of Abberbury (precentor of Lichfield) received a licence to assign to Walter and his successors as bishops, a messuage held of the king for 1d.,[9] presumably a different property and perhaps that belonging already to

the bishopric. Shortly afterwards Walter conveyed to Thomas, presumably as feoffee, the messuage granted to him by Moeles.[10] At the same time the bishop received a licence to crenelate his houses in his dwelling-place in Strand, both those held in right of his bishopric and those built by him of stone and lime on his freehold plot, and also to build and crenelate a stone turret in the angle of his dwelling towards the east by the river Thames.[11] Langton, whose great wealth and support for the policies of Edward I had aroused deep dislike, was imprisoned by Edward II from 1307, when the temporalities of his bishopric were seized, but was restored in 1312, in which year he dated a charter at the stone cross, most likely meaning his house near the cross.[12] In 1321 John of Langton, clerk, whose relationship to Walter, if any, is unknown, received a licence to grant to the bishop to enlarge his house, a plot of land 7 perches by 4 adjoining the inn, and held of the bishop of Worcester for 12d. a year,[13] but a few months later Walter died there. A liberal benefactor of his diocese, he left all his property in the Strand to his episcopal successors.

By 1358 the messuage included six shops by the church of St Mary, let on lease by the bishop for 64s. a year.[14] Given that the bishops were often referred to as bishops of Chester, and that their inn was usually called Chester Place by themselves and others in the early 16th century, this was certainly the Chester Inn to which Thomas Hoccleve, a clerk of the privy seal, referred as his dwelling in *De Regimine Principum*, completed c.1412.[15] Bishops of Coventry who were not royal ministers commonly let their London inn to men who were: in 1381 the inn was occupied by John Fordham, keeper of the privy seal and bishop-elect of Durham, when the London mob broke in and stole barrels of wine from the cellar;[16] in 1424 John Stafford, treasurer of England, sealed a deed at the inn, and may have been living there.[17] From 1450 the bishops of Coventry were instructed to maintain only five residences, which included the inn on the Strand.[18] In 1535 the bishop's mansion there with its tenements was valued at £10 12s. a year, 40s. being paid to a bailiff.[19] Despite appeals to the king and Thomas Cromwell,[20] the bishop was forced to exchange his house on the Strand with Edward Seymour, then Viscount Beauchamp, for property in Kew in 1537; Seymour may have already been living in the inn, because his child was

1 *Survey of London*, XVIII. 121–3; TNA, C 66/3153, no. 4.

2 Pevsner, *London 6: Westm.* 379.

3 See was successively Lichfield, Chester, Coventry. Known officially as Bp of Chester until early 12th cent., unofficially much later, Bp of Coventry from mid 12th cent., Coventry and Lichfield from 1228: *Handbk of British Chronology*.

4 Worcs. & Herefs. RO, 821/BA 3814, f. 1050.

5 Strype, *Survey*, I, bk IV, 105; TNA, DL 25/149; DL 27/67; above, Manorial, Soke of Leic.

6 *Tax. Eccl.* (Rec. Com.), 14, 20b.

7 *DNB*.

8 TNA, CP 40/134, rot. 203.

9 *Cal. Pat.* 1301–7, 373.

10 TNA, CP 25/1/148/37/323.

11 *Cal. Pat.* 1301–7, 367.

12 BL, Add. Ch. 5485.

13 TNA, C 143/149, no. 13; *Cal. Pat.* 1321–4, 12.

14 TNA, E 149/14, no. 9. Inq. calls him John, but presumably Rog. de Northburgh.

15 Erroneously confused with inn of chancery called Strand inn nearby by John Stow and many subsequent writers.

16 *Anonimalle Chronicle*, ed. Galbraith, 141.

17 *Cal. Close*, 1422–9, 133.   18 *Cal. Papal Reg.* X. 471.

19 *Valor Eccl.* III. 128.

20 *L&P Hen. VIII*, XII(1), p. 357 (nos 806–7), p. 363 (nos 820–1), p. 526 (no. 1139); XIII(1), p. 76 (no. 223).

23. *Old Somerset House c.1720, a bird's eye view from the Thames, after the property, Chester Inn, had been enlarged by the acquisition of the neighbouring Worcester Place and remodelled, first for Protector Somerset in the mid 16th century and later as a royal residence.*

baptised in the chapel there before the exchange had formally taken place.[1] It was confirmed to Seymour, then earl of Hertford, and his heirs by Act of Parliament in 1539, and consisted of the capital messuage called Chester Place, with gardens, orchards, courts and other buildings, and also 13 tenements adjoining called Chester Rents.[2] Seymour became Lord Protector in 1547 on the accession of his nephew, Edward VI, and received the title of duke of Somerset.

Somerset Place

In 1547 Somerset enlarged the site of his inn, acquiring Worcester Place, which lay on the west side, together with the advowson, buildings, and churchyard of the church of St Mary of Strand, which lay on the east;[3] the church was demolished by the middle of 1548. At about the same time he also acquired the Strand inn, which lay between the church and the river[4] and in 1550 added the Goat inn, which had stood on the east side of the church and had a large garden behind.[5] From 1548 Somerset began building a new house farther up the site on ground formerly occupied by Chester Rents and the church and churchyard, and by 1550 Chester Place was also known as Somerset Place. The original hall of the inn, which seems to have lain close to the river,[6] may not have been demolished until some time later.[7] The later history of Somerset House will be treated as part of the account of the royal palaces in a later volume.

DURHAM INN

The bishop of Durham's inn near Charing was probably

his London residence when Richard Poore was bishop (1228–37), since during the ensuing vacancy of the see in 1237, Henry III housed the papal legate in the 'bishop's house at London'.[8] The bishops also had land on the north side of the Strand by the 1220s, later known as Durham Garden, which stood next to property in the parish of the Holy Innocents (later part of St Margaret's parish).[9] Bishop Walter of Kirkham (1249–60) was granted a rent of 4s. from property held of Westminster Abbey and given to the Pied Friars (below), near, or possibly adjoining, that garden.[10] The bishop was assessed in 1291, apparently in error, for rents valued at 10s. in the parish of St Clement Danes.[11] The bishop's house was described as in the parish of St Martin-in-the-Fields in 1309 when it was burgled.[12]

The bishop had a bailiff for his liberty in London in 1307,[13] and in 1345 the keeper of the bishop's 'manor of London', as his inn at Charing Cross was often called, received wages of 2d. a day, together with the profits of the garden and curtilage.[14] In 1373–4 John Rous, citizen of London, was appointed as keeper for 4d. a day and the profits of the garden.[15] The bishop was presented in the 1390s for not repairing the paving of the highway and the waste along the road outside his gate, the muddy plot being a danger to carts as well as pedestrians.[16]

In 1380 Thomas Hatfield, bishop 1345–81, granted in trust to John Henley, Hugh of Westwick, William of Beverley and John atte Lee, clerks, a significant part of his inn. The grant consisted of two chambers in the house (a vaulted chamber under the chapel and a solar by the entrance to the chapel) towards the north; the

---

1 *L&P Hen. VIII*, XII(1), p. 233 (no. 494).

2 TNA, E 315/34, no. 101; *L&P Hen. VIII*, XIV(1), p. 404 (no. 868).

3 Below, Worcester; Religious Hist.: Pars (St Mary Strand).

4 TNA, E 326/11959; E 315/48, no. 285. No doc. evidence for his acquisition of Strand Inn has been found.

5 Below, other Eccles., Abbey of Combe. Strand Inn reserved for treatment under Law Cts and Lawyers' Inns.

6 Wyngaerde, *View*.

7 *Cal. Pat.* 1549–51, 430–2; S. Thurley, *Somerset House:*

Palace of England's Queens, 1551–1692 (London Top. Soc., forthcoming 2009).   8 *Close R.* 1234–37, 479–80.

9 BL, Add. Ch. 10657.

10 TNA, C 145/78, no. 1; *Cal. Close*, 1313–18, 503; below, Other Eccles. Ests, Pied Friars.

11 *Tax. Eccl.* (Rec. Com.), 14, 20b.

12 *Cal. Pat.* 1307–13, 237.

13 C.M. Fraser, *Hist. of Antony Bek* (1957), 108.

14 *Cal. Close*, 1343–6, 532.   15 *Cal. Pat.* 1377–81, 584.

16 *Pub. Wks in Med. Law*, II (Selden Soc. XL), 60–1.

24. *Durham House, the main gatehouse from the Strand, c.1790, shortly before demolition.*

vestibule of the chapel with two chambers adjoining; all the inn with its houses or buildings lying on the east side of the north gate, inhabited by William of Beverley; a quarter of the garden within the garden wall, extending from the garden entrance northwards as far as the highway, 160 feet by 140; and a piece of waste 'outside the manor' opposite its north gate, perhaps the later garden on the north side of the Strand. The clerks were instructed to find 12 chaplains to celebrate divine service for 60 years within the inn for the souls of the bishops of Durham.[1] In 1537 the eastern part of Durham Place between the main gate and Ivy Lane, lying north of the inn's garden, was the site of Durham Rents, so the grant of 1380 may have been made with the intention of erecting houses for letting to support the chantry.[2] Bishop Thomas also loaned a sum of money to the abbey of St Albans to be repaid within 15 years after his death, to maintain chaplains celebrating in the inn's chapel for

his soul and that of the late king, which was paid over in 1387.[3] Before 1400, Beverley's executors granted a great messuage and garden to Sir Thomas Shelle, which may be his holding in the inn.[4]

Thomas Longley, bishop of Durham, who was chancellor of England in 1407, was using his London inn by 1427.[5] By 1516 the inn was usually called Durham Place, and was occupied by Cardinal Wolsey while York Place was being rebuilt. Wolsey subsequently also held the bishopric of Durham from 1523 to 1529, and bought hangings from his predecessor's executors: eight pieces with stories of Priam, Paris and Achilles, Jupiter, Pluto and Ceres, Hannibal, Virtue and hunting, some of which had been hung in Durham hall.[6] By 1509 Humphrey Coke or Cooke, the king's master carpenter, was keeper of Durham Place and bailiff of Durham Rents in the Strand,[7] where he had a lease for years of a tenement.[8] Several other craftsmen who worked for the king also

1 *Cal. Pat.* 1377–81, 611.
2 Below, Durham Rents.
3 *Cal. Close,* 1381–5, 554; 1385–9, 28, 440.
4 TNA, C 145/274, no. 6.   5 *Cal. Close,* 1422–9, 337.

6 *L&P Hen. VIII,* II, pp. 730, 765, 884; IV(3), pp. 2765, 2767.
7 J. Harvey, *Eng. Mediaeval Architects* (rev. edn 1984), 64–5; TNA, SP1/25, frame 208.
8 TNA, C 1/757/17; C 1/616/48.

lived in the Rents by 1514,[1] and by the 1520s one or more printers lived and worked there.[2]

In 1535 the bishop's property at Charing Cross consisted of his mansion with rents and farms there amounting to £18 1s. 4d. a year; his steward and bailiff, William Hebbistwayte [Hebelthwaite], received a fee of 15s. 2½d.[3] In 1536 the bishop gave the Durham property to Henry VIII in an exchange. The king received Durham Place with all its buildings, garden, orchard, fishponds, and stables, lately occupied by Thomas Boleyn, earl of Wiltshire, and all the other messuages and lands in St Martin's (Durham Rents) and in the parish of St Margaret Westminster (Durham garden), to the value of £18 18s., free of all encumbrances except leases; the bishop received Cold Harbour in Thames Street (in the City), of which George Talbot (d. 1538), 4th earl of Shrewsbury, was the tenant for life. The exchange was confirmed by Act of Parliament.[4] Durham Rents consisted of 20 tenements and 2 messuages with gardens lying between Durham Place and Ivy lane: the first tenement and the two messuages were held for 20s. by Humphrey Cooke, and the 19 other tenements were let for rents of between 10s. and 33s. 4d.[5] In 1537 the Crown leased the Rents to William Hebelthwaite together with Durham garden on the north side of the Strand, for 21 years at £20 a year,[6] but in 1544 sold them both in fee with other lands to William Forth or Ford on behalf of Nicholas Fortescue, groom porter of the king's household, for £220, subject to the lease to Hebelthwaite.[7]

Durham Place

The main part of the inn, Durham Place, with the mansion and other buildings in the courtyard, remained in the Crown's hands until 1603, serving as an auxiliary palace. In 1540, during a tournament held at the Palace of Westminster for Anne of Cleves, Durham Place was used for suppers and banquets for the king, queen, and nobles;[8] in 1546 the French embassy to London had to be found alternative accommodation because Durham House had been damaged by fire;[9] a mint was established there by the beginning of 1549.[10] Durham Place was included in the grant of lands made in 1550 to Princess Elizabeth in fulfilment of Henry VIII's will, to hold for life until a marriage was arranged for her.[11] After she became queen she used the house to accommodate foreign visitors and courtiers, including Sir Walter Raleigh who lodged there for 20 years, occupying in 1600 a house by the gateway to the Strand. Grey, Lord Chandos, also occupied a house nearby in 1603.[12] However, in 1558 Queen Mary had granted the reversion of Durham Place back to Cuthbert, bishop of Durham, and his successors.[13] The grant was never cancelled, and the bishops therefore resumed possession in March 1603 on Queen Elizabeth's death; the tenancies she had granted also ended with her death, and occupants such as Raleigh had to surrender possession to the bishop.[14] Although the bishop had lost possession of Durham Rents, the inn was still a large urban property, with the principal house and chapel, two courtyards, a garden, a large gatehouse with lodgings, and stables along the Strand frontage to the west. Parts of this assemblage were soon granted away, and their history is covered below after the main house.

Durham House

A plan drawn up in 1626 shows the layout of the principal mansion, which had an outer court with gatehouse to the Strand, and an inner court enclosed on the south and east by the medieval mansion. The hall range lay parallel with the river, partly screened from it by a lower block through which stairs descended to the water. Other ranges including the chapel lay at right angles between the courts and a garden all along the east side.[15] The view from the river drawn by Hollar in 1630 shows that the hall and ranges to the river were of stone and that the east ranges ended to the south as a tall block and a tower.[16]

As in earlier decades the house continued to be used to house important visitors to Court: the commissioners of Archduke Albert in 1604 during negotiations for a peace treaty between the kings of England and Spain and the archduke;[17] the duke of Lennox by 1606; and in 1619 three sets of ambassadors, from France, Savoy, and the States (Holland), and three agents, for the kings of Spain and Bohemia and the archduke. In 1623 the house was being fitted up for the grandees accompanying the prince and infanta of Spain, using furnishings from the royal wardrobe, and the French ambassador was again lodged there in 1626:[18] the bishop claimed he had given up 30 of the best rooms to the ambassador at the king's request, crowding himself and his family into the worst.[19] Various courtiers also occupied lodgings in the house: Viscount Conway by 1632 until at least 1639,[20] and Lord Keeper Coventry lived there from 1625 to his death in 1641.[21]

1 *Hist. King's Works*, III. 40, 204.
2 *DNB* sv. Wyer, Rob.   3 *Valor Eccl.* V. 300.
4 TNA, E 305/1/A3; *L&P Hen. VIII*, X, pp. 459–60.
5 TNA, SC 12/3/13; SP 1/25, frame 208.
6 TNA, E 315/209, f. 65v.
7 *L&P Hen. VIII*, XIX(1), p. 621 (no. 1035/41); TNA, E 318/10/447; CP 25/2/27/185/36Hen8/Mich. Below for later hist. of Durham Rents and Garden.   8 *L&P Hen. VIII*, XV, p. 300.
9 Ibid., XXI(1), p. 694.   10 *Cal. Pat.* 1548–9, 303.
11 Ibid. 1549–51, 240; 1550–53, 90–1.
12 Wheatley, 'Durham Ho.' 158–9.

13 *Cal. Pat.* 1557–8, 400.
14 'Egerton Papers', *Camden Soc.* XII (1840), 377.
15 Plan reprod. in Wheatley, 'Durham Ho.', opp. p. 150, and in *Survey of London*, XVIII, 92.
16 Drawing by W. Hollar, engraved 1808, pub. by W. Herbert and R. Wilkinson (Guildhall Libr., Main Print Colln, Pr.W2/STR).
17 Hist. MSS Com. *8th Rep.* App. I, pp. 95a, 98a.
18 *Trans. Devonshire Assoc.* XXXV (1903), 565, 573–4.
19 Wheatley, 'Durham Ho.' 151–5.
20 *Cal. SP Dom.* 1631–3, 282; 1635, 3; 1625–49, 603.
21 Wheatley, 'Durham Ho.' 160.

25. *Royal Society of Arts and no. 6 John Adam Street, two of the few surviving houses of the Adelphi scheme, designed by Robert and James Adam 1772–4, and built on Durham Yard, part of the inn of the bishops of Durham.*

At the suggestion of the king, the bishop granted the house to Philip Herbert, 4th earl of Pembroke, and his heirs in return for an annual rent-charge of £200, which was still being paid (to the Ecclesiastical Commissioners) in 1937;[1] the grant was confirmed by Act in 1640.[2] Pembroke apparently intended to rebuild, but the scheme was never carried out, probably because of the outbreak of the Civil War.[3] In the 1640s and 50s Pembroke allowed French Protestants to meet at Durham House;[4] parliamentary soldiers were also quartered there during the Commonwealth,[5] and in 1650 Parliament paid £200 to the earl for the use of the house by the State.[6] Pembroke died in 1650, succeeded by his son as 5th earl. The latter is said to have demolished the house in the 1660s, leasing the site in building plots used for new houses.[7] Although that might be thought to be when the street called Durham Yard was laid out east-west across the site and although William Faithorne's plan of Westminster published in 1658 still shows the old mansion and garden, a case put that year to parliamentary commissioners suggests that much new building had already been made on the foundations of the ancient house and outbuildings, and refers to the site as Durham Yard.[8]

Lord Pembroke sold the property in 1677 to Sir Thomas Mompesson, whose assignees sold it in 1716 to trustees of Sir John Werden, and it later passed to Charles Beauclerk, 2nd duke of St Albans, who had married one of Werden's daughters. After the death of George, the 3rd duke, without a male heir, his title and property devolved upon George Beauclerk, a descendant of the 1st duke. He devised the estate to his aunt, Charlotte Beauclerk, who married John Drummond, successor to the founder of Drummond's Bank, and it was still in the hands of her descendants in 1937.[9]

In 1682 there was one principal street, Durham Yard, running from east to west across the site to Ivy Bridge Lane, and a street joining it from the Strand gate. Houses were built on the south side of Durham Yard with gardens sloping to the river, but there were also wharves by the river front for commercial use, and soon most of the site had courts of little houses occupied by small trades and artisans. By the mid 18th century Durham Yard had become a slum, and nearly all the buildings were in ruins by 1767.[10] In 1768 the trustees of the 3rd duke of St Albans granted a 99-year lease of the property to the Adam brothers, Robert, James, and William, who built the Adelphi on the site. They obtained an Act in 1771 permitting them to reclaim and embank part of the Thames adjoining the site, on which they built vaulted wharves with the residential streets above, most of it completed by 1772. Financially the enterprise was nearly disastrous for the brothers, but architecturally the Adelphi was a great success, publicizing and popularizing the new Adam style, used there in external decoration as well as for the interiors.[11]

1 *Survey of London,* XVIII. 93; Wheatley, 'Durham Ho.' 160–1.   2 16 Chas I, c. 23.
3 *Survey of London,* XVIII, 93.
4 *Procs. Hug. Soc. London,* XXIV (1983–8), 232–9; below, Religious Hist.: Foreign Chs.
5 *Survey of London,* XVIII, 93.   6 *Cal. SP Dom.* 1650, 26.

7 *Survey of London,* XVIII. 93–4; Wheatley, 'Durham Ho.', 160–1.   8 BL, Add. MS 36223, f. 263.
9 *Survey of London,* XVIII, 94 n.
10 Morgan, *Map of London* (1682); *Survey of London,* XVIII. 94.
11 J. Summerson, *Georgian London* (1978 edn), 137–40.

Sales to the Earl of Salisbury

In 1603, Bishop Tobias Matthew (1583–1606) leased to the Crown for 80 years a 66-foot strip along the eastern border of his garden, parallel to Ivy Lane, and in 1604 the king assigned this to Sir Robert Cecil, created earl of Salisbury in 1605, for inclusion in the grounds of the house he had built on part of the neighbouring Carlisle inn.[1] Also in 1603, the bishop leased to his son, Toby Matthew, and to Dudley Carleton the gatehouse with rooms, lodgings, and buildings on the west side of the gate, presumably including the site of the former stables destroyed by a major fire in 1600, with access to the water conduit in the outer court, the gardens and orchard, and the Thames watergate. In 1605 Matthew and Carleton assigned all or part to Sir Thomas Leigh and Thomas Spencer.[2] In 1607 and 1608 Robert Cecil acquired their interests in property fronting the Strand and in the ruined stables (probably not rebuilt), and on the site began building Britain's Burse or the New Exchange.[3] Matthew's successor, Bishop William James (1606–17) made a grant in fee farm to Salisbury in 1609 of part of the inner court, to provide a passage at the rear of the new Burse to be joined at its western end by another at right angles leading to the riverbank, where a landing place was to be constructed which required the removal of some of the domestic offices. High walls were to be erected to separate those portions from the bishop's own residential part of the buildings. The arrangement is shown clearly on the 1626 plan. Under the deed separate stables for the use of the bishop were to be built on the west side of St Martin's Lane, presumably on Salisbury's estate there.[4]

The site of the New Exchange, the plot leading to the Thames, and the strip included in Salisbury House were held by the earls of Salisbury at an annual feefarm rent of £40, paid to the bishop until 1648 when William, earl of Salisbury, bought it out for £480.[5]

Salisbury's New Exchange was built in the Strand as a western counterpart to the Royal Exchange in the City of London. A design for it was drawn by Inigo Jones, but as the finished building differed considerably from Jones's design and records are unreliable, the extent of his involvement is not clear.[6] The king opened the Exchange in April 1609, giving it the name Britain's Burse, and Inigo Jones was paid for the entertainment provided for the king, which included speeches and songs.[7] It was intended as a shopping centre for fancy goods, serving the upper-class clientele passing along the Strand from City to Court. After a slow start it became a financially successful enterprise by the outbreak of the Civil War,[8] and, particularly after the Great Fire in London, became the seat of much trade and a fashionable resort, but lost popularity in the 18th century and was demolished in 1737.[9]

Salisbury's servant, Thomas Wilson (1560?–1629), knighted 1618, keeper of the records and author, supervised the building,[10] and in 1608 Salisbury leased to him a house behind the Burse at the western end next to the wall dividing York Garden from Durham Yard.[11] In 1615 Wilson leased his house to Sir Robert Cotton, antiquary and collector of manuscripts, for 21 years, although he was also still living in Durham Yard during this period.[12]

Bishop of Durham's Garden

In 1536 the bishop's property on the north side of the Strand consisted of a new tenement and a cottage held by Henry Romyng, the king's smith, for 5s., three new tenements held by Robert Tomson for 5s., and a cottage and garden held on an annual tenancy by Darby Laghyn and valued at 20s.[13] All this property was let to William Hebelthwaite with Durham Rents (above) in 1537, but in 1542 Henry Romyng obtained an 80-year lease from the Crown of his new tenement and cottage, for 36s. 8d. a year; the tenement was later known as the Black Bull inn and stood until c.1680.[14] The freehold of the whole property was granted to Nicholas Fortescue in 1544.[15]

EXETER INN AND ESSEX HOUSE

In the 1190s Henry Marshall, bishop of Exeter, built a chapel for the use of his bishopric on land in Longditch street he had acquired from Geoffrey Picot,[16] and presumably had a residence there, though nothing further is known of it. Although a small piece of land along the Strand was recovered in 1239 in a law-suit against a later bishop of Exeter,[17] it was probably not land of the bishopric, and there is no record of the bishops having a residence in the area before 1324, when Bishop Walter Stapleton acquired the property of St Sepulchre's priory, comprising 5 messuages, including that held for life by William de Bereford, in St Clement Danes, and 10s. 10d. rent in Westminster.[18] He also

1 *Trans. Devonshire Assoc.* XXXV (1903), 563, 578–9.

2 Wheatley, 'Durham Ho.' 159.

3 *Trans. Devonshire Assoc.* XXXV (1903), 563–4, 579–80; below.

4 *Trans. Devonshire Assoc.* XXXV (1903), 565; L. Stone, 'Inigo Jones and the New Exchange', *Archaeological Jour.* CXIV (1959), 106; below, Later Creations, Salisbury.

5 *Trans. Devonshire Assoc.* XXXV (1903), 580.

6 Summerson, *Archit. in Britain*, 115, 186.

7 Hist. MSS. Com. 9, *Salisbury*, XXIV, pp. 90, 168; Wheatley, 'Durham Ho.' 156.

8 Stone, *Crisis of Aristocracy*, 360.

9 Wheatley, 'Durham Ho.' 156. Detailed treatment under Economic Hist. in a later vol.

10 *DNB*.

11 TNA, SP 14/40, no. 22A; Wheatley, 'Durham Ho.' 158.

12 *Cal. SP Dom. 1619–23*, 424; BL, Cotton Ch. XXX. 24, ff. 1, 32.

13 TNA, SC 12/3/13.

14 *L&P Hen. VIII*, XVIII(1), p. 548 (no. 982); TNA, E 315/235, f. 117; *Survey of London*, XVIII. 126–7.

15 TNA, E 318/10/447.

16 *Eng. Episcopal Acta*, XII, *Exeter 1186–1257*, ed. F. Barlow (1996), 196.

17 *Cur. Reg. R.* XVI. 208.

18 Below, Other Eccles. Ests, Priory of St Sepulchre.

acquired a plot of land belonging to the honor of Leicester and lying between his property and the Thames, measuring about 140 feet along the waterfront and 140 feet deep on the east side, and enclosed it into his inn.[1] When he was murdered by a mob in 1326 he was said to be building a 'fair tower' at his house by the Thames, using stone from Holy Innocents' church.[2]

In 1338 the bishop granted to John of St Paul, king's clerk and later archbishop of Dublin, the tenement with its shops, houses, garden and orchards which had belonged to William de Bereford, together with the chapel of St Thomas annexed to it. This tenement clearly made up a substantial part of the Exeter property, stretching from the highway near St Clement Danes to the wall of the river, and extending from the property of the bishops of Bath on the west to an old dyke.[3] When the archbishop died in 1362 his tenement was described as a messuage with an adjoining garden and 7 shops, valued at 66s. 8d.[4] However, the bishop of Exeter still had a residence there, and reserved access to the chapel in 1338. In 1369, in addition to his inn, the bishop held 48s. in rents from 8 shops, described as 6s. each from cottagers.[5] In the 15th century a tenement on the property, formerly let to Peter Stucley, clerk, was let in 1472 on a 90-year lease to William Milford for 40s. a year,[6] and Milford Lane ran through the western part of the property from the Strand to the Thames by 1556, suggesting that the tenement was the one formerly occupied by Bereford and John of St Paul.[7] By the 1530s more than eleven additional houses or shops on the property were let by the bishop,[8] who in 1535 received £48 8s. 4d. in rents from London, including St Clement Danes.[9] The tenements were known as Exeter Rents and let in the early 16th century to William Daunce.[10]

Exeter Place was occupied by the duke of Norfolk in 1542.[11] In 1548, under instructions from the king, the bishop granted the mansion and all its appurtenances to Sir William Paget, KG, the king's principal secretary and later Lord Paget of Beaudesart, and his heirs in free socage. The king also granted to Paget a parcel of land from the garden of the Middle Temple, stretching 130 feet southwards from the back of tenements belonging to Exeter Place, and about 70 feet wide adjoining the east side of Exeter garden.[12] The inn was often known as Paget Place.

Paget died in 1563, succeeded by his son Henry, Lord Paget, who died without male issue in 1568, having conveyed the house to feoffees to be sold within two years of his death. The Spanish ambassador was lodging there in 1569, but was forced to move when the feoffees sold the inn to Robert Dudley, earl of Leicester, for £2,500.[13] During Paget's ownership, part or all of the property in Milford Lane was sold off separately: a house and garden newly-built in 1556 was apparently already in other hands, and later became the rectory of St Clement Danes,[14] and premises including a watermill were conveyed in 1564, possibly the mansion and wharf at the bottom of Milford Lane conveyed in 1568.[15] In 1581 four messuages next to Milford Lane, formerly part of the Exeter estate, had been held by William Evans since at least 1569 in free socage, and occupied by labourers or craftsmen.[16]

Leicester House

Leicester built a two-storeyed banqueting house in the garden by the river in 1575,[17] and possibly made other improvements to the inn, now called Leicester House. Several inventories of the contents of the inn made during the earl's lifetime and after his death list the wealth of furnishings, pictures, and other possessions; the value in 1588 was £3,297,[18] and his collection of pictures was the first really large collection recorded in England.[19] A detailed inventory of his goods in the house taken in 1590 describes a hall, 42 chambers, the high gallery, which contained several portraits and framed maps, the low gallery, four wardrobes (rooms), kitchen, buttery, pantry and larder, lodge, chapel and vestry, armoury, and banqueting house. Apart from Lady Leicester, the earl of Warwick occupied several of the chambers, as did Lady Rich, and the Rich wardrobe included maps and portraits.[20] Leicester bequeathed the house, failing issue from his illegitimate son Robert Dudley, to his stepson Robert Devereux, earl of Essex, but on Leicester's death in 1588, his widow Lettice took possession without licence, for which she was pardoned in 1589 and allowed to remain in possession.[21] She leased to Christopher Browne, in consideration of long service by his father Richard to the earl of Leicester, the messuage and other rooms then occupied by Richard, together with the tennis court, to hold for 40 years or the term of her life.[22] Lettice married Sir Christopher Blount, Leicester's former master of horse, in 1589, and

1 TNA, C 135/6.

2 J. Leland, *Antiquarii Collectanea*, I. 468.

3 *Cal. Pat.* 1338–40, 127; *Year Bk 18 Edw. III* (Rolls Series), p. 89; *Cal. Close*, 1343–6, 580.

4 TNA, C 135/174, no. 3.

5 TNA, E 149/29, no. 1.

6 *Cal. Close*, 1485–1500, 340.

7 Burghley Ho. MSS, cal. NRA 6666, 80/27.

8 TNA, C 1/884/76.

9 *Valor Eccl.* II. 291.

10 TNA, C3/52/74.

11 *L&P Hen. VIII*, XVII, p. 555 (no. 997).

12 *Cal. Pat.* 1547–48, 295.

13 GEC, *Complete Peerage*, X. 276–80; A. Kendall, *Rob. Dudley, Earl of Leicester* (1980), 121; TNA, C 2/Eliz/C10/46.

14 Burghley Ho. MSS, cal. NRA 6666, 80/27, 5/25.

15 TNA, CP 25/2/171/6Eliz/Trin. [Cal. only – doc. missing]; 171/18&19Eliz/Mich.; 172/22Eliz/Trin.; E 210/10346.

16 TNA, C 142/406, no. 13; CP 25/2/171/11Eliz/Trin.

17 Kendall, *Rob. Dudley*, 151.

18 BL, Harl. Roll D. 35, m. 16.

19 Stone, *Crisis of Aristocracy*, 714.

20 TNA, E 178/1446.

21 TNA, C 66/1316, m. 20.

22 TNA, C 146/9306.

they were granted the house by the queen in 1590 to hold on payment of £161 a year to the Exchequer in settlement of Leicester's debts to the Crown;[1] in 1592 Blount was appealing to Burghley for some relief from his debts, possibly referring to payment of Leicester's obligations.[2]

Essex House

By 1593 the house was also known as Essex House,[3] and Robert Devereux, 2nd earl of Essex (6th creation), was living there. In February 1601 it was the scene of his surrender after his abortive rebellion.[4] Both he and Blount were executed for treason, but Lettice continued in possession of Essex House until her death in 1634, and various family members also lived there. Her daughter Dorothy (d. 1619), wife of Henry Percy, earl of Northumberland, was living there with her husband by 1602;[5] later residents included Lettice's granddaughter Lucy and her husband James Hay, Lord Hay, later earl of Carlisle, famous for his culinary exploits, which included a feast at Essex House for the French ambassador in 1621, involving 100 cooks employed for 8 days concocting 1,600 dishes, at a total cost said to be £3,300.[6] In 1627 Lettice granted a lease to the earl of Carlisle and his wife of the rooms formerly occupied by Northumberland, including the long high gallery, for 11 years or her lifetime, at £90 a year, but after the rent was not paid, she had to go to court in 1631 to get possession.[7]

After Lettice's death the house passed to her son Robert Devereux, 3rd earl of Essex, who in 1639 leased specified parts of it for 99 years at a token rent to his sister Frances and her husband Sir William Seymour, earl, later marquess, of Hertford.[8] Lord Essex, Lord General of the parliamentary forces, died at Essex House in 1646: his heirs were his sister Frances and Sir Robert Shirley, son of his other sister Dorothy.[9] The Hertfords continued living at Essex House, and in 1654 the property, described as 29 messuages, a wharf, and 5 acres of land, was conveyed to trustees to secure the debts of Lady Hertford and her son Viscount Beauchamp.[10] Mid 17th-century depictions of the house suggest it was largely the work of Leicester; it stood south of an irregular forecourt behind a row of tenements but at the north end of the long plot: Hollar shows the main part of the house with a compact and apparently 16th-century courtyard plan, with two-storeyed ranges rising to four storeys at the south-east corner. The east range extended north to the Strand and may have had a flat roof, and another wing stretched west. The compact form meant

that most of the land was devoted to terraced gardens with 17th-century style parterres; Leicester's banqueting house still stood by the river.[11]

In 1660 Lord Hertford was restored to the title of duke of Somerset held by his ancestor, but died that year. His duchess continued at Essex House, which was rated on 58 hearths in 1674.[12] Tenements fronting the Strand and buildings in the court were let on long leases: one house in the court was let to the common lawyer Sir Orlando Bridgeman, Bt (d. 1674), chief baron of the Exchequer and lord chief justice of Common Pleas in 1660, and lord keeper of the great seal 1667–72.[13] He was using his house at Essex House as his London residence by 1665, and complained to the duchess that although he valued the benefit of being in some sense under her roof, his rent had been raised several times to £58 a year, which he felt was more than it was worth, as in addition he had to hire a coach-house and stable elsewhere bringing the cost to *c*.£80; it would also cost him £500 to put the house in good repair.[14] Possibly it was rebuilt, as in 1670 it was referred to as 'new',[15] but Ogilby and Morgan's map suggests that it had been altered rather than completely renewed. It shows that east range of the courtyard was wider, the north range had gone and the courtyard had been reduced to a passage from the forecourt.[16]

The duchess died at Essex House in 1674, bequeathing to her granddaughter Frances and the latter's husband Sir Thomas Thynne use of the apartment they had in Essex House for six months.[17] Thynne and Sir William Gregory, baron of the Exchequer, were her executors. They sold Essex House and 7 tenements fronting the Strand to Dr Nicholas Barbon for £13,450, and some other tenements near the house to Thomas Cox for £850.[18] By 1679 Barbon had demolished the house and other buildings, except the part occupied by Bridgeman, and laid out Essex Street along the line of the former entrance to the house and court, with a cross street from Milford Lane to the Middle Temple, erecting some houses and wharfs on part and leasing the rest to others for building. Shortly afterwards he sold on all the ground rents and reversion of the site, including two wharfs, two vaults, and some stables, except for a building then under construction to be used as part of the Middle Temple, and the house and ground occupied by Lady Bridgeman, which was to be conveyed to her. The old tenements fronting the Strand held by tenants on 21-year leases remained, except for a couple for which the tenants' interests were bought out, in order to

1 Guildhall MS 111, vol. 14, ff. 138, 170–2.
2 HMC 58, *Bath V*, p. 224.
3 Ibid., pp. 254, 261–2.
4 Ibid., pp. 277–81; *Cal. SP Dom.* 1601–3, 11.
5 GEC, *Complete Peerage*, IX. 734.
6 Stone, *Crisis of Aristocracy*, 561.
7 TNA, C 78/515, no. 7.
8 *Coll. Top. et Gen.* VIII. 309–12.
9 HMC 58, *Bath IV*, p. 219.
10 Ibid., pp. 222–6; TNA, CP 25/2/617/1654/Easter.
11 *Hollar's London*, Plate 5.
12 HMC 58, *Bath IV*, p. 255.
13 *DNB*.
14 HMC 58, *Bath IV*, p. 255.
15 Ibid., pp. 269–70, 359–60.
16 Ogilby & Morgan, *Map of London* (1677).
17 HMC 58, *Bath IV*, p. 235.
18 Ibid., p. 357.

widen the former entrance to the house and create Essex Street.[1]

LLANDAFF'S INN

William of Radnor, bishop of Llandaff, was granted permission for life in 1263 to lodge in the close of the king's hermitage at Charing when visiting London,[2] and in 1280 the king granted to the bishop's successor, William de Breuse, with the consent of Edmund, earl of Leicester, the lord of the fee, permission to lodge in the inn of the priory of St Sepulchre, Warwick, near the church of St Clement Danes, for life.[3] Subsequently, however, Edmund granted to the bishop a plot of land near the church of St Mary of Strand, on which the bishop had built two houses by his death in 1287, the main one north of the other. In 1311 Edmund's son Thomas, earl of Lancaster, granted to William's successor, John of Monmouth, a plot of land 98 feet by 12 belonging to his soke of Leicester, on the west side of the bishop's houses and next to the church.[4] In 1373 the bishop's property there, described as his inn and garden near the Strand, was in the hands of the king for a debt owed by Bishop Roger of Cradock,[5] and was still in the king's hands in 1382 at the bishop's death. In 1399 the inn was given into the keeping of Thomas, bishop of Llandaff, who had to pay 60s. a year to the Exchequer, the amount at which the property was valued.[6]

In 1479 the bishop's garden lay on the south side of a tenement just inside the parish of St Clement Danes:[7] assuming it adjoined the bishop's inn, this would place the inn south of the churchyard of St Mary and of the later Goat inn, stretching eastward to the parish boundary, and with its garden straddling both parishes. No further reference to Llandaff's property has been found, and the bishopric did not hold property in Westminster in 1535.[8] The location of the inn and garden suggests that it had become the chancery inn called Strand Inn by the early 16th century; it may have been let to lawyers by the bishops at an earlier date.

NORWICH PLACE AND YORK HOUSE

The bishop of Norwich had a house in London by 1237, when the keeper of his property was ordered by the king to repair the quay of the bishop's buildings, suggesting that this was the inn by the Thames near Charing.[9] In 1369 Bishop Thomas Percy was occupying his inn at Charing Cross, and also received 13s. 4d. rent in the

parish of St Martin-in-the-Fields, presumably from buildings or gardens in the inn.[10] At his death in 1425, Bishop John Wakeryng held the inn which with its gardens was valued at 40s. a year after fees to the keeper, with ten cottages annexed to it valued at 20s. a year,[11] but by the time his successor was translated to another see in 1437, the inn was said to include five cottages valued at 100s. a year.[12]

The inn stood on the west side of its site, with a gateway from the Strand leading to the hall of the inn, which also included a chapel, gardens on the east, and access to the river on the south via stairs in the middle of the river frontage.[13] The five cottages were apparently the tenements which stood on the east side of the gate fronting the Strand by the late 15th century when they were let on lease. In 1520 they were rebuilt as seven tenements, and with vacant ground between them and Durham Place were leased to Robert Hale and his wife Alice and 12 new houses built. The 19 tenements were known as Norwich Rents:[14] tenants included the printer Richard Pynson, where he was succeeded by Robert Wyer, printer, c.1530.[15] Hale was presumably 'Hule', keeper of the bishop's inn, who was one of five people in St Martin's with goods of over £20 in 1522, being assessed on £40.[16]

In 1536 Henry VIII granted the bishop a house in Canon Row in exchange for Norwich Place, which he then granted to his close companion Charles Brandon, duke of Suffolk, reserving the rights of William Hale, Richard Hale and his wife Catherine to the keepership of the inn, which included the profits of the garden.[17] Suffolk died there in 1545, succeeded by his under-age son Henry, but both Henry and his brother and heir Charles died on the same day in 1551.[18]

In 1557 Nicholas Heath, archbishop of York and lord chancellor, bought the rights in the inn, known as Suffolk Place, of Lady Frances, duchess of Suffolk, daughter of the 1st duke, and of the heirs of her two sisters, the premises being described as 50 messuages, 10 cottages, 4 stables, and 7 gardens in St Martin-in-the-Fields, and the queen granted the inn to the archbishop and his successors in frankalmoign; it was thereafter usually known as York House.[19]

After Elizabeth's accession the mansion was not occupied by the archbishops; it was sometimes used by the Crown for housing official guests and courtiers,[20] but in general seems to have been let to successive chancellors

1 TNA, C 78/1210, no. 1.
2 *Cal. Pat.* 1258–66, 246–7.
3 Ibid. 1272–81, 370–1.
4 Ibid. 1307–13, 286; TNA, DL 42/2, f. 217, no. 11; C 143/72, no. 3.
5 *Cal. Fine R.* 1369–77, 217.
6 Ibid. 1399–1405, 32; TNA, E 364/33, m. 1.
7 TNA, C 54/333, m. 7d.
8 No Westm. property listed in *Valor Eccl.*
9 *Close R.* 1234–7, 488.
10 TNA, E 149/29, no. 2.

11 TNA, E 153/1019, [m. 2].
12 Ibid. /1026, [no. 3].
13 *Survey of London*, XVIII. 51, 55, 57; *L&P Hen. VIII*, IV(2), 1869 (no. 4242).
14 *Survey of London*, XVIII. 57–8.
15 *DNB* sv. Wyer.
16 TNA, SP 1/25, frame 205.
17 *Survey of London*, XVIII. 51.   18 TNA, C 142/96/29.
19 TNA, CP 25/2/74/630/3&4P&M/Hil; *Cal. Pat.* 1555–7, 439.
20 HMC 58, *Bath V*, 216; Stone, *Crisis of the Aristocracy*, 461.

26. *York Water-gate in Embankment Gardens. Built by Nicholas Stone in 1626–7, it was the grand Thames river entrance to the gardens of York House, which was demolished c.1676 for Buckingham Street.*

or keepers of the great seal. Sir Nicholas Bacon, lord keeper 1558–79, occupied it, and his son Francis was born there in 1561. In 1600 the trial of the earl of Essex, after his Irish *débâcle*, was held in the great chamber in York House, attended by *c.*200.[1] The lord chancellor, Sir Thomas Egerton, died there in 1617. His successor as lord keeper, Francis Bacon, succeeded him in the house,[2] taking a lease from the archbishop in 1617 for 21 years. Following his dismissal from office for alleged corruption, Bacon, then Viscount St Albans, assigned his lease to George Villiers, duke of Buckingham, for £1,300 in 1622.[3]

In 1593 the archbishop drafted a grant to Edwin and Miles Sands of the custody of York House in the Strand at a fee of £3 10*d.* a year, granting them also the gatehouse, a rent of 3*s.* 4*d.*, and the porter's lodge and garden house.[4] In 1596 Edward Coppinger obtained a lease from the archbishop of a strip of ground in York House garden at the rear of York Rents, measuring 300 feet east–west from Durham wall up to the hall door by the great gate, and 70 feet from York Rents southwards. He divided the ground into plots to correspond with the tenements in the Rents and sublet them to the occupiers: most were used to increase their accommodation as the Rents were only *c.*20 feet deep.[5] The 19 tenements of York Rents were held by 11 lessees *c.*1618, who renewed

their leases every 3, 5, or 7 years; in 1618 they paid a total of £230 to the archbishop in entry fines.[6]

In 1624 the archbishop surrendered the inn with York Rents to the king, who, wishing to grant it to the duke of Buckingham, pointed out that it had not been used as a bishop's residence for a long time. As the archbishops only received £11 a year for the house, which was in bad repair in any case, it was insisted that they would benefit from the surrender, for which they received lands in Yorkshire valued at £140 a year and a house in Canon Row provided by the duke; the surrender was confirmed by Act of Parliament.[7]

Buckingham remodelled the house, sometimes known as Buckingham House during his occupation, but the demolition of old and decaying walls was not enough to create adequate rooms for state occasions. As he could not afford to demolish it all and rebuild in a modern fashion, rooms were adapted instead, under the supervision of Sir Balthazar Gerbier, who had a dwelling beside the gatehouse[8] and was employed by the duke as keeper of his collections and architectural adviser. Gerbier's work, carried out in 1624–5, was mainly decorative, and included a marble cabinet and a great chamber, both of which were paved. Although the duke also had Wallingford House in King Street as a residence, York House with its state rooms and fine garden became

1 HMC 58, *Bath V*, 269.
2 *Cal. SP Dom.* 1611–18, 514; *Letters of John Holles 1587–1637*, I (Thoroton Soc. Rec. Series 31, 1975), 156.
3 TNA, C 78/218, no. 13; R. Lockyer, *Buckingham: Life and Political Career of Geo. Villiers, 1st duke of Buckingham* (1981), 118–19.

4 *Cal. SP Dom.* 1591–4, 325.
5 *Survey of London*, XVIII. 58.   6 TNA, C 3/324/74.
7 Lockyer, *Buckingham*, 213; 21 Jac. I, c. 30; *Letters of John Holles 1587–1637*, II (Thoroton Soc. Rec. Series 35, 1983), 295; *Cal. SP Dom.* 1623–5, 202, 301.
8 TNA, E 178/5973.

his principal London house, used especially for ceremonial occasions. The main approach was from the river Thames, where an appropriate entrance was created in 1626 with a new water-gate imitating one of Serlio's designs for city gates. It may have been designed by Nicholas Stone, who is credited with building it.[1]

One of the attractions of York House was the magnificent art collection which Buckingham assembled there, from 1621 commissioning Gerbier and others to scour Europe for paintings, sculptures and other rarities. His position as favourite of James I and then chief minister of Charles I ensured that English ambassadors around Europe also sought marbles and paintings for him. At his death in 1628 he had well over 300 pictures, in particular of the Venetian school – a collection superior to that of the earl of Arundel. Buckingham also admired Caravaggio and those influenced by him, including Orazio Gentileschi whom he lured to York House in 1625, where the painter decorated the grand saloon ceiling, and also acquired for York House most of Sir Peter Paul Rubens's famous collection.[2]

The duke was assassinated in 1628, and York House passed to his widow Catherine for life as part of her jointure. In 1631 she asked for help in getting the king to pay the money he owed to Gentileschi so that the latter would leave England and his lodgings in York House; the duchess claimed she had to keep a family at her Chelsea house to look after her laundry owing to lack of room at Charing.[3] The estates of the duchess, who had married Randall MacDonnell, 2nd earl of Antrim, were sequestered in 1644. On her death in 1649 the property passed to her son George, 2nd duke of Buckingham,[4] but he had fought for Prince Charles in 1648 and escaped abroad, forfeiting his estates.[5] Much of the art collection went abroad with him and he sold over 200 paintings at Antwerp in 1648.[6]

Parliament granted York House to Thomas, Lord Fairfax, the parliamentary general, in satisfaction of various arrears due to him.[7] The 2nd duke returned to England in 1657, persuaded Fairfax's daughter Mary to marry him, and took up residence at York House. At the Restoration his estates were returned to him, but he moved to Wallingford House which became his London residence, letting York House for state and ceremonial purposes. It was used by Spanish, Russian, French, and Portuguese ambassadors; in 1671 the king and queen were entertained there with the French ambassador,[8]

and in 1672 the conferences of the commission treating with the Portuguese ambassador were held there.[9] In 1662 Buckingham demanded a rent of £400 for lodging the Russian ambassador,[10] but even charging as much as £450 a year, he was still out of pocket because so much had to be spent in repairs, and early on he considered rebuilding.[11] He was granted a licence to rebuild York House and other houses in 1664, though it was only in 1672–3 that he granted a building lease of York House, which was then demolished. Buckingham, George (later York Buildings), Villiers and Duke streets and Of Alley (later York Place) had been laid out by 1674; Villiers Street was approximately on the line of the main gate to the Strand. A terrace walk was formed along the river bank with the York water-gate in the centre.[12] Like most of the duke's estates, the property was heavily mortgaged, and was probably sold before Buckingham died in 1687.

York Rents were sequestered with the rest of York House during the Commonwealth and sold in lots in 1653, but the freehold was returned to the duke in 1660. The Rents were broken up when York House was divided into building plots in 1674, and most seem to have been rebuilt. Some were demolished to make entrances from the Strand into Villiers and Buckingham streets and George Alley (later Court).[13]

WORCESTER INN

The bishops of Worcester had an inn in the Strand by 1208, and may have had property nearby for much longer:[14] the land which Bishop Alhwine received from King Burghred in 857 seems to have lain in the heart of *Lundenwic*.[15] The church of St Mary of Strand, which apparently belonged to the cathedral priory of Worcester by 1100, was perhaps built on part of it.[16] The site of the bishop's inn, although near that church, was acquired later and there is no known tenurial connection between the two properties. The inn's origins lie in a residence built by the royal clerk, Godfrey de Lucy, on land at the Strand bought sometime before he became bishop of Winchester in 1189. In 1204, shortly before his death, Godfrey granted this house with its buildings and rents to the abbey of Lessness (Kent), subject to the right of his son John de Lucy to hold them for life paying 6s. 8d. to the abbey. Abbot Fulk and the convent of Lessness and John de Lucy sold their rights in the property to Bishop Mauger of Worcester for 50 marks,

1 Colvin, *British Architects*, 396–7, 561.

2 Lockyer, *Buckingham*, 409–11; Stone, *Crisis of Aristocracy*, 719–20.

3 *Cal. SP Dom.* 1631–3, 123.

4 *Cal. Cttee Comp.* I. 254.

5 *DNB*.

6 Lockyer, *Buckingham*, 462.

7 BL, Add. Ch. 1800.

8 *Cal. SP Dom.* 1671, 43.

9 Ibid. 1672–3, 629–30.

10 Ibid. 1661–2, 500.

11 *DNB*; *Survey of London*, XVIII. 57.

12 *Cal. SP Dom.* 1663–4, 612; NRA 11231, cal. of Bateman Hanbury MSS (Northants. RO), BH(K) 1154–1165; *Survey of London*, XVIII. 57, 61.

13 *Survey of London*, XVIII. 59.

14 Worcester Inn has no connection with the later Worcester Ho., for which see above, Carlisle Inn.

15 Sawyer, *A.-S. Charters*, no. 208; below; Religious Hist.: Intro.

16 *Cartulary of Worcester Cathedral Priory* (PRS LXXVI), pp. l, 41; below, Religious Hist.: St Mary le Strand.

presumably before 1208 when the bishop fled abroad.[1] In 1212 the bishopric received rent of 28s. 3d. a year from London;[2] if 12s. 6d. of this came from its London soke (as in 1303), the remainder may all have derived from the Strand and the church of St Mary of Strand, probably arising from some of the plots later resumed by the bishops in the 13th and 14th centuries.

In 1222, after a successful claim for service by Bishop William de Blois of Worcester, Richard son of Edward, also called Richard Aylward, granted and quitclaimed to the bishop the messuage with free access which he held of the bishop in socage for 18d. service; it lay on the Strand, in the parish of St Mary of Strand, next to the bishop's demesne land, and stretched from the highway to the Thames; the bishop and the priory gave him 100s. for the grant.[3] At about the same time Bishop William paid 4 marks to Everard de la Welle (?Atwell) for a grant of his land in St Mary of Strand, lying between the land of the bishop and the land of the priory of Coventry, and extending from the highway to the Thames, for which the bishop was to pay a penny to Everard and his heirs and 16d. to the unnamed lord of the fee;[4] possibly this was the tenement for which the bishops paid 16d. to the soke of Mohun c.1300.[5] The bishop may have used the acquisition to enlarge his house.

During a vacancy of the see in 1266, Henry III granted the episcopal houses near the church of St Mary to his half-brother, William de Valence, for a lodging.[6] The bishop was residing there in 1282 when its chapel was mentioned,[7] but parts of his property were held by tenants. In 1278 Robert the cooper held a plot of land between the highway and the Thames lying on the west side of the bishops land next to the Savoy estate; this was granted to the holder of the Savoy in 1294, who paid 24s. a year to the bishop for it.[8] The property of the bishops in the Strand may have been augmented by the lands of Peter fitzAlan, citizen of London, which Henry III granted to his clerk Godfrey Giffard in 1265;[9] Giffard subsequently became bishop of Worcester in 1268, and the messuage in Strand parish which he granted successively to Alan of Huntingfield for life, and to Richard the parson of St Mary of Strand for life before 1278,[10] may have been part of that property rather than the houses on the south side of the Strand. In 1281 the bishop paid 40s. to Alan's sister and heir Maud of Huntingfield for a

quitclaim of the messuage.[11] This augmentation would account for the high amount of rent the bishop received from the parish of St Mary, recorded in 1291 as £4 5s. 6d.[12] In 1294 the bishop also claimed right to the assize of bread and of ale for his tenants in the parish, claiming he and his predecessors had held them from time immemorial without interruption, but a jury found the assizes were part of the king's farm of London.[13] In 1302–3 the bishop received £3 15s. 6d. rent from his manor near the stone cross (in the Strand), in addition to his sokage in London of 12s. 6d.[14]

Two other parts of the Strand property were held by tenants by the early 14th century. One was a plot of land 7 perches by 4 held by John of Langton, clerk, for which he paid 12d. a year to the bishop and suit of the bishop's 3-week court.[15] The other was plot 99 by 53 feet, with a lane 240 feet long and 11 wide leading from the plot to the Thames with a chamber built over it at the end next to the river; it lay between the bishop's tenement and Langton's, and was held by Nicholas of Kertling and his wife Christian from the bishop and the chapter of Worcester, apparently free of rent. Bishop Walter Reynolds (1307–13), chancellor from 1310, who frequently resided in London, resumed the plot and lane from the Kertlings in 1308, paying them 20 marks,[16] probably to enlarge his house: the rental income from the property had been considerably reduced by 1373. His successor obtained the plot formerly of Robert the cooper on the west side of the inn in 1316 from Thomas earl of Lancaster, for anniversaries for the earl's parents.[17] At Bishop William de Lenne's death in 1373 the bishop's inn was not valued because he resided there, and the only other property mentioned were three shops annexed to it and valued at 30s. a year; these were said to be in St Clement Danes, and may have been part of Giffard's property rather than the inn.[18]

Like other bishops' houses, the inn was often occupied by royal officials and ministers. In 1339 Edward III granted the bishop of Worcester's houses in the Strand to his treasurer, William de la Zouche, dean of York, during a vacancy in the see;[19] the chancellor, Sir Robert de Bourchier, was dwelling there in 1340–1,[20] and his successor, Sir Robert Parving, lodged there in March 1343.[21] In August that year the bishop granted to William of Netherton for life the office of keeper of his

1 Worc. RO, 821/BA 3814, ff. 52–v., 103; HMC, *14th Report, pt. 8, MSS of D & C of Worcester* (1895), 194; *Eng. Episc. Acta, VIII, Winchester 1070–1204*, 162–3. Names of witnesses indicate Strand nr Westm. is meant.

2 *Pipe Roll 14 John* (PRS, NS, XXX, 1954), 60.

3 Worc. RO, 821/BA 3814, ff. 104v–105; TNA, CP 25/1/146/6/39.

4 Worc. RO, 821/BA 3814, f. 105.

5 WAM 50638.

6 *Cal. Pat.* 1258–66, 562.

7 *Reg. Godfrey Giffard*, II. 149.

8 TNA, DL 29/1/3, m. 13d.

9 Grant recorded with other Strand grants in Liber Albus of bps, Worc. RO, 821/BA 3814, f. 103. FitzAlans held property in St Clement Danes.

10 TNA, CP 40/31, rot. 67d.; CP 40/33, rot. 56.

11 Worc. RO, 821/BA 3814, ff. 48v.–9, 104v.

12 *Tax. Eccl.* (Rec. Com.), 14.

13 *Plac. de Quo Warr.* (Rec. Com.), 475.

14 TNA, SC 6/1143/8.

15 TNA, C 143/149, no. 13; above, Chester Inn.

16 Worc. RO, 821/BA 3814, ff. 103v.–104v.; *Cal. Pat.* 1307–13, 148; TNA, C 143/74, no. 7; CP 25/1/149/39, no. 24.

17 *Cal. Pat.* 1313–17, 441; TNA, C 143/111, no. 9.

18 TNA, E 149/36, no. 1.

19 *Cal. Pat.* 1338–40, 176.

20 *Cal. Close*, 1339–41, 657; 1341–3, 267.

21 *Ibid.* 1343–6, 97.

manor next to the Thames, and collector of rents in and outside the City of London, receiving annually in return 40s. and a robe.[1] In 1386 another chancellor, Thomas Arundel, bishop of Ely, was lodging there.[2]

In 1398 the bishop granted the custody of his mansion with all the easements of its houses between the great gate of the mansion and the Savoy, and a vacant plot between the gate and the Savoy 30 feet by 18, with all issues from the gardens and stanks, to Henry Cambridge, citizen and fishmonger, who was to build on the plot, and provide 'herbs' from the gardens for the bishop's household when in residence, paying a pound of pepper at Michaelmas.[3] In 1435–6 the bishop paid £48 and promised an additional £46 13s. 4d. for the construction of a row of 8 houses on the Strand property.[4]

In 1535 the bishop, Hugh Latimer, held rents of £6 2s. at the Strand, from which his bailiff was paid 6s. 8d.,[5] and resided in the inn, then known as Worcester Place. In 1546 his successor was forced by Henry VIII to exchange his property in the Strand and land elsewhere for the property of the Carmelite Friars in Fleet Street, formally completed in May 1547. Worcester Place was granted at farm to Sir Ralph Sadler, royal administrator, in 1546 for £10 a year, and in fee the following year.[6] The day after the latter grant, Sadler conveyed the property to Edward Seymour, duke of Somerset,[7] who held the adjoining Chester Place. Worcester Place and the advowson of St Mary were confirmed to the duke in 1550 after his rehabilitation,[8] but after his attainder and execution in 1552, the property returned to the Crown as part of Somerset Place.

Some of the inn's buildings were presumably demolished to enable Somerset to enlarge Chester Inn, perhaps forming the stable yard, since the gatehouse to Worcester Place, as well as the houses fronting the Strand, remained untouched. The rents for seven of these amounted to £5; two of them were let for 70 years in 1528 for 26s. 8d., and two tenements and gardens in 1532 for 60 years at 33s. 4d. A tenement on the west side of the gatehouse of Worcester Place was let by the Crown for 21 years in 1559, and others in reversion in 1573, one abutting the former wall of the bishop's mansion on the south, another on the bishop's garden.[9] Access to stables in the Savoy over land formerly of the bishop of Worcester through an old gate to the Strand was granted by the Crown in 1574.[10]

YORK PLACE

The property which later became York Place had its origins in the late 12th century, when Richard fitz Neal (Richard of Ely), treasurer to Henry II and Richard I, acquired land and buildings between King Street and the Thames, to the north of Endive Lane, which led to the Thameside wharf of Enedehithe. It is not certain whether he was living there in 1177 when he wrote the *Dialogus de Scaccario*.[11] After he became bishop of London in 1189, he granted his property to his kinsman William of Ely, who succeeded him as treasurer in 1196, and his heirs, in return for rendering annually a two-pound wax candle to Westminster Abbey on the feast of Translation of St Edward; the grant was confirmed by the abbot of Westminster in 1196, and by the king in 1200.[12] William also acquired another messuage at Endith from Marwanna daughter of William, possibly the messuage in William's close which Roger Enganet quitclaimed to him in 1201.[13] By 1217, after his dismissal from office, his property by the Thames consisted of several buildings and a courtyard, with a stable outside the court but adjoining it; it probably also housed some of the treasurer's clerks.

About 1220 William granted his houses, courtyard, and stable to Westminster Abbey, with provision for him to continue to live there for payment of the wax candle.[14] Between 1222 and 1224 the abbey granted the property to Hubert de Burgh, justiciar of England and later earl of Kent, together with liberty of a chapel for use of his household, to hold for a three-pound wax candle.[15] Before 1227 Hubert also acquired from William's son Ralph all his buildings, grange, and meadow within the two gateways of Hubert in Westminster, described as the houses with meadow adjoining the court and houses of Hubert on one side of the road within the gates, and 2 houses and the grange with a meadow which adjoined his stable on other side of the way, all held of Westminster Abbey for a wax candle on St Edward's feast and a penny at Pentecost. Hubert also paid William 6 marks and 5s. for a grant of the land he had acquired from Geoffrey de Crace lying beside the Thames, with the service of a tenant, for which Hubert was to pay 6d. service to the lord of the fee and a penny to William. He also acquired land and a garden between the highway and the Thames from Odo the goldsmith for 10 marks, and adjoining land from Roger of Ware, held for 18d. to Westminster Abbey and 6d. to Henry *de capella*.[16] The stables apparently stood on land belonging to a messuage on the Charing side of the mansion, and Hubert paid a penny to the holder of that messuage;[17] the mansion also included an orchard or garden.

After his fall from power Burgh was permitted in 1234

1 Worc. RO, 821/BA 3814, f. 104v.
2 *Cal. Close,* 1385–9, 136, 151.
3 *Cal. Pat.* 1399–1401, 343.
4 C. Dyer, *Lords and Peasants in a Changing Soc.: Ests of Bpric of Worc., 680–1540* (1980), 172.   5 *Valor Eccl.* III. 219.
6 TNA, E 318/19/968; E 328/43; BL, Add. Ch. 40224; *Cal. Pat.* 1547–48, 114, 258, 260.
7 TNA, E 326/12005; above, Chester Inn.
8 *Cal. Pat.* 1549–51, 430–2.

9 Ibid. 1558–60, 346; 1572–5, 35–7 (no. 103).
10 TNA, DL 25/3604; *Cal. Pat.* 1572–5, 252 (no. 1329).
11 Richardson, 'William of Ely', *TRHS,* 4th ser., XV (1932), 47–8: Rosser, *Medieval Westm.* 18–21, 89.
12 *Westm. Charters,* p. 164; *Rot. Cart.* 49.
13 *Westm. Charters,* p. 273; TNA, CP 25/1/282/4, no. 23.
14 *Westm. Charters,* p. 275.   15 WAD, f. 347.
16 TNA, C 52/34, nos 3–6.
17 WAM 17376.

27. *Whitehall Palace from the Thames in the 17th century. On the right is the medieval hall and chapel, built when the site was York Place, and in the middle Inigo Jones's banqueting house built for James I.*

to keep his private property including that in Westminster,[1] but shortly afterwards he gave all his property in St Margaret's parish for religious purposes in redemption of a vow to go to the Holy Land, and his feoffees conveyed it to Walter Gray, archbishop of York, for 400 marks. Walter granted it to the see of York and his successors as archbishops in 1245, confirmed by the king. Gray may well have built a new residence there, as he was building extensively in York at that time. Three years later he granted out two houses next to Charing for 10s. a year, retaining the right to accommodation when required, and another two houses the following year.[2]

York Place

The inn with its court, stables and garden, known eventually as York Place, remained the property of the archbishops of York until 1529. Members of the royal family resided there from time to time, and as some archbishops also held royal office, the inn served quasi-administrative functions. The archbishops did not always occupy the inn: for six years to 1267 it was in the hands of a keeper, and included a curtilage used for grazing worth 2s. a year, and a garden whose crop was valued at 5s., while the rest of property produced annual rents of 20s. 3d.[3] Edward I, who occupied the inn for several periods during the 1290s while building work was carried out in Westminster Palace, paid for repairs at York Place; after 1297 he paid for major building work there as well. The king used at least 4 chambers; there was also a chapel and chaplain's lodging, hall, pantry and buttery, watergate, and a garden. From 1303 to 1307 he

also had rooms built for his second wife and baby daughter, including the queen's hall, privy chamber, little chamber, maid's room, and wardrobe. A new hall, a chapel for the princess, and the great chamber were wainscotted, and the hall and king's great chamber were tiled.[4] Further building took place in the 15th century, most likely by George Neville, archbishop 1465–76, for a new range on the south side of the mansion including a large hall, some subsidiary chambers, a cloister, and alterations to the chapel and boundary walls; it also included replacement in brick and stone of a 14th-century timber building.[5] A gateway from King Street called the Court Gate probably also dated from the 15th century.[6]

Thomas Wolsey became archbishop of York in 1514 and quickly began rebuilding the inn on a palatial scale, including the great hall, the great or watching chamber and the vaulted undercroft on which it stood, and the chapel; he probably started building the privy kitchen, and most likely built or rebuilt the great kitchen which stood to the north of the hall. An armoury, a gallery, a dining chamber, and a cloister are also mentioned in accounts for 1515–16; by 1519 visitors traversed eight rooms to reach the audience chamber. Work was done by Henry Redman, chief mason of Westminster Abbey and later of the king, Richard Russell (d. 1517), carpenter, Thomas Stockton, the king's chief joiner, Barnard Flower, the king's glazier, with leadwork by John Burwell, the king's sergeant plumber. Work was still underway at Wolsey's fall, and his carpenter, James Nedeham, was paid by the king for a bridge or landing-stage (the privy

1 *Close R.* 1231–4, 443.
2 *Reg. Walt. Gray, Archbp of York* (Surtees Soc. LVI, 1870), 199–200, 257–8; TNA, C 52/34, no. 1; *Cal. Chart. R.* 1226–57, 284.
3 *Cal. Inq. Misc.* I. 112; TNA, CP 40/26, rot. 133d.
4 S. Thurley, *Whitehall Palace* (1999), 2–3.
5 Ibid., 4.
6 *Hist. King's Works*, IV. 302.

bridge) completed early in 1531.[1] Wolsey also increased the size of the site of York Place; in 1519 he received a grant from Henry VIII of a plot of land between King Street and the Thames on the north side of York Place known as Scotland, and in 1520 he bought from William Lytton the remainder of a 24-year lease of five tenements and their gardens stretching between King Street and the Thames on the south side, granted to Lytton in 1511 by Westminster Abbey.[2]

Despite Wolsey's protests that York Place belonged to the archbishopric and not himself, on his fall from power in 1529 he was forced to surrender it to the king, a grant formally completed in 1530 with a fine describing it as a messuage, 2 gardens and 3 acres.[3] Thereafter it became the Palace of Whitehall and part of the Crown's estates.[4] The archbishops of York later acquired Norwich Place (above).

OTHER ECCLESIASTICAL ESTATES

ABBEY OF COMBE

Richard of Hedersete acquired a number of properties in and around Westminster, including a messuage in St Mary of Strand and 4 shops in St Clement Danes obtained from Walter Wolward and his wife Joan, for which Richard sought their warranty in 1276.[5] In 1289 Prince Edmund, as earl of Leicester, made a claim against Richard for a messuage in St Mary of Strand, presumably because it was held of the honor of Leicester.[6] Richard also had land in Westminster which he granted to the abbey of Vale Royal, with a 6s. 8d. quitrent from a tenement in St Mary of Strand held by Robert of Aldenham.[7] Although there is no further evidence for Richard's ownership of the remainder of his holdings in the Strand, it seems to be the property which Henry le Waleys was licensed in 1293 to grant to the abbot and convent of Combe, described as one messuage in the parish of St Clement Danes and another in the parish of St Mary of Strand; the messuages were held of the honor of Leicester for 11s. 10d. a year and suit of court, and were valued at 6 marks.[8] The connection with Richard is suggested by the quitclaim in 1298 by Luke of Ware and his wife Joan to Henry le Waleys of their right in 6 marks rent in St Mary of Strand and St Clement Danes:[9] Luke and Joan had brought a suit against Richard for the property in 1284, and Joan may have been Wolward's wife or daughter.[10] In addition, in 1313 Gregory of Norton, son of Joan Wolward, released all his right in the lands Joan had granted to Richard Hedersete in the soke of Leicester at the stone cross, that is, on the south side of the Strand, and at the same time quitclaimed to Combe all the lands the abbey held at the stone cross.[11]

Combe Abbey continued to hold the premises until the Dissolution. By 1534 the messuage in the parish of Strand was an inn and garden called the Goat, and that in St Clement Danes was let as two tenements with gardens and a stable. The two parts of the estate lay on the south side of the Strand, separated by another tenement; the Goat lay between the east side of the church of St Mary and the boundary of Strand parish, and its garden behind stretched eastwards behind its neighbour and behind the other Combe property in St Clement's parish.[12] Shortly before the Dissolution, the Goat was leased to Richard Yeoman, innholder, for 41 years at a rent of £4 rising to £5 after 13 years, and the other property to Nicholas Gravenor (or Gravener), citizen and leatherseller, for 60 years at 33s. 4d.[13] The quitrent due to the honor of Leicester was represented by a payment of 12s. a year to the bailiff of the Savoy, receiver of rents of the duchy of Lancaster.[14]

In 1539 Henry VIII granted the Combe estate for life to Mary Fitzroy, duchess of Richmond and Somerset, widow of his illegitimate son.[15] Subject to the duchess's life interest, the rents were sold in 1543 to Thomas Brooke, merchant tailor of London, and John Williams, followed by the freehold in 1544.[16] The two men with the duchess sold the Goat to John Skutt, merchant tailor, for £80 in 1546, to be held of the king for knight service and 8s. a year.[17] The freehold of the other property, in St Clement Danes, was sold to the lessee, Nicholas Gravenor, in 1546.[18] In 1547 Skutt sold the Goat and its garden to William Gyes of Strand and his wife Christian. By the end of 1548 the eastern end of the Goat's garden must have been incorporated into Bath Place, probably while in the ownership of Sir Thomas Seymour; Seymour bought the tenement next to the Goat and

1 *Hist. King's Works*, IV. 301, 305.
2 *L&P Hen. VIII*, III(1), pp. 176, 218; TNA, E 40/13404.
3 J.J. Scarisbrick, *Henry VIII* (1971 edn), 313; TNA, CP 25/2/27/181/22HENVIIIEASTER.
4 Reserved for treatment under Royal Palaces in a later vol.
5 TNA, CP 40/13, rot. 38d.; /24, rot. 66d.
6 Ibid. /78, rot. 60d.; /81, rot. 51, 69d.; /83, rot. 165.
7 Below, Abbey of Vale Royal.
8 *Cal. Pat.* 1292–1301, 14, 140; TNA, C 143/19, no. 16.
9 TNA, CP 25/1/148/36/284.

10 TNA, CP 40/41, rot. 60; /43, rot. 69d.; /38, rot. 72; /55, rot. 116.   11 *Abbrev. Plac.* (Rec. Com.), 317.
12 TNA, E 326/11959; E 303/16, no. 35.
13 TNA, E 318/5/179. Only 100s. was listed in 1535: *Valor Eccl.* III. 55.   14 TNA, DL 29/287/4712.
15 *L&P Hen. VIII*, XIV(1), p. 595 (no 1355).
16 TNA, E 318/5/179; *L&P Hen. VIII*, XIX(2), p. 319 (no. 527/42); XXI(1), p. 693 (no. 1383/110).
17 *Cal. Pat.* 1547–48, 222; TNA, E 326/12061; E 328/164.
18 *L&P Hen. VIII*, XXI(1), p. 692 (no. 1383/110).

made a new lane from the Strand to the Thames, which apparently ran across the gardens of the Goat and the Strand Inn.[1]

William and Christian Gyes sold the Goat in 1550 to Edward Seymour, duke of Somerset, in exchange for a former Leicester college property (the Cage) on the north side of the Strand; they were allowed to continue living in the Goat until they received possession of their new property, which was tenanted, at which time they would also be allowed a month to take down the old stables, lofts, and chambers at the back of the Goat, which were excluded from the sale.[2] The inn itself was not incorporated into the site of Somerset's new house, though the remaining garden apparently was.[3] After Somerset's attainder and execution in 1552, the Goat returned to the Crown and thereafter was let for periods of 21 years, forming part of the Crown's Somerset House estate. In 1567 it was called the George, and lay between two other tenements, with the garden of Somerset Place on its south side.[3]

ABBEY OF VALE ROYAL

Richard of Hedersete acquired several properties in Westminster, St Mary of Strand, and St Clement Danes, some of which later passed to the abbey of Combe (above). In 1299 he granted to the king property in Westminster, Islington, and London, to be given to the abbey of Vale Royal, which included 2½ acres in Westminster held of St James's Hospital for 5s. a year, 2½ acres held of Master William de Wanden for 5s. a year, and a quitrent of 6s. 8d. a year from property held by Robert of Aldenham in St Mary of Strand.[5] Part of the grant comprised 2½ acres which Roger of Purley had given to his daughter Elizabeth, wife of William Spinoch, and their issue, and which Richard had acquired by c.1280.[6]

In 1535 Vale Royal held 40s. annual rent in the suburbs of London, which included property in Shoe Lane, near Fleet Street, out of which they paid 9s. a year to St Giles's Hospital.[7] At the Dissolution the abbey held 5 acres in three parcels in St Martin's field, which they had leased to Hugh Lee in 1536 for 60 years. Lee showed his lease in the court of Augmentations in 1546,[8] but despite this the land was 'discovered' as concealed in 1573.[9] In 1583 a 21-year Crown lease was granted to Ann Farrant, who immediately assigned it to Robert Wood of Smithfield, yeoman.[10] In 1590 the Crown sold to Henry Best and John Wells a large amount of land including the 5 acres, to hold of the manor of East Greenwich in free socage.

Best and Wells immediately conveyed the 5 acres to Roger Wood, sergeant at arms, son of the lessee.[11] Roger Wood later conveyed the land to his father-in-law, Robert Carr, and in 1634 Carr's grandson, Sir Edward Carr, and Wood's son, Sir Robert Wood, sold 4 acres to Mountjoy Blount, earl of Newport, who used it for the garden of Newport House.[12]

CHURCH OF ST BOTOLPH WITHOUT ALDERSGATE

In 1403 John Bedford, clerk, and Richard Gaynesburgh, citizen, granted in mortmain to the parson and church-wardens of St Botolph without Aldersgate a garden containing two tofts and 2½ acres in Charing to keep the anniversary of Alice Colwell in the church.[13] In 1502 the churchwardens brought a suit against the abbot of Westminster, because after the appropriation of their church by the deanery of St Martin le Grand, which in turn had been granted to Westminster Abbey, the abbot had dispossessed them of a toft and 1½ acres of the land;[14] the outcome of the suit is unknown but it was probably unsuccessful, as the parish's property in 1548 consisted of only the five tenements with gardens in Charing Cross Street (western end of the Strand), leased to John Russell, the king's master carpenter, in 1542 for 70 years, at a rent of 26s. 8d.; 4s. a year was paid for Alice Colwell's obit.[15] The property lay in the parish of St-Martin-in-the-Fields, opposite the inns of the bishops of Durham and Carlisle, between the Strand on the south and Covent garden on the north, and on the west side of the former garden of the Pied Friars belonging to Westminster Abbey.

In 1548 the freehold was sold by the Crown to John Hulson and William Pendred as agents for Russell.[16] By 1564, when Russell wrote his will, the property consisted of ten tenements on the west side of the site with a garden plot on the east. He bequeathed it all to his wife Christian for life, then the six westernmost tenements to his daughter Elizabeth and the other four new tenements and the garden to his daughter Dorcas, with remainders to each other and their brothers Francis and Henry; Russell died by July 1566.[17] Dorcas Russell quitclaimed her share to Hugh Overend and Richard Wilson in 1574.[18] The property has not been traced further.

COLLEGE OF ST MARY AND ST STEPHEN

In 1348 Edward III founded a college to serve the free chapel of St Mary and St Stephen within the Palace of

1 TNA, E 318/29/1645, [m.2]; above, Episcopal Inns, Bath.
2 TNA, E 41/198; E 328/173; below, College of St Mary Newark.   3 Above, Episcopal Inns, Chester.
4 *Cal. Pat.* 1566–9, 93; 1572–5, 35–7 (no. 103); TNA, E 315/203, f. 2v.
5 *Cal. Pat.* 1292–1301, 437; TNA, C 143/29, no. 4.
6 TNA, CP 40/31, rot. 148d.; /34, rot. 35; /38, rot. 64d.; /47, rot. 26; /83, rot. 74; /87, rot. 15; E 40/1538.
7 *Valor Eccl.* V. 208.
8 TNA, E 315/104, f. 186; LR 1/43, f. 62.

9 TNA, E 178/1397.
10 TNA, C 66/1225; LR 1/42, f. 313.
11 TNA, LR 1/43, f. 97; C 54/1365.
12 *Survey of London*, XX. 3–4.
13 *Cal. Pat.* 1401–5, 308; TNA, LR 2/241, f. 120.
14 TNA, C 1/258/64.
15 TNA, LR 2/241, ff. 120, 124, 126.
16 *Cal. Pat.* 1548–9, 36.
17 TNA, PROB 11/48, f. 403v.
18 TNA, CP 25/2/171/16ELIZ/HIL.

Westminster, to include a dean and 12 secular canons as well as vicars, clerks and choristers. They were assured an income of £500 a year, with any shortfall from their revenues being made up by the Exchequer.[1]

The Foundation Endowment and the Precinct

In 1353 the king granted to the college sites near the chapel and Westminster Hall, and land and houses lying within the fee of the palace north of the hall, which included buildings used for stabling the king's horses, the king's garden which adjoined the stables, and the inn which had formerly belonged to the earl of Kent,[2] which lay on the north side of the garden. Also included were tenements which Roger de Heyton, the king's surgeon, had held of the king, and which probably lay near the site of the later woolstaple.[3]

The garden and Kent's inn later formed the site of the houses for the canons, but it is not clear whether this was intended from the start, or whether the king's grant of the property was initially just to add to their revenues. Shortly afterwards in 1353 the woolstaple, a market for wool set up by the king and under the management of the mayor and corporation of the City of London, was established at Westminster, and some of its buildings and the road to the woolbridge, the staple's wharf on the Thames just north of the palace and the privy bridge on the Thames, were on the college's property; the college received from the Exchequer the rent paid from the staple to the king.[4]

The remainder of the precinct forming the college's endowment consisted of the king's garden and stables, lying on the north side of the courtyard outside Westminster Hall. The house of Roger de Heyton, the king's surgeon, also given to the canons, was within the fee of the palace, but its location is uncertain. It probably lay near the palace gate, and was later used for the woolstaple, but it is also possible that it was a property carved out of the earl of Kent's inn, lying in King Street near St Stephen's alley.

The houses for the canons, later known as Canon Row, were apparently being laid out in 1394, and the road known as Canon Row, which ran northwards from the palace yard between King Street and the Thames, was not then in existence but had probably been planned. The 'new great gate of the canons' was mentioned in 1394, and is the forerunner of St Stephen's Alley, but the access there to King Street is likely to predate the ownership by the canons.[5] The 13 houses for the dean and canons were laid out on the east side of the later Canon Row with sites that stretched back to the Thames. The row would allow for 13 sites of roughly equal frontages

of 34–35 feet each, and some sites were of that width in the 18th century.[6]

In 1437 the college complained that the part of their endowment which came from rents from the staple had greatly reduced in value and the Exchequer only made up the difference with assignments. They asked for lands of an alien priory instead, which was granted,[7] though 18 years later they complained how little they had received from that manor (in Yorkshire).[8] The college surrendered to the king the six woolhouses in the Staple on the north side of the road later called Long Woolstaple, lying between the woolbridge and the college's storehouse, possibly in return for the priory. These houses were then granted out by the king but surrendered back in order that they could to be sold to the college for the chantry of William Prestwyk, canon.[9] In 1469 the dean and canons were granted a licence to make a permanent grant to the vicars, clerks and choristers of the college of a rent-charge of 7 marks a year from their messuages, gardens, lands, tenements and shops in the New Rent in a lane running east–west with a gate at each end, later known as St Stephen's Alley, which still had the gates in 1547.[10]

The college received licences in 1521 and 1529 to rebuild their property on the south side of the Long Woolstaple. In 1521 they were permitted to rebuild all the houses on the south side of the road between the stone wall bordering the Thames and the weighhouse, using the wall of the palace courtyard as a support and putting in windows and doors as necessary; they were also allowed to put pales with posts and gates within the palace 10 ft from the wall to enclose and give access to their tenements,[11] thus incorporating the palace wall into the houses. The licence was partially repeated in 1529, when they were permitted to rebuild their property between the weighhouse and the bell-tower, with permission to enlarge the houses towards the tower upon the wall where necessary.[12]

Since its foundation the college had had to accommodate visitors to the palace, and by the sixteenth century churchmen and courtiers attending court were often housed by the canons; among those staying or living in Canon Row were Thomas Cranmer (1533), Thomas Howard, duke of Norfolk (1534, 1536), Thomas Lord Wriothesley, Lord Privy Seal (1544), William Paget, secretary of state (1545). Some of the canons, who often had greater benefices elsewhere, seem to have leased out their houses in Canon Row.[13]

Other Property of the College

In 1535 the college's property in Westminster was valued at £145 10s. 4d. in rents and leases, with one

1 *VCH London*, I. 566.
2 Below, Secular Inns, Earl of Kent.
3 *Cal. Chart. R.* 1347–1417, 133–7; TNA, C 135/126, no. 2.
4 *Cal. Close*, 1369–74, 398.
5 Below, Secular Inns, Earl of Kent.
6 Detailed hist. of hos in Canon Row reserved for treatment in a later vol.

7 *Cal. Pat.* 1436–41, 125.
8 BL, Harl. Roll N.19.
9 *Cal. Pat.* 1436–41, 123; 1441–6, 143–4.
10 Ibid. 1467–77, 150–1; TNA, E 315/105, f. 44v.
11 TNA, C 66/636, m. 20.
12 Ibid. /654, m. 7.
13 Below.

payment to the abbey of 13*d.* from a tenement in King Street. From the various grants made of the college's property from the late 1540s a summary of their holdings shows that in addition to the 12 canons' houses and a storehouse or counting house in Canon Row, they had at least 13 messuages in St Stephen's Alley plus the gatehouses; ten more including the Helmet inn and brewhouse on the east side of King Street, and the Chequer inn and alley on the west side; nine in the Long Woolstaple and two others on the north side of the palace; and 16 other properties in St Margaret's parish. There was also a messuage and buildings in St Martin-in-the-Fields, leased out with land.[1] The college's properties which were not in the original royal endowment were probably given to the college by Westminster residents for religious purposes such as obits.[2]

Disposal of the College's Estate

After the dissolution of the college in 1547, most of the canons' houses were sold by the Crown. However, the 3rd house from the southern end, which was held by Dr William Knight, archdeacon of Richmond and canon of St Stephen's, for life in 1535–6, had already been granted away by Henry VIII in 1536 to the bishopric of Norwich, in exchange for the latter's house in the Strand, to take effect after Knight's death.[3] It was occupied by Sir John Thynne and his successors from 1550 to 1737. The 4th, 5th, and 6th houses became the site of Hertford House, later bought by Sir Henry Montagu (d. 1642), 1st earl of Manchester; it subsequently became the site of Manchester Buildings. The 7th, 8th, and 9th houses were the site of Wharton House, residence of Philip Wharton, Lord Wharton, in 1589, and belonged to Henry Fiennes, earl of Lincoln, in 1616. It was later known as Dorset House and was replaced by Dorset Court by 1764. At the northern end of the row the 13th house seems to have been the residence of Anne Seymour, duchess of Somerset, widow of the Lord Protector. She had married Francis Newdigate (d. 1582), who bought a house in Canon Row from Lord Hunsdon, and at her death in 1587 she left the house to her eldest surviving son, Edward Seymour, Lord Hertford. Next to that house, the 11th and 12th houses, which were apparently bought by the earl of Derby in 1552, formed the site of Derby House. That remained for some time in the ownership of the earls but by 1674 was used as the office of the lords commissioners of the Admiralty, and as secretary to the commissioners Samuel Pepys had lodgings there.[4]

The college's other property was largely sold off in the mid 16th century in small groups of up to half a dozen tenements, mainly to pairs of purchasers either for themselves or as agents on behalf of others.[5]

COLLEGE OF ST MARY IN THE NEWARK, LEICESTER

The inhabitants of an almshouse in Leicester received assistance from property in the eastern end of Westminster, which can be traced back to the late 14th century. John French held several properties including his inn in St Clement Danes, as well as in St Mary of Strand. In his will in 1384 he left the Angel on the Hope in St Clement Danes with its annexed tenements for the support of a lamp in the parish church; the Swan on the Hope and another inn or messuage, both in St Mary of Strand, were to be sold to support chaplains in St Clement's after death of his wife, Maud of Kent.[6] He also held the tenement next to the Angel known as St Mary Inn, which may have been his dwelling.[7] The supervisor of the will was Thomas Hervey of Kidwelly, and by 1398 all French's property had passed into the hands of Hervey and his wife Maud: the latter had granted the property to feoffees to hold for Thomas and herself, which suggests that Hervey had married French's widow.[8] In 1391 Thomas and Maud also acquired from Nicholas Blake a toft in St Clement Danes which lay on the west side of St Mary Inn;[9] in 1407 that inn was apparently occupied by Maud.[10]

At his death in 1398 Hervey's property in Westminster consisted of four inns, the Angel, the Swan, the Fleur-de-lys, and St Mary Inn, and a messuage and garden, plus the toft. In his will he left all his lands and tenements in the parishes of St Mary of Strand and St Clement Danes except the Angel brewhouse to his wife Maud for life, and then to John of Gaunt, duke of Lancaster, and his heirs on condition they paid a rent-charge of £20 a year for the support of the poor in the almshouse of the new College of St Mary in the Newark, Leicester.[11] In 1410 Maud granted property including the Angel to Gaunt's son, King Henry IV (as duke of Lancaster), who then granted them back to her for life, with remainder to the collegiate church of St Mary Leicester in frankalmoign, for the maintenance of the poor in the college's almshouse. The property consisted, in St Mary of Strand, of the Swan on the north side of the Strand with a garden, a cottage and a shop adjoining, which paid a service of 4*s.* 6*d.* to the cellarer of Westminster Abbey and had formerly belonged to John French,[12] the Fleur-de-lys with 3 cottages and 3 shops, which lay a little to the east of the Swan at the corner of the lane leading to St Giles (Little Drury Lane); and, in St

1 From TNA, E 318, particulars for grants, by letters pat.
2 E.g., BL, Cotton Faust. B. VIII, ff. 40–1v.
3 TNA, C 65/144, no. 17.
4 Acct of Westminster Precinct, Canon Row, reserved for treatment in a later vol.
5 From TNA, E 318, particulars for grants.

6 Newcastle MSS, Ne D 4719.
7 Guildhall MS 9171/1, f. 124v.
8 Ibid., ff. 386–87v.
9 Newcastle MSS, Ne D 4719.
10 Ibid., Ne D 4724.
11 Guildhall MS 9171/1, ff. 386–87v.   12 TNA, SC 11/458.

Clement Danes, of a messuage with a garden and dove-cote, a messuage called St Mary Inn with a garden, 3 cottages and 2 shops adjoining, and another next to it on the east called the Angel with 3 cottages and a shop adjoining.[1] The college had taken possession by 1432, and possibly by 1417.[2] By 1498 St Mary Inn had lost its separate identity, probably by being absorbed into the Angel, still held by the college, but alternatively it may have been amalgamated with the New Inn property on the west.[3]

The college granted out its property on long leases. In 1432 the Swan was being held by Robert Nyk for a term of years,[4] and when the College was dissolved in 1548 the Swan on the Hope inn with a garden and a cartway or lane belonging to it was let for 37s. 6d. The Fleur-de-lys was leased to William Normanton, clerk, master of Chancery at his death, from 1440 for 95 years at 26s. 8d. a year, with a covenant to repair the messuage and shops and rebuild the garden walls, thatching them with reeds;[5] Normanton was living there in 1451,[6] and in his will of 1459 instructed his executors to sell the lease at his death.[7] It was later known as the Cage, and in 1548 also as Chichester Place, probably because it had been occupied by the bishop of Chichester in the 1530s.[8] The Angel inn with a garden and 4 cottages or shops was let to several tenants for a total of £5 6s. 8d. by 1548, and a house with a garden and stable, which lay between Wych and Hollow lanes, west of Lyons Inn, formerly let to John Pemberton, master of Chancery, was let in 1486 to Richard Blackwell, another master, for 99 years at 40s.[9] The college at its dissolution was receiving a total of £10 10s. 10d. a year from this estate.

The Crown sold the freehold of the four properties to William Gyes of St Mary of Strand and Michael Puresey of Leicestershire in 1548, to hold in socage subject to the existing leases.[10] In 1550 Edward Seymour, duke of Somerset, bought the leases of the house near Lyons Inn and of the Cage from the former college's lessees, and assigned them to William Gyes in exchange for the Goat Inn, which he required to enlarge Somerset Place.[11]

In his will of 1558 William Gyes of St Clement Danes left all his freehold in St Clement Danes and Strand to his wife Christian, except for three houses adjoining the east side of Gyes's inn called the Angel on the Hope, occupied by John Bright, butcher, Madder Wysbecke the French-man, and William Wright, hosier. After Christian's death, all except the three houses were to remain to his sons Michael and Erasmus and their issue to hold as one

moiety each, and with remainders to each other or to Gyes's sisters. The three houses excepted from the arrangement were bequeathed to his sister Joan Leache for life, then to her children for 21 years, with remainder to Gyes's sons.[12]

The property eventually all devolved on Michael Gyes, who barred the entail and left it to Margaret, wife of John Mules (Mewles) by 1588.[13] Mules later sold the freeholds to various buyers.

COVENT GARDEN AND LONG ACRE

This estate, which derived from three landholdings, Covent Garden, Tocksgarden, and Longacre, reached its fullest extent in the 16th century under the ownership of Westminster Abbey, before its acquisition in the 16th century by the 1st earl of Bedford (below, Later Creations: Bedford).

Covent Garden

The area known as Covent Garden was probably assigned to the cellarer and gardener of Westminster Abbey from an early date: plots on its southern border granted out in the 12th and 13th centuries paid quitrents to the cellarer in the 14th century and later. Though the main part may always have been in demesne, land on the east side along Aldwych Street (Drury Lane) was granted away in fee at an early date by the Abbey, which later re-acquired it.[14] Property in the Strand was bounded on the north by the wall of the garden of the abbot of West-minster c.1220 and throughout the 13th century, also referred to as the great garden of the monks.[15] By the mid 13th century there was a gate on the east side of the garden into Aldwych Street, and the abbey was granted rents from a messuage on the north side of the gate and from two on the south side.[16] There may also have been a gate on the west side of the garden near the later Little Chandos Street.[17]

Tocksgarden

Property on the west side of Aldwych Street belonged to members of the Tocke family in the early 13th century, and a garden later called Tocksgarden with five messuages was the subject of a suit 1229–31 between members of a leading London family that produced a number of aldermen and mayors in the 13th century. Two-thirds were held by Peter fitzRoger, who claimed that his grandfather Alan had bought the land and granted it to his second son, Roger fitzAlan (sheriff

1 *Cal. Pat.* 1408–13, 171, 187–8.
2 WAM 18889; 18890.
3 Newcastle MSS, Ne D 4740; below, Secular Inns, New.
4 WAM 18890 5 *Cal. Close*, 1447–54, 238–9.
6 TNA, C 54/302, m. 27d.
7 TNA, PROB 11/4, f. 144v.
8 *L&P Hen. VIII*, VI, p. 338; XII(2), p. 160; XIII(2), p. 401; TNA, C 78/21, no. 9.
9 *VCH Leics.* II. 50; TNA, E 315/68, f. 323; E 41/198; DL 29/224/3567.

10 *Cal. Pat.* 1547–8, 299–300; A.H. Thompson, *Hist. of the Hosp. and the New Coll. of the Annunciation of St Mary in the Newarke, Leicester* (1937), 211–12.
11 TNA, E 41/198; E 328/173; above, Abbey of Combe.
12 TNA, PROB 11/41, f. 33.
13 TNA, C 2/Eliz/M3/39.
14 Below, Tocksgarden.
15 WAM 17136; 17539.
16 WAM 17366; 17086.
17 *Survey of London*, XXXVI. 19.

1192–3, mayor 1212–14), and one third was held by Alan's great-grandson Peter fitzAlan, who claimed the other two-thirds on the grounds that his grandfather Peter fitzAlan, the eldest son, had been in possession in the late 12th century and that the whole property should pass to the eldest son's heirs. Henry Bocointe, another Londoner, also claimed rights in the property for unstated reasons.[1] Peter fitzAlan was successful in getting part of the property, including two messuages formerly held by Wakerilda of Aldwych, from his cousin in 1233 to add to his third, possibly giving him two thirds, and he relinquished his right in the remaining part.[2] Henry Bocointe then claimed again against both parties; in 1233, however, he quitclaimed his right in Peter fitzAlan's share to the holder for 60s.,[3] but succeeded in winning his suit against Peter fitzRoger for the other part in 1235, by duel on Tothill fields.[4] The two parts thereafter passed separately. The location and extent of both is not precisely known, but indications are that they probably formed some or all of the parcels later known as Longacre and Elmfield. It is possible, however, that they lay slightly south of this, and part may been used to increase the size of Covent Garden in the Middle Ages.

The part that Peter fitzAlan won from Peter fitzRoger lay between the garden of Henry de Castello on the north and Peter fitzRoger's garden on the south, and stretched next to a field called Layfield up to the street next to Goldenacre. The latter seems to have lain on the west side of St Martin's Lane near St Giles's Hospital, but Layfield has not been identified. Peter fitzAlan is not recorded in the area thereafter; the only possible trace of the property is a grant by John son of John fitzPeter (d. 1290), citizen and alderman, who in 1297 acknowledged to Hamo heir of William Atwell his grant of 'Cokkesgarden' for a rent of 61s. 8d., a property otherwise untraced; Hamo's successors held Elmfield in the late 14th century.[5]

The part that Bocointe acquired lay on the north side of the garden of the abbot and convent, presumably Covent Garden.[6] Shortly afterwards he granted it to Henry of Belgrave for a quitrent of 2½ marks to him and his heirs, and 2s. 6d. a year to Westminster Abbey, and Belgrave made a demise in feefarm to Thomas Bittaille for 20s. a year, of part of the garden he held of Henry Bocointe called Tockesgarden. This was then described as the part from the crest of the ditch up to Aldwych Street, with the houses which Belgrave had built on the east side fronting the street, formerly taken from the

messuage of Richard Tocke.[7] Belgrave later released and quitclaimed to Westminster Abbey all the garden he held of Bocointe, presumably after some grant to them by Bittaille or his successors, with the abbey to pay the 2½ marks annually to Bocointe's heirs.[8] Henry Bocointe's widow Grace, who had married Roger de la Donne, received the rent of 2½ marks as dower, and as a widow granted her life interest in it to Sir Adam of Stratton; Bocointe's heirs, Joan, Margaret, and Margery, the daughters of his son Ranulf, granted Stratton the reversion of the rent in 1272.[9] In 1283 the abbey granted Stratton some quitrents in the City of London in exchange for a release to them of the rent from Tocksgarden, which was quitclaimed to them by Bocointe's heirs.[10] The fact that Tocksgarden is not mentioned again strongly suggests that it was thereafter either included in Covent Garden, or formed the 7 acres of arable or pasture which was let with Covent Garden in 1416–17 and was later known as Longacre. This land lay along the north side of Covent Garden between Drury Lane and St Martin's Lane.

Covent Garden and Longacre

During the 15th and early 16th centuries the abbey leased out Covent Garden and the 7 acres adjoining for £5 6s. 8d. a year, the last such lessee being Richard Weston, under-treasurer of England, in 1530.[11] In 1536 Henry VIII acquired the freehold of Covent Garden and the 7 acres from Westminster Abbey by exchange.[12] Weston had conveyed his leasehold interest to Henry Dingley, who in 1535 had granted a sub-lease of his term for 36 years to Richard Browne, a royal servant. Browne was ordered by the Court of Augmentations to quit his lease for the king's convenience, and in 1537 was granted an annuity of £10 for life in compensation; in 1538 Dingley also received a similar annuity.[13]

Anthony Denny, bailiff of the king's manor of Westminster, was appointed keeper of Covent Garden in 1542,[14] and rendered accounts annually for the rent of £5 6s. 8d. The accounts for 1547–8 recorded that the land had been reserved for the king's use and that sheep had been grazing there; these may have belonged to Edward Seymour, earl of Hertford,[15] to whom grants of land including Covent Garden were made in July 1547 to support his new rank of duke of Somerset.[16] After Somerset's execution the lands returned to the Crown, to be granted by the king in May 1552 to John Russell, earl of Bedford, keeper of the privy seal, and to his male heirs in free socage.[17]

---

1   *Cur. Reg. R.* XIII. 390–1; XIV. 300; XV. 81.
2   TNA, CP 25/1/146/9/110.   3   Ibid., 146/8/100.
4   WAM 17444; TNA, CP 25/1/146/10/129.
5   Below, Secular Inns, Clement's.
6   WAM 17444.
7   WAM 17431.
8   WAM 17355.
9   TNA, E 40/2618; E 40/1568.
10 TNA, E 40/2485; WAM 17481.

11 WAM 18889; TNA, SC 11/458; C 1/736/47.
12 TNA, C 65/146, no. 12.
13 *L&P Hen. VIII,* XIII(1), p. 583 (no. 1520); XIV(1), p. 594 (no. 1355); TNA, C 1/736/47.
14 *L&P Hen. VIII,* XVII, p. 692 (no. 1258).
15 *Survey of London,* XXXVI. 21.
16 *Cal. Pat.* 1547–8, 130–1.
17 Ibid. 1550–3, 298. Later hist. below, Later Creations, Bedford.

FRATERNITY OF ST MARY

The fraternity or guild of the Assumption of St Mary, based in the church of St Margaret, was the leading institution of its kind in late medieval Westminster, in some ways a surrogate town council.[1] Its members were holding property for the guild's purposes by 1431, when they paid 6s. quitrent to the cellarer of Westminster Abbey from three tenements in Our Lady's Alley, King Street;[2] the guild is thought to have been founded shortly before this.[3] The fraternity was incorporated in 1440 with a licence to acquire in mortmain lands to the value of 10 marks a year, and another licence was granted in 1474 for lands to the same value; both were confirmed in 1502 with licence to acquire another 10 marks a year, specifically to maintain a chaplain in St Margaret's for the souls of the royal family and guild members.[4] Property acquired by the guild, through intermediaries, included a tenement in King Street and one in Tothill Street by 1450,[5] a toft or vacant plot in King Street from Richard Walshe in 1455,[6] and a messuage and 2 shops with adjoining gardens in the parish of St Mary of Strand by 1457.[7] In 1466 Nicholas Norton, heir of William and Joan Norton, quitclaimed to the guild the Maidenhead or Pelican in King Street and a rent-charge of 13s. 4d. paid by the new work of Westminster Abbey from the Saracen's Head, King Street,[8] presumably granted to the fraternity by William, and in 1474 David Selly's feoffees conveyed to the guild the Rose and another messuage in King Street after the death of Selly's widow Cecily,[9] followed by the unexpired part of the lease of the Belle in King Street.

In 1474 the guild's property consisted of 2 tenements in Tothill Street from which they received 60s. a year, the Maidenhead in King Street (£5 a year), 8 tenements in Our Lady's Alley including the gatehouse (£7 10s.), 2 tenements in King Street (63s. 4d.), tenement in Tothill Street (26s. 8d.), seven tenements at Strand, annexed to the Swan (75s. 4d.), 10½ acres and a garden plot, mainly in Eyefield (11s. 6d.), the Rose (10 marks) and other tenements (£3 3s. 4d.) all in King Street, a tenement and garden (20s.) and two tenements and a garden given by Richard Saxilby, parish priest of St Margaret's (13s. 4d.), all in Longditch. They also received the quitrent of 13s. 4d. from the Saracen's Head, and 6s. a year which John Randolf paid for use of the entrance of Our Lady's Alley.

At that time they were also negotiating for the purchase of Richard Wylly's house in Tothill from his widow for 50 marks, with a fine of £10 to the abbey.[10]

In 1531 the guild had to sell the Rose with its cottages and gardens built in Rose Alley to Henry VIII,[11] who also acquired 14 acres in St Margaret's from them in 1536,[12] but at its suppression in 1548 the guild still had an income of £55 10s. 4d. from its property, mainly in Westminster,[13] granted on long leases. The property included in Tothill Street: the Swan inn, leased for 40s. a year,[14] 3 tenements (28s.), a tenement with shops and cellars (16s. 8d.),[15] 2 messuages and a gatehouse and barn, a messuage with shops, and 3 messuages with a garden and close (53s. 4d.);[16] in King Street: the Maidenhead with buildings, shops (60s.),[17] the Unicorn inn (26s. 8d.),[18] the Sun inn, and messuages, buildings and shops in Our Lady's Alley on the east side of King Street; in Longditch: an alley with messuages, stables, gardens and plots given by Lady Morland c.1508, and another messuage there; 2 messuages in St Margaret's parish, 2 messuages at Strand let for 20s.,[19] and 5 other messuages in St Mary of Strand.

Most of the property was sold in feefarm by the Crown in parcels of one or two messuages between 1548 and 1553. The Swan in Tothill Street and the Unicorn in King Street became part of the Maynard estate (below). Three messuages and a close in Tothill Street and the Sun in King Street were bought for Richard Castell, and passed to Christ's Hospital (below).

HOSPITAL OF ST GILES IN THE FIELDS

The leper hospital of St Giles, founded by Queen Matilda (d. 1118),[20] lay in its own parish created from land formerly part of Westminster manor. Over the centuries it acquired parcels of land and quitrents in Westminster and elsewhere given by lay landholders or bought by the hospital. Most of the parcels in Westminster lay in the vicinity of the hospital: just south of its precinct near the later Covent Garden, along the highway that became Drury Lane, in St Clement Danes, in the fields west of the hospital, along St Martin's Lane, and at Charing Cross.[21] Several early grants of land were made in fee by the hospital for quitrents, and over the centuries the hospital had some difficulty obtaining their rents. In 1498 the master of Burton Lazars, who exercised the keepership of the hospital, obtained two years arrears from Sir John

1 Rosser, *Medieval Westm.*, 285–93.
2 WAM 18890; TNA, SC 11/458.
3 H.F. Westlake, *Parish Gilds of Mediaeval England* (1919), 84–5.
4 *Cal. Pat.* 1436–41, 448; 1461–7, 460; 1494–1509, 280.
5 LMA, Acc. 110/1.
6 WAM 17774.
7 TNA, C 143/452, no.5.
8 *Cal. Close*, 1461–8, 365; WAM 17898.
9 TNA, E 40/1461, /1463, /1464; C 1/66/320.
10 WA, Vol. of Accts of guilds of St Mary and St Mary Ronceval. Guild also had 2 tenements in Kensington and property in City of London.

11 *L&P Hen. VIII*, V, p. 202; TNA, E 40/1563.
12 TNA, E 326/5899.
13 *Chantry Cert.* 65 (no. 139).
14 TNA, E 315/68, f. 137.
15 Ibid., f. 315v.
16 Ibid., f. 298v.; Guildhall MS 12993.
17 TNA, E 315/68, f. 302v.
18 Ibid., f. 137.
19 TNA, E 318/27/1527.
20 *VCH Middx*, I. 206.
21 BL, Harl. 4015, passim: hosp.'s cartulary which includes Westm. deeds from late 12th cent. to 1327, with later entries of court cases concerning land.

Ryseley and his wife for New Inn in St Clement Danes and the concession that the hospital was entitled to the annual rent of 6s. 5½d.[1] The hospital was also entitled to 30s. rent from Clement's Inn in 1532.[2] In 1535 the hospital was entitled to 9s. a year from the abbey of Vale Royal for land in the suburbs of London, probably the parcels they held in St Martin's field.[3]

In 1536 Henry VIII gave to Burton Lazars land in Leicestershire in exchange for what was apparently all St Giles's land in Westminster, all held by tenants under leases: 25 acres in St Giles's field and 10 acres by Colmanhedge, said to be in St Giles's parish but apparently in the part of Westminster which became St Anne, Soho; 10 acres called the marshland (next to the hospital's orchard); conduit close of 5 acres; the White Hart, the Rose, and the Vyne with closes, probably all in St Giles's parish.[4] The later history of these parcels is reserved for treatment under the Crown's estates.

HOSPITAL OF ST JAMES

The hospital of St James, founded in the 12th century,[5] acquired messuages, lands, and rents in the vills of Westminster and Eye up to the 15th century, some in the fields adjoining the hospital, but also at Charing Cross, Strand, St Clement Danes, Knightsbridge, and Ebury. The recorded acquisitions up to the end of the 13th century were in fairly small parcels, of one or two acres or of 2–5s. rent, for which the hospital usually paid a small quitrent;[6] the hospital also owed fealty and suit of court to the abbot of Westminster for some of its land by the 1360s.[7] In 1242 the king granted that the leprous maidens of St James might hold their lands with various rights and liberties.[8] Some land was held in chief of the king, possibly part of a foundation grant for the hospital. In 1306 the hospital was granted a licence to retain a messuage, 22 acres of land, 2 acres of meadow and 14s. rent in Westminster and Fulham, which it had acquired from William de Wanden. This included 18 acres that William had held of the hospital and 8 acres in Westminster acquired from Hugh the marshal, which he had held of the hospital for service of 8s. a year. The hospital received the licence in return for supporting a chaplain to celebrate daily in the king's chapel at the Mews.[9]

In 1412 the hospital held £20-worth of land in chief of the king,[10] in addition to land held of others. In 1449 Henry VI granted the hospital and its lands to the provost and college of St Mary, Eton, to take effect after the death of the warden, and the warden's residence became the town house of the provost.[11] It was also used as a town residence by the bishop of Chichester in 1491, and by the bishop of Norwich when he was warden of the hospital. Its demesne was let in one unit, and the great garden on the east of the hospital was let in 1454. In 1531 Eton College granted to Henry VIII the site of the hospital and its land in Westminster, except for a messuage in Westminster in which Thomas Brightman dwelt, receiving in exchange lands in Kent and Suffolk. The land covered 185½ acres: 64 acres lay south of the highway in which the hospital stood, running from Charing Cross to Aye or Eye hill, and 96 acres lay north of that highway; 18 acres lay in 2 closes at Knightsbridge; 5 acres in Thames mead and a half acre in Chelsea mead both lay in Ebury in the angle between the Thames and the Westbourne river; 2 acres lay in Fulham.[12]

By 1537 the bailiwick of St James in the Fields had been created to manage the king's property, not only the former hospital and its lands but also some of the other land in Westminster the king had acquired by purchase and exchange. The king's bailiff, William Moraunt, accounted for the property in 1537–8: the former hospital's demesne lands and farm buildings in the hospital precinct had been leased to Thomas Arnold for £18 a year by Eton in 1521, with tolls of the fair and with a dovecot, stable and chamber over.[13] There is no indication that St James's Park had been created by then, although a grant in 1536 of annuities to four women, who had been among the residents of the hospital as sisters of St James, stated that the hospital had recently been inclosed and made into a park and manor.[14] In June 1540 it was said that the king had imparked 20 acres of meadow and 28 acres of arable, and the other houses and buildings out of the property leased to Arnold, for which he was allowed £7 6s. reduction in his rent, and the king's bailiff had received the tolls of the fair for 2 years.[15] The Palace of St James was built on the site of the hospital buildings.[16]

HOSPITAL OF ST MARY OF BETHLEHEM, BISHOPSGATE

The hospital of St Mary of Bethlehem at Bishopsgate had acquired a tenement at Charing Cross by 1403, valued at 6 marks (£4) and let for 20s. a year.[17] Its provenance is

1 Newcastle MSS, Ne D 4740.
2 Ibid., Ne D 7, p. 3 (intro to Bdl. A21).
3 *Valor Eccl.* V. 208.
4 TNA, SC 12/3/13, mm. 5d.–6.
5 *VCH London*, I. 542.
6 *Beauchamp Charters*, 108; BL, Harl. MS 4015, f. 181v.; WAM 17108, 17087; *Cur. Reg. R.* XIV. 339; TNA, CP 25/1/147/14/250; 147/15/254; 147/18/330; 147/19/357–8; 147/19/365–6; 147/20/376; 147/20/399; 147/20/400.
7 WAM 50700.
8 *Cal. Chart. R.* 1226–57, 269.
9 TNA, C 143/61, no. 11; *Cal. Pat.* 1301–7, 484–5.

10 *Feudal Aids*, VI. 487.
11 *Cal. Pat.* 1446–52, 296; *VCH London*, I. 545.
12 TNA, E 41/216; *L&P Hen. VIII*, V, pp. 201, 276, 287–8; *VCH Middx*, IX. 99.
13 TNA, SC 6/Hen8/2102. Hist. of bailiwick will be treated under Crown's Estates in a later vol. Fair will be treated under Economic Hist. in a later vol.
14 *L&P Hen VIII*, X, p. 325.
15 TNA, REQ 2/12/95.
16 To be treated under Royal Court and Govt in a later vol.
17 *32nd Rep. Char. Comm.* pt VI (Parl. Papers, 1840 (219), XIX(1)), p. 477.

unknown, though as it had a substantial stone-built house c.1500, it may be the place and garden which Henry, Lord Beaumont, granted to the king in 1368, which cannot otherwise be accounted for.[1] Later tradition asserts that lunatics were kept there before being moved to Bishopsgate by 1377,[2] but there is no evidence for this. The master and brethren of the hospital leased the property, described as a tenement called the stone house with three other recently-built houses, to Thomas Wood, his wife Joan, and Joan's heirs, in 1545 for 99 years at £3 a year, with a covenant to repair the paving of the highway outside it.[3]

The property was bounded by the Chequer inn on the east, the highway on the south and the Mews on the west and north in the late 15th century. In the 17th century, however, the mayor and citizens of London, as governors of the hospital, brought suits in Chancery and Star Chamber to try to recover two pieces of land on the west and north of their property which been granted by the Crown in 1557 and 1568, the latter as concealed land,[4] but which they claimed had originally belonged to the hospital. They do not appear to have been successful in regard to the land on the west, but the property on the north, which extended eastwards to St Martin's Lane, was held by two men who surrendered it to the hospital in 1649 in return for a lease. The land had to be recovered through the courts in 1759, however, after the hospital's clerk failed to re-enter the property on expiry of the lease in 1728.[5]

In 1647 the governors granted a new 31-year lease of the main part of their property to the tenant, Olave Buck, esquire, for a fine of £40 to be paid in 1648, and a rent of £26 a year for ten years, then £30 a year, in consideration of Buck's expenditure in repairing the messuages he inhabited; £50 more was to be spent rebuilding another part, and the adjoining messuage was to be demolished and replaced within a year with a 4-storeyed brick house at a cost of at least £300. In 1670 the governors had to get a decree to repossess on the grounds of non-payment of the rent.[6] The hospital also acquired from an unknown source a house in Vine Street by 1736, which was later sold to the Crown with the Charing Cross property.

In 1830 the estate at Charing Cross, consisting of five houses used for commercial purposes, was conveyed to the Commissioners of Woods and Forests for the creation of Trafalgar Square. In exchange the hospital

was given freehold property on the south side of Piccadilly, for which the hospital paid £9,538 for the difference in value. The new estate consisted of nos 181–95 Piccadilly, stretching from the west side of St James's churchyard to Duke Street, and south to Jermyn Street with a corresponding frontage on the south side of Jermyn Street, let on various leases for a total rental of £2,045; the western side of the estate was occupied by Fortnum & Mason's premises.[7] After 1948 ownership of the estate passed to the board of governors of the united Bethlem Royal Hospital and Maudsley Hospital and their successor trustees, and from 1999 to the South London and Maudsley NHS Charitable Trustees.[8]

HOSPITAL OF ST MARY RONCEVAL

The origins of the hospital of St Mary Ronceval lie in an estate at Charing belonging to the earls of Pembroke.[9] Before 1199, the elder William the Marshal granted part or all of this estate to one of his household clerks, Master Joscelin, before 1199, reserving the right for the earl and his men to lodge there when attending on the king. Joscelin, who was known as Joscelin of the Exchequer by 1198, and also as Joscelin the marshal, deputised for the earl at the Exchequer.[10] William died in 1219, succeeded in the earldom by his son William Marshal (d. 1231), who granted to the Augustinian priory of St Mary at Roncevalles, Spain, his houses at Charing, together with adjoining houses and curtilages which had formerly belonged to William Briwere (d. 1226), a grant confirmed by Henry III in 1232.[11] By 1236 the priory had opened a daughter house at Charing where William's brother, Gilbert Marshal, earl of Pembroke, sealed a charter.[12] Its activities are unknown, but like the mother house it may have included the shelter of pilgrims, who came to the shrine of St Edward at Westminster.[13]

The integrity of the hospital's property suffered because of the distance from the mother house. In 1280 Laurence of Westminster, chaplain, recovered land measuring 100 feet by 60 against the prior of Ronceval[14] on the latter's non-appearance at the hearing,[15] and in 1293 the hospital had to justify its claim to a toft in Westminster disputed by Adam son of Walter Scot.[16] The tenements and rents of the priory were held of the soke of Mohun for 4s., paid to the abbot of Westminster as holder of the soke c.1300.[17] In 1341 the lands formerly of the brothers of the hospital of Ronceval were in the

1 TNA, E 40/2489; below, Secular Inns and Ests, Beaumont.

2 From John Stow: E.G. O'Donoghue, *Story of Bethlehem Hosp.* (1914), 67.

3 *32nd Rep. Char. Comm.* pt VI, 477.

4 *Cal. Pat.* 1555–7, 407; 1566–9, 227 (no. 1376).

5 *Survey of London*, XX. 11–14; *32nd Rep. Char. Comm.* pt VI, 478.

6 TNA, C 78/738, no. 16.

7 *32nd Rep. Char. Comm.* pt VI, 478–9.

8 Inf. from Bethlem Royal Hosp. archivist and web site (www.bethlemheritage.org.uk), 19 Jan. 2006.

9 For an acct. of the hosp. see Rosser, *Medieval Westm.* 310–21.

10 D. Crouch, *William Marshal* (1990), 146; *Westm. Charters*, p. 106.   11 *Cal. Chart. R.* 1226–57, 167–8.

12 *Cal. Papal Reg.* I. 164.

13 Rosser, *Medieval Westm.* 310–11.

14 Often spelt Rounceval.

15 TNA, CP 40/31, rot. 51d.; /32, rot. 35; /33, rot. 61.

16 Rosser, *Medieval Westm.* 311: possibly the origin of 'Scotland' which adjoined hosp. site on south.

17 WAM 50683.

king's hands, and 6*s*. 8*d*. was received from the holding at the corner next to the cross at Charing for the herbage there.[1] In 1382 the king, having been informed that the hospital stood on his land giving him sole rights to dispose of the custody, had appointed Nicholas Slake, one of his clerks, as warden of the hospital, but in 1386 the prior of Ronceval successfully claimed his rights under the grant by the earl of Pembroke.[2] The Crown presumably again took control under the alien priories legislation in 1414, if not earlier.

In 1422 the hospital had a master and brothers caring for poor or infirm people. The vicar of St Martin-in-the-Fields then complained that the master and brothers had, under various papal letters, unlawfully withheld tithes and oblations belonging to him. The letters were sent to Rome where they were found to be forgeries, and the archbishop of Canterbury was ordered by the Pope to publicly burn the letters and restore the tithes to the vicar.[3] The hospital had probably resorted to such methods because of financial need, as in 1423 the Pope granted dispensations for those giving alms for the maintenance and repair of the chapel of Ronceval, whose buildings were in decay.[4] Some citizens of London included Ronceval in their bequests, including the distribution of pennies amongst the poor and infirm of the hospital in 1458.[5]

In 1474 a fraternity or guild of the hospital of St Mary Ronceval by Charing Cross was founded by letters patent to maintain a chaplain there, and in 1478 the king granted to the master and brothers and sisters of the guild the custody and advowson of the chapel or hospital of St Mary and all its lands and oblations, to maintain the chaplain and two additional chaplains celebrating divine service, and to care for the poor people who came there.[6]

The site of the hospital was on the bend of the highway at Charing Cross, facing the cross and St Martin's Lane, and stretching south-east to the Thames; by the 16th century it included an almshouse, chapel and churchyard, and gardens. The extent of the hospital's site has been roughly determined from deeds and later plans. The street frontage extended northwards from and including the later no. 8 Charing Cross to approximately the centre of the modern Northumberland Avenue. It had a great gate to the street and the churchyard was surrounded by a lime-washed mud wall. The churchyard and chapel were at the northern end of the property, and the rest of the grounds extended in a south-easterly direction towards the river behind the sites of nos 1–15 Whitehall and the hermitage; a wharf gave access to river. The almshouse may have adjoined the royal property on the south-west, as it was later commandeered for use of the king's works.[7]

Later History

In 1531 Henry VIII acquired 3 tenements and a wharf belonging to the hospital, confirmed to him by Act of Parliament in 1536, in exchange for which the guild received property in St Clement Danes formerly belonging to St John of Jerusalem. The king's acquisition presumably included the almshouse, which was being used as payhouse for the king's works at Whitehall in 1531; it was divided into various rooms, and included a study, a counting-house and lodgings for the surveyor. In 1539 the building was referred to as the 'plumerye', but later the storehouse and works moved into buildings on the Scotland property and the almshouse was used as the office for the clerk of works.[8] By 1537 the Crown had leased out the 3 tenements and wharf, receiving rent of 46*s*. 8*d*. from John Reed for a great tenement and the wharf, and 16*s*. 8*d*. from Richard Harrison for a tenement, described in 1550 as the long shop; the remaining tenement, the almshouse, occupied by the king's works, was valued at 46*s*. 8*d*.[9] In 1539 the Crown issued a new lease of the 3 tenements and wharf to John Reed, a member of the king's household.[10]

Burials continued in the chapel at least to the end of 1541, but in 1541–2 it was dismantled and the tabernacle of Our Lady was taken out and set up in St Margaret's church.[11] The fraternity of the chapel of St Mary of Ronceval formally surrendered the chapel, churchyard, lands and all possessions to the king in 1544.[12] In 1548 the Court of Augmentations was still paying £8 a year from the revenues of the former fraternity for a priest and clerk in St Margaret's church.[13]

According to the later patent, Henry VIII verbally granted the whole to Sir Thomas Cawarden, gentleman of the privy chamber, as a reward for his attendance and for devising engines of war for use against the French. In 1550 Cawarden received the formal grant, which gave the first detailed description of the whole property, valued at £12 6*s*. 8*d*. a year. It comprised the chapel and the parcel of land adjacent to it called the churchyard (1½ roods), held by Cawarden; the almshouse 80 feet long from north to south and 23 feet wide; and the messuage, wharf, stable, cellars, solars, and land called the backside, held by John Reed (Rede, Reade), MP for Westminster in 1547;[14] Reed also held a garden 108 feet by 104 which was bounded on the north by the churchyard and on the east by an entry which led straight from Reed's messuage to the Thames. Another messuage was

---

1 TNA, E 372/186, m. 16.
2 *Cal. Inq. Misc.* IV. 97–8.
3 *Cal. Papal Reg.* VII. 238, 282.
4 Ibid., 251.
5 *Somerset Med. Wills* (Som. Rec. Soc. XVI), 181–5, 268.
6 *Cal. Pat.* 1476–85, 114.
7 *Survey of London*, XVIII. 4.

8 *Hist. King's Works*, III. 22, 24.
9 TNA, SC 6/Hen8/2102; SC 12/3/13; E 315/191, f. 163.
10 *L&P Hen. VIII*, XV, p. 561 (no. 1032).
11 *Survey of London*, XVIII. 4.
12 *L&P Hen. VIII*, XIX(2), p. 355 (no. 590).
13 *Chantry Cert.*, p. 65 (no. 139).
14 Merritt, *Early Modern Westm.* 64.

held by John Young, and the long shop was held by Richard Harrison. The rest of the property was made up of gardens: three, measuring 150 feet by 50, 123 feet by 45, and 126 feet by 84, were held by Richard Attsell, and another, 102 feet by 84, by Hugh Haward, and the property was bounded on the west by a common sewer (watercourse). The grant, which included all reversions of the property and all the lead there, was made to Cawarden and his heirs and assigns, to hold of the king in socage as of his honour of Westminster by fealty only, rendering yearly 12*d*. for the chapel and churchyard, 4*s*. 8*d*. for the almshouse, 4*s*. 8*d*. for the premises held by Reed, 4*s*. 8*d*. and 2*s*. 8*d*. for Attsell's 3 gardens, 2*s*. for Haward's garden, 3*s*. 4*d*. for Young's messuage, and 20*d*. for the long shop.[1]

Before his death in 1557 John Reed purchased the freehold of the whole property from Cawarden,[2] and built four new houses to the east of his own residence.[3] Under his will, Reed, by then keeper of the king's and queen's wardrobe at Westminster, left to his nephew Robert Reed and his wife Elizabeth for their lives the house they were living in and another adjoining, and after their deaths the two houses and another four on the east side were to pass to Robert's three sons, John, Robert, and Henry, and their male issue. He left his own capital messuage or dwelling called Ronceval within its great gates to his wife Alice to hold for life.

The will included a schedule of the rooms and goods given to his wife, and indicates that he had converted the chapel into his dwelling. There were apparently 3 storeys in the chapel each with 3 chambers, and another house next to it with about 6 chambers, a hall with a counting-house over it, and a parlour. The house may have adjoined the great gate, which had 2 chambers and a garret over it. There were also two kitchens, called great and north, with a chamber over each, and chambers occupied by John Parker, Sir Walter Hungerford, Mr Cooke, and Mr Burridge, and the chamber next to the garden gate which he bequeathed with furnishings and £20 to Alice, daughter of William Rawlinson.[4] Reed also acquired a garden on the north side of the Strand on which nine tenements and gardens later stood, as well as the Cage in St Mary of Strand.

Robert Reed senior died in 1567, leaving all his property to his wife Elizabeth for life, and then entailing it on his eldest son John, with remainders to his other children.[5] Elizabeth, who married John Hill, a neighbour, died in 1577. John Reed took possession but died later that year leaving a daughter, and the property passed under the entail to Robert's second son Robert. In

1578 the description of the property was similar to the 1550 grant, but it specified that the capital messuage and curtilage with chambers, solars and stables in which Robert Reed then lived had been constructed from the former chapel, the churchyard, and the almshouse.[6]

Reed may later have moved away, since before 1587 Robert Reed of Creek (Norf.) let an inn called the Angel, which stood on the western side of the Ronceval site and was very likely the principal house, to John Pemmerton, who sublet several rooms in the inn.[7] The estate seems to have remained intact until 1605, when Robert Reed sold part, described as 10 messuages and 3 gardens,[8] to Sir Francis and Sir George Fane, probably as a marriage portion for their sister, Frances, who at about this time married Sir Robert Brett, gentleman usher of the privy chamber and king's sergeant. Brett was the first occupier listed for a house at Charing Cross in 1604, and his son was christened there in 1607 with Prince Henry as a godfather.[9] In 1608–9 Reed apparently sold the remainder of the Ronceval site, described as 3 messuages and two gardens, to Henry Howard, earl of Northampton,[10] as in 1612 Brett claimed in a law suit to be in possession of all the property granted to Cawarden except the part inclosed into Northampton's house and garden.[11]

In 1613 Brett sold his house to Lord Northampton together with 10 messuages near Charing Cross occupied by tenants, and Brett and a trustee released and quitclaimed to Northampton 12 messuages, 10 cottages, and 12 gardens in St Martin-in-the-Fields.[12] Brett seems to have retained possession of his own dwelling and possibly other houses under a lease for 60 years, said to have been granted by the earl to Brett in 1604.[13] He continued to live in his house, and bequeathed the leasehold interest to his wife in his will proved in 1620. The will also transferred all his freehold property to his executors, and a subsequent transaction shows that this included three messuages on the west side of Northampton House, apparently reserved out of the sale to Northampton and acquired by the earl later. The whole of this property on the west side was given by the earl to his hospital at Greenwich.[14]

KNIGHTS HOSPITALLER

In 1338 some of the former Templar property valued at £7 5*s*. 2*d*. a year was given with the Temple church and churchyard to the Knights of the Hospital of St John of Jerusalem to hold of the Crown, paying to the Exchequer any profits in excess of £10 a year.[15] The prior and knights in 1339 granted to the keeper of their church of

1 *Cal. Pat.* 1549–51, 111–12.
2 TNA, C 142/182, no. 23.
3 TNA, REQ 2/31/57.
4 TNA, PROB 11/39 (PCC 51 Wrastley).
5 TNA, PROB 11/49 (PCC 35 Stonard), image 363/297.
6 TNA, C 142/182, no. 23; *Survey of London*, XVIII. 4.
7 TNA, C 3/215/52.   8 TNA, CP 25/2/323/3JAS1/HIL.

9 *Survey of London*, XVIII. 5.
10 Below, Later Creations, Northumberland Ho.
11 *Survey of London*, XVIII. 5.
12 Ibid.; TNA, CP 25/2/324/11JAS1/MICH.
13 *Survey of London*, XVIII. 6 n.
14 Ibid., 4; below, Later Creations: Trinity Hosp.
15 Below, Knights Templar.

New Temple the land called Ficketsfield and Coterells garden nearby for the maintenance of himself and the church.[1] The Hospitallers' estate in the area included property along the highway within the bars, in the parish of St Dunstan in the West, as well as outside in St Clement Danes and the beerhouse or brewhouse and cottages in St Martin-in-the-Fields near Charing Cross.[2]

In 1540 the hospital of St John of Jerusalem, Clerkenwell, was dissolved and the following property within Westminster passed to the Crown: the Brewhouse and 11 cottages at Charing Cross; Ficketsfield (15 a.); the Ship inn near Temple Bar and the 6-acre Cupfield used with it; 15 tenements on the south side of the Strand near Temple Bar; 4 tenements and a garden near Temple Bar; a tenement on the north side; 5 tenements next to the Angel north of the church of St Clement Danes; a messuage on the north side; a garden and barn on the north side of the Strand. In 1542 the Ship and Cupfield, both near Lincoln's Inn fields, were granted by the Crown to the Guild of St Mary Ronceval for knight service of 56s. a year in compensation for the 3 tenements and wharf on the Ronceval site taken by the Crown,[3] but the property returned to the Crown in 1544 when the guild was suppressed.[4] In 1558 the hospital was refounded as St John of Clerkenwell,[5] but the few properties in St Clement Danes re-granted to the hospital returned to the Crown under Elizabeth. Some smaller properties were sold on by the Crown, but most of the former hospital's property in Westminster was granted on Crown leases during Elizabeth's reign.[6]

KNIGHTS TEMPLAR

The Knights Templar acquired land by the Thames within the liberties of the City of London, bordering on St Clement Danes, which became the site of the New Temple c.1161; it had a churchyard by 1163, and a church eventually dedicated in 1185, lying within the liberty of the City of London. The lord of the fee was apparently the earl of Leicester, but it is not known whether he was directly concerned with their acquisition of the site.[7] Henry II granted to the Templars the nearby church of St Clement Danes c.1173,[8] and by 1185 in addition to 70s. received from that church and 6d. from the chapel of the Holy Innocents, they received rents from several houses and tofts near the New Temple, both inside and outside the bar which marked the boundary between the City of London's jurisdiction and St Clement Danes parish, later known as Temple Bar.

Gilbert Basset had granted them 17s. 10d. from seven tofts at Charing, and a man called David gave 3s. 4d. from a toft at the Strand. Henry II granted them 2s. 7d. from Baldwin the younger in the *gara regis*, probably land in the highway near the church of St Clement Danes, and 1d. from the land of Browning. Robert de Watenville granted them 5s. from a croft and a pound of cumin from land by the Thames, all held of the honor of Leicester. Rents of 15s. came from 3 houses which with a vacant house were also probably west of the bar; another 29s. 10d. from property of the honour of Leicester may also have lain in St Clement Danes.[9]

In 1251 Geoffrey Blundel and his wife Felicia granted to the Templars 43s. 4d. annual rent in the parish of St Martin's, Westminster, to hold of the heirs of Felicia for a penny, in return for which the grantors and the heirs of Felicia would be received into the benefits of the Temple.[10] The rents came from land with a frontage of 105 feet to the highway stretching to the Thames with a frontage there of 132 feet, which Geoffrey and Felicia had granted to William the tiler. William had granted it to Geoffrey of Hyde by 1257, paying 40s. to the Templars and 3s. 4d. to the building of the church of St Mary Westminster (the Lady chapel in the abbey);[11] it may be the site of the tofts at Charing of 1185. In 1303 a licence was granted for Robert the Dorturer to grant to the Templars a messuage in Charing street, parish of St Martin-in-the-Fields, which he held of them for 40s.,[12] presumably the same property.

By the time the order of the Knights Templar was dissolved in 1312, the knights also held a garden in St Clement Danes next to the Temple, granted to them by Peter or his son, from which Peter son of Meilania had granted 4s. a year to St Mary Southwark before 1188,[13] and a tenement in the parish of St Mary of Strand from which 2s. 8d. a year was claimed by St James's Hospital.[14] The pope intended the Templars' lands to go to the Knights Hospitallers of St John of Jerusalem, but the New Temple and its associated rents were amongst lands taken by Edward II for other purposes.[15] The manor of the New Temple, as it was known, was initially granted to Aymer de Valence, earl of Pembroke, but in 1314 Thomas of Lancaster forced Pembroke to relinquish the manor to him with all the lands and rents in the suburbs of London and Middlesex as part of Thomas's earldom of Leicester.[16] When Lancaster was executed in 1322 he held rents of £4 9s. with the New Temple, as well as Ficketsfield (by the later Lincoln's Inn), valued at 15s.,

1 BL, Cotton Nero E. VI, f. 26v.
2 BL, Lansd. 200, and Cotton Claud. E. VI, Hosp.'s lease bks from 1490s on, give details of various properties.
3 TNA, C 66/706, m. 11.
4 Above, Hosp. of St Mary Ronceval.
5 *Cal. Pat.* 1557–8, 314.
6 To be treated under Crown's Estates in a later vol.
7 *Rec. Templars*, p. lxxxix.
8 BL, Cotton Nero E. VI, f. 52v.
9 *Rec. Templars*, 13–15.

10 TNA, CP 25/1/147/17, no. 313.
11 WAM 17157.
12 *Cal. Pat.* 1301–7, 134; TNA, C 143/44, no. 5.
13 BL, Cotton Nero E. VI, f. 31; *Cal. Close*, 1307–13, 468. Garden held of earl of Leic. by Peter: might be the later Ficketsfield, or the later Temple garden.
14 *Cal. Close*, 1307–13, 483.
15 McKisack, *Fourteenth Cent.* 292.
16 *Cal. Pat.* 1313–17, 184–5; TNA, DL 42/2, f. 217; McKisack, *Fourteenth Cent.* 67.

which may have once belonged to the Templars. Edward II is said to have returned the manor to Pembroke for life, but he subsequently granted it to Hugh Despenser the younger, presumably in 1324 when the prior of the hospital of St John of Jerusalem handed over to Despenser the New Temple and rents of £6 13s. 4d.[1] After Despenser's execution the manor passed into the hands of Edward III. In 1332 it was granted into the keeping of Walter of Langford, king's clerk, for life for £24 a year.[2] Subsequently the churchyard and other consecrated places valued at £12 4s. 1d. were reunited with the Temple church and given to St John of Jerusalem. In 1338 the remainder of the property, including the rents outside the bar, valued at £7 5s. 2d., was granted to St John of Jerusalem to hold with the church and churchyard in frankalmoign, paying to the Exchequer any profit in excess of £10 a year.[3]

PIED FRIARS

The Pied Friars, or Friars of St Mary of Areno, Mother of Christ, came to England c.1267 and received a royal licence to acquire lands. In 1268 the king confirmed a grant to the friars by one of his clerks, William of Plumpton, of two messuages and the chapel of St Margaret the Virgin in the parish of the Holy Innocents (in the Strand), which William had acquired from the priory of St Sepulchre, Warwick, and from Robert de Lisle, to hold of the king in frankalmoign in order to found an oratory.[4] In 1269 Godfrey the prior and the brothers were granted a garden in the vill of Westminster by Alice widow of William the carpenter and a man probably called Thomas, and the latter also quitclaimed to the brothers two messuages and a curtilage.[5] The claim by the prioress of Kilburn on this grant suggests that this was the property later described as a manse or dwelling-house granted to them by Sir William Arnaud, Kt, and held of Westminster Abbey for 3s., since an inquisition in 1317 found that Arnaud's property had formerly been held by several tenants who had granted rent charges to the bishop of Durham (4s.) and the priory of Kilburn (3s.).[6] Other quitclaims were made to the friars by Margery of Boxley in a messuage in Westminster in 1269,[7] and by William of Aldenham in a messuage and curtilage and in a penny rent from a house in the parish of the Holy Innocents.[8] In 1270 the king granted to the friars a plot of land 225 feet by 37 beside the highway in the parish of the Holy Innocents, lying on the west side of their church, so that they might enclose and build on it.[9]

With the death of the last friar, Hugh of York, in 1317, the order died out in Westminster and their property passed to the Crown. The abbot of Westminster then claimed their dwelling-house, which seems to have included a garden, as the abbey thereafter received rents from the former garden of the Pied Friars. A cottage and garden adjoining the Pied Friars' garden was let by the cellarer and was later also called Pied Friars, but it is not certain whether it had actually been part of the Friars' estate. In 1354 the abbey let to Roger Stowey of Charing and his wife Joan a garden described as a parcel of the Pied Friars, for 8s. to the sacrist. In 1408 the gardens called the Pied Friars were being let for 33s. 4d. to the sacrist, who paid the 3s. to the priory of Kilburn in that and subsequent years.[10] In 1524 both the garden and the cottage adjoining it were let to Thomas Bradley, and after the dissolution of Westminster Abbey the two plots, one the tenement and garden called Friars Pyes measuring 61 feet along the Strand by 193 feet back to Covent Garden, and the other the ground and buildings next to it with some cottages, measuring 329 feet along the Strand, 132 feet at the west end and 184 feet at the east, were granted in 1541 by the Crown to John Russell, 1st Baron Russell and later earl of Bedford, reserving the rent of 3s. 5d.[11]

The remainder of the friars' property was not mentioned in 1317, and its location is uncertain. Some of the chronicles reporting the murder of Walter Stapleton, bishop of Exeter, in 1326, record his body being thrown into an abandoned cemetery formerly belonging to the Pied Friars, Stapleton having taken stone from their chapel to build his house.[12] Elsewhere the cemetery and chapel is identified as the church of the Holy Innocents, and it is probable, therefore, that at some point the friars had acquired the parish church as well as the adjacent chapel of St Margaret Virgin.[13]

PRIORY OF ST SEPULCHRE, WARWICK

A house of Canons Regular of the Holy Sepulchre, founded at Warwick in 1109 by Henry de Beaumont, first earl of Warwick, held property in the street of St Clement's, probably at the west end of the Strand, in 1239, when the prior recovered seisin of a plot 20 feet by 15 against William de Briwere, bishop of Exeter.[14] In 1242 the prior recovered two messuages in the parish of 'St Peter in Westminster', probably the north side of the Strand opposite the Savoy, for which he gave the tenant 15s. 4d., and by the 1240s the priory also held the appropriated church of St Clement Danes.[15] This church was

1 TNA, C 135/6 [last item]; E 40/1469.
2 *Cal. Fine R.* 1327–37, 298.
3 *Cal. Pat.* 1338–40, 99. Later hist. above under Knights Hospitaller.   4 TNA, C 53/57, m. 10.
5 TNA, CP 25/1/147/24, no. 469 (RH side missing; endorsed with claim by prioress of Kilburn and another).
6 TNA, C 145/78, no. 1.
7 TNA, CP 25/1/147/23, no. 469.
8 WAM 17134.

9 *Cal. Pat.* 1266–72, 447.
10 WAM 17166; 19660; 19700.
11 TNA, E 305/4/C14; below, Later Creations, Bedford.
12 Thos Walsingham, *Hist. Anglic.* (Rolls Ser) I. 182; John Leland, *Antiquarii Collectanea*, I. 468; above, Episcopal Inns, Exeter.
13 Below, Religious Hist.: Par. Chs (Holy Innocents).
14 *Cur. Reg. R.* XVI. 208.
15 Ibid., XVII. 188; below, Religious Hist.: Par. Chs.

the property of the Knights Templar in 1219, who also held land and rents in the parish, adjoining their New Temple site. As both the church and land near the Temple was later in the hands of the priory, all held of the honor of Leicester, they may have received the property directly from the Templars, who had an association with the Holy Sepulchre.

The priory granted all or part of their land opposite the Savoy to William of Plumpton, who in 1268 granted it to the Pied Friars,[1] and in 1281 William had to bring a suit to get the prior to render the service claimed by the earl of Leicester from his holding.[2] By 1278 Prince Edmund, earl of Leicester, had given the priory custody of his hospital of St Clement,[3] which existed near the New Temple in 1229 when the king gave 20s. to its prior.[4]

The priory's property in St Clement's apparently consisted of one substantial tenement and 4 smaller ones, and may be the inn in which the bishop of Llandaff was granted residence for life in 1280 by the king with the consent of Edmund.[5] A large house there was occupied by William de Bereford in 1324: he had been the acting prior in the 1280s and held this dwelling for life.[6] In 1291 the priory was taxed on rents of £2 2s. 8d. in St Clement Danes, as well as the appropriated church valued at £2.[7]

In 1324 the priory's property in St Clement Danes consisted of 5 messuages, which the priory granted with the advowson of the church, 10s. 10d. rent in the vill of Westminster, and a carucate of land in Haringey to the bishop of Exeter in exchange for 8 acres and the advowson of Snytenfield (Warws.). The 5 messuages, including the one held for life by William de Bereford, were valued at £4 19s. 6d. net and held of the honor of Leicester for a service of 3s. 10d. a year.[8] The property from which the rent came was not identified, but probably comprised the land in the Strand near the church of the Holy Innocents and the Pied Friars' property, opposite the Savoy.

OXFORD AND CAMBRIDGE COLLEGES

BRASENOSE COLLEGE, OXFORD

The property which was conveyed to Brasenose College in 1524 is first recorded in 1348 as a tenement held by Walter Arderne, barber, which stretched from the north side of the Strand to Covent Garden, possibly once part of a larger property belonging to his father Roger, since the latter's other son, also Roger, held a messuage, shop and moiety of a garden on the west side of Walter's property in 1348.[9] Walter was succeeded by his son John by 1368. John died shortly before 1395, leaving a widow Agnes but no children, and instructed in his will that his two messuages in St Mary of Strand opposite the bishop of Worcester's inn were to be sold.[10] The property owed an annual quitrent of 20d. to the cellarer of Westminster Abbey, paid in 1407 and 1417 by Master Richard Gatyn.[11] By 1432 the property had passed via Richard Ockley to Richard Parys,[12] and in 1448 Parys and his wife granted it to Ralph Lee (or Leigh), who granted it in 1457 to William Martyn and others.[13] Robert Martyn paid the quitrent for the two tenements late of William Martyn in 1486.[14] In 1508 Richard Sutton, a lawyer for the Privy Council and steward of Sion Abbey, bought the tenements to form part of his grant to Brasenose College, Oxford, of which he was co-founder. He leased the property to the college in 1519 and shortly afterwards

released it to them, with a formal conveyance in 1524. In 1520 the property was an inn known by the sign of the Hart, renamed the White Hart by 1524; it was in some decay, and the college paid £30 to Sutton for rebuilding it. The inn was let for £5 a year, and the tenant in 1547 was Thomas Gent.[15] In 1582 the tenant was Humphrey Gosling, lessee of the neighbouring Covent Garden pasture, and he was succeeded by his widow's son John Daunson or Danson, who also leased several pastures in St Martin-in-the-Fields.[16]

In the 16th century the inn included several buildings and a garden,[17] and in the 17th century a passage through the inn led to a back road (White Hart Street) which linked Drury Lane and Covent Garden. In 1662 the commissioners under the Act for improving the streets of London and Westminster wanted to buy the property to replace it with a new street into the Covent Garden area: the college and their tenant Henry Browne resisted for some years, claiming it was unnecessary to take the whole site, and only in 1673 did the commissioners succeed in buying it, for £1,700. The inn and its buildings were demolished and Catherine Street laid out on the site.[18]

CORPUS CHRISTI COLLEGE, CAMBRIDGE

The dean and chapter of Westminster, instituted by Henry VIII to replace the dissolved abbey of West-

1 TNA, C 53/57, m. 10.   2 TNA, CP 40/43, rot. 123.
3 TNA, DL 42/2, f. 217, no. 3.   4 *Cal. Lib. R.* 1226–40, 160.
5 *Cal. Pat.* 1272–81, 370–1.
6 *VCH Warws.* II. 97–8; below.
7 *Tax. Eccl.* (Rec. Com.), 13, 17.
8 *Cal. Pat.* 1321–4, 390; TNA, C 143/167, no. 4; CP 25/1/286/33, no. 257. For later hist., above, Episcopal Inns, Exeter.   9 TNA, DL 42/11, f. 24; Newcastle MSS, Ne D 4703.
10 *Cal. Inq. Misc.* VI. 37–8.

11 WAM 18888; 18889.   12 WAM 18890.
13 TNA, CP 25/1/152/93, no. 142; CP 25/1/152/95, no. 183.
14 TNA, SC 11/458.
15 *Brasenose Quatercentenary Monographs*, VI (Oxford Hist. Soc. LII, 1909), 12, 15; IX (ibid. LIII, 1909), 137, 178, 201; *DNB*.
16 WAM 17212; BL, Lansd. 71, no. 22; *Survey of London*, XXXVI. 22.
17 TNA, C 3/60/7.
18 *Survey of London*, XXXVI. 35.

minster, were given the obligation to support 20 students at the universities of Oxford and Cambridge. To discharge this obligation, in 1545 the dean and chapter surrendered back to the king property including 3 messuages and 2 gardens in Longditch in the parish of St Margaret's, Westminster.[1] This property was then sold by the Crown and came into the possession of Robert Hulson or Hollson, citizen and merchant tailor of London. In 1562, apparently at the persuasion of Dr Matthew Parker, archbishop of Canterbury, Hulson granted to the Crown the 3 messuages in Longditch, which the Crown then granted to the·master and scholars of the college of Corpus Christi and St Mary the Virgin, Cambridge, and their successors, to support three 'Canterbury scholars' of whom the dean and chapter of Canterbury had the nomination.[2] The college's possession of the property, described as a chief messuage and 2 other messuages with 2 gardens, was challenged by Richard Ravenor, who had tenants in the property,[3] and the college was unable to collect the rents until 1565, when it was given possession until Ravenor could recover at common law, which he does not appear to have done.[4]

In 1639 the master and fellows petitioned the king for permission to rebuild their Westminster property, which they described as being in a ruinous state and harbouring the poor.[5] In 1873 the college's property consisted of 25 dwellings in Parker Street, which had been rebuilt c.1856, and nos 10–13 Princes Street (Storey's Gate), of which no. 13 was a public house; all were let on 40-year leases at a total annual rent of £385. The Canterbury scholars still received £60 a year from the property.[6] The college sold most of its property there, in Princes Street and Central Buildings, between the two world wars, and had disposed of the whole estate by 1939.[7]

MAGDALEN COLLEGE, OXFORD

The property which eventually passed to Magdalen College, Oxford, is first recorded in 1371, when Robert Parker of Thorlestone (Derbys.) granted all his lands in St Clement Danes together with the guardianship and marriage of his daughter and heir Agnes, and all his lands in St Clement Danes after his death, to secure a loan of 20 marks.[8] With his wife Margaret or Margery he made another grant in 1373 of their tenements with

houses built there in St Clement Danes and St Mary of Strand.[9] Parker made yet another grant of his daughter's marriage and his lands to John Walsh, citizen and goldsmith of London, in 1377,[10] and in 1381 John Holest and his wife Agnes, possibly Parker's daughter, released and quitclaimed to Walsh all right in the property, described as a messuage and 7 shops.[11] In 1382 Walshe granted the premises in St Clement Danes to John Stegeyn or Stygayn,[12] and the property, now described as a messuage and 11 shops, was settled on Stegeyn and his wife Alice in 1391,[13] but after his wife's death Stegeyn's feoffees conveyed the property to Christopher Tildesley, citizen and goldsmith, in 1398.[14] In 1414 Tildesley was among a group of neighbours presented for throwing dung into Holwey (Hollow) Lane and blocking it.[15]

In 1421 Tildesley and his wife conveyed the messuage and 11 shops for £100 to Richard Lightfoot,[16] with whom Tildesley had had business dealings in 1410.[17] Lightfoot granted an annuity of 40s. from the property to Henry Felawe (Goodfelawe) and his wife Margery, his kinswoman, in 1426,[18] and in his will in 1428 left to his wife Margery for life her dower and 4 marks a year out of his land in St Clement Danes.[19] By 1432 Lightfoot's widow had married William Byle, who was holding the property, and Lightfoot's feoffees paid 20s. service to the duchy of Lancaster.[20] In 1435 a settlement was made whereby the feoffees conveyed the messuage, called the Chequer, with three shops on the west side of the gate to Margery and William, the shops for the life of Margery only and the inn for the lives of both Margery and William, and after their deaths ownership was to pass to David Lightfoot and his male heirs.[21]

In 1438 David Lightfoot conveyed 13 messuages in St Clement Danes to Master Peter Stucley, clerk, and others:[22] the beneficial owner is unclear, but they may have been feoffees for John Stafford, bishop of Bath and Wells, who in 1441 granted a five-year lease of the Chequer and the three shops to William Byle.[23] Stucley was presented for obstructing Hollow Lane in 1443 with dung and sand and may have been living in part of the premises.[24] The bishop died that year and the property remained in the hands of his feoffees until they conveyed it in 1452 to John Audley, son and heir apparent of James, Lord Audley,[25] who conveyed it in 1455 to William Waynflete, bishop of Winchester, and his feoffees, with lands in Hampshire acquired from the

1 TNA, E 305/7/D42.
2 *Cal. Pat.* 1560–3, 223; J. Lamb, *Masters' Hist. of the Coll. of Corpus Christi Camb.* (1831), 102.   3 TNA, C 3/40/44.
4 TNA, C 78/29, no. 28.
5 Lamb, *Coll. of Corpus Christi Camb.* 175.
6 *Universities Commission* [C-856], 1873, XXXVII, p. 169.
7 Inf. from college archivist.
8 Macray's Cal. Temple Bar 41–2, 62.
9 Ibid. 65 (& 72(1)).   10 Ibid. 18, 61.
11 Ibid. 55; TNA, CP 25/1/151/76, no. 44.
12 Macray's Cal. Temple Bar 35, 56; *Cal. Close,* 1381–5, 436.
13 Macray's Cal. Temple Bar 17, 19; TNA, CP 25/1/151/79, no. 121.

14 Macray's Cal. Temple Bar 13, 32–4, 43, 51.
15 TNA, KB 9/205/1, m. 18.
16 Macray's Cal. Temple Bar 8, 49, 69; TNA, CP 25/1/152/87, no. 39.
17 Macray's Cal. Temple Bar 38, 62–3.
18 Ibid. 14, 30, 39.
19 Ibid. 30.
20 Ibid. 67.
21 Ibid. 16, 37; *Cal. Close,* 1435–41, 42.
22 Macray's Cal. Temple Bar 12.
23 Ibid. 59.
24 TNA, KB 9/243, m. 12.
25 Macray's Cal. Temple Bar 40.

same source.[1] The bishop successfully established his right to hold the property for 20s. a year to the duchy of Lancaster, against a claim by the Crown in 1472 that the Chequer on the Hope with eight tenements had been built without licence on part of the king's waste in St Clement Danes; it was then granted into his custody.[2]

Waynflete demised the property to the president and scholars of his newly-created college of St Mary Magdalen at Oxford in 1456,[3] but did not release it formally to them until 1483: as with his other endowments, he apparently preferred to keep financial control.[4] In 1469 the property consisted of the Chequer inn and brewhouse and 11 tenements, giving a total rent of £15 13s. 4d.[5] The brewhouse was rebuilt c.1491.[6] In 1535 the college received rents totalling £13 7s. 10d. from its property near Temple Bar, and paid a fixed rent of 20s. to the Savoy hospital, representing the service to the duchy.[7] In the 17th century the property formed a block of buildings fronting the Strand on the south and Holywell Lane on the north, with Pissing Alley forming the western boundary,[8] and in 1683 consisted of the Chequer and its tenements, producing a rent of £6 18s. 8d., and the Black Dog tavern, the Lamb, an apothecary's shop, the Rainbow, and 3 other tenements with a rental of £8 8s. 8d.[9] In 1834 the buildings were nos 285–91 Strand and nos 37–42 Holywell Lane; no. 285 Strand was a public house called the Angel and Sun. The rental totalled £194 11s. 4d.[10] The college retained ownership until the site was bought by the London County Council and demolished in the 1890s to create the Aldwych.

THE QUEEN'S COLLEGE, OXFORD

The property given to the Queen's College in 1482 was put together in the 14th century. In 1312 John of Sudbury granted to his daughter Christian la Baignour a messuage on the south side of the highway at Tothill, and in the following year the moiety of plot or garden nearby.[11] Christian granted both to William of Marham, who in 1347 granted them with the other moiety of the plot to Robert of Baildon, king's sergeant at arms.[12] In 1351 William Husseborne acquired the plots and added messuages and land adjoining on the east side, so that by 1395 the property measured 186 feet on the north side, along the highway (Tothill Street), 174 feet on the east

side, against the road to the common pasture of Tothill, 108 feet on the south side, by the road opposite the chapel of St Mary Magdalen, and 174 feet on the west side.[13] The holding passed from William Husseborne and his wife Julian to their son William, also called Salisbury, citizen of London, and in 1391 he conveyed it to Richard Arnald, citizen and goldsmith.[14] Arnald granted it in 1395 to Richard Stanley, esquire, and his wife Cecily, but in 1396, Cecily, now widowed, and her sons conveyed it to Robert Eland and others;[15] it then passed through several groups of feoffees, and was known in 1410 as the Vyne.[16] In the mid 15th century Richard Walshe of Cheshire conveyed it to feoffees, who in 1464 conveyed it to William Chardyn (or Jarden), tailor, when it was a brewery called the Katherine Wheel with a messuage and 9 cottages and gardens.[17]

In 1482 William and his wife Joan granted the property to the provost and scholars of the Queen's College, Oxford, for anniversaries in the college chapel, payments to the poor, 4 marks annually to a priest to celebrate in St Margaret's, Westminster, and 40 marks to the master of Eton and his successors.[18] The property, described as in 1464 with the other messuage now called the Dragon, was conveyed to William and Joan to hold for life, after which it would remain to the college.[19] After William's death Joan married Hugh Morland, and they surrendered the lease to the college, who granted them £10 a year for life.[20]

In 1509 the college leased the whole estate in Tothill Street for 31 years to William Bate of Westminster, brewer, who was to pay £10 16s. 8d. during the life of John Morland, and £9 thereafter, and to repair and maintain the buildings, gardens, and the adjoining pavements.[21] In 1535 the college's property in Westminster was valued at £7 16s. 8d. a year, from which they paid £3 for the anniversaries and 20s. to Robert Tyffen.[22] By 1547 the Katharine Wheel, also known as the Brasen Tenement, a corruption of *tenementum brasineum* (i.e. brewhouse), and the Green Dragon were let separately, the former with a cottage and garden, and the latter with 8 cottages and gardens, for terms ranging from 39 to 60 years. In 1629, however, Joseph Bradshaw took leases of both parts of the estate for 40 years and put up a new wall dividing the two parts, at the same time assigning land from the Dragon to the Katharine Wheel. He then sold

1 Macray's Cal. Temple Bar 20, 22, 52; *Cal. Close*, 1454–61, 67, 103.

2 TNA, C 145/326, no. 3; *Cal. Fine R.* 1471–85, 53; Macray's Cal. Temple Bar 1, 3.

3 Macray's Cal. Temple Bar 9, 21.

4 Ibid. 44; V. Davis, 'Wm Waynflete and the Educational Revolution of the 15th cent.', in *People, Politics and Community*, ed. J. Rosenthal and C. Richmond (1987), 49.

5 Magdalen Coll., deeds, Temple Bar 71.

6 Magdalen Coll., Index Leases, EL/1, f. 81v.

7 *Valor Eccl.* II. 280; TNA, DL 29/287/4713.

8 Magdalen Coll., Maps 45; Ogilby & Morgan, *Map of London* (1677).   9 Magdalen Coll., deeds, 129/33.

10 Magdalen Coll., MS D-Y 353.

11 Bodl., MSS DD Queens Coll., nos 1741–2.

12 Ibid., nos 1745–6.

13 Ibid., nos 1747–50.

14 Ibid., no. 1753.

15 Ibid., nos 1751, 1754–5.

16 Ibid., nos 1756–8.

17 Ibid., nos 1759–60.

18 Ibid., no. 1766.

19 Ibid., no. 1767.

20 Ibid., nos 1768–70.

21 Queen's Coll. Archives, 4N 2.

22 *Valor Eccl.* II. 229.

the two leases to different assignees, who renewed the leases as they stood, leading later to legal wrangles regarding the extent of each part.[1] By the 17th century the rent of each part was £13 6s. 8d.,[2] and these rents remained the ground rent paid to the college until the 1860s. The leases issued by the college in the 18th and 19th centuries were for 40 years, renewable at the lessee's request after 14 years, with an entry fine of one and half year's rack rent paid on each renewal.[3] The rack rent, obtained by the head lessee from his tenants, naturally increased over the period; in the late 17th century it was £178, with an additional £89 in prospect when the leases expired,[4] while in 1740 it was £314 from which the landlord paid only land tax and the ground rent, repairs being the responsibility of the tenants.[5] In the 1750s the lessee obtained £360 net of ground rent, land tax, insurance, and sewer tax,[6] and £353 net in 1794.[7] After renewal in 1809 the rents were £605 gross.[8] In 1823 the college wanted to use a higher rack rent, nearly double the usual rate; whether they achieved this is not clear, but

on the next renewal in 1837 the college received £1,300. In 1823 the lessee asked for and obtained a single lease with a new description and plan.[9] The property was again divided in 1852, but the two parts were leased together in 1865, when the fine was £1,552 10s.[10]

In 1867 the college and their lessee agreed to sell the freehold of the northern half of the property to the Metropolitan District Railway Company; the amount of money paid to the college was settled by arbitration in 1869 at £3,100.[11] It formed the site of St James's Park station, and the headquarters of London Transport. The college bought a small property in St Ermin's Hill adjoining their remaining estate in 1903, but in 1916 the London Electric Railway Company began negotiations to buy the college's remaining property for offices, under the London Electric Railway Act of 1914, and this was concluded in 1917 for £16,600. Subsequently the college purchased a leasehold house in Conduit Street in 1946, and two freeholds in Brook and South Molton streets in 1927, all still the property of the college in 1999.[12]

SECULAR INNS AND ESTATES

Like the episcopal inns, secular inns were substantial private houses, each with a hall, service buildings and lodgings arranged round a courtyard, usually entered by a gatehouse from the street; only later was the term used for commercial premises which might include high status lodgings, public victualling houses and lawyers' inns. Private houses might bear names, such as the Angel on the Hope or the Rose, and by the 16th century many forms of commercial premises, including workshops and retail shops, were also known by a name, with a sign outside to identify them, a custom eventually confined to public houses and taverns.

ALMAYNE

Richard, earl of Cornwall and brother of Henry III, was granted 30 oaks from Windsor by Henry in 1234 for his houses at Westminster, which presumably he was then building on land north of the palace precinct; the land itself may once have been part of the precinct granted to him by the king. In 1256, Richard was elected king of the Romans, the title borne by Holy Roman Emperors before they had been crowned by the pope, but was commonly styled king of Germany, since this was regarded as the emperors' principal domain. Thereafter, his property was known as Almayne, derived from the French name for Germany. In 1264 Londoners led by Hugh le Despenser, the baronial justiciar, attacked

Richard's manor at Westminster, razing it to the ground and uprooting all his orchards.[13] Richard granted the property to his eldest son Henry, probably before leaving for Germany in 1268. In 1270 Henry granted his estate at Westminster, with its buildings, gardens, quays, and rents to Westminster Abbey for a light on the shrine of King Edward the Confessor, and the grant was confirmed by the king.[14] The property was thereafter subsumed into the abbey's estates.

Almayne lay south of Endive Lane, between King Street and the Thames. There was a gateway to King Street, and part of the estate lay between the street and the Clowson ditch, but it is not certain whether the main house lay east or west of the Clowson. Parts of the estate, probably all fronting King Street, had been granted out for reserved rents before the abbey acquired it, and John le Blund quitclaimed 11s. rent from the property to Westminster Abbey.[15] In 1300 the abbey granted out a messuage between the highway and Clowson, and another leased by them was quitclaimed in 1305. The rents were assigned to the sacrist, who in 1306 granted a lease for life to Thomas Grigge of 2 messuages on the south side of the Almayne gates, stretching back to the stream running from the Thames to the close bridge, where King Street crossed the Clowson stream, for 10s. a year. The whole of Almayne was apparently assigned to the sacrist, who accounted for mowing the meadow of

1 Queen's Coll. Archives, 4N 12.
2 Ibid., 6, 9.
3 Ibid., 44.
4 Ibid., 13c.
5 Ibid., 27.
6 Ibid., 33, 34a and b.
7 Ibid., 40a.
8 Ibid., 44.
9 Ibid., 52–60, 65–8.
10 Ibid., 77.
11 Ibid., 78–80.
12 Queen's Coll. Archives, inf. from keeper.
13 N. Denholm-Young, *Richard of Cornwall* (1947), 126, 132.
14 WAM 17360; *Cal. Chart. R.* 1257–1300, 146.
15 WAM 17466.

Almayne in 1349–50. On the south side of the property the boundary with the estate of the earl of Kent was marked by a ditch in 1394.

BEAUMONT

Henry de Beaumont, Lord Beaumont, a French kinsman of Edward I, for whom he fought against the Scots in 1307,[1] held property in Westminster by 1327, including land north of Charing Cross and on the west side of King Street.[2] He died in 1340, and his son and heir John, Lord Beaumont, died in 1342 holding in Westminster a messuage and garden and 36 acres, a toft with meadow and pasture adjoining, another toft with adjoining meadow, and a third toft, with a total value of £10 10s. and all held of Westminster Abbey or St Giles's Hospital.[3] John's son and heir Henry, aged 2 in 1342, received livery of his lands in 1360,[4] and in 1368 granted to Edward III his place and garden next to the cross at Charing and enclosed by a wall;[5] the location is uncertain, but there is a strong possibility it was the stone house granted to the hospital of St Mary of Bethlehem (above). Henry died in 1369, and his son John was knighted in 1377 and received his lands in 1382–3. He died in 1396 holding a toft and croft in St Martin-in-the-Fields, a croft and half an acre of land next to Charing Cross, 8 acres next to the Mews, 3 next to St James's hospital, 7 in St Giles's parish and 10 said to be in Tyburn parish (St Marylebone). His son and heir Henry, then 16 years old,[6] was knighted in 1399 and summoned to Parliament as Lord Beaumont in 1404. He paid 8s. 2d. quitrent to the cellarer of Westminster Abbey in 1407 for 8 acres land and 5d. for 1 acre near St Edward's water (the river Tyburn), and died in 1413 holding 18 acres of land and 3 acres of meadow in the vill of Westminster of the abbot for fealty and 16s., and 4 acres in Tyburn of the earl of Arundel.

His estates eventually passed to his son John, born 1410, knighted 1426 and summoned to Parliament as Lord Beaumont in 1432. Distinguished both in war and at court, John was created Viscount Beaumont in 1440, the first viscountcy in England, but was killed in 1460. His son and heir William, Viscount Beaumont, had been known as Lord Bardolf since 1449, inheriting through his mother, the granddaughter of Thomas Bardolf, Lord Bardolf, the latter's barony and estates. As a Lancastrian supporter, Beaumont was attainted in 1461 and again in 1471, being reinstated the second time in 1485, but was found insane and from 1487 was placed with his lands in the custody of John Vere, earl of Oxford, dying in 1507 without issue. His widow Elizabeth married Lord

Oxford and in 1509 the king granted the Westminster property to Elizabeth for life as part of her dower, for payment of 53s. 4d. a year. She died in June 1537,[7] whereupon the land reverted to the Crown, and thenceforth, as 'Beaumont's lands', formed part of the Crown's estates in Westminster.

In 1468 the garden of Lord Beaumont lay on the west side of King Street, and in 1486 Robert Rede paid 8s. 7d. to the cellarer for what was called Beaumont's lands. In 1538 the Crown leased 29 acres to William Jennings, groom of the king's chamber, for 21 years at a rent of 55s., reduced shortly afterwards to 33s. 4d. when 7½ acres of arable on Stonehill was enclosed into Hyde Park. Of the remainder, 10½ acres lay in Brookshot next to the Tyburn at Piccadilly, and 11 acres near Charing Cross and in the common field of St Martin's. Jennings purchased 18 acres of it in free socage in 1554.[8]

BERNES' (BOSHAM'S) INN AND DRURY HOUSE

The origins of the large estate later known as Bernes' or Bosham's inn lie in landholdings in St Clement Danes along the highway called Aldwych Street in the 13th century, and later Drury Lane. The inn was sited on Drury Lane itself, on the site later occupied by Fortescue's Place and Drury House. In the early 13th century Walter son of Cecily held land of the hospital of St Giles along Aldwych Street, which he granted to Martin son of William (Martin Muxelebroth). In 1258 Martin granted back to the hospital his right to the land, in Aldwych field, together with 22d. rent received for a messuage. The land was bounded by the land of the hospital, probably the parish boundary, on the north, and land of Hugh the clerk of St Clement Danes on the south, and stretched from the highway to Ficketsfield, the site of the later Lincoln's Inn Fields.[9] Hugh the clerk received a quitrent from three houses in Aldwych Street, whose site was part of Bosham's inn by the late 14th century, so Muxelebroth's land may have extended to the three houses.[10]

Another landholding that later became part of the estate belonged to the family of Atwell (*de fonte*).[11] In the thirteenth century Robert Everard held a property in Drury Lane from the hospital of St Giles for 8d. a year, perhaps that granted to the hospital by Muxelebroth. Robert's son William *de fonte* inherited this and acquired another in Drury Lane from Westminster Abbey for which he paid another 8d. a year to St Giles. The two holdings were presumably contiguous; in the second half of the 13th century (probably *c.*1280) the

1 GEC, *Complete Peerage*, II. 59–60.
2 BL, Harl. MS 4015, f. 160; WAM 17610.
3 TNA, C 135/66, no. 32.
4 GEC, *Complete Peerage*, II. 61.
5 TNA, E 40/2489.
6 TNA, C 136/91, no. 12.

7 GEC, *Complete Peerage*, II. 61–4.
8 Below, Later Creations, Jennings.
9 BL, Harl. MS 4015, f. 135 and v.   10 Below, New Inn.
11 Possibly descended from Ewerard or Everard *de fonte*, who with his son John witnessed grants in the parish *c.*1190 and *c.*1220: *Westm. Charters*, 237–8 (no 396).

hospital remitted part of each rent, so that William thereafter owed a total of 13*d.* a year.[1] William Atwell, who witnessed grants in the area from the 1270s, held other property in the parishes of St Clement Danes and St Giles, including that later known as Clement's Inn and the field known as St Clement's or Clement's Inn field behind it.[2]

William died between 1294 and 1297,[3] but the property in Drury Lane did not pass with his other estates to his son Hamo, and was not recorded again until 1370, when it was in the hands of John de Bernes, citizen and mercer and mayor of London 1370–1, together with the three houses in Aldwych Street formerly of Hugh the clerk.[4] Bernes evidently lived on the property, as the messuage was known for many years afterwards by his name, and he also held what was for this area a very large amount of land, some 96 acres in the northern part of the Westminster. The provenance of the land is not certain. It consisted of 52 acres arable and 12 acres called (in one series of deeds) Pantersmead between St Giles's Hospital and the Tyburn, parcels of 20, 3, and 5 acres arable in the same area, and the 2-acre Mewscroft adjoining the Mews at Charing Cross. In the 15th century the owners of Bernes's Inn paid 6*s.* 8*d.* to the cellarer of Westminster for land and meadow called Penteslands,[5] so possibly Bernes had acquired the holding that William Pente inherited from his father Thomas, consisting of 55 acres land, 10 acres meadow and 6 acres pasture in 1327.[6] Bernes bequeathed his lands, rents, and tenements in London and the suburbs to be sold to create a loan chest in the Guildhall; the inn and the 96 acres were conveyed by his executor John Dane, citizen and mercer, to feoffees for John Bosham, citizen and mercer, in 1382.[7] At the same time Bosham also acquired the Clement's Inn property, as well as messuages in St Mary of Strand from Andrew son of Geoffrey of Tettesworth in 1383, and 3 acres in St Clement's field from the New Inn estate: 2 acres opposite Bosham's gate on the east, and an acre at the end of his great garden.[8] His estate in the vill of Westminster was therefore one of the largest in lay hands, and he seems to have inhabited Bernes's inn, later known as Bosham's inn, turning the site of the three houses in Aldwych

Street into a new garden on the south-east side of the inn, measuring within its walls 138 feet along the highway and 144 feet on the north-west side.[9]

Bosham's wife and children predeceased him, and at his death in 1393 his feoffees and executors disposed of his lands in two large parcels, though possibly also with some smaller disposals, such as the tenements in St Mary of Strand, which may have been included in the property that Thomas Hervey left to the College of St Mary Newark, Leicester.[10] Bosham's executors conveyed the inn and the 96 acres, with 2 acres and a toft, and the 3 acres in St Clement's field, to Richard Ryngstede, citizen and mercer, in 1405.[11] Ryngstede had a house in London but also occupied Bosham's inn and its lands, where he had corn growing at his death in 1408. He left the property to his wife Catherine for life, and then to his son John, to whom his feoffees conveyed it in 1420.[12] By 1426 John and his sister were dead, and the property had passed to Richard's brother William Ryngstede of Dynham (Norf.) to be sold under the terms of Richard's will. The inn and land, let to Sir John Kyghley, Kt,[13] were conveyed by William to Edmund Winter, esquire, in 1428.[14]

Winter let the chamber on the south side of the great gates of the inn and another called the garret over the gates to a tenant for life in 1439.[15] In 1442 he conveyed the inn with an acre adjoining and the land in Westminster to feoffees for the use of Sir John Fortescue, justice and political theorist.[16] Later the same year the feoffees holding Clement's Inn granted a great walled garden adjoining Bosham's inn to Fortescue, and his feoffees granted to Clement's Inn a meadow, garden and cottage lying east of Bosham's inn, presumably to rationalise the layout of the two holdings.[17]

Fortescue's Place

Fortescue acquired the inn for his own residence, and it later became known as Fortescue's Place, and the road as Fortescue's (Foscues) Lane. His support for the Lancastrian cause led to his attainder in 1462; he lived abroad until 1471, and his estates in Middlesex and elsewhere, presumably including the inn, were granted by the Crown to John, Lord Wenlock.[18] The attainder was

---

1 BL, Harl. MS 4015, f. 196 (endorsement in margin). This was quitrent that Drury Ho. owed to man. of St Giles (estate of former hosp.) in 17th cent. Copy of this entry made *c.*1618 by steward of man., endorsed 'proving tenure of Drury ho. and other tents in Drury lane late inher. of Sir Hen. Drury Kt': Craven Papers 144.

2 Below, Clement's Inn.

3 TNA, CP 40/119, rot. 150.

4 Newcastle MSS, Ne D 4708; Guildhall MS 25121/887.

5 E.g. WAM 18888–18890.

6 *Cal. Close*, 1327–30, 123. Thos Pente was also called Pentecost, so probably inherited from Pentecost de Hereford. Pentecost obtained a messuage, 57 a. land, 10 a. pasture, and 54*s.* rent from Ralph Somer 1276: TNA, CP 25/1/148/26, no. 45. There are not many holdings of over 50 a. in manor of Westm., making it likely that they represent the same holding.

7 *Cal. Husting Wills*, pt. 2, 180; *Cal. Letterbk H*, 2, 287; Craven Papers 59, deed 6 Ric. II; *Cal. Close*, 1392–6, 107.

8 Below, New Inn.   9 Guildhall MSS 25121/1839; /889.

10 Above, Other Eccles. Ests.

11 *Cal. Close*, 1402–5, 486–7. Below, Clement's Inn, for other parcel.

12 Guildhall MS 9171/2, f. 121v.; Craven Papers 59, deed 8 Hen V.

13 Craven Papers 59, deed 1428.

14 *Cal. Close*, 1422–9, 445; Craven Papers 59, deeds 5 Hen VI, 7 Hen VI, 12 Hen VI.

15 Craven Papers 59, deed 17 Hen VI.

16 Ibid. 59, deeds 20 Hen VI. The land later passed to Mercers' Co.: below.

17 Ibid. 59, deeds 11 May 20 Hen VI; TNA, C 146/3154.

18 *DNB*; *Cal. Pat.* 1461–7, 192; 1467–77, 99.

reversed in 1473, but though Fortescue did not die until 1479, some of his property including that in St Clement Danes was apparently in the hands of his nephew, John Fortescue, in 1472,[1] who was definitely in possession in 1477.[2] Fortescue, esquire of the body to Edward IV and Richard III, later joined Henry Tudor and was knighted in 1485; he remained in possession of the inn until his death in 1500. His widow Elizabeth and her husband Sir Edward Howard in 1504 let the inn, garden and orchard with its courts and yards to Sir Robert Drury of Hawstead (Suff.), former MP and speaker of the House of Commons, for 20 years or the life of Elizabeth; Sir John Fortescue's son, also John, made another lease to him for 20 years to start on Elizabeth's death.[3] In 1508 John Fortescue released and quitclaimed the freehold to Drury and his heirs, and Drury settled it on feoffees for the use of his wife Anne in 1510.[4] John Fortescue sold the land and meadow associated with Bernes separately; in 1511 he and his wife Phillippa conveyed 20 acres land, 40 acres meadow, and 60 acres pasture in Westminster, St Giles, and St Martin-in-the-Fields to Richard, bishop of Norwich, and others as feoffees for the anniversary of Joan Bradbury, and the property was later conveyed to the Mercers' Company for that purpose.[5]

Drury House

Sir Robert Drury died in 1535, succeeded by his son Sir William Drury, esquire of the body to Henry VIII, and an MP and privy councillor under Mary.[6] He died in 1558, and Drury House apparently passed to his brother Sir Robert for life. The latter died in 1577 and the house then passed to Sir William's heir, his grandson William. The latter was knighted c.1576, and was an MP in 1584, but he amassed large debts, principally to the Crown in his capacity as receiver for Essex, Hertfordshire, and Middlesex, and was forced to go abroad in 1587. On his death in 1590 he still owed the Exchequer over £3,000, leading to seizure of his property by the Crown. His principal sureties, led by Sir Nicholas Bacon, compounded with the Crown, and Sir Nicholas was granted a lease of Sir William's estates, including Drury House, for 200 marks a year until the debt was repaid. Sir William's widow Elizabeth married Sir John Scott and they and Bacon acquired the wardship of the heir, Robert (knighted c.1591); the Scotts held Drury House

during Lady Scott's lifetime. Sir Robert presumably took possession on her death in 1599; the final part of the debt to the Crown was waived in 1605.[7]

Sir Robert's children predeceased him, and on his death in 1615 Drury House passed under his will to his cousin Sir Henry Drury and his heirs. Sir Henry died in 1618, succeeded by his son William, who sold off the Drury House estate in parcels 1622–5. The house, its court, outbuildings and garden were sold in two parts to Gabriel Barbor, who sold both in 1631 to William Craven, Lord Craven; some houses around the court and fronting the highway were sold separately or included in the sales of Drury gardens.[8] Drury stables, on the north-west side of the house, which had been developed as Reindeer Yard, were sold to John Holles, earl of Clare (d. 1637), in 1623.[9] The gardens had been leased in 7 plots in 1600 and largely built over;[10] the plots were sold to Jeffrey Prescott, citizen and merchant taylor, the earl of Clare, Silvanus Taylor, citizen and lorimer, George Lord Carew, later earl of Totnes, James Necton of Grays Inn, George Rolfe, citizen and merchant taylor, and John Fishbourne, citizen and vintner.[11] In 1630 Clare bought Prescott's plot, which lay between Reindeer Yard and the garden plot he had bought, and he or his son built or converted houses there into a dwelling, known as Clare House by 1638.[12]

Drury House and Craven House

Lord Craven's estates were confiscated by Parliament in 1650.[13] Drury House was then being used as the headquarters of one of the parliamentary committees, the trustees for the sale of estates forfeited for treason, usually known as the Drury House trustees,[14] but part of the main house had been let by Craven before he went abroad.[15] When he returned to England with Charles II in 1660 and his estates were restored, he offered the house to Queen Elizabeth of Bohemia, enabling her to come to England; she remained in residence until early 1662.[16] Craven did building work on the adjoining land to the south-east, where Craven House was built, and may have altered Drury House as well. On Hollar's plan of the west central district, drawn in the 1650s or 60s, Drury House appears as a compact gabled house, apparently of the 16th or 17th century, standing detached with courtyards or gardens on the north-east and south-east, and no

1 Craven Papers 59, deed 12 Edw IV.
2 *Hist. Parl. 1439–1509*, Biogs (1936), 349.
3 Craven Papers 59, deed 19 Hen VII; ibid. 144, deed 19 Hen VII.
4 Ibid. 59, deeds 23 Hen VII, 2 Hen VIII.
5 TNA, CP 25/2/27/278/2HENVIII/HIL; below, Mercer's Co.
6 Inf. on Drury fam. from *Hist. Parl. Biogs*, 1509–1558; ibid. 1558–1603; R.C. Bald, *Donne and the Drurys* (1959); Sir John Cullum, *Hist. of Hawsted*, in Nichols, *Bibliotheca Topographica Britannica*, V.
7 Bald, *Donne and the Drurys*, 110; *Cal. SP Dom.* Add. 1580–1625, 461.

8 TNA, C 54/2556, no. 10; C 54/2632, no. 16(2); C 54/2511, no. 5.   9 Newcastle MSS, Ne D 4765.
10 P. Croot, 'Before and After Drury Ho.', *London Top. Rec.* XXVIII (2001), 23–54.
11 TNA, C 54/2511, nos 6, 7, 9, 10, 14; C 54/2557, no. 24; Newcastle MSS, Ne D 4765.
12 For later hist. of Clare's property, below, Clement's Inn.
13 Below, Later Creations, Craven.
14 *Cal. Cttee Comp.* I. 467.
15 Craven Papers 144, deed 1650.
16 M.A.E. Green, *Elizabeth, Electress Palatine and Queen of Bohemia* (1909 edn), 376, 402–3, 405, 409.

28. *Craven House, Drury Lane, c.1810, probably viewed from the north-east or from the stable-yard at the rear of the house; the attic storey and other alterations show signs that the residence built for Lord Craven between 1663 and 1674 had been converted by then into lodgings and workshops.*

obvious gatehouse to Drury Lane.[1] This cannot be recon-ciled with the footprint shown on Morgan's map of 1682, where Drury House is shown with a larger, long block at right angles to a smaller one (perhaps that drawn by Hollar) and with an obvious entrance to Drury Lane.[2] The south-eastern corner had a greater variety of small buildings, which were still owned by the Barbors in the 1660s and 1671 when Lord Craven acquired them, and built Craven House, later sometimes known as Bohemia House, on the site. This was a large, perhaps triple-pile house with a hipped roof and at least two of its four storeys articulated by rows of pilasters, and seems to be related in style to Craven's Berkshire houses, his country seat at Ham(p)stead Marshall and his hunting lodge, Ashdown House; the architect, William Winde, may have been involved in all three projects.[3] Lord Craven died in 1697 and his estates passed according to a strict settlement made in 1674.[4] Drury House and its build-ings, excluding the south-east end and Craven House, passed to his first cousin's great-grandson, William Craven, on whom the Craven barony also devolved;[5] the rest, Craven House and 3 other small houses, passed to Sir Anthony Craven, Kt and Bt, a grandson of the earl's cousin.[6] Sir Anthony's sons predeceased him, so on his death in 1713, Craven House was reunited with the Drury House portion under the 1674 settlement, and the whole site then descended with the Craven barony.

Drury House was replaced with Craven Buildings in 1723. Craven House and adjoining property were also

let for building in 1724, but this does not seem to have been carried out, possibly because of bankruptcy of the builder,[7] and Craven House was occupied as several tenements by the late 18th century; the odd arrangement of windows in its attic storey and linking the remaining dormers seen in contemporary prints may have been alterations done to light workshops.[8] The eastern corner near Stanhope Street was sold to the duke of Newcastle for the creation of Newcastle Street in 1784,[9] and four new houses were built by the Craven family fronting the street. Craven House was demolished in 1803 and formed the site of the Olympic Pavilion, later Theatre. The whole estate was acquired by the LCC in 1898 for the formation of Kingsway and all the buildings were demolished by 1904.[10]

CLEMENT'S INN AND CLARE ESTATE

William *de fonte* (Atwell) held several properties in the vill of Westminster and in the parishes of St Clement Danes and St Giles, and was witness to grants in the area from the 1270s. He held property in Aldwych Street (Drury Lane), partly inherited from his father Robert (son of) Everard,[11] and a messuage and land to the north of the church of St Clement Danes, for which he owed service of 30s. a year and suit of court to the hospital of St Giles.[12] That messuage, which was known as Clement's Inn by 1404, was presumably William's dwelling, as in 1279, at the request of the Carmelite Friars, he was granted freedom from livery by the king's officers in his

1 *Hollar's London*, Plate 5.
2 Morgan, *Map of London* (1682).
3 Colvin, *British Architects*, 1135; *VCH Berks*. IV. 179, 504.
4 TNA, C 112/205, no. 13.
5 GEC, *Complete Peerage*, III. 502.
6 For Craven geneaology see *Yorks Archaeological Jour*. XIII (1895), 441–80.
7 Craven Papers 144, agreement 1724, papers 12726, 1728;

282, papers 1726.
8 Guildhall Libr., Print Colln, Pr.W2/DRU, cat. nos p542005x, p5418253.
9 Newcastle MSS, NE D 4919–28; 4871.
10 C. Gordon, *Old Time Aldwych, Kingsway and Neighbour-hood* (1905), 27–30.
11 Above, Bernes' Inn.
12 BL, Harl. MS 4015, ff. 136v.–7.

houses in the street opposite the north side of St Clement's church.[1] William was also granted land called 'Cokkesgarden' in St Clement Danes by John son of John fitzPeter, alderman of London, for 61*s*. 8*d*. a year; he died between 1294 and 1297 when 'Cokkesgarden' was quitclaimed to his son Hamo and his heirs.[2]

Hamo paid the 30*s*. service to St Giles for the property which then consisted of a messuage, 10 acres of land, and 8 cottages,[3] but William's land in Aldwych Street and possibly elsewhere may have been divided amongst others; his widow Agnes granted parcels of 5 acres and 4 acres to his daughters Olive and Catherine in 1307,[4] and in 1310 John Atwell, possibly Hamo's brother or uncle, quitclaimed to Hamo and his wife Isolda a tenement next to Hamo's in St Clement Danes. At a court held for St Giles's Hospital, probably 1315–16,[5] it was stated that Hamo had died in the war in Scotland, leaving as heir his eight-year-old son John, who was put into the guardianship of his mother. A relief of 30*s*. was paid to the hospital on John's behalf, on the understanding that it would be remitted to Hamo if he returned.[6] It seems that he did indeed return, as in 1317 Hamo and his wife Isolda made a grant of land in St Clement Danes, and in 1330 Hamo made another grant which his son and heir John quitclaimed at the same time. There are no further references to John, but Hamo continued to witness deeds and put in claims on property in fines, the last known being in 1348.[7]

Reference to the garden formerly of Hamo in 1351 suggests that he died about then. Possibly his son had predeceased him, as in 1368 it was stated that the 30*s*. service paid by William *de fonte* and William's son Hamo had subsequently been paid by John Clerk and his wife Joan, William Furrard and his wife Margaret, and John Farnham and his wife Agnes. The latter couple received a moiety of a messuage, 2 shops, and 20 acres of land in St Clement Danes and Kentish Town (St Pancras) from Edward Lauvoyr and his wife Olive in 1351.[8] This seems most likely to be the messuage near St Clement's church and the land in St Pancras (later known as Cantlowes close) that was thereafter conveyed with it. In 1368 John Walsh, citizen and goldsmith, was sued for the 30*s*. service,[9] and moieties of this property belonged to Walsh and his wife Margaret, and to Richard

Shirstoke and his wife Margaret in 1382, when both couples conveyed their shares to John Bosham and his wife Felicity.[10] Bosham also acquired an inn in Aldwych Street, where he lived, and other property in Westminster.[11]

In 1398 Bosham's executors conveyed 2 messuages, 16 acres of land and 10 of meadow in Kentish Town, St Clement Danes, and St Giles-in-the-Fields, to new feoffees.[12] In 1401 the property was conveyed to seven men who all worked in the king's chancery, including the master of the rolls,[13] and in 1403 to Richard Palmer, rector of St Clement's, Thomas de Sireston and John Thorlethorp.[14] In 1404 the master of Burton Lazars, as keeper of St Giles's Hospital, successfully brought a suit against the three for non-payment of the service of 30*s*. a year on a messuage, 3 gardens and 8 acres in St Clement Danes, claiming that Sireston had closed the gates of the buildings against him when he attempted to distrain for the arrears owed.[15] Sireston was living there at his death in 1404, when it was known as Clement's Inn. He was one of the five auditors of the Exchequer, and Thorlethorp was his clerk and executor, and succeeded him as auditor. Sireston's will, written in the inn, was witnessed by four other clerks,[16] which suggests that Sireston, like other royal officials, may have been housing his clerical staff in his household. Thorlethorp seems to have succeeded to the property, as in 1412 he held in fee property valued at £6 13*s*. 4*d*. in the vill of Westminster,[17] and in 1424 he was referred to as the holder of the house and garden near Clement's well;[18] he left office in 1427.[19]

Clement's Inn passed into the ownership of Richard Barre or Barry, citizen of London, whose daughter Margaret married William Cantlowe, citizen and mercer, and later alderman and MP,[20] to whom the property passed. Cantlowe probably possessed it by 1442, as he was one of the feoffees who granted a great walled garden to the feoffees of the nearby Bosham's inn, which only he and his heirs warranted, receiving on the same date an acre of meadow lying south of Clement's Inn meadow.[21] He was named as the holder in 1457, and he paid the 30*s*. service to St Giles's Hospital in 1463.[22] Cantlowe, knighted in 1461, died in 1464 leaving his property in St Clement Danes to his wife Elizabeth for life, then to his son William. By 1486 it had passed to the

1   *Cal. Pat.* 1272–81, 299. Approx. site of later Clement's Inn. Ho. was by St Clement's well, hence possibly his name.

2   BL, Harl. MS 4015, f. 133 [dated from TNA, CP 25/1/148/34, no. 243]; CP 40/119, rot. 150.

3   BL, Harl. MS 4015, ff. 136v.–7.

4   TNA, CP 25/1/149/39, nos 6–7.

5   Source dated only 9 Edward, but because of Hamo's age, and gaps in refs to him in St Clement Danes, Edw II's reign more likely than Edw III.

6   BL, Harl. MS 4015, ff. 136v.–7.

7   TNA, DL 42/11, f. 24d.

8   TNA, CP 25/1/150/64, no. 280.

9   BL, Harl. MS 4015, ff. 136v.–7.

10 *Cal. Close*, 1381–5, 200; TNA, CP 25/1/151/76, nos 46, 48; 151/77, no. 51; C 146/1423.

11 Above, Bernes' Inn.

12 *Cal. Close*, 1392–6, 109; 1396–9, 291–3.

13 *Cal. Close*, 1399–1402, 475; Williams, *Early Holborn*, no. 1502.

14 *Cal. Close*, 1402–5, 173.

15 BL, Harl. MS 4015, f. 137v.

16 Guildhall MS 9171/2, f. 46v.

17 *Feudal Aids*, VI. 489.

18 Newcastle MSS, Ne D 5023.

19 *Officers of the Exchequer*, comp. J.C. Sainty (L & I Soc. Special Ser. 18, 1983), 116.

20 *Hist. Parl.* 1439–1509, biogs. (1936), 152–3.

21 Craven Papers 59, deeds 11 May 20 Hen VI; TNA, C 146/3154; BL, Add. Ch. 40052; above, Bernes' Inn.

22 Newcastle MSS, NE D 4664; TNA, C 146/6188.

latter's son, Sir John Cantlowe, who leased Clement's Inn to Master William Elyot, clerk, and John Elyot for 80 years at £4 6s. 8d. a year, including six chambers outside the south gate of the inn and two gardens adjoining, one with a dovecot and one with a barn and stables, a gatehouse and Clement's Inn close, which together stretched from the road on the north side of St Clement's church northwards to the parish boundary, and were bounded on the east by Ficketsfield and another tenement of his held by the Elyots, and on the west by New Inn, by the garden of Sir John Fortescue (later Drury Ho.), and by another tenement which Cantlowe had leased to the Elyots.[1] Sir John died shortly afterwards without issue and the inn passed to his uncle Henry Cantlowe, merchant of the Staple, who himself died in 1490. It then passed with other Cantlowe property successively to Henry's son Richard (d. 1517), to his grandson John who died in 1520 without issue, and to Henry's daughter Joan and her husband Oliver Wood.[2]

The property was then inherited by the Woods' only child, Margaret, and her husband Sir William Mantell (d. 1529); in 1531 she married Sir William Hawte, and in that year they sold their property in St Clement Danes and St Pancras to Sir William Holles, Kt, former mayor of London, consisting of the house of Clement's Inn valued at £6 13s. 4d., a tenement held by the principal of the inn valued at £1 13s. 4d., six other tenements valued at a total of £7 18s. 8d., including eight gardens, and a close called Clement's field containing 14 acres with a stable, barn, and waste ground, valued at 40s., all in the parish of St Clement Danes, together with Cantlowes close near Tottenham Court in St Pancras.[3] Holles also bought the remainder of the Elyots' lease at about the same time, and in 1540 he bought from Sir Thomas Elyot, Kt, a freehold tenement called the Plough, which seems to be that on the east side of the inn, and ten other tenements held by tenants.[4] Sir William died in 1542, leaving his property in St Clement Danes and St Pancras to his wife Elizabeth for life, and then to his second son William,[5] later Sir William Holles, MP. The latter acquired the Lamb inn with its stable and garden lying between Clement's Inn and the highway in 1544, and in 1570 conveyed all his property in St Clement Danes to feoffees.[6]

Holles was succeeded in 1591 by his grandson John Holles, knighted 1593, created Baron Haughton in 1616 and earl of Clare in 1624. In 1612 Sir John bought the freehold of property between New Inn and Drury House, which improved access from Drury Lane to

Clement's Inn field, and in the 1620s and 1630s bought parts of the Drury House estate which also adjoined the field on the west, as well as land in St Giles's parish on the north side of the field. On his death in 1637 his son John succeeded to the title and to the estate. The 2nd earl lived in a mansion in Drury Lane, built on part of the Drury House estate (above), and began building development on Clement's Inn field. Complaints were made in 1638 about Clare building on his land, but in 1640 his lessee received a licence to build on part of Clement's Inn field, alter highways and make sewers.[7] Clare Street was inhabited by 1644, and Clare had a market house built in 1647: his right to hold a market on three days each week was confirmed in 1657, and again by Charles II in 1662.[8] By 1650s there were 86 new houses built on the land, and the whole estate was built over by 1680.[9] He died in 1666, succeeded by his son Gilbert (d. 1689), 3rd earl, and the latter's son John, 4th earl. John also inherited the large estates of his great-uncle, Denzil Holles, Lord Holles of Ifield, in 1691, and successfully petitioned for the resurrection in himself of his father-in-law's title of duke of Newcastle-upon-Tyne in 1694. He had no legitimate male issue, and in 1707 he settled the Holles estates, including the property in St Clement Danes, in tail male on his sister's son, Thomas Pelham (later Pelham-Holles), and his male issue, with successive remainders to Thomas's brother Henry and others. Thomas Pelham inherited on the duke's death in 1711, and was created duke of Newcastle in 1714. In the 1760s the Clare Market estate, as it was known, was Newcastle's biggest single source of income, with annual revenue of nearly £5,000 gross.[10]

After Thomas's brother Henry died in 1754, Thomas, who had no children, persuaded the king to grant him the creation of duke of Newcastle-under-Lyne with remainder to his sister's son, Henry Fiennes-Clinton, 9th earl of Lincoln, who was married to Henry Pelham's daughter Catherine, having settled the estates to include the latter and their issue in 1741.[11] Lincoln, who was High Steward of Westminster from 1759 until his death, succeeded as 2nd duke in 1768, and the St Clement Danes property was included in a settlement on the marriage of his eldest son Henry in 1775.[12] The trustees were empowered to sell estates and reinvest, and some property was sold 1787–91 to raise money to create Newcastle Street, running from Stanhope Street to the Strand to open up access to the estate, and further sales were made by auction in 1792 in 94 lots.[13] The 2nd duke

1 Newcastle MSS, Ne D 4638.
2 BL, Add. MS 5521, no. 4 (p. 8, f. 5v.); Newcastle MSS, Ne D 7, Bdl A21, no. 9; Ne D 4641.
3 Newcastle MSS, Ne D 4643; TNA, CP 25/2/27/181/23HENVIIIHIL.
4 TNA, CP 40/1106, carte rot. 13d.
5 *Memorials of the Holles Fam.* (Camden Soc. 3rd ser. LV, 1937), 21; TNA, PROB 11/29, f. 100v.
6 TNA, CP 25/2/27/185/36HENVIIIMICH; CP 25/2/171/12ELIZHIL.

7 *Cal. SP Dom.* 1639–40, 477.
8 Newcastle MSS, Ne A 530, 536, 541, 545, 547; *Acts and Ordinances of the Interregnum, 1642–1660*, II. 1233; TNA, C 66/3013, no. 4.
9 Morgan & Ogilby, *Map* (1677).
10 R.A. Kelch, *Newcastle: a Duke without Money* (1974), 37, 71, 179.
11 Newcastle MSS, Ne D 110–112; LMA, C/96/1295.
12 Newcastle MSS, Ne D 166.
13 LMA, C/96/1313, copy of Private Act 55 Geo. III, c. 38.

was succeeded by his second son Thomas Pelham-Clinton as 3rd duke in 1794, but he died the following year succeeded by his son Henry (b. 1785). Most of the freehold of the estate seems to have been sold during the 1790s and early 19th century.

CONVERS

John le Convers, king's sergeant, was given freedom from livery by the king's stewards in 1270 for his property near the stone cross in the Strand; the strip of land 25 feet by 9 feet he acquired near the stone cross in 1289 was probably to enlarge his holding there, which seems to have lain at the western corner of the Strand and Little Drury Lane.[1] He also acquired a large holding of land in the vill of Eye at Knightsbridge by 1290, to which he added another 3 acres in 1306, and exchanged 2 acres with the abbot of Westminster for 2 acres adjoining other land of his, presumably to rationalize his holding there.[2] Between 1285 and 1293 John and his wife Joan acquired from John son of Richard Wolward 10 acres in Chelsea and 44s. rent in Westminster from tenements near Westminster Palace, paid by Ralph the vintner (20s.), William of the infirmary (16s.), and John Cardoil (8s.).[3] John and Joan also acquired houses, gardens and paths at the close bridge after the death of Henry of Westminster, son of Master Alexander, the king's carpenter, and were granted houses by George the falconer. They granted to William of Sandford and his wife Alice, John's daughter, the rent from the latter houses, the houses at the close bridge, and rents paid by Ralph the vintner and Julian Cardoil, but shortly afterwards Alice, then a widow, granted to her father a tenement belonging to the palace in exchange for a third of the tenement which had once belonged to Henry of the palace (probably Henry son of Alexander).[4]

In 1309 John and Joan granted to their son Ralph a messuage and 80 acres in Knightsbridge, Chelsea, Brompton, and Eye, which Ralph then granted back to them to hold for their lives for 40s. a year.[5] By 1317 John and Joan also held for the term of their lives land in the manor of Eye at Tyburn and Pourtelane for which they paid 20s. 10d. a year.[6]

Convers was dead by June 1324 when his widow granted the messuage near the stone cross in the parishes of St Mary of Strand and St Clement Danes to John of Langton, clerk.[7] Convers's son Ralph is presumably the Ralph Convers of Newcastle-upon-Tyne whose son John while a minor married Amy of Langton; a divorce was pronounced in 1347, after the birth of a daughter Joan.[8] John then married Denise of Wedeshale, widow of

John of Pelham, in 1348, and took possession of the lands of her former husband in Eye at the Hyde.[9] Both John and Denise died of the plague and his property was inherited by his sister Christian or Christine and her husband Peter of Alnmouth, despite unsuccessful claims by John's former wife Amy, daughter Joan and the latter's husband, John Porter, who enfeoffed Henry of Shenefield in some of the lands.[10]

In 1350 Alnmouth and his wife sold Convers's estate in Knightsbridge, described as 3 messuages, 91 acres land and 10s. 2d. rent in Knightsbridge, Kensington, Chelsea, and Eye, with the Hyde to Westminster Abbey through the latter's nominees, acquired for the anniversary of Prior Nicholas of Litlington.[11] John of Langton quitclaimed all right in these lands in 1351, as did Henry of Shenefield, cook, in 1353.[12] The land was presumably subsumed into the demesne land of the manor of Ebury.

EARL OF KENT'S INN

This property within the precinct of the Palace of Westminster can be traced back to Master Odo the goldsmith, keeper of works to Henry III. Odo held land in Westminster by the beginning of the 13th century, including some in Longditch and at Endith, the latter later forming the nucleus of the inn of the archbishops of York, and he was reeve in the abbey's manor of Westminster in the second decade of the 13th century. By 1218 he was appointed keeper of works for the palace and began extensive repairs to the buildings, the riverside quay and precinct wall, followed by major rebuilding in the 1230s and 1240s.[13] He was presumably granted this property within the precinct during his keepership, and by 1236 it was his principal property, with a private chapel for his household for which he paid 4s. a year to the sacrist of Westminster Abbey in lieu of oblations to St Margaret's, and he was granted the privilege of having a chantry in his chapel while it remained in the ownership of himself and his heirs.[14] Between October 1241 and Easter 1242 his office passed to his son, Master Edward of Westminster, who also inherited Odo's property soon afterwards.

The houses were described as being near the sluice, presumably the close bridge where the Clowson passed under King Street, but probably lay back from the highway. In 1244 Master Edward, who was Henry III's clerk, keeper of works, and general administrator at Westminster, was granted as a mark of favour the right to run a pipe for water to his house from the king's supply to Westminster. Edward died early in 1265, and his house was granted to Peter de Montfort, who was given freedom from livery there in March 1265,[15] but

---

1 *Cal. Pat.* 1266–72, 455; TNA, CP 25/1/148/32, no. 176; WAM 17090.
2 TNA, CP 40/83, rot. 21; WAD, f. 108; WAM 4779.
3 WAM 17475; 17547.
4 WAM 17491; 17544.
5 TNA, CP 25/1/149/39, no. 16.
6 TNA, SC 6/919/14.
7 TNA, CP 25/1/149/51, no. 312.

8 WAM 9282.
9 WAM 4767; 4782*; above, Manorial Ests, Eye.
10 WAM 4780.
11 TNA, CP 25/1/150/64, no. 288; WAM 5406; Harvey, *Westm. Abbey Ests*, 419; above, Manorial Ests, Eye.
12 *Cal. Close*, 1349–54, 365, 614.
13 *Hist. King's Works*, I. 494.
14 WAM 17333.   15 *Cal. Pat.* 1258–66, 413.

Montfort was killed at the battle of Evesham later that year and the king granted the messuage to Sir Roger Leyburn, Kt,[1] to whom Edward of Westminster's son and heir Odo later quitclaimed.[2] The messuage was described as lying between the court of the king of England and the court of the king of Germany (Almayne) and between the house of John the cook and that of the archdeacon of York, stretching from the highway to the Thames. The houses of John and the archdeacon most likely fronted the highway, as the latter had been taken out of the estate: in 1272 Master Edward's younger son Thomas of Westminster quit-claimed to Robert Burnell, archdeacon of York, all right in the houses of his father which his brother Odo had sold to the archdeacon.[3] The grant to Leyburn also included another messuage probably on the south-west side. Despite the wording it is not clear whether these houses were completely alienated from the estate, and it is likely that all such grants were made at the behest of the king, who used the property near the palace to house his ministers and officials. Nor is it clear whether the grants above represented the whole of this property, or if Master Odo, who was king's remembrancer by 1273 until shortly before his death c.1291,[4] was still occupying part: a path 7 ft wide at the southern end of the property for access to the highway was reserved to Odo and his heirs from the grant to Leyburn, but this may have been just for the benefit of other tenants.

Sir Roger died in 1271 and the main property passed to his son William Leyburn, but by 1281 seems to be the house of Otho de Grandison,[5] who had served Edward I overseas before his accession, and returned to England in 1274, a trusted and confidential servant of the king; a royal council was held in his house outside the palace in 1292. He eventually left England in 1307.[6] The house later passed to the king's brother, Edmund of Wood-stock, earl of Kent, who also held for life a messuage formerly of Walter of Bedewynde, king's clerk, probably the houses at the close bridge which Edward II granted to his brother in 1321 after they were surrendered to the king by John of Ockham, wardrobe clerk and later baron of the Exchequer from 1317.[7] After Edmund's execution for treason in 1330, Queen Isabella, widow of Edward II, obtained a grant of his Westminster property,[8] but on the fall of Roger Mortimer later that year the queen had to surrender her acquisitions,[9] which presumably included Kent's inn. An extent of Kent's property in

Westminster taken at the beginning of 1331 described Otho's former messuage, of which part was held of the abbot of Westminster by the service of 2s. a year (perhaps part of the 4s. paid to the sacrist by Odo the goldsmith), as having no value beyond the outgoings because the house was ruinous and in need of repair. The other messuage was valued at 13s. 4d. a year.[10] The property may then have remained in the king's hands until in 1353 it formed part of the endowment of the college of St Stephen's chapel. It was bounded on the north by Almayne, near the northern end of the later Canon Row, and given that the canons also held the site of St Stephen's alley, with tenements on either side extending to King Street, it is likely that the alley was the entrance to the inn. Its extent southwards is not known. The buildings were still standing in 1362 when the king paid for repairs to the roof.[11]

HUNGERFORD INN

Sir Walter Hungerford, steward of the household to Henry V and an executor of Henry's will, acquired a messuage at Charing Cross in the parish of St Martin-in-the-Fields, conveyed for the use of him and his heirs by Sir Robert Chalons and his wife Blanche in 1425.[12] It had formerly been two tenements held for 18d. each, but in 1420–1 Chalons held it of Westminster Abbey for a quitrent of 3s. to the chapel of St Mary, which Hunger-ford was paying by 1422–3.[13] In 1425 Westminster Abbey leased to Hungerford a plot of land, presumably adjoining the messuage, for 90 years at the nominal rent of a red rose, on which he had built a new house by 1426.[14] He was one of the very few laymen to own a substantial mansion in Westminster in the medieval period, and his property at Charing Cross was referred to as Hungerford Inn by 1444.[15] It was settled on him for life and on his male issue in 1429.[16] Sir Walter, Baron Hungerford from 1426, was treasurer of England 1426–32, and a leading member of the Council, as well as chief steward of the duchy of Lancaster.[17] He died in 1449 and the inn and the barony passed to his eldest son, Sir Robert Hungerford.[18] Robert died in 1459 and was succeeded by his son, also Robert, summoned to Parliament as Lord Moleyns from 1445, having married Eleanor daughter and heir of Lord Moleyns (d. 1429). Robert's devotion to the Lancastrian cause led to his attainder in 1461; he was captured and executed in 1464. His son and heir Sir Thomas was also attainted,

1 *Cal. Chart. R.* 1257–1300, 55.
2 TNA, E 40/2508.
3 *Cal. Close,* 1268–72, 566.
4 D. Crook, 'Early Remembrancers of the Exchequer', *Bulletin of Institute of Hist. Res.* 53 (1980), 21–2.
5 *Cal. Pat.* 1272–81, 435.
6 *TRHS,* 3rd ser., III (1909), 125–95.
7 TNA, C 135/23 [f.5]; *Cal. Pat.* 1317–21, 568; Tout, *Chapters,* II. 270.
8 *Cal. Pat.* 1327–30, 506.
9 McKisack, *Fourteenth Cent.* 101–2.

10 TNA, C 135/23, [f. 5].
11 *Hist. King's Works,* I. 525. For later hist. of site, above, Other Eccles. Ests (Coll. of St Mary and St Stephen).
12 TNA, CP 25/1/152/88, no. 24.
13 WAM 23213; 23226; *Survey of London,* XVIII. 40.
14 WAM 23214.
15 WAM 17171B.
16 *Cal. Close,* 1429–35, 44.
17 J.S. Roskell, 'Three Wiltshire Speakers', *Wilts. Arch. Mag.* 56, 301–41.
18 *Cal. Fine R.* 1445–52, 143.

and executed in 1469.[1] Hungerford Inn, sometimes called Lord Moleyns' Inn, was granted to Anne Neville, dowager duchess of Buckingham, for life in 1462, and she occupied it with her 2nd husband Walter Blount, Lord Montjoy (d. 1474). She died in 1479; a grant in reversion had been made to her son John Stafford, earl of Wiltshire, but he predeceased her, and the holder of the inn is unknown until 1485.[2]

Sir Thomas Hungerford's only child Mary married Sir Edward (later Lord) Hastings. On the accession of Henry VII the attainders were reversed in her favour and her husband was summoned to Parliament as Lord Hungerford, but Thomas's brother Walter (d. 1516), who fought on the Tudor side at Bosworth and was knighted in 1485, received most of the Hungerford estates including the inn at Charing Cross. He was succeeded by his son Sir Edward, who occupied the inn with his second wife Agnes, to whom he left his goods there, but after his death in 1522 she was convicted of murdering her first husband John Cotell, and was hung at Tyburn in 1523.[3] Sir Edward's son, Walter, esquire of the body to Henry VIII, settled his lands including Hungerford inn with its garden in 1529.[4] He was created Baron Hungerford of Heytesbury by 1533,[5] but was accused of many crimes of both treason and perversion, and executed in 1540 with his patron Thomas Cromwell. His widow Elizabeth, who married Sir Robert Throckmorton, held Hungerford inn until her death in 1554.[6] The attainder on Sir Walter was reversed in 1554, and his eldest son Walter, gentleman pensioner to Queen Mary, received a grant of the reversion of the inn in fee tail for knight service; he also received a grant of Hungerford Place (or Inn) and the adjoining garden then in the tenure of John Reed, to hold in free socage, possibly to take account of the two parts of the property, one part held in freehold of the former Westminster Abbey, and the other held by lease, although no connection with the former abbey estates was mentioned.[7]

Hungerford House and Market

In 1583 Sir Walter, his son and heir Edward, and his half-brother Edward re-settled the Hungerford Inn property, described as 2 messuages, half an acre of land and a wharf, a plot of land 264 feet long and 96 wide next to the Thames, and a lane from the plot to the Thames;[8] a further settlement was made in 1585.[9] No image or record of what the property looked like then has been identified. Sir Walter died in 1596, having quarrelled bitterly with his second wife: his son had presumably

predeceased him, as he left all his property to his brother Edward, from whom his widow had to recover some dower. Edward died without issue in 1607, seized of Hungerford Inn and garden all held in free socage. It passed to his adopted heir and great-nephew Edward Hungerford (1596–1648), the son of Sir Walter's daughter Lucy and her husband Sir Anthony Hungerford of Black Bourton (Oxon.), a descendant of the 1st Lord Hungerford.[10] A fine was levied in 1608 settling the property in tail male.[11]

In 1628 Sir Edward granted a lease of five messuages there to Simon Greene, who probably built the alley running to the river known as Greene's Lane, which first appears in rate books that year. Sir Edward Hungerford died in 1648 and the property passed to his royalist half-brother Sir Anthony Hungerford, whose son, another Sir Edward (1632–1711), renowned for his profligacy, was the last occupant of the house.[12] In 1664 Sir Edward settled Hungerford House, including a 200-year term in the house to the trustees to raise £10,000 after his death for his daughter Rachel; the remainder was vested in his son Edward, but the latter died under age without issue, after which an additional £20,000 was to be settled on Rachel. In 1677, however, Hungerford obtained an Act of Parliament which enabled him to grant building leases for 50 years, reserving in all £400 a year in rent. At the same time he began borrowing large sums from Sir Stephen Fox, amounting to £10,000 by 1679, secured on the property with a covenant to rebuild so that the property would be worth £1,500 a year. In 1679 he obtained letters patent giving him the right to hold a market at Hungerford House on three days a week,[13] and bought some adjoining property in York Buildings to add to the site of the market place. In 1680 Hungerford conveyed the freehold of the market to Fox, and obtained a release from his daughter's husband and trustee of her portion and title in the property. In 1681 Hungerford received £29,000 from Fox and conveyed Hungerford House to Fox's feoffee, but a further £1,000 was paid in 1683 secured on the House and the market. The final sale of Hungerford Buildings and market to Fox took place in 1684; a fourth of the purchase belonged to Sir Christopher Wren, and under a covenant he and his heirs were entitled to the benefit of a fourth part of the market as well. Fox had obtained a new 40-year lease in 1678 from the dean and chapter of Westminster of the property adjoining Hungerford's freehold called the Lyon with a garden and tenements, suggesting he was considering long-term involvement rather just

1 K.B. McFarlane, *Nobility of Later Medieval Eng.* (1973), 126–8.
2 *Cal. Pat.* 1461–67, 196; 1467–77, 346.
3 *L&P Hen VIII*, III(2), p. 1203.
4 TNA, CP 25/2/51/367/21HENVIII/Mich.
5 *L&P Hen. VIII*, VI, p. 553.
6 *Survey of London*, XVIII. 43; GEC, *Complete Peerage*, VI. 627.
7 *Cal. Pat.* 1553–4, 94–5.
8 TNA, CP 25/2/172/25&26ELIZ/Mich.
9 BL, Add. Ch. 40085.
10 TNA, C 142/306, no. 160; GEC, *Complete Peerage*, VI. 626.
11 WCA, Acc. 181/1.
12 Erroneous belief that ho. burned down 1669 based on misidentification of 'Lady Hungerford's ho.', which was in Durham Yard, by Latham & Mathews, eds, *Pepys Diary*, IX. 535n.
13 *Cal. SP Dom.* 1678 & Add. 1674–9, 305, 308, 334.

29. *Hungerford Market from the Thames c.1847, and I.K. Brunel's Hungerford footbridge of 1841–5 spanning the river. The market was opened on part of Hungerford Inn and adjoining buildings c.1680. The riverside stairs and quay were extended into the river c.1830, and a new market house opened in 1833.*

lending capital to Hungerford, but it is not clear at what point he decided to buy the property.[1] In 1685 Fox and Wren obtained further letters patent enabling them to sell grain at the market.[2]

After Fox's death, his widow and trustees, together with Wren, sold the Hungerford estate and market to Henry Wise in 1718, who also took a new lease of the Westminster property adjoining. In 1730 the annual income from the market and buildings was just over £1,900, which included seven ground rents of c.£190; most of the rest was from rack rents in Hungerford Street, the Strand, the east and west sides of the market, the meal-wharf, Hele Alley, the market house and vaults, and two rents in York Buildings.[3] The property remained in hands of Wise's descendants until 1830, when the Hungerford Market Company acquired it. The water-stairs and quay were then constructed in granite 150 feet farther into river than the old embankment, and the neighbouring Villiers Street wharf was bought to provide access through Villiers Street to the Strand. Part of the neighbouring property on the west side, Charles Court, was also added to the original site and the line of Hungerford Street was moved farther east so that it led to the great hall of the market, which was designed by Charles Fowler, architect of Covent Garden market, as a very long structure with a great hall lined with shops on two levels and a fish market beyond by the river. It was opened in 1833. In 1851 Hungerford Hall was erected for lectures and shows but was destroyed by a fire which also caused considerable damage to the market hall. In 1862 the whole property was bought by the Charing

Cross Railway Company for the formation of Charing Cross station.[4]

MAUDUIT

William Mauduit (d. 1194), the king's chamberlain, acquired property in Westminster from the 1180s, including a messuage in Longditch from Adam of Westminster and his wife Maud, daughter of Robert of Deerhurst, held of Westminster Abbey for a rent 10*d.* paid to the almonry; land in Longditch adjoining that messuage from Alexander son of William the priest and his wife Alice; and half an acre of meadow in Lousmede just to the north from Peter son of Thomas the mariner.[5] His son Robert, also king's chamberlain, continued the acquisition of property from the 1190s, including land in Tothill west of his house, from the sons of Ralph of Tothill, and, from Westminster Abbey, the houses, land and meadow in Longditch which William the abbot's usher had given to the abbey and which Robert thereafter held for a service of 11*s.* a year to the infirmerer.[6] At about the same time the abbot also granted to Robert licence for a chapel in his house.[7] Robert added to his estate 4*s.* in quitrents from 3 tenants from Adam of Westminster, two messuages and a meadow in Longditch adjoining his land from Pavia of Longditch, and an acre of meadow in Lousmede adjoining his garden from Julian widow of Robert Testard, whose son Richard then granted him 3 acres in Tothill. Another 3 acres in Tothill from Edward son of Leviva meant that by c.1215 his land extended from his house in Longditch (now Storey's Gate) along Tothill Street to a path leading from Tothill

1 Acct based on C. Clay, *Public Finance and Private Wealth* (1978), 178–82.
2 TNA, C 66/3265, no 4.
3 WCA, Acc. 181/1.
4 *Survey of London*, XVIII. 43–5. Hist. of sta. reserved for

Comms, and of mkt for Economic Hist.
5 *Beauchamp Charters*, pp. 107, 110–11.
6 *Beauchamp Charters*, pp. 111, 114–15; *Westm. Charters*, p. 162.
7 *Westm. Charters*, p. 163.

to St James's Hospital, approximately by the later Guards' Chapel.[1] Robert's wife Isabel also acquired property, 2 messuages from John Testard, and 7s. 8d. in quitrents from John son of Edward the reeve, in order to grant them to maintain the lights on the altar of St Mary in Westminster Abbey.[2]

Robert died in 1222 and his son William (d. 1257) inherited the estate and chamberlainship. In 1234 he acknowledged that he owed the abbot service of 21s. 10d. from 14 tenants on his Westminster estate, in return for which arrears of the service were acquitted.[3] One of these holdings, a messuage in Tothill, reverted to him and was granted out again for a quitrent of 4s.[4] He was succeeded by his son William, who in 1263 inherited the lands and title of the earldom of Warwick through his mother Alice, daughter of Waleran (Beaumont) de Newburgh, earl of Warwick, and the Mauduit estate in Westminster thereafter passed with the estates of the earldom. William died in 1268 without issue, and his estates and earldom passed to his sister's son, William Beauchamp of Elmley.[5] In 1281 Joan daughter of Robert of Barking claimed a service from the earl for a free tenement in Westminster, and in 1291 the master of St James's Hospital claimed two holdings from the earl, which the earl had resumed because they had been granted without licence to the hospital, against the statute of mortmain.[6] William died in 1298, holding in the vill of Westminster a messuage and 8 acres of arable, valued at 53s. 4d. a year and held of the abbot of Westminster by suit of court and 14s. 10d. a year.[7] It passed to his son and heir Guy, earl of Warwick, who in 1315 added to his estate a piece of land in Lousmede called Lousacre from Sir Edward Charles, held of St James's Hospital for 8d. a year.[8] Guy died in 1315 holding the messuage and 8 acres as well as 10s. rent, for which he owed the abbot 15s. a year and suit of court, and an acre of land and half an acre of meadow in Westminster held of St James's for 8d. a year. The messuage with its close and the meadow was valued at 60s., and the land at 12d. an acre. He was succeeded by his infant son Thomas.[9] In 1344 Thomas granted his estate in Westminster to Westminster Abbey in exchange for rent of 41s. in Hanslope (Bucks.); the estate was described as a toft called Mauduitsgarden, a croft called Mauduitscroft, an acre of arable and a half of meadow in Lousmede held of St James's, with rent of 7s. 6d. from 6 tenants.[10]

In 1350 the abbey let the Mauduit estate including the rents to Roger Belet for 40 years at 41s. a year, though a vacant plot on Tothill Street which was part of the estate was leased to him separately for 60 years at 12d.; Belet already held three of the tenements from which the 7s.

6d. rent came.[11] In 1398 Robert Chaundler was the lessee of the garden formerly of Robert Mauduit for 41s. paid to the inner treasurer, who paid the 11s. to the infirmerer and 6s. 4d. to the cellarer. Mauduit's garden continued to be so identified in the abbey's accounts: in 1465 it was a messuage also called Caleys.[12] By 1490 part of the holding was a close called Conyngarth,[13] which Westminster Abbey leased in 1509 to Anthony Legh or Lee and his wife Emma for 30 years; it was described as part of Caleys or Mauduit's garden, and included the ditch surrounding the garden, and the rent was 20s.[14] In 1531 Petty Caleys, which had been let to John Lord Berners, a member of the king's household and deputy in Calais, was among the lands obtained by Henry VIII. Berners had to fight to get what he regarded as adequate compensation from the Crown: he claimed that the 10 acres might be nearer 20, and that he had spent more than a £100 on it; it had been marsh ground, lying open, and overflowed at every tide (via Longditch), the drainage cost more than £100 and he had raised the site by 2 feet. The garden had been raised more than 3 feet, and the paling of the ground and about the house cost him £50, even though it was his own timber. He had also rebuilt the outer gatehouse, stable and barn at a cost of £50 or more; other repairs and expenses made the summer before he went to Calais cost over £100. He had bought the lease of the upper house and ground from Anthony Lee for £50, and he felt sure the king would give him £400 in ready money, which was less than he would accept from anyone else, since he could let it for £10 a year profit for the rest of his term. He was assured by Cromwell that he would not lose by his sale to the king, and he commented that he knew well all others who have lands or houses taken from them were well rewarded.[15] The estate was incorporated into the south-eastern corner of St James's Park.

By the 15th century, and possibly by 1350, the street frontage had been let separately from Maudit's garden. Only the latter, mainly open ground, was granted to Henry VIII, while the rest of the estate remained in the tenants' hands, possibly for quitrents and was not separately identified in the abbey's accounts. In 1495 the abbey obtained quitrents of 18d. and 9d. from Hartshorn in Tothill; rent of 100s. from herbage and pasture in Lousmede; 33s. 4d. for a croft at the end of Tothill; 12d. for an acre arable at the pinfold; 20s. for a croft; 33s. 4d. for a stable and a small garden next to the Hartshorn let with the croft. The annual total from the Mauduit property was thus £7 14s. 4d. in rent and 27d. in quitrents.[16]

1 *Beauchamp Charters*, pp. 108–9, 112–13, 116–18; TNA, CP 25/1/146/2, no. 21; 146/4, no. 59; WAM 17318.
2 *Westm. Charters*, 185–6, 258–9, 187.
3 TNA, CP 25/1/146/9, no. 111.
4 WAM 17394.   5 GEC, *Complete Peerage*, XII. 367–8.
6 TNA, CP 40/43, rot. 114d.; /45, rot. 42d.; /87, rot. 13, 25d., 121d.   7 TNA, C 133/86, no. 1.
8 BL, Add. MS 28024, f. 48–v.   9 TNA, C 134/49 [f. 3].
10 *Cal. Pat.* 1343–5, 246; WAM 17635–7; 17123.
11 WAM 17652–3.   12 WAM 17788.
13 WAM 17892.
14 WAM 17959.
15 *L&P Hen. VIII*, V, pp. 406, 533–4.
16 WAM 23121A.

MERCERS' COMPANY

Joan Bradbury, widow of Sir Thomas Bradbury, lord mayor of London (d. 1509), left lands for the endowment of a chantry in the church of St Stephen, Coleman Street (City of London) and for coals for the poor of that parish. Her feoffees, including Richard, bishop of Norwich, and Richard Broke, acquired from John Fortescue and his wife Phillippa *c.*120 acres in the vill of Westminster and in St Giles-in-the-Fields in 1511, which had been held successively in the 14th century by John Bernes and John Bosham with their inn in St Clement Danes.[1] In 1516 the feoffees conveyed the land, held of the abbot of Westminster for 6*s.* a year, with 29 acres in Marylebone to the Mercers' Company of London, who had received a licence to acquire in mortmain lands for the uses specified by Joan. The Mercers took possession of the land in 1529, after Joan's death, holding under the ordinances she had made for the management of the chantry in 1523.[2]

In 1536 the Mercers were forced to exchange with the king the bulk of their estate in Westminster, consisting of Conduit mead, an adjoining close of 24 acres, and another 3-acre close, all held by the Corporation of London on lease, 42 acres in several parcels, 3 acres of arable at the claypits, 11 acres in the common field and in St Martin's field, and 3 acres of pasture in a close near the Mews. They received instead the manor of Hasyllyngfeld (Kent). The Mercers were then left in Westminster with only the 10-acre close called Elmfield, which lay between Covent Garden and the parish of St Giles.[3] In 1820 that land was said to be 8½ acres near Long Acre.[4]

In 2006 the Lady Bradbury estate, as it was known, was still in the ownership of the Mercers' Company, described as the largest property holding in single ownership in Covent Garden. It comprised 6 blocks of buildings between the north-west side of Long Acre and Shelton Street, a mix of shops, warehouses, offices, cultural spaces, and residential flats.[5]

MOTE

The origins of the estate later known as the Mote lay in the 13th century. Joan Charles, widow of William Charles, held land in the vills of Westminster and Eye *c.*1280,[6] and at her death *c.*1305 held a messuage and 32 acres of land in Westminster, for which she rendered

10*s.* to Westminster Abbey, 5*s.* to St James's Hospital, 5*s.* to St Margaret's church, Westminster, and 10*d.* to Master William of Wanden. Her heir was her son Edward Charles.[7] In 1309 Edward's feoffees conveyed a messuage and 30 acres in Westminster to Edward and his wife Alice and his heirs,[8] and in 1314–15 Edward sold an acre called Lousacre near St James's Hospital to Guy Beauchamp, earl of Warwick.[9] Edward died in 1329 holding a messuage with an adjoining close and 19 acres, of which William Charles, the 16-year-old son of Edward's second son William, was heir.[10] In 1332 John of Waltham was in possession of messuages and lands in the vills of Westminster and Eye by the grant of William Charles, and granted them to Sir John de Stonor, Kt, chief justice of common pleas, to whom William Charles released them in 1334, presumably on coming of age.[11] A third of a messuage and 30*s.* was held by Joan wife of Roger of Solehull as dower and released to Stonor in 1346.[12]

At his death in 1354 Stonor was said to hold a messuage and 60 acres of Westminster Abbey for fealty and 10*s.*, which passed to his son and heir John.[13] John died in 1361, when his son and heir Edmund was 15 years old. Edmund received seizin of his land in 1365 and died in 1382 holding a rent of 20*s.* a year from four shops held by Ralph Steynour and his wife Alice and their son Maurice; the rest of the property was not listed.[14] His two surviving sons were both minors: the heir, John, died in 1383, succeeded by his brother Ralph. Custody of all the Stonor property in Westminster, except that held by Steynour and Sir John Salisbury, was granted by the king to Hanekin de Grys, yeoman of the king's chamber, in 1386. Ralph was 21 in 1390, when the property consisted of a tenement called the Mote, 46*s.* 8*d.* in rents, and a barn and 60 acres, all held of Westminster Abbey for service of 12*s.* 6*d.*[15] Ralph conveyed all his estates including his lands and rents in Westminster and Charing to feoffees in 1390,[16] but was killed in Ireland in 1394, leaving two infant sons, Gilbert (d. 1396) and Thomas. Ralph's property in Westminster, valued at 73*s.* 4*d.*, was granted by the king to Ralph's widow Joan as part of her dower.[17] Thomas Stonor received seizin of the estates in 1415, and in 1417 all or part of the Westminster land was farmed to Robert Charryngworth.[18] The property in Westminster was conveyed to Thomas and his heirs by his feoffees in 1422.[19] Thomas Stonor died in 1431: by his will he gave

1 TNA, CP 25/2/27/178/2HENVIII/Hil.; above, Bernes' Inn.
2 *Endowed Chars London,*VI. 696; TNA, C 142/29, no. 85; Watney, *Middx & Herts N&Q,* I. 88–91.
3 TNA, SC 12/3/13.
4 *Endowed Chars London,* VI. 696.
5 Inf. from Mercers' Co. via website (www.mercers.co.uk, 13 Jan. 2006).
6 WAM 4832; BL, Harl. MS 4015, f. 144v.; TNA, CP 40/88, rot. 29.   7 *Cal. Inq. p.m.* IV. 203.
8 TNA, CP 25/1/149/39. no. 1.
9 BL, Add. MS 28024, f. 48–v.

10 *Cal. Close,* 1327–30, 468.
11 Ibid. 1333–7, 339; TNA, CP 40/292, rot. carte 2.
12 TNA, CP 25/1/150/62, no. 238.
13 TNA, C 135/128, no. ll. Inf. on Stonor fam. from *Stonor Letters and Papers,* ed. C.L. Kingsford (Camden Soc., 3rd ser., XXIX, 1919), intro.; *Hist. Parl.* 1386–1421, III. 483–5.
14 TNA, C 136/21, no. 13.   15 TNA, C 136/64, no. 8.
16 *Cal. Close,* 1389–92, 291.
17 Ibid. 1392–6, 339; TNA, C 136/85, no. 5.
18 *Stonor Letters* (Camden 3rd ser., XXIX), 29.
19 *Cal. Close,* 1422–9, 42.

the guardianship of his son and heir Thomas, aged 7, to Thomas Chaucer, and gave his wife Alice dower in the manor of the Mote, valued at 10 marks.[1] Alice married Richard Drayton in 1432, and they gave a rent from the land in Westminster and elsewhere for ten years for the maintenance of one of Stonor's daughters, Isabel, in 1432. Drayton was paying the quitrents to Westminster Abbey in 1450.[2] Both died in 1468, when presumably the Mote passed to Thomas Stonor. He died in 1474, succeeded by his eldest son William.

In 1478 Sir William Stonor, KB, granted the Mote and its land to John Sant, abbot of Abingdon, and his abbey;[3] a fine as part of the conveyance described it as the manor of the Mote with 8 messuages, a garden, 100 acres of land, 20 acres of meadow in the vill of Westminster and the parishes of St Giles-in-the-Fields and St Martin-in-the-Fields.[4] In 1490 the property was temporarily in the hands of the king because of the abbot's rebellion, and was granted to Hugh Vaughan, gentleman usher.[5] In 1495 the abbot paid 11s. quitrent from the Mote, its adjoining tenements, and land in St James's field, to the warden of the chapel of St Mary in Westminster Abbey.[6] In 1538 the abbot of Abingdon formally completed an exchange with Henry VIII whereby he conveyed to Henry the manor of Kensington and all Abingdon's lands in Westminster and Strand,[7] the king having already bought out the abbey's lessee of the Mote (below).

The messuage, known as Charles in 1355, and Mote in 1390, was also referred to as Stonors.[8] It lay on the west side of the later King Street, and possibly stretched back as far as Longditch, as well as running to the north behind other property in King Street. It included a garden, and a ditch on at least one side. It is not clear whether and for how long the site had a mansion house, referred to in 1473, or whether the Stonors or the abbots of Abingdon ever resided there. The 4 shops that Ralph Steynour held by 1382 fronted King Street and were later acquired by Westminster Abbey; Sir John Salisbury may have been holding the main dwelling. The 60 acres lay in the northern part of Westminster and were included by the king in the bailiwick of St James after 1536. They were let to George Sutton, and continued to be let by the Crown during the 16th century.[9] There was also a garden in St Martin-in-the-Fields, on the west side of Covent Garden.

NEW INN

The property later known as New Inn is first recorded in

the 13th century when Hugh the clerk of St Clement's held three houses on the north side of Aldwych Street (later Drury Lane), where it turned north-westwards, with an acre in St Clement's field at the east end of the houses, for which he paid 2s. a year to St Giles's Hospital; the houses were granted to William the Dauber for a quit rent of 5s. 4d., which Hugh granted to St Paul's in perpetuity, confirmed by his son Guy.[10] Hugh probably also held the nearby messuage with 2 acres in St Clement's field, for which St Giles's received 7s. a year, and which was in the possession of Guy in 1253.[11] Guy's son and heir William de la Purye (Pirie) granted the messuage and 3 acres to Hamo de la Barre by 1300, and it was settled on Hamo, his wife Christian and the latter's heirs.[12] In 1313 the premises were in the possession of Walter de Enemere and his wife Christine, and settled on them and Christine's heirs,[13] and in 1334 the property and all the goods in it were settled on Walter de Enemere, possibly a different man, his wife Desiderata, and his heirs.[14] Walter had died by 1347 when Desiderata and her husband Walter de Bickele, skinner, granted the messuage and 3 acres to William Credil, clerk,[15] to whom Enemere's heirs granted their right for 20 marks.[16] William Credil sold the property to Simon de Orgemount, butler to Sir Bartholomew de Burghash, who in 1351 sold it to Henry de Boresworth or Boseworth, citizen and vintner of London. Henry was dead by September 1375, leaving a wife Alice,[17] who in 1389 with her husband William Badby quitclaimed her dower in the messuage and 3 acres to Henry's son and heir Henry de Boseworth, citizen and mercer.[18]

By 1391 Henry had sold the 3 acres to John Bosham, whose inn lay to the north-west of Boseworth's property.[19] In 1403 the master of the hospital of St Giles brought a claim against Boseworth and John Roland, clerk, possibly his tenant, for the 9s. service owing from the property, which was 12 years in arrears. The arrears were assessed at £4 17s. 6d. and Boseworth agreed to allow the master to distrain, but the latter could not recover the service for the land because Boseworth was no longer the holder.[20] In 1415 Boseworth granted his remaining property there, described as a messuage with houses, mansions, gardens, tofts, fences and ditches, to Thomas Joly, citizen and armourer, Thomas Dorkynghole known as Armourer, and Thomas Robellard, citizen and armourer; Robellard released to the other two in 1421.[21] In 1422 Joly and Dorkynghole granted the premises to five feoffees,[22] who later that year conveyed it

1 *Stonor Letters* (Camden 3rd ser., XXIX), 47–9.
2 Ibid., 50–1; WAM 23226.   3 *Cal. Close*, 1476–85, 218.
4 TNA, CP 25/1/152/98, no. 67.
5 *Cal. Pat.* 1485–94, 316.   6 WAM 17127.
7 TNA, CP 25/2/52/372/29HEN8/Hil.   8 WAM 17657–8.
9 Later hist. to be treated under Crown's Estates in a later vol.
10 Guildhall MSS 25121/887–888. 3 hos became part of adjoining Bosham's Inn by 1370: above, Bernes' Inn.
11 TNA, CP 25/1/147/18, no. 327.
12 Ibid. 25/1/148/36, no. 293; Newcastle MSS, Ne D 4683.

13 TNA, CP 25/1/149/43, no. 111.
14 Newcastle MSS, Ne D 4696, 4697.
15 Ibid., Ne D 4701.
16 TNA, CP 25/1/150/62, no. 231.
17 *Cal. Husting Wills*, pt 2, 172–3.
18 TNA, CP 25/1/289/55, no. 184.
19 *Cal. Close*, 1392–96, 109.
20 BL, Harl. MS 4015, f. 133v.
21 Newcastle MSS, Ne D 4705; 4725; 4727.
22 Ibid., Ne D 4728–4731.

to John Gedney, citizen and clothworker of London, and his feoffees.[1] In 1443 Gedney granted all his lands in Middlesex including the property in St Clement Danes to Joan Large widow, whom he married, Thomas Staunton, and other feoffees; they granted it back to Gedney for life in 1444,[2] and in 1446 he also acquired a small toft or garden 82 feet by 126 feet formerly belonging to Maud Hervey, which was incorporated into the east side of his property.[3]

After Gedney's death in 1449 the remaining feoffee quitclaimed to Staunton and Joan Large, and at her death in 1462 Joan left the land and tenements now called the New Inn to her son Richard Turnaunt.[4] By 1465 the inn was occupied by a principal and fellows, presumably a society of common lawyers, who paid a rent of £6 a year to Turnaunt, less an allowance for repairs.[5] In 1474 Turnaunt and his feoffees conveyed the New Inn with its buildings and gardens and the toft to Turnaunt's only child Thomasine, wife of John Ryseley (knighted 1485), to hold for life.[6] In his will of 1486 Turnaunt confirmed the grant to his daughter, with remainder to her issue.[7] By 1498 the New Inn estate also included all the smaller properties on the west side between the inn and Bosham's Inn,[8] which had comprised a tenement and garden, a tenement, solar and stable, and 5 shops with a garden in the 1390s.[9]

In 1505 the property was resettled by Thomasine and her husband on the latter and his heirs,[10] shortly before Thomasine died without issue. Sir John Ryseley died in 1512, instructing his executors to sell the New Inn,[11] and they with the executors of Turnaunt and his widow sold it in fee in 1517 to Sir John Fyneux, chief justice of king's bench, for £40; Fyneux conveyed it to feoffees for the use of his will.[12] It passed to his son and heir William who in 1548 sold it for 100 marks to Edmund Smyth of London and his wife Alice, described as his Great House and messuage called the New Inn and all its buildings, valued at £4 a year net, lying between the Angel and the garden of Clement's Inn on the east, the house of Sir William Drury on the west, the highway on the south and the field called St Clement's Close on the north.[13] The fine described it as a messuage, 3 gardens, an orchard, and 2 acres of land.[14] From 1548 he granted successive tenants of Clement's Inn field access across his land from the highway to the field via a gate on the west side of the inn,

though from 1575 the agreement was subject to cancellation at a week's notice if Smyth wished to build by the gate.[15] From 1547 Smyth also held a lease from Magdalen College, Oxford, of 3 tenements in St Clement Danes where he later dwelt,[16] and in 1554 he also bought a messuage and garden in St Clement's from John Fitz, his wife Anne, and John Gardener.[17]

Smyth made a settlement in 1560 on himself for life with successive remainders in tail to his second son John and then to other children with a trustee to hold for the life of Edmund's (second) wife Agnes,[18] but in 1578 Edmund granted the New Inn to his daughters Lucy and Margaret and to their heirs, and in his will also granted them his leasehold dwelling in the parish; he died by November 1579.[19] However, a settlement made by Edmund's son John in 1584 on his marriage included all the lands in St Clement Danes conveyed to John in the 1560 settlement, described as 5 messuages, 14 gardens, and half an acre of land.[20] Eventually John brought a claim in Chancery against his sisters in 1595 for the property: they claimed that the enfeoffment of 1560 had never been fully executed, and that Edmund had left the property to them when John had left his post as officer of common pleas and gone abroad against his father's wishes.[21] The decision is unknown, but John seems to have been confirmed in the reversion of the property after his sisters, as in 1609 he sold his reversion of the New Inn itself to the Benchers of the Middle Temple for £133 6s. 8d., while his sisters sold them their life interest for £90.[22] In 1612 Sir John Holles, owner of Clement's Inn field, paid £250 each to Margaret Smyth, spinster, and John Smyth for the freehold of the rest of the estate, lying between New Inn and Drury House and consisting of a messuage and piece of ground, 2 messuages with gardens, a messuage with 2 gardens, and 7 individual gardens, held by ten tenants.[23] Thereafter it remained part of Holles's estate.[24]

ROSAMOND

In 1308 the king granted Sir John Benstede, keeper of the wardrobe and a justice of common bench,[25] licence to crenellate his dwelling in Eye called 'Rosemont', and freedom from livery by the king's stewards.[26] The messuage apparently lay in the manor of Westminster near Tothill and Eybridge, and its origin is uncertain; it

1 Ibid., Ne D 4732.
2 Ibid., Ne D 4737; *Cal. Close*, 1447–54, 89–90.
3 Newcastle MSS, Ne D 4735.
4 Guildhall MS 9171/5, f. 327v.; Newcastle MSS, Ne D 4737.
5 TNA, C 1/45/35.
6 Newcastle MSS, Ne D 4738.
7 TNA, PROB 11/7, f. 193.
8 Newcastle MSS, Ne D 4740.
9 Ibid., deeds in bdl. D21.
10 TNA, CP 25/1/152/101/Mich 21 Hen 7.
11 Williams, *Early Holborn*, no. 1490.
12 Newcastle MSS, Ne D 4742–4744.
13 Ibid., Ne D 4745–4747.
14 TNA, CP 25/2/61/473/1Edw6/Hil.

15 Newcastle MSS, Ne D 4647.
16 Magdalen Coll., Index Leases, EL/3, p. 176; EL/5, f. 64; EL/6, ff. 247, 321v.
17 TNA, CP 25/2/74/629/1Mary/Trin.
18 Newcastle MSS, Ne D 4748.
19 Ibid., Ne D 4750; TNA, PROB 11/61, f. 327.
20 Newcastle MSS, Ne D 4751–2.
21 TNA, C 2/Eliz/F1/33.
22 Williams, *Early Holborn*, no. 1473. Later hist. treated under Law Cts and Legal Inns.
23 Newcastle MSS, Ne D 4756–8, 4753–4.
24 Above, Clement's Inn.
25 *Oxford DNB*.
26 *Cal. Pat.* 1307–13, 58, 61.

may have been the messuage, 40 acres of land and 4 acres of meadow in Westminster and Eye in which Hugh de Arderne and his wife Alice held a third as Alice's dower, relinquishing it to Benstede in 1309.[1] Benstede also acquired from John of the Hyde a messuage, 45 acres of land and 2½ acres of meadow in Eye in 1312, and from Henry le Keu 2 acres adjoining Benstede's land by Tothill in 1316.[2] He was also leased houses and gardens in Eye by Luke of London, rector of St Benet Fink, prior to 1317.[3]

Benstede died in 1323, holding a messuage called Rosamond, 12 acres of land, an acre of meadow, and 4 acres of pasture in Westminster, held of the abbot for 10s. a year and suit at Westminster; 2 acres in Westminster held of Walter Fraunceys without service; and 43 acres of land and an acre of meadow in Eye, held of the manor of Ebury for 4s. and suit at Ebury. He was survived by his second wife Petronilla (d. 1342) and his son Edmund, a minor.[4] Benstede's property in Westminster and Eye was granted in 1324 to Master Robert de Ayleston during the heir's minority,[5] and Edmund sought possession of his lands in 1333.[6]

By 1355 the manor of Rosamond and its lands in Westminster and Eye were in the possession of John of Chichester, citizen and goldsmith of London, who conveyed them to Thomas of Baldeswell, also a goldsmith.[7] In 1358 Thomas's messuage and garden were valued for debt at 3s. 4d., 72½ acres of arable in Westminster and Eye at 48s. 4d., 7½ acres of meadow at 37s. 6d.; he had a cow and corn on the property.[8] In 1361 he

conveyed the manor to another goldsmith, Richard Weston, who sold it to Westminster Abbey via nominees.[9]

Materials from a demolished house at the manor of Rosamond were used by the almoner for building shops in Tothill Street in 1362–3.[10] The arable seems to have lost its identity as part of Rosamond, but the site of the buildings and adjacent land was still referred to as Rosamond into the 16th century, and lay in the south-west corner of the later St James's Park: in the 1330s a ditch leading to Rosamond manor lay westward from the lane from Tothill to St James's Hospital, and a lane to Rosamond lay at the west end of Tothill. Rosamond was assigned to the cellarer and gardener by 1407, and that office paid the service to the abbot and to the manor of Ebury, amounting to £10 10s. in 1535.[11] The herbage of Rosamond was used by the abbey in 1407,[12] and in 1417 Rosamond consisted of a croft let for 8s., its garden let for 5s., 5 acres meadow nearby let for 26s. 8d., and another croft let for 6s. 8d.[13] Buildings apparently still existed there at the end of the 15th century, since 19 loads of stone were carried from 'Rosamond's bower' in 1500 for work on the abbey church.[14] In 1520 a close or pasture called 'Rosemonds-bore' lay between the extension of Tothill Street on the south and the ditch leading towards land of St James's Hospital on the north in 1520.[15]

The land called Rosamonds was granted by the abbey to Henry VIII in 1531, and incorporated into the newly-created St James's Park.[16]

LATER CREATIONS

GROSVENOR ESTATE

What was to become the Grosvenor estate after the marriage of its child-heiress to Sir Thomas Grosvenor, Bt, in 1677, had its origins in 1623, when James I sold the freehold of the site and lands of the manor of Ebury to John Trayleman and Thomas Pearson for £1,151 15s. Although this estate continued to be referred to as the 'manor' of Ebury, neither the courts nor views of frankpledge were included, nor were there any copyholds or rents of assize belonging to it any longer. Ebury had thus become a freehold estate rather than a manor.

Some land in the former manor was not included in the sale, being disposed of by the Crown elsewhere,[17] and though wastes were specified in the grant, a claim in 1682 by the owner of the estate to waste along the highway was not successful.[18]

The grant covered all the property which had been leased to Richard Whashe, including two closes in Longmore in the vill of Westminster and the wastes and watercourses. Also included in the sale were several other freeholds in the vills of Eye and Westminster

1 TNA, CP 25/1/149/40, no.38.
2 Ibid., 149/42, no. 87; CP 40/215, rot. 1 (carte).
3 TNA, CP 40/220, rot. 1 (carte).
4 *Cal. Inq. p.m.* VI. 285–7; *Cal. Close,* 1323–7, 229.
5 *Cal. Fine R.* 1319–27, 279.
6 TNA, C 135/37, no. 5.
7 WAM 17660.
8 TNA, C 145/177, no. 21.
9 WAM 17664–5; 17667; 17678; Harvey, *Westm. Abbey Ests,* 422.

10 Rosser, *Medieval Westm.* 72.
11 *Valor Eccl.* I. 421.
12 WAM 18888.
13 WAM 18889.
14 WAM 23577.
15 WAM 18000.
16 TNA, E 211/72.
17 *Survey of London,* XXXIV. 416; above, Manorial, Manor of Eye.
18 *Cal. Treas. Bks,* 1680–85, I. 583, 644–5.

30. *Belgrave Square from the south-west in 1982, showing the grandest square of the Grosvenor family's Belgravia estate, developed from c.1812 and distingushed by large stuccoed houses.*

purchased by Henry VIII from Westminster Abbey and others in 1536.[1] Those lands, all bought from Westminster Abbey unless noted otherwise, consisted of the following in the vill of Westminster (which included Knightsbridge): 4 acres of meadow in Longmore; 14 of arable in St Margaret's; 4 of arable and 1 of meadow in 'humber' in the vill of Westminster bought from William Jennings; 1 of arable in St Martin's, identified *c.*1663 as Sawpit acre opposite St James's; 20 acres in Millbank (Market meadows), with the horseferry and the road there; 3 near the Mews at Charing Cross and 1 of Beaumont's lands adjoining it. Lands said to be in St Martin's but with the vill not specified were: a half acre bought from Nicholas Fisher, 20 acres from Sir William Essex, and an acre from John Lawrence. Lands obviously in Ebury were: 3½ acres of arable in St Martin's lying in the Brache and Ayefeld bought from Sir Hugh Vaughan; 6 in St Martin's in Eyburyfeld and the Brache bought from John Norris; 2 at Eycross; 2 of meadow and one moor in Thames meadow; 6 acres of meadow in Chelsea mead and Thames mead. Another 37 acres, mainly arable, lay in various unspecified locations. Such vagueness, and the fact that the location of most open-field arable was only roughly known, led to disputes in the 17th century.

The sales were in feefarm, fixed at a perpetual annual rent of £38 7s. 10d. – £21 5s. 8d. for Ebury and £17 2s. 2d. for the other lands. Offered for sale during the Commonwealth,[2] the rent returned to the Crown in 1660 and in 1663 was granted by Charles II to the earl of Sandwich.[3] It was still being paid by the estate to the earl's descendants in the 1920s.

Trayleman and Pearson immediately conveyed all the

premises to trustees for Sir Lionel Cranfield, earl of Middlesex and master of the Court of Wards, for £1,501 15s. In 1623 Cranfield's trustees conveyed Sawpit acre in Westminster, east of the later St James's Street, to Thomas Howard, Viscount Andover, created earl of Berkshire in 1626, for 3,000 years at 2s. 8d. a year, and it formed part of the site of Berkshire House.[4] Cranfield sold the freehold of the rest to Hugh Audley in 1626 for £9,400, together with Lynde's moiety of the Crown lease of the manor of Ebury (above). One or two small parcels in Westminster were sold by Audley, but the bulk of the land passed under a settlement he made shortly before his death in 1662 to his great-nephew Alexander Davies, with the 20 acres at Millbank going to Alexander's brother Thomas. Shortly afterwards Thomas sold his holding to his brother for £2,000.[5]

Alexander Davies settled his estates on his issue with a life interest for his widow Mary; in default of issue surviving to 21 years, the estates would be divided between his brothers.[6] He died of the plague in 1665, leaving a 7-month-old daughter Mary, and early in 1666 his widow married John Tregonwell,[7] who then held the Ebury estate in his wife's right. Under an Act of 1675,[8] several fields in the Mayfair portion, known as the Hundred Acres, were held in dower by Mrs Tregonwell, forming *c.*56 acres in the western part. In 1677 Mary Davies was married to Thomas Grosvenor, who paid £1,000 for the reversionary rights which Tregonwell had acquired should Mary die under-age. The total annual value of the estate in 1677 was £2,170, but a third of this was paid to Mrs Tregonwell in dower, and after annuities the clear income from the remainder was £824.[9] Under a settlement made in 1694, Mary Grosvenor

1 *Ebury plan c.*1663.

2 TNA, E 308/3/21, m. 49.

3 TNA, C 66/3032, no. 8, m. 6.

4 Gatty, *Mary Davies,* I. 43.

5 *Survey of London,* XXXIX. 2–3.

6 *Cal. SP Dom.* 1670 (& Add. 1660–70), 720–1.

7 Gatty, *Mary Davies,* I. 169–70.

8 Below, Sales.

9 *Survey of London,* XXXIX. 3–4.

received a life interest in the whole estate except for the third held by her mother. Although she did not die until 1730, Mary was adjudged insane in 1705 and the revenues were controlled by the court of Chancery. By an Act of 1711 the estate was settled on Sir Thomas's son and heir Richard in tail male, and Richard was allowed to grant building leases for up to 60 years of land in London in which his mother held a life interest, except for the third held by Mary Tregonwell as dower. The dower land passed to the Grosvenors on Mary Tregonwell's death in 1717. Building development, on the Hundred Acres in Mayfair, began in 1720.[1]

The estate remained in the Grosvenor family, generally subject to family settlements, and passed with the baronetcy and the subsequent peerage titles: the 7th baronet, Sir Richard Grosvenor, was created Baron Grosvenor in 1761, and Viscount Belgrave and Earl Grosvenor in 1784; Robert, 2nd Earl Grosvenor, was created marquess of Westminster in 1831; and Hugh Lupus, 3rd marquess, was created duke of Westminster in 1874. After the death of the 2nd duke in 1953, control and management of the estates passed to the Grosvenor trustees,[2] and by the late 20th century the Westminster estate belonged to the Grosvenor Group Limited, an international property company of which the duke of Westminster was the major shareholder.[3]

SALES OF LAND

Several pieces of the estate were disposed of after Davies's death, mainly to pay his debts. In 1666 Tregonwell sought an Act to allow him to sell Goring House, which Davies had already agreed to sell to Henry Bennet, Lord Arlington, just before his death, claiming that Alexander had intended by its sale to build his mansion at Horseferry, but had died, much in debt, before he could do so. Davies's brothers, Thomas and William, petitioned the House of Commons against Tregonwell's bill, claiming that Alexander had settled Goring House with his other lands on his only child, Mary, with remainders to the petitioners, and that the house was mortgaged and charged with annuities. They wanted to ensure that the money from the sale was secured to the heirs, and obtain some control over Tregonwell's actions regarding the estate.[4] The bill received a second reading and was sent to committee,[5] but perhaps because of opposition by Davies's brothers, nothing further came of it. Another bill vesting certain lands in trustees for sale for payment of debts, which had the agreement of Davies's relations and trustees as well as the Tregonwells,[6] was introduced in 1675 and received royal assent the same year.[7] Under the Act, Goring House with *c.*20 acres adjoining it, 7 in

Mayfair north of the line of Brick Street, 22 in Knightsbridge (repurchased by the Grosvenors in 1763), and 5, which later formed the north-west corner of Green Park, were sold.[8] The last of those parcels was probably the confirmation of the Crown's purchase from the estate *c.*1669 of a close of 4½ acres near Piccadilly to enlarge St James's Park.[9] Later sales included 35 acres sold by Sir Thomas Grosvenor in 1681 for £3,400 to the earl of Arlington, apparently at the king's request, and 2½ acres by the Westbourne river sold to the Royal Hospital, Chelsea.[10]

Major sales took place in the 1920s and 1930s, largely to provide for the death-duties likely to fall upon the estate when the 2nd duke died. To avoid depressing the market by mass land sales upon the event, the duke's advisers recommended preliminary piecemeal selling of a few particularly valuable sites, and investing the proceeds. On the Millbank estate the duke had leased land at peppercorn rent to Westminster City Council for working-class housing in 1928, and between 1929 and 1934 he sold the rest of the Millbank estate to a property company for over £900,000.[11] However, he was very reluctant to sell any part of Mayfair or Belgravia, and not until 1930 did he agree to do so. In 1930–2 the freeholds of the Connaught Hotel, Mayfair House (both in Carlos Place), Claridge's (Brook Street), Fountain House (Park Lane), nos 139–140 Park Lane, no. 32 Green Street, and nos 415, 417, 419 Oxford Street were sold. Other sales occurred in Pimlico (notably the Victoria Coach Station site), and after the 2nd duke's death in 1953 all the Pimlico properties south of Buckingham Palace Road were sold to pay death duties which reportedly amounted to £17 million.[12]

Despite the few sales in Mayfair in the 1930s, the 2nd duke kept the Mayfair and Belgravia parts of the estate intact as far as possible, and repurchased some sites when they became available: St George's Vestry Hall, Mount Street, in 1930; St Anselm's Church, Davies Street, in 1939; and the Connaught Hotel, Carlos Place, and no. 32 Green Street, both repurchased after 1945. After death duties had been paid off in the 1960s, the estate maintained an active management policy for the remainder of the London estate in Mayfair and Belgravia, and was also successful in retaining power of management when faced with the leaseholders' right to buy their freeholds under the Leashold Reform Act, 1967.[13]

PETERBOROUGH (GROSVENOR) HOUSE, MILLBANK

Alexander Davies began speculative building on his estate at Millbank, south of the horseferry, laying out a

1 *Survey of London*, XXXIX. 4–6.
2 Ibid., 79–80.
3 *Grosvenor: Annual Report & Accounts, 2003.*
4 *Cal. SP Dom.* 1670 (& Add. 1660–70), 720–1.
5 *CJ,* VIII. 661, 646, 648.
6 HMC, *9th Rep.* App. II, 64a.
7 27 Car. II, no. 2 (Private).
8 *Survey of London*, XXXIX. 3; Gatty, *Mary Davies,* I. 178–80.
9 *Cal. Treas. Bks,* 1669–72, 197.
10 *Survey of London*, XXXIX. 4; below, Buckingham Ho.
11 *Survey of London*, XXXIX. 76 and n.
12 Ibid., 78–9.
13 Ibid., 80–2.

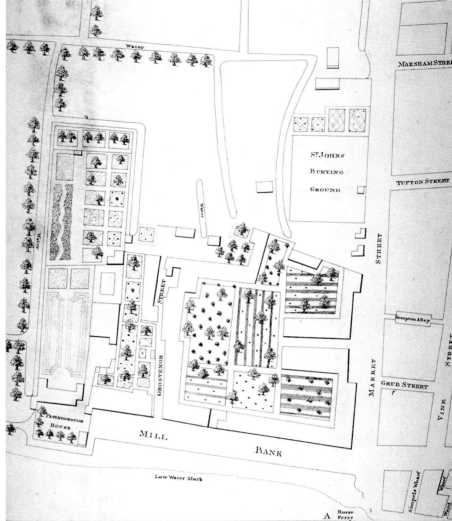

31. *Plan of Peter-borough House and gardens, Millbank, drawn in 1807. Also known as Grosvenor House, it was built in the mid 17th century but reconstructed 1731 by Sir Richard Grosvenor, and was a residence of the Grosvenor family until 1808.*

street along the river bank and letting land for building houses. At the south end of the new street he built a large mansion for himself, which was still unfinished at his death in 1665. It was referred to *c.*1670 as Horse Ferry House, but by 1682 was usually known as Peterborough House and then, in the 18th century, as Grosvenor House.[1] It was presumably the house on Millbank for which Lord Peterborough was rated at £10 in 1673, while Mr Tregonwell was rated at £6 for a house in same row; Henry Mordaunt, 2nd earl of Peterborough, was the occupant in the Tregonwells' bill of 1675. In 1683–4 Lord Peterborough was still rated for the big house, Sir Thomas Grosvenor for another house some nine houses away, and Mrs Tregonwell next door but two to Sir Thomas.[2]

Peterborough House became the London home of the Grosvenor family, who first occupied it in 1719. In 1731 Sir Richard Grosvenor, 4th Bt, completely reconstructed

the house at a cost of £2,000. On his succession in 1755 Sir Richard Grosvenor, 7th Bt, bought the lease of no. 45 Grosvenor Square, which he occupied until his death, as Earl Grosvenor, in 1802, and the Millbank house was let. In 1789 Lord Grosvenor bought back the lease of the Millbank house as a home for his son and heir Lord Belgrave, who remained there after his father's death rather than moving to no. 45 Grosvenor Square.[3] The Grosvenors moved back to Mayfair in 1808, and the Mill-bank house was demolished in 1809.[4] Just before it was demolished it was represented as a two-storeyed brick house with basement and dormers, a south façade with giant angle pilasters, a decorated frieze and sculpture in alcoves with paterae over them, and an irregular west side. The façade decoration may have been the work of William Thomas who altered the house in 1789.[5] The irregularity, together with evidence of the plan published in 1807, suggests that the building incorporated earlier

1 *Cal. SP Dom.* 1670 (& Add. 1660–70), 720–1; *Survey of London*, XXXIX. 3.

2 Gatty, *Mary Davies*, I. 183–4; Morgan, *Map of London* (1682).

3 *Survey of London*, XL. 158–9, 240; Gatty, *Mary Davies*, I. 183.

4 *Survey of London*, XXXIX. 43.

5 Colvin, *British Architects*, 1035.

fabric. In 1807 the house stood in formal gardens which still had a character of *c*.1700. It seems that, although the house was twice altered, at least elements of Lord Peterborough's property was still identifiable.[1]

GROSVENOR HOUSE, MAYFAIR

A proposal from the late 1790s to build a large penitentiary on open ground south of the Millbank house was probably the reason for the Belgraves' decision to look for a house in Mayfair *c*.1800. They registered their interest in Gloucester House, Upper Grosvenor Street, although the lease would not expire until 1830, so that the Grosvenor Board would have to consider it as a presumed future Grosvenor family residence when considering lease renewals nearby. This large detached house with 13 main rooms in 1761, had been built 1731–2 on the south side of Upper Grosvenor Street, and also had an extensive frontage to Park Lane, with views south and west over Hyde Park; the gardens sloped southwards from a terrace at the rear. The lease had been acquired in 1738 by the 3rd duke of Beaufort, who also leased land to the south to preserve the views, and was used as that family's London home until 1761, when they sold the house and most of its contents to Prince William Augustus, duke of Cumberland. After Cumberland's death in 1765 his executors assigned the lease to his nephew, Prince William Henry, duke of Gloucester, brother of George III, and the house was then generally known as Gloucester House. When the duke of Gloucester died in 1805 negotiations began to obtain the house for Lord Grosvenor; the purchase was agreed at a compromise price of £20,000, and the lease was assigned in 1807;[2] Lord Grosvenor, after spending large sums on extensive alterations, including external stucco, bow windows and redecoration, moved there in 1808. Renamed Grosvenor House and altered many times, sometimes lavishly, it remained the family's principal London residence until 1916. It was demolished in 1927,[3] and replaced by the speculator, A.O. Edwards, with a large block, still called Grosvenor House but containing a hotel and service flats and entered from Park Lane.[4]

BEDFORD ESTATE

The estate in Westminster belonging to the earls, later dukes, of Bedford was created in the 16th century from three landholdings: Covent Garden, Tocksgarden, and Longacre.[5] Together they formed the Covent Garden estate granted in 1552 to John Russell, earl of Bedford, which also included the Friars Pyes garden fronting the Strand. The bounds of this estate were then given as St Martin's Lane on the west, Fortescue Lane (Drury Lane) on the east, the Strand ('Strondway') on the south and Elmfield on the north, but the southern boundary was only approximate, since the estate only touched the Strand at the Friars Pyes garden. In the late 16th century Covent Garden, excluding Longacre, was estimated to consist of about 40 acres, the boundaries being Drury Lane, Floral Street, St Martin's Lane, and a line drawn south of Chandos Place, Maiden Lane, and Exeter Street.[6]

The estate remained in the ownership of the Russell family for nearly 400 years, with only small alienations.[7] The 1st earl lived at Russell Place, formerly the inn of the bishops of Carlisle, on the south side of the Strand, where he died in 1555, and the acquisition of both Friars Pyes and Covent Garden were probably principally to supplement the garden and grazing facilities for his household; by 1564 stables had been built on Friars Pyes fronting the Strand, which lay almost opposite Russell Place.[8] The 1st earl was succeeded by his son Francis, who also lived and died at Russell Place, and who let out all the estate not occupied by his stables.[9] Some small sales were made between 1560 and 1565 and in 1570 to his eastern neighbour Sir William Cecil, Lord Burghley, who was enlarging Burghley House on the north side of Strand.[10] The earl also granted Cecil liberty to open a door into Covent Garden for himself and his family to walk there; certain other local inhabitants had similar privileges.[11] In 1585 the estates were settled on the 2nd earl's eldest son Francis and his male heirs, with remainder to the 2nd earl's brother. The 2nd earl died in 1585, succeeded by his grandson Edward, a minor, whose wardship was granted in 1586 to Ambrose Dudley, earl of Warwick, and his wife Anne, Edward's aunt. Since Russell Place had to pass on the 2nd earl's death to his eldest grandchildren, Elizabeth and Anne Russell,[12] a new house was built for the 3rd earl in the

---

1 Guildhall Libr., Print Colln., cat. nos p5405517 (watercolour by Geo. Shepherd 1809), p 540443X (plan pub. 1810 by Geo. Smith). Other more idealized views in Wakefield Collection, Guildhall Libr., are difficult to reconcile with Shepherd's and Smith's.

2 *Survey of London*, XL. 239–40.

3 Ibid., XXXIX. 43; XL. 239–50.

4 Pevsner, *London 6: Westm.* 553.

5 For earlier hist., above, Other Eccles. Ests (Covent Garden; Pied Friars).

6 *Survey of London*, XXXVI. 19; TNA, C 142/435, no. 118.

7 Unless otherwise stated, acct below based on very full hist. of est. in *Survey of London*, XXXVI. 21–7.

8 TNA, PROB 11/48, f. 403v.; above, Episcopal Inns (Carlisle).

9 *Survey of London*, XXXVI. 23.

10 Burghley Ho. cal., NRA 6666, 5/21, 5/31–3, 5/37, 93/2; below, Burghley Ho.

11 *Survey of London*, XXXVI. 23.

12 TNA, C 142/211, no. 183.

32. *The piazza laid out on the Earl of Bedford's Covent Garden estate in the 1630s to designs by Inigo Jones, and enclosed by houses with arcaded ground floors, with St Paul's church on the west side. The view of c.1750 looks south towards Southampton Street, laid out across the site of Bedford House, and Covent Garden market is well established in the middle.*

1580s on the site of the stables and the western side of Friars Pyes fronting the Strand, with new stables behind.

The 3rd earl came of age in 1593, and although he greatly increased the income from the estate, it had been encumbered by his long minority, to which was added a fine of £10,000 for complicity in the earl of Essex's rebellion. In addition, therefore, to developing parts of the estate, the 3rd earl also began selling property fronting the major roads. From the late 1590s leases were granted of plots fronting St Martin's Lane and Drury Lane, and many of these were later granted away in feefarm, so that the earls had little control over subsequent development there. Two plots in Longacre were sold to Robert Cecil, earl of Salisbury, and in 1615 the earl, in collaboration with the lessee of Mercers' Company's land on his northern boundary, laid out the street called Long Acre; grants continued to be made there in feefarm during the 17th century. The open ground in the middle of Covent Garden remained and was let, with the earl retaining the right to pasture eight cows there. Between 1610 and 1613 the central close was reduced slightly and enclosed with a brick wall, which marked the extent of the Covent Garden estate built in the 1630s. By 1618 only this central 'great pasture' was still grazing land, enclosed by the brick wall. The rest of the estate outside the wall was either built over or occupied as gardens, with the south block occupied by Bedford House, and houses on Friars Pyes

and on the south side of the later Maiden Lane and Chandos Street.[1]

The earl had no son, and the heir apparent, his uncle Sir William Russell, Baron Russell of Thornhaugh, intervened, compelling him to enter into bonds not to sell. After Lord Russell's death, the earl formally vested lands including Covent Garden in trustees in 1617 for the next heir apparent, the earl's cousin Francis, Lord Russell, but in 1619 the earl conveyed Bedford House, Friars Pyes, Covent Garden and Longacre with other property to Lord Russell for immediate possession, in exchange for an annuity of £1,695; Lord Russell let Bedford House back to the earl for life. The 3rd earl died in 1627, and his cousin Francis succeeded to the earldom.

In 1629 Charles I granted to the 4th earl a warrant for a licence to build both a new church and the area of Covent Garden with uniform and decent houses, in accordance with the Commission for Buildings proclamation of 1625 and with a plan drawn up by the King's Surveyor, Inigo Jones.[2] In 1631 the earl paid £2,000 for the licence to build houses for gentlemen and those who could afford them, one family per house, in Covent Garden and Long Acre. It included permission to demolish or repair existing buildings, and divert ways and passages, but little was done to areas already built, the main effort being in the central open area of *c.*20 acres, where streets and a piazza enclosed by an outer rectangle of streets was laid out in 1631–7.[3] The houses

1 *Survey of London*, XXXVI. 23–4, 33, 266–9.
2 D. Duggan, ' "London the Ring, Covent Garden the Jewel of that Ring": New Light on Covent Garden', *Archit. Hist.* 43

(2000), 141. For St Paul's Ch, below, Religious Hist.: Par. Chs.
3 *Survey of London*, XXXVI. 26–7.

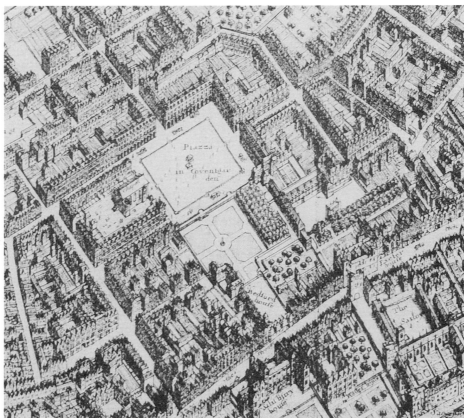

33. *Bedford House and the piazza in a detail from Hollar's view of c.1660. The main entrance to Bedford House was through a gatehouse on the Strand, but the mansion's main part lay behind, facing east to a long courtyard; its gardens extended north to a terrace overlooking the piazza, with other buildings and an orchard to the east.*

in the surrounding area were less uniform and more conventional in their lay-out, with gables to the street, than in Jones's piazza, where continuous terraces of houses linked by ground floor-arcades were inspired by continental models.

Between 1641 and 1668 the 5th earl sold at feefarm many of the remaining properties in Long Acre, Drury Lane, and Chandos Street, but the earls retained control over the central portion, which, with the addition of Bedford House in the Strand, became the parish of St Paul, Covent Garden, in 1646.[1] The 5th earl also obtained the right to hold a market in 1670, which greatly altered the character of the estate, despite efforts to exclude unpleasant trades. In time the market became the most lucrative part of the estate, and many surrounding buildings were gradually taken over by it.[2]

The estate passed with the earldom and later dukedom of Bedford until 1918. In 1913 the 11th duke made a provisional agreement to sell, which passed to Sir Joseph Beecham, the wealthy pill manufacturer and philanthropist. The sale was delayed by Beecham's death, but was completed in 1918 for £2 million to the Covent Garden Estate Company, whose directors were Sir Joseph's sons, Sir Thomas and Henry Beecham. All the property except for a house recently bought by the duke, and St Paul's Institute omitted by mistake, were

sold to the company, consisting of 231 properties, 5 victuallers' licences, 3 feefarm rents, and various market rights. Sir Thomas Beecham withdrew from his musical career for three years to devote himself to sorting out the estate, selling over £1 million-worth of property, including Bow Street Magistrates' Court and police station, and Drury Lane Theatre, and increasing the revenue of the remainder including the market. The purchase money to the duke was paid off in 1922 and a public company, Beecham Estates and Pills Ltd, was floated in 1924 to exploit the remainder of the estate combined with the pill-making business. In 1928 the latter business was sold and the company was renamed Covent Garden Properties Company. The market and nearby property were sold to the newly-established Covent Garden Market Authority in 1962.[3]

BEDFORD HOUSE

Bedford House, built as a residence for the 3rd earl, was the administrative centre of the Bedford estates from c.1586 to 1700. The earl was living there with his guardians in 1590, and it remained the London residence of the earls until the death of the 5th earl (1st duke) in 1700. His grandson and successor Wriothesley preferred to live in his mother's house in Bloomsbury: Bedford House and its outbuildings which had grown accretively

1 *Acts and Ordinances of the Interregnum, 1642–60,* I. 814–17.
2 *Survey of London,* XXXVI. 35–6; *Cal. SP Dom.* 1670 (&

Add. 1660–70), 101.
3 *Survey of London,* XXXVI. 50–2.

around courtyards and a garden were demolished 1705–6, and the site laid out for building as Southampton Street.

The 16th-century house was timber-framed. It had at least 45 rooms and closets in 1643 and included a gabled range with great gates, an agent's office, and a top-floor gallery along the Strand front. Behind lay a long yard and north of that a garden. The yard formed the forecourt to a long west range, perhaps containing the great hall, and north of that a large two-storeyed building, where the family had its lodgings. The latter had been altered or replaced by 1673, when the property had 60 hearths.

OTHER ESTATES

BERKELEY ESTATE AND DEVONSHIRE HOUSE

In 1664 Edward Hyde, earl of Clarendon, and his son Henry, Viscount Cornbury, sold part of their freehold Crown grant to John Berkeley, 1st Lord Berkeley of Stratton, consisting of some 5 acres of Stonebridge Close and 3 acres of Penniless Bench adjoining it, both fronting south on to Piccadilly.[3] Lord Berkeley had a mansion built at the south end of his eight-acre site, fronting Piccadilly with gardens stretching behind, possibly finished early in 1665. Designed by Hugh May, Berkeley House was architecturally important and conspicuous, almost the first house seen on the western approach to the West End and London. The earliest depiction of it is on Ogilby & Morgan's map of 1681–2, and this and a description by John Evelyn (who laid out the garden) indicate that it was a compact house in May's usual fashion, built of brick and stone and with a pediment over the centre of its nine-bayed front. Remarkable and influential – most immediately on the design of Buckingham House – were its quadrant wings in the Palladian manner linking the house to service pavilions on the Piccadilly frontage and enclosing a forecourt.[4]

Lord Berkeley also acquired the large Brick Close and Hay Hill farm to the north of this site. Charles, Lord Clifford, son of the earl of Burlington, apparently purchased the farm and 33 acres of Brick Close from Thomas Lee in 1675 for £2,500,[5] and he and Berkeley jointly mortgaged it,[6] but only Lord Berkeley was rated for the land from c.1675 and Clifford's interest is not recorded thereafter.[7] The field lay on the north side of

the Tyburn, separated from the Berkeley House gardens by a small enclosure called Little Brookfield.

Lord Berkeley died in 1678, succeeded by his son Charles (d. 1682), and his second son John (d. 1697), with his widow Christian (d. 1698) retaining a life interest in the estate. In 1691 Lady Berkeley and John Lord Berkeley leased for building small parcels of land formerly part of the garden of Berkeley House, lying on the west side of the newly-formed Stratton Street,[8] and Lady Berkeley let the house itself to Princess Anne from 1692 to 1695 for £600 a year.[9] Soon after the princess left, Lord Berkeley negotiated to sell the house with two parties, William Cavendish, 1st duke of Devonshire, and John Sheffield, marquess of Normanby, creating such confusion that each thought they had bought it: a Chancery suit settled the matter by 1697, when Devonshire was first rated on the house, for which he paid £11,000.[10]

Though some freehold sites were sold for building as Brick Close was developed, the Berkeleys retained most of the estate, which passed successively to John's brother William, 4th Lord Berkeley (d. 1741), and the latter's eldest son John, 5th Lord Berkeley. A clause in the sale of Berkeley House bound Lord Berkeley and his heirs not to build on their land north of the house, within the breadth of the garden, which might cause annoyance to the occupants of the house.[11] Probably for that reason, in 1718 Berkeley and Devonshire took a long lease from the Curzon family of the part of Little Brookfield that lay at the north end of the garden,[12] and when building began to spread on the estate, Berkeley Square was created the breadth of the garden with no building on its south side, to honour the clause. Building on the east side of the square began in the late 1730s and on the west in the

1 Ibid., 205–7; Colvin, *British Architects*, 891–2.
2 *Hollar's London*, Plate 5.
3 TNA, C 66/3065, no. 17; Johnson, *Berkeley Sq.* 38–9; below, Clarendon.
4 Summerson, *Archit. in Britain*, 174, 245–6; R.T. Gunther (ed.), *The Architecture of Sir Roger Pratt* (1928), 139–40, 261; D. Pearce, *London's Mansions* (1986), fig. 107. For Buckingham Ho., below, Buckingham.

5 TNA, C 54/4429, no. 19.
6 WCA, Cal. deeds, 10/20.
7 Johnson, *Berkeley Sq.* 58; below, Jennings.
8 LMA, O/10/1–3.
9 *Cal. SP Dom.* 1691–2, 245, 381; Colby, *Mayfair*, 31.
10 Colby, *Mayfair*, 33.
11 Ibid.
12 Johnson, *Berkeley Sq.* 62.

34. *Devonshire House, Piccadilly, the front and forecourt c.1890, after removal of the outside staircase which originally led to the 1st-floor entrance. Designed by William Kent and built in the 1730s, its austere exterior gave no indication of its spacious and richly decorated formal rooms.*

early 1740s (the north side belonged to the Grosvenor estate); Bruton, Hill, and Charles streets were also built on the estate.[1] Lord Berkeley had a London house at no. 16 Berkeley Square in 1773.[2]

The 5th Lord Berkeley died in 1773 without male heirs and the barony became extinct. By his will he left his freehold estate in Middlesex in trust for the benefit of Anne daughter of Dr Henry Egerton, bishop of Hereford, for her life or until she married. She died unmarried in 1803 and under Berkeley's will the estate passed to Frederick Augustus, 5th earl of Berkeley, a distant relative. The estate then passed with the earldom until the death of the last earl in 1942. By c.1950 the freehold of the estate belonged to Samuel Estates Ltd,[3] but by the 1980s many parts belonged to pension funds and insurance companies.[4]

DEVONSHIRE HOUSE

After its purchase by the duke of Devonshire, Berkeley House became known as Devonshire House, but was destroyed by fire in 1733. A new brick house was built on the site for the 4th duke, designed with rich interiors but a notably austere main façade and service wings by William Kent between 1734 and c.1740.[5] That house, famous as a centre of high political and social life in the 18th and 19th centuries, was altered by the architects James Wyatt (1776–90) and Decimus Burton (1834). Sold by the 9th duke in 1920 for £750,000,[6] it was demolished at the end of 1924,[7] and both the site and the gardens were built over.[8]

BUCKINGHAM (GORING, ARLINGTON) HOUSE

Buckingham House and its predecessors were built on land formerly part of the manor of Ebury, a large part of which had been the Mulberry Garden, together with roadside waste.

The Mulberry Garden

In 1611 the lessees of the manor of Ebury sold back to James I their interest in two pieces of land enclosed with a brick wall lying by the highway opposite the west wall of St James's Park, with another piece outside the wall and next to the highway, totalling 4½ acres.[9] By 1614 King James had created a mulberry garden there supporting silkworms,[10] as part of an unsuccessful scheme to reduce the import of silk. The Crown retained the freehold of this land when the remainder of Ebury was sold in feefarm in 1623.[11] In 1628 Charles I granted the keepership of the garden, with the fee of £60 a year, to Walter Aston (d. 1639), 1st Baron Aston of Forfar, for his life and that of his son. By 1638 Aston had a house there, the earliest on the Buckingham House site, built on a rood of waste between the garden and the highway, opposite the wall of St James's Park.

In 1640 George, Lord Goring (earl of Norwich from 1644), paid Lord Aston £1,000 to surrender his interest in the Mulberry Garden and house to the king, who for £400 and surrender of the annual £60 fee, made a grant in socage for 10s. a year to trustees for Goring of the 4½

1 Pevsner, *London 6: Westm.* 498.
2 Johnson, *Berkeley Sq.* 193.
3 Ibid., pp. xiv, 154, 177, 193–4.
4 S. Green, *Who Owns London?* (1986), 108, 154, 170.
5 Colvin, *British Architects*, 217.
6 *Oxford DNB* sv. Cavendish, Victor.

7 Colby, *Mayfair*, 36–7, 43.
8 Colvin, *British Architects*, 201, 1189; Pevsner, *London 6: Westm.* 503.
9 TNA, E 214/1154.
10 *Ebury map*, 1614.
11 Above, Grosvenor.

35. *Devonshire House, Piccadilly, late 19th-century photograph showing its opulent interiors as remodelled in the 19th century, which formed the setting for formal entertainment.*

acres, the house and its site, and the watercourse beside it (which ran alongside the highway), with liberty to enclose the watercourse with a wall and to remove the trees and silkworms.[1] Either because Goring was attending Queen Henrietta Maria in Holland or because of the outbreak of the Civil War, a patent was never issued for the grant,[2] and in 1651 the Mulberry Garden was surveyed by Parliament as part of the king's possessions; it is not clear if Goring was actually using it as part of the gardens to his main house, built on adjoining land (below). The garden property consisted of a four-storeyed house of timber and tile in one range, with the hall and kitchen in two adjoining ranges of three storeys, and attached was another decayed two-storeyed range. A small gardener's house of brick and lead adjoined Lord Goring's house, and a shed was used as a washhouse supplied by water through lead pipes. The waste on which the buildings stood was enclosed with a brick wall. Part of the former mulberry garden was also enclosed

with a brick wall, and part was paved with Purbeck stone, running 88 ft in length at the back doors of Goring's house and 10 to 16 ft wide. Other parts of the ground were used for a bowling alley, or were 'meanly' planted with several varieties of fruit trees, and another was planted with whitethorn as a wilderness or maze. Particulars for sale were drawn up in 1651 for Anthony Deane, Goring's grandson,[3] but it is not clear if this sale was concluded. The freehold in any case returned to the Crown in 1660. In 1654 the Mulberry Garden was being used as a 'place of refreshment' for fashionable society.[4]

Goring returned to England in 1660 and petitioned Charles II for completion of the grant of the Mulberry Garden made to him in 1640. This was granted but as a long lease rather than in fee.[5] When Henry Bennet, Lord Arlington, acquired Goring House in 1665, he seems to have acquired the lease of the Mulberry Garden as well; in 1672 he received a new Crown lease of the garden for 20s. a year.[6] Although the rent was included in a list of

1 Bodl. MS Bankes 55, ff. 5–6.
2 *Cal. S.P. Dom.* 1660–1, 182.
3 TNA, E 317/Middx/41; E 320/L2.

4 *Diary of John Evelyn*, ed. E.S. de Beer, III (1955), 96–7.
5 *Cal. Treas. Bks,* I. 83.
6 *Cal. Treas. Bks,* III. 1313.

feefarms to be sold in 1698,[1] in 1760 the Crown ascertained that the property, which then formed part of the site of Arlington's house and garden,[2] was a Crown leasehold held under a 99-year lease granted in 1672.[3]

Goring (Arlington) House

The freehold land belonging to Goring was part of a conveyance in 1623 by Thomas Browne and his wife Elizabeth and William Phillipps and his wife Anne to William Blake, citizen and vintner of London. The property, in Westminster, Knightsbridge, Kensington, and Chelsea, was described as 3 messuages, a dovehouse, 3 gardens, 30 acres of land, 20 of meadow, and 20 of pasture, and it included 4 acres in Ebury field and half an acre nearby, said to lie beside the footway from Charing Cross to Chelsea.[4] The half acre lay on the south side of the Mulberry Garden, and in the 1650s was claimed by owner of the Ebury estate to be part of Crowfield (formerly Ebury Field). However, Blake's ownership is supported by the earliest extant map of Ebury of 1614, where the half acre is marked as 'Poules', as was the 4 acres in Ebury field which were also part of Blake's purchase.[5] Even in the 1660s ownership was unclear and 'Poules' was interpreted as referring to the dean and chapter of St Paul's as lords of the manor of Knightsbridge,[6] but as that manor actually belonged to the dean and chapter of Westminster, St Paul's ownership of 'Poules' seems unlikely. More probably it derives from Powell: a David Powell held land in Knightsbridge in 1577,[7] which may have included parcels in Ebury.

William Blake (d. 1630), knighted in 1627, was resident in Kensington by 1606 and built up a large estate there and in Westminster and Chelsea. Despite sales before his death, he still left c.370 acres to his heirs.[8] In 1629 he laid the foundation of a house on the half acre next to the Mulberry Garden, but was ordered to stop building by the Privy Council as it would overlook the garden and St James's Park.[9] However, a house was standing there by 1640, and probably in 1634 when Blake's son William conveyed the messuage and 4½ acres to trustees for George, Lord Goring. Goring either enlarged Blake's house, by the addition of another 'pile' of building on the south side,[10] or demolished and replaced it with a new building for his residence.[11] He also increased the grounds; in 1640 he agreed with Hugh Audley, owner of the Ebury estate, for the purchase for c.£7,000 of upper and lower Crowfields, part of the former manor of Ebury, which lay on the west side of his house and the Mulberry Garden. He may have used a small part to increase the site of his house, but most was

converted into gardens and orchards, enclosed with brick walls, and included the 4 acres acquired from Blake which lay on the western edge of this part of Crowfields. However, since Goring did not pay the balance of the purchase by the agreed date (1642), the land later reverted to Audley. Goring also enlarged the site (presumably before 1642) by taking in nearly 3 acres of waste along the footpath on the south side of the house and adjoining fields. By the 1650s this land had been built up with, from east to west, the laundry yard, the entrance and courtyard, the fountain yard and terrace walk, some kitchen gardens and cherry garden, and the messuage known as Prince Henry's slaughter house, which in 1652 was a four-roomed house with a yard and pond surrounded by a brick wall.[12] In 1652 the amount of Crowfield included in the grounds of Goring House was being established, presumably at the request of Hugh Audley: the terrace walk and a small part of the fountain garden were taken from Crowfield, with the equivalent parts of the kitchen gardens on the west side as far as the slaughter house.[13]

In 1636 Goring had mortgaged the site of his house to John Denny, a maternal kinsman, for £2,531. Goring was abroad in the early 1640s, but returned in 1647 to compound for his estates. Having fought for the king in 1648 and been captured and released, he went abroad in 1650. Before departing he and his trustees released his equity of redemption to Edward Denny, son and heir of John, giving him ownership of the property, apparently to clear his debt to Denny. Confusion over the location of the half acre, and therefore over ownership of Goring House, led to suits between Hugh Audley and Edward Denny. As he did not have adequate evidence of title, Denny brought a suit in the Chancery court against Audley in 1653 to try to establish his ownership of the half acre, but the judgement gave possession to Audley, who had to pay £1,100 to Denny. The fine of 1654 in settlement described the property as a messuage, garden, 4 acres land (in Ebury field) and 2 acres pasture.[14] After Audley's death in 1662 the freehold of both Goring House and the gardens passed with the Ebury estate to Alexander Davies.[15]

In 1649 Audley leased to Anthony Cogan the great garden (Goring Garden) of 20 acres enclosed with a brick wall for 20 years at a rent of £80 and 100 pippins or 10s., and in 1656 8 acres of pasture called Mulberry Garden field, which seems to be the field on the north side of the Mulberry Garden, for 19 years for £21. In 1661 Cogan sold the remaining years in his leases to Charles II, with the Crown paying the rents to Cogan

1 *Cal. Treas. Bks*, XIII. 312.
2 Below.
3 *Hist. King's Works*, V. 134.
4 *Ebury plan c.*1663.
5 *Ebury map*, 1614.
6 *Ebury plan c.*1663.   7 E.g. TNA, E 211/657.
8 *Survey of London*, XLI. 58; TNA, WARDS 5/30/433. For Chelsea estate: *VCH Middx*, XII. 127.

9 *Acts of PC*, 1628–9, 366.
10 *Ebury plan c.*1663.
11 TNA, C 78/980, no. 2.
12 TNA, C 78/980, no. 2; E 317/Middx/27; Bodl. MS Bankes 42, ff. 5–6.
13 TNA, E 317/Middx/28.
14 *Ebury plan c.*1663; Gatty, *Mary Davies*, I. 103–4, 106.
15 TNA, C 78/980, no. 2.

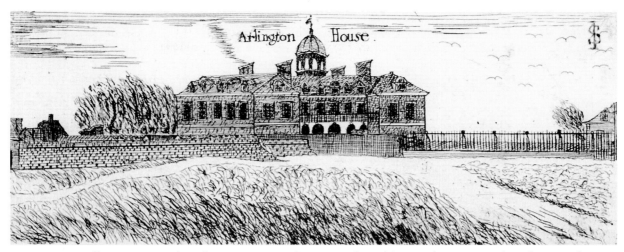

36. *Arlington House, viewed across Green Park, c.1680. The etching, not by an expert draughtsman, shows the H-plan house with central arcade and cupola, built in 1674 after its predecessor was burned down. It was apparently depicted before the highway in front was moved behind the house in 1682. The house was demolished and replaced by Buckingham House in 1705.*

who paid them to the ground landlord.[1] By 1668, however, Crown ministers were considering whether to buy the rented land or surrender it back to the owner of the Ebury estate.[2] Perhaps because of Lord Arlington's interest in the property, the Crown's tenant, Dr Morison, was ordered in 1670 to deliver possession of Goring Garden back to the owner.[3]

Henry Bennet, secretary of state, Lord Arlington from 1663 and earl of Arlington from 1672, was living in Goring House by March 1665,[4] and in May agreed with Alexander Davies to pay £3,500 for Goring House and gardens.[5] Davies died before the sale could be completed, and as his estate was held in trust for his infant daughter, an Act was obtained in 1675 to enable the sale to go ahead.[6] By 1672, Arlington had also bought out the interests of the heirs of the Goring family in both Goring House and the Mulberry Garden (George Goring had died in 1663 and his son Charles, 2nd earl of Norwich, in 1671).[7] Meanwhile the house burned down in 1674 and was rebuilt by Arlington, as an H-plan house with an arcade between its hipped roofed wings and a central cupola.[8] It was eventually known as Arlington House, though Arlington himself still dated a letter at 'Goring House' in 1677.[9]

In 1681 35 acres lying east and north of Arlington House were sold by Sir Thomas Grosvenor to the earl of Arlington for £3,400, apparently at request of the king.[10] Arlington then granted 33 acres of this to the king to enlarge St James's Park, for which he received a plot of land for building in the angle of Piccadilly and St James's

Street, the site of Arlington Street.[11] The purchase also enabled him to arrange for the closure of the road that ran from Tothill to Hyde Park Corner along the west side of St James's Park and divided the park from the Mulberry Garden and Arlington House, replacing it with a new road west of Goring great garden and away from his house, approximately along the route of the modern Grosvenor Place. Consent to the move was conveyed by St Margaret's vestry to Lord Arlington in July 1682, after they had sought the advice of Sir Christopher Wren in the matter.[12]

Arlington's only child, Isabella, was married to Henry FitzRoy, acknowledged by Charles II as his son, and created duke of Grafton in 1675. On Arlington's death in 1685 Arlington House passed to Grafton, and on the latter's death in 1690 to trustees for his young son.[13] In 1702 the trustees sold the house to John Sheffield, 3rd earl of Mulgrave, created duke of Buckingham and of Normanby in 1703,[14] who entirely rebuilt the house.

Buckingham House

Buckingham employed William Winde as architect for the building of his new house, which was completed by 1705, but the initial design may have been the work of William Talman, who had previously enjoyed the duke's patronage. The plan with quadrant colonnaded wings seems to have been influenced by Berkeley House,[15] but the introduction of a balustraded attic to screen the roof was new to London mansions; with its attic and wings Buckingham House became the prototype of many early

1 *Cal. Treas. Bks*, VII. 1542.
2 *Cal. Treas. Bks*, II. 225, 411, 522.
3 *Cal. Treas. Bks*, III. 704, 763.
4 *DNB*; *Diary of John Evelyn*, ed. E.S. de Beer, III (1955), 404.
5 Gatty, *Mary Davies*, I. 167.   6 Above, Grosvenor.
7 GEC, *Complete Peerage*, IX. 772, 776; below.
8 TNA, C 78/980, no. 2; Guildhall Libr. Print Colln, Pr.W2/GRE/par., cat. no. p5415527.

9 *Cal. SP Dom.* 1677–8, 297.
10 *Survey of London*, XXXIX. 4; BL, Crace Maps, Portf. X, no. 30*.
11 *Cal. Treas. Bks*, VII. 211; TNA, C 66/3232, no. 7.
12 *Catalogue of Westm. Recs.* ed. J.E. Smith (1900), 192.
13 *DNB*, s.vv. Bennet, Hen.; Fitzroy, Hen.
14 GEC, *Complete Peerage*, II. 398.
15 Above, Berkeley.

18th-century country houses.[1] Both Goring House and the rebuilt Arlington House had faced roughly south-east, fronting the footway to Chelsea; Buckingham House was built on a new north-easterly axis aligned with, though not centred on, the avenue called the Pall Mall in St James's Park, thereby making the park into a grand setting for the house. The site of the house also incorporated the old road from Tothill to Hyde Park, as the two-storeyed pavilions at the ends of the two curved wings must have covered the former road,[2] and more than half the house was built on the former Mulberry Garden.[3] The house also encroached on the park itself: the duke was ordered to comply with the queen's permission, which was to take in only a ditch and a little land in front of his house to make a straight line.[4]

Buckingham died at his house in 1721, and his widow offered to lease the house and contents to the prince and princess of Wales, considering it too good for a private individual, but her price of £3,000 a year was thought too high.[5] After her death in 1742, since Buckingham's last legitimate son had died in 1735, the house passed under his will to his illegitimate son, Charles Herbert, who took the surname Sheffield and was created a baronet in 1755.[6] In 1760 he sought a renewal of the Crown lease of the Mulberry Garden, due to expire in 1771, but after some negotiations offered to sell the whole property to the Crown instead, and in 1762 it was acquired by George III for £28,000.[7]

The subsequent history of the house is reserved for treatment under Royal Palaces.

BURGHLEY (EXETER) HOUSE, STRAND

William Cecil, Lord Burghley, Elizabeth I's chief minister, began acquiring property in the Strand in 1550, when he was Edward VI's principal secretary. By 1561 he had built up a small estate on the north side of the Strand on which he had his London residence, known in 1571 as Burghley House. Cecil acquired his first lease in 1550 from the master of the Savoy, of a messuage in Savoy Rents, which lay opposite the Savoy, for 31 years at £4 a year.[8] In 1559, by then principal secretary to Elizabeth I, he acquired the lease of a nearby house with curtilage and garden, also opposite the Savoy, built by Sir Thomas Palmer c.1552 on property belonging to the rector of St Clement Danes; in 1561 the rector conveyed to Cecil's trustees the freehold of all the

rectory property there, consisting of Palmer's house and the parsonage house.[9] Meanwhile in 1560, on the east side of the rectory property, Cecil acquired a garden and barn formerly belonging to the priory of St John of Jerusalem, and beyond that a messuage called the Hartshorn and garden formerly of the duchy of Lancaster. Acquired in 1545 by John Taylor, this property had been sold in 1556 to Sir William Paget, Lord Paget of Beaudesert,[10] who in turn sold them to Cecil.

Cecil rebuilt or enlarged Palmer's house for his own use, using the western part of Paget's ground for the east end of his brick house.[11] In 1561 the queen granted Cecil another duchy property, east of the Hartshorn, called the Flower de Luce with 3 cottages and a garden, straddling the boundary between the parishes of St Clement Danes and St Mary of Strand.[12] Cecil also acquired two pieces of ground from the earl of Bedford, one on the west side of his house taken from the former Friars Pyes garden, and the other a strip of Covent Garden, 78 feet wide, running along the north side of his property, with right of access and use of Covent Garden, at that time open land. He enclosed the strip into his garden with a brick wall, from which projected three banqueting houses, one at either end and one in middle. In 1673, the southern frontage of the Cecil estate, along the Strand, was 385 feet, while on the northern side it was 481 feet. After his elevation to the peerage as Baron Burghley in 1571, his mansion became known as Burghley House, and under his eldest son Thomas, earl of Exeter from 1605, as Exeter House.[13] The property passed thereafter with the earldom and later marquessate of Exeter.

A ground plan of the house dated to the 1560s shows a rectangular building around two internal courts, with a small private garden, tennis court, and bowling alley on the east, and the formal garden behind with an orchard east of that behind an unused part of the estate.[14] In Hollar's plan of the area it is shown with an additional storey at each angle, forming a compact house which projects slightly into the Strand, a garden behind and an alley of trees leading towards Drury Lane.[15] Lord Burghley later built a smaller house attached to the north-east corner of his mansion and over part of the private garden, which he granted to his younger son, Sir Robert Cecil, for life with two other houses;[16] it was probably the house known in the 17th century as Cecil House, and later as Little Exeter House. A house built at

1 Colvin, *British Architects*, 1010, 1133; Summerson, *Archit. in Britain*, 245–6.

2 Grosvenor Estate plan of 1675, reprod. in Gatty, *Mary Davies*, I. plate IX; Morgan, *Map of London* (1682); Rocque, *Map of London* (1741–5).

3 *Hist. King's Works*, V. 134.

4 *Cal. Treas. Bks*, XVIII. 379.

5 *Hist. King's Works*, V. 134.

6 GEC, *Complete Peerage*, II. 398–9.

7 *Hist. King's Works*, V. 134.   8 TNA, E 210/10230.

9 *Cal. Pat.* 1555–7, 122; EH, Survey of London, notes from Burghley Ho. MSS, 5/17, 5/26–8; below, Religious Hist.: Par. Chs (St Clement Danes).

10 *L&P Hen. VIII*, XIX(1), p. 629, no. 1035/107; *L&P Hen. VIII*, XX(1), p. 59 (no. 125/31); TNA, E 318/11/492, m. 4; CP 25/2/61/473/1Edw6/Mich.; notes from Burghley Ho. MSS, 5/5; Cal. of Burghley Ho. MSS, NRA 6666, 80/21; above, Manorial (Soke of Leic.); Other Eccles. Ests (Knights Hospitaller).

11 Notes from Burghley Ho. MSS, 5/18.

12 Below, Religious Hist.: Par. Chs (St Mary of Strand).

13 *Survey of London*, XXXVI. 35, 223; plate 10 (plan of 1673).

14 Plate X in *Patronage, culture and power: the early Cecils*, ed. P. Croft (2002).

15 *Hollar's London*, Plate 5; *Survey of London*, XVIII. 125.

16 EH, Survey of London, notes from Hatfield Ho. MSS, Cecil fam. and est. papers, 184/5.

37. The north side of the Strand, painted in the 1880s, showing the typical shops and offices on narrow plots which had lined the Strand since the late 15th century, often concealing aristocratic mansions behind. Some fronts are 18th-century and of brick, others belong to earlier timber-framed buildings.

the eastern end of the estate, adjoining the White Hart, was later occupied by Lord Exeter's 3rd son, Sir Edward Cecil (d. 1638), Viscount Wimbledon, and known as Wimbledon House; it was probably this house for which Inigo Jones designed an entrance, if not more.[1] In 1627 a fire burnt part of Exeter House and the adjoining houses, which were rebuilt.[2]

In 1671 the 4th earl's son and heir, John, Lord Burghley, on whom Exeter and Little Exeter houses had been settled, petitioned for a licence to build over the site of the houses, garden and stables. Exeter Street was built running east–west through the garden, and the southern end of Burleigh Street was laid north–south joining the Strand at the western edge of the estate.[3] Exeter Change was built on the site of Exeter House, jutting out on the street frontage as the mansion had done previously. It was used for various entertainments,[4] and later became a famous menagerie of wild animals, but was demolished in 1830 to widen the Strand.[5] The remainder of the site was used for Exeter Hall, built in 1830–1 to a neoclassical design by J.P. Gandy-Deering, as a centre for Evangelical activity, which became the focal point of many philanthropic and religious societies.[6] The building was purchased in 1889 by the YMCA, but was demolished in 1909 to make way for the Strand Palace hotel, which had a narrow front to the Strand but was extended in

1928–30 and given a memorable Art Deco entrance, parts of which survive in the Victoria and Albert Museum.[7] At the eastern end of the estate Wellington Street was formed 1833–5 after the destruction by fire of the English Opera House (later the Lyceum Theatre) in 1830, and a new theatre was built on Lord Exeter's estate on the west side of the new street, completed in 1835.[8] All or part of the estate was sold in the 1850s.[9]

CHRIST'S HOSPITAL

Christ's Hospital foundation acquired three principal groups of property in Westminster, two by bequest and one by purchase: the Westminster estate given by Richard Casteler in his will of 1555; the Long Acre estate bought in 1682 with a bequest from Thomas Stretchley; and the Soho estate derived from a gift by John and Frances West in 1720. Some subsequent small acquisitions were managed with those estates.

Westminster Estate

Christ's Hospital's earliest property in Westminster was acquired through a bequest to the mayor and corporation of London as governors of the hospitals of Edward VI. The donor was Richard Castell, Cassener, or Casteler, cordwaner of Westminster, son of James Cassener of Pepeling near Calais, where Richard had a

1 Colvin, *British Architects*, 590.

2 C. Dalton, *Life and Times of Gen. Sir Edw. Cecil, Vct Wimbledon* (1885), II. 108, 288, 310–11; J. Husselby and P. Henderson, 'Location, Location, Location! Cecil House in the Strand', in *Archit. Hist.* 45 (2002), 186.

3 *Survey of London*, XXXVI. 223; Guildhall MS 9800/2.

4 *Middx County Rec. Sess. Bks 1689–1709*, 181.

5 *Survey of London*, XVIII. 125.

6 Colvin, *British Architects*, 405, 702; Guildhall Libr., Print Colln, Pr.W22/STR, cat. no. p7522629.

7 Pevsner, *London 6: Westm.* 366.

8 *Survey of London*, XXXVI. 43, 227.

9 Cal. of Burghley Ho. MSS, 47/7; LMA, E/BER/CG/T/V/PO1.

brother and sister still living in 1548.[1] A charitable bequest which Richard gave to the parish of St Margaret's was subsequently referred to as Castell's charity, and his bequest to Christ's Hospital as Casteler's.

Richard Castell had built up an estate in Westminster towards the end of his life. In 1544 he bought the 'manor' or liberty of the Round Woolstaple, of a net value of £13 14s. 8d., from William Middleton for £192 5s. 4d.[2] By that date comprising 12 messuages, 5 gardens and 2s. quitrent from another house nearby, it lay just east of King Street near New Palace Yard, forming the entrance to the former woolstaple buildings and wharf. Richard also purchased three small groups of former religious property in St Margaret's from the Crown through agents in 1549–50. In 1549 John Royston, citizen and pewterer, and William Pendred, citizen and founder, bound themselves to him in £200 to purchase from the king three messuages with shops, cellars, and solars, in King Street, one of them occupied by Castell himself by lease, and two other messuages nearby in the Long Woolstaple, all formerly belonging to St Stephen's college; and a messuage called the Sun in King Street, and four others with a garden and close in Tothill Street, all of which had belonged to the fraternity of St Mary in St Margaret's church. In the event it was John Hulson of London, scrivener, and Pendred who conveyed and released to Castell in 1549 the messuages in King Street and Long Woolstaple, to hold of the king of the manor of East Greenwich in free socage.[3] The property in Tothill Street was purchased from the Crown in 1550 by William Place and Nicholas Spakeman, haberdasher, and conveyed by them to Castell to hold by the same tenure.[4]

In his will of 1555, Richard Castell otherwise Casteler (d. 1559) devised the 3 houses in King Street including his own dwelling to his wife Catherine and her heirs outright, and the remainder of his property in Westminster to his wife for life, to remain thereafter to the mayor and citizens of London as governors of the hospitals, out of which they were to pay £8 a year to the churchwardens of St Margaret for the poor and distribute the rest for the benefit of the poor of the hospitals. He asked Richard Grafton, grocer, one of the governors, to assist his wife and oversee the will.[5] Grafton was the first treasurer of Christ's, which was just being founded at that time, and Castell may have indicated he wanted to benefit Christ's in particular. In 1567 Castell's widow Catherine and her husband Robert Morecock confirmed to the hospital the

Sun with its garden and closes, to be held for the use of Catherine for life, and then to remain to the hospital;[6] the property passed to the hospital on Catherine's death in 1576.[7] The rentcharge to the parish of St Margaret's was paid by the hospital until it was redeemed in 1889.[8]

The Casteler gift was augmented by gift and purchase. In 1585 the governors bought from John Lawrence of Hackney the messuage with shops and solars adjoining the east side of their Tothill property.[9] The White Horse alehouse in New Palace Yard, given by Dame Anne Alston by will of 1694 for the support of poor children,[10] lay near to the hospital's houses in Long Woolstaple and was administered with Casteler's gift. All the Casteler property in the Round and Long woolstaples and the Alston gift were sold 1735–40 to the Commissioners for Building Westminster Bridge to form part of the approaches to the new bridge,[11] but the governors continued to develop and add to the Tothill property, mainly in the 19th and 20th centuries, by small purchases of adjoining property. Building on the Tothill property had begun in the 1670s and 1680s, principally by Christ's lessee Sir Edward de Carteret, who built Carteret and Park streets on the site. The latter became the eastern end of Queen Anne's Gate in 1874.[12] The hospital took a 999-year lease of a house in Dartmouth Street from the earl of Dartmouth in 1754, which they demolished to give additional access through to Park Street,[13] and bought the freehold of several houses on the west side of Dartmouth Street in 1829 and 1840.[14] In 1925 the hospital bought back Broadway Chambers, no. 40 Broadway, on the western corner of Carteret Street, part of the original Tothill bequest which had been acquired by the Metropolitan District Railway and sold on by them in 1870.[15] The hospital also bought no. 32 Queen Anne's Gate, backing onto St James's Park, in 1932,[16] and in 1948 no. 4 Queen Anne's Gate (formerly no. 2 Dartmouth Street).[17] In the mid 1970s the hospital sold some freehold to meet financial needs, including nos 4–12 Queen Anne's Gate in 1976, but the Westminster estate still included most of Queen Anne's Gate (part of which was formerly Park Street), Old Queen Street, and Carteret Street.[18] The freehold of no. 32 Old Queen Street was sold in 2003.[19]

Long Acre Estate

Thomas Stretchley in his will of 1678 left property in several counties to Christ's Hospital, with £5,200 to buy additional property which would bring the total value to

1 Guildhall MSS 13013–14; TNA, CP 25/2/27/185/36HENVIII/HIL.

2 TNA, CP 40/1123, carte rot. 22; CP 25/2/27/185/36HenVIII/HIL.

3 Guildhall MS 13007; *Cal. Pat.* 1549–51, 128–9.

4 *Cal. Pat.* 1549–51, 409; Guildhall MS 12996.

5 TNA, PROB 11/42B, f. 295 (PCC 37 Chaynay).

6 Guildhall MS 13008.

7 *Survey of London*, X. 78–9.

8 *Endowed Chars London*, V. 342; Guildhall MS 13117.

9 Guildhall MS 13012.

10 TNA, PROB 11/432, f. 162.

11 Guildhall MSS 13048, 13051.

12 *Survey of London*, X. 78–80.

13 Guildhall MS 13084.

14 Guildhall MSS 13103–5.

15 Guildhall MS 13106.   16 Guildhall MS 13113.

17 Guildhall MS 13108.   18 Green, *Who Owns London?*, 33.

19 Christ's Hospital, *Annual Review 2003–2004*, p. 15 (via website, www.christs-hospital.org.uk, 10 May 2005).

£380 a year. The will was proved in 1681, and in 1682 the hospital bought from Edward Proby messuages and stables and other buildings called Northumberland Stables in Long Acre, in the parish of St Martin-in-the-Fields, leasing back to Proby a substantial newly-built house and a barn; they issued four leases of the rest to him for rebuilding.[1] The three-storeyed house, called the White House in 1682, lay at the western end of the property and fronted north-west on to Long Acre; it had oak wainscotting and shutters, 2 marble chimney-pieces and 11 marble hearths, and piped water to a 'fountain' in the great parlour. From the late 1680s until 1756 it was known as the Bagnio, and was later nos 15 and 15a Long Acre.[2] Christ's original estate in Long Acre stretched from the site of no. 15 north-eastwards probably as far as the later no. 23, and possibly included nos 24–5, which the hospital owned by 1866. By that date the site also included Conduit Court.[3] The estate stretched back from Long Acre to Hart (later Floral) Street and included properties which later fronted that street.[4] No. 26 Long Acre with houses in Banbury Court and no. 30 Floral Street, which was freehold in other hands in the 1780s and 1876, was acquired by Christ's by 1935.[5] In 1937 the hospital sold by auction a 99-year building lease of all its Long Acre property,[6] and in the second half of the 20th century its leaseholders, Capital & Counties, developed nos 18–26 Long Acre and nos 28–30 Floral Street, considered generally to be part of Covent Garden.[7]

Soho Estate

In 1720 John and Frances West conveyed to Christ's Hospital their property in London for the education, support and apprenticing of poor children. A major part of this gift was land and houses in the parish of St James, Westminster, lying either side of Rupert Street north of Richmond Street and in Hedge or Hays Lane and Edmund's Court.[8] In 1806 the property consisted of 9 houses on the north side of Richmond Street; 12 houses on the west side of Prince's (formerly Hay) Street, later Wardour Street, one of them formerly two houses at the corner of Richmond Street; 14 houses in Rupert Street, 6 of them on the west side with coachhouses, sheds, and a warehouse behind in Archer Street, and 7 with stables, a coachyard and coachhouses, probably on the east side; and 11 houses in Edmund's (later Tisbury) Court.[9] Shaftesbury Avenue, created by the Metropolitan Board of Works in the 1870s, maintained the line of the north side of Richmond Street which it absorbed, giving Christ's property a frontage to the new road. In 1905

Christ's let the block fronting Shaftesbury Avenue between Rupert and Wardour streets, on which were built the Queen's and Globe (later renamed Gielgud) theatres. In the mid 1970s, in addition to selling some properties in its Westminster estate, the hospital also sold off part of the Soho estate: properties in Wardour Street, nos 1–7 Brewer Street, nos 52–4 Rupert Street, and nos 1–4 Tisbury Court. At the end of 1985 it got back possession of the block leased in 1905,[10] but in 2002–3 sold the two theatres to reinvest in property funds.[11]

CLARENDON ESTATE

In 1664 the king granted to Edward Hyde, earl of Clarendon, Lord Chancellor, and his son Henry, Viscount Cornbury, the freehold of three closes amounting to c.30 acres in the bailiwick of St James, surrendered by Queen Henrietta Maria and her trustees. The closes, Stonebridge close, Penniless Bench, and Stone Conduit close, lay together along the north side of the later Piccadilly and stretched north and west to the Tyburn.[12]

Clarendon sold the western half of Stonebridge close to Sir William Pulteney, the rest of that close and a third of Penniless Bench to John, Lord Berkeley of Stratton,[13] and about two-thirds of Stone Conduit close to Sir John Denham, retaining the remaining parts of Penniless Bench and Stone Conduit close, c.8 acres, between the Berkeley and Denham portions. On this site, standing back from the highway and opposite the top of St James's Street, he built a great mansion called Clarendon House; the foundation was laid and a brick wall made around the site by August 1664, apparently using stone intended for the repair of St Paul's.[14] Completed in 1667 and designed by Roger Pratt, who was knighted the following year. It was among the most innovative and widely copied houses of its day. Its appearance, with a symmetrical plan, two storeys of equal height and, to catch a magnificent view, balustraded flats on the hipped roofs reached from central cupola, is most accurately portrayed in an engraving in the Crace Collection of the British Museum.[15] John Evelyn, who described it under construction, estimated the cost at £50,000, extra expense having been caused by replacing three of the City of London's water pipes through the site with new lead ones, and by foundations where a pond had been filled. The house was of vast proportions; it had 101 hearths in 1666. Clarendon later characterized its building as a 'rash enterprise that proved so fatal and mischievous to him': its grandeur led people to think that his funds must have been obtained by fraud and

1 Guildhall MS 12868, pp. 3, 14, 33, 22v.
2 Ibid. MS 13886.   3 Ibid. MSS 13890, 13892.
4 E.g. ibid. MS 13891.   5 Guildhall MSS 13887, 13889.
6 Ibid. MS 13893.   7 Green, *Who Owns London?*, 33.
8 Guildhall MS 12817, copy of deed of release and confirmation by Wests.
9 Guildhall MS 12817, 3rd Schedule to Act 1806 settling charity.

10 Green, *Who Owns London?*, 33.
11 *Christ's Hospital: Annual Review 2002–2003*, p. 210 (via website, www.christs-hospital.org.uk, 22 Apr. 2004).
12 *Cal. SP Dom.* 1663–4, 613; TNA, C 66/3065, no. 17.
13 Above, Berkeley.
14 Johnson, *Berkeley Sq.* 39–40.
15 Colvin, *British Architects*, 828–9; Summerson, *Archit. in Britain*, 140–1.

38. *Clarendon (later Albemarle) House, Piccadilly, designed by Sir Roger Pratt for the 1st Earl of Clarendon in 1664–7; one of the first new mansions to be built along Piccadilly, and although it was demolished as early as c.1683, it was widely copied.*

treason. In 1667 he fell from power and went into exile in France to avoid prosecution.[1]

The house was occupied by the duke of Ormond in 1670, who continued there until at least 1674.[2] Soon after Clarendon's death in 1674, his son sold the house for £25,000 to Christopher Monck, 2nd duke of Albemarle, who obtained a confirmation of the royal grant to Clarendon, as the parish had been wrongly stated;[3] the house was often known thereafter as Albemarle House. In 1683 it was sold to a syndicate of bankers and builders for c.£35,000 and demolished.[4] The syndicate was led by three citizens of London, John Hind, goldsmith, Cadogan Thomas, merchant, and Richard Frith, bricklayer, who also bought the 99-year lease that Clarendon had obtained in 1667 from the Corporation of London of the 27-acre Conduit Mead estate.[5] Relatives of Hind also acquired the Hay Hill farm lands. The site of Clarendon House and its gardens, and the southern part of Conduit Close were together known as Albemarle Ground, and parts were let by the syndicate on building leases; Dover, Bond, and Stafford streets and most of Albemarle Street had been laid out by 1684.[6] The syndicate began selling parts of the freehold from 1684, sometimes to the lessees including Sir Thomas Bond and Henry Jermyn, Lord Dover.[7]

CONDUIT MEAD

In 1536 Henry VIII acquired from the Mercers' Company a meadow called Conduit Mead with two adjoining closes, totalling 27 acres in the parish of St Martin's and valued at £4 13s. 4d., which had been part of Lady Bradbury's chantry and were leased to the corporation of the City of London with the right to convey the water from the conduit to the City.[8] The conduit heads lay near the main London road (Oxford Street) to the east of the Tyburn river, with the meadows in a broad band from the road southwards along the eastern bank of the Tyburn, with a narrow band of land running north-eastwards from the southern end. The freehold was granted to the City by the Crown to hold for a feefarm of £4 as part of the Royal Contract estates in 1628, and was retained by the City thereafter, principally because of the conduit's importance for the city's water supply. In 1651 Parliament arranged the sale of the £4 feefarm as part of King Charles's estates, and it seems to have been sold to the City as it was not mentioned thereafter.[9]

The meadows, which abutted the Clarendon House estate on the south, were leased by the City to Edward Hyde, earl of Clarendon, in 1666 for 99 years at £8 a year, with a second lease in 1667. The leases passed with Clarendon House and were eventually bought by a syndicate which began serious building development of both estates.[10] Conduit Mead estate was built over by c.1730: New Bond Street was laid out roughly north–south, and Conduit Street along the north-easterly band. The freehold of the estate remained in the possession of the City corporation, but owing to a decision to issue

1 Johnson, *Berkeley Sq.* 76–7.
2 *Cal. SP Dom.* 1670 (& Add. 1660–70), 56; 1671, 101; 1673–5, 251.
3 *Cal. SP Dom.* 1675–6, 409; *Cal. Treas. Bks*, V. 211.
4 HMC, *7th Rep.* App. 481a.; Johnson, *Berkeley Sq.* 80.
5 Johnson, *Berkeley Sq.* 41, 86–8; below, Conduit Mead.
6 Johnson, *Berkeley Sq.* 81, 102–5.

7 Ibid., 107–8. Development of site will be treated in a later vol.
8 TNA, SC 12/3/13; above, Secular Inns and Ests (Mercers).
9 TNA, E 308/3/21, m. 53; I. Doolittle, 'The City's West End Estate', *London Jour.* VII(1) (1981), 20.
10 P. Booth, 'Speculative Housing and the Land Market in London 1660–1730', *Town Planning Rev.* 51 (1980), 388–9; Johnson, *Berkeley Sq.* 41, 86–8; above, Clarendon.

perpetual leases in the mid 18th century, the corporation did not develop the estate itself and was also unable to benefit from rising property prices, except in a few cases where a new lease was required. The Property Act of 1925 converted the extant leases into 2,000-year terms, and though some leases were resumed by the corporation for failure to comply with terms, and others revised in return for dispensation from legal requirements for renewal, most were still in their original form in the 1980s.[1]

CRAVEN ESTATE

William Craven, earl of Craven, had three separate property holdings in Westminster. One was Drury House, acquired in 1631, where he had a residence.[2] The other two holdings were the estate he inherited at Charing Cross, and land he acquired at Pesthouse Close.

Charing Cross

Sir William Craven, lord mayor of London 1610–11, in his will proved in 1618 left large cash legacies to be invested in lands for his sons, to be held by his wife Elizabeth while they were minors. Amongst other property, Elizabeth purchased most of the capital messuage at Charing, in St Martin-in-the-Fields, called the Brewhouse with its houses and wharves, held by 7 tenants and formerly belonging to the hospital of St John of Jerusalem; she settled it on herself for life and then for use of her second son Thomas and his heirs. Lady Craven died in 1624 while her eldest son, William, was still a minor, and the Brewhouse, held of the king in common socage, was valued at £6 a year,[3] though a survey for the court of wards did not record the settlement on Thomas, but listed the Brewhouse among lands descending to William and valued it at £10 a year.[4] The estate was administered by Elizabeth's brothers, Sir William and Sir George Whitmore, as trustees and executors until her eldest son, William, knighted and created Baron Craven in 1627, came of age in 1629.[5] From 1624 the rents for the Charing Cross estate were received for the use of Thomas Craven and amounted to c.£160 a year, including £60 paid for the Brewhouse itself c.1630.[6] Thomas Craven died in 1637, and the value of his lands and legacies was divided amongst his surviving brothers and sister, with William, Lord Craven, taking possession of the lands at Charing Cross.[7]

Lord Craven was abroad with the court of James I's daughter, Elizabeth, queen of Bohemia, when Civil War broke out, and remained there with the permission of Parliament. He was accused of treason after consorting with the exiled Prince Charles (later Charles II) in Holland in 1650 and his estates were confiscated.[8] His property in the Strand, held by various tenants on 7-year leases, was sold in eight lots. The houses and stables fronting the Strand included the Salutation tavern, built over the entrance to Spur Alley, and houses called the Swan, the Crown, and the Greyhound; other houses and cottages lay either side of Spur Alley, with houses and stables in Brewers Yard.[9] In 1663 there were at least 19 tenants on the estate.[10] The two alleys ran from the Strand to the Thames between the Hungerford estate on the east, and the later Northumberland House estate on the west.[11] Craven recovered his estates in 1660; in 1665 he was created earl of Craven, and his barony was extended to include the male descendants of his first cousin.[12] In 1678 Craven bought the freehold of most of the property which had been excluded from Elizabeth Craven's purchase of 1620, consisting of six messuages in Brewers Yard.[13]

Craven died in 1697. The earldom became extinct, but his estates and barony passed to his cousin's great-grandson, William Craven of Combe Abbey.[14] On the latter's death in 1711 the estates and title passed successively to his sons William (d. 1739), 3rd baron, and Fulwar (d. 1764), 4th baron, and then to their first cousin William (d. 1769), 5th baron. He was succeeded by his nephew William (d. 1791), 6th baron, who was created earl of Craven (2nd creation) in 1801.

In the 1730s the 3rd baron redeveloped the Strand property, demolishing the houses in Spur Alley and Brewers Yard. A new street, Craven Street, was laid out along the line of Spur Alley and leased in building plots in the early 1730s, and the land on the east side of Brewers Yard, now renamed Brewer's Lane, was divided into plots used for stabling, reducing the width and length of the lane. Land at the south end of Craven Street was let as a wharf. When the leases were renewed from 1789, the street was extended southwards by four houses, and a grant made of a wharf which fronted onto an embankment made into the river.[15] The east side of Brewer's Lane was taken for Charing Cross station in 1862, and the remaining alley was later renamed Hungerford Street.[16] The wharf at the southern end of Craven Street remained until Victoria Embankment was

---

1 *London Jour.* VII(1) (1981), 15–27; Green, *Who Owns London?*, 48, 60.

2 Above, Secular Inns and Ests (Bernes' Inn).

3 Craven Papers 281, wills of Sir Wm Craven 15 Jas, and Eliz. Craven 1624; Craven Papers 279, ff. 6–9.

4 TNA, WARD 5/27, bdl. 3.

5 Craven Papers 59, acquittance 26 Dec. 1629; Craven Papers 280, receipts Dec. 1629 and 1630s; GEC, *Complete Peerage*, III. 500.

6 Craven Papers 42.

7 Ibid. 281, inv. 20 May 1637.

8 *Oxford DNB*; Craven Papers 152.

9 *Cal. Cttee Comp.* II. 1619, 1621–2, 1624–6; *Survey of London*, XVIII. 30.

10 Craven Papers 60, ind. 23 Oct. 15 Car II.

11 Morgan, *Map of London* (1682).

12 GEC, *Complete Peerage*, III. 500.

13 *Survey of London*, XVIII. 30.

14 NRA 11231, Cal. of Bateman Hanbury MSS (Northants RO), BH(K) 1243; BH(K) 1244.

15 *Survey of London*, XVIII. 31–2.

16 Ibid., 40.

created 1862–70; part of the Craven property was taken to extend the street to the new embankment road.[1]

Pesthouse Close

During the plague of 1665 the earl of Craven rented a 4-acre close in St Martin-in-the-Fields, acquired by the Crown from the Mercers' Company in 1536,[2] as the site for a pesthouse and burial ground; it was enclosed by a brick wall and had rooms for a physician and a surgeon, and a later description said it had 36 small houses for plague victims. In 1671 Craven bought the freehold of what was then called Pesthouse Close from James Baker for £280, and in 1687 he conveyed it to his heir apparent, Sir William Craven, and his heirs in trust to maintain it for the relief of poor inhabitants of the parishes of St Clement Danes, St Martin, St James, and St Paul afflicted with plague, and for a burial ground. After his death in 1697 it descended with his other Westminster property. By the early 18th century the area around the close was built up and in 1722–3 the 3rd Lord Craven tried unsuccessfully to get a Bill through Parliament which would allow him to buy out the interests of the four parishes and build on the land. He was finally successful in 1734, as by then fears of plague epidemics had subsided; in any case putting plague victims in a then heavily-populated area was seen to be impractical. Craven purchased a site in Paddington on which to build another pesthouse, and Pesthouse Close was immediately built over with houses, market buildings and shops in Marshall Street, Dufours Place and Broadwick Street, except for a small area in the north-east corner which was leased to St James's parish for 500 years to enlarge the parish's adjoining burial ground.

Between 1774 and 1791 the Craven estate was enlarged by the purchase of part of the Lowndes estate adjoining on the west side as far as Carnaby Street, including Carnaby or Marlborough market. Some houses on the east side of Marshall Street were sold to St James's vestry. In 1820–1 Carnaby market was closed, and the area cleared for rebuilding. The Craven family still held property there c.1960.

JENNINGS (MAYNARD) ESTATE

William Jennings, groom of the king's chamber, who sold 4 acres of arable and an acre of meadow in St Martin-in-the-Fields to Henry VIII in 1536,[3] was granted a Crown lease in 1538 of Beaumont's lands, consisting of 8½ acres arable and 2 acres of meadow in Brookshot (next to the Tyburn), 3 acres next to Charing Cross, half an acre of arable nearby, and 5 acres arable

and 2½ acres meadow in St Martin's field.[4] In 1541 he had a lease from Westminster Abbey of the Boarshead inn in King Street including shops, and a tenement called the Steyre with a cellar.[5] He also held a lease of Market meadows in 1544.[6] In 1553 Francis and Anthony Vaughan released and quitclaimed to him a messuage, 2 cottages, 3 gardens, a barn and appurtenances in Tothill Street,[7] which seems to be the property that later became the White Hart, lying between the north side of Tothill Street and St James's Park wall.[8] In 1554 Jennings with John Green purchased from the Crown in free socage all but 3½ acres of Beaumont's lands, and three parcels in the manor of Ebury which had been leased together by Westminster Abbey in 1520 to Elizabeth Vincent, widow:[9] Brick Close, north of the Knightsbridge road (Piccadilly), Priors Croft by the road to Ebury, and Priors Hope (1½ a.) near the Thames.[10] Jennings was still a groom of the royal chamber in 1556 when the king and queen asked the dean and chapter of Westminster to grant him a new lease of the Boarshead, where he was then dwelling.[11]

Shortly before his death in 1558 Jennings settled 8 messuages, 6 gardens, 40 acres of land, 40 of meadow and 40 of pasture in the city of Westminster, Tothill, and the parish of St Martin-in-the-Fields, giving George Kendall, husband of his daughter Joan, the profits and use for life. In his will he bequeathed the lands to George and Joan's son Henry Kendall and his issue, with remainders to their other children. His property included the White Hart and the Saracen's Head in Tothill, residences at Lambeth and in the leasehold Boarshead, and other leaseholds included Thames meadow and property in Tothill Street and St Margaret's churchyard. He also left his 'brickhills' to be sold: these were presumably brick kilns as he also bequeathed 20 loads of bricks to the restored abbot of Westminster for his building work.[12]

In 1580 Henry Kendall sold the lands in Westminster to Thomas Pierson, usher of Star Chamber, for £1,180, including the former Beaumont's lands, the parcels from Ebury, the White Hart and the Saracen's Head in Tothill; he also sold an inn called the Swan with Two Necks in Tothill Street, and the Unicorn or Cannocks House in King Street, both of which had been part of the estate of the fraternity of St Mary.[13] Pierson died in 1590, and his property passed to his daughters and their husbands, Susan and Henry Maynard and Mary and William Bowyer. In 1601 the Bowyers seem to have released to the Maynards their share in the Westminster property including 60 acres in St Margaret's and St Martin's.

1 Thames Embankment Act, 25 & 26 Vic. c. 93.
2 Acct based on *Survey of London*, XXXI, 196–208.
3 TNA, E 326/5868.
4 TNA, E 326/7173; Above, Secular Inns and Ests (Beaumont).
5 TNA, SC 12/12/6.
6 TNA, E 315/216, f. 133.
7 TNA, CP 25/2/61/475/7EDWVI/EASTER.

8 Guildhall MS 13057.
9 WAM 4823.
10 TNA, E 305/3/B44; E 318/40/2169; *Cal. Pat.* 1553–4, 505.
11 WAM 18056.
12 TNA, CP 25/2/74/630/5&6P&M/Mich.; PROB 11/42A, f. 86v.
13 *Cal. Pat.* 1547–8, 411–13; TNA, E 315/68, f. 137; C 54/1108.

Maynard, who was secretary to Sir William Cecil, Lord Burghley, and sheriff of Essex, was knighted in 1609,[1] and he sold 2 acres of Beaumont's lands near Charing Cross to Robert Cecil, earl of Salisbury, that year.[2] All Maynard's property in Westminster, described as 10 messuages, 10 gardens, 10 orchards, 6 acres of land, 6 of meadow, and 50 of pasture, had been settled in 1608 on Henry for life, and then on his eldest son William and his male heirs. Sir Henry died in 1610, holding with his wife Susan the inn called the White Hart in Tothill Street, the Lamb House, and four other houses in St Margaret's parish, and land, meadow, and pasture in St Margaret's and St Martin's, held by Elizabeth, Lady Knyvett, for life. The land included Brick close, Priors croft (later Pimplico), and Priors hope, marked on a plan of Ebury of 1614 as belonging to Sir Henry Maynard.[3]

Sir William Maynard received a baronetcy in 1611, an Irish barony in 1620, and an English barony (of Estaines Parva) in 1628.[4] In 1628 he let 3 acres in St Martin's Field, described as Swan Close, to William Ashton, and in 1640 sold the freehold to the earl of Northumberland for £200.[5] He had also built 20 houses in Tothill Street by 1634.[6] He died in 1640 holding the White Hart inn in Tothill Street with its buildings, barns, land and garden; the Saracens Head and six small tenements nearby; the Lamb House and the four other houses, one of them the site of Kitter's yard in Petty France in 1650, all in St Margaret's and valued at £3 a year; and lands and tenements in St Martin's valued at 40s. All his property was left to his wife Anne for life, then passed to his son William, Lord Maynard.[7] The latter was paying an annual quitrent to the dean and chapter of Westminster of 3s. 2d. for the Tothill Street tenements in 1649.[8]

Lord Maynard was impeached in 1647 but the prosecution was dropped in 1648.[9] In 1650 he leased the messuage, barn, stables and other buildings and garden and orchard in Kitter's Yard to Colonel William Herbert for 40 years,[10] but in 1653 sold nearly all his Westminster estate to Gervase Andrewes, citizen and goldsmith: an agreement between them allowed Maynard to redeem the lands, but he apparently did not do so. The property was described in detail and indicates the amount of building that had taken place in Tothill Street, White Hart Yard, Turnagain Lane, and Kitter's Yard. There was also a messuage and newly-built farm with 33 acres of meadow and pasture in the fields near Hyde Park and Stone Bridge (in the later Piccadilly) in St Martin-in-the-Fields, let to Ralph Gerrard. The property excepted from the sale was Priors Croft by the road from Eyebridge to Ebury.[11]

Andrewes died in 1654 leaving the farm and 33 acres to his widow Winifrid and her heirs in lieu of dower out of his other lands. The remaining property bought from Maynard was left to Winifrid as executor to pay legacies and an annuity of £24 a year.[12] Though contested by his son John Andrewes and a daughter Sarah, wife of John Hamond, the will was upheld. Before probate Winifred married Thomas Lee of the Middle Temple, a royalist who at the Restoration became Chester Herald. The Lees had difficulty with Gerrard over non-payment of his rent from 1657, and the lease expired. Gerrard was also accused of committing waste and defacing the bounds. He claimed that he had a lease for 33 years from 1639 with liberty to dig and take brick-earth, loam, sand and gravel. He also claimed that Andrewes had promised to renew the lease for 31 years on condition he enclosed a piece of ground on the farm with a brick wall and planted it as a garden or orchard, built two new rooms, repaired all buildings and enclosed the yard with a brick wall; he had spent £150 on this work, and there had been no buildings when he took the lease. He was prepared to pay the rent if they renewed the lease. The decision is not known, but Gerrard was still rated in St Martin's for 31 acres under 'Hyde Park corner to Knightsbridge' in 1661. He was dead by February 1662 and was succeeded in the rate books by John Emblin, brickmaker, rated in 1663 at 'Garratts Hall'; his brickmaking enterprise was said to be near Stonebridge and near Piccadilly from 1665 to 1673, occasionally described as 'Jarratts kiln'.[13]

Lee sold 3 acres to the Crown in 1669 for enclosure into St James's Park, at the north-east end of the modern Green Park, for £197.[14] In 1675 he conveyed the farm and 33 acres, still described as lately built, to Charles Boyle, Lord Clifford, son and heir of Richard Boyle, earl of Burlington, for £2,500, excluding from the sale the pasture enclosed into Green Park and 2 acres nearby in Brookshot on the south side of Piccadilly.[15] Shortly afterwards Clifford and John Berkeley, Lord Berkeley, jointly mortgaged the property,[16] and it apparently passed into the possession of Berkeley, who was rated for Brick close from the late 1670s. Lee died 1677 leaving his remaining 2 acres to his grandchild Deborah King.[17]

LEICESTER HOUSE

A small estate in St Martin-in-the-Fields was created by Robert Sidney, 2nd earl of Leicester, in the mid 17th

1 TNA, PROB 11/75, f. 86v.; Johnson, *Berkeley Sq.* 14; GEC, *Complete Peerage*, VIII. 599.

2 *Survey of London*, XXXIV. 339, 416.

3 TNA, C 142/319, no. 195; PROB 11/115, f. 312v.; *Ebury plan c.1663.*

4 GEC, *Complete Peerage*, VIII. 599.

5 *Survey of London*, XXXIV. 416; below, Leicester Ho.

6 Stone, *Crisis of Aristocracy*, 362.

7 TNA, C 142/615, no. 129.

8 *Acts and Ordinances of Interregnum*, II. 262–71.

9 GEC, *Complete Peerage*, VIII. 599.

10 TNA, C 107/185, bdl. 14 (deed 20 July 1651); *Cal. SP Dom.* 1655–6, 276.

11 TNA, C 54/3708, no. 18: acreage given as 330 in error.

12 TNA, PROB 11/246, f. 215v.

13 Johnson, *Berkeley Sq.* 17–20.

14 *Cal. Treas. Bks*, III. 197, 240, 313.

15 TNA, C 54/4429, no. 19.

16 WCA, Cal. deeds, 10/20.

17 Johnson, *Berkeley Sq.* 58; above, Berkeley.

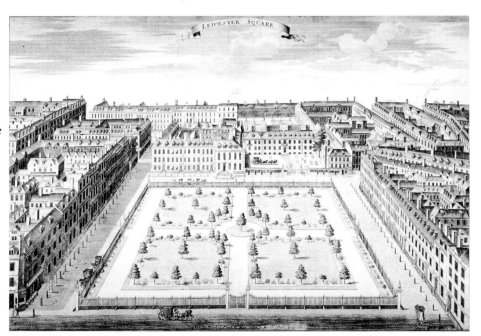

39. *Leicester House in the mid 18th century, facing south over former fields, by then formalized into Leicester Square; by then the whole area had been heavily built up with three- and four-storeyed town houses.*

century, from 3 acres formerly belonging to Westminster Abbey and 4 acres of Beaumont's lands.[1] Beaumont's 4 acres lay in two parcels in St Martin's Field, separated by the 3 acres of Westminster Abbey, and during the 16th century the Crown leased out the 3 acres together with an acre of the Beaumont's lands, accounted for under the bailiwick of Neat. In 1623 those 4 acres were included in the sale by the Crown of the freehold of Ebury and Neat to Lionel Cranfield, earl of Middlesex, who sold it all in 1626 to Hugh Audley.[2] Audley sold the 4 acres in 1630 to Lord Leicester for £160: the earl built Leicester House in the 1630s on the northern half, while the remainder became known as Leicester Fields.[3]

The inhabitants of St Martin's objected to building by the earl on land over which they had common rights, and the privy council arbitrated between the parties, setting limits for the wall of the house and gardens and designating a path across the field, part of which was to be turned into walks and planted with trees, with spaces left for the inhabitants to dry their clothes. These alterations were to be made at earl's expense, in addition to which he was to pay to the parish in perpetuity £3 a year in recompense of the Lammas common in the field to which the parishioners were entitled. The king granted Leicester licence to build in 1631.[4]

In 1648 the earl acquired the remaining 3 acres of the Beaumont's lands, which adjoined the east side of his house and land. The freehold had become part of the Maynard estate,[5] and the 3 acres, described as Swan Close in 1628, were sold by William, Lord Maynard, in

1640 to the 10th earl of Northumberland for £200, who sold them to his brother-in-law, Lord Leicester, in 1648.[6] In 1671 Lord Leicester received licence to build on Leicester Fields and the bowling green adjoining, with a pardon for building already started. Leicester Square was laid out south of Leicester House, which formed the north side; the 3 acres acquired in 1648 formed the site of the east side of Leicester Square and Bear, Green, and Castle streets to the east.[7]

On the death of the 2nd earl in 1677, his heir contested probate of the will against the executors and tried to upset the building leases granted by his father. The estate was held in Chancery until he confirmed the leases and paid certain sums: Leicester House was conveyed to the 3rd earl's trustees in 1681 and Leicester Field to the trustees to hold for the use of the tenants in 1682. The earl and his eldest son then resettled the estate in tail male.[8] The 3rd earl increased the revenue from the estate by letting the western part of Leicester House garden for building, and shops and a tavern were also built in front and to the east of the courtyard;[9] he died in 1698 succeeded by his only legitimate son, Robert (d. 1702), as 4th earl. On the marriage of his eldest son Philip in 1700, the 4th earl confirmed the entail of the London estate by settling it after his death on his son in tail male. Philip succeeded him as 5th earl but died without issue in 1705. Under the entail Leicester House and the rest of the estate passed to Philip's brother John, 6th earl. In 1735 the 6th earl purchased the major part of the former Military Ground, which lay on the north side of the Leicester estate, and died in 1737 bequeathing the

---

1 Above, Secular Inns and Ests (Beaumont). For Leicester Ho., Strand, above, Episcopal Inns (Exeter).
2 Above, Manorial (Manor of Eye).
3 *Survey of London*, XXXIV. 418.
4 *Acts of PC*, 1630–1, 394; *Cal. SP Dom.* 1629–31, 453.

5 Above, Jennings.
6 *Survey of London*, XXXIV. 416, 418.
7 Ibid., 424; TNA, C 66/3127, no. 25; *Cal. SP Dom.* 1670 (& Add. 1660–70), 154; 1671, 63.
8 *Survey of London*, XXXIV. 418–19.   9 Ibid., 446, 454.

Military Ground to his younger brother Jocelyn, who succeeded him as 7th earl. Jocelyn died in 1743 leaving only an illegitimate daughter, Ann Sidney. In default of legitimate male heirs, the estate devolved on the only surviving legitimate descendants of the 4th earl, Mary, wife of Sir Brownlow Sherard, and Elizabeth, wife of William Perry, who took possession in 1743 as joint tenants each holding a moiety.

In 1744 Lady Sherard sold her moiety of Leicester House to her sister, but the joint tenancy of the rest of the estate continued until 1789. Lady Sherard died in 1758, leaving her share to Anne Howard, widow of Sir William Yonge, Bt, for life, with remainder to their son Sir George Yonge, Bt and MP. Sir George sold his remainder to his sister's father-in-law James Stuart Tulk (d. 1775). Elizabeth Perry died in 1783 leaving her estates heavily mortgaged, and by her will left her estate in Middlesex to her executors to sell to pay her debts. Following a petition in Chancery, a certificate of partition of the estate, excluding Leicester House, was made with the holders of the other moiety in 1788, and confirmed in 1789, making it possible to sell Perry's estate; it was sold in 29 lots to 16 different purchasers or groups of purchasers. The Tulk share continued in the family but was gradually subdivided amongst heirs into about a dozen separate holdings by the mid 19th century.[1]

Leicester House

Leicester House stood at the northern end of the Leicester estate facing down the southerly slope which had an open aspect stretching as far to the royal mews; it was mainly built between 1631 and 1635, though work continued for some time afterwards. Lord Leicester claimed the house cost him £8,000 in building and furnishing it, and he sent back many items for it from Paris where he was ambassador 1636–41.[2] In 1648 Leicester House included outbuildings, gardens, and orchards,[3] and in 1675 the house was rated for 55 hearths.[4] Inventories of the house and contents exist for the 1640s and 1677 listing the goods, furniture and pictures by room, which give an idea of the size and style of the house, and the style of life conducted within it, but do not allow for a plan of the interior; in addition to the main part of the house there were rooms described as being in the new buildings.[5]

The 2nd earl retired to Penshurst in the 1640s, and rarely visited the house thereafter. It was occasionally let in the 1660s and 70s, notably to the king's aunt, Queen Elizabeth of Bohemia, who died there in 1662, to the French ambassador 1668–70, and to Ralph Montagu, later 1st earl and 1st duke of Montagu, 1674–6. Philip, 3rd earl of Leicester, regularly used the house, and his

successor repaired and refurnished it 1698–1700, but subsequent earls apparently did not use the house much. In 1718 it was let to George, Prince of Wales (later George II), when he and his family were turned out of St James's Palace after a quarrel with his father, George I. He also occupied the neighbouring Savile House, linked by a covered passage during his occupancy, and left on becoming king in 1727. In 1742 the house was let to George II's son, Frederick, prince of Wales, who similarly moved there after a quarrel with his father, occupying the house from 1743 until his death in 1751. His widow continued there until 1764 and continued to pay rent and rates for it until 1767. It was then let to Simon, Earl Harcourt, until 1774, and then to Ashton Lever, a naturalist whose collections were on display to the public there until 1788. The house was sold by Elizabeth Perry's executors in 1789 and demolished c.1791–2. Views of the house made in the 18th century suggest that, up to the time the house was demolished, the exterior remained very plain despite the lavish interiors created for the prince of Wales and described in 18th-century inventories, and some remodeling of the north façade at that date. The house was of brick, two storeys above a semi-basement, and seems to have retained its somewhat irregular late 17th-century ten-bayed façade with projecting wing, enclosing the west side of a walled forecourt; if there was an east wing it must have gone c.1710. The small shops built in the 17th century lay against the forecourt wall until c.1794, and stables to the north-east followed the boundary of the Leicester and Salisbury estates.[6]

NORTHUMBERLAND HOUSE

Northumberland House, formerly known as Northampton House then Suffolk House, stood at Charing Cross until 1874, and was built in the early 17th century on parts of two estates, the Rose Inn and Ronceval Hospital.[7]

The Rose Inn Estate

On the east side of the hospital of St Mary Ronceval lay a freehold property, which in 1559 was a private inn called the Rose, owned and occupied by John Best. Although no record of his acquisition of the inn has been found, Best was probably living there by 1548 when he served William Morant, gentleman of the king's cellar, and was known to dwell at Charing Cross.[8] By 1552 Best was also leasing several parcels of former Westminster Abbey land in St Martin's and St Margaret's from the Crown,[9] and in 1554 received from the Crown the grant of the freehold of an inn called the Swan and 4 cottages on the north side of the highway near Charing Cross, which had been purchased by Henry VIII.[10]

1 Ibid., 420.
2 Ibid., 441–2.　　　　3 BL, Add. MS. 32683, f. 39.
4 Survey of London, XXXIV. 441n.
5 Ibid., 443; BL, Add. MS. 32683, ff. 16–36, 101.

6 *Survey of London*, XXXIV. 444–52.
7 Above, Other Eccles. Ests (Hosp. of St Mary Ronceval).
8 TNA, PROB 11/32, f. 99 (PCC 13 Populwell).
9 TNA, E 315/223, f. 294v.　　　10 *Cal. Pat.* 1553–4, 151.

40. *Northumberland House and Charing Cross, looking south from St Martin's Lane across Trafalgar Square before Northumberland House was demolished in 1874 to make way for Northumberland Avenue. Northumberland House was one of the few great houses to be built in one campaign; its original, elaborately decorated gateway had survived several remodellings of the courtyard mansion built c.1610.*

By the time of his death in 1559, Best had evidently done a great deal of building at the Rose. In that year he bequeathed to Thomasine his wife for life as her dwelling his new building over the gate of the Rose, consisting of 2 great lodgings with the garret over them, the new kitchen, and the old house between the two; the hangings of red and blue in the two lodgings were to remain with the property. She also received the chamber over the parlour adjoining the new lodging with a place of easement for life, paying 40s. to the tenant of the Rose, and was to receive £10 a year from profits of the Rose. The Rose itself was devised to Best's brother Robert and his heirs.[1]

Robert Best received licences from the Crown to sell lands in St Martin's in 1562,[2] and in 1564 to sell the Swan and other lands to Thomas Huycke, LL.D, master in Chancery.[3] The Rose, which was not held of the Crown, was probably sold to Huycke at about the same time, and a fine for part of Best's property, described as a messuage and 2 acres, was dated 1571.[4] In 1573 Huycke sold to William Cooke, clerk in the court of Wards and Liveries and brother-in-law of Lord Burghley, the messuage or inn called the Rose together with 2 curtilages and its buildings, barns, and stables, and also another messuage next to the Rose, the way or entry leading from the Rose's barn and stables into two gardens lying together towards the Thames, and those two gardens and a pond adjoining them, all lying on the south side of highway leading to Charing Cross. Later that year Cooke brought an action against George Bell of

London, ironmonger, who as a kinsman had residual rights in the property under John Best's will,[5] and in 1575 Bell released to Cooke all his rights in 2 messuages, 2 curtilages, 2 gardens, an orchard and 1 acre of land in St Martin's.[6]

Cooke died in 1589 bequeathing to his wife Frances for life his mansion house and garden where he dwelt in St Martin's, which was to go to his eldest son William after her death.[7] Mrs Frances Cooke and her son Sir William were rated from 1599 to 1604 for adjoining properties near Charing Cross, but their names were replaced by that of Henry Howard, 1st earl of Northampton, who in 1605 bought the Cookes' property described as 2 messuages, a cottage, 3 curtilages, 2 gardens, and 2 acres in St Martin's.[8]

Northampton House

Between 1606 and 1613 Northampton acquired various properties adjoining the Rose, and built a new house there c.1608.[9] In 1606 he obtained a 60-year Crown lease of half the ditch or stream which ran between the ground of the Rose on the north and east and the Crown's land called Scotland into the Thames, and abutted partly on ground belonging to the Christopher, which was held for life by Anne, widow of Humphrey Cooke,[10] and was the inheritance of Michael Apsley; in 1611 he was granted it in perpetuity.[11] In 1608–9 he bought from Robert Reed 3 messuages and 2 gardens out of the Ronceval property, which probably formed about the western third of the site of Northampton House and garden.[12]

1 TNA, C 3/11/76.
2 *Cal. Pat.* 1560–3, 381, 419.
3 Ibid. 1563–6, 139 (no. 614).
4 TNA, CP 25/2/171/13&14ELIZ/MICH.
5 TNA, C 2/Eliz/C15/23.
6 TNA, CP 25/2/171/17ELIZ/HIL.

7 TNA, PROB 11/74, f. 362v.
8 *Survey of London*, XVIII.10.
9 Below.
10 No relation of Wm Cooke.   11 TNA, LR 1/55, f. 123.
12 *Survey of London*, XVIII. 10; above, Other Eccles. Ests (Hosp. of St Mary Ronceval).

Northampton bought most of the rest of the Ronceval estate from Sir Robert Brett in 1613, and he bought ground at the southern end of Hartshorn Lane, on the east side of his house, from Michael Apsley, which he had formerly held for a term of years: much of the foundation of his banqueting house and garden walls stood on Apsley's land.[1] Most of the ground purchased, however, was bequeathed by the earl in 1614 to Trinity Hospital, Greenwich.[2]

At his death in 1614, Northampton held Northampton House and its gardens, the mansion house on the Ronceval estate and its wharf and various other houses and ground, houses formerly belonging to Apsley's property, the messuage of Anne Cooke adjoining the east side of Northampton House, the two moieties of the water ditch or stream 159 ft long bounding his property with a part of Scotland by the ditch, all enclosed with a wall into his garden. Northampton House, valued at £10, was held by unknown service (reflecting the freehold status of the Rose); the remaining property was held of the king in socage.[3] Ownership of Northampton House and gardens passed to Northampton's nephew Thomas Howard, 1st earl of Suffolk, and the house became known as Suffolk House. He died there in 1626, succeeded by his son Theophilus, 2nd earl (d. 1640), and grandson James, 3rd earl. In 1642 Suffolk House passed to Algernon Percy, 10th earl of Northumberland, on his marriage to Lady Elizabeth Howard, daughter of the 2nd earl of Suffolk, on payment of £15,000 to the Howards. Thereafter the house was usually called Northumberland House.[4]

Northumberland House

Earl Algernon died in 1668, and Josceline, the 11th earl, in 1670, leaving as heir his 3-year old daughter Elizabeth Percy. After her death in 1722, her property passed to her 3rd husband, Charles Seymour, 6th duke of Somerset, to whom she was married in 1682. In 1748 the house was inherited by his son, Algernon Seymour, the 7th duke, who was created earl of Northumberland in 1749 and died a year later. The earldom passed to his son-in-law, Sir Hugh Smithson, who took the surname Percy and was created duke of Northumberland in 1766.[5] Additions were made to the property with the purchase of no. 1 Whitehall, adjoining the house on the west in 1742–3, to prevent subsidence of the turret there, and nine houses in Charing Cross Street opposite the house c.1750 to build stables. At about the same time the duke acquired a Crown lease of part of Scotland Yard adjoining the river, to open the view and extend the gardens to the riverside. The 3rd duke obtained the freehold of the latter in 1827, in exchange for the stables on the north side of the road, required for the formation of Trafalgar Square and its environs. He also purchased property on the east side of the house in 1821 from Trinity Hospital Greenwich.[6]

The estate passed with the dukedom of Northumberland until in 1874 the Metropolitan Board of Works bought the whole of the duke's property at Charing Cross for the formation of Northumberland Avenue, and the house was demolished.[7]

The House

Building of Northampton House began between 1606 and 1612. It was a rare example of a house along the riverside built *de novo* during the 17th century, although it did not have access to the river until much later. A courtyard house of brick with stone dressings and with corner towers, instead of a gatehouse and flanking ranges or tenements to the Strand, it was also unique among the Strand houses in having a symmetrical street front, 162 feet long, with an central entrance through an elaborate frontispiece in Anglo-Flemish style, which was apparently thought so remarkable that it survived all later alterations. It was perhaps the work of Bernard Janssen who was said by Vertue to have been the surveyor, and its detail resembled that at Audley End (Essex) where the earl of Northampton was also involved.[8] The south range was lower but had a basement because of the fall of site. The great hall partly filled it and extended into the eastern range, which like the western one had a very large oriel window on the top floor at the south end.[9] After the property had changed hands and been renamed Northumberland House, the southern part was extensively altered in 1649–52 under the supervision of the surveyor Edward Carter,[10] and the south range was given new state rooms and a south staircase by John Webb c.1655–9.[11] In 1749–52 Daniel Garrett made the street front classical and added south wings of two storeys over a basement, which contained state rooms including a ballroom and gallery, the latter completed by James Paine in 1757.[12] Robert Adam redecorated the state rooms in 1770–5.[13] A major fire in 1789 destroyed the upper storeys of the north range, which was rebuilt with the towers reduced in height.[14] Thomas Cundy refronted the south range in 1818–24, and, after a fire, Salvin created another ballroom in 1869. Fragments from the building survive in various

1 TNA, C 78/226, no. 6.
2 *Survey of London*, XVIII. 10–11, 23; below, Trinity Hosp.
3 TNA, C 142/384, no. 161.
4 *Survey of London*, XVIII. 11.
5 Ibid., 13–15.
6 Ibid., 13–16; below, Trinity Hosp.
7 *Survey of London*, XVIII. 20.
8 Colvin, *British Architects*, 569.
9 *Survey of London*, XVIII. 17, pl. 2a (drawing by Hollar), fig.

3 (plan by Rob. Smythson).
10 J. Wood, 'The architectural patronage of the 10th Earl of Northumberland' in *English Architecture Public and Private: essays in honour of Kerry Downes*, ed. J. Bold and E. Chaney (1993), 58–74.
11 Colvin, *British Architects*, 1097.
12 Ibid., 412, 769.
13 Ibid., 49.
14 *Survey of London*, XVIII. 16–18.

locations.[1] Hawksmoor and Samuel Ware may also been involved with work on the house.[2]

SALISBURY ESTATE

Sir Robert Cecil, created earl of Salisbury in 1605, built a house on the south side of the Strand, treated under the bishop of Carlisle's inn, and a commercial venture nearby called Britain's Burse on part of the bishop of Durham's inn.[3]

In 1609 Salisbury bought land on the east side of St Martin's Lane from the 3rd earl of Bedford in fee farm, consisting of two garden plots at the north end of the lane near Longacre, and built a range of stables there. His accounts suggest a sizeable building, which had access into the common garden to water horses in the Longacre.[4] The property seems to have extended southwards down St Martin's Lane from the junction with the later Long Acre street to just short of New Street; the stables were later replaced with houses and yards.[5]

Also in 1609 Salisbury bought about 2½ acres on the west side of St Martin's Lane in St Martin's field, from Sir Henry Maynard, which had formerly been part of Beaumont's lands; it lay between the later Cecil Court on the north and Hemmings Row on the south.[6] At about the same time Salisbury also bought two adjoining closes totalling nearly 7 acres, which all became known as Swan Close. The purchases gave Lord Salisbury the whole of the west side of St Martin's Lane from the north end by the parish boundary at the later Newport Street, south to St Martin's new burial ground. In 1613 the 2nd earl leased land at the northern end of the lane to John Waller who had carried out building along the lane by the 1650s.[7] Most of this property was owned by the Salisbury Settled Estates in 1966.[8]

TRINITY HOSPITAL, GREENWICH

Henry Howard, earl of Northampton, founded a hospital at Greenwich for poor men, and by his will of 1614 ordered that after obtaining incorporation his heir, Thomas Howard, earl of Arundel, was to endow the hospital with lands in Kent, and messuages and gardens in St Martin-in-the-Fields recently bought from Sir Robert Brett (the Ronceval estate), Michael Apsley, and Sir Edward Montague (the Christopher).[9] He also directed that the Mercers' Company should nominate the inmates, choosing 12 from Greenwich and 8 from Shotesham (Norf.), his birthplace.[10] In 1615 James I by letters patent granted incorporation of the hospital to house a warden and 20 poor men,[11] and Lord Arundel conveyed the property to the hospital for its support.[12]

Although the Mercers' Company may have played a more active role in granting leases in the 17th century,[13] by 1821 the company superintended the management of the property and regulated allowances to the almspeople and officers, but no part of the income ever passed through their hands. All transactions were in the corporate name of the hospital, leases were under the seal of the warden, and rents were received and disbursements made by the warden.[14]

In 1821 an Act empowered the warden and poor of the hospital to sell property in St Martin's to Sir Henry Percy, 3rd duke of Northumberland.[15] The property sold was intermixed with property of the duke, who offered £16,038 for it and also met the expenses of the Act and conveyance.[16] In 1834 the hospital's remaining property at Charing Cross consisted of five houses at nos 4–8 Charing Cross, and two commercial premises and five houses in Trinity Place.[17] In 1871, under an Order of the Charity Commission, the hospital's property at the southern end of Trinity Place, which formed part of the sites of the house of Charles Stanhope, 7th earl of Harrington, and a bank, were sold to Lord Harrington for £7,600. The remainder of the property at Charing Cross, consisting of nos 4–8 Charing Cross and nos 1–5 Trinity Place, was acquired under compulsory powers by the Metropolitan Board of Works for street improvements (Northumberland Avenue) in 1875, for £51,622.[18]

The hospital's property at Charing Cross originally lay either side of Northumberland House. On the west side lay Angel Court, later Trinity Place, formerly part of the hospital of St Mary Ronceval. It included the residence of Sir Robert Brett (d. 1620), who he continued to occupy under lease after selling the property to Lord Northampton, succeeded by his widow Anne, who married Francis Cottington, later Baron Cottington, in 1623. Cottington occupied the house until his death in 1634. Later occupants included the earl of Cleveland 1635–8, and Lord William Hamilton, earl of Lanark, 1640–1. The lease passed to Sir Roger Palmer by the 1640s, and to Palmer's brother Sir James in 1657. By 1648 Angel Court, occupied by 12 tenants, had been built on part of the property, and the great house was let to Nathaniel Impes by 1658. The lease passed to Sir James's son Philip, who transferred it to his brother Roger, earl of Castlemaine and husband of the king's mistress Barbara Villiers; in 1666–7 Castlemaine petitioned for the king's help in obtaining renewal of the lease from the Mercers' Company. Houses on the site were rebuilt by the lessee in the early 18th century.[19]

1 Pevsner *London 6: Westm.* 356–7.
2 Colvin, *British Architects*, 499, 1090.
3 Above, Episcopal Inns (Carlisle; Durham).
4 *Survey of London*, XXXVI. 267.
5 Ibid., XX. 121–2.
6 Ibid., XXXIV. 339, 416; above, Jennings.
7 *Survey of London*, XXXIV. 343–4; XX. 116.
8 Ibid., XXXIV. 341.   9 Above, Northumberland Ho.
10 TNA, PROB 11/123 (PCC 55 Lawe), image 628/561.
11 *Endowed Chars London*, II. 248.
12 Ibid. 250, 254.
13 *Survey of London*, XVIII. 5.
14 *Endowed Chars London*, II. 249.
15 2 Geo. IV [Private Act c. 39].
16 *Endowed Chars London*, II. 256.   17 Ibid. 257.
18 Ibid. 309.   19 *Survey of London*, XVIII. 5.

RELIGIOUS HISTORY

THIS CHAPTER is devoted to the religious life of the inhabitants of Westminster and the institutions and buildings which served it. It excludes, however, the institutional history of the abbey of Westminster and of the collegiate church which succeeded it, already covered in *VCH London* I,[1] and the history of the abbey buildings and the precinct, reserved for treatment in a later volume on settlement and growth. Instead, it restricts itself to discussion of the abbey's achievement of a national role and its impact upon the religious life of Westminster as a whole, primarily through its parish church, St Margaret's. It also considers the other parish churches established within the area covered by the modern city, a few going back to medieval times but most dating from the later 17th century and later. There is also discussion of the Roman Catholic and protestant churches which developed after the Reformation and of a distinctive feature of Westminster's religious life, the royal chapels. Like the abbey, the royal chapels will only be considered in relation to the wider religious life of Westminster; full treatment of their institutional life and buildings is reserved for a later volume on royal palaces. The chapter concludes with a section on non-Christian faiths.

The parish church accounts begin with the two most important medieval churches, St Margaret's and St Martin's. The rest of the medieval and 18th-century parish churches follow in alphabetical order. District chapelries and parishes created in the 19th century are placed under the civil parishes from which they emerged, followed by chapels of ease and proprietary chapels. Roman Catholicism is also arranged under embassy chapels, the cathedral and parish churches; and Protestant Nonconformity by denomination, most arranged alphabetically with groupings of other congregations and missions at the end.

INTRODUCTION

This introduction focuses upon the achievement of the abbey's national role and the privileged ecclesiastical jurisdiction which accompanied it and gave the abbot exclusive control under the pope of the abbey and its parish. It examines the emergence of the medieval parochial system in the area covered by the modern city and its transformation in the 16th century with the Reformation and the creation of the great Palace of Whitehall.

THE IMPACT OF THE ABBEY

Westminster Abbey was the focus of the settlement which developed near its walls and remained fundamental to that settlement's history throughout the Middle Ages. The abbey's foundation can with reasonable certainty be attributed to Dunstan, probably in 959 when he was bishop of London. Though the monk Sulcard, historian of the abbey in the late 11th century, claimed that a church was founded on Thorney island in the early 7th century and refounded in the 8th by Offa king of Essex, there is little to support this apart from some 8th and 9th century finds on the site.[2] The most informative source for Dunstan's foundation is the so-called *Telligraphus* (charter) of Æthelred II, probably an early 12th-century forgery but likely to incorporate authentic traditions. This tells us that the bishop paid King Edgar 120 *mancuses* of gold for the church and received permission to establish a small Benedictine monastery, probably for 12 monks. Dunstan also purchased land from private individuals to endow the church, to the amount of £200; the king sold him 5 hides at Westminster from the royal demesne.[3] Little is known of the monastery from the death of Edgar in 975 until the accession of Edward the Confessor in 1042, apart from the brief burial there of King Harold 'Harefoot' in 1040. This, however, was the period when the abbey received an endowment which by 1042 was valued at *c*.£80 a year, and which included Westminster, valued at £12. Although it was not thus outstandingly rich, it was certainly not the poor and insignificant foundation presented by King Edward's biographer. When Edward

1 Published in 1909, 433–57; updated in *Religious Hos of London and Middx*, ed. C.M. Barron and M. Davies (2007), 51–70.

2 Above, Gen. Intro.: Settlement.
3 Harvey, *Westm. Abbey Ests*, 341–2, 346, 352–4, 358–9; Robinson, *Gilbert Crispin*, 167–8.

41. *An aerial view of Westminster Abbey from the north-east, with the cloisters, school, and other buildings beyond, and the parish church of St Margaret, Westminster, beside it on the north side.*

decided to make it his place of burial, he rebuilt the church and greatly enhanced its endowment, making it one of the richest monasteries in the kingdom.[1]

THE CULT OF EDWARD THE CONFESSOR

Although a Life of King Edward was written and a few miracles noted shortly after his death in 1066, his cult and the growth of his shrine as a place of pilgrimage were slow to develop.[2] Interest in him quickly declined, even among the monks, none of whom 15 years after his death was sure which was his tomb. In 1102, with the renewal of interest in things English, Edward's grave was opened, possibly to confirm its location with a view to creating a shrine. The body was found uncorrupted. In 1118, Henry I's first wife, Edith/Matilda, a princess of the ancient English royal house and Edward's great-great niece, was buried next to the king.

A crucial role in the promotion of Edward's cult was played by Osbert of Clare, monk and perhaps prior of Westminster *c.*1120 and prior again in the 1130s. Osbert was leader of a faction anxious to defend the abbey's rights and privileges, which they believed were diminishing under Abbot Herbert (1121–36). They resorted to fabrication, both of charters to support the abbey's rights and of history to enhance its standing. The

development of Edward's reputation for sanctity was an important part of this activity. The king's canonization would give the charters attributed to him authority, and would generate income through pilgrimage to his tomb. Osbert quarrelled with Herbert and was banished from the monastery, but on his return in 1134 as prior campaigned in earnest for Edward's canonization. He preached on Edward's anniversary, and encouraged the development of miracles among men and women of standing. By 1138 he had produced a new Life of St Edward incorporating all the miracles he could find, and had composed Edward's three charters for the abbey.

Although they were backed by King Stephen, Osbert's attempts to secure Edward's formal canonization by the pope did not succeed. The cult declined again and nothing further was done until 1160, when the newly installed abbot, Laurence, obtained the support of the King Henry II and the English bishops for a renewed petition to the pope. In 1161 Pope Alexander III authorised canonization. Edward's remains were translated to a new shrine in the presence of the Henry II in 1163, and a new and definitive Life of the king was written by Aildred of Rievaulx. Edward's cult never gained a large popular following, but it continued to receive royal support, above all under Henry III (1216–72). In 1245 Henry

---

1 Harvey, *Westm. Abbey Ests*, 20–4.
2 Following account based on F. Barlow, *Edward the Confessor* (1989 edn), 258–84.

initiated an opulent and ambitious new building campaign, in which he was to invest heavily for the rest of his reign, and which culminated in 1269 in the translation of the Confessor's remains to a new and splendid shrine behind the high altar. The cult thus lay at the heart of the abbey's newly-achieved role as a favoured royal church, a role which ultimately affected all aspects of religious life in Westminster.[1]

THE ABBEY'S PARISH AND LIBERTY

Besides acting, in however limited a way, as the focus of cult, the abbey had pastoral responsibilities. From earliest times, there were presumably a number of households dotted around the manor of Westminster, farming the land, some of whom would have worshipped in the pre-conquest minster and initially in the early abbey church. By the early 12th century, however, the growth of a lay community around the abbey and palace made a separate parish church desirable. That the local population still had a degree of involvement with the abbey as late as the earlier 13th century is indicated by burial within the abbatial church and by pious donations of property to the community's new Lady chapel; such involvement declined by the mid 13th century as royal patronage increased. The abbey's royal role, as marked out by Henry III and his successors, excluded humbler local residents, who by the late 15th century were prominent in rebuilding the parish church of St Margaret.[2]

The abbey's parishioners are recorded as having worshipped on the north side of the abbey's nave,[3] until 1121x36 when a church dedicated to St Margaret of Antioch stood in the abbatial cemetery.[4] It was presumably built by the monks, to accommodate the parishioners whom they wished to remove from the abbey church. Almost certainly, it was quite new when it entered the record, although a 14th-century tradition attributed the foundation of a church of St Margaret to King Edward the Confessor.[5] Worship in the abbey probably continued until the early 12th century; indeed the abbey was still thought of as the mother church in the 1190s, when St Margaret's was described as a chapel, even though by then it had given its name to the parish.[6]

As early as 1170, the abbey claimed exemption for its parish of St Margaret's from diocesan synodal dues payable to the archdeacon and demanded by the bishop.[7] In 1189 the monks obtained a papal bull exempting the church of St Margaret from having any archbishop or bishop saying mass or holding a synod there, probably a response to claims made by the bishop.[8] The dispute between the abbey and the diocese

42. *The shrine of St Edward the Confessor, king of England 1042–66, in Westminster Abbey.*

continued until the definitive decision made in the abbey's favour by the papal judges delegate in 1222. Thereafter the abbey precinct and its parish formed a privileged ecclesiastical liberty; cure of souls and all other spiritual authority was vested in the abbot, who was answerable only to the pope.[9] The former diocesan, the bishop of London, was to have no jurisdiction over the inhabitants of the liberty, whether clerical or lay; the abbot and monks could call upon any bishop they wished for crucial ritual and pastoral activities such as consecrating the abbot, dedicating churches, chapels and altars, ordaining monks and secular clergy, confirming children and blessing the holy oils.

Apart from the abbey precinct, the liberty was confined to St Margaret's parish, with its church, chapels and other dependencies.[10] Within this area from time to time the abbot had problems exercising his extensive jurisdiction. In 1342 his right of visitation of the hospital of St James was challenged by royal officials,[11] and in 1394 the college of the chapel of St Stephen in the Palace

1 P. Binski, *Westminster Abbey and the Plantagenets* (1995), esp. 10–89.

2 Rosser, *Medieval Westm.* 47n, 256–60, 263.

3 Ibid., 251 *n.*2.

4 BL, Harl. Ch. 84.F.46.

5 H.F. Westlake, *St Margt's Westm.* (1914), 3–4; Rosser, *Medieval Westm.* 251n.: St Margt was a Saxon cult.

6 *Eng. Episcopal Acta XII: Exeter 1186–1257*, ed. F. Barlow (1996), 196; *Westm. Charters*, 106, 163.

7 *Letters and Charters of Gilbert Foliot*, ed. Morey & Brooke, 302–3.   8 *Westm. Charters*, 87.

9 *Acta Stephani Langton* (Cant. and York Soc. L), 69–73.

10 Above, Gen. Intro., Boundaries & Local Govt (Parishes).

11 *Cal. Pat.* 1340–3, 456–7.

of Westminster successfully obtained exemption from the abbot's jurisdiction for the members of the college and their chapel, precinct and houses (Canon Row).[1] Nevertheless, the abbey and its parochial clergy clearly dominated the vill of Westminster, within which there were only four other churches, two of which were small and one only fleeting.

As a parish church presumably founded by the monks and within their precinct and manor, St Margaret's and its tithes belonged to the abbey before formal appropriation was necessary. The tithes within the vill of Westminster had belonged to the abbey before the creation of the parish church, and had been assigned, as was usual with monastic tithes, to the office of the almoner before 1086.[2] When the church was instituted, the almoner continued to receive the tithes, becoming *de facto* rector of St Margaret's.[3]

Royal involvement in the churches of Westminster extended beyond the abbey and in particular to the parish church. Henry III named his eldest daughter, born in 1240, Margaret, presumably after Edward the Confessor's great-niece Margaret of Scotland, soon to become a saint herself. Although the parish church was named after a different Margaret, the virgin martyr of Antioch, the latter may have been regarded as a namesake, at least before Margaret of Scotland's canonization. At all events, Henry gave vestments to St Margaret's church in 1252.[4] He also established a chaplain for his daughter, with a salary of 60s. in a chapel dedicated to St Margaret in 1241.[5] The location of this church is something of a mystery. It seems odd to refer to the parish church in this way at this late date; it is possible therefore that there was a chapel dedicated to St Margaret in the old abbey church, then still standing, or that the chapel in question was that which lay next to the church of Holy Innocents.[6] In 1268 the sum was paid to a chaplain celebrating in St Margaret's church, but earlier that year the king had granted the chapel of St Margaret to the Pied Friars, so the chaplaincy may have been moved.[7] By 1268 Henry had also appointed a chaplain to celebrate commemorative masses for his daughter Katherine (d. 1257) at a hermitage at Charing.[8]

THE MEDIEVAL PARISHES

Besides the abbey's church of St Margaret, there were four other medieval parish churches in the area which was to become Westminster: St Martin-in-the-Fields, St Mary of Strand, St Clement Danes and Holy Innocents. They were all concentrated in the east, in or near the Anglo-Saxon *wic*. St Martin's lay at Charing by the bend of the river, the others along the Strand. The earliest church in the area was probably St Martin's which perhaps originated on a cemetery in the conversion period and later served the *wic*. While St Martin's is the only church with firm archaeological evidence that it lay on an early and important ecclesiastical site, the possibility that at least one of the other churches may also have had its origins in the *wic* cannot be discounted. In particular, St Mary of Strand may have been associated with land granted to the bishop of Worcester by the Mercian king Burghred in 857. That land, which had belonged to Ceolmund, the royal reeve or *wic gerefa*, lay *in vico Lundonie* not far from the City's west gates (Newgate and Ludgate), almost certainly in the very heart of the *wic*. In the 880s Bishop Wærferth of Worcester seems to have played an important role in the establishment of the walled city as the main settlement; although he then received a new estate at Queenhithe, it is possible that he retained an interest in the earlier site on the Strand. His church of St Mary of London, in existence by 1100, is perhaps to be identified with St Mary of Strand.[9]

St Clement Danes, like St Martin, may also have been associated with a burial ground, but in this case one which had probably developed only well after the abandonment of the *wic*.[10] In fact, none of the Strand churches appears in the record until the 11th or 12th century, when they were in the patronage of important magnates and communities established in the area, including the abbot of Abingdon, the earl of Leicester, the bishop of Worcester, and the Templars. By the earlier 12th century, they seem to have been organised by the bishop of London as a deanery, under the parish priest of St Martin's, clearly the most important church.[11]

The abbey, however, retained an interest in the churches which had been built on its estate which in the 10th and 11th centuries may still have extended along Fleet Street. By the late 12th century, already in a jurisdictional dispute with the bishop, it was evidently

1 *Cal. Pat.* 1391–6, 553; *Cal. Papal Reg.* IV. 462; BL, Cotton Faust. A. III, ff. 293–314.

2 *Westm. Charters*, 109; G. Constable, *Monastic Tithes: from their Origins to the Twelfth Century* (1964), 201, 207, 225.

3 Below, Par. Chs, St Margt.

4 *Cal. Lib. R.* 1251–60, 40.

5 *Cal. Pat.* 1232–47, 252.

6 Rosser, *Medieval Westm.*, 251 n.2; below, Par. Churches: Holy Innocents.

7 *Cal. Lib. R.* 1267–72, 45.   8 Below, Royal Chapels.

9 Sawyer, *A.-S. Charters*, nos 208, 346, 1628; M. Biddle, 'A City in Transition', in *Atlas of Hist. Towns* III: *City of London*, (1989), 29; below, St Mary le Strand.

10 Above, Gen. Intro. Boundaries, Parishes; below, St Clement Danes.

11 *Book of the Foundation of St Bartholomew's Church in London*, ed. N. Moore, Early Eng. Text Soc. 163 (1923), 47; below, St Martin.

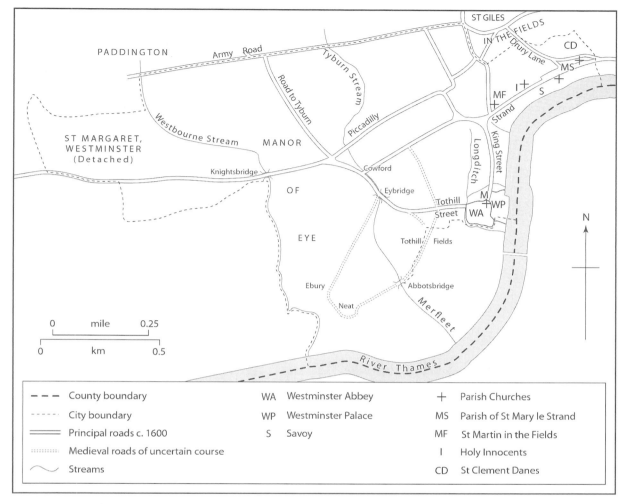

43. *Medieval Parish Churches of Westminster.*

exploiting its rights to the full. One interesting expression of this was Bishop Gilbert Foliot's confirmation of pensions and other financial rights in some 20 churches in the City and diocese of London. Those churches included St Martin-in-the-Fields and St Clement Danes and the Fleet Street churches of St Dunstan-in-the-West and St Bride, St Martin's pension of 20s. being the largest, again a mark of its superior income and status. The origins of these dues are likely to have been complex and various. Those payable from the churches in the Strand and Fleet Street may have been in recognition of the abbey's continuing lordship of the area. Significantly, no due was payable from the church of St

Mary of Strand, which by the 12th century lay within the liberty of the honor of Leicester.[1]

One of the Strand churches, probably that latest in origin and with the smallest parish, failed to survive. Holy Innocents has been mistakenly confused with St Mary of Strand, but its separate existence is beyond doubt. In the 13th century, its parish fell victim to the abbey's determined exploitation and enlargement of its rights, and the church, granted to the Pied Friars, disappeared when they gave up the house.[2] Thereafter, the parish arrangements of the vills of Eye and Westminster appear to have remained fairly stable until the 1530s.

THE 16TH AND 17TH CENTURIES

The Reformation and the religious changes of the mid 16th century made fundamental alterations to Westminster in a number of ways: to the nature and role of

Westminster Abbey, to the religious and cultural life of the parishes, to the size of some parishes, and to religious organization in Westminster. The presence of the court

---

1 Above; Gen. Intro.: Boundaries, Duchy of Lancaster; Parishes; Landownership: Manorial Estates, Soke of Leicester.

2 Above, Gen. Intro.: Boundaries, Parishes; Landownership:

Estates of Medieval Origin, Other Eccles. Estates (Pied Friars); below, Holy Innocents.

and government also had fundamental influences on religious life in Westminster at a time of radical religious change imposed by the State. At parish level religious change of the 16th century was experienced slightly differently in St Margaret's from St Martin's, two parishes whose history, inhabitants and outlook were distinctly different, but all the parishes in Westminster were affected in a wider way by the royal presence.[1]

The first significant effect was not, however, the result of religious change nor of the dissolution of the monasteries, but of Henry VIII's creation of his major palace at Whitehall. In 1534 Henry VIII ordered the abbot of Westminster to arrange with the vicar of St Martin-in-the-Fields for all parishioners of St Margaret's who lived north and east of his palace to worship henceforth in St Martin's, and a few months later ordered the vicar and churchwardens of St Martin's to do the same,[2] to avoid having possibly infected corpses carried past the palace for burial at St Margaret's. The new arrangement was confirmed by letters patent in 1542 when the king granted to the parish of St Martin's all the houses and other tithable places which had hitherto belonged to the parish of St Margaret between St Clement Danes and the royal Palace of Westminster, so that the inhabitants would become inhabitants of St Martin's and receive sacraments and pay tithes and dues there; this was stated to be not only to avoid carrying corpses past the palace but also to recompense St Martin's for the loss of tithes through the imparking of lands for St James's Park.[3] Such high-handed changes by the king were later echoed by the powerful Lord Protector, Edward, duke of Somerset, when he demolished St Mary Strand to incorporate the site of church and churchyard into his enlarged inn, Somerset Place, in 1548; it was later said that he had intended to found a new church for the parish, but was executed before he could so.[4] In Elizabeth's reign, St Mary's parishioners were instructed to join St Martin or St Clement Danes, but the strength of parochial identity, and the ability to continue some form of parochial worship and organization using the Savoy chapel, meant that a quasi-parish survived for 160 years, to be rewarded by a new church under Queen Anne (below).

BISHOPRIC OF WESTMINSTER

Though Westminster Abbey lost much of its land in Westminster by forced exchange with the Crown in the 1530s, the abbey itself was only dissolved early in 1540. Later that year Henry VIII created the bishopric of Westminster, reconstituting the former monastery as a cathedral church, with bishop, dean, and 12 prebendary priests: Thomas Thirlby, dean of the Chapel Royal, became the first bishop, and William Boston, the former abbot, became the first dean, using his family name of Benson. The new diocese included the new city of Westminster and the whole county of Middlesex except the parish of Fulham.[5] The names and salaries of all the minor offices were also given, and included 10 readers, at least 39 scholars taught grammar in the school, 20 students of divinity to be supported at Oxford and Cambridge, 12 petty canons to sing in the choir with 12 laymen and 10 choristers, and 12 almsmen; lands were assigned to the dean and chapter to meet the estimated cost of alms, repairs, mending the highways, and servants' wages.[6] In 1550, however, the bishop surrendered the bishopric to Edward VI.[7] It was abolished largely for political reasons and the diocese reunited with that of London. The bishop of London was also given jurisdiction over areas formerly exempt from his authority: the cathedral church of Westminster and its precinct, the parishes of St Margaret and Paddington, the sites and chapels of St Stephen within Westminster palace, the royal house of Durham Place with its chapel and Durham Rents, and other formerly exempt religious houses in London and Middlesex. He also received the advowson of the vicarage of St Martin Charing, and the house called the convict prison of Westminster (Gatehouse prison) with a little house and garden adjoining it, but none of the other buildings including the former bishop's dwelling; he had to pay £5 a year to the bailiff of the liberty of the bishopric of Westminster, and £6 1s. 8d. to the keeper of the convicts there.[8]

An Act was passed in 1550 to preserve the abbey as a separate cathedral church within the London diocese, but retaining its Henrician charter. After the accession of Mary the dean and chapter continued in office, though 9 of the 12 Edwardian prebendaries were deprived, until it was dissolved in September 1556, when Queen Mary refounded the monastery and granted to it the abbey and precinct, the rectory and church of St Margaret and various properties surrendered by the dean and chapter.[9] After Elizabeth's accession the collegiate church was refounded in 1560 with a dean and 12 prebendaries, all priests, and given the abbey, precinct, St Margaret's rectory, the tithes of the rectory of St Martin-in-the-Fields, the advowson of the free chapel of St Mary Magdalene, Tothill, and various manors, lands and quit-rents.[10] The abbey and the church and parish of St Margaret's remained exempt from the jurisdiction of any archbishop or bishop, while St Martin's remained within the spiritual jurisdiction of the bishop of London.

---

1 Section based on Merritt, *Early Modern Westm.* 25–69, who has detailed acct of religious changes.

2 TNA, SP 1/87, pp. 27–8; SP 1/90, pp. 140–1.

3 TNA, C 66/706, m. 11.   4 Below, St Mary of Strand.

5 *L&P Hen. VIII*, XVI, p. 174 (no 379/30).

6 *L&P Hen. VIII*, XVI, p. 154–5 (no 333); above, Landownership: Manorial (Manor of Westm.).

7 TNA, E 305/19/G23.

8 *Cal. Pat.* 1549–51, 171, 262–3.

9 Ibid. 1555–7, 348–50; Carpenter, *Ho. of Kings*, 118–120, 122.

10 *Cal. Pat.* 1558–60, 397–403; above, Landownership: Manorial (Manor of Westm.).

INFLUENCE OF THE CENTRAL GOVERNMENT

Crown and Court to the 1640s

The settling of the Court and diplomatic contacts in Westminster from the 16th century created a political community in the town, and religious practices in Westminster became significant, and opinions a matter of government scrutiny. The political nature of religious activity in the 16th and 17th centuries gave the Westminster pulpits a greater significance, and led to attempts by the government to control access to them. Ben Jonson was examined by the attorney-general about the authorship of some anti-government verses, which he thought were written by a divine from Christ Church Oxford who had preached at St Margaret's.[1] The most notorious case was that of Dr John Everard, parish lecturer at St Martin-in-the-Fields and opponent of the Spanish marriage proposed for Charles, prince of Wales; in 1621 Dr Everard was imprisoned for preaching against the Spanish match, and about six months later was still petitioning the king for release from the Gatehouse. In 1622 he was committed to the Marshalsea and was still there early in 1623.[2] In all he was imprisoned on six or more occasions, but was also as frequently pardoned, presumably through highly-placed support, and also retained the support of St Martin's vestry.[3] One of his auditors complained that Everard was a sectary who had infected him with pernicious doctrines,[4] but apparently unjustly; his transgressions were political not religious.

The experience with Everard and other preachers of a puritan outlook, no doubt encouraged the Crown to alleviate the problem by assuming the right to appoint lecturers and others at St Martin's. On the death of the lecturer at St Martin's in 1627, the king attempted to place one of his chaplains, Humphrey Peake, in the post. The vestry objected strongly, and a compromise was only reached, and Peake appointed, after the king accepted the parish's right to chose freely without royal intervention. However, when Peake left in 1633, the king then recommended to William Laud, bishop of London, that Alexander Levingston have the place,[5] and Laud passed on the request to the vestry, acknowledging their right to chose, but urging that they accept the king's wishes, which they did. Laud also presented one of his own chaplains, William Bray, to the living of St Martin's, which also became vacant that year, because although the parish had accepted Peake, they had then raised funds to support other lecturers more to their liking, including Everard, and two notorious puritans, Thomas Foxley and Abraham Grymes.[6]

At the other end of the religious spectrum, Roman Catholicism in Westminster also presented the government with unique problems, especially in the 17th century. The residence in the capital of foreign envoys permitted to hold Catholic services for their households, as well as the Catholic consorts of the Stuart kings with their households, meant the constant and aggravating presence of Catholics near the Court, giving credence to the fear that the monarchs themselves might be Catholics. It also gave English Catholics the opportunity to attend mass. The presence of Roman Catholics, therefore, was not only perceived as a political threat to the Crown and the established religion, as it was under Elizabeth I, but increasingly, particularly under Charles I and James II, the presence of Roman Catholics in Westminster exacerbated the relationship between the king and his subjects as a whole. Despite this, recusancy was not as severely punished in Westminster, where Catholics included aristocrats close to the Court, as elsewhere, and only in the 1620s, when politics entered matters, did the Privy Council take steps to reduce what was seen as tacit support for Catholicism.[7] In 1626, for example, the king expressed concerned about the number of his subjects who were attending mass in the chapel of the French ambassador in Durham House, the residence of the bishop of Durham.[8] Efforts to apprehend the English attenders, said to number more than 100, led to a fracas between the constables and the ambassador's servants. The bishop was aggrieved at being blamed for all this, having given up 30 of the best rooms in the house for the ambassador at the king's request, and crowding himself and his family into the worst, while the ambassador's servants colluded in assisting English papists to attend mass and escape by water.[9]

The presence of the Crown had disadvantageous implications for parish life; in 1630, as part of measures against the plague, the Privy Council forbade burials in the churchyard or church of St Margaret's, permitting them only in a new burial ground, which lay away from the palace and abbey.[10] Royal servants could be difficult to control; the curate at St Clement Danes, for example, complained to Archbishop Laud that a royal servant he had presented for drunkenness and incontinence retaliated with a warrant from the Earl Marshal and threats of Star Chamber.[11]

On the other hand, proximity to national government could be beneficial. Those who appealed to the Crown might offer the local parishes unusual means of financial assistance to secure their suit. In 1608 two men successfully offered £100 to repair the church and paving in St Martin's to obtain pardon from penalties imposed by

1 *Cal. SP Dom.* 1628–9, 360.
2 Ibid. 1619–23, 233, 294, 439, 531.
3 Merritt, *Early Modern Westm.* 338–9.
4 *Cal. SP Dom.* 1637–8, 166.
5 *Cal. SP Dom.* 1633–4, 2–3.

6 Merritt, *Early Modern Westm.* 344–6.
7 Below, Rom. Cathm.   8 *Acts of PC*, 1625–6, 347.
9 Wheatley, 'Durham Ho.', 150–5.
10 *Acts of PC*, 1629–30, 314.
11 *Cal. SP Dom.* 1637, 569–70.

the Privy Council.[1] The large amount of Crown land gave parishes a supportive landowner to whom they could appeal. In 1606, for example, St Martin's used the increase in the size of its parish to support a petition for an acre of Crown land behind the Mews for a new churchyard.[2] In 1684, the Crown was involved in granting the land for St James's church and churchyard,[3] while in 1680 St Martin's petitioned for the grant of the tolls from the hay market to compensate the parish for land taken to widen St Martin's Lane,[4] and again received funds to purchase additional land for the churchyard.[5]

Though the creation of royal gardens and parks took land out of cultivation and tithes, the Crown did make some compensation for this. In 1662 the vicar of St Martin's, Dr Hardy, petitioned for a consideration since the king had converted to gardens several acres in the parish at Lower Crowfield, which had formerly paid tithes; he was granted £18 in lieu of four years' tithes, to be continued annually.[6]

Parliamentary Intervention in the 1640s and 1650s

The church in Westminster was also affected by the conflicts of the civil war and interregnum, when Parliament interfered in church affairs much as the monarch had done. There were presentations in the city for rejecting the Book of Common Prayer in 1642 and 1643.[7] A number of ministers were sequestrated in 1643, included Hall of the new church of St Paul, Covent Garden, for being with the royalist army; Smith in St Clement Danes: and Geoffrey Sharpe, lecturer at St Martin's.[8] Parliament made an order in January of that year to supply St Martin's and St Paul's with suitable ministers;[9] later Dr Wincop of St Martin's and Mr Price of St Paul's were among those named in the ordinance for calling an assembly of divines to settle the government of the church.[10] St Paul's was made parochial and its bounds set down in 1646.[11]

In 1645 an ordinance was passed appointing a committee drawn from the Lords and Commons to manage the estate of the collegiate church of Westminster and dispose of the rents; the dean and all but one of the prebendaries had become delinquent or deserted their charge, leaving the college with no government, and the school, almsmen, and officers with no means of subsistence. The committee was empowered to handle rents, to let for up to three years, and to place almsmen in vacancies. Allowances were to be made from the

revenues to preachers in the abbey.[12] In 1649 an Act for the abolition of the dean and chapter made provision for the upkeep of St Margaret's.[13] The school and almshouse belonging to the collegiate church were excluded from the Act for abolishing the dean and chapter, and a separate Act was passed in 1649 to continue and maintain them. Named governors were appointed to manage the goods and revenues and became the holders of the abbey, its cloisters, storerooms and workshops, and the profits from funerals held there; the dean's house with its outbuildings; the college's garden and orchard; the schoolhouse and library; lodgings for scholars and officials' service rooms; the almshouses; Tothill fields, and all the property formerly belonging to the dean and chapter. The governors were incorporated and could let any houses not required for the scholars or officials.[14]

The Westminster parishes were also caught up in the demand of the Church to reassess the way tithes were calculated in the City of London; this issue was, however, resolved by the Crown more to the benefit of the inhabitants than the churchmen. Both the representatives of the City and the London clergy had agreed to accept the king's arbitration in the matter by 1635, but the king was slow to act, not wishing to antagonize the City further during a difficult political period, and suits by residents against tithes increased. The clergy petitioned the king again in 1638, this time joined by the Westminster clergy from St Margaret's, St Martin's, St Clement Danes and the Savoy chapel, making complaints of inadequate income, since much formerly tithable agricultural land was now covered by houses whose residents paid only a few pennies at Easter, and that the king's delay had removed all opportunity of improvement. The parishioners in Westminster however, refused to accept royal arbitration, despite admitting they paid no tithe on new buildings, but wanted all tithe disputes left to the law. Royal orders imposed a tithe of 2s. in the £ on rents in Norwich in 1638, to enormous opposition, but in the end the matter was dropped in London because of more pressing political events in Scotland, after which the civil war intervened.[15] The issue of tithes remained at the forefront of many residents' concerns; in 1660 an Act received royal assent for making St Paul's parochial, and inhabitants petitioned that they were entitled to be tithe-free as the earl of Bedford was bound to endow the parish. When the area had been made parochial in 1646, they had had great taxes levied on them to support the minister, and this had been incorporated in the 1660 Act without the consent of the majority of the precinct.[16]

1 *Cal. SP Dom.*, Add. 1580–1625, 507.
2 TNA, C 66/1711, m. 20.
3 Below, Par. Chs, St James.
4 *Cal. SP Dom.* 1679–80, 554.
5 Ibid.1682, 71.
6 Ibid. 1661–2, 374; 1664–5, 225.
7 *Middx County Rec.* III. 80, 85.
8 *Walker Rev.* 49, 57.

9 HMC, *5th Rep.* 68.
10 *Acts and Ordinances of the Interregnum, 1642–60*, I. 182.
11 Ibid. 814–17.
12 Ibid. 803–5.
13 Ibid. II. 100, 104.   14 Ibid. II. 256–77.
15 C. Hill, Economic Problems of the Church (1968 edn), 280–7; *Cal. SP Dom.* 1637–8, 399, 414–15.
16 HMC, *7th Rep.* App., p. 137b.

Royal involvement in presenting to Westminster's livings continued after 1660. In 1689 at St Paul's, Covent Garden, the outgoing rector in 1689, promoted to the bishopric of Chichester, recommended as successor a certain Mr Williams, in preference to Dr Samuel Freeman; the patron, the earl of Bedford, when asked by the Crown to present, named both, and the Crown then picked Freeman.[1] About 1691 rules were proposed for church preferments in Westminster; only ministers of London and Westminster were to hold prebends at the abbey. St Margaret's, because it was attended by peers and MPs, required a good preacher, and so its minister was always to be one of the prebendaries.[2] From 1695 no disposal of prebends in Westminster was permitted when the king was abroad.[3]

The presence of the court and national government had cultural implications for the church as for society as a whole. Noblemen's households often contained chaplains and scholars, and in the 1680s Thomas Tenison, vicar of St Martin's, sought to establish a library for the benefit of such cultivated residents. He claimed there were no stationer's shops in Westminster or London fully furnished with books of all learning, and the only libraries allowing public use were the king's in St James's Palace, to which access not easy; Sir Robert Cotton's, chiefly books on the antiquities of England; and the dean and chapter's, allegedly inconvenient for all inhabitants because of its 'remote situation'. With the support of the churchwardens Tenison created a public library for students in a building near the new churchyard, and provided for its maintenance.[4]

Because of new building in the northern part of the parish, the church and vestry of St Martin's had indeed become a central focus of the City and its liberties. In 1676, of the parishes which recorded their figures, St Martin-in-the-Fields contained 16,672 conformists, 195 papists and 251 nonconformists; St Mary le Savoy had 210, 6, 8; and St Paul Covent Garden 790, 64, 6.[5] About 1723, even after the creation of two new parishes, the parish of St Martin remained the most populous; it was then computed that the number of families served by each parish under the jurisdiction of the bishop was St Martin 3,700; St Paul 500; St James 3,000; St Anne 1,500; St Clement Danes 1,700; St Mary le Strand plus the Savoy 300.[6]

CHURCH BUILDING IN THE 18TH CENTURY

If the presence of the court and government in Westminster was a constant factor in Westminster's religious life, a more pressing perennial problem was church accommodation. The small medieval parish churches were ill equipped to accommodate the influx of potential parishioners brought by urban growth, and ad hoc rebuilding and the provision of additional chapels of ease only partially met the deficiency. When the problem became of acute concern to the government, towards the end of the 17th century with the growth of the newly-licensed nonconformist congregations, creation of chapels gave way to the creation of new parishes by an official body, creating the parochial structure that still existed in the 21st century. The new parishes had a wider significance, though, as they were also civil authorities, and so became the framework for much of Westminster's local government until 1900.

As mentioned above, St Martin's parish was particularly affected by population growth. The initial response, the rebuilding of St Martin's church, was followed by the building of a chapel of ease to serve the earl of Bedford's Covent Garden estate. In 1646 this became a new parish, St Paul's, Covent Garden.[7] From 1670 efforts were made to create a new parish and church for the bailiwick of St James; the church of St James was eventually opened in 1684, and another, St Anne, in 1686, both made parochial by Acts of Parliament and taking large chunks of St Martin's parish.[8] Despite this drastic reduction, St Martin's still had more Anglican chapels than any other London parish in 1714: six, together with an almshouse chapel and two royal chapels.[9] In 1690 the churchwardens and inhabitants of St Mary Savoy petitioned the Treasury for the Savoy chapel and churchyard to become the parish church for themselves and the inhabitants of the Savoy precinct after the death of the master of the Savoy, with a suitable allowance from the hospital's revenues settled on their minister, but were unable to get leave to apply for an Act to effect this.[10]

By 1710 pressure to reform the Church of England and to fight the spread of nonconformity had brought the need for adequate church accommodation to the fore. After surveying the parishes in and around London, Parliament, with royal approval, decided that 50 new churches were required, to be financed by an additional tax on coals imported into London, with a commission set up to decide on the sites for the

1 *Cal. SP Dom.* 1689–90, 258, 276, 279, 311.
2 Ibid. 1691–2, 49.
3 Ibid. 1694–5, 379.   4 BL, Add. MS 38693, ff. 147–8.
5 *Compton Census of 1676*, ed. Whiteman, 40, 56–7. St CD not recorded; St Margt not under bp of London.
6 Guildhall MS 9550.
7 Below, St Paul.
8 Below, St Martin.
9 Paterson, *Pietas Lond.* 153; below, St Martin.
10 *Cal Treas. Bks*, III. 896.

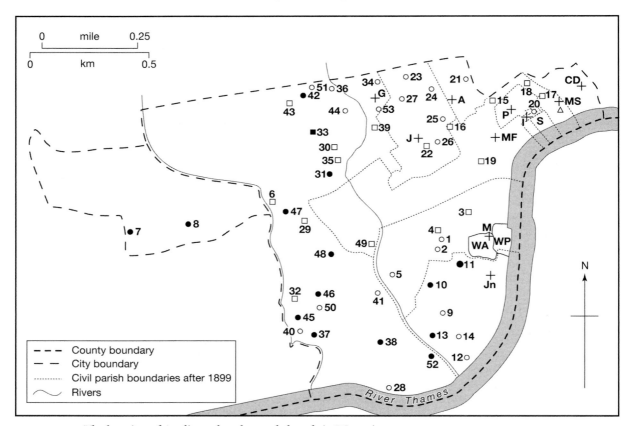

44. *The location of Anglican churches and chapels in Westminster.*

churches. The commission was established by an Act passed in 1711, and began work that year,[1] and under a further Act was to continue until its work was completed.[2] The commissioners received powers to contract for sites for churches, churchyards, and parsonage houses; to erect churches, and to make chapels into parish churches; to treat with the patrons of existing parishes; to appoint select vestries for the new churches; and make a perpetual division of parish rates. Burials within the new churches were forbidden.

Although far fewer than fifty churches were ever built under the commissioners, Westminster benefited widely from the scheme. The ministers and vestries of the six existing Westminster parishes (St Margaret, St Martin, St Clement Danes, St James, St Anne, and St Paul), together with those from St Mary le Strand worshipping at the Savoy chapel, and those of the Broadway chapel in St Margaret and the King Street chapel in St James, were asked to number their inhabitants, to indicate the need for new churches and to suggest sites. By the end of 1711 it had been decided that new churches should be built in the parishes of St Anne, St Clement Danes, St Margaret, and St Mary le Strand. Consideration was given to making Tenison's chapel in King Street parochial but dropped when Archbishop Tenison opposed it, but it was decided that the parishes of St James and St Martin should be divided into four.[3] Several sites for a new

church in St Martin were considered but it was not until 1720 that a site near Hanover Square was finally adopted.[4] Elsewhere, there was disagreement over how the parish of St Clement Danes might be divided, but a site in Millbank was chosen for a new church for St Margaret. Progress thereafter slowed down, through difficulties both in obtaining sites and with the actual building work, as well as the commissioners' financial problems. In the end only three churches were built in Westminster by the commissioners: St Mary le Strand, consecrated in 1724, whose parish included some houses on the north side of the Strand taken from St Clement Danes and St Martin;[5] St George's Hanover Square, also consecrated in 1724 to serve a parish taken out of St Martin; and St John's, Smith Square, built in 1728, to serve about half of St Margaret's parish. The church of St Martin-in-the-Fields was also rebuilt at this time, but not with the assistance of the 50 new churches commissioners: it was necessary to get its own Act of 1720 which allowed for rating and its own commissioners.

Population growth continued, but during the 18th century church accommodation was largely supplemented by chapels of ease and proprietary chapels, particularly in the more fashionable residential areas. In the period 1780 to *c*.1812 there were still four chapels in St Martin's parish – Long Acre, Oxendon, Tavistock,

1 *Fifty New Chs*, pp. ix–xiv.
2 10 Anne, c. 11.   3 *Fifty New Chs*, 149, 151.
4 Ibid. 81.
5 Ibid. 100.

+	**Parish Churches (pre-1800)**		
A	St Anne, Soho	M	St Margaret, Westminster
CD	St Clement Danes	MF	St Martin in the Fields
G	St George, Hanover Square	MS	St Mary le Strand
I	Holy Innocents (lost)	△	St Mary Strand (medieval site)
J	St James, Piccadilly	P	St Paul, Covent Garden
Jn	St John, Westminster		

	Extra-Parochial		
WA	Westminster Abbey Precinct	S	Savoy Chapel
WP	Westminster Palace Precinct		

Daughter Churches and Chapels

●	Daughter churches (standing)	■	Founded as proprietary chapels
○	Daughter churches (demolished)	□	Proprietary chapels (demolished)

M	**St Margaret, Westminster**	J	**St James, Piccadilly**
1	Medieval Tothill Chapel	24	St Luke, Berwick Street
2	Christ Church, Victoria Street	25	St Peter, Great Windmill Street
3	Duke Street Episcopal Chapel, Storey's Gate	26	St Philip, Lower Regent Street
4	Queen's Square Chapel (later St Peter's Episcopal Chapel)	27	St Thomas, Kingly Street
5	St Andrew, Ashley Place	**G**	**St George, Hanover Square**
		28	All Saints, Pimlico
	Knightsbridge and St Margaret's Detached	29	Belgrave or St John's Chapel, Halkin Street
6	Knightsbridge (Trinity) Chapel/Holy Trinity Church	30	Berkeley Chapel, Chesterfield Hill
7	Holy Trinity, Prince Consort Road	31	Christ Church, Down Street
8	All Saints, Ennismore Gardens (now Russian Orth.)	32	Eaton Episcopal Chapel, Coleshill Street
		33	Grosvenor Chapel, South Audley Street
Jn	**St John, Westminster**	34	Hanover (St George's) Chapel, Regent Street
9	St Mary the Virgin, Tothill Fields	35	Mayfair or Curzon Chapel
10	St Stephen, Rochester Row	36	St Anselm, Davies Street
11	St Matthew, Great Peter Street	37	St Barnabas, Pimlico
12	Holy Trinity, Bessborough Gardens	38	St Gabriel, Warwick Square
13	St James the Less, Thorndike Street	39	St George's Chapel, Albemarle Street
14	St John, Causton Street	40	St John the Baptist, Pimlico Road
		41	St John the Evangelist, Wilton Road
MF	**St Martin-in-the-Fields**	42	St Mark, North Audley Street (now secular use)
15	Long Acre Episcopal Chapel	43	St Mary, Park Street (Park Street Chapel)
16	Oxendon Chapel	44	St Mary, Bourdon Street
17	Russell Court Chapel, Drury Lane	45	St Mary the Virgin, Bourne Street
18	St John the Evangelist, Broad Court (formerly Tavistock Chapel)	46	St Michael and All Angels, Chester Square
19	St Matthew, Spring Gardens (formerly Spring Gardens Chapel)	47	St Paul, Wilton Place
20	St Michael, Burleigh Street	48	St Peter, Eaton Square
		49	Charlotte (later St Peter's) Chapel, Palace Street, Buckingham Gate
A	**St Anne, Soho**	50	St Philip, Buckingham Palace Road
21	St Mary the Virgin, Charing Cross Road	51	St Saviour, Oxford Street
		52	St Saviour, St George's Square
J	**St James, Piccadilly**	53	Trinity Chapel, Conduit Street
22	St James Chapel, York (Duke of York) Street		
23	St John the Baptist, Great Marlborough Street		

and Spring Gardens. In St George's there were five for which the rector was patron – Charlotte Street, St George, Albemarle Street, Mayfair, Trinity, and Five Fields, and four for which the patron was not given – Belgrave, Dudley, Berkeley, Park Street. In St James there were three – Berwick, King Street, and St James's chapel.[1]

19TH CENTURY TO THE PRESENT

By the early 19th century lack of church accommodation was an increasing problem once again, with newly-built suburbs spreading over Belgravia and Pimlico, while areas built up in earlier centuries in the eastern part of Westminster became overcrowded slums, with little support for church provision of any kind. Nothing reflected the Church of England's institutional formality more than its difficulty in responding to population growth and providing places of worship. While myriad nonconformist groups and undesignated congregations, mainly of an evangelical persuasion, registered front rooms, back rooms, shops, and warehouses all over Westminster for religious worship in the late 18th and early 19th centuries,[2] many of which later developed into formal affiliations with purpose-built chapels, the Church of England struggled to catch up with the thousands of new residents for whom there was no possibility of being able to attend an Anglican church.

1 Guildhall MS 9557, ff. 26, 28, 33, 43.

2 Below, Prot. Nonconformity, passim, and Undesignated.

CHURCH EXTENSION

Part of the problem was addressed by the provision of district chapelries, many being built in Westminster with the aid of grants from the Church Building Commission. In 1818 the commissioners asked bishops for parishes where population exceeded church accommodation by 20,000 or more: 25 were identified including the parishes of St George, St James, and St Martin-in-the-Fields.[1] Another parliamentary grant in 1824 was applied to areas where population exceeded accommodation by 15,000 or more, which included the joint parish of St Margaret and St John.[2] Churches built with the aid of the first grant included St Philip's, Regent St, built in 1819–22; St George's, Regent Street, known as Hanover Chapel, 1823–4; St Peter's, Eaton Square, 1824–7; St Mark's, North Audley Street, 1825–7; and St Michael's, Burleigh Street, Strand, 1832–4.[3] Churches built with aid from the later grant were St Mary the Virgin, Vincent Square (1835–6), St Luke's, Berwick Street (1837–9), St Paul's, Wilton Place (1840–2), Christ Church, Broadway (1842–3), All Saints, Ennismore Gardens (1848–9), St Matthew's, Great Peter Street (1849–50), Holy Trinity, Bessborough Gardens, Pimlico (c.1851), St Andrew's, Ashley Place (1853–5).[4] Some grants were for very small, 'token', amounts, such that given to Holy Trinity, which was mainly funded by Revd W.H.E. Bentinck, canon of Westminster.[5] Several other new churches were provided by private donation. St Stephen's, Rochester Row, in a slum area, was the gift of Baroness Angela Burdett-Coutts in memory of her father, and the most expensive church in London at that time;[6] St Barnabas, Pimlico, was paid for by an appeal to the congregation of St Paul's, Knightsbridge, by their vicar to fund a church in a poor area; St James the Less, Pimlico, was paid for by the daughters of J.H. Monk, bishop of Gloucester and Bristol.

Many of the churches in newly-built Belgravia and Pimlico were erected on sites provided by the Grosvenor family or Thomas Cubitt, keen to provide amenities to attract middle-class residents, but unusually there was difficulty in the 1840s in finding the site for a district church in Knightsbridge, a smallish area with several landowners.[7]

URBAN PROBLEMS

While new district churches were being provided to serve the suburban areas in St George's in the western part of Westminster, the older established areas in the east had severe social and economic problems which made it difficult to spread the Christian message at all. The problem of church provision in growing towns was addressed nationally by a parliamentary committee in 1858. It interviewed the rector of St Clement Danes, a parish which then had a population of c.17,000 of whom 10,000 were too poor to contribute towards church rates, its questions suggesting surprise at finding so many poor in the Strand area. St Clement's church held 1,350, with only c.200 free seats suitable for adults. The church was a old one, not built under any of the special Acts, and while the parish had been unfortunate not to get a second church in the early 18th century, when it was more prosperous, by the 1850s it had little means of supporting even the one it had. The church's income was falling: pew rents once contributed over £200 a year, but with many people refusing to pay, this had fallen to £100, and was applied to church rates and churchwarden's expenditure. The minister was supported by the Easter offerings of c.£230, the ground rent of £27 from the former rectory house, and interest of about £18 a year on money received when the old churchyard was sold to King's College Hospital. The parishioners had increased the offering since the rector's arrival by c.£100, and it mainly consisted of very small sums of 1s. to 2 gns, with only six offerings of £10 or more, three of them from local businesses. The minister's income had been severely reduced by the loss of burial fees worth £150–200 a year; after paying rent, since he did not inhabit the rectory house, he had less than £200 to live on, derived from voluntary offerings, for the charge of 17,000 people. The minister paid £40 towards the stipend of one of his curates and the Additional Curates' Society a further £60; another curate was paid £100 by the Pastoral Aid Society. Asked about the moral and religious feeling in the parish, he stated there was a frightful amount of infidelity, a crying evil, and many residents had little idea of the existence of God. There were few dissenters in the parish, who could hardly keep open the one chapel they had, while there were several houses of ill-fame, and much overcrowding with sometimes 15–16 people to a room. He felt that more curates would help, as much had been done with the additional curate he had: people chiefly wanted house to house visits and care and attention shown to them by the parish clergy. The recent arrival of a City missionary, whose £70 annual stipend was largely met by a private individual, had also helped. Clare market, which traded on Sundays all during the morning service, was a 'great evil', but free sittings were well used in the evening, and evening services for the poor had been recently started in the parish school. The rector wanted to have the pews in the church removed, as the free seats were well used, more would attend if all seats were free, and an additional 200 could be seated if the pews were lowered and reorganized. When asked if the pew-holders would perhaps

1 Port, *Six Hundred Chs*, 30.
2 Ibid., 96 and n.
3 Ibid., 136–7.
4 Ibid., 156–7.

5 Hobhouse, *Cubitt*, 223; below, Par. Chs (St John; St Geo.).
6 Below, Par Chs, St John's (Other Chs).
7 Below, Knightsbridge (All Saints).

45. *St Martin-in-the-Fields parish from the north-east, showing both the richly detailed elevations designed by James Gibbs in 1720, and the some of the work contributed in 2001–8 by Eric Parry Architects, who redeveloped the northern burial vaults as the St Martin's Centre, top-lighting them from a circular feature shown.*

pay for a new church to avoid losing their pews, he thought not, because so many of the householders and owners of businesses in the parish actually lived elsewhere, and there were comparatively few respectable people in the parish, Even the 7,000 not poor included many infidels and shopkeepers in the Strand. He had hoped to build a new church but could not get the funds. Those who lived and attended church outside the parish did not wish to support the church at their place of work. St Clement's included some of the worst streets in London, near the church, such as Wych Street, Holywell Street, and Clare Market, and without more clergy and increased church accommodation, the minister was unable to cope with the immense amount of spiritual destitution in his parish. He was, he felt, in a painful position.[1]

All this was in marked contrast to the experience of the minister of St George, Hanover Square. He could report that pew rents in his church amounted to £950 for 700 sittings, of which a third went to provide a second evening service, and the rest to church expenses. There were about 300 open sittings for adults out of the accommodation of 1,200, the rest let in pews. The poor were not admitted to the pews, but sat in open seats in the middle aisle or against the wall in the body of the church or the galleries. When it was commented that this was so as to make a marked distinction between the poor

and the rich in that house of God, he replied, 'Yes, certainly'.[2]

The committee concluded that there were parishes in the metropolis which could be described at present as unmanageable, having populations exceeding 10,000 and being comparatively poor. These included St Clement Danes, a parish which had been overlooked in all recent measures of church extensions, with great poverty and urgent demand for a new church in the neighbourhood of Clare market and Lincoln's Inn Fields. Also St Martin's had a population of 17,770 and St Anne's Soho 17,335: a good measure of church extension would be to erect a church near Leicester Square, where the two parishes met, creating a district of about 8,000 taken from each. The number of benefices with a population of over 5,000 were listed by the committee, and included 20 in Westminster: most had one church, though St George's, Hanover Square, St Paul's, Wilton Place, with St Barnabas, and St James, Piccadilly, had two or three.[3]

Other parishes in a more fortunate position, with only limited slum areas, perhaps found it easier to make improvements, and doubtless an energetic and charismatic incumbent could make an even greater difference. Several incumbents of Anglican and other churches drew huge crowds, such as G.H. Wilkinson at St Peter, Pimlico, or Dr John Cumming at the Church of Scotland, Crown Court. Some incumbents not only drew crowds when

1 *Mins of Evidence and Rep. Sel. Cttee on Means of Divine Worship in Populous Dists.* HC, 387 (1857–8), IX, pp. 113–18.

2 Ibid., pp. 237–8.
3 Ibid., 577, 579, 585.

they preached, but like F.W. Farrar at St Margaret's also made vast improvements in the nature of parochial life, the role of the clergy, and the lot of the poor.[1]

CHURCH ATTENDANCE

Concern about religious activity led to detailed surveys of accommodation and attendance during the mid and later 19th century, beginning with the religious census of 1851. The official population of the five districts that made up Westminster was 233,345 in 1851. Anglican church accommodation totalled 47,718, and recorded attendance was 54,538 at all the services on the census Sunday; nonconformist accommodation was 17,845 and attendance 21,663; Roman Catholic accommodation 2,890 and attendance 7,850; Jewish accommodation 622 and attendance 140; Scottish and foreign language churches 150 and attendance 4,380. The attendance at the census was in most cases lower than the average (also asked for), because of very bad weather on the morning of census Sunday. Several Anglican ministers, in the western half of Westminster, mentioned that they were filled to capacity during fashionable society's 'Season' from Easter to July, when upper-class pew-holders were resident in London, but far lower at the rest of the year.[2] The incumbent of St Matthew, Spring Gardens, felt that the reduction of private residences in favour of government offices had reduced church attendance in his area, and while civil servants might stay in the area during the week, their family home was in the newer suburbs where they attended church.[3]

In 1886 the Church of England had 51 churches and chapels offering public worship; attendance totalled 23,740 in the morning, 20,382 in the afternoon and evening. In 1903, when attendance had fallen to 15,965 and 12,094 respectively, it still had 51 places of worship, together with 13 Anglican missions operating in poorer parts of the city with a further Sunday attendance of 1,340. Seven of these were in St Margaret's and St John's, two in St Clement Danes, two near Covent Garden in St Paul's and St Martin's, one in St Anne's, and one in St Gabriel's district in the southern part of Pimlico. Anglicans represented about 58 per cent of the total religious attendance. In 1903 Nonconformist worshippers numbered 11,471, about 23 per cent; Roman Catholic 7,705, about 15 per cent, and foreign Protestant services was 286. Attendance at Jewish services was 699 and at other, mainly Christian, services 760.[4]

TWENTIETH-CENTURY CHANGES

All faiths suffered a decline in attendance as a result of population changes: residents, especially church-going ones, moved out from the centre to new suburbs, and places of worship gradually amalgamated and closed. In 1913 there were still 48 Anglican churches and chapels, and 12 missions, but these had been reduced by 1970 to 23 churches and district chapels and 3 extra-parochial churches (Westminster Abbey, the Savoy chapel, and King's College chapel, Strand), and by 1995 to 19 churches. St Clement Danes was by then also extra-parochial, having become the RAF church.

Similarly the major Nonconformist sects also declined in the course of the twentieth century, and although four new sects appeared in Westminster, three of them after 1950, by 2008 only ten places for public worship by nonconformists were still open: Congregationalists (2), Salvation Army (2), Baptists, Methodists, Society of Friends, Christian Scientists, Spiritualists, and the Emmanuel Evangelical Church.

For Roman Catholics one new church opened in Pimlico to serve the population there, but in the 1970s two others closed. Although the number of long-term residents declined, the remaining churches were in demand to serve foreign Catholics living and working in Westminster, as well as English Catholics working in Westminster who attended weekdays masses, especially on holy days.

Among non-Christian faiths, the long-established Jewish population also declined, and by the late 20th century the only synagogue within the city of Westminster was at Knightsbridge. Several other non-Christian faith groups had also appeared in the city. The Baha'i faith had a place of worship by 1944, and Muslims by 1979, both of which continued worship in the city in 2000. Buddhists also had a centre in Westminster by 2006.

While the number of churches and church-goers declined in Westminster because of a reduction in residents and other causes, some churches in Westminster found new roles in the life of the city. The prominence that churches in Westminster had in national and international religious history, also meant that movements in Westminster could lead to a new direction for some Anglican churches. The most significant of these was the astonishing ministry of Revd H.R.L. Sheppard, vicar of St Martin-in-the-Fields 1914–26, and later dean of Canterbury, known universally as Dick Sheppard, an appropriately informal style for a man who fought against the formality and institutionalization of the Church of England, trying to establish a church based on

1 Below, accts of individual chs.

2 E.g. TNA, HO 129/3, 1/1/1 (f. 92), 1/1/3 (f.94), 2/1/5 (f.100), 3/1/6 (f.108); /4, 2/1/8 (f.21); /6, 2/1/2 (f.5), 2/1/4 (f.7).

3 TNA, HO 129/5, 1/1/2 (f.2).

4 Att. figs for individual congs given in sections below are taken from following sources: 1851 from TNA, HO 129/; 1886 from *The British Weekly*, 5 Nov. 1886, p. 3; and 1903 from Mudie-Smith, *Rel. Life.*

fellowship and care for other human beings. He abolished pew reservations, instituted a daily eucharist and threw open the church day and night: during the First World War troops could rest and shelter there, and he opened the crypt for shelter during air raids. After the war he kept the crypt open for anyone in need, establishing St Martin's as a centre for the needy which continued into the 21st century with its Social Care Unit, founded by Revd Austen Williams, vicar 1956–84. Sheppard's willingness to allow the first complete service to be broadcasted from St Martin's in 1924, after Westminster Abbey and St Paul's were unwilling, together with the social role he established for St Martin's continued by his successors, made St Martin's the pre-eminent *local* church for the capital, while the abbey and St Paul's had more national roles. The social role he established for St Martin's, so unusual in his time, by the end of the 20th century had become the norm for the Anglican Church. Another initiative of Sheppard's which went on to be of wider influence in the Church was the group he set up in 1917 with William Temple, then rector of St James, Piccadilly, known as Life and Liberty, which aimed to renew the Church of England through reforms and more self-government, and led in 1919 to the establishment of the National Assembly of the Church of England.[1]

Though not as influential as the work of St Martin's, other churches in Westminster found similar roles appropriate to central London parishes. The Scottish Church at Crown Court gave support to Scots visiting or newly arrived in London in the 19th century. Several Anglican and Nonconformist churches included services and support for foreign communities in Westminster, such the Chinese, and Catholic churches provided foreign-language masses for the large number of Catholics from Eastern Europe brought to London by the expansion of the European Union. Although financial support for local churches was always difficult to find, many churches also included suitable non-religious activities to augment their income and support their pastoral work, particularly concerts, as at St Peter, Eaton Square, and at St Martin-in-the-Fields, where a professional chamber orchestra, the Academy of St Martin-in-the Fields, was created in 1958 out of the tradition of music in that church.

RELIGIOUS BUILDINGS

Westminster was served by five parish churches during the Middle Ages,[2] although only at St Margaret's is medieval work extant, and this not of its original 12th-century fabric but from the Perpendicular rebuilding begun in the 1480s.[3] Financed by a wealthy, determined and pious parish community, St Margaret's enjoyed a more complete renovation programme than its parochial neighbours, being entirely rebuilt during a forty-year period. Subsequent restoration has erased much of the detailed evidence of this campaign, but the original plan and profile remain intact and are typical of the period. Although work on St Margaret's continued well into the reign of Henry VIII, few religious building projects of a public nature were initiated in the early 16th century. Instead, activity was confined to royal or courtly endeavour within private palaces, some of which represented the earliest experiments in England with the latest Renaissance theories of decoration, then arriving from the Continent. The Chapel Royal within St James's Palace from 1540 is a rare survivor of this type, its painted and moulded ceiling based on Serlio's Fourth Book of Architecture.[4] Ecclesiastical building in Westminster dwindled still further under Edward VI and the queens Mary and Elizabeth, with lavish memorials and tombs becoming the chief expressions of pious donation under the later Tudors. Several monuments from the later 16th century and early 17th were installed in St Margaret's, and incorporate conventional Renaissance motifs, as well as the kneeling rather than recumbent figures then popular because of Netherlandish influences.

The coronation of James I, which more-or-less settled earlier religious strife, also ushered in a flurry of extension and repairs to Westminster parish churches. This was particularly marked at St Martin-in-the-Fields, where the burgeoning of the population gave cause to extend the nave westward, and to add north and south aisles and a new chancel.[5] But it was the appointment of Inigo Jones to the post of Royal Surveyor in 1615 that inspired a revolution in architectural ideas. Many of Jones's most important buildings were erected in Westminster. Amongst them was St. Paul's, Covent Garden, the first new Anglican parish church to be built in London for nearly a century, and an entirely new kind of church, erected as an integral part of London's first residential square to which the vernacular character of its Tuscan style was well suited.[6] Jones's influence can be seen at the Broadway chapel, St Margaret's, *c*.1630,

1 *DNB* and *Oxford DNB*, sv. Sheppard; A. Saunders, *St Martin-in-the-Fields* [n.d.], 18, 20.

2 Below, St Margaret's, St Martin-in-the Fields, St Clement Danes, St Mary le Strand, Holy Innocents.

3 Section based on accts of individual chs and chapels below,

where detailed evidence can be found.

4 Pevsner, *London 6: Westm.* 600; Summerson, *Archit. in Britain*, 52–3.

5 Below, St Martin.

6 Below, St Paul.

although Laudian taste may have dictated the inclusion of Gothic tracery in a design that otherwise obeyed Renaissance principles.[1]

From the later 17th century new building burgeoned in Westminster: development spread first north into Soho with medium-sized houses, then westward into St James's and Mayfair with mansions and garden squares for the aristocracy and gentry. Classical styles were well established but, while Jonesian idioms continued to be used, contemporary French and Italian classicism, particularly the precise and elegant Baroque of Christopher Wren, became alternatives for church architects. At first religious building projects concentrated on improving access to existing churches and repairing the damage many had suffered during the Civil War. The west tower of St Clement Danes (now surviving as its lower stages) dates from this period, a mixture of lingering Gothic with Y-tracery and angle buttresses and tentative Mannerism, with doorcase and obelisks derived from Jones's work at St Paul's cathedral. Toward the end of the century new buildings generally fell into one of three categories. The first comprised purpose-built dissenters' chapels which began to appear in the older, more heavily populated districts from 1672. Although none survives from this early period, accounts confirm they were of a conventional type: square, brick-built preaching halls, well-lit and fitted with large galleries on three sides. The second group was French Huguenot chapels, of which between 1685 and 1700 nearly a dozen were built in Soho to serve its substantial refugee population of largely professional classes.[2] In the third category were the works designed by or involving Wren: the Chapel Royal at Whitehall, the complete rebuilding of the ancient St Clement Danes, and churches for two new parishes carved out from the greatly over-populated parish of St Martin-in-the-Fields. Of those, St James, Piccadilly, built for Lord St Albans's suburban development to the north of Pall Mall, exemplified Wren's ideal church. Its internal configuration, with windowed aisles below vaulted galleries, was one of Wren's more innovative solutions to the spatial needs of town congregations and remained influential throughout the 18th century.[3]

The Act for Building Fifty New Churches of 1711 bestowed three buildings on Westminster, all conspicuous beacons for the faithful and all exemplars of the new more confident Baroque favoured by the Act's High Church, Tory authors. Compared to the style of Wren, these churches displayed more muscularity and a greater interest in the dramatic possibilities of space and volume. The intention for each was to supply the accommodation the existing parish churches were unable to meet. Two were located within established districts, although planned development in the area around St

John the Evangelist, Smith Square, only began after the church had been built. Outside the remit of the Act, St Martin-in-the-Fields was completely rebuilt at the expense of the parish in 1722–4 to replace a much extended but severely dilapidated medieval predecessor. The architect was James Gibbs, who pioneered here the combination of a giant Corinthian hexastyle portico with what Gibbs himself called a "Gothick" steeple emerging from behind the pediment – a formula that became the model for many larger town churches of the 18th and early 19th centuries throughout Britain and the Empire.

Despite new churches and new parishes, religious accommodation in Westminster continued to suffer pressure from an expanding population. For Anglicans, much of the need was met by proprietary chapels. These privately financed establishments quickly became an integral part of the West End development, many set amidst in smart residential areas while the less affluent neighbourhoods were usually served by chapels of ease. Of the former, Grosvenor Chapel, 1730, is the sole survivor, a neat brick building with Doric porch. Its steeple sits above a pediment in a manner derivative of Gibbs, but its simpler Classicism reflected the contemporary Palladian revival which was favoured by the Whig aristocracy.

Nonconformity continued to flourish in Westminster, especially in the second half of the century as buildings for New Dissent began to appear, including chapels for the Baptists, Methodists and Unitarians. Congregations were often transitory, loose associations, but after 1740 purpose-designated buildings, both new and remodelled, accounted for a much larger proportion of registrations, generally indicating the denominations' increased confidence as well as access to greater financial support. In terms of style, the new chapels shared much with their Anglican counterparts, and many, too, were built in the wealthy suburbs of Mayfair and Piccadilly; none has survived. The end of the 18th century also saw the first significant Roman Catholic church built in Westminster since the Reformation, for a native rather than ambassadorial, foreign or royal congregation; the first purpose-built synagogue, however, the Western Synagogue by R. Abraham, was not built until 1827 although the Jewish community had met and worshipped in the Covent Garden area since the 1760s. The Roman Catholic Our Lady of the Assumption and St Gregory, Warwick Street, Soho, was designed in 1789 by Joseph Bonomi, himself a Catholic who had worked with the Adam brothers and was primarily known as a country house architect. While the consciously modest brick façade may have been a response to the recent anti-Catholic Gordon Riots, it also drew on the austere neo-classicism then popular on the Continent and

---

1 Below, St Margt (Christ Church); J. Harris and G. Higgott, *Inigo Jones: Complete Architectural Drawings* (exhibition catalogue, 1990), 16, 298–302.

2 Below, Foreign Chs (French Protestant).
3 Summerson, *Archit. in Britain*, 197.

employed by Bonomi at the contemporary St James, Great Packington (Warws.).

Like their forerunner of the previous century, the Church Building Acts of 1818 and 1819 were intended to address the lack of metropolitan church accommodation, but they also aimed at controlling the social and political degradation that the shortfall was believed by the establishment to underpin. From the first Act, Westminster gained five new churches, more than any of London's borough. A further eight were built with grants from the second Act, again the maximum number allocated within London (Islington and Bethnal Green also got eight churches).[1] This generous provision illustrates the enormous population growth Westminster was experiencing in the early 19th century as new residential districts were developed and civic and commercial improvement schemes attracted more and more people to the capital. The style chosen for the first five churches was predominantly classical, a distinctively cosmopolitan preference as church extension in the provinces tended to favour the superficial 'Commissioner's Gothic'. The three Mayfair churches were provided on the area's perimeter, as much of it had already been built over, and St Michael's, Burleigh Street, the only Gothic church of this first group, was slotted into Nash's West Strand improvements.[2] Only St Peter, Eaton Square, could be built on a more prominent site, being the first church on the Grosvenor's Belgravia estate.

Churches built with grants from the second Act were entirely of the Gothic Revival, several designed by those leading architects favoured within High Church, Ecclesiological circles. Half were sited close to areas of extreme poverty, in Soho and the area around the new Vauxhall Bridge Road. They were large, seating at least 1,200, and generally followed High Church plans with distinct aisles and chancels and liturgical fittings. Most were in the correct 13th- or 14th-century native style preferred by the High Church. Few churches of this grant phase survive. An especially unfortunate loss was Holy Trinity, Bessborough Gardens, by Pearson, 1849. Primarily funded by the ritualistic Archdeacon Bentinck of Westminster its cruciform plan with crossing tower, raised chancel and stone spire was praised by Pugin and Scott for its stylistic purity and by the Ecclesiologists, with reservations, for its liturgical correctness.

Provision for Anglican worship in Victorian Westminster was also initiated privately. On the Grosvenor estates of Belgravia and particularly Pimlico, Thomas Cundy II, estate surveyor from 1825, designed four new district chapelry churches within Cubitt's rapidly progressing developments. All are of Kentish ragstone with stone spires, variously detailed as Early English, Geometric or Decorated. Ferrey's St Stephen, Rochester Row, an extremely costly Puginian edifice with flowing

46. *The Anglican church of St James the Less, off Vauxhall Bridge Road, in the parish of St John, Westminster, interior with font. Church and furnishings were designed by G.E. Street in 1859, who created what was perhaps the most architecturally inventive of the many district churches built for Westminster during the 19th century.*

tracery of the Lincolnshire type, was financed by Baroness Burdett-Coutts, and accompanied by schools and vicarage. G.E. Street's only church in Westminster, St James-the-Less, Pimlico, was the area's first example of Italianate polychromatic brickwork, boldly illustrative of the architect's theories on Continental forms and colour, established in *Brick and Marble in the Middle Ages*, 1855.

From the 1860s to the end of the century, Anglican church architecture in Westminster was dominated by A.W. Blomfield, son of C.J. Blomfield, the reformer bishop of London and founder of the permanent Ecclesiastical Commission in 1835.[3] His work was typical of later 19th-century Gothic Revival, often reliant on red brick or rich polychromy and an eclectic mix of English and Continental motifs, and some of his plans were experimental, for example the wide, aisleless St John the Baptist, Great Marlborough Street. Most of Blomfield's

1 Port, *Six Hundred Chs*, 134–5, 150–7.
2 Pevsner, *London 6: Westm.* 372.

3 A. Saint and C. Brooks, eds, *The Victorian Church* (1995), 34.

work in Westminster, however, was devoted to the extension or redecoration of existing churches, representing a shift in focus from *c.*1870 away from financing new buildings and toward alterations in response to dropping church attendance. In fact, 1876 saw the first demolition of a 19th-century Anglican chapel without replacement.[1]

Throughout the 19th century, nonconformity remained a vigorous alternative to the established church in Westminster, although in contrast with what was happening elsewhere in England it was responsible for few buildings. Sixteen new chapels were built under Victoria, mostly for Congregationalists and Methodists, and mostly in the southern districts of Pimlico and Victoria. Their style and size varied from the established classical box to fashionable and monumental buildings by renowned architects, such as the Norman Romanesque King's Weigh-House Chapel by Waterhouse, 1889, and secular late Flemish Gothic French Protestant Church by Aston Webb, 1891.

Despite the Emancipation Act of 1829, Roman Catholic building in Westminster did not begin in earnest for another fifteen years, probably because chapels which had become securely established during the previous century still operated. Catholic architect J.J. Scoles designed the church of the Immaculate Conception in Mayfair in 1844, in lush French late Gothic which contrasted with the contemporary preference for English styles. The most important new work was Westminster Cathedral, begun 1895, the supreme example in Britain of late Victorian Byzantine revival and the *chef d'oeuvre* of its Catholic architect, J.F. Bentley. Conceived with the help of the energetic Cardinal Vaughan, it too made clear a bold diversion from contemporary Anglican work, even that carried out by Anglo-Catholic architects such as G.F. Bodley (Holy Trinity, Prince Consort Road, 1901) or Ninian Comper (Grosvenor Chapel fittings, 1912), who developed a rich Perpendicular idiom.

The chief development in 20th-century Westminster was demolition and adaptation. What began as a trickle in the 1870s had swelled to a flood of closures and demolitions even before the First World War, and encompassed as many non-conformist chapels as Anglican churches. World War II further decimated Westminster's stock of religious buildings, but more recent commercial and social pressures have also played their part: Thomas Cundy III's polychromatic All Saints, Grosvenor Road, 1869, was bombed during the War, restored in 1955, but then demolished to make way for council housing in 1980. Despite such widespread demolition, exacerbated by the over-zealous Victorian focus on the superficial benefits of a dynamic church building with little or no thought to the realities of future sustainability, several strikingly original yet respectful contributions were made during the last century. Notable are H.S. Goodhart-Rendel's work at St Mary's Bourne Street, 1925–8, and the additions to S.P. Cockerell's Georgian tower at St Anne's Soho by the Westwood Partnership, 1989.

Other denominations and faiths continued to build, or built on a nationally significant scale for the first time. The Methodists chose a remarkably important site for their magnificent Beaux-Arts Methodist Central Hall, by Lanchester and Rickards, 1905, which is prominently counter-posed to Westminster Abbey. The Third Church of Christ Scientist in Mayfair, also notable Edwardian Baroque, was also designed by Lanchester and Rickards, whereas the Ninth Church of 1926–30 is a sedate complex in Early Christian style by Sir Herbert Baker and Scott. One of the most remarkable of all Westminster churches, H.O. Corfiato's neo-classical Notre-Dame de France 1951–5, was designed to recall its late 19th-century predecessor, which had been converted from an 18th-century panorama, and illustrates a familiar Westminster story of the adaptation of an existing building to religious use.

PARISH CHURCHES

ST MARGARET, WESTMINSTER

The church of St Margaret of Antioch, in being by 1121x36,[2] served the parish attached initially to the minster and later to the abbey of St Peter. That parish, presumably in existence from *c.*959, was confined to, but not coterminous with, the manor of Westminster. As described in the proceedings before the papal judges delegate in 1222, it excluded the church and cemetery of St Martin, an area of uncertain extent. It also excluded the Strand parishes, St Clement Danes and St Mary of

Strand, parts of which lay outside the abbot's manor. Outside the manor of Westminster, Knightsbridge, Westbourne and the chapelry of Paddington, all described as members of the vill of Westminster in the reign of Edward I, were said to 'pertain' to the parish of St Margaret, although their limits are not described.[3] From the 13th to the 16th century the parish also contained a chapel of ease at Tothill (below).

Because the abbot later acquired the advowson of St

---

1 Below, St James (St James' Chapel, Duke of York St).
2 BL, Harl. Ch. 84.F.46; above, Intro., for foundation and

exemption.
3 Above, Gen. Intro.

47. St Margaret's parish church, Westminster, dwarfed by the north transept of the Abbey, showing the west porch added to the medieval church in the 1890s and the tower rebuilt in the 18th century.

Martin's, the only other early church in the manors of Westminster and Eye, some uncertainty may have arisen about the boundaries between the two parishes. A definitive separation was made in 1534–5, when Henry VIII ordered parishioners north of his palace to worship henceforth in St Martin's.[1] Thereafter, St Margaret's was bounded on the east and south by the Thames, and its northern boundary stretched from the Thames through the middle of the modern Horse Guards and St James's Park to the Tyburn, which formed the western boundary. A small area of Westminster, comprising the parts of Knightsbridge and Hyde Park west of the Westbourne river, remained as a detached part of St Margaret's parish; its churches are treated separately below. St Margaret's continued to serve the whole of this parish, with the assistance of the New Chapel and some proprietary chapels, until the consecration of St John the Evangelist, Smith Square, in 1728. From that date the half of the parish south of the abbey precinct and south-east of Greencoat Place was served by St John's.

The church and parish of St Margaret were exempted from the jurisdiction of the diocese of London from the 12th or 13th century until the dissolution of Westminster Abbey in 1540.[2] The parish was then included in the diocese in which it lay, that is, initially the short-lived bishopric of Westminster, and from 1550 the diocese of London.[3] In 1560 the new collegiate church of St Peter again acquired extra-diocesan status, and St Margaret's parish became a peculiar of the dean and chapter of Westminster under the patronage of the Crown. This continued until the Ecclesiastical Commissioners Act of 1840, whereby the parish became independent of the dean and chapter and was incorporated into the diocese of London. In 1973, in accordance with the Westminster Abbey and Saint Margaret Westminster Act of the previous year, St Margaret's ceased to be parochial, and the church and churchyard together with the part of the parish occupied by the Houses of Parliament were placed under the jurisdiction of the dean of Westminster, as the royal peculiar of Westminster Abbey with the

1 TNA, SP 1/87, pp. 27–8; SP 1/90, pp. 140–1.
2 Above, Gen. Intro.

3 *Cal. Pat.* 1549–51, 171; 1553–4, 119–21.

church of St Margaret, with the Queen as Visitor. The remainder of the parish not incorporated into the Close of Westminster Abbey was divided between the parishes of St Martin-in-the-Fields and St Matthew, Westminster.[1]

RECTORY, VICARAGE, AND ADVOWSON

The rectorial tithes belonged to the abbey from the parish's foundation.[2] The vicarage, the ordination of which to serve the cure of an appropriated church was generally required after 1215, existed by 1254, and by 1317 had certainly been appropriated and assigned to the sacrist.[3] In fact, this arrangement may date back to the early 12th century; the grant 1121x36 by the abbot of £3 from the church towards the expenses of the high altar of the abbey, paid to the sacrist whose responsibility such expenses were,[4] may represent the ordination of a vicarage or its appropriation. The grant pre-dates the period when vicarages were specified as such, and the church may well have been served by chaplains throughout the 12th century.[5] That was almost certainly the case in the early 13th century when named chaplains of St Margaret's frequently witnessed charters. The creation of a vicarage and assignment to the sacrist may as compensation for the building of the church on a part of the abbey precinct assigned to the sacrist to maintain the abbey's worship.[6] In 1254, although the abbot was nominally patron of the church and vicarage, the appointment of chaplains to serve the cure was made through the sacrists.

In 1254 the abbot as patron took 20s. a year from the church of Westminster, and 2 marks from the vicarage.[7] In 1291 the church with the chapel of St Katharine, Paddington, was valued at £20, and the vicarage at £8.[8] Although leases of 1512 and 1528 refer to the almoner as rector,[9] in 1535, he merely received £4 a year from the corn and hay tithes, and the sacrist was said to hold the rectory 'valued at £24 a year',[10] evidence perhaps that an informal division of income had been abandoned or overlooked. The vicarage of St Margaret's is not mentioned again. In 1542 the king granted the rectory of St Margaret's to the dean and chapter of the newly-created collegiate church, which succeeded the abbot and convent in the abbey buildings.[11] In 1548 they received £26 13s. 4d. from the rectory and provided a curate to serve the parish.[12]

The rectory passed to the refounded monastery in

1556, and back again to the dean and chapter in 1560,[13] when Elizabeth I confirmed the extra-diocesan and extra-provincial status of the collegiate church of St Peter and its precinct. This became in effect a royal peculiar, and St Margaret's was therefore subject only to the dean and chapter; the rectory was appropriated by the chapter and the benefice was served by one of the canons as curate.

Under the Ecclesiastical Commissioners Act of 1840 the rectory of St Margaret's was removed from the dean and chapter and annexed to the canonry in Westminster Abbey held by the current curate, Revd Henry H. Milman, and his successors, who thereafter became rectors; the advowson belonged to the Crown. One of the prebendal houses was transferred from the dean and chapter to provide accommodation for the rector, and arrangements were made for the division and application of finances for the canon as member of the chapter and rector of the parish. Provision was also made for the stipend and accommodation for the minister of Broadway Chapel, a daughter church of St Margaret's.[4] By the 1970s the reduction in the number of residents in the parish meant St Margaret's was no longer financially viable as an independent parish church, and under an Act of 1972, its parochial responsibilities were ended and the church was placed once more under the dean and chapter of Westminster, the incumbent of St Margaret's still being designated rector.[15]

After 1560, the chapter continued to let the parsonage to those serving as curates, generally for the term of their life. In 1618, William Murray, then curate, held by lease from the chapter a residence called the Ancres House, abutting upon the south side of the chancel, together with all tithes, offerings, and fees pertaining to the vicarage. He surrendered these rights for a new appointment for life as rector with the cure of souls of the parishioners, receiving 20 marks a year for maintenance and all the fees for marriages, baptisms, burials and other church services; for this he was to preach on the first Sunday of each month and on four other occasions each year.[16] Similar appointments were made of Isaac Bargrave, DD, in 1622, Vincent Pearse, in 1626, Gilbert Wimberley, S.T.P. (later DD), in 1631 and 1641.[17] Later curates also received the tithes, including a sum from the Crown for the tithes from Kensington House (later Palace) from 1694.[18] In 1768 the dean and chapter granted an 18-year lease to the churchwardens and

---

1 *Cal. Pat.* 1558–60, 397–403; Guildhall MSS 9537/2, f. 101v.; 9557, f. 29; Smyth, *Church and Par.* 3; P. Holland, *St Margt's Westm.* (1993), 90.   2 Above, Intro., Parishes.

3 *Val. of Norwich*, ed. Lunt, 359; WAM, Sacrist's accts (only extant from 1317); WA, Liber Niger, f. 140v.–2.

4 BL, Harl. Ch. 84 F.46. Assignment to sacrist indicated in endorsement in later hand.

5 R.A.R. Hartridge, *Hist. of Vicarages in the Middle Ages* (1930), Chap. 2 and App. A.

6 Rosser, *Medieval Westm.* 254.

7 *Val. of Norwich*, ed. Lunt, 359.

8 *Tax. Eccl.* (Rec. Com.), 17.

9 WAM 17967; 18040.

10 *Valor Eccl.* I. 412–13.

11 *L&P Hen. VIII*, XVII, pp. 392–6.

12 *Chantry Cert.* 65.

13 *Cal. Pat.* 1555–7, 348–50; 1558–60, 397–403.

14 Smyth, *Church and Par.* 3; Holland, *St Margt's*, 165–6.

15 *St Margt's, Westm Abbey: A concise Guide.*

16 WAM 18134; 18135.

17 WAM 18139; 18144; 18164.

18 *Cal Treas. Bks*, X. 514.

others, feoffees for the poor of St Margaret's, of all the great tithes belonging to the parsonage of St Margaret's, and all the seats in the middle chancel of the church and burials fees for that area, in return for 53*s.* 4*d.* to the chapter, repairs to the middle chancel, and 13*s.* 4*d.* or 6*s.* 8*d.* to the curate for every adult or child buried there. This replaced a similar lease of 1747.[1] In 1851 St Margaret's had an endowment of £8 8*s.* in tithe, and received fees of £240 and Easter offerings of £98.[2] In 1887 the incumbent received £15 for commuted tithes in St Margaret detached (Kensington and Knightsbridge).[3]

MEDIEVAL CHURCH LIFE

The names of curates serving the parish church are known from *c.*1200.[4] In 1268 Henry III paid a chaplain there an annual salary of 60*s.*, presumably a continuation of the service for his daughter which he had established in 1241 for the same fee at the unlocated chapel of St Margaret's.[5] This chaplain appears to have been an addition to the parochial clergy, since there is no other indication of royal control of patronage in St Margaret's in the Middle Ages. In 1381 the parochial curate was assisted by four other celebrants, Simon, William, Nicholas, and John, with Thomas the clerk.[6] In 1416 the sacrist leased the vicarage to John Latener for 20 years at a rent of £13 6*s.* 8*d.*: John was to act as parish priest, or to supply another priest if he became infirm.[7]

A rent charge of 2*s.* was due to church of St Margaret from land at Endith granted to sacrist by Richard son of John son of Edward the reeve *c.*1230, and one of 5*s.* from land held at her death by Joan Charles in 1305.[8] In 1366 William de Hussebourne received licence to alienate 20*s.* rent in Longditch in the vill of Westminster to the abbot and convent, to provide a daily wax light at masses at St Margaret's high altar.[9] By the late 15th century such grants, as well as obits, seem to have been channelled though parish fraternities or guilds.

Residents of Westminster formed at least eight guilds in association with the parish church, of which the principal was the fraternity of the Assumption of the Virgin Mary, usually referred to as the guild of St Mary, founded not long before 1431 and confirmed as a corporation in 1440. The guild had a number of important functions in relation to the local community, one of which was to provide masses for its deceased members, and by the late 15th century it had a guild chapel with 3 altars in the parish church, and supported 3 permanent chantry priests.[10] Other lesser guilds were dedicated to St

Cornelius (by 1498), St John (in 1500), St George (*c.*1509), the Holy Trinity (by 1510), Corpus Christi (by *c.*1514), St Christopher, and St Anne (both mentioned 1517).[11] Only St Cornelius is known to have been incorporated, in 1514, enabling it, like St Mary's guild, to hold property.[12] These guilds are mainly known about from bequests made to them, their donations to the church, or attendance in various ways at funerals or saints' festivals.

The original church was probably rebuilt to some degree *c.*1300 to accommodate an increased population, and from 1399 to 1428 the sacrist, as vicar, paid for a new, enlarged chancel, with the parishioners subscribing over £8 for a newly-glazed east window.[13] A chapel of St Nicholas existed in the church in 1482.[14] In the 1480s the parishioners decided to build a new church, possibly an indication of their desire for a major public building in the town.[15] The designer and first master mason was probably Robert Stowell (d. 1505), master of the abbey masons, and the work was supervised by leading parishioners. What was finally achieved by the time of its dedication in April 1523 was a large and fashionable parish church in conventional Perpendicular style built to a coherent design and symmetrical except for the north-western position of the tower. The chancel was one of the last parts to be rebuilt, in 1517–18: although it was the responsibility of the monks as rectors, the parishioners gave a donation of £30, possibly to spur them on.[16] The monks paid £160 for the chancel, but the cost of the church to the parishioners was *c.*£2,000. Though there may have been some large benefactors, such as Lady Mary Billing, said to have been responsible for the south aisle, the accounts show that the vast majority of parishioners contributed, doubling and then quadrupling the usual income of the churchwardens during periods of building; fund-raising activities were organized, such as a parish lottery and a children's may game, as well as the benevolences drawn up with lists of subscribers, house-to-house collections, and contributions from the parish guilds. A new peal of five bells was hung 1527–8; three were cast out of the old set, the Assumption guild provided one more, and the last was made from pewter pots, latten basins and the like, collected in the parish and then delivered to the bell-founder.[17]

Tothill Chapel

The chapel of St Mary Magdalen, Tothill, was mentioned in the reign of Henry III, *c.*1230 and *c.*1250,[18] but the date of its foundation is unknown. It stood on the south

1 Guildhall MS 2032.
2 TNA, HO 129/4, 2/1/12 (f. 26).
3 *Return of Tithes Commuted and apportioned*, H.C. 214 (1887), LXIV. p. 123.
4 Rosser, *Medieval Westm.* App. II, lists curates occurring in records *c.*1200–1556, to whom should be added Alexander *c.*1230 (WAM 17161).
5 *Cal. Pat.* 1266–72, 261; above, Intro.: Abbey's Par.
6 *Ch in London* 1375–92, 38.   7 WAM 17730.
8 WAD, f. 351; *Cal. Inq. PM.* IV. 203 (Mote estate).
9 *Cal. Pat.* 1364–7, 229.
10 Rosser, *Medieval Westm.* 285–7 and n.; above, Landownership, Other Eccles. Ests (Fraternity).
11 Rest of para. based on Rosser, *Medieval Westm.* 273n, 282–5.
12 TNA, C 66/622, m. 28.
13 Rosser, *Medieval Westm.* 263–4.
14 *Cal. Close*, 1476–85, 271.
15 Rosser, *Medieval Westm.* 264.   16 Ibid. 268.
17 Ibid. 270–1.   18 WAM 17401, 17406.

side of Tothill street, west of the junction with the road leading into Tothill fields and thence to Neat. Walter 'parson of the church of Tothill' is mentioned in 1278,[1] and William Crouches, warden of Tothill chapel, exchanged with William Albone for a church in the diocese of Ely in 1371. The right of presentation belonged to the abbot, except during vacancies of the abbacy when it passed to the Crown.[2]

By the early 16th century the chapel was sometimes referred to as the free chapel of St Mary Magdalen and St Armill, or just St Armill's.[3] During a vacancy of the abbacy in 1532, Henry VIII granted the chapel to John Hulston of Westminster for life, with its appurtenances and with liberty of bread and service and anciently accustomed *acommodicat*, as had been held by Philip Tymmys.[4] The advowson was granted back to the refounded abbey in 1556, and to the collegiate church of St Peter in 1560.[5] When it ceased to be used for worship is unknown, but by 1599 the 'chapel of St Armill' was no longer standing and the site, known as St Ermin's hill, was being let to an almshouse charity by the dean and chapter.[6]

Private Chapels

Leading residents received licences to have private chapels on their property in the parish, with the right to oblations reserved to the parish priest of St Margaret's: Henry Marshal, bishop of Exeter, in Longditch in 1190s;[7] Robert Mauduit in Longditch in 1190s, remaining under jurisdiction of the parish priest;[8] Hubert de Burgh, who c.1222 took over the property and chapel of William of Ely, treasurer of king in 1190s, by the Thames,[9] later the inn of the archbishops of York who had a chapel there in 1326;[10] Odo the goldsmith of Westminster, surveyor of the king's works, by the Thames in 1230s;[11] and John de Lovecote, a chantry in his chapel dedicated to St John Baptist in 1285.[12]

CHURCH LIFE AFTER 1540

The refounded chapter continued to appoint curates, generally for life. Curates appointed in the 1620s and 30s were required to preach on the first Sunday of each month and on four other occasions each year.[13] Gilbert Wimberley (d. 1653), curate from 1631,[14] also held a

prebend in Wells Cathedral from 1632, and was sequestered in 1644, when the House of Commons appointed Samuel Gibson,[15] still minister in 1645–6.[16] Dr Wimberley's sub-curate, Robert White, serving the cure in Wimberley's absence in 1636, appealed to Archbishop Laud for assistance against two Catholic priests who were seeking to convert sick parishioners.[17] During the Commonwealth, lecturers at St Margaret's included Seth Wood, later a Congregational minister, and Edward Pearse, prolific author and divine, ejected in 1662; both were also lecturers at the abbey.[18]

From 1614, St Margaret's had an important role as the parish church of the Houses of Parliament. In that year, as a political gesture the Commons held a service there, imitating the service held at the abbey by the monarch and the Lords on the opening of Parliament. St Margaret's was used for state services from 1660, but by the time such services were abolished in 1859 official attendance had already ceased except for certain special occasions. The relationship meant that St Margaret's received funds from Parliament for repairs from the 17th century up to 1845; between 1734 and 1815 the grants amounted to £25,370, and another £10,855 up to 1845. All MPs were automatically parishioners of St Margaret's since the Palace of Westminster lay within the parish boundary.[19]

Many of the alterations made during and after the 17th century were to suit MPs as well as local parishioners. In the last two-thirds of the 17th century a large three-decker pulpit was installed, as well as new seats and galleries, and a Speaker's pew. One gallery was erected sometime after 1644,[20] and another in 1681–2 to designs by Wren and at the cost of Sir John Cutler, with several pews intended to be let to persons of quality for the benefit of the poor of the parish; the two best in the 4th row were let for £3 a year each in 1682.[21] When the 17th-century galleries taken down in 1758, the parish paid £21 a year instead to the poor,[22] and the children of the Grey Coat School, who had occupied galleries flanking the chancel, were seated at the back of the new aisle galleries.[23] A beautification programme begun in 1692 provided the east end with armorial glass and liturgical furnishings,[24] and by 1714 the church was described as having a large chancel, fine altar-piece, two

1 TNA, CP 40/24, rot. 72.
2 *Cal. Pat.* 1370–4, 55.
3 Possibly St Armel, a popular Welsh saint, suggesting connection with accession of Hen VII: *London Top. Rec.* XXIV. 117.   4 TNA, C 66/661, m. 4.
5 *Cal. Pat.* 1555–7, 348–50; 1558–60, 402.
6 *Endowed Chars London*, V. 230.
7 *Westm. Charters*, 106.
8 Ibid. 163.
9 Ibid. 101; WAD, f. 347.
10 *Cal. Pat.* 1324–7, 284.
11 WAM 17454.
12 WAD, ff. 352v.–3.
13 WAM 18134; 18135; 18139; 18144; 18164.

14 WAM 18139; 18144; 18164.
15 *Walker Revised*, 62–3; *Fasti Ecclesiae Anglicanae 1541–1857*, V *Bath & Wells* (1979), 92.
16 *Cal. SP Dom.* 1645–7, 427, 437, 448, 460.
17 Ibid. 1636–7, 109.
18 *Calamy Revised*, 384, 542; *DNB* sv. Pearse. List of mins. to 1895 in Hennessy, *Novum Rep.* 438–9.
19 Smyth, *Church and Par.* 5–6, 26; Holland, *St Margt's*, 148; below, Ch Fabric.
20 Friedman, *Georgian Par. Ch*, 88.
21 TNA, C 93/42/35.
22 *Endowed Chars London*, V. 242.
23 Friedman, *Georgian Par. Ch*, 88–9.
24 Ibid. 90.

large galleries, a large organ-gallery and organ, and a tower 85 feet high with 6 large bells.[1] In 1714 prayers were held each week on Wednesdays and Fridays, as well as holy days, and lectures included an annual sermon on All Souls' day for which Mrs Joan Barnet (d. 1674) left a rent charge of 20s., still being paid in 1899.[2] Several occasional sermons were delivered on public state days and before members of the House of Commons. The minister in 1714 was Dr Nicholas Only, with Robert Dobyns as curate and lecturer. The parish at that date included the new chapel in Tothill fields (Broadway), and those in Duke Street near Storey's gate, and Queen's Square, with six chapels in the almshouses and hospitals in the parish.[3]

The huge 18th-century programme of repair and restoration was directed by the vestry and it was their taste which was expressed, although the House of Commons, which had petitioned for the rebuilding of the tower, supplied most of the funds. The first phase of work, from 1757 until *c*.1760, included an elaborate new Speaker's pew, a polygonal chancel and an imported 16th-century east window complete with painted glass and stone tracery. Another phase, carried out under S.P. Cockerell in 1792–1802 improved the structure and embellished some of the earlier work. Cockerell rebuilt the aisles and the upper part of the nave, decorated the chancel, pulpit and organ galleries with carved Gothic woodwork, and replaced the Speaker's seat yet again.[4]

The appointments to the incumbency of St Margaret's were often political ones, and during the 18th century many incumbents were non resident. Dr Charles Fynes (later Clinton), curate 1796–1828, was also rector of Cromwell (Notts.) where he usually resided. In 1820 he set aside the vestry's elected choice of lecturer, Revd Isaac Saunders, minister of Broadway Chapel, whom Fynes accused of being too 'methodistical' and evangelical to share his pulpit. The parishioners felt that as they paid the lecturer they should be able to select him, but Fynes pointed out that no-one could lecture from the pulpit without the sanction of the incumbent and a licence from the dean and chapter. The vestry then chose the other candidate, whose first lecture was greeted by a disturbance in the church, and Fynes brought a law suit against one of the tradesmen whom he accused of being a ring-leader.[5]

Several incumbents of the 19th century were more parochially-minded and active locally in different ways. Henry Hart Milman, curate (later rector) 1835–49, worked among the poor of the Tothill slums, served on many local boards and committees, and, a pioneer in slum clearance work, actively supported the schemes of the Westminster Improvement Commissioners; a noted

scholar, he was later dean of St Paul's. In 1851, when the church seated 1,649, attendance ranged from 950 (a.m.) to 250 (evg),[6] but under Frederic William Farrar, rector 1876–95, a dynamic parish priest, St Margaret's saw an unprecedented religious revival, with congregations rising in 1886 to 1730 (a.m.) and 1362 (p.m.).[7] Farrar raised £30,000 to restore and refurnish the church's interior and the derelict churchyard. Assisted by a team of able curates he organized the work of the over-populated parish, completely changing the concept of parochial work there and made St Margaret's the centre of a vigorous religious life. He built a mission hall, taught in church schools, founded clubs and societies, and gave popular lectures on various literary subjects. He kept in constant contact with his voluntary workers, including the 60 Sunday school teachers whose schools were one of the show-pieces of the London diocese. He also kept in touch with problems in his parish and presided over meetings of district visitors, and supported the Salvation Army because of the problems of drink, crime, and prostitution he saw in his parish. Despite all that work, Farrar was also an internationally famous preacher, preaching 120 sermons a year, and filling St Margaret's, where he regularly preached on Sunday mornings, and the abbey in the evenings. His preaching made St Margaret's one of the best-known parishes in the diocese, but he was passed over when a new dean was required in 1881, because his vehemence worried the queen, and only became dean in 1895 when he was 65.[8]

By 1903 attendance had declined to 542 (a.m.) and 776 (p.m.). Missions were also being held in New Tothill Street (60 a.m.) and Lewisham Street (31 p.m.).[9] The church lost its parish in 1973 but continued to offer weekly Sunday services.

Although from 1876 all financial support from MPs was on a purely personal basis, the connection with St Margaret's continued to be valued. In 1984 the Speaker launched an appeal to raise funds for repair and restoration of the stonework and roof, and £1 million was raised within a year enabling the work to be started in 1986.[10] Three of the rectors before 1973 were also chaplains to the Speaker of the House of Commons, and since that date all the rectors have also held that post.

CHURCH FABRIC

Before its replacement by the present building, the church founded in the 12th century and probably partly rebuilt *c*.1300 comprised a nave and north aisle, 'St George's aisle', and the chancel which apparently opened into two side chapels, the Lady chapel on the north and Trinity chapel on the south.[11] Rebuilding began in 1486–8 with a south aisle, which was probably

1 Paterson, *Pietas Lond.* 146–9.
2 *Endowed Chars London*, V. 344.
3 Paterson, *Pietas Lond.* 146–9.
4 Friedman, *Georgian Par. Ch*, 79–95, 101–10.
5 Smyth, *Church and Par.* 128–33.
6 TNA, HO 129/4, 2/1/12 (f. 26).

7 *Brit. Weekly*, 5 Nov. 1886, p. 3.
8 Smyth, *Church and Par.* 168–72, 180–1.
9 Mudie-Smith, *Rel. Life*, 105.
10 Smyth, *Church and Par.* 210–11; Holland, *St Margt's*, 92, 145.
11 Rosser, *Medieval Westm.* 265, 266n.

the widening of an earlier one (perhaps the St George's aisle) as existing rafters were extended to cover it; it was in use in 1490. In 1492 the king gave the parishioners licence to demolish his building called the Poultry, granting them the site in frankalmoign, to allow them to enlarge the east end of the church.[1] In 1494 work was being carried out on the choir, which was then boxed in so that the side chapels could be demolished and the new south aisle, and probably the existing or renewed north one, could be extended eastwards without disrupting use of the church. Roofing was carried out in 1497–8, 1499–1500 and 1501, as the work progressed. The structural walls and arcades were probably completed by 1500; the following year the new chapels at the eastern ends of the aisles were paved and the windows inserted in the west end and north aisle. The completed roof was tiled in 1502–3. Richard Russell, carpenter, installed the carved nave ceiling, with rosettes in the panels, in 1503. A battlemented parapet with gargoyles was added, and the interior was paved 1503–4. The chancel and north-western tower were left unfinished for 10 years; the foundation stone of the tower was laid in 1515, with Thomas Redman (d. 1516) the master mason, succeeded by his son Henry, and completed by 1523.

The church as restored to approximately its medieval design is rectangular with tall eight-bayed arcades down the length of the church, a clerestory over, a timber roof on corbelled wall shafts, and no structural division between nave and chancel. The tracery was not accurately reconstructed.[2] The tower, rebuilt by John James in a papery Gothick manner, was part of an extensive restoration which was begun by James in 1735–7, and included replacing the roof and refacing the original Kentish rag and Reigate and Caen stone dressings in Portland stone, a refacing that has been replaced at least once. The necessary work was continued in 1757–8 by Kenton Couse, but all his work and the embellishments made by S.P. Cockerell, 1799–1802, were removed by Sir George Gilbert Scott in the 1870s, except for the carved reredos of 1758.[3] Scott, who also retained the fine 16th-century stained glass, re-used in successive east windows, designed new furnishings and replaced the roof again. In 1891 and 1894 respectively an elaborate western porch and south-eastern one were added by J.L. Pearson. The east end was lengthened by *c.*6 ft in 1905–6. The fittings are of many dates and origins, and the stained glass, also of many periods, is considered among the most interesting in any London parish church.

Churchyard   Many well-known people were buried in the church or churchyard, including William Caxton

1491; John Skelton, poet laureate, 1529; Sir Walter Raleigh 1618; Admiral Blake 1661; John Pym 1661; Wenceslaus Hollar 1677. The church contains many monuments to public figures.[4] In 1881–2 all the tombstones, except for the table tomb of Alexander Davies (d. 1665), were removed, and the churchyard and the abbey churchyard were turfed over and laid out as a public garden, together amounting to *c.*2¼ acres, maintained by the local authority.[5]

POST-REFORMATION CHURCHES AND CHAPELS

In 1711 it was decided to build two new churches in the parish of St Margaret as part of the fifty new churches in London, and although the dean and chapter offered land in Tothill fields, a site in Millbank was chosen for one of them, which became St John's, Smith Square (below). The chapter requested that the new chapel in Tothill Street become the other,[6] but this did not happen, and the chapel, known later as Broadway chapel, remained a daughter church of St Margaret's, rebuilt as Christ Church (below) in 1843. The parish was also served in the 18th and 19th centuries by proprietary chapels in Duke Street, New Way, and Queen's Square, as well as the Chapel Royal in Whitehall Palace. A temporary church, St Mark's, was opened in Tothill fields in 1848, replaced by the permanent St Andrew's, Ashley Place, in 1855. The proprietary chapels disappeared in the course of the 19th century as district churches came into being, and the district churches themselves closed immediately after the Second World War.

Christ Church, Great Chapel Street, Victoria Street

Christ Church was built as the successor to the nearby Broadway or New chapel, which originated in a donation of £400 made by George Darell (d. 1631), prebendary of Westminster, towards building a chapel on Tothill fields to serve local inhabitants.[7] Donations were obtained from parishioners, and part of the parish's additional burial ground was chosen as the site. Because it was near the Palace of Westminster, the dean and chapter sought permission from the Privy Council. The shell was complete by 1636, but the vestry continued to pay for work, including a compass ceiling, 12 capitals, and a black and white marble font; pews were added in 1638, and a rate for completion levied in 1639. The font was made by Nicholas Stone in 1641 and was later moved to St Margaret's church.[8] Delay in opening the chapel was probably because no provision had been made to support a minister, but in December 1642

1 *Cal. Pat.* 1485–94, 389.
2 For description of building and furnishings see Pevsner, *London 6: Westm.* 207–9.
3 Friedman, *Georgian Par. Ch,* 79–96.
4 Clarke, *London Chs,* 173–5. Mons described in Pevsner, *London 6: Westm.* 209–10.

5 Pevsner, *London 6: Westm.* 210–11; LCC, *Burial Grounds,* 5.
6 *Fifty New Chs,* 4, 7, 106–7, 148.
7 Acct of chapel based on P. Guillery, 'The Broadway Chapel, Westm.: a forgotten exemplar' (*London Top. Rec.* XXVI, 1990), 97–133.
8 Pevsner, *London 6: Westm.* 208.

House of Commons ordered Sir Robert Pye, one of Darell's trustees, to open the chapel, and first minister was probably financed from the former Westminster Chapter estate, of which Pye was chairman. In 1652 Pye gave eight houses in Petty France in trust to maintain minister, on condition that he and his heirs had right of nomination. He also had a gallery and several pews built for his tenants' use. Onesiphorus Rood, chaplain to House of Lords in the 1640s, was appointed curate in 1648.[1]

The chapel's Palladian design was remarkable for the 1630s, and was probably directly influenced by Inigo Jones, who may have been consulted by the Privy Council; some of the craftsmen employed there had also worked on the architect's queen's chapel, St James's Palace. The style was Palladio's version of the Tuscan, also used by Jones for example at St Paul's Covent Garden. Brick-built brick with stone dressings, the building was low with slightly-projecting transepts. The classical windows were filled with Gothic tracery and stained glass (destroyed during Commonwealth) possibly the result of pressure from Laudian elements in the Westminster chapter. The centralized interior, which had no obvious orientation and no chancel, was novel; columns and groined ceilings over the central vessel and transepts defined a cross-in-square plan. Additions made after the Restoration included a communion table and rails, and north and south and possibly west galleries.

In 1714 it was a chapel of ease to St Margaret's; daily prayers were held, and it was maintained by £50 p.a. given by Edmund Pye; several charity sermons preached during the year. The minister was Dr George Smalridge, bishop of Bristol, and Thomas Bowyer was lecturer and curate.[2] In 1721 the parishioners took the dean and chapter to court over their right both to the site and to nominate the minister. In 1724 the chapel was briefly considered for conversion into one of the fifty new churches, but was eventually demolished to make way for a new church.

Christ Church, of ragstone with a north-west tower designed in Early English style by Ambrose Poynter in 1841, was consecrated in 1843, and was paid for by subscriptions from parishioners, and donations from the dean and chapter, Commissioners of Woods and Forests, and the Church Commissioners. It was assigned a district from St Margaret's in 1844,[3] and was endowed from the canonry attached to that church, an endowment increased to £500 p.a. in 1866. The patron was rector of St Margaret's and the benefice was united to St Peter, Eaton Sq., c.1953. The church was designed to seat 1,246 free, and 304 others, but in 1851 the attendance was 700 (a.m.), 600 (evg), and much less in 1886 (151 a.m., 342 p.m.) and 1903 (154 a.m., 122 p.m.). The church was closed in 1952 and demolished in 1954. A vicarage designed by Seddon was built on part of the churchyard between 1869 and 1888, and was also demolished in 1954.[4] The churchyard became public garden at the corner of Victoria Street and Broadway.

St Andrew, Ashley Place, Victoria Street

Built with a grant from the Church Building Commissioners in 1853–5 to 13th-century style designs by G.G. Scott, it served a district chapelry of St Margaret's from 1856,[5] and was endowed out of the canonry attached to that church, whose rector was patron.[6] Its value was £503 and pew rents. Consecrated in 1855, the church had seating for at least 1100, 600 of them free.[7] Evening services were mostly choral in 1871.[8] Attendance in 1886 was 415 (a.m.) and 1128 (p.m.); in 1903, 335 (a.m.) and 187 (p.m.). It was closed after Second World War and demolished c.1953.[9]

St Mark's Temporary Church Located in Tothill fields and licensed in 1848 until a permanent church was built, it was paid for by the incumbent, assisted by private subscriptions and had 400 free seats. Its attendance in 1851, when it was said to be closing, was 140 (a.m. and p.m.). It was presumably replaced by St Andrews.

Proprietary Chapels

Duke Street Episcopal Chapel Located in Storey's Gate and founded by Mr Higgins and private subscribers in 1709, it was used by residents of Duke and Charles streets and Crown Court.[10] It was one of three proprietary chapels in dispute with the dean and chapter in 1748, and was still privately owned in 1851, when the income was from pew rents; it seated c.250; attendance was then 70 (a.m.) and 25 (aft.).

New Way Chapel, off Great Almonry Street Probably a former Presbyterian chapel,[11] and shown on Rocque's map of 1745, in 1748 it was one of three proprietary chapels in dispute with the dean and chapter.[12] It was called the Duke of York's chapel in 1813.[13]

Queen's Square Chapel (St Peter's Episcopal Chapel)[14] Founded in 1706 in Queen Anne's Gate by Charles Shales for the use of neighbouring tenants,[15] it was used as Queen Sq. mission hall 1872–86, and as a parish room

1 *Calamy Revised*, 417.   2 Paterson, *Pietas Lond.* 204–6.

3 *London Gaz.* 20 Nov 1844, p. 4409.

4 Pevsner, *London*, I (1973 edn), 487; Pevsner, *London 6: Westm.* 723n; *Crockford* (1951–2).

5 *London Gaz.* 1 Aug 1856, p. 2661.

6 Guildhall MS 19224/385.

7 Port, *Six Hundred Chs*, 156–7.

8 *Mackeson's Guide* (1871).

9 Port, *Six Hundred Chs*, 156–7.

10 Paterson, *Pietas Lond.* 73–4.

11 Below, Prot. Nonconf., Presbs.

12 *Survey of London*, X. 139.

13 *Regency A to Z*.

14 Except where stated, acct based on *Survey of London*, X. 139–41.

15 Paterson, *Pietas Lond.* 248.

48. *Knightsbridge Chapel in the late 18th century, facing south-west onto Knightsbridge highway and showing the new front of 1789 as a clear addition to the earlier chapel of 1699.*

by Christ Church, 1873–82; it went into secular use after 1886.[1] Proposals for its establishment were made between the dean and chapter of Westminster and, presumably, Shales; the estimated income from pew rents was £170, and the expenses were to include £50 to the minister, £10 to the charity school, ground rent £60, and £50 to the clerk and others and for repairs. The building was to be invested in trustees including the minister, who was to be licensed by the chapter, and Shales was to be perpetual patron. The chapel trustees were to form a vestry, to let pews, and excess of profits over expenses was to be paid to the minister. The chapel lay on the N side of the stable yard (Queen Sq. Mews) above coach-houses belonging to the square. Probably with a bell turret over its gabled east end and with two storeys of round-headed windows on the west, it was described as a neat building with gallery and pulpit in 1714, where prayers were held daily and Edw. Oliver was minister.[2] In 1748 the chapel was one of three in dispute with the chapter over the disposal of money collected at communion; the ministers then in office were said to be unlicensed. Thos Baker was minister in 1748 and in 1759, with John Maddox assisting; Wm Bailey was minister in 1842. It was called St Peter's Episcopal chapel from 1844 when the minister was Dr John Flowerdew

Colls. Jas Kelly, formerly of Charlotte chapel (St Geo.), was minister 1848–55, and also patron 1855. In 1851 it had seating for 400, 40 free; attendance was then 180 (a.m.), 125 (evg). Although it was listed in directories 1855–69, no further incumbents were given, and it was apparently closed by 1870. It included a ragged school, until 1871.

KNIGHTSBRIDGE (ST MARGARET'S DETACHED)

Knightsbridge Chapel (Holy Trinity)

The lazar house at Knightsbridge, founded by William and Agnes Thomson shortly before 1474, included a chapel for the use of the founders and other inmates, built on a site leased from the abbot of Westminster and subsequently from the dean and chapter of Westminster.[3] In 1629 William Laud, bishop of London, with the consent of the vicar and churchwardens of St Martin-in-the-Fields, granted a licence to the inhabitants of Knightsbridge village to rebuild the decayed hospital chapel, which they were using as their main place of worship, to use as a chapel of ease on condition they attended their respective parish churches (St Margaret and St Martin-in-the-Fields) at least once a quarter and at Easter. It was finished and consecrated five years later,[4]

1 *Survey of London*, X. 137–41.
2 Paterson, *Pietas Lond.* 248.
3 Guildhall MS 9171/6, ff. 254v.–5; TNA, C 1/52/274–7. For

hosp., see *Rel. Hos of London and Middx*, ed. C.M. Barron and M. Davies (2007), 322–3.
4 *Survey of London*, XLV. 41; Paterson, *Pietas Lond.* 127–8.

but was in use by 1633, possibly 1631, when nine men from the congregation certified to Bishop Laud that they would comply with the gesture of kneeling at communion, after discussions with Nathaniel White, described as the curate of Trinity chapel at Knightsbridge.[1] It was intended that pew rents would provide an income to cover maintenance and the curate's stipend, but the rents were apparently inadequate from an early date.[2] Henry Walker, journalist and preacher, was minister at Knightsbridge in 1650,[3] leading to a protest by the inhabitants against his ministry as he had formerly been a 'writer of weekly news'.[4] George Cooke was minister in 1653.[5] The chapel's status was rather anomalous, since although licensed as a chapel of ease to St Martin's, in which parish it stood, most of the area it served was in St Margaret's, and the site belonged to the dean and chapter of Westminster, who were sometimes described as the patron.[6] However, it became more or less a proprietary chapel: the lessees of the lazar house estate in the late 17th and 18th centuries sub-let the chapel, with the chapter appointing the under-tenant as minister.

In 1699 the inhabitants of Knightsbridge began rebuilding the chapel, but were unable to meet the cost and petitioned William III for assistance in finishing it,[7] presumably because the king then lived nearby at Kensington Palace. The outcome is unknown, but since Nicholas Birkhead, goldsmith of London and lessee of the lazar house estate from 1668, is widely attributed with the rebuilding in 1699, it seems likely that the inhabitants had to turn to him for assistance instead. The chapel was described in 1714, when Robert Hicks was minister, as a 'fair chapel of ease', still kept in good repair, with prayers and sermon twice every Sunday, and communion once a month.[8] Other ministers or curates there included Humphrey Peirsehouse in 1747, succeeded by Dr Anselm Bailey by 1763,[9] who was still there in 1780; he was succeeded by John Gamble.[10] The chapel was enlarged, giving it 300 seats, refronted and repaired in 1789,[11] presumably by Dixon Gamble, lessee from 1788. It had a central entrance from the street, with stairs nearby to the galleries on three sides, a central cupola over the entrance with a bell given by the lessee, Mary Birkhead, in 1733, and an organ built by Hancock in 1770.[12]

Hibbert Binney, minister from 1833, found the chapel dilapidated and uncomfortable, and tried to regularize its status and rebuild on a larger scale, to no avail. Interest in providing increased church accom-

modation led the Church Building Commissioners to offer £2,000, but the opening of St Paul's, Wilton Place, in 1843 obviated the need for a new church at the east end of Knightsbridge,[13] and the grant was eventually used for All Saints, Ennismore Gardens. Binney, who lived in Berkshire, complained in 1851 that, despite claiming the patronage, the dean and chapter completely neglected repairs, and commented that it was extraordinary that despite the fact that it was consecrated, they should treat it as a proprietary chapel, letting it out for many years to the highest bidder. He thought this was probably the reason there was no district attached. In 1851, when attendance was 330 (a.m.), 100 (p.m.), the only endowment came from a charge of £30 on land forming part of the former lazar estate; other more irregular income came from pew rents or contributions, amounting to *c.*£120.[14]

With the increase in the local population, the desirability of rebuilding the chapel led to a committee being formed in 1859. The chapel was demolished and Holy Trinity church built on the site. The benefice, of which the dean and chapter of Westminster were patrons, was formed as a consolidated chapelry and a district was assigned out of St Paul, Wilton Place, and All Saints, Ennismore Gardens, in 1866;[15] it was united with All Saints, Ennismore Gardens, in 1970. The living, staffed by a vicar and curate, was valued at £350.[16]

The church, consecrated in 1861, seated 600 and cost £3,600, met by subscriptions.[17] Designed by Raphael Brandon and Henry M. Eyton in Early Decorated style, it stood north–south on its narrow site on the north side of the highway, flanked by two public houses. The site dictated lofty proportions, the need for a clerestory glazed from end to end, and a south entrance with a large Geometrical window over.[18] Despite local protests, the church was replaced by a new building in Prince Consort Road and the old church demolished in 1904.[19]

Holy Trinity, Prince Consort Road The new church, designed in 1901 as one of G.F. Bodley's last works, was not completed until 1906.[20] A fine version of a 14th-century hall church, its street front had a stone-faced gable with elaborate traceried windows and bellcote, and behind a broad wagon-roofed nave, aisles, and an outer aisle. Bodley designed most of the fittings, including the triptych reredos executed 1911–12, and was commemorated in a monument by E.P. Warren, 1910.[21]

1 *Cal. SP Dom.* 1631–3, 231.
2 *Survey of London*, XLV. 41.
3 *Oxford DNB.*
4 Hist. MSS. Com. *4th Rep.*, p. 188.
5 *Cal. SP Dom.* 1652–3, 342.
6 Guildhall MS 9556, p. 38.
7 *Cal. SP Dom.* 1699–1702, 200.
8 Paterson, *Pietas Lond.* 127–8.
9 Guildhall MS 9556, p. 38.
10 Guildhall MS 9557, f. 40.
11 J.N. Brewer, *Beauties of Eng. & Wales*, X (1816), 158–9.

12 *Survey of London*, XLV. 41.
13 Ibid.
14 TNA, HO 129/4, 2/1/13 (f. 27).
15 *London Gaz.* 6 Feb. 1866, p. 680.
16 *London Diocese Bk* (1970 edn), 95.
17 *Survey of London*, XLV. 41.
18 Eastlake, *Gothic Revival*, App. p. 111.
19 *Survey of London*, XLV. 42.
20 RIBA Drawings Collection, catalogue of Bodley drawings PB391/1(1&3).
21 Pevsner, *London 3: NW.* 455.

All Saints, Ennismore Gardens

The first church in the area was Brompton chapel (later Brompton School) in Montpelier Street. Founded in 1769, it had stuccoed walls, a pediment, cupola, and Venetian chancel window.[1] In 1845, E.W. Harness, then minster, assisted in obtaining the site for a new church to north, which became All Saints Ennismore Gardens.[2]

Consecrated in 1849, All Saints was assigned a district which extended from Kensington Palace Gardens to Albert Gate and included the barracks and streets on the south side of Kensington Road, a socially mixed area with the very poor in crowded areas near the barracks. It had income from tithes, fees, a portion of a stall in Westminster Abbey, and pew rents, put at £400 c.1870.[3] The rector of St Margaret's was patron.

The church, which was built with money from the Church Building Commissioners and private subscriptions, provided 500 free seats and 800 others. In 1851 it was said to be thinly attended except during the Season, and the average attendance was 700 (a.m.), 300 (evg), plus 100–130 Sunday scholars.[4] Attendance in 1886 was still quite good at 501 (a.m.) and 353 (p.m.), and in 1903 was 404 (a.m.) and 126 (p.m.). When Canon Anthony Deane was vicar early in the 20th century he found that, because the many distinguished parishioners were absent in the country at weekends, most of the congregation came from outside the parish.[5] When the church closed in 1955, its district was merged with that of Holy Trinity, Prince Consort Road, the church was then leased to the Russian Orthodox Church, who dedicated it to the Assumption and All Saints and later bought the freehold.[6]

The building, designed by Lewis Vulliamy c.1846 and built 1848–9, follows the pattern of a north Italian early Christian basilica with Lombardic gable and a campanile (added in the 1870s) and very tall galleried interior with cast-iron columns. The fashionable style extended to decoration in the apse by Owen Jones, replaced in a protracted scheme of embellishment which began in the 1890s and included new vestries and seating, the formation of a chancel, moving the organ, and organ case and screen designed 1920 by Joubert but not completed until 1928. The decoration was by Heywood Sumner, C. Harrison Townsend 1892, and Derwent Wood 1911.[7]

ST MARTIN-IN-THE-FIELDS

The earliest securely datable reference to the church, as St Martin of Charing, occurs c.1180x1187, when, together with St Clement Danes, it was among some 19 churches, many in London, confirmed by Bishop Gilbert Foliot as paying a pension to the monks of Westminster.[8] A chaplain of St Martin's, however, attests a charter which may be earlier, though still in the reign of Henry II (1152–89), and a canon of St Bartholomew's, writing c.1180, tells of an unchaste priest called Wymond who had governed the church for many years.[9] He is perhaps to be identified with Wymund, a prebendary of Neasden at St Paul's in the early 12th century, who is mysteriously described as decanus in Lincoln, perhaps an error for London.[10]

St Martin's was certainly parochial by 1200. Although the extent of the medieval parish is in some doubt, by then it included the settlement by the Thames at Charing and probably also the vill of Eye, the largely unsettled area between the Tyburn and the Westbourne which was definitely part of the parish in the late 13th century (below). The first known reference to its full parochial name, St Martin-in-the-Fields, occurs in 1269.[11]

From 1534 on the order of Henry VIII, the church served the whole of the vill of Westminster north of a line running roughly east–west from the Thames through the later Horse Guards, as well as the vill of Eye. In the mid 17th century the parish was reduced when Covent Garden and its inhabitants were assigned to the new church of St Paul, by 1646 a separate parish.[12] From the later 17th century the parish was reduced still further with the creation of three new parishes, St James, St Anne, and St George,[13] until by 1724 only an irregular area running from the parish church and the riverside near Charing Cross westwards to Buckingham Palace remained. About half of this was taken up by two palaces and two royal parks, and by the mid 19th century St Martin's was known as the Royal Parish.[14]

ORIGINS

The church may have existed long before it emerges in

1 Pevsner, *London II*, 247.

2 *Survey of London*, XLV. 186.

3 *Mackeson's Guide* (1871).

4 TNA, HO 129/4, 2/1/8 (f. 21): 1851 not counted as curate could not attend because of weather.

5 Pevsner, *London 3: NW*. 465; Clarke, *London Chs*, 187.

6 *Survey of London*, XLV. 189; below, Foreign Chs (Russian Orthodox).

7 Pevsner, *London 3: NW*. 465; Clarke, *London Chs*, 187.

8 BL, Cotton Faust. A. III, f. 253v.; *Westm. Charters*, no. 211; for text and an earlier dating, c. 1163–81, see *Letters and Charters*

of Gilbert Foliot, ed. Morey & Brooke, 489–90: above Religious Hist., Intro.

9 *Westm. Charters*, no. 404; *The Book of the Foundation of St Bartholomew's, London*, ed. N. Moore, Early Eng. Text Soc. 163 (1923), 47; BL, MS Cotton Vesp. B IX, f. 67v.

10 D.E. Greenway, *Fasti Ecclesiae Anglicanae, 1066–1300*: I, *St Paul's London*, p. 63; *Bk of Fdn of St Bart*. 47.

11 TNA, C 66/87, m. 14.

12 *Cal. SP Dom*. 1639, 217.

13 Below.

14 TNA, HO 129/5, 1/1/3 (f. 3).

the written record.[1] The crucial evidence is provided by finds from around or under the present church made in 1725 and 2005–7. They comprise three stone coffins, probably late Roman, and some seven earth burials, together with accompanying grave-goods, including jewellery, glass cups and a hanging bowl, mostly from the late 6th or 7th century and suggestive of relatively high status. One of the stone coffins was certainly in situ, as may have been the others, although the latter had both been reused. All three and one earth burial were aligned north-south, while other earth burials were aligned east-west. Although no remains of the pre-Gibbs church have been found, there is evidence from early 18th-century plans that it was on a different alignment, shared by the east-west burials and by the medieval cemetery above them.

The most plausible interpretation of the evidence is that it represents a Romano-British cemetery with burials aligned north-south, last used in the late 4th or early 5th century and brought back into use in the late 6th or 7th. The reuse of the stone coffins, although occasionally mentioned by Bede in connection with the burial of high ecclesiastics and royal men and women, is very rare, if not unique, in pre-Viking Anglo-Saxon cemeteries.[2] In this instance it may well have been associated with a church established on the site in the conversion period (i.e. shortly after the establishment of the London see at St Paul's in 604). The church's dedication and the extra-mural cemeterial site have parallels in developments at Canterbury after the establishment of the Gregorian mission there in the early 7th century.[3]

Although there is no known evidence of burial on the site between the 7th century and the 12th, it is possible that church and cemetery continued to serve the developing *wic*, especially after the disappearance of the cemetery at Covent Garden and of dispersed burial at the edges of the settlement.[4] Although they perhaps suffered temporary abandonment during the apostasy of the East Saxon kings (after 616) and again during the Viking attacks on the *wic* in the later 9th century, the church and cemetery's evident importance in 1222, when they were expressly excluded from the abbot's exempt jurisdiction, suggests that they survived or came back into use.[5] The reference is a puzzling one, but should probably be taken to mean a parochial institution, not simply the church and its immediate environs;[6] St Martin's was certainly parochial by then.[7] The church's importance for the bishop is, moreover, confirmed by his appointment of

49. *St Martin-in-the-Fields parish church, designed by James Gibbs in 1720, west front from Trafalgar Square; this front was originally seen obliquely from the narrow St Martin's Lane which was built up on both sides. As the population of St Martin's increased it became more significant as a parish church within Westminster, and by the 20th century was sometimes styled the parish church for London.*

Wymond, priest of St Martin's, as dean of the neighbouring churches (presumably those along the Strand and Fleet Street), well before 1180.[8]

Besides the settlement at Charing, the parish appears from early times to have included the vill of Eye, which apparently had no place of worship within its bounds, apart from a chapel at the abbot's house at Neat, in existence by the early 14th century. Land in Eye was described as in the parish *c.*1280.[9] Since, as the judgement of the papal judges-delegate makes clear, Eye was not in St Margaret's parish in 1222, it was presumably

1 The following section was contributed by Alan Thacker and depends for archaeological information and analysis upon Martin Biddle. 1725 excavations (1725): London, Soc. of Antiquaries, Min. Bk. 1718–32, I, pp. 151, 170; MS 268, f. 63 [p. 119]; BL, Add. MS 4025, ff. 76–7; BM, Dept. of Ethnography 45 C (Hans Sloane, Catalogue of Miscellanea, f. 183. See also *Medieval Archaeology* 51 (2007), 255–8; 52 (2008), 342–6.

2 Bede, *Ecclesiastical History of the English People*, ed. R. Mynors and B. Colgrave (2nd edn, 1991), pp. 367, 394.

3 Nicholas Brooks, *Early History of the Church of Canterbury*

(1984), 16–30.

4 Above, Gen. Intro.; *Medieval Archaeology* 52 (2008), 346–8.

5 *Acta Stephani Langton* (Cant. and York Soc. L), 69–73; above, Religious Hist.: St Margaret's.

6 Reference to the appropriated church (*ecclesia*) of Staines in the same document clearly refers to a church and its parish.

7 WAM 17141, 17142. Cf. ibid. 17152, 17153; WAD f. 136v.–137.   8 *Bk. of Fdn of St Bart.* 47.

9 WAM 17160; WAD, f. 334–v.

already by then in St Martin's. The relatively substantial pension confirmed as payable to the abbey in the 1180s (20s. as against 5s. from St Clement Danes), may also suggest that the parish was a large one. Given that Eye did not pass to the abbot until 1097, it is reasonable to suppose that it had never been in the parish of St Margaret's and even before the Conquest was, as later, connected with St Martin's.

Taken together, the extensive and perhaps scattered nature of the thirteenth-century parish, and the fact that the church was of sufficient importance to be the seat of the local dean in the 12th century and to be retained by the bishop in 1222, suggest that St Martin's may originally have served a large area west of the City and the *wic*, in some ways analogous with the perhaps later parish of an extramural City church, St Andrew Holborn. Its links with Eye are of especial interest here, since Eye contained the hundredal meeting place, the Ossulstone.[1] St Martin's may thus have been an important church in the 10th century if not before, but one whose rights and standing had been progressively eroded by the establishment of Westminster within its ancient *parochia*.

These arguments are not without their problems. It is curious, perhaps, that there is no mention of St Martin's in any of the surviving records from before 1200 (above all in the abbey's own fabrications), and that there are so few references to the parish in the numerous charters issued before the later 13th century. Two of the three properties described as in St Martin's parish in the earlier 13th century are associated with the soke of Mohun, as is another property so described *c.*1250, part of the Templars holding at Charing. There is indeed a possibility that the church belonged to the soke; when granted by Reynold de Mohun to Robert Beauchamp, probably *c.*1245 and certainly prior to 1252, it was said to include the advowsons of churches within the City of London and without, between the Fleet bridge and Charing. The churches thus so specifically referred to are limited in number and include St Martin's.[2]

The abbey was clearly trying to extend its control in the early 13th century in all sorts of ways, including by acquiring the soke of Mohun, which seems to have been the chief lord of land at Charing, and by trying to enforce claims on the two parish churches which lay within its lordship of Westminster, St Martin's and Holy Innocents. It did not entirely succeed with St Martin's, as far as ecclesiastical jurisdiction went, but it did with Holy Innocents.

One reading of this evidence might be that, whatever its early history, there was no longer a church at St Martin's after the Viking attacks and that its emergence

in the records *c.*1200 reflects a relatively recent creation as an estate church of the lords of Mohun, with a small parish not unlike the nearby Holy Innocents. The problems with this interpretation include the status implicit in Wymond's position as dean and in the exclusion from the abbey's exemption of 1222. Above all, there is the parochial connection with Eye; it is difficult to see what parish Eye would have belonged to before 1222, if not St Martin's.

PATRONAGE, INCOME, AND PROPERTY

By the 1240s the abbot had acquired the patronage and a share of the rectorial tithes; a vicarage was in existence but it is not clear who was rector.[3] Nor is it clear who was patron, or who was entitled to the rectorial tithes; before the 1240s the exemption of the church and churchyard from the spiritual jurisdiction of the abbot in 1222 presumably reflects an origin outside the abbey's control. The abbey, however, must have acquired the rectory by 1275, when it obtained papal permission to appropriate St Martin's to support hospitality for its guests, an arrangement confirmed by the bishop of London, who instituted a perpetual vicar.[4] By 1318 the church had been assigned to the prior, who thereafter presumably presented to the vicarage.[5] The nature of the abbey's jurisdiction over St Martin's was, however, complex. It continued to receive the pension of 20s., which was paid to the sacrist in 1275.[6] In 1534 Henry VIII described the abbot as a 'person proprietary' at St Martin's, distinguishing his role there from his role at St Margaret's, where he was ordinary (i.e. had spiritual jurisdiction).[7] Before this, the relationship between the two parishes had not perhaps been fully determined, although when Henry VIII moved residents from St Martin's to St Margaret's, parishioners were clearly aware that they belonged to one parish or the other. Despite Henry's ruling of 1534, uncertainties over the parochial boundaries remained, and emerged in law-suits concerning land ownership in the northern part of the vill of Westminster.[8]

After the Dissolution, the advowson of the vicarage passed to the Crown, and was granted in 1541 to the newly-created bishopric of Westminster as part of its foundation grant.[9] When that bishopric was abolished in 1550, the advowson was given to the bishopric of London, a grant confirmed in 1554.[10] The bishops of London thereafter continued to own the patronage until the Interregnum, when John Rogers obtained right of presentation under the Great Seal in 1653. Between 1661 and 1756 presentations were generally made by the Crown,[11] except for those by the archbishop of Canter-

1 Above, Gen. Intro.: Boundaries and Local Government (Manor and Liberty of Westm.).

2 Above, Landownership: Manorial (Soke of Mohun).

3 Guildhall MS 25509; above, Rel. Hist., Intro.

4 WA, Mun. bk III, pp. 58–60.

5 *Cal. Pat.* 1317–21, 220.

6 WA Mun.bk III, pp. 58–60.   7 TNA, SP 1/87, pp. 27–8.

8 E.g. TNA, E 178 /1391; Gen. Intro: Boundaries, Parishes.

9 *L&P Hen. VIII*, XVI, pp. 242–4 (no. 503/33).

10 TNA, E 305/19/G22; *Cal. Pat.* 1549–51, 262–3; 1553–4, 119–21.

11 Hennessy, *Novum Rep.* 294.

bury and the bishop of Norwich in 1717.[1] The bishop of London presented in 1776 and thereafter.[2]

In the 1240s the church was valued at 10 marks (£6 13s. 4d.), with the vicarage at 5 (£3 6s. 8d.),[3] while in 1291 the church as a whole was valued at £10.[4] The rectory and pension were put at £5 6s. 8d. in 1535,[5] and the rectory, tithes and a close and barn in Petty France were let for 49 years from 1539 for £4 6s. 8d.[6] After the Dissolution, the king granted the rectory of St Martin's to the newly-created collegiate church of Westminster in 1542, and thereafter the rectorial tithes remained part of the dean and chapter's estate.[7] In 1607 the dean and chapter raised £9 on an annual rent charge on the lease of the rectory of St Martin's to augment the stipend of the choir of Westminster Abbey.[8]

The portion assigned to the vicar in 1275 comprised a cell (*arca*) on the north side of the church where the vicars had been accustomed to dwell, the small tithes, offerings, altar dues, and a third of the great tithes; the vicar was to pay all regular diocesan dues and a third of any extraordinary dues, except the pension of 20s. hitherto paid to the sacrist and now included in the rectory.[9] The vicar's portion of the church therefore amounted to £3 6s. 8d. in 1291.[10] In 1315 the vicar renounced his claim for tithes in the manor of Neat and Ebury (the area of Westminster between the Tyburn and Westbourne rivers), after a suit against the abbot before the papal judges.[11] In 1535 the perpetual vicarage was valued at £12, considerably more than the rectory.[12] In 1662 the vicar petitioned the king for compensation for the tithes from several acres in St Martin's which the king had taken for gardens, and in 1665 a warrant was issued to pay to the vicar £18 for 4 years' allowance in lieu of tithes for Lower Crowfield close, taken into the King's Physic (Mulberry) Garden, to be continued annually.[13] In 1780 the vicarage was valued at £500, and the first fruits at the 1535 value of £12. In 1851, the benefice's income included £280 from glebe, £475 from fees and dues, and an Easter offertory of £98. Additional fees of £222 came from the cemetery. The curate's stipend was paid from the income.[14]

The vicarage, which stood at the north-east corner of the churchyard, was apparently new in 1579, when Thomas Davyes was accused of taking framed timber from the site where the vicar was building. It was rebuilt in 1666–7. The vicarage in St Martin's Place was part of improvements made in 1830, along with the vestry hall and schools, all designed by John Nash; the house itself was paid for by Dr George Richards, vicar 1824–34.[15] The vicarage and the rest of the north range was restored in 2008 as part of the church's refurbishment.

MEDIEVAL CLERGY AND CHURCH LIFE

William chaplain of St Martin's, who witnessed a charter c.1175, was also designated priest of St Martin's c.1190 and probably served the church.[16] William the chaplain was vicar of St Martin of Charing sometime between 1222 and 1242, when he gave a quitrent to the abbey for an annual service for a former almoner.[17] John Hocclive became the first perpetual vicar when the church was appropriated in 1275.[18] In 1299 Aleyn, then vicar or chaplain, was arrested and held in Newgate, possibly in connection with treasure trove said to be in the church and claimed by the king.[19] He or a later vicar was in prison in 1307, when the bishop ordered the rector of St Mary at Strand to provide pastoral care and receive dues during the vicar's absence.[20] In 1357, the vicar, John of Barsham, travelled to Rome on spiritual matters.[21] Thomas Skyn was vicar in 1363 when he exchanged benefices with John Atwater.[22] John was vicar in 1381 when he paid 3s. 4d. poll tax,[23] but in 1383 exchanged benefices with William Foucher or Fogere, who left in 1384 by exchange with John Jakes.[24] A series of exchanges in 1393–4 led to four different men as vicar in less than a year: John Wimbledon exchanged with Nicholas Sprot, succeeded by John Larke, then John Martyn.[25]

There was a fraternity of St John Baptist in St Martin's church by 1474, and in the 1520s.[26] In 1536 the churchwardens of St Martin's sold to the king 1½ acres in St Margaret's,[27] possibly held by the parish for an obit. In 1548 only two obits were recorded: one for 20 years, worth 10s. a year, given by Christian Norris, and a rent

1 *Reg. Parker*, I (Cant. & York Soc. XXV), 293; Hennessy, *Novum Rep.* 294; TNA, Inst. Bks; *Calamy Revised*, 427.

2 *London Diocese Bk.*

3 Guildhall MS 25509. Same valuation in 1254: *Val. of Norwich*, ed. Lunt, p. 359.

4 *Tax. Eccl.* (Rec. Com.), 17; WA, Liber Niger Quat., f. 142.

5 *Valor Eccl.* I. 412. Pension not included in other valors of period: TNA, SC 12/19/30; SC 12/36/28.

6 TNA, E 303/19, no. 85.

7 *L&P Hen. VIII*, XVII, pp. 392–6 (no. 714/5); *Cal. Pat.* 1555–7, 348–50.   8 WA, Mun. bk VII, f. 1.

9 WA, Mun. bk III, pp. 58–60.

10 *Tax. Eccl.* (Rec. Com.), 17.

11 WAD, f. 105.   12 *Valor Eccl.* I. 433.

13 *Cal. SP Dom.* 1661–2, 374; 1664–5, 225.

14 Guildhall MS 9557, f. 33. TNA, HO 129/5, 1/1/3 (f. 3).

15 *Survey of London*, XX. 55; Pevsner, *London 6: Westm.* 325–6.

16 *Westm. Charters*, 245; *Beauchamp Charters*, 111. He had 2 sons, Alexander and Salomon, the latter probably also a priest.

17 WAM 17143B; 17144 (dated by d. of witness).

18 WA, Mun. bk III, pp. 58–60.

19 TNA, SC 8/328 (no. E.873); SC 8/313 (no. E.64); *Cal. Pat.* 1292–1301, 431, 479. Refs to Pat. R. noted by TNA on binding. Treasure probably grave gds from Saxon burials.

20 *Reg. Baldock* (Cant. & York Soc.), 53.

21 *Cal. Pat.* 1354–8, 566.

22 Hennessy, *Novum Rep.* 293.

23 *Ch in London*, 1375–92, 36.

24 *Cal. Pat.* 1381–5, 304, 387.

25 Hennessy, *Novum Rep.* 293; *Cal. Pat.* 1391–6, 317. Subsequent vicars as listed in *Survey of London*, XX. 128, and Hennessy, *Novum Rep.* 293–4.

26 Guildhall MS 9171/6, f. 254v.–5; Merritt, *Early Modern Westm.* 22n.

27 TNA, E 326/5425.

50. *The old parish church of St Martin-in-the-Fields, demolished c.1720, from the west showing the aisles added in the early 17th century, and the rebuilt tower and cupola of 1668–72. A small church, tucked away in the narrow St Martin's Lane, and without the open aspect which the creation of Trafalgar Square in the 1820s gave to the 18th-century church.*

charge of £1 6s. 8d. a year for a morrow mass priest given by Humphrey Cooke, the king's master carpenter.[1] Parishioners of St Martin's were also members of the guild of St Mary Ronceval, which lay close to St Martin's parish boundary and the church, and many probably belonged to fraternities in St Margaret's church.[2]

The abbot had a chapel, dedicated to St Mary, in his house at Neat, referred to as the chapel of *Insula c.*1230;[3] it had an image of St Mary in 1323,[4] and may have served local residents.

MEDIEVAL CHURCH BUILDING

Although St Martin's was parochial by the 13th century, little is known about the medieval church, which, except for the tower, was rebuilt in 1607. Records made when the church was altered in the 16th-century suggest that it was built of rubble, repaired with brick, and had chancel and nave under one roof.[5] Money was bequeathed in the 1460s or 1470s towards the making of St John's aisle and the porch of the church,[6] and at about this time a steeple was being considered or built, probably the north-west tower (recased and with a post-medieval cupola) shown in a view made *c.*1710.[7] In the early 16th century St John's aisle and chapel had pews, and may have been divided from the rest of the church; similarly, St Cuthbert's chapel had stairs, pews, and a door or doorway, suggesting some physical division. At that time there was also an altar of Our Lady of Pity, and possibly a Jesus altar.[8] In 1525 the rood loft was carved and embellished with images of Jesus, Mary and the 12 prophets,

and the porch was rebuilt in brick and tile; the church itself was partially re-tiled and the floor re-paved. The pre-Reformation church had bells, an organ, and pews for the parishioners, some coloured glass in the windows, and a whitewashed interior.[9] Probably as the result of the increase in the urban population of the parish when the boundary was formally redrawn in 1542, the walls were repaired and perhaps rebuilt, and aisles added or extended to enlarge the building overall.[10]

POST-REFORMATION CLERGY AND CHURCH LIFE

Robert Beste, a former Franciscan who became vicar of St Martin's in 1539, possibly a royal appointment, was a supporter of Protestant reform, and St Martin's quickly complied with reformation policy, removing images, and introducing Protestant services, even replacing window glass showing the Trinity, and consistently exceeding the bare minimum required to ensure Protestant conformity. Communion pews were built and the rood loft destroyed in the early 1550s.[11] From 1553, however, St Martin's also acted swiftly to restore Catholic materials and worship, and paid for rebuilding the rood loft. Beste continued English services until ejected in 1554. He was replaced by Thomas Welles, who had strong Catholic sympathies, and who was in turn was deprived on Elizabeth's succession when Beste then returned. Protestant practice was being reintroduced in 1560 and the rood loft was removed again early in 1561.[12] Beste continued until his death in 1572, and

1 *Chantry Cert.* 64; Merritt, *Early Modern Westm.* 20, 22.
2 Merritt, *Early Modern Westm.* 24.
3 WAD, f. 638.
4 TNA, E 210/6937.
5 *Survey of London,* XX. 19.
6 *Cal. Chancery Procs. t. Eliz.* (Rec Com), II, xliv–xlv [C 2].

7 TNA, C 1/52/277.
8 *Survey of London,* XX. 20; Merritt, *Early Modern Westm.* 21–2 & n.
9 *Survey of London,* XX. 20.
10 Merritt, *Early Modern Westm.* 29–30.
11 Ibid. 50–1, 53–4.   12 Ibid. 62–3, 66–7.

seems to have set the Protestant tone in St Martin's. His successors were all university graduates and many were connected to the Court.[1]

The parish continued to increase in size, and included many committed Protestant gentry. In 1600 a group of parishioners wrote to Sir Robert Cecil with a proposal to establish a lectureship, to supplement the deficiencies of their ageing vicar, Thomas Knight. They eventually obtained the departure of Knight and his replacement by Thomas Montford, a former chaplain in ordinary to the queen and a learned and frequent preacher, together with a lecturer, the strongly puritan Robert Hill, in 1602. Together they inaugurated a sustained programme of thoroughgoing religious reform in the parish, supported by a number of lay activists; Montford remained until his death in 1633. Initiatives to provide widespread religious instruction in the parish were also introduced, including a systematic programme of catechism ward by ward, and a rota system for Easter communion, in response to the growing population.[2]

In 1544 the vicar was assisted by two curates; none was listed 1561, and one in 1574.[3] Dr Montford was assisted by a curate in the early 17th century. During Elizabeth's reign a number of clergymen other than the vicar preached at St Martin's, and visiting preachers, many of them distinguished churchmen, continued to be a feature during the early 17th century. From 1609 sermons were also preached in the churchyard in the summer, to reach a larger audience than the church could accommodate. After Hill left in 1613 the character of the lectureship was contested; the lecturer Hamlet Marshall was appointed on the recommendation of the earl of Suffolk, but did not please many who therefore did not contribute towards his stipend. Parishioners resisted the idea of a fixed levy, feeling that a voluntary contribution would ensure that the lecturer had to be good to survive, and thereafter the vestry resisted attempts to transform their lectureship into a sinecure for protégés of local aristocrats, normally supporting more radical puritans in the period up to the civil war.[4] Dr John Everard, parish lecturer from 1617, preached strongly anti-Catholic rhetoric during the period of the Spanish Match, 1621–2, leading to his imprisonment on six or more occasions. The importance of the pulpit so close to the palace led to royal interference in the clergy at St Martin's on several occasions, and although St Martin's acquiesced in Laudian reforms, railing in the communion table in 1630, the vestry objected strongly to interference with their right to choose their lecturers, and after being persuaded to accept a royal nominee in 1627, they then raised funds to support other lecturers of a more puritan outlook.[5]

In 1640, John Wittie of St Martin's, gardener, left the minister reading morning prayer 40s. a year during the term that remained in his property in Covent Garden; if (as happened about two years after his death) morning prayer ceased to be read, the money was to go to the poor.[6] Thomas Case, who was lecturer 1641–2, later became a member of the Westminster Assembly and rector of St Giles-in-the-Fields.[7] Geoffrey Sharpe, lecturer at St Martin's and St Andrew Undershaft (City), was ejected from both in 1643 for seditious utterances against Parliament.[8]

CHURCH ACCOMMODATION IN THE EARLY 17TH CENTURY

In the 1590s major internal changes were made to enable the congregation to hear the preachers better, with the replacement in timber of the stone piers and arches. By the early 17th century the parish's population had outgrown the church, and between 1606 and 1609 the parishioners enlarged it by adding a chancel at the east end, extending the body of the church on the north and south sides to provide aisles, and westward by about 20 feet in line with the outside wall of the tower, adding a great west door.[9] The growing population included many prominent courtiers who took an interest in the church. Among them was Sir George Coppin, clerk of the Crown in the court of Chancery, reputedly a prime mover in the enlargement, who in 1608 asked the king's secretary, another benefactor of the parish, to consider an offer made by two men under threat of punishment by the Crown, to pay £100 towards repair of the church for a pardon.[10] James I, Henry, prince of Wales, and many courtiers contributed to the rebuilding. To raise money the parishioners wrote to leading residents, such as the earl of Salisbury; they pointed out that the parish was the place most frequently used by the king and greatly inhabited by noblemen and gentry and their households, so that the church being small could not accommodate half the inhabitants and was often so crowded that many were in danger of stifling and infection. The parishioners had made contributions according to their means to enlarge the church to give it more room and air, and to enclose a new churchyard with a brick wall, but could not meet the costs without the assistance of the lords and principal men of the parish. They asked Salisbury to contribute 'as much as God shall incline your heart to', and he gave £20 in 1608.[11] The north and south galleries were also enlarged in the 1620s and 30s.[12] Despite the additions the church remained inadequate for the growing population. Claiming that their population had trebled, the parish

1 Ibid. 309.
2 Ibid. 310–12, 316, 319.
3 Guildhall MSS 9537/1, f. 67A; /2, f. 98; /3, f. 31.
4 Merritt, *Early Modern Westm.* 314–16.
5 Above, Rel. Hist.: Intro., 16th and 17th cent. (Influence of Central Govt).
6 TNA, C 93/23/11.
7 *Calamy Revised*, 104.
8 *Walker Revised*, 57.
9 *Survey of London*, XX. 20–1.
10 *Cal. SP Dom.* Add. 1580–1625, 507.
11 Hist. MSS. Com. 9, *Salisbury*, XXIV, p. 158.
12 *Survey of London*, XX. 22; Merritt, *Early Modern Westm.* 219.

petitioned Charles I *c.*1626 to allow them to convert a hallway in Durham House into a chapel of ease,[1] apparently without success.

Though the funds and support obtained from the nobility and gentry were essential for St Martin's, the role of courtiers in the church was by no means welcomed by all parishioners of lower rank, and resulted in a dispute over the accounts and allocation of pews. Seating in the church, with the difficulty of achieving a balance between social rank and the status of parochial officeholders, was a continual problem for the vestry.[2]

CHURCH LIFE AFTER THE RESTORATION

At the Restoration, Gabriel Sangar, vicar from *c.*1650, was ordered to give possession to Dr Nathaniel Hardy, presented by Charles II; Sangar continued as a nonconformist preacher in the Strand area.[3] On Hardy's death in 1670, the bishop of London presented Dr Thomas Lamplugh, royal chaplain-in-ordinary, and archdeacon of London since 1664, who successfully petitioned the king for a dispensation to hold the rectory of Charlton (Oxon.) with St Martin's.[4] Lamplugh was promoted to the bishopric of Exeter in 1676, and his successor, Dr William Lloyd, a former canon of St Paul's, was presented by Charles II, but was promoted to the bishopric of St Asaph in 1680. He was succeeded by another prominent churchman, Thomas Tenison, who not only contributed significantly to London's vibrant ecclesiastical life in this period, but worked tirelessly to improve the religious life of St Martin's at a time of great population growth. He provided a library for the use of clergymen and scholars in the parish, which included a number of chaplains in the aristocractic households. In 1681, he formed a Society of Young Men in the parish, composed of communicants who met on the third Sunday each month. Each meeting began with prayers and bible reading, and attenders paid 6*d.* each meeting for the poor, and 3*d.* for swearing. At the major festivals, the meeting took a collection to cover the rent of the room, with the rest going to the poor.[5]

Tenison's parishioners included national figures, and he became enthusiastically involved in the heated Romanist debates of the 1680s, publishing increasingly contentious pamphlets against Catholicism; after the accession of James II, St Martin's became an Anglican bastion and Tenison the leader of the London clergy. Following the creation of St Anne's parish in 1678, Tenison also agreed to Parliament's further division of the parish to create St James-in-the-Fields, later St James, Piccadilly, in 1685, of which he became the first

rector. In 1691 he was nominated to the see of Lincoln, and resigned from St Martin's and St James's in 1692.[6] Tenison, characterized as the only Englishman who preached from the heart, was said to have accepted the bishopric because he was tired from the effort he had put into serving the two churches.[7]

In 1714 prayers were held twice a day; the morning prayers in summer were maintained by a gift of Dr Willis, an eminent physician of the parish, the rest by the parish. Holy communion was held twice on the first Sunday of the month and on major feasts, and once on other Sundays. A charity sermon was given on the third Sunday of each month, maintained by contributions for the relief of the poor children of the parish. The vicar was assisted by joint lecturers, Dr Edmund Gibson and George Hudson, and a minister, Robert Grisedale,[8] who had been there 21 years in 1715.[9]

In 1715 the vicar, William Lancaster, apparently responding to episcopal concerns over the licensing of preachers in the parish, observed that neither of the ground landlords of Russell Court and Trinity chapels would agree to lease the site nor alienate them to the church, so the bishop could suppress them if the preachers were unacceptable; since, however, the two chapels had been of great use and the ministers gave general satisfaction, he hoped the bishop and his officers would not do anything to alarm the landlords.[10]

In 1780 there were three services daily and four on Sundays, communion service every Sunday and twice on the major festivals and first Sunday in the month. About 200 children were catechised twice a week in Lent.[11]

In 1851, when St Martin's was described by the vicar as the Royal Parish, there were 700 free and 800 other seats, and attendances were 1500 (a.m.); 750 (aft.); 1300 (evg). The vicar commented that he thought the seating, given by parish clerk, much below the actual, but assumed the attendances to be correct, which he would otherwise have estimated as 1,600 plus 400 scholars.[12] In the 20th century St Martin's found a new role as the parish church for London, discussed above in the introduction to Religious History.

CHURCH REBUILDING

Rebuilding of the tower on safety grounds was considered from 1657, but only took place in 1668 when it was reconstructed in stone by Richard Ryder. It was given a cupola designed by Wren in 1672.[13] The interior, redecorated in 1688 and again in 1701, was wainscotted to head height in oak in 1708. In 1714, when 8 newly-cast bells were hung in the 90-foot high tower, the church

1 *Cal. SP Dom.* 1625–6, 525; Merritt, *Early Modern Westm.* 321–2.
2 *Survey of London*, XX. 20, 22; Merritt, *Early Modern Westm.* 215–21.
3 *Calamy Revised*, 427; Hennessy, *Novum Rep.* 294 (gives Hardy as Nich.). Below, Prot. Nonconf.
4 *Cal. SP Dom.* 1670 (& Add. 1660–70), 295.
5 BL, Add. MS 38693, f. 137.   6 *Oxford DNB.*

7 HMC, *7th Rep.*, p. 204b.
8 Paterson, *Pietas Lond.* 150–3.
9 Bodl., MS Rawl. B. 376, f. 84.
10 Ibid.
11 Guildhall MS 9557, f. 33.
12 TNA, HO 129/5, 1/1/3 (f.3).
13 Colvin, *Brit. Architects*, 892, 1161; *Survey of London*, XX. 23.

was considered to be very much decayed and dark. It had a fine organ, monuments to leading figures, and several capacious galleries, but still not could not accommodate the great and increasing local population. Despite its reduction by the creation of three new parishes, St Martin's was still the second most populous parish within the London bills of mortality. Rebuilding the church was being considered by 1714,[1] as surveyors in 1710 advised that the weight of the roof had pushed the walls outward and, despite tying-in with iron cramps, it would not long survive.[2] After appeals to the commissioners for the fifty new churches, the queen, and in 1717 to Parliament, eventually, in 1720, an Act was passed for rebuilding the church, and levying a rate on the parishioners for up to £22,000. Commissioners were appointed to manage the project; they were also authorized to buy land from Westminster Abbey to enlarge the churchyard, and required to provide accommodation in the new church for the owners of Northumberland House comparable to that in the old.[3] A temporary church was built on part of the churchyard and notice was given that bodies and monuments could be removed from the old church and churchyard. Remaining monuments were later re-erected in the crypt of the new church.[4] The rebuilding commissioners, seven men and the two churchwardens sought contributions from the owners and occupiers of lands and tenements within the palaces and verges of Whitehall and St James.[5]

The new church, designed by James Gibbs in 1720 and built 1722–4 at a cost of £33,662, was consecrated in 1726. Gibbs's novel and influential design combined a giant west portico and elaborate steeple in a single composition.[6] In the view along the narrow St Martin's Lane, portico and steeple, containing a peal of 12 bells, most recast in 1725 and first rung in 1727, made the church's presence felt amongst the street's houses. Gibbs treated the other elevations richly as they could be seen from St Martin's Passage (north) and the churchyard, which was protected by fine contemporary railings, but it was not until a hundred years later that the length of the church was revealed and became a memorable feature of the new Trafalgar Square. The galleried interior was a variation on two of Wren's designs, and relied for much of its effect on fine plasterwork by G. Bagutti and C. Wilkins. The narrow chancel was flanked by two boxes, one for the royal family, the other for the royal household. The seating in the nave was temporary until 1799 when the present box pews were installed. The organ, with a case was given by George I as compensation for not serving as churchwarden,[7] was later moved to Wotton-under-Edge (Glos.) and other furnishings have been added, but the communion rails and font are original. Most Victorian alterations, including the choir stalls installed during alterations by Sir Arthur Blomfield and Sons in 1887, were removed during the renovation programme of 2001–8, executed to designs by Eric Parry Architects at a cost of £36 million. The brick-vaulted crypt beneath the church, converted into a café in 1987, was enlarged and linked to reconstructed burial vaults and the vestry hall to the north to create a shop, public spaces, and better social care and office accommodation for the St Martin's Centre.[8] The entrance to the public areas was designed as a transparent rotunda with lift and staircases in St Martin's Passage, with a large light-well to the east.

Churchyard   In 1606 the parish petitioned the king for an additional burying-ground because their churchyard was so overcrowded and unhealthy and were granted an acre at the rear of the Mews on the west side of St Martin's Lane opposite the church.[9] Additional land was sought in 1668,[10] and in 1680 the parish was to be compensated for part of the churchyard taken to widen St Martin's Lane.[11] The compensation, however, was slow in coming and in 1682 the vicar and parishioners had to petition the king to speed up its payment, since without it they could not pay off their debt of £700 to Dr Nicholas Barbon, for extra land for burial.[12]

In 1895 St Martin's churchyard covered a third of an acre, paved in stone, with trees and seats supplied by the Metropolitan Public Gardens Association, and maintained by the vestry. A large piece called the Waterman's churchyard on the south side of the church was taken for public improvements in 1831, and the bodies moved to the vaults.[13]

NEW CHAPELS AND CHURCHES

The first chapel of ease for St Martin's was St Paul's, Covent Garden, opened in 1638, whose district became a new civil parish in 1646.[14] In 1676 the vestry leased Oxendon chapel from Richard Baxter for £40 p.a.; it was fitted up for Anglican services at the expense of the pew-holders and maintained as a chapel of ease until St Martin's was rebuilt in 1726.[15] St James's church was opened in 1684 and St Anne's in 1686, both made parochial by Acts which gave them large chunks of St Martin's parish.[16]

In 1714 St Martin's had more chapels of ease than any other London parish: Horse Guards, Knightsbridge,

1 Paterson, *Pietas Lond.* 150–3.

2 *Survey of London*, XX. 24.

3 Archit. acct follows Clarke, *London Chs*, 181–2; *Survey of London*, XX. 24–5; Pevsner, *London 6: Westm.* 291–2. Colvin, *Brit. Architects*, gives many additional refs.

4 *Survey of London*, XX. 24; described in detail on pp. 30–54.

5 Bodl., MS Rawl. B. 362, f. 87.

6 Clarke, *London Chs*, 181–2.

7 *Survey of London*, XX. 27.

8 Above, Rel. Hist.: Intro., (Twentieth-Century Changes), for work of the Centre.

9 TNA, C 66/1711, m. 20; C 66/2632, no. 2.

10 *Cal. SP Dom.* 1667–8, 243.

11 Ibid. 1679–80, 554.

12 Ibid. 1682, 71.

13 LCC, *Burial Grounds*, 5. Other bur. grounds will be treated under Pub. Svces in a later vol.   14 Below, St Paul.

15 *Survey of London*, XX. 102–3.   16 Below.

Oxendon chapel, Russell Court chapel, Spring Garden, and Trinity chapel in the fields at the upper end of Dean Street. There were also the royal chapels at St James and Whitehall and a private chapel in Hog lane almshouses.[1] Despite the creation of St James's and St Anne's parishes, in 1711, when the vestry computed the parish's population at about 19,600, the commissioners for building fifty new churches considered that St Martin's still required more accommodation.[2] It was not until 1725, however, that the church of St George, Hanover Square was opened and much of St Martin's parish assigned to it.[3] Even so, there was still the need for four chapels of ease in 1780: Long Acre, Oxendon, Tavistock, and Spring Gardens.[4]

In the 19th century the problem of overcrowding was again addressed and new churches were created. Spring Gardens chapel was given to St Martin's by the Crown for a chapel of ease in 1829, and consecrated as St Matthew in 1832. In 1833 the vicar of St Martin's took over the proprietary Tavistock chapel as a chapel of ease, and it was consecrated in 1855 as St John the Evangelist. St Michael, Burleigh Street, was built in 1830s with a parliamentary grant, and a district was assigned in 1848.[5] St Matthew closed *c.*1880, St Michael *c.*1905, and St John between 1913 and 1970.

St John the Evangelist, Broad Court, Drury Lane

The church originated as the proprietary Tavistock chapel, built in 1763 to replace Russell Court, by the Russell family to serve the Bedford estate.[6] John Glen King, D.D., was licensed as reader and preacher 1774.[7] Leased by Revd Thos Webster 1825, it taken over in 1833 by Dr George Richards, vicar of St Martin's, who also bought the freehold; on his death he gave it to parish trustees for worship, a school, or charitable purposes. The parish repaired it, raising *c.*£1,600 by voluntary rate. The chapel's income came from pew rents, voluntary rate, and collections.[8] It was consecrated in 1855 as St John the Evangelist, and a district chapelry was assigned to it out of St Martin's.[9] The benefice was valued at £310 in 1894, and patrons, presumably parish trustees, included Sir W. James (1871) and Lord Northbourne (1894), who presented a pulpit from Penshurst (Kent).[10] It was united with Holy Trinity, Kingsway (St Giles-in-the-Fields) *c.*1940 with the bishop of London and Lord Northbourne as patrons.

In 1851, when attendance was 133 (a.m.), 72 (evg), the church seated 1,001 (360 free), but it was rearranged by William Butterfield before consecration in 1855, to seat 900, all free in 1871. Butterfield created a choir and vestry 1883, and the church seated 500 in 1894. In 1886 attendance was 202 (a.m.), 21 (p.m.), and in 1903 95 (a.m.), 67 (p.m.). The church was still open 1935, but closed *c.*1940.[11]

St Michael, Burleigh Street, Strand

Built with a grant from Church Building Commissioners, it was designed by J. Savage in a Gothic style, 1832–4. It was consecrated in 1833 as a chapel of ease to St Martin's and a district was assigned in 1848. The benefice was valued at £240 in 1871, £300 in 1894; the vicar of St Martin's was patron. Originally seating 934, with 449 free, in 1851 only 150 were free.[12] In 1851 attendance was 480 (a.m.), 600 (evg), and in 1903 114 (a.m.), 186 (p.m.). In 1866 it had a surpliced choir. Still open in 1871, it was apparently closed for a period, reopening 1886. In 1894 seated 890 all free.[13]

The benefice was united with St Paul's, Covent Garden, 1905, because of falling population in both parishes. The vicarage house became St Paul's clergy house. The church was closed 1905, and sold and demolished 1906. Some fittings and proceeds of sale of site were used for St Michael, Sutton Ct (Chiswick).[14]

Other Chapels

Long Acre Episcopal Chapel (also called Hanover chapel, St Mark's chapel).   This chapel of ease was built on a site leased to the parish by the Mercers' company in 1760.[15] Morning and afternoon preachers were licensed in 1760 and 1784.[16] Methodists from Orange Street used it from *c.*1778 by agreement with St Martin's, and were still there 1814, presumably sharing the chapel.[17] In 1851 Anglican attendance was 195 (a.m., including 111 Sunday scholars), 141 (evg). The chapel, which was supported by the pew rents, seated *c.*750.[18] It was apparently sold *c.*1855 after St John's, Broad Ct, opened.[19]

Oxendon Chapel, Oxendon Street, Haymarket.   It was built in 1676 behind the street frontage for Richard Baxter,[20] but when prevented from preaching there in 1678 he offered it to St. Martin's as a chapel of ease, the vicar paying the ground rent.[21] In 1714 only daily

1 Paterson, *Pietas Lond.* 153.
2 *Fifty New Chs*, 149.
3 Ibid. 81; above, Rel. Hist.:Intro. (Ch Bldg in 18th Cent.).
4 Guildhall MS 9557, f. 33.
5 Below.
6 *Mackeson's Guide* (1871); McMaster, *St Martin-in-the-Fields*, 333–4.
7 Guildhall MS 9557, f. 33.
8 TNA, HO 129/5, 2/1/2 (f. 11).
9 *London Gaz.* 14 Aug. 1855, p. 3083.
10 *Mackeson's Guide* (1871, 1894).
11 *Crockford* (1935, 1940).

12 TNA, HO 129/5, 1/1/4 (f. 4); Port, *Six Hundred Chs*, 136–7; *London Gaz.* 26 Dec. 1848, p. 4665.
13 *Mackeson's Guide* (1866, 1871, 1894).
14 *Survey of London*, XXXVI. 224; *VCH Middx*, VII. 92; below, St Paul.
15 McMaster, *St Martin-in-the-Fields*, 339.
16 Guildhall MSS 9556, p. 39; 9557, f. 33.
17 Wilson, *Dissenting Chs*, IV. 22–3.
18 TNA, HO 129/5, 2/1/1 (f. 10).
19 McMaster, *St Martin-in-the-Fields*, 339.
20 Below, Prot. Nonconf. (Presbs.).
21 Wilson, *Dissenting Chs*, IV. 52–4.

morning and evening prayers were held, with sermons on Sundays; the congregation went to the parish church for communion. A weekly Friday lecture was maintained by the congregation.[1] Morning and afternoon preachers were licensed 1747, and a preacher 1774.[2] By 1807 chapel was vacant and leased by Scotch Presbyterians under Revd Geo. Jerment.[3]

St Matthew, Spring Gardens, Charing Cross   Originally called Spring Gardens (sometimes Garden) chapel, the second of that name,[4] it was designed by G. Salter and built in 1731 for Sir Edward Southwell at corner of Spring Gardens and New Street, on his estate leased from the Crown.[5] In 1763 it was worth £60–80.[6] Preachers, generally for morning and afternoon, were licensed in 1746, 1763 and 1786, and an afternoon preacher and reader in 1793.[7] From 1792 there was a dispute between the Southwells and the vicar of St Martin's over right of presentation.[8] Southwell's lease of the site expired in 1828, and in 1829 the Crown gave the chapel to St Martin's as a chapel of ease, served by a curate.

Consecrated in 1832, the chapel had income of £188 from pew rents, and £42 from other sources in 1851, when attendance was 199 (a.m.). The curate complained that the attendance was not a criterion for judging the need for a church, as without an assigned district he was unable to establish the chapel as the place of worship for an area beyond Spring Gardens, and attendance had fallen over the previous decade as offices had replaced residents nearby.[9] In 1871 it was worth under £150 of which £30 was from endowment and pew rents.[10]

The plain classical brick building had an irregular plan with the north-eastern corner sliced off because of the configuration of the streets, and the sanctuary was in an east apse, in which a window and reredos were erected in 1805 when the chapel was cleaned and beautified.[11] In 1851 it seated c.370, with only c.20 free,[12] and in 1871 400, none free. The church closed between 1879 and 1881,[13] and was part of the area acquired c.1882 by the Commissioners of Works for new Admiralty offices. The chapel housed Admiralty records in the 1890s, but was cleared by 1910 as part of site for Admiralty Arch.[14]

Trinity Chapel, Conduit Street   See below, St George's: New Churches and Chapels, Other Chapels.

Proprietary Chapels

Russell Court Chapel, Drury Lane   Originally a nonconformist chapel, when the lease expired 1706 it was let to 'gentlemen of Her Majesty's Playhouse' and others, who repaired and opened it as an Anglican chapel of ease for St Martin's. The Drury Lane theatre held a benefit to raise funds, to cynical amusement.[15] In 1715 the vicar of St Martin's, William Lancaster, told the bishop he and his neighbours had purchased the chapel and the lease from the duke's tenant, who had formerly sublet it to 'Mr Burgesses Meeting House' for £36 a year. St Martin's spent c.£700 on it and Dr Smith, presumably the minister, was said to have brought great interest and reputation to it. The lease had expired some time before and, though the duke had said he would make a present of it to the parish, he died before this was done; the steward allowed them to continue there for £5 a year, but neither he nor the duke's guardians would allow it to be brought under church jurisdiction or leased.[16] In 1714 and c.1723 prayers were held twice a day on Sunday by morning and afternoon preachers.[17] A reader was licensed 1747, but the chapel was said to have been demolished by c.1770 when a new chapel was built in Broad Court, and was certainly closed by 1780.[18] In 1810 the site belonged to St Mary le Strand (below), and was used as a burial ground.

Spring Garden Chapel.   A private chapel said to have been built for foreign ambassador, perhaps that fitted up by the Spanish ambassador at his house in Old Spring Garden which he left 1693.[19] It was then used briefly by French Protestants, but by 1714 had become a proprietary Anglican chapel leased by the minister, James King, from the proprietor, and served as chapel of ease in St Martin's for those living around Charing Cross and St James's Park. In 1714 prayers and sermon were held on Sundays only and on holydays, but not communion.[20] Perhaps closed and demolished by Sir Edw. Southwell when he rebuilt areas of Spring Gardens, as he built a new chapel there 1731.[21]

Tavistock Chapel   See above, this section: St John the Evangelist.

1 Paterson, *Pietas Lond.* 215.
2 Guildhall MSS 9556, p. 39; 9557, f. 33.
3 Wilson, *Dissenting Chs,* IV. 52–4; below, Nonconf, Presbs.
4 Below, Spring Gdn chapel.
5 *Survey of London,* XX. 61.
6 Guildhall MS 9556, p. 39.
7 Ibid. MSS 9550; 9557, f. 33.
8 *London Top. Rec.* XIV (1928), 53; *Survey of London,* XX. 63.
9 TNA, HO 129/5, 1/1/2 (f. 2).
10 *Mackeson's Guide* (1871).
11 *Survey of London,* XX. 61; *Mackeson's Guide* (1871).
12 TNA, HO 129/5, 1/1/2 (f. 2).
13 *Mackeson's Guide* (1881–2).
14 *London Topog. Rec.* XIV (1928), 53 and plate 8; *Survey of London,* XX. 63.
15 Wilson, *Dissenting Chs,* III. 568–72.
16 Bodl., MS Rawl. B. 376, f. 84.
17 Paterson, *Pietas Lond.* 251; Guildhall MS 9550.
18 Guildhall MS 9556, p. 39; above, St John the Evangelist.
19 *Cal. SP Dom.* 1693, 433.
20 Paterson, *Pietas Lond.* 261–2.
21 Above, St Matthew.

HOLY INNOCENTS

The parish church of the Holy Innocents originated as a chapel, granted as part of a small estate by Gilbert of Ghent to the abbot of Abingdon in 1086, and stood mid-way along the Strand on its north side, opposite the gates of the abbot's mansion[1] Its short-lived parish, first recorded in the early 13th century, had certainly been extinguished by the early 14th if not some 50 years earlier.[2]

The chapel has been confused from the time of Stow with the medieval church of St Mary of Strand, which lay nearby but on the south side of the highway, outside the vill of Westminster, and was never claimed by the abbot.[3] The error derives from changes in the dedication of the abbot of Abingdon's chapel in two papal bulls to the abbey, of 1146 and 1152; the second, probably through scribal error, referred to the chapel as St Mary's.[4] There is, however, so much evidence to show that Holy Innocents continued in use as a parish church well into the 13th century, and was known as a ruined building in the early 14th (below), that it cannot be the church of St Mary of Strand.

In 1185 John de Sobire of the chapel of the Innocents paid 6*d.* for the church to the Knights Templar, possibly in acknowledgement of patronage.[5] Richard was chaplain *c.*1190, but in 1198 it was called the *church* of the Holy Innocents. The church was referred to as the white church in the 1190s, and by the time it was abandoned it was built of stone.[6] The first known reference to the parish occurs in 1219,[7] and a chapel next to the church of the Innocents is mentioned in 1222.[8]

As with the other churches in Westminster, Henry III took an interest in Holy Innocents church, in 1241 granting a 50-lb candle to the church for Holy Innocents day.[9] It is also possible that the chapel of St Margaret, in which in 1241 he established a chaplain for his daughter Margaret on an annual salary of 60*s.*, was the chapel next to the church.[10] There was a chapel of St Margaret in the parish of the Holy Innocents in 1268, when it was granted to the Pied Friars with two messuages in that parish as their London house.[11]

Sometime probably in the 1240s the abbot of Westminster successfully brought a suit against John of the Temple, parson of the Holy Innocents, before the papal judges delegate, concerning 8 messuages which he claimed were in St Margaret's parish and hence in his ecclesiastical liberty,[12] perhaps a result of the judgement in 1222, which set the extent of St Margaret's parish, but left a question over the boundary up to the chapel next to the church of the Innocents.[13] Since the church also lay in the area included in St Margaret's parish, it seems to have ceased to be a parish church, with possibly only the chapel next to it continuing as the chapel of St Margaret. The part of the parish south of the Strand was probably united to St Clement Danes.[14] The use of the parish designation continued, however, for several decades longer.

The Pied Friars' property seems to have included the main church and churchyard.[15] When the order died out in 1317, their property passed to the abbey and was assigned to the sacrist, and the church and chapel were not apparently used again. The church was clearly abandoned in 1326 when accounts of the murder of Walter Stapleton, bishop of Exeter, relate that he was temporarily buried at a derelict ecclesiastical site, variously called the church of the Holy Innocents and the churchyard of the Pied Friars.[16]

ST ANNE, SOHO

St Anne's was the latest of the three new parish churches established in the 17th century. In 1676, shortly after building started on St James's church, the vestry of St Martin-in-the-Fields was informed that the bishop of London, Henry Compton, wished to give £5,000 towards a second new church in the parish; the money

1 BL, Cotton Claud. C. IX, f. 138.

2 For extent and location of parish, see above, Gen. intro.: Boundaries, Parishes (Strand).

3 E.g. C.N.L. Brooke and G. Keir, *London 800–1216: The Shaping of a City* (1975), 140.

4 BL, Cotton Claud. C. IX, ff. 170–1.

5 *Rec. Templars*, 13. Templars had also acquired property that became the Temple *c.*1150, church of St Clement Danes, and property nearby. Honor of Leicester links Templars, Gilb. of Ghent, and Henry son of Reiner: above, Landownership: Manorial (Soke of Leic.).

6 TNA, CP 25/1/146/5, nos 4–6; 282/6, no. 19; *Westm. Charters*, 165.

7 TNA, CP 25/1/146/5/6.

8 *Acta Stephani Langton* (Cant. & York Soc. vol. L), 69–73.

9 *Close R.* 1237–42, 374.

10 *Cal. Pat.* 1232–47, 252; cf. WAM 17135; above, Intro.

11 TNA, C 53/57, m. 10; *Cal. Chart. R.* 1257–1300, 89; above: Landownership; Ests of Med. Origin, Other Eccles. Estates (Pied Friars).

12 WAD, ff. 346v.–7; J.E. Sayers, *Papal Judges Delegate in the Province of Canterbury* 1198–1254 (1971), 180.

13 *Acta Stephani Langton* (Cant. & York Soc. vol. L), 69–73.

14 Above, Gen. Intro.: Boundaries, Parishes (Strand).

15 Above, Landownership: Ests of Med. Origin, Other Eccles. Ests (Pied Friars).

16 *Annales Paulini* (*Chronicles of Edw. I and Edw. II*), I. 317; Thos Walsingham, *Historica Anglicana* (Rolls Ser.), I. 182; J. Leland, *Antiquarii Collectanea*, I. 468. Stapleton said to have taken stone from ch to rebuild his inn in St Clement Danes.

51. *The parish church of St Anne, Soho, in 1828, showing the west front and unusual tower designed by S.P. Cockerell in 1803 to replace the early 18th-century original.*

may have been his, or disposed of by him on behalf of a benefactor.[1] The bishop also decided on the site adjoining Wardour and King streets, obtaining the lease from two building speculators in exchange for land in Kemp's field, which the vestry had held under lease for use of the poor since 1674. The freehold was not obtained, but the site was appropriated to sacred uses under the Act of Parliament of 1678 which established the parish (to come into existence the following year), together with its boundaries, and those of the church, churchyard and glebe land.[2]

The absence of any record of payments by St Martin's vestry suggests that Bishop Compton was handling the finances and building work between 1678 and 1684, and in 1685 he took steps to finish the church. A twelve-man commission established to supervise the work was given authority to seek an Act to raise money from the inhabitants and owners in the prospective parish. An Act of 1685 authorized the bishop to appoint 30 inhabitants who, together with the rector and two churchwardens, were to supervise completion and were allowed four years to raise the money.[3] Although the interior fittings and the spire were not completed, the church of St Anne was consecrated in 1686; the dedication was probably chosen by the bishop in honour of his pupil, Princess Anne, the future queen.

BENEFICE, ADVOWSON, AND PROPERTY

The benefice was established as a rectory of which the bishop of London was patron until 1953. The district assigned in 1856 to the chapelry of St Mary, Charing Cross Road, was reintegrated in 1933.[4] In 1935 the benefice was united with that of St Luke, Berwick Street (in St James's parish), which was closed.[5] The Act of 1678 established the bounds of the rector's glebe fronting King Street (later Shaftesbury Avenue), and

1 Acct based on *Survey of London*, XXXIII. 256–74. Add. inf. is footnoted.
2 30 Chas II, c. 7 (private).

3 1 Jas II, c. 20.
4 Below.
5 Guildhall MS 19224/171.

adjoining the churchyard. Valued in 1747 and 1780 at £400, in 1851 the benefice had an income of £755, including rents from houses of *c.*£500 and other endowments of £55 a year.[1] In 1942 the glebe consisted of the sites and buildings of nos 61–73 (odd) Shaftesbury Avenue, let on two 999-year leases of 1899 and 1901 for a total of £623 a year. St Anne's was closed after bombing in 1940 and the benefice united with those of St Thomas's and St Peter's (both from St James's) in 1953;[2] St Anne's was reopened later (below), to serve the united benefice. From 1942, £500 a year from its income was distributed among six other benefices of which the bishop of London was patron.

Rectory House and other Buildings

The Act of 1685 provided for building a rectory house, but this did not take place within the time limit in the Act, and the first rector used a rented house. In 1705 a faculty was obtained by the parish and a house, later no. 58 Dean Street, was built partly on a piece of the churchyard north of the east end of the church and partly on the site of the watch-house. This rectory house was sold in 1861 and the bishop of London and Queen Anne's Bounty bought Monmouth House, no. 28 Soho Square, from the Crown for £2,540 in 1862. The house had been built in 1775 on part of the site of the 17th-century Monmouth House, and although the bishop's surveyor reported that the house was unnecessarily large, both it and the terms were so good that he thought it desirable to attach it to the living. By 1895 a boys' club room had been built at the rear, which adjoined a passage called Bateman's Buildings to the west.[3] In 1935 the house was sold and demolished, and the rector moved to St Anne's House, no. 57 Dean Street, adjoining the churchyard, until this, too, was demolished and replaced by a rectory house as part of the new church complex.[4]

CHURCH LIFE

In 1699 William III presented the church with the organ, apparently built by Renatus Harris, from the queen's chapel in St James's Palace. The parish had petitioned the Crown for the organ, and though it was given as a free gift, the parish paid for repairs to the ceiling of the chapel in 1700.[5] A fashionable congregation attended the church in its early years, some coming from St James, and the prince of Wales (later George II) worshipped there 1718–19. In 1714 the rector had an assistant and a lecturer; services were held four times a day, with communion twice a month.[6] In 1780 services were held three times on Sundays and twice on weekdays, with communion again twice a month; children were catechised every Sunday from January to June. A joint

lecturer and curate was licensed in 1782; his successor received a stipend of £52 10*s.* in 1791, and £80 in 1807 and 1813.[7]

After resistance by some parishioners, an Act was passed in 1802 to rebuild the church; 24 inhabitants were nominated to be trustees with the rector, churchwardens and overseers, and given the power to raise a rate of up to 6*d.* in pound; they completed the steeple, watch-house, engine house, and vestry room and repaired the church, with some redecoration and stained glass for the east window. Further major rebuilding was carried out in 1830–1, under Robert Abraham, to replace the defective roof and face the walls in Roman cement, and the east front was altered. In 1851 the church seated 1,144, of which 184 were free; attendance in 1851 was not recorded.

After Nugent Wade became rector (1846–90), the ensuing years were marked by dissension in the vestry over his supposed Puseyite sympathies. From 1866 radical alterations were made to the church, to designs by A.W. Blomfield: a chancel was formed out of one bay of the nave, raised up from the remainder, and the apse was reserved as a sacrarium; a low screen of carved oak across the church at the first pillar from the east created a choir with choir stalls, separated from the side aisles by screens. A reredos and super-altar in marble and alabaster were installed. The pews in the nave and aisles were cut down and the seating rearranged; the gallery seats were lowered. In the 1860s Wade also built up the fame of St Anne's for its choral services; the original organ had been replaced in 1795 by one built by Robert and William Gray of New Road, and this was enlarged in 1868 by J.W. Walker and Sons, and possibly moved at this time from the gallery at W. end to S. side of the chancel.[8] In 1886 attendance was 386 (a.m.), 463 (p.m.), and in 1903 366 (a.m.), 526 (p.m.).

The Sisterhood of St John the Baptist, an Anglican order founded at Clewer by Harriet Monsell, had a mission in 1862 at no. 9 Rose Street, Soho, with Mrs Monsell as Sister Superior, and ran a school for the parish in St Anne's Court.[9] Mission services were held in St Anne's schools, Dean Street, in 1903: attendance 86 a.m.

A small charity of unknown origin existed by 1836, consisting of an annual charge of 50*s.* paid to the churchwardens from the estate of Newport Market, and applied towards the general expenses of St Anne's church together with the pew rents and burial fees. When the market was purchased by the Metropolitan Board of Works for improvements in 1879, the parish received £83 for the rent-charge, which was invested in stock. In 1899 the annual dividend of £2 5*s.* 8*d.* con-

1 TNA, HO 129/13, 1/1/2 (f. 2).
2 Guildhall MS 19224/171.
3 Ibid.; *Survey of London,* XXXIII. 113, 275–6.
4 *Survey of London,* XXXIII. 275–6.

5 Paterson, *Pietas Lond.* 27–8; *Survey of London,* XXXIII. 266.
6 Paterson, *Pietas Lond.* 27–8.   7 Guildhall MS 9557, f. 25.
8 *Survey of London,* XXXIII. 265–7.
9 TNA, ED 7/79.

tinued to be applied towards church expenses.[1] After the benefice of St Luke's was united to St Anne's in 1935, £200 a year formerly paid by the Ecclesiastical Commission to St Luke's for lay assistance was granted to St Anne's for similar work.[2]

After the parish was united with St Thomas's and St Peter's in 1953, the intention was to use St Thomas's church for services and sell the site of St Anne. However, partly in consequence of London County Council's policy to maintain or increase residential use of Soho, it was decided in 1956–7 to reinstate a church at the old site. Under a Private Act in 1965, the rector (in whom the steeple and burial ground were vested) and the London Diocesan Fund (in whom were vested the sites of rest of the church and St Anne's House, no. 57 Dean Street) were authorized to clear the church site, retaining the steeple, and to build a new church there to serve the united benefice. A mixed-use scheme of 1965 was superseded by a joint scheme of 1976 for the church and the Soho Society, in turn succeeded in 1980 by a new version of the mixed-use scheme which was finally carried out in 1989–91.

CHURCH FABRIC

Begun by August 1677, the church was apparently completed 1685–6, except for the spire and interior fittings. Wren and William Talman were involved with the commission to complete the church and one of them probably designed it. Talman certainly provided a design for the west tower in 1714 but it is not known if this was used for that built in 1718.[3] The nave of five bays had north, south and west galleries reached from stairs in vestibules flanking the apsidal chancel. The church was externally plain, extremely so on the hidden north side, although the south front with the main entrance was more elaborate. In 1714 it was described as a large church of brick, with fine monuments and stately galleries, situated in a pleasant churchyard.[4]

In 1801 the tower was demolished as unsafe. It was replaced by one designed by S.P. Cockerell, completed in 1803 and still surviving. The bell-stage of the upper part is stone-faced and conventionally neoclassical but it bears a bulbous lead spire apparently indirectly inspired by some of Wren's but bearing four clock faces.

St Anne's was severely damaged by enemy action in 1940–1, when only the tower and walls survived; the walls at the east end were demolished to window-sill height and the site was de-consecrated in July 1953. In 1989–91 new buildings designed by the Westwood Partnership (Jan Piet and Julian Luckett) for the church and Soho Society replaced the shell of the nave. In 2002 it

housed a small parochial chapel, a rectory, premises for the Soho Society, and 20 flats for the Soho Housing Association. The new parts were blended carefully with Cockerell's tower: seen from the west they spread out like a nave with flanking courtyards. The chapel, a plain room to be subdivided as required, was decorated only by its fittings.[5] Parish registers exist from 1686.[6]

Churchyard The churchyard originally abutted both Dean and Wardour streets, but the Dean Street (east) end was taken for the rectory and other parish buildings in 1705. A strip 8 feet wide on the west side was lost to Wardour Street in 1901. The churchyard had access from the church entrance in Dean Street, and from doors in Old Compton Street and Shaftesbury Avenue; a way from Wardour Street was opened *c*.1871. A bone house was built in 1801 in the SW corner for remains disinterred for new graves. By 1851 the three-quarter-acre churchyard was 'horribly' over-crowded with bodies, which caused much dissension in the parish between those wanting a new burial ground, and those, led by the rector and churchwardens, wanting to continue burials at St Anne. Under metropolitan legislation, however, the ground was closed anyway in 1853, and new facilities for burial were obtained at the London Necropolis, Woking. In 1892 the churchyard was reopened as a garden by the Metropolitan Public Gardens Association, and leased to Strand District Board of Works who maintained it; in 1901 it was leased to Westminster City Council for 999 years.[7]

DISTRICT CHAPELRY

St Mary the Virgin, Charing Cross Road

After an appeal for funds, the rector of St Anne purchased the former Greek church in Hog Lane (later Charing Cross Road) from Baptists in 1850 to provide a chapel of ease for St Anne.[8] The large meeting room with galleries was refitted by P.C. Hardwick, who removed the eastern portion of the galleries to make a small chancel, enclosed with a low screen. The chapel, which seated 600, all free, was consecrated in 1850. In 1851 it was served by the curate of St Anne's and services were held twice daily; attendance was then 80 (a.m.), 130 (evg.). The site included a school and house for clergy and schoolmaster.[9] Said to be thronged by the poor, it was more ritualistic than St Anne and despite hostility among some parishioners, continued to play its part in the Oxford Movement. In 1856 gifts of £1,500 from Mary Shepherd and £1,000 from John Charles Sharpe were transferred to Queen Anne's Bounty and parish trustees to endow a minister and enable St Mary's to be

1 *Endowed Chars London*, V. 1, 6. [amount misprinted as £50 in Rep.]   2 Guildhall MS 19224/171.

3 Colvin, *Brit. Architects*, 1012, 1161.

4 Paterson, *Pietas Lond.* 27–8.

5 Pevsner, *London 6: Westm.* 391–2.

6 Registers 1686–1940 in WCA.

7 *Survey of London*, XXXIII. 274–5.

8 Section based on W.H. Manchee, 'First and Last Chapters of the Ch of "Les Grecs", Charing Cross Rd', *Procs. Hug. Soc. London*, XVI (1937–41), 140–58; *Survey of London*, XXXIII. 283–4.

9 TNA, HO 129/13, 1/1/1 (f. 1).

turned into a district chapelry; a district was allocated in 1856. The patronage was also surrendered by the rector of St Anne to the parish trustees (who included the rector), and in 1899 they also held £1,500 in stock with an income of c.£58. The other endowed fund was held by Queen Anne's Bounty who paid the dividends to the vicar of St Mary's.[1]

Though most of the large congregation were poor, the church had wealthy supporters who subscribed towards rebuilding to designs by R. Herbert Carpenter and W. Slater, to match the ritualistic leanings of its clergy. Work began in 1869 with a 6-storeyed clergy house, including common room, choir, and vestry, on the site of no. 11 Crown Court, the former St Martin's charity house. No. 10 Crown Court and the eastern end of the

church were then demolished, 1872–3, to make way for a new chancel, 1872–3. Of 2 bays, with 12 steps up to the altar, this structure abutted Crown Street (later Charing Cross Road), and was entered through the clergy house on its north side. Tall and plain school buildings were then added to the clergy house, allowing the site of the old school house to be used for a north aisle, completed in 1874. The whole group of buildings, Gothic except for the school, soared above its neighbours. Although a new nave was planned, the old one survived until condemned as dangerous and replaced in 1900.

In 1886 attendance was 247 (a.m.), 650 (p.m.), but had fallen in 1903 54 (a.m.), 109 (p.m.). The church closed in 1933, and was sold to found churches in new suburbs. The site was used for St Martin's School of Art.[2]

ST CLEMENT DANES

The church of St Clement Danes, founded on land in the middle of the highway belonging to the king, existed by 1173 when Henry II granted it to the Knights Templar.[3] Its origins probably go back at least to a community of pre-Conquest Danish settlers. That is suggested both by its name and its dedication; St Clement's legend has a seafaring element appropriate to a Scandinavian community. That a Danish community had certainly settled in London by the earlier 11th century is apparent from the fate of the body of King Harold I Harefoot (d. 1040), the presumed son of the Danish king, Cnut (1016–40). First buried in St Peter's Westminster, it had been exhumed and flung into the Thames, and was said to have been recovered and buried in a Danish cemetery in London.[4] It is possible that the church of St Clement Danes was associated with that cemetery.

The parish, first recorded in the 1190s,[5] lay partly in the eastern extremity of the vill of Westminster and partly in the liberty of Leicester.[6] It was united with St Mary le Strand c.1953. The church was among those which Bishop Gilbert Foliot of London confirmed to the monks of Westminster as liable to pay them a small pension (of 5s.), a grant confirmed by two subsequent bishops in the early 13th century,[7] and probably reflecting the abbot's secular authority over the part of the parish lying in the vill of Westminster.[8]

ADVOWSON AND STATUS

The Templars still held the church in 1219,[9] but by the 1240s it belonged to the Austin canons of the priory of St Sepulchre, Warwick, who had appropriated it and established a vicarage.[10] The priory also held property opposite the church, next to the Temple, and may have received both from the same source.[11] In 1277 a papal decree in a suit between the prior and canons of Warwick, and Hugh called English, a brother of the Holy Sepulchre, Jerusalem, confirmed that the church was the property of the priory.[12] In 1324 the priory received a licence to alienate the advowson of St Clement Danes and their property in the parish to the bishop of Exeter, in exchange for property in Warwickshire, and the grant took place in 1325.[13] The bishop made his first presentation to the rectory that year,[14] and his successors held the advowson until forced to surrender the bishopric's London property to the Crown in the 1540s.

In 1547 the king granted the advowson to the Lord Protector, Edward Seymour, duke of Somerset.[15] It returned to the Crown on Somerset's attainder, and in 1552 the king granted it to Sir Thomas Palmer, Kt, with other property in compensation for losses in fighting the king's wars.[16] By 1556 Palmer had been attainted for treason, and the advowson was in the hands of the

1 *Endowed Chars London*, V. 9–10.
2 Registers 1850–1932 at WCA.
3 BL, Cotton Nero E. VI, f. 52v.
4 *Chronicle of John of Worcester*, ed. R.R Darlington and P. McGurk, II (1995), 528–30.
5 WAM 17078; *Westm. Charters*, pp. 237–8; N.J.M. Kerling, *Cartulary of St Bartholomew's Hosp.* (1973), 55 (no. 486).
6 For bounds see above, Gen. Intro.: Boundaries, Parishes (Strand Pars).
7 BL, Cotton Faust. A. III, f. 253v.; above, Intro.
8 No record found of receipt of the 5s. by abbey; *Acta Stephani Langton* (Cant & York Soc. vol. L), 69–73.

9 *Bk of Fees*, I. 272.
10 Guildhall MS 25509, f. 85.
11 Above, Landownership: Other Eccles. Ests (Priory of St Sepulchre).
12 TNA, E 315/42, no. 257. Not clear if Hugh was member of Warwick community, or from another Holy Sepulchre ho.
13 TNA, C 143/167, no. 4; CP 25/1/286/33, no. 257; above, Landownership: Episcopal Inns (Exeter).
14 *Reg. Baldock* (Cant. & York Soc.), 276.
15 *Cal. Pat.* 1547–48, 131.
16 Ibid. 1550–53, 236.

52. *The parish church of St Clement Danes from the south c.1720, before Aldwych was created c.1900 and left it isolated on an island site in the highway. The south porch, part of Wren's design for the nave rebuilt in 1680–2, was removed in 1813.*

Crown again, who presented to the living in 1557 and 1559.[1] In 1560 Queen Elizabeth granted the advowson in fee simple to Thomas Reve and Nicholas Pynde of London, to hold of the manor of E. Greenwich in socage;[2] they probably obtained it on behalf of Sir William Cecil, the queen's principal secretary, as their charter of sale to him was dated the following day.[3] He made the next presentation to the living, in 1589.[4] The advowson then passed to his eldest son Thomas Cecil, Lord Burghley and later earl of Exeter, who presented in 1602, and thereafter it remained part of the estates of the earls, later marquesses, of Exeter, though presentation was sometimes made by others, particularly trustees in whom the advowson was vested.[5] In 1617 Lord Exeter granted the right to the next presentation to Richard Smith;[6] it passed to a Mr Cary and may have then passed to the king, as Charles I presented in 1634 despite the petition of William, earl of Exeter, asking the king to confer the right on him, 'to prevent controversies'.[7] The benefice was united with that of St Mary le Strand after World War II, to which the marquesses of Exeter (later the Burleigh House Preservation Trust) presented alternately with the Lord Chancellor.[8]

A vicarage existed in the 1240s, when the church had been appropriated, and the prior of St Sepulchre, Warwick, presented John de Cotes to the vicarage in the 1260s; his successor successfully claimed the right to present the next vicar in 1289.[9] After the sale of the advowson to the bishop of Exeter, however, the rectory was no longer appropriated, and no vicar or vicarage is recorded thereafter.

INCOME, PROPERTY AND RECTORY HOUSES

Income The Templars received 70s. from the church in 1185.[10] It was valued at 6 marks (£4) in 1219, in the 1240s, and in 1254, and the vicarage at 2 marks (26s. 8d.).[11] Hugh called English had apparently received £60 from the church over three years by 1277 which he had to return to the priory.[12] In 1291 the church was taxed at £2,[13] and in 1341 only a fifth of this came from great tithes.[14] The rector in 1381, William atte Cross, paid 7s. 8d. poll tax.[15] In 1535 the rectory was valued at £52 7s. 1d. net.[16] The rector received £31 a year in 1548.[17]

Fees for burials, including those in the chancel and chapels in the church, for ringing bells, and for other church functions were set down at the end of Elizabeth's reign, but higher fees were being charged in the 1620s, and non-parishioners paid double. The rector also received an entry fine of 6s. 8d. for seats in the chancel.[18] An allotment of 2s. in the £ was made to maintain the minister in the 1630s.[19] In 1650 tithes amounted to £300 a year, based apparently on a rate on houses, as 86 new houses on the Clare estate had not been so rated.[20] In 1871 the offertory amounted to c.£200 a year and there was no endowment.[21]

1 Ibid. 1555–7, 122.
2 Ibid. 1558–60, 302.
3 WCA, 10/136.
4 Hennessy, *Novum Rep.* 128.
5 E.g. Cal. Burghley Ho. MSS, Cecil 21/2 and /3; TNA, CP 25/2/386/9JASI/Hil.
6 Cal. Burghley Ho. MSS, Cecil 16/6.
7 *Cal. SP Dom.* 1631–3, 474; 1633–4, 530.
8 *London Diocese Bk* (1970, 1980, 1995 edns).
9 TNA, CP 40/76, rot. 68.   10 *Rec. Templars*, 13.

11 *Bk of Fees*, I. 272; Guildhall MS 25509, f. 85; *Val. of Norwich*, ed. Lunt, p. 359.   12 TNA, E 315/42, no. 257.
13 *Tax. Eccl.* (Rec. Com.), 17.
14 *Inq. Non.* (Rec. Com.), 198.
15 *Ch in London, 1375–92*, 36.
16 *Valor Eccl.* I. 433.
17 *Chantry Cert.* 68.
18 TNA, E 178/5482.
19 *Cal. SP Dom.* 1637–8, 167.
20 *Home Counties Mag.* I. 115.   21 *Mackeson's Guide* (1871).

Property and Parsonages   In 1233 John the parson of St Clement Danes held a plot of land on the south side of the Strand not far from the church, but it is not known whether this was in his own right or in that of his church.[1]

In the 1540s the rector, John Rixman, leased for an unknown term both the tithes and other income belonging to the rectory, and the parsonage house and its two adjoining gardens, in separate leases to John Chauntrell, citizen and vintner; the house and gardens, which were not occupied by the rector, lay on the north side of the Strand opposite the Savoy. In 1548 the leases were assigned by Chauntrell's widow Alice and her husband William Harper to Thomas Fisher.[2] By 1556 the site contained the parsonage house, occupied by a tenant, and another house with a curtilage and garden built by Sir Thomas Palmer, and occupied by him until his attainder. In 1556 the rector leased everything except the parsonage house to James Basset, gentleman of the queen's privy chamber, for 80 years at 40s. a year, and the Crown as patron ratified the lease.[3] The lease was assigned in 1559 to Sir William Cecil, and in 1561 the new rector William Harward granted the freehold of both the parsonage and adjoining house to Cecil's trustees as part of the site for Burghley House.[4] In 1560 the queen granted Cecil a licence to grant lands to the value of £4 a year to William Harward and his successors, to hold in frankalmoign, presumably in compensation for the rectory property.[5]

In 1564 Margery Chesshire, widow, conveyed to the rector and his successors a messuage and garden in the parish, and in 1567 William and Agnes Pedley conveyed a messuage to him; one or both may have been used as a rectory house.[6] In 1650 the parsonage house was inhabited by the minister, George Masterson,[7] who also had custody and use of the goods in the house belonging to the sequestered rector, Dr Richard Dukeson, valued at £10 3s. 6d., but had to pay support to Dukeson's wife.[8] The 17th-century rectory house apparently stood in Milford Lane, where in 1851 a parochial charity infant school was built on its site and leased to the school trustees.[9] The rectors had ceased to live in the parish by the 1830s,[10] possibly because it was considered insalubrious, and in 1871 the rector resided in Bloomsbury at

Russell Square with office accommodation in the parish at no. 14 Clement's Inn.[11]

MEDIEVAL CLERGY AND RELIGIOUS LIFE

Priests and chaplains of St Clement Danes were mentioned in 1185 and in the 1190s.[12] Rectors are mentioned in 1233 and in 1292 when the incumbent was John, grandson of Richard the marshal.[13] Others included the long-serving incumbents John of Horton (1328 until after 1348) and William atte Cross (by 1369 until his death in 1392).[14] The king ratified the estate of the rectors, Richard Palmer (1396–1407) and William Wykes (1407).[15] John Castell, rector 1425–30, received permission to farm out the income of his benefices for five years.[16] John Green, rector 1434–45, was granted papal dispensation to hold several benefices including St Clement Danes.[17] Master Roger Bowle, rector 1445–63, also held the prebend of West Thurrock in the royal free chapel of Hastings.[18] John Rixman, rector 1540–57, served the cure with the assistance of one curate in 1548.[19]

The court of chancery was occasionally held in the church, 1346–48.[20] In 1398 Thomas Hervey requested burial in the chapel of the Holy Trinity in St Clement's, and left 10 marks for the upkeep of the chapel and the belfry of the church.[21] In 1406 Henry IV granted to the rector and parishioners a plot of land 200 feet by 24 on the north side of the churchyard, for 2s. a year to the Crown, with licence to enclose and build to support the maintenance of a continuous light before the image of the Holy Trinity and other church uses.[22]

By the mid 15th century the fraternity of St Clement's maintained a morrow mass priest in the church to pray for the souls of its members, and by 1468 received bequests from parishioners.[23] Seven tenements were given to the fraternity towards maintenance of their priest, from which £10 rent was received in 1548. Two were built by Roger Bowle, rector, by 1463, on the land given by Henry IV; three were given by William Beckingham in honour of the Five Wounds with a payment of 5d. a year to the poor, and two others also paid 4s. each to nine poor,[24] the latter possibly being those said to have been given by Alice Newton, widow, in the mid 15th century.[25] Henry VIII gave 6s. 8d. to the

1 TNA, CP 25/1/146/9, no. 103.
2 WCA, 10/137; TNA, E 318/1/19.
3 *Cal. Pat.* 1555–7, 122.
4 Cal. Burghley Ho. MSS, Cecil 5/17, 5/26–28.
5 *Cal. Pat.* 1560–3, 64.
6 TNA, CP 25/2/171/6&7ELIZ/Mich.; CP 25/2/171/9ELIZ/East [Cal. only – doc. missing].
7 *Home Counties Mag.* I. 115.
8 *Home Counties Mag.* I. 115; *Cal. Cttee Comp.* I. 523.
9 *Endowed Chars London*, V. 42.
10 Guildhall MS 19224/216.
11 *Mackeson's Guide* (1871).
12 WAM 17078; *Westm. Charters*, pp. 237–8 (no. 396); Kerling, *Cart. of St Bartholomew's Hosp.* 55 (no. 486).
13 TNA, CP 25/1/146/9, no. 103; CP 40/93, rot. 63d.

14 *Reg. Baldock* (Cant. & York Soc.), 276, 285; Hennessy, *Novum Rep.* 127; *Cal Close*, 1354–60, 63; 1369–74, 103; Hennessy, *Novum Rep.* 127: remaining rectors as listed therein.
15 *Cal. Pat.* 1396–9, 259; 1405–8, 247.
16 *Cal. Papal Reg.* VII. 435.
17 Ibid. X. 334.
18 Hennessy, *Novum Rep.* 128; *Reg. Bourgchier* (Cant. & York Soc. LIV), 205.
19 *Chantry Cert.* 68.
20 *Cal. Close*, 1346–9, 174, 178, 243, 547, 551.
21 Guildhall MS 9171/1, ff. 386–87v.
22 *Cal. Pat.* 1405–8, 191.
23 Guildhall MS 9171/6, ff. 63, 88, 113v.
24 *Chantry Cert.* 68.
25 TNA, E 315/67, f. 318.

fraternity in 1538.[1] Bowle's two tenements were sold by the Crown in 1548, and another messuage said to have been given by Bowle for the fraternity priest and the two tenements given by Alice Newton were all sold in 1549.[2]

The churchwardens also received rents from cottages in the parish of St Giles-in-the-Field, and in St Clement's from 5 small cottages built together at the east end of the churchyard and from a divided tenement called the Horse Shoe, given for a priest in the church, which passed to the Crown as concealed lands and were granted in socage in 1572.[3] The parishioners had built a parish room in the churchyard by 1548, used for parish meetings, with under-rooms let rent-free to the poor.[4]

CLERGY AND CHURCH LIFE AFTER THE REFORMATION

Throughout the late 16th and early 17th centuries the rectors were assisted by one curate,[5] as was the minister in 1650.[6] Ralph Jackson, STB, rector 1557–9, was also master of the Savoy at his death in 1559,[7] when he was succeeded by William Harward, rector 1559–89, who also held the vicarage of Cowfold (Chichester dioc.).[8] Essex House had pews in the church in 1639.[9] Disagreement between the clergy and parishioners over fees grew in the early 17th century. Thomas Tuke, then curate, was said to have defaced the table of fees then in use in the church, and an enquiry was held in the 1620s to establish the amounts.[10] Richard Dukeson, rector 1634–78, was sequestered in 1643, accused of charging unwarranted fees and preventing preaching; he was then imprisoned in Gatehouse prison for lying to the Speaker. He had a pass to go to the king in Oxford with a petition for peace from the parishioners of St Clement Danes, Westminster, and St Martin-in-the-Fields, but was found to be carrying letters (presumably from royalists).[11] Dukeson's curates also had problems with the parishioners; John Rhodes, curate in 1637, appealed to Archbishop Laud for assistance when brought before the Lord Chamberlain in revenge by someone he had admonished for drunkenness and incontinence,[12] while Smith, curate in 1643, was, like Dukeson, summoned before Parliament in 1643.[13]

After Dukeson was sequestered in 1643, the parishioners petitioned for Richard Vines to be rector, and he was minister there by September 1644. However, because of his frequent absences on church business, the

parish petitioned again in 1647 for a settled minister.[14] In 1649 the living was in the hands of George Masterson by order of the Committee for Plundered Ministers, and he received permission to use Somerset House chapel on Thursday afternoons.[15] In the 1650s the marquess of Hertford, who was living in Essex House, paid 20s. a quarter to Masterson for preaching in the parish church.[16]

Dukeson was reinstated at the Restoration and held the living until his death. Richard Willis was chosen lecturer in 1692 and became a well-known preacher there, following which he became a chaplain to William III in 1694, and a prebendary of Westminster in 1695.[17] In 1714 the rector was assisted by two joint lecturers. Prayers were held three times on Sundays, including evening prayers, started, despite much opposition, by a local tradesman and maintained since his death about 20 years earlier by some 'well-disposed' parishioners. Holy communion was held every Sunday and sermons preached on every holy day; a monthly lecture on the first Sunday of the month was maintained by a parish society for the use of the poor.[18]

During Dukeson's time a new tower was built, and in 1680–2 a new church was paid for by the parishioners and gifts. In 1697 the churchwardens and parishioners petitioned the Middlesex justices for an additional poor-rate, which they obtained, as the parish had spent nearly £15,000 on their new church and were nearly £4,000 in debt.[19] Gifts included £200 from Richard Shalmer, a parishioner, in 1698.[20] Despite this recent expenditure on their church, the parish made a proposal for a new church on the site of Grange Inn, near the additional burial ground, which was accepted by the Commissioners for Fifty New Churches in 1711 but was never carried out, possibly because of the cost of buying out the freehold and leasehold interests.[21] Soon afterwards the Vestry decided on improvements to the existing church (below). In 1723 services were held twice on Sundays, with communion every Sunday; there was one curate.[22] During the 18th century the church continued to be served by one or two curates and lecturers, paid £40 or £50. In the early 19th century Dr Rennie, curate, received £70, and his successor in 1810, John Sheppard, £84. A Sunday afternoon lecturer was licensed in 1811.[23]

The social problems of the parish and financial

1 *L&P Hen. VIII*, XIII(2), p. 524.
2 *Cal. Pat.* 1547–48, 301; 1548–49, 421; 1549–51, 8–19; TNA, E 318/33/1866; E 315/67, f. 318.
3 *Cal. Pat.* 1569–72, 346.
4 *Chantry Cert.* 68.
5 Guildhall MSS 9537/1, f. 67A; /2, f. 98.; /3, f. 31; /4, ff. 6, 68; /6, f. 128.
6 *Home Counties Mag.* I. 115.
7 *Cal. Pat.* 1557–8, 141; 1558–60, 249.
8 Ibid. 1558–60, 5.
9 *Coll. Top. et Gen.* VIII. 309–12.
10 TNA, E 178/5482.
11 *Walker Revised*, 46.
12 *Cal. SP Dom.* 1637, 569–70.
13 *Walker Revised*, 57.
14 HMC, *6th Rep. App.* 7a, 146a, 201b–202a.
15 *Cal. SP Dom.* 1649–50, 401; *Home Counties Mag.* I. 115.
16 HMC 58, *MSS Bath at Longleat*, IV. 357.
17 *DNB*.
18 Paterson, *Pietas Lond.* 67–9.
19 *Middx County Rec. Sess. Bks 1689–1709*, 176.
20 TNA, C 93/46/28 [3rd inq].
21 *Fifty New Chs*, 149, 153, 156.
22 Guildhall MS 9550.
23 Guildhall MSS 9556, p. 28; 9557, f. 20.

difficulties faced by the rector were reported to a parliamentary committee in 1858.[1] In 1871 the rector was assisted by two curates and a mission curate, and the parochial school children sang at services.[2] In 1880 the rector received annually for sermons from the parochial charities, 40s. (New Year's day), 20s. (Ladyday), 20s. (Good Friday), and 42s. (Good Friday and Christmas day). The curate received 10s. 6d. for reading prayers on Good Friday and Christmas day, for which the churchwardens received 42s. towards lighting the church and other church purposes.[3] Attendance in 1886 was 212 (a.m.), 353 (p.m.), and in 1903 114 (a.m.), 200 (p.m.).[4]

Left in ruins after being bombed in 1941, in 1953 the church was handed over to the keeping of the Air Council and a world-wide appeal launched for its rebuilding. Some £250,000 was raised and in 1958 the church was reconsecrated as the central church of the Royal Air Force, with shrines containing books of remembrance inscribed with the names of RAF men and women who died on active service. The church commemorated those who died at Holy Communion and held an annual memorial service. Endowed with a fine organ by Harrison and Harrison, in 2008 it had choral services of holy communion or matins every Sunday.

Seven of the eight bells made famous by the nursery rhyme, and the oranges and lemons chime inaugurated in 1920, were destroyed in 1941.[5]

Missions Clare Market mission chapel stood in Horse Shoe Court at the north end of Clement's Inn by 1866, served by a missionary curate provided by the Bishop of London's Fund, who also owned the building. It seated 300, all free; services were held twice on Sundays and once on weekdays; the surplice was worn for preaching. The mission had ceased by 1894,[6] but was apparently re-started there or in another building, as attendance in 1903 at Clare Market mission was 14 (p.m.). In 1871 the boys' schoolroom of St Clement Danes parochial school, no. 45 Stanhope Street, was used for mission services on Thursday evenings in winter;[7] it is perhaps to be identified with the mission room in Stanhope Street which in 1894 seated 100, with services twice on Sundays.[8] In 1903 attendance at another mission, held by the Inns of Court in Drury Lane, was 22 (p.m.).[9]

CHURCH FABRIC

The medieval church, which had a western tower, appear to have been almost fully oriented so that it stood on the north side of the Strand and at a slight angle to it and to the churchyard wall. When rebuilt in the 1680s the new church followed the same line, whereas the new church of St Mary-le-Strand followed the line of the highway.[10] At the time of its rebuilding St Clement's had a nave with one north aisle and two south ones, a chancel and a 17th-century west tower. Few other details are known; in the 1390s it included the chapel and image of the Holy Trinity, to the right of the high altar, and also a belfry.[11] A new aisle was being built in 1468; a south door is mentioned in 1473; and the high cross, perhaps a crucifix over the high altar, was being painted in 1470.[12] In the 1470s there was an image of St John the Baptist, and in the choir marble stones for decoration and covering tombs, presumably in the floor.[13] The church was repaired at the cost of the parish in 1608, 1616, and 1631–3,[14] and in 1628 had more than one chapel, a new vault for burial, and a peal of 5 bells.[15]

The tower was rebuilt 1668–70 in an unsophisticated artisan style by Joshua Marshall and Stephen Switzer,[16] and was retained when the church was rebuilt on advice given by surveyors in 1679. The rest was demolished in 1680, under a contract made by the churchwardens with John Shorthose and Edward Pearse, masons, who agreed to rebuild under the supervision of Sir Christopher Wren, Surveyor of the King's Works. They were to preserve the battlements of 650 feet for reuse as well as the stone, bricks, and window ironwork, to construct the foundations, walls, windows, and pillars ready for the roof, and to case the new walls in Portland ashlar, using the old materials for their core.[17] The new church was completed in 1682, with work by the carpenters Henry Pierson and John Green and the plasterer Robert Powell. At the east end the walls of the nave were continued as quadrants flanking a shallow apse, an unusual and baroque solution to the problem of the restricted site. Inside the galleries wrapped round the quadrant ends and Corinthian columns rose from them to support arches and groin-vaulted aisle ceilings. The plasterwork in the centre and apse was by Robt Powell and Edward Goudge. In 1714 the following were thought noteworthy: a fine dial, clock and portico, a beautiful steeple, 116 ft high, containing 9 bells, the altar-piece, and a fine chancel paved with black and white marble.[18]

As part of the improvements agreed c.1711, the tower was raised by 25 feet in 1720, and the original octagonal lantern replaced by an elegant steeple 50 feet high and of three diminishing stages, designed by James Gibbs with Townsend as mason. The interior was sumptuously

1 Above, Rel. Hist., Intro. (Urban Problems).
2 *Mackeson's Guide* (1871).
3 *Endowed Chars London*, V. 65–6.
4 *Brit. Weekly*, 5 Nov 1886, 3; Mudie-Smith, *Rel. Life*, 105.
5 Inf. from pamphlets available in the ch.
6 *Mackeson's Guide* (1866 and later edns); TNA, ED 3/27.
7 TNA, ED 3/27.   8 *Mackeson's Guide* (1894–5).
9 Mudie-Smith, *Rel. Life*, 106.
10 *Civitas Londinum. Plan of London circa 1560–70, by Ralph*

Agas (London Top. Soc. 1905), now known as the woodcut map.
11 Guildhall MS 9171/1, ff. 386–87v.
12 Ibid., /6, ff. 31v., 63, 127v.
13 Ibid., ff. 113v., 171.
14 Paterson, *Pietas Lond.* 67–9.
15 TNA, E 178/5482.
16 Pevsner, *London 6: Westm.* 289–90.
17 BL, Add. Ch. 1605.
18 Clarke, *London Chs*, 176–7; Paterson, *Pietas Lond.* 67–9.

fitted, the columns were fluted and the capitals gilded. A glory painted by Kent was erected over the altar, but was taken down in 1725 by order of the bishop following an allegation that the figure of St Cecilia was a portrait of the Stuart Pretender's wife with some of her family. Carving on the altar was done by James Richards, and there was also fretwork and wainscotting, and a south gallery.[1] In 1866 the altar-piece was of carved wainscot of the Tuscan order; the church seated 1,500, 350 of them free, and there were 10 bells and an organ by Smith, rebuilt by Robson.[2] Repairs and redecoration by H. and P. Currey were carried out 1897–8, when the pews were lowered. The interior except for the fine Wren pulpit was destroyed by bombing in 1941, and was convincingly reconstructed for the RAF in the 1950s, to designs based on drawings and photographs of the 17th-century work by W.A.S. Lloyd of W. Curtis Green, Sons and Lloyd; it reopened in 1958 with the addition of RAF badges set into the floor, new furnishings and glass, and a chapel in the crypt.[3]

Churchyard and burial grounds The medieval churchyard lay east and west of the church,[4] by the 17th century part of an island of buildings between Aldwych Street and its continuation as Butcher Row on the north and the Strand on the south. In 1802 a large portion was taken for improving Temple Bar and the Strand, but the parts not needed were returned to the parish in 1811 to be used for burials,[5] which continued until the churchyard was closed in 1853. In 1895 the churchyard covered a quarter-acre, and was not well-kept, suffering from mud thrown up by passing vehicles;[6] it was later paved over. Since 1945 war memorials to RAF officers have been placed west of the church, which now forms an island between the carriageways of the eastern end of Aldwych and the Strand.

Ground belonging to John Reade near Lincoln's Inn grange became the new churchyard of St Clement Danes between 1593 and 1609.[7] In 1674 the bishop of London granted the parish a licence to build houses and shops on a strip 18 feet wide along the north side of the new churchyard from which the rents were to be used for the benefit of the poor, and the vaults underneath used for burials.[8] The new churchyard lay along the south side of Portugal Street in 1745, with an entrance in Carey Street.[9] In 1895 the Portugal Street cemetery was called the 'green-ground' and was crowded with bodies. King's College Hospital had taken the whole ground: a corner of the hospital was built on part, and the remainder, nearly half an acre between the hospital and Portugal Street, formed the entrance drive and grass plot for the hospital.[10]

ST GEORGE, HANOVER SQUARE

St George's was the last of the new parishes to be created out of the parish of St Martin-in-the-Fields. In 1720 the commissioners for building fifty new churches in London agreed to build one of the new churches for St Martin's near Hanover Square. The site for the church was given by General William Steuart, who was to have a pew in the south gallery, and the commissioners decided on a design from John James, with some alterations to keep the cost under £10,000. Complaints were made by the residents in 1723 about the slowness in finishing the church,[11] which was eventually consecrated in 1725. The new parish took much of the area of St Martin's, but was then largely unbuilt; in 1730 the boundary around the parish measured over 8 miles, but the area it enclosed contained only about 1,432 houses.[12]

ADVOWSON, BENEFICE, AND RECTORY HOUSE

The Crown appointed the first rector in 1725 but thereafter patronage was vested in the bishop of London, who usually presented except in 1774 (Dr Henry Reginald Courtenay).[13] Under the Act to create the new parishes, a large but rich parish like St George's did not receive any part of the parliamentary fund for the living, and the benefice was funded solely from an annual rate producing £350, of which the curate was to receive £80 and the rector the residue.[14] A curate was licensed in 1728, and curates were licensed as lecturers in 1771, 1800, and 1805. The curate received £60 in 1791, and £126 in 1811.[15]

The living was valued at £300 c.1730,[16] £800 c.1760,[17] and between £800 and £1300 in 1780.[18] In 1851 it included an endowment of £10 ground rent from a small house, and fees and dues of £800 plus £450 gross, a net income of £900.[19] A rectory house was provided by the commissioners, who bought the lease of no. 15 Grosvenor Street, and its freehold in 1724. It remained the site of the rectory for St George's until 1937; the house was said to have been rebuilt in 1826 at a cost of £3,960.[20] In 1960 the parsonage house was no. 24 South

1 Clarke, *London Chs*, 176–7.   2 *Mackeson's Guide* (1866).
3 Clarke, *London Chs*. 176–7.   4 TNA, LR 14/300.
5 TNA, C 54/8889, no. 13.   6 LCC, *Burial Grounds*, 5–6.
7 TNA, C3/466/14.
8 Craven Papers, vol. 144.
9 Rocque, *Map of London* (1741–5).
10 LCC, *Burial Grounds*, 5–6.
11 *Fifty New Chs*, 81–2, 82, 87–8, 102.

12 *New Remarks of London, collected by Company of Parish Clerks* (1732), 260–3.
13 *Fifty New Chs*, 136; Guildhall MSS 9550; 9556, p. 31; BL, Eg. Ch. 8193.   14 *Fifty New Chs*, 121.
15 Guildhall MSS 9550; 9557, f. 26.   16 Ibid. MS 9550.
17 Ibid. MS 9556, p. 31.   18 Ibid. MS 9557, f. 26.
19 TNA, HO 129/3, 1/1/2 (f. 93).
20 *Survey of London*, XL. 35–6.

Audley Street, when improvements were made.[1] After St Mark's district church closed in 1974, the ground and first floors of the former vicarage of St Mark's, no. 13 North Audley Street, were adapted as the rectory of St George's.[2] That building had been sold by 2007, and the rectory in 2008 was at no. 2a Mill Street, behind the church.

CHURCH LIFE

In the 1730s, under the first rector, Andrew Trebeck (1725–59), prayers were held twice daily. The church had a good organ and one bell; the organist, Dr Rosengrave, was described as the best in England, and had an annual salary of £50.[3] The church served a rapidly expanding and fashionable area in the 18th century. Among many eminent parishioners, one of the most outstanding was the composer, George Frideric Handel, who came to live in nearby Brook Street (the present no. 25) in 1723, remaining until his death in 1759: he attended the church from its opening, had a pew there, and assisted the church in musical matters, such as choosing the organ and organist.[4]

In 1780 services were held twice each day and four times on Sundays; communion was held monthly and on the great festivals; there were 250–500 communicants. No children were catechised.[5] In 1851 the church seated 430 free, 800 other, and was filled (attendance 1150 (a.m.), 550 (aft.), 850 (evg.).[6] It remained popular until the 20th century: attendance in 1886 was 697 (a.m.), 711 (p.m.), but 259 (a.m.), 206 (p.m.) in 1903. The decline was probably the result of social change with the movement of residents away from the immediate neighbourhood. St George's, however, continued to be a popular church for fashionable London weddings, as well as serving the reduced residential population of Mayfair; a communion service and a sung eucharist were held each Sunday. It also serves both residents and visitors in other ways, with musical recitals and concerts, and by hosting many of the performances for the annual Handel Festival.[7]

CHURCH FABRIC

The church has features in common with St Martins-in-the-Fields and St George's, Bloomsbury, chiefly the Corinthian temple front, which here projects onto the pavement and is prominent in the planned layout of Hanover Square and the streets leading out of it.[8] The side elevations and, in particular, the pedimented west bays of the nave were also designed to be seen in an oblique view from the square and, less so, from the south. As at St Martin's, a tower, in this case based on Wren examples, rises just behind the portico, and in the

53. *The parish church of St George, Hanover Square, designed by John James and built in 1721–5 within the development begun by the first Earl of Scarborough c.1713. The six-columned portico, which was intended to be crowned by a giant statue of George I, projects over St George Street, laid out c.1715 and still with houses of that period.*

original design for the façade incorporated a giant statue of George I, of the type realised at Hawksmoor's Bloomsbury church. The interior is quite plain with a segmental tunnel-vault above the nave, and transverse barrel-vaults on Corinthian columns above the galleries, which are carried on pillars. The fittings are mostly of the 1720s, some like the reredos with a Last Supper painted by William Kent, in their original state, others combined with woodwork made when A. Blomfield formed the chancel in 1894. Sir Reginald Blomfield created the east chapels in 1926 and baptistery in 1935. An incongruous note is struck by the superb stained glass of c.1525 attributed to Arnold van Nijmegen, which was brought from the Carmelite church in Antwerp and installed in the Venetian east window by T. Willement in 1841.

1 Guildhall MS 19224/255.
2 *Survey of London*, XL. 105.
3 *New Remarks of London* (1732), 260–3.
4 *Oxford DNB*; inf. from ch website (www.stgeorgeshanoversquare.org).

5 Guildhall MS 9557, f. 26.
6 TNA, HO 129/3, 1/1/2 (f. 93).
7 Inf. from ch website (www.stgeorgeshanoversquare.org).
8 Archit. acct follows Pevsner, *London 6: Westm.* 479–81; Colvin, *Brit. Architects*, 567.

Churchyard There was no churchyard around the church, and a site for a burial ground near the later Mount Street was bought from Sir Richard Grosvenor for £315 in 1723. Another burial ground was later opened in Bayswater Road.[1]

OTHER CHURCHES AND CHAPELS

By 1750 the parish church had been augmented by five chapels: Grosvenor (South Audley Street); Mayfair or Keith's (Curzon Street); Berkeley (Charles Street); Trinity (Conduit Street); and Five Fields (near the boundary with Chelsea).[2] The rector was the patron of Trinity chapel; the remainder were then proprietary chapels. Charlotte Street chapel was opened in 1766, and by 1780 was in the patronage of the rector, as was the Mayfair (Curzon) chapel and, by 1787, Five Fields. St George's chapel, Albemarle Street, was opened by 1811, again with the rector as patron. Other proprietary chapels included Park Street from 1763, Dudley by 1802, and Belgrave, Halkin Street, from 1812.[3] Many proprietary chapels later became chapels of ease to St George's, and subsequently district churches.[4]

In 1818 St George's parish was amongst those where the population exceeded church accommodation by 20,000 or more. District churches built in the parish with the aid of a parliamentary grant included St George's or Hanover chapel, St Mark's, St Peter's, and St Philip's. Subsequently Holy Trinity and St Paul's were built with the aid of the grant for areas where population exceeded accommodation by 15,000.[5]

Christ Church, Down Street, Mayfair

A district chapelry was formed 1865 from St Geo.'s parish.[6] The patron in 1871 and 1970 was the bishop of London, and the income of the benefice was £600 in 1871.[7] The ragstone, Decorated style church of 1865 was fairly lavish as befitted the area. It was designed by F. & H. Francis with nave and north-eastern transept, and the polychrome interior embellished with foliage carving, and much stained glass which survives. Enlarged in 1868, it was only partly finished in 1871 when half the seats were free. It was much rebuilt after a fire in 1906 to designs by R.L. Hesketh, which included an arts and crafts style gallery.[8] Attendance in 1886 was 377 (a.m.), 312 (p.m.), and 314 (a.m.), 154 (p.m.) in 1903. By 2000 it was no longer used for Anglican services; the Ethiopian Orthodox Church used it for Sunday services.

Hanover (St George's) Chapel, Regent Street

A district chapelry was formed from St George in 1835.[9] The patron was the rector of St George's, and the value of the benefice was £700 in 1871. The duke of Westminster made a substantial contribution to the incumbent's income from 1879. In 1851 attendance was 1,500 (a.m.), 910 (aft.); in 1886: 502 (a.m.), 375 (p.m.).

The church's building costs were paid by St George's parish, with a grant from the Church Building Commissioners and the church was consecrated in 1825. The building, which stood a matter of yards from St George's on the west side of Regent Street, between Hanover and Princes streets, was designed 1821–5 by C.R. Cockerell, who also repaired it in 1845–6. It received critical acclaim. The Regent Street front was bold with an Ionic portico and flanking towers, the central space planned like a classical atrium, top-lit from a dome and with two tiers of galleries, and the detail scholarly.[10] It seated 1,580, 726 of them free. By 1851 free seats had increased to 800 with 860 other: the minister complained that the free seats were usually full, but some pews were not let as even the wealthiest objected to paying pew rents.[11] In 1871 it seated 1,600, 750 of them free.[12] The incumbent asked the Grosvenor Estate for aid to improve the chapel in 1881, but it was decided to sell the site and rebuild the chapel on a more appropriate site. An Act was obtained 1891 to demolish and sell, despite strong opposition against loss of a fine building; proceeds of the sale were used for the costs and endowment of St Anselm, Davies Street (below). The church was demolished in 1896 after St Anselm opened.[13]

St Anselm, Davies Street, Oxford Street

St Anselm replaced Hanover chapel (above) as district church, and built with the proceeds of that chapel's sale on a site between St Anselm's Place and Weighhouse Street given by the duke of Westminster. The patron was the rector of St Geo.'s, and benefice was valued in 1907 at £550.[14] Some fittings were transferred from Hanover chapel. The integrated church and vicarage were designed in Neo Byzantine style by Balfour and Turner and built in stock brick 1894–6; the church was consecrated in 1896.[15] It seated 800 in 1907,[16] but was never popular: attendance in 1903 was 384 (a.m.), 160 (p.m.), and it was found expensive to maintain by 1923. Because

1 *Fifty New Chs*, 90–1, 99; LCC, *Burial Grounds*, 5. Reserved for treatment under Local Govt: Pub. Svces.
2 Ibid. MS 9556, p. 31, 41, 46.
3 Ibid. MS 9557, ff. 26, 43.
4 Below.
5 Port, *Six Hundred Chs*, 30, 136–7, 96, 156–7.
6 *London Gaz.* 8 Aug. 1865, p. 3874.
7 *Mackeson's Guide* (1871); *London Diocese Bk* (1970 edn).
8 Pevsner, *London 6: Westm.* 479; *Mackeson's Guide* (1871).
9 *London Gaz.* 23 June 1835, p. 1193.

10 G.L. Carr, 'C.R. Cockerell's Hanover Chapel', *Jnl of Soc. of Archit. Historians*, 39 (1980), 265–85.
11 TNA, HO 129/3, 1/1/1 (f. 92).
12 *Mackeson's Guide* (1871).
13 *Survey of London*, XL. 76–7; Port, *Six Hundred Chs*, 136–7; G. Clinch, *Mayfair and Belgravia* (1892), 60.
14 *Crockford* (1907 edn).
15 Acct based on *Survey of London*, XL. 77; Pevsner, *London 3: NW*, 299.
16 *Crockford* (1907 edn).

of population decline in the 1930s, the Church Commissioners decided to divide the district between St George and St Mark and close the church in 1938; the site was sold back to the Grosvenor Estate and the church demolished 1939. Building and decorative materials as well as fittings were used in a new church of St Anselm, Belmont (Stanmore) to which the church's endowments also passed. Wall monuments were transferred to St Mark.

St Barnabas, St Barnabas Street, Pimlico

A district chapelry formed from St Paul, Knightsbridge, 1866,[1] it was endowed with £200 p.a. from the Common Fund.[2] In 1871 the income was £231 and the patron was the vicar of St Paul (thereafter the bishop of London). The church was built in a poor part of parish after appeal by W.J.E. Bennett, then vicar of St Paul's. Sir F.A. Gore Ouseley, the clerical musician, gave the organ and paid for the choir; matins and evensong were sung daily. The buildings, including a school and clergy house, were designed by Thomas Cundy II, with assistance from Bennett, 1847–50.[3] The church, which seated 550 (all free in 1871), was of ragstone rubble in the Early English in style, with a long nave and chancel, both aisled, a south porch, and NW tower with spire. Thought by *The Ecclesiologist* to be a model of excellence, it was pioneering in the Anglo-Catholic movement, but its ritualism immediately attracted public criticism. The church was later given lavish fittings, decoration and stained glass, chiefly by G.F. Bodley, C.E. Kempe and N. Comper for Revd A. Gurney who made it fashionable from the 1880s. Attendance in 1886 was 382 (a.m.), 683 (p.m.), and in 1903 was 474 (a.m.), 279 (p.m.). Still in use in 2008, it retains its High Church character and is shared with the parish of St John Chrysostom (Eastern Rite Roman Catholic).[4]

St John the Baptist, Pimlico Road Served from St Barnabas, the chapel had opened by 1871, with 3 Sunday services and a children's service.[5] Attendance in 1886 was 315 (a.m.), 214 (p.m.) and in 1903 304 (a.m.), 246 (p.m). Still open in 1913, it closed in the mid 20th century. Its altar and reredos were installed in St Barnabas (above) as the altar of St John the Baptist.

St Gabriel, Warwick Square, Pimlico

The site was given by the Grosvenor Estate under a local Act,[6] and a district was assigned 1853 from St Peter's, Eaton Sq.[7] The patron was the duke of Westminster. A

Kentish ragstone church of 1851–3 by Thomas Cundy II in early Decorated style with NW tower and spire, it was consecrated in 1853.[8] Altered by J.P. St Aubyn in 1887–8, it was enlarged and beautified in 1895–7, when outer aisles, a south-eastern chapel, and west porch were added by Arthur Baker, with lavish chancel decoration by Messrs Powell, and other fittings and stained glass by J.F.Bentley and C.E. Kempe.[9] Attendances in 1886 were 744 (a.m.), 643 (p.m.), and in 1903 535 (a.m.), 357 (p.m.). The church was still in use 2008.

St Mark, North Audley Street, Mayfair

Built by the parish with a grant from Church Building Commissioners and consecrated 1828.[10] A district was assigned from St George's, 1835, and the rector was patron.[11] The benefice, which included part of St Anselm's district from 1938, was reunited with St George's 1974. The church of 1825–8 was designed by John Gandy (later Deering) in Greek style, its narrow front with an Ionic portico in antis and a Tower of the Winds type of lantern above; its galleried interior seated 1,510 (784 free),[12] but by 1851 1640 (940 free).[13] In 1878 Sir Arthur Blomfield modified the galleries and roof timbers, and inserted Romanesque arcades; the good ensemble of fittings were provided then and later.[14] In 1892 it seated 1,350.[15]

Attendances in 1851 were 1,112 (a.m.), 390 (aft.), 571 (evg.); in 1886 447 (a.m.), 349 (p.m.); and in 1903 272 (a.m.), 142 (p.m.). The church was closed 1974, but was used by the Commonwealth Church from 1995 to 2007. Planning permission for commercial use, which would include extensive repairs, was being sought by the diocese of London in 2008.[16]

St Michael and All Angels, Chester Square, Belgravia

The church was built on the Grosvenor estate with a district assigned from St Peter, Pimlico.[17] Largely paid for by the patron, the marquess of Westminster. The Middle Pointed style ragstone building by Thomas Cundy II, 1844–6, has a Low Church plan with broad transepts and galleries, plus a north-west tower and spire. Double chancel aisles were added by T. Cundy III in 1874–5, the north ones being enclosed as a meeting room c.1970. A Gothic war memorial chapel was added in a different style in 1920–1 from designs by Sir Giles Gilbert Scott. There was some modernization in 1993.[18] Attendances in 1886 were 1,800 (a.m.), 1,046 (p.m.)

1 *London Gaz.* 10 Aug. 1866, p. 4459.
2 Ibid. 14 May 1867, p. 2766.
3 *Mackeson's Guide* (1871).
4 Inf from Ch website (www.melkite.org.uk).
5 *Mackeson's Guide* (1871).
6 13 & 14 Vic. c. cvii (Local).
7 *London Gaz.* 21 June 1853, p. 1737.
8 Hobhouse, *Cubitt*, 218.
9 Pevsner, *London 6: Westm.* 767; Clarke, *London Chs*, 188.

10 Acct based on *Survey of London*, XL. 105–8.
11 *London Gaz.* 23 June 1835, p. 1193.
12 Port, *Six Hundred Chs*, 136–7.
13 TNA, HO 129/3, 2/1/6 (f. 101).
14 Clarke, *London Chs*, 183–4; Pevsner, *London 6: Westm.* 481.
15 Clinch, *Mayfair*, 61.
16 Below, Prot. Nonconf., Other; Pevsner, *London 6: Westm.* 481.   17 *London Gaz.* 11 Sep. 1846, p. 3254.
18 Pevsner, *London 6; Westm.* 733.

54. *The district church of St Michael, Chester Square, one of the Gothic churches designed for the Grosvenor Estate by Thomas Cundy in the mid 19th century.*

and in 1903 922 (a.m.), 471 (p.m.). A third of seats were free in 1866.[1] The church was still in use 2008.

St Paul, Wilton Place, Knightsbridge

The district was assigned from St George's, 1843,[2] parts later being assigned to Holy Trinity, St Barnabas, St George, and St Peter, Pimlico. The patron was the bishop of London. In 1871 the income of £1,500 derived from endowment and pew rents.[3] The large brick Perpendicular style church of 1840–3 by Thomas Cundy II, built on the Grosvenor estate with a grant from Church Building Commissioners, seated 1,520 (540 free).[4] Although the church was galleried and pre-Tractarian in spirit, the first Vicar, W.J.E. Bennett, a High Churchman, introduced many ritualistic features and fittings. Bennett resigned 1851, after a long struggle with Bishop Blomfield. The surpliced choir was

dispersed, and the credence, lectern and candlesticks were removed. In 1870–1, however, the chancel was enlarged and refitted by R.J. Withers, who added a porch and designed the clergy house.[5] The chancel was given a south chapel in 1889 instead of a vestry and porch, and extended eastwards in 1891 by Bodley, who designed many of the High Church fittings and decoration.[6] St Luke's chapel was added by Sir A. Blomfield by 1894.[7]

Attendance in 1886 was 1,140 (a.m.), 1,027 (p.m.); and in 1903 710 (a.m.), 350 (p.m.). At the end of the 19th century, it succeeded St George's as the most popular church for fashionable weddings, because it allowed rehearsals to provide newspaper copy.[8] The parish had two sisterhoods: St Mary and St James had a mission at no. 16 Kenniston St, in 1871, and the London Branch of St Margaret, East Grinstead, had a mission house at no. 15 Westbourne St in 1894. Still in use 2008, the church maintains its Anglo-Catholic tradition.

St Peter, Eaton Square, Belgravia

Founded in 1827 as a chapel of ease for St George's, it was assigned a district from St George in 1830, which stretched from Knightsbridge to Vauxhall Bridge Rd.[9] It became a parish in 1844, and the boundaries were adjusted with those of St Paul's Knightsbridge in 1846; parts were also taken to form St Michael and St Gabriel. The patron was the bishop of London. The living was united with Christ Church, 1954, when half of St Andrew's parish was also included.[10]

In 1851 the income derived from pew rents (£1100), fees (£160), and Easter offerings (£175). In 1851 the church seated 1,795 (805 free),[11] and in 1871 2,000 (800 free).[12] Attendance in 1851 was 1,200 (a.m.), 600 (aft.), which had risen in 1886 to 1,800 (a.m.), 1,727 (p.m.), but dropped dramatically by 1903 (809 a.m.; 509 p.m.).[13] The rise in numbers was due to the extraordinary ministry of G.H. Wilkinson, vicar 1869–83, and later bishop of Truro and of St Andrew's. Despite alterations, the building of the daughter church of St John, Wilton Road, and the creation of a mission church in St Peter's chapel, Buckingham Gate, St Peter's was then crowded out, with some of the congregation standing or using camp-stools.

The church had been built, after lengthy planning by St George's vestry and a competition in 1819,[14] to Greek style designs with a giant Ionic portico and west tower by H. Hakewill, 1824–7, after a Gothic design was rejected. The Church Building Commissioners contributed about a quarter of the cost. Consecrated in 1827, it was gutted by fire and restored in 1836 by Hakewill's son, J.H..

1 *Mackeson's Guide* (1866).
2 *London Gaz.* 23 Nov. 1843, p. 4043.
3 *Mackeson's Guide* (1871).
4 Port, *Six Hundred Chs*, 156–7; Pevsner, *London 6: Westm.* 734.   5 *Mackeson's Guide* (1871)
6 Clarke, *London Chs*, 184–5, 498.
7 *Mackeson's Guide* (1894).
8 Colby, *Mayfair*, 66.

9 Hobhouse, *Cubitt*, 143–4; *London Gaz.* 27 July 1830, p. 1583.
10 Inf. in ch.
11 TNA, HO 129/3, 3/1/2 (f. 104).
12 *Mackeson's Guide* (1871).
13 TNA, HO 129/3, 3/1/2 (f. 104); *Brit.Weekly*, 5 Nov. 1886, p. 3; Mudie-Smith, *Rel. Life*, 105.
14 Colvin, *Brit. Architects*, 330, 510.

55. *St Peter, Eaton Square, provided as a chapel for Belgravia in 1824–7, and created a district church in 1844. The interior was recreated in 1988–91, after a fire, to echo the original neo-classical design by Henry Hakewill.*

Hakewill, to the original drawings. The simple interior was made Italian Romanesque by Sir Arthur Blomfield, 1872–5, who added a chancel, nave arcades and clerestory, new seating and in 1894–5 a south chapel. After being gutted in an arson attack 1987, the interior was remodelled 1988–91 by Braithwaite Partnership, who removed almost all the earlier work.[1] Reopened 1991, and reconsecrated 1992, the fittings are Anglo-Catholic in tone, with sanctuary lamp, tabernacle, and there is a sung eucharist with a professional choir. The organ of 1992 filled the west wall above entrance, with choir stalls at the west end of nave. The church was still in use in 2008, maintaining a liberal Catholic tradition as an 'inclusive church' to encompass a broad range of Anglican belief.

St John the Evangelist, Wilton Rd, Vauxhall Bridge Rd
This chapel of ease to St Peter's was designed by A.W. Blomfield and consecrated 1874. With an organ by Lewis (1876), 8 bells, and sanctuary lamps, it seated 800, all free. All Souls' chapel by Temple Moore was dedicated 1893. In 1894 the church was served by a curate-in-charge and an assistant in 1894, holding 5 services on Sunday; the offertory was £1645 p.a.[2] Attendance in 1886 was 648 (a.m.), 263 (p.m.), and 472 (a.m.), 318 (p.m.) in 1903. Still there in 1947, it had been demolished by 1952.[3]

St Mary the Virgin, Bourne Street, Pimlico
The church was said to have opened 1874 as chapel of ease to St Barnabas, Pimlico,[4] though it was united to St

Paul's, Wilton Place by 1896.[5] It was given a parish and consecrated in 1909, the patronage vested in trustees.[6] The red brick building of 1873–4 by R.J. Withers is in Early English Gothic style, with flèche, a clerestoried nave with low aisles, an apse, and an ingenious polygonal porch and north chapel added by H.S. Goodhart-Rendel, 1927, who provided some of the high-quality largely Anglo-Catholic Baroque fittings in the interwar period; others were designed by S. Gambier-Parry *c.*1908–10.[7] In 1894 when served by 2 assistant curates, it had 6 Sunday services, at which surplices and eucharistic vestments were worn. The church seated 520 (all free).[8] Attendances in 1886 were 500 (a.m.), 660 (p.m.) and in 1903 220 (a.m.), 138 (p.m.). Services maintained the Anglo-Catholic tradition in 2008.[9]

St Saviour, St George's Square, Pimlico
The district chapelry was formed 1864 out of St Gabriel, Pimlico.[10] The patron was the marquess, later duke, of Westminster, jointly with the dean and chapter of Westminster after the benefice was united with St James the Less (below, St John's par.) between 1966 and 1970. The large ragstone church was built in 1863–4 to designs by Thomas Cundy II in mixed Gothic style, with a north-west tower and meagre spire, and was consecrated in 1864. In 1882 W.H. Romaine-Walker, son of the first vicar, embellished the church and removed the galleries.[11] In 1871 it was staffed by a vicar, curate, and 3 sacristans, with services in surplices (eucharistic vestments by 1894). A sisterhood was established in parish, under direction of the Association of St Denys,

1 Hobhouse, *Cubitt*, 493; Pevsner, *London 6: Westm.* 735.
2 *Mackeson's Guide* (1894).   3 *Crockford* (1947, 1952).
4 Clarke, *London Chs*, 191.
5 *Crockford* (1896, 1907).
6 Ibid. (1926); *London Diocese Bk* (1970).
7 Clarke, *London Chs*, 191; Pevsner, *London 6: Westm.* 732–3.
8 *Mackeson's Guide* (1894).
9 Inf. from ch website (www.stmarythevirgin.org.uk).
10 *London Gaz.* 30 Aug. 1864, p. 4210.
11 Clarke, *London Chs*, 190; Pevsner, *London 6: Westm.* 767.

Warminster.[1] Attendance in 1886 was 522 (a.m.), 781 (p.m.), and in 1903 458 (a.m.), 400 (p.m.). The church was still in use 2008.

All Saints, Grosvenor Rd, Pimlico A temporary iron building provided by Geo. Cubitt in 1860,[2] seating 500, and a permanent church was built 1869–71 on the same site and consecrated 1871 as a chapel of ease to St Saviour, Pimlico.[3] It was a large Early English style church designed by Thomas Cundy III, in polychrome brick, with aisled nave, polygonal apse, south chapel, north vestry and an almost-detached south-west tower with spire. Attendance in 1886 was 327 (a.m.), 368 (p.m.), and in 1903 227 (a.m.), 280 (p.m.). Closed 1940, and damaged during Second World War, the church was restored and rededicated 1955.[4] Still open 1970, it has been demolished and replaced by Darwin House flats c.1980.[5]

Holy Name A mission church, opened by 1871 at no. 2 Aylesford Street, Grosvenor Road, seating 300, it had a Sunday morning communion service, and evening mission service, with a communion service for children on Saturday.[6] Attendance in 1903 was 206 (a.m.), 54 (p.m.). Still there 1913, it had closed by 1926.[7]

Other Chapels

Dudley Chapel A reader was licensed 1801, with stipend of £50 p.a.; a morning and afternoon preacher was licensed in 1802, and a successor in 1808.[8] Its location is unknown.

St Philip, Buckingham Palace Rd, Belgravia Opened c.1888, it had a vicar and curate, who by 1894 held 3 Sunday services.[9] Attendance in 1903 was 59 (a.m.), 116 (p.m.). Used by Russian Orthodox Church 1923–54,[10] it still had Anglican services in 1940, but no clergy were listed in 1947, 1952,[11] and it was demolished in 1954.[12] A parsonage at no. 162 Buckingham Palace Road was built 1892, with a small church hall at rear.[13]

Trinity Chapel, Conduit Street, Mayfair A *portatile* or 'moveable' tabernacle used by James II on Hounslow

Heath, was re-erected in fields of north Westminster as chapel of ease to St Martin-in-the-Fields by vicar, Dr Tenison, c.1689. By 1708 streets nearby were being built,[14] and in 1714 the chapel stood at the upper end of (Old) Bond Street. It was described as beautiful and stately chapel covered with slate, with large galleries and stately pews and other fittings,[15] so presumably the original building had already been reconstructed or replaced by one built in brick, on the site which was later on the south side of Conduit Street, close to its junction with Bond Street. About 1710 the chapel was long, with a pedimented west front, tower over, and projections on the east side.[16] Prayers were held twice a day in 1714, sermons twice on Sunday and communion on the 3rd Sunday of the month. A weekly lecture on Wednesday was maintained by private benefactors.[17] The chapel lay on private land, whose owner had to be prevailed on not to demolish it.[18] It was retained and refronted c.1775 in neoclassical style to accord with houses on flanking plots built and apparently designed by John Mecluer, district surveyor of St Clement Danes and adjoining parishes. During the 18th century the chapel was served by curates and preachers, with two services on Sunday.[19] After the creation of St George's, Hanover Sq., the rector appointed the preachers and ministers.[20] By 1804 the chapel had been rebuilt or refaced and had a neoclassical façade the width of one of the 18th-century houses which flanked it along Conduit Street.[21] In 1851 the chapel seated 1,000, of which 100 were free; attendance was then 476 (a.m.), 356 (evg.).[22] It continued in use until 1877 when it was demolished to make way for a shop.[23]

Proprietary Chapels

Belgrave Chapel (St John), Halkin Street, Belgrave Square Built 1812 to designs by Sir Robert Smirke,[24] it seated 1,100 in 1894. The patronage was vested in trustees.[25] Two morning preachers and a reader and afternoon preacher were licensed in 1812 or 1813.[26] In 1871 it remained a proprietary chapel in district of St Paul, Knightsbridge, with services on Sun. and Wed., and communion once a month.[27] Attendance in 1886 was 350 (a.m.), and in 1903 was 88 (a.m.), 53 (p.m.). It had closed by 1913.

1 *Mackeson' Guide* (1871, 1894).
2 Hobhouse, *Cubitt*, 235.
3 *Mackeson's Guide* (1866, 1871).
4 Clarke, *London Chs*, 190; Pevsner, *London I* (1973 edn), 485.
5 *London Diocese Bk* (1970); Pevsner, *London 6: Westm.* 781.
6 *Mackeson's Guide* (1871).
7 *PO Dir.* (1926).
8 Guildhall MS 9557, f. 26.
9 *Mackeson' s Guide* (1894).
10 Below, Foreign Chs.
11 *Crockford* (1940, 1947, 1951–2).
12 Pevsner, *London 6: Westm.* 733.
13 Ibid. 748.
14 *Middx County Rec. Sess. Bks 1689–1709*, 332.
15 Paterson, *Pietas Lond.* 277–8.

16 L. Knyff and J. Kip, *Bird's-eye view of Burlington House on Piccadilly, looking north; with figures and a horse-drawn cart and coach in the foreground*, c.1710 (Guildhall Libr. Main Print Colln, Pr.W2/PIC, p5395285).
17 Paterson, *Pietas Lond.* 277–8.
18 Bodl., MS Rawl. B. 376, f. 84.
19 Guildhall MS 9550.
20 Guildhall MSS 9556, p. 41; 9557, f. 26.
21 P. Jeffery, 'Trinity Chapel, Conduit Street', *Trans Ancient Mons Soc.*, 39 (1995), 80–1.
22 TNA, HO 129/3, 2/1/1 (f. 96).
23 *Mackeson's Guide* (1866 and later edns); Clinch, *Mayfair*, 63.
24 J. Elmes, *Metropolitan Improvements* (1831), 153–4, plate
25 *Mackeson's Guide* (1894).
26 Guildhall MS 9557, f. 26.   27 *Mackeson's Guide* (1871).

Berkeley Chapel   Built 1750 by the Berkeley family on their estate, on the corner of Charles Street and Chesterfield Hill, Berkeley Sq., the chapel was designed by William Jones, architect of the Rotunda in Ranelagh Gardens, Chelsea, in a Greek style with cupola and Doric porch.[1] A minister licensed 1755, and a preacher and reader in 1790.[2] Revd Sydney Smith preached there when he came to London c.1802, his fresh and racy preaching filling seats and the pockets of the proprietor.[3] The chapel was acquired in 1850 by Francis Tate, who lived in Hastings but was also the minister in 1851, when he calculated the income from pew rents at c.£800, but the expenses that year considerably more. The chapel seated c.900, including 20 free seats, but attendance was 399 (a.m.) and 129 (aft.) with no evening service. Average morning attendance was 600 for the 4 months of the London Season, 300 the rest of year.[4] By 1856 Tate was vicar of Axminster (Devon), and had installed Dr Lee of Lambeth, minister 1856–8, who described the chapel as fashionable but unsatisfactory for worship, plainly decorated and upholstered with pink velvet and hangings on brass rods; a large stove, which dwarfed the communion table, was the chief ornament, placed in the centre aisle on cold days. It had a select and eminent congregation of peers and their families.[5] In 1866 the chapel was said to be 'a place of worship exclusively for the upper classes', with no free seats.[6] In 1876 a visitor described its cheerful fire in the stove in the centre of the middle aisle, which was carpeted in 'cozy Brussels'. It had recently been fashionably redecorated, with pews cut down and the east wall and pulpit multicoloured. The chancel was raised, and the organ moved from the 3-storeyed west gallery to behind the choir at the east end, where the tiny altar was over-draped, and a mixed choir squeezed into the too-small chancel.[7] In 1894 the patron was Revd H. Cart, and the minister H.T. Cart. Attendance in 1886 was 315 (a.m.), 62 (aft.), but had fallen to 64 (a.m.), 26 (p.m.) in 1903. It was demolished in 1907.[8]

Eaton Episcopal Chapel, Coleshill Street (later Eaton Terr.), Belgravia   A chapel existed near the boundary with Chelsea by 1746, when William Rothey was licensed as preacher or minister at the 'new chapel near Chelsea'; it may also have been 'new chapel' referred to in 1742.[9] William Williams was licensed as minister 1760, and in 1787 the rector of St George's presented Dr Richard Sandilands as minister.[10] It may be same as the Five Fields chapel which stood in the fields east of the Westbourne stream and just south of the king's road to Chelsea, though that did not appear to be on the Eaton

chapel site in 1745.[11] The Five Fields chapel was still so-called in 1823 when it lay on the east side of Fivefields Lane.[12] The lane seems to have become Coleshill Street by 1862, when Eaton Episcopal chapel stood on or near the site, on the south side of the junction with the later Eaton Gate.[13] Still a proprietary chapel in 1871, in 1886 it had an attendance was 250 (a.m.), 340 (p.m.). It had closed by 1894.

Grosvenor Chapel, South Audley Street, Mayfair[14]   The chapel was planned by 1723 when Sir Richard Grosvenor sold land adjoining the proposed site to the parish of St George's for a burial ground, but because of delays by the vestry the foundation stone was only laid in 1730, after Grosvenor had granted a 99-year building lease to four builder-proprietors. Grosvenor later sold to the vestry the freehold, ground rent and reversion of the chapel. In 1751 one of proprietors, Robert Andrews, Sir Richard's agent and lawyer, acquired the interests of the other three; a Revd Mr Andrews, presumably a relative of the owner, was minister up to 1793. James Trebeck, presumably a relative of the rector, was licensed as afternoon preacher in 1751. A reader was also licensed in 1759.[15] The chapel became a chapel of ease to St George's by Act 1831, and was consecrated 1832, the rector appointing as minister his curate, Evan Nepean, who continued until 1873. Dick Sheppard was minister in 1913 before moving to St Martin-in-the-Fields. The rector and churchwardens of St George's were patrons and in 1873 the income, from pew rents, was c.£1,000. Attendance in 1851 was 1,000 (a.m.); 500 (aft.); in 1886 35 (a.m.), 157 (p.m.); and in 1903 96 (a.m.), 69 (p.m.).

The chapel was probably designed by one of the proprietors, Benjamin Timbrell, and was built in 1730–1 of yellow brick with round-headed windows, a pedimented front with tetrastyle Tuscan porch and, above, a tower with octagonal bell-stage and spire. There were galleries on two sides and a west organ gallery, a shallow chancel, and a large carved central pulpit. In 1851 chapel, including children's gallery, seated 1,200, of which 400 were free.[16] In 1877 the pulpit was moved, pews were cut down, and choir stalls added. In 1912 Sir Ninian Comper started an incompleted scheme: he screened the 18th-century chancel from the rest, creating a nave and Lady chapel, but retained the fine pilastered reredos behind his Lady altar, the plastered ceiling, and the original galleries and organ case by Abraham Jordan given in 1732 by Sir Richard Grosvenor. There are numerous wall tablets, many to eminent residents, because the chapel vaults functioned as a burial place for parish. The chapel still in use in 2008.

1 Colvin, *Brit. Architects*, 564; Colby, *Mayfair*, 74.
2 Guildhall MS 9557, f. 26.
3 *DNB*.
4 TNA, HO 129/3, 2/1/5 (f.100).
5 Colby, *Mayfair*, 74–5.   6 *Mackeson's Guide* (1866).
7 C.M. Davies, *Orthodox London* (1876 edn), 36–7.
8 Colby, *Mayfair*, 74–5.   9 Guildhall MS 9550.
10 Guildhall MSS 9556, p. 31; 9557, f. 26.
11 Rocque, *Map of London* (1741–5).
12 *Regency A to Z*.
13 Stanford, *Map of London* (1862–5).
14 Acct based on *Survey of London*, XL. 298–301.
15 Guildhall MS 9556, p. 31.
16 TNA, HO 129/3, 2/1/3 (f. 98).

56. *The Curzon, or Mayfair, proprietary chapel, Curzon Street, before demolition in 1899. A fashionable place of worship for residents during the London Season, it had been notorious for clandestine marriages in the 1730s and 1740s soon after it opened.*

Mayfair (Curzon, Keith's), Chapel, Curzon Street   Built *c.*1730, with prayers twice a week,[1] it was famous for clandestine marriages in the 1740s, and the large income that the minister, Alexander Keith, received from fees was a matter of comment. In 1742, 700 marriages performed there against 40 at St George's; the rector, Andrew Trebeck, brought a suit against Keith and he was committed to Fleet prison in 1743, dying there in 1758. Until the Marriage Act, 1754, marriages continued performed by Keith's assistants at his nearby house on the corner of Queen Street, known as the Little chapel. By *c.*1759 James Trebeck was licensed preacher together with a reader.[2] The rector of St George's was patron by 1772 when he presented Dr John Baker.[3] In 1851 the chapel, called Curzon chapel, was the property of Earl Howe and seated 900 of which 300 were free. Attendance in 1851 was 635 (a.m.), and 298 (aft.);[4] in 1886 it was 151 (a.m.), and 95 (p.m.). The chapel was demolished in 1899 and the site used for Sunderland House.[5]

St George's Chapel, Albemarle Street, Mayfair   Said to have been built or licensed in 1811, when the rector of St George's presented William Cockburn as minister,[6] it was described in 1851 as a proprietary chapel belonging to Revd W.W. Ellis, whose income came from pew rents. It was then full at both morning and evening services, seating 1,200, of which 200 were free.[7] In 1896 the annual income was £200.[8] Attendance was, however, low out of Season. The church was described as very fashionable, with a service at 9 p.m. allowing the congregation to dine first, arriving at church in full evening dress. Well-known singers such as Dame Clara Butt sang there. It closed 1904.[9]

St Mary, Park Street, Mayfair (Park Street chapel)[10]
The chapel was built 1762–3 in a classical style with portico and cupola, on a site at the south-eastern corner of Park and Green streets leased from Grosvenor Estate by Wm Timbrell and John Spencer, carpenters, under agreement with Revd Pulter Forester, who paid half the cost. In the late 18th century two joint morning preachers were licensed, each receiving stipend of £30 p.a., and a reader and afternoon preacher were licensed 1801.[11] On the expiry of the lease *c.*1822, Lord Grosvenor and his successors became its proprietors, appointing ministers and maintaining it until closure. Attendance in 1851 was 527 (a.m.); 296 (aft.); the minister noted that morning services were full during the Season when the pew renters were in London. The chapel seated 925, of which 207 were free. The proprietor received the pew rents and paid for all repairs and expenses, providing the minister with a rent-free house (no. 51 Green St) and £400 p.a., from which he paid the clerk.[12] There was a minister and curate in 1871.[13] Demolished in 1882, it was replaced by St Mary's, Bourdon St.

St Mary, Bourdon Street, Berkeley Square[14]   Built as a mission church to serve the poor of the Bourdon Street area at the request of the rector of St George's, on a site provided by the Grosvenor Estate, it replaced St Mary's Park Street. The red brick church, with south-west tower, clerestoried nave and single aisle, was built in 1880–1 to Early English Gothic designs by Sir Arthur Blomfield, and seated 300; the cost (over £1,000) was met by the duke of Westminster. Opened in 1882, it was served from St George's. In 1894, when it seated 400, all

1 *New Remarks of London, collected by Company of Parish Clerks* (1732), 260–3.   2 Guildhall MS 9556, p. 31.
3 Guildhall MS 9557, f. 26.
4 TNA, HO 129/3, 2/1/4 (f. 99).
5 Colby, *Mayfair*, 73.
6 Guildhall MS 9557, f. 43.
7 TNA, HO 129/3, 2/1/2 (f. 97).

8 *Crockford* (1896).
9 Colby, *Mayfair*, 79–80.
10 Acct based on *Survey of London*, XL. 255–6.
11 Guildhall MS 9557, f. 26.
12 TNA, HO 129/3, 1/1/3 (f. 94).
13 *Mackeson's Guide* (1871).
14 Acct based on *Survey of London*, XL. 58–60.

free, three services were held on Sunday, one on other days; surplices were worn.[1] Attendance in 1886 was 410 (a.m.), 272 (p.m.); and in 1903 174 (a.m.), 95 (p.m.). Dick Sheppard was incumbent 1911–13 and filled the church. It was used by the Dutch Reformed congregation from Austin Friars (City) 1940–54. The lease was then surrendered to Grosvenor Estate and the church demolished shortly afterwards.

St Peter's Chapel (Charlotte chapel), Charlotte (later Palace) Street, Buckingham Gate   In 1766 Dr William Dodd, a successful and fashionable preacher, one of the king's chaplains since 1763, invested his wife's legacy and lottery prize totalling £2,500 in building Charlotte chapel, Pimlico, named after the queen. Debt forced him to dispose of most of his interest in the chapel in 1776, shortly before he was hung for forgery.[2] In 1780 the rector of St George's appointed the morning and afternoon preachers, the latter receiving salary of £50 p.a. in 1785.[3] It was called Charlotte Episcopal chapel in 1850, but St Peter's chapel in 1851, when it was a chapel of ease to St Peter's, Eaton Square, though apparently still a proprietary chapel. The incumbent, Thomas Norton Harper, had recently become a Roman Catholic and left the country, leaving the chapel without a minister.[4] By

1871, when the proprietor was Revd S. Wilkinson who owned the adjoining school, established that year,[5] there were two services on Sunday, one on Wednesday, and communion twice a month. The chapel, which seated 900 (none free) derived its income from pew rents and collections.[6] Attendance in 1903 was 466 (a.m.), 182 (evg.). It was still a chapel for St Peter's Eaton Square in 1926, but had gone by 1935.[7] The chapel was apparently demolished by 1927.[8]

St Saviour, Oxford Street   Built on the corner with Lumley Street by (Royal) Association in Aid of Deaf and Dumb it ministered primarily to over 2,000 deaf and dumb in London, secondarily to local inhabitants.[9] S. Smith, vicar-designate 1871, was chaplain to the association. The site was given by the duke of Westminster on a 60-year lease. Built with an adjoining clergy house and lecture hall below in 1870–4 in the Gothic style by Sir Arthur Blomfield, it seated 150, all free and opened in 1873.[10] Attendance in 1886 was 36 (a.m.), 80 (p.m.); in 1903 it was 16 (a.m.), 126 (p.m.). The Grosvenor Estate refused to renew the lease and bought out the Association in 1922, when the church closed. The proceeds were used to build a replacement, St Saviour's, Armstrong Rd (Acton), to which the fittings were removed.[11]

ST JAMES, PICCADILLY

Inhabitants of the bailiwick of St James petitioned Parliament unsuccessfully for a separate church and parish as early as 1664, and a bill of 1670, connected with Henry Jermyn, 1st earl of St Albans, similarly failed to proceed because of opposition from Dr Nathaniel Hardy, vicar of St Martin's, and the vestry. The earl offered the site for a church, churchyard, and minister's house between Piccadilly and Jermyn Street, part of the leasehold in St James's fields he held of the Crown,[12] presumably as part of his building plans for the estate.[13] He petitioned the Crown for the freehold of the site in 1674, necessary if the church was to be consecrated and used as a parish church,[14] and although he did not obtain the freehold at that time, building went ahead with the earl meeting the greater part of the cost. The freehold of the church site was eventually granted in 1684 after Lord St Albans and Dr Thomas Tenison, the new vicar of St Martin's, had again petitioned the Crown;[15] the grant included the site of the church, land on the north and

west sides of the church for the churchyard, a house and land where the rectory was later built, and houses and land fronting Piccadilly and Jermyn Street to endow the living.[16] St Albans having died that year, the grant was made to his nephew and heir, Thomas Jermyn, Lord Jermyn, who passed the deeds to the bishop of London before consecration. The church was used as a chapel of ease to St Martin, until the Act of 1685 which created the parish of St James. Dr Tenison, vicar of St Martin's, became the first rector of St James's in 1685.[17]

ADVOWSON, BENEFICE, AND INCOME

In 1685–6 the patronage of the rectory was vested in the bishop of London and Lord Jermyn, who had every third turn. In 1700 Lord Jermyn conveyed his third share to Henry Compton, then bishop of London, and his heirs in trust, to be nominated by the bishops of London. Presentations were made by the bishop of London in 1729, 1750, 1759, and 1802, and by Hatton Compton in

1 *Mackeson's Guide* (1894).
2 *DNB.*
3 Guildhall MS 9557, f. 43.
4 TNA, HO 129/3, 3/1/1 (f. 103).
5 TNA, ED 7/84.
6 *Mackeson' Guide* (1871).
7 *Crockford* (1926, 1935).
8 *PO Dir.* (1927).
9 Acct based on *Survey of London*, XL. 179–80.

10 *Mackeson' Guide* (1871 Add; 1894)
11 *VCH Middx*, VII. 38.
12 *Survey of London*, XXIX. 29, 31.
13 Pevsner, *London 6: Westm.* 584.
14 *Cal SP Dom.* 1673–5, 384.
15 Ibid. 1683–4, 72.
16 *Cal. Treas. Bks*, 1680–5, II. 1123–4; *Survey of London*, XXIX. 33.
17 *Survey of London*, XXIX. 32–3.

57. *The parish church of St James, Piccadilly, from the south-east, an unusual view of the east end usually obscured by buildings. The church was designed by Wren in 1684 for a parish newly established in 1664 to serve an area with an increasing population.*

1733 and Edward Compton in 1763. The living was valued at £400–500 in 1723 and £700 in 1780.[1] In 1850 it consisted of endowments of £487 from the glebe and £27 from other sources, fees of £364, and Easter offerings of £253. From this the rector paid £160 towards the curates' stipends, who also received payments from fees and from the parish, and mortgage payments of £104 a year to Queen Anne's Bounty for the new parsonage.[2]

Rectory House

A rectory house built 1685–6 in the north-east corner of the churchyard was demolished in 1846, a new one being built on the site, designed by John Henry Hakewill, for which the rector borrowed £1,600 from Queen Anne's Bounty. That house was destroyed by a bomb which fell in the churchyard in 1940, and a new rectory was built 1955–7. Designed by Austin Blomfield, it incorporated a church hall at basement level and a vestry room.[3]

CHURCH LIFE

The foundation stone of the church was laid by the earl of St Albans and the bishop of London, in 1676. The new parish was responsible for paying for its completion, for part of the cost of the church, and for building the rectory house. Described in 1714 as one of the latest and finest in London, the large auditory church cost over £7,000. Prayers were held 3 times daily, catechising every Thursday, communion every 2nd Sunday of the month and every Sunday between Palm and Trinity Sundays. It was served by the rector and a preacher assistant.[4] In 1723 services were held twice on Sundays with communion on the second Sunday of the month.[5] In 1780 services were held three times a day, and communion monthly and on the great festivals. Children were catechised in Lent.[6]

The church seated 460 free, 940 other, in 1851. Attendances (plus Sunday scholars) were then 1282 + 74 (a.m.), 682 + 72 (aft.), 943 + 30 (evg.); 65 also attended the evening service held at the girls' school in Marshall Street, which seated 70, all free.[7] In 1903 attendances had fallen to 439 (a.m.), 545 (p.m.). St James continued to serve a shrinking population in the 20th century, as houses were turned into offices and many of its daughter churches closed. Still in use in 2008, it provided an inclusive church for the local community of residents, workers, and visitors to the West End; few of its congregation actually lived locally. Services, of communion, eucharist, or prayers, were held six days a week. The church and its ancillary rooms were also widely used for community events, concerts, and meetings.[8]

1 Guildhall MSS 9550; 9557, f. 28; TNA, Institution Bks.
2 TNA, HO 129/6, 2/1/1 (f. 4).
3 *Survey of London*, XXIX. 53; Guildhall MS 19224/286.
4 Paterson, *Pietas Lond.* 113–14.   5 Guildhall MS 9550.

6 Guildhall MS 9557, f. 28.
7 TNA, HO 129/6, 2/1/1 (f. 4).
8 Inf. from ch website and Parish Profile (www.st-james-piccadilly.org).

CHURCH FABRIC

The church took many years to complete. The tower and wooden spire were unfinished at consecration in 1684, their completion delayed until 1700 by concerns over structural stability.[1] The design was by Sir Christopher Wren, who had more scope on the open site than he did when planning most of his City churches. He considered that at St James's he had solved the problem of enabling the largest possible number to see and hear the preacher. The five-bay church, of red brick with stone dressings, had galleries on square piers with columns above; the columns carried both the barrel vault over the nave and subsidiary barrel vaults over each bay above the galleries. The east end was lit by a two-storeyed window, the upper part of which was Venetian, and some of the fittings (many of which survive) were carved by Grinling Gibbons. Wren had provided a central cross-axis with doors from Piccadilly and Jermyn St; the north one was removed by Thomas Hardwick who repaired the church in 1803–4, the other went in 1856.

Sums were borrowed from Queen Anne's Bounty for repairs or alterations to the church in 1866, 1880, 1916, and 1967–9.[2] The roof and some of the interior were destroyed by incendiary bombs in 1940–1, and carefully restored 1947–54 by Sir Albert Richardson, who reversed some of the early alterations. The interior of the church housed many memorials, listed by the Survey of London in 1960.[3]

Churchyard

The churchyard in 1684 consisted of two pieces of land, one on the west fronting Jermyn Street, the other on the north separated from Piccadilly by several buildings. It was lit from 1688–9. In 1747 the northern churchyard was enlarged by Act of Parliament with a piece which was part of the rector's endowment, in return for £27 a year, and by another Act in 1762 a piece of Crown land with two houses on it was incorporated into the churchyard and consecrated after the houses were demolished. From at least the middle of the 18th century the northern churchyard was apparently paved and burials made in vaults underneath the paving.[4] In 1895 St James's churchyard, of half an acre, was described as a dreary ground which might be made very attractive. The part with most burials had been considerably raised above the rest; the part on N. side was entirely paved, often with gravestones.[5] After the Second World War Viscount Southwood provided money to make the western churchyard into a garden of remembrance,

opened in 1946.[6] From the late 20th century the church-yard was used for a market and a café.

OTHER CHURCHES AND CHAPELS

The northern part of the parish of St James was quickly developed into a densely populated area. Church accommodation was supplemented by Archbishop Tenison's chapel in King Street opened in 1687 and by a chapel in Berwick Street, probably opened in 1708. Both later became district churches after rebuilding, the former as St Thomas's in 1869, and the latter as St Luke's in 1839. In 1714 there were said to be three chapels, the third being the extra-parochial St James's, whose identity is uncertain.[7] In 1780 the rector of St James nominated the preachers at the three chapels.[8]

Other new district churches were St Peter, Great Windmill Street, consecrated in 1861, and a temporary church formed in Great Marlborough Street in 1865, for which St John the Baptist was consecrated in 1885. In the southern part of the parish a chapel of ease, St Philip's, was opened c.1820 in Waterloo Place, and a proprietary chapel was opened in a former noncon-formist chapel in York Street as St James's chapel in 1833. The latter closed in 1876, and St Philip's by 1914. St John the Baptist closed in 1937; St Luke's was amal-gamated with St Anne, Soho, in 1935, and St Peter closed in 1954. When St Anne was closed because of bomb damage in the Second World War, St Thomas remained the only Anglican church in the northern part of the parish, but it too was closed in 1973, services having restarted in St Anne's.[9]

St John the Baptist, Great Marlborough Street

The district, formed in 1865, was united to St Thomas, Kingly St, in 1937.[10] Services were held in a room behind no. 49 Poland St, and 1867–9 in the conservatory of the Pantheon. In 1869 nos 49 and 50 Great Marlborough Street were purchased and a temporary iron church opened at the rear. When it closed at the end of 1884, services were held in a mission room in Cambridge Street, while a permanent church was built, most of the cost being met by a grant from the Commissioners of Woods and Forests. The new church, consecrated in 1885, was designed by A.W. Blomfield as an aisleless rectangle which incorporated vestries flanking the chancel and a north-west tower. It was screened by a quite elaborate free Perpendicular-style façade in red brick and stone. Attendance was only 68 (a.m.) and 98 (p.m.) in 1886, and 99 (a.m.) and 131 (p.m.) in 1903. It was closed and demolished 1937.

---

1 Archit. acct follows *Survey of London*, XXIX. 31–2, 34–6, and Pevsner, *London 6: Westm.* 584–5.
2 Guildhall MS 19224/286.
3 *Survey of London*, XXIX. 47–51.
4 Ibid. 51–2.
5 LCC, *Burial Grounds*, 5.
6 *Survey of London*, XXIX. 52.
7 Paterson, *Pietas Lond.* 113–14.
8 Guildhall MS 9557, f. 28.
9 Based on accts of chs below.
10 Para. based on *Survey of London*, XXXI. 262–3.

St Luke, Berwick Street, Soho

In 1707 rector of St James proposed that parish should purchase the lease of the former French Huguenot chapel in Berwick St to use as chapel of ease.[1] Probably opened in 1708, it was apparently rebuilt by the parish *c.*1711. In 1714, when it was described as very beautiful and large, of brick and tile with two galleries, communion table, and organ, it was served by a minister and a lecturer. Prayers were said twice daily, with sermons on public feasts.[2] There were morning and afternoon preachers in 1747, and in 1799 the combined morning and afternoon preacher and reader received a salary of £200.[3]

The lease was renewed 1765 and there were extensive repairs 1765–7, a room being added to the west of the chapel, used for services for poorhouse children. The organ from Tenison's chapel was acquired 1766. There were further repairs 1794 under Thomas Hardwick, and the freehold was purchased 1801–2.[4]

Gerrard Andrewes, rector of James 1802–25, bought £2,000 in stock raised from subscriptions and offertories at St James, part of which by his will proved in 1825 was to be used to make Berwick St chapel free for the poor. The annual income of £55 was later used towards stipend of the vicar of St Luke's.[5] The increase of poor in the area reduced the congregation. The chapel was demolished *c.*1835, and replaced by St Luke's, consecrated 1839. The cost, raised by grant and public subscriptions, and believed to be *c.*£14,000, included the purchase of additional land. A district was assigned 1841, described as the most densely populated in London, with the rector as patron. The incumbent's income in 1851 after deduction of expenses was *c.*£130, including an endowment of £106. Attendances (excluding scholars) were then 292 (a.m.), 51 (aft.), 332 (evg.).[6] Attempts to charge low pew rents for about half the sittings were gradually abandoned because of the district's poverty and by 1863 all were free. Valued at £300 in 1871, the benefice was served by a vicar and curate.[7] Attendances in 1886 were 338 (a.m.), 413 (p.m.), and in 1903 52 (a.m.), 37 (p.m.).

The new church of 1838–9 by Edward Blore was a Decorated Gothic box, set parallel to Berwick Street and entered on the east side. The seven-bay aisles arcades were of timber, and a dais at the south end served as a chancel, accommodating choir stalls and sanctuary. Renovations in the 1860s cost £1,600.[8] It opened with *c.*1,540 seats of which *c.*937 were free,[9] but in 1851 seated 1,306 of which 234 were free for adults and 600 for children in the deep north school gallery;[10] in 1871 it

seated 800, all free.[11] The benefice was united to St Anne, Soho, 1935, and the church was closed and demolished in 1936.

St Peter, Great Windmill Street, Soho

There were plans for a new church in the area as early as 1854; public subscriptions were raised and a curate appointed in 1858. The cramped site, formerly nos 4–6 on the east side of Gt Windmill St, cost £6,000 and the church £5,500. Because of the district's poverty, funds were raised from outside sources, the largest contribution from the earl of Derby.

Designed by Raphael Brandon in a continental version of First Pointed Gothic style, the church was built 1860–1 with only the west end visible. Brick-faced inside and out, it had a lofty clerestoried nave, meagre aisles, and an apsidal chancel flanked by vestry and the base of an unfinished south-eastern tower. A district was assigned 1865. The church was frequently attended by Lord Salisbury, and daily by W.E. Gladstone when living in London. The attendance of 420 (a.m.), 180 (p.m.) in 1886, had dropped to 103 (a.m.), 129 (p.m.) in 1903.[12] The living was united with those of St Anne and St Thomas 1953, and the church was closed in 1954 and demolished.

St Thomas, Kingly Street, Regent Street

The chapel originated as Archbishop Tenison's chapel built to meet rapid growth in northern Westminster. Tenison, then rector of St James's, built a tabernacle and charity school in 1687, having purchased a sub-lease of Crown land on the west side of King (later Kingly) Street, extending back to Swallow Street.[13] The chapel, consisting of one large room, opened 1688, of timber on a brick foundation, costing £900 paid for out of a large charitable benefaction in Tenison's hands. The site was enlarged 1690 on the north and used for houses for the master and under-master and a playground; in 1692 Tenison petitioned the Crown for the freehold, which was granted, except for unbuilt land fronting Swallow Street (leased for 99 years). In 1700 Tenison, then archbishop of Canterbury, vested his freehold and leasehold in trustees, and presented £500 to endow chapel as public Anglican chapel for the parish. Rents from the endowment and pew rents were to be used for the upkeep of the chapel, services, stipends of clergy, and to support the school.[14] Tenison and his successors had Visitor's rights.

In 1702 the severely-decayed chapel was demolished with the under-master's house behind to form the site of a new chapel, the cost of which was met by lending the £500 at interest and a mortgage on an adjacent freehold.

1 Except where footnoted, based on *Survey of London*, XXXI. 226.   2 Paterson, *Pietas Lond.* 39–40.
3 Guildhall MSS 9556, p. 36; 9557, f. 28.
4 TNA, C 54/7756, no. 13.
5 *Endowed Chars London*, V. 176.
6 TNA, HO 129/6, 1/1/1 (f.1).
7 *Mackeson's Guide* (1871).

8 Ibid.
9 Port, *Six Hundred Chs*, 156–7.
10 TNA, HO 129/6, 1/1/1 (f. 1).
11 *Mackeson's Guide* (1871).
12 *Survey of London*, XXXI. 32.
13 Acct based on *Survey of London*, XXXI. 180–5.
14 Hist. of sch. to be treated under Educ. in a later vol.

58. *St Philip, Lower Regent Street, a chapel of ease to St James, Piccadilly, and built 1819–20 in keeping with Nash's Regent Street design.*

The new brick proprietary chapel, which had a broad front with a pedimented centre to Kingly Street, opened 1702 before its consecration. Sir Isaac Newton (a trustee) paid for a dial in the chapel 1705. A smaller building at western end housed vestry, chapelkeeper, and school. In 1711 Tenison was unwilling for his chapel to be made to be parochial as one of the new churches for St James, and it remained proprietary until 1869.[1]

The south wall and roof were taken down in 1713 to repair defects and some fittings rearranged. After reopening, the chapel was described in 1714 as very spacious with an excellent organ, fine capacious galleries on both sides, a large altar-piece and a chancel paved with marble. Prayers were held four times each day, and communion on the last Sunday each month; prayers and a sermon were held on Christmas and other holy days.[2] In 1723 there were two Sunday services with communion on alternate weeks.[3] In 1747 morning and afternoon preachers and a reader were licensed.[4]

Much needed repairs and reseating were done in 1805. The Tenison trustees obtained a new lease of the Swallow Street ground in 1814, but in 1824 surrendered sites in Regent Street in exchange for small annuity from the Crown, retaining the freehold of land north of no. 172 Regent Street, with its valuable frontage (leased to Crown for 99 years from 1821 and bought by the Crown in 1902). The small vestry and school building was replaced by an entrance from Regent Street, with lobby, new rooms, and school above behind a façade designed by C.R. Cockerell and built by the New Street (Regent Street) commissioners 1824. The chapel was redecorated inside by Thos Hardwick.[5]

By the middle of the century the congregation had declined as the neighbourhood became commercialized. Its poverty lowered the income from pew rents and in 1850, despite a reduction in clergy stipends, the chapel could not meet current expenses. To increase income the trustees converted the Regent Street entrance into a shop and dwelling in 1854, altering the two remaining rooms to make a new south entrance from Tenison Court.

Negotiations with Ecclesiastical Commissioners from 1853 to turn the chapel into a district church were completed 1869. The chapel's preacher and its reader became the first vicar and curate. The commissioners acquired the site itself, but the trustees retained the rest of the property until 1902, paying most of the income to the church, which was consecrated in 1869 as St Thomas's and assigned a district from St James in 1870.[6] Restoration work 1903–4, under W.J. Parker, included a new entrance from Tenison Court, new gallery staircases, and roof repairs; a south-eastern memorial chapel was probably added then. St Thomas's was a centre of liturgical experiment c.1960, which involved re-arrangement of some furnishings.[7]

St Thomas's was united with the district of St John the Baptist, Gt Marlborough St, in 1937, and by 1954 had become the only Anglican parish church in wide area between Regent Street and Charing Cross Road. After reopening of St Anne, however, it was declared redundant and demolished in 1973.[8]

Other Chapels

St James's Chapel (Location uncertain: possibly the forerunner of St Luke's). Two curates of St James were licensed as joint morning preachers in 1793. A reader and afternoon preacher was licensed in 1795.[9]

St Philip, Lower Regent Street   A chapel of ease was built 1819–22 on Crown land site opposite Carlton Street, obtained by the bishop of London and the rector with a covenant to keep the building the same colour as those adjoining.[10] Designed by G.S Repton, it was built for his brother Revd Edward Repton.[11] The stuccoed façade in

1 *Fifty New Chs*, 5, 9.   2 Paterson, *Pietas Lond.* 126–7.
3 Guildhall MS 9550.
4 Guildhall MS 9556, p. 36.
5 *Survey of London*, XXXI. 183–4, figs 24–5.
6 *London Gaz.* 8 Feb. 1870, p. 737.
7 *Survey of London*, XXXI. 185.
8 Ibid.; Pevsner, *London 6: Westm.* 388.
9 Guildhall MS 9557, f. 28.
10 TNA, C 54/10109, no. 2.
11 Colvin, *Brit. Architects*, 801.

Greek style was grand with raised end bays, a Doric portico and, over it, a tower based on the temple of Lysicrates in Athens. Consecrated c.1820, it cost £19,272, obtained from private benefactions, sale of pews (£6,000), Church Building Commissioners (£2,000), and mortgage, and it seated 1,500 (500 free). The income was £400. Attendances in 1851 were recorded as 700 (a.m.), but were said to vary seasonally from 300 to 1,300. By 1886 they had fallen to 133 (a.m.), 121 (p.m.), and by 1903 to 59 (a.m.), 34 (p.m.). The chapel had gone by 1914.[1]

Proprietary Chapels

Tenison's Chapel   See above, St Thomas

York Street Chapel (St James's) A former nonconformist chapel, licensed in 1833 on the application of the proprietor, the earl of Romney, it was used as an Anglican proprietary chapel thereafter. In 1851 it seated 480 or 550, all rented and giving income of c.£400. Attendance in 1851 was 250 (a.m.), 70 (aft.). The morning average, however, was 33, the congregation being much greater during the Season.[2] In 1865 the chapel was let to Revd A. Stopford Brook, notorious as a spokesman of Broad Church principles. His ministry started in April 1866 and attracted a large and fashionable congregation. When his lease expired in 1875, he moved to Bedford chapel, Bloomsbury, and this chapel closed 1876.[3]

ST JOHN THE EVANGELIST, SMITH SQUARE

St John's, Smith Square, was built under the Act for building 50 new churches,[4] to provide an additional church in the parish of St Margaret's, which was then divided, creating the new civil parish of St John. The site at Millbank was chosen in 1711, and the design by Thomas Archer in 1713.[5] Because the site was low-lying and marshy there were difficulties over the foundations, which caused settlement problems and adjustments to the design up to completion in 1728. The quality of the original bricks also gave cause for concern.[6] Though by the summer of 1715 it was stated that the church was nearly ready for the roof,[7] the residents were petitioning in 1723 for the church to be finished and brought into use.[8] The sites for a burial ground and the minister's house were being sought in 1725–6,[9] and the church was not consecrated until June 1728.[10]

The benefice was a rectory to which a canonry of Westminster Abbey was attached from 1840. Before this the rector received a stipend of £100 and the rectory-house and garden,[11] while in 1851 the income was £359, but a third of the emoluments of the canonry was paid to the incumbents of 2 district churches.[12] In 1894 the value of living was £300 with a house.[13] The Crown was patron. The benefice was united to St Stephen, Rochester Row, by 1952.[14]

CLERGY AND CHURCH LIFE

For the first hundred years of its existence, St John's was served by rectors who were pluralist and largely non resident, delegating their duties to curates. One was dean of Lincoln, another was successively bishop of St David and of Bath and Wells; another obtained licence to be absent from his parish for 21 years, assigning his stipend and rectory house to his curate.[15] Under the rectorship of John Jennings, formerly the curate at St John's, and prebendary of Westminster from 1837 and archdeacon of Westminster from 1868, St John's had an active rector deeply concerned with his parish and the difficulty of reaching the increasing number of poor parishioners. Soon after his arrival he instituted a Sunday evening service in addition to the morning and afternoon services of his predecessors, and he was instrumental in founding and endowing St Mary, Tothill fields, and the other 4 district churches within St John's. When he arrived there was one church, a rector seldom resident, one curate, and a small Sunday school in a hired room; when he died in 1883 he left 6 churches, each with National and Sunday schools, and 17 clergy, serving a population which had doubled during his ministry.[16] Attendance in 1851 was 1277 (a.m.), 864 (aft.), and 1267 (evg.). In 1903, despite the several district churches, it was still 675 (a.m.), 627 (evg.).[17]

After its destruction by bombing during World War II, the church was not used for religious services again. It was replaced by St John's, Causton Street.[18]

CHURCH FABRIC

The church, characteristic of Thomas Archer and influenced by buildings he had seen in Austria and Germany, was the most baroque of London's 50 new churches. Its

1 TNA, HO 129/6, 2/1/4 (f. 7); Port, *Six Hundred Chs*, 136–7; *Mackeson's Guide* (1871); *Old OS Map* 61 (1914).
2 TNA, HO 129/6, 2/1/2 (f.5); 2/1/3 (f. 6) (2 returns, one by min, one by curate).
3 *Survey of London*, XXIX. 118.
4 Above, Rel. Hist.: Intro. (Ch Bldg in 18th cent.).
5 *Fifty New Chs*, 7, 19–20.
6 Archit. acct follows Friedman, *Georgian Par. Ch*, 33–57; *Fifty New Chs*, 21, 23, 36.

7 *Fifty New Chs*, p. xxv.   8 Ibid. 99, 101.
9 Ibid. 131–3, 138.   10 *Mackeson's Guide* (1871).
11 Smith, *St John Evangelist*, 72, 87.
12 TNA, HO 129/4, 1/1/1 (f. 2).
13 *Mackeson's Guide* (1871, 1894).
14 *Crockford* (1952 edn).
15 Smith, *St John Evangelist*, 79–88.
16 Ibid. 91–3.   17 No figs recorded for 1886.
18 Clarke, *London Chs.* 181; below.

59. *The parish church of St John the Evangelist, Smith Square, from the north-west. One of the parishes churches built with a grant from the Commission for Building Fifty New Churches 1713–28, it was designed by Thomas Archer as the centrepiece of a new development.*

design was influenced by its position at the centre of the irregular square, which lay in an area of Tothill fields laid out from *c.*1686, and the consequent need for four main façades. The four towers were intended to be seen from all sides, and were thought to give the structure greater stability. The entrance porticoes were north and south, the N one forming a *point-de-vue* at the end of the street leading into the square from the direction of the abbey; the east and west ends were subsidiary with attached porticoes of pilasters. This arrangement meant that the church was entered at the sides, under the galleries flanking the nave and, as at St George's Bloomsbury, the sanctuary lay at right angles to them. After the church was gutted by fire in 1742 with the loss of the elaborate fittings, a bland Palladian interior with galleries on three sides was created by James Horne in 1744–5; in the mid-19th century it seated 1,900, with 1,100 free in 1851 and 1,000 in 1871.[1] Altered in 1824–5 by W. and H.W. Inwood, and again by William Butterfield in 1884, the church was burnt out in 1941. In 1965–9 it was restored as a concert hall by Marshall Sisson who used giant Corinthian columns in accordance with evidence for its

original appearance, but placed seats facing west; the crypt was adapted to accommodate changing rooms and a restaurant. An organ case of 1733 from St George, Great Yarmouth (Norfolk), was installed in 1993.[2] It was still in use as a concert hall in 2008.

Churchyard   The church yard around the church originally extended a little way to the south which was taken to form the road in Smith Square; the remainder, less than a quarter-acre, became a railed enclosure around the church. A supplementary burial ground on the south side of Horseferry Road was consecrated in 1727.[3] A parish hall, designed by Sir Edwin Lutyens in 1905, was built at no. 7 Tufton Street; by 2003 it had become Faith House, used by the Society for Promoting Christian Knowledge.[4]

St John, Causton Street, Vauxhall Bridge Rd   Built 1956–8 and designed by Caröe & Robinson, it was a small church over a hall.[5] It was closed between 1964 and 1968,[6] and in 2001 was used by Fairley House School.

1 *Mackeson's Guide* (1871).
2 Pevsner, *London 6: Westm.* 680–1; Clarke, *London Chs,* 181.
3 LCC, *Burial Grounds,* 5. Burial grounds reserved for treatment under Pub. Svces.

4 Pevsner, *London 6: Westm.* 720.
5 Pevsner, *London 6: Westm.* 716; Clarke, *London Chs,* 181.
6 *PO Dir.* (1962, 1968 edns).

OTHER CHURCHES AND CHAPELS

Four daughter churches were built in the mid 19th century to serve district chapelries formed from St John's: St Mary the Virgin, Tothill fields, consecrated in 1837, St Stephen, Rochester Row, consecrated in 1850, St Matthew, Great Peter Street, in 1851, and Holy Trinity, Bessborough Gardens, in 1852. A fifth, St James the Less, Thorndike Street, served a chapelry formed in 1862 from St Mary's. St Mary's and the nearby St Stephen's were built to meet the needs of the overcrowded and slum area of Tothill, the former with a grant from the Church Building Commissioners, the latter through a private benefactor; similarly, St Matthew's was designed to work in a poor and largely slum area. Holy Trinity and St James the Less, in the western part of the parish, were built to serve the newly-built suburbs.

St Mary's closed shortly after the First World War, and Holy Trinity did not reopen after being burnt out in the Second World War. St John's, Causton Street, was built as a district chapelry in the 1950s, to replace St John's Smith Square, but closed a decade later. St James's, St Matthew's, and St Stephen's continued in use in 2008.

Holy Trinity, Bessborough Gardens, Vauxhall Bridge Road

Built on Crown land on west side of Bessborough Gardens 1849–51, the church was paid for by W.H.E. Bentinck, canon and later archdeacon of Westminster, with only a token grant from the church building commissioners. It cost over £10,000, an informal act of patronage which compensated for the chapter's official lack of pastoral responsibility for the area.[1] A district chapelry was assigned in 1852 from St John and St Mary, Tothill fields, and patronage was transferred to the dean and chapter of Westminster in 1853.[2] The church had 500 free seats 1866, 750 in 1871, when its value was £374 (weekly offerings), £600 (endowment), and a house.[3] In 1868 Bentinck left £5,000 to the dean and chapter, the income to be divided between the vicar (3/5ths) and curate (2/5ths). In 1899 income of £147 was paid annually to vicar, from which 2/5ths was paid towards £160-salary of the junior curate; the senior curate's salary (£200) mainly provided by grant from Westminster Spiritual Aid Society.[4]

J.L. Pearson's first London church, it was of Bargate stone with Bath stone dressings and in 14th-century Gothic style with cruciform plan and elegant spire; its liturgical arrangements with raised chancel etc. provoked admiration from contemporaries.[5] Attendance in 1886 was 313 (a.m.), 279 (p.m.); in 1903 226 (a.m.), 148 (p.m.). Burnt out in the Second World War, it did not reopen and was demolished by 1973.[6] A garden was laid out on the site in the 1980s.[7]

St James the Less, Thorndike (formerly Garden) Street, Moreton Street

A district chapelry formed 1862 from St Mary's, Westminster, its patron was the dean and chapter, jointly with duke of Westminster by 1980, after the benefice united with St Saviour, St George's Square. The church, paid for by the Misses Monk in memory of their father, J.H. Monk, bishop of Gloucester and Bristol, was designed in 1859 for a poor neighbourhood, and consecrated in 1861. It had an endowment of £500 by 1866, when the surplice was worn in the pulpit and all seats were free.[8] Attendance in 1886 was 323 (a.m.), 237 (p.m.); in 1903 211 (a.m.), 162 (p.m.). It was still in use in 2008.

The building was the first London work of G.E. Street, and the embodiment of the discoveries he had made on his European tours. North Italian influences predominate in the patterning of red and black brickwork and the bold tower, which is linked to the west end of the church by a short passage and rises as a landmark above the neighbouring houses. The nave with aisles, transeptal chapels and apsed chancel lies parallel to the street, and forms a group with the school (1861–4) and later infant's school by A.E. Street (1890, now parish hall). The interior is rich with polychrome materials, historiated carving, ornate furnishings, and stained glass designed by G.E. Street.[9]

St Mary the Virgin, Tothill Fields

The church was built 1835–6, with a grant from the Church Building Commissioners, to Gothic-style designs with a steeple by E. Blore. Consecrated in 1837, it seated 1,219 (806 free).[10] A district chapelry was formed 1841 from St John's with the rector as patron.[11] By 1851 it had a permanent endowment of £200 p.a.[12] Attendance then 697 (a.m.), 477 (aft.), dropped to 223 (a.m.), 180 (p.m.) in 1903. The chapelry was united to St Stephen's, Rochester Row, by 1926,[13] and the church had been demolished by 1927.[14] There was a neighbouring vicarage at no. 21 Vincent Square.[15]

1 TNA, HO 129/4, 1/1/(deleted) (f.7); Hobhouse, *Cubitt*, 223; Port, *Six Hundred Chs*, 156–7.
2 *London Gaz.* 9 July 1852, p. 1916; 2 Dec. 1853, p. 3547.
3 *Mackeson's Guide* (1866, 1871).
4 *Endowed Chars London*, V. 392.
5 A. Quiney, *John Loughborough Pearson* (1979), 24–6, 280; Eastlake, *Gothic Revival*, App. p. 81; Hobhouse, *Cubitt*, 223; above, Rel. Hist.: Intro. (Rel. Bldgs).
6 Eastlake, *Gothic Revival*, App. p. 81; Pevsner, *London I* (1973 edn), 502.   7 Hobhouse, *Cubitt*, 493–4.

8 *Mackeson's Guide* (1866, 1871).
9 Eastlake, *Gothic Revival*, App. p. 108; Clarke, *London Chs*, 188–9; Pevsner, *London 6: Westm.* 766–7; *Architectural Hist.* 23 (1980), 86–94.
10 Port, *Six Hundred Chs.* 156–7; Harris and Bryant, *Chs and London*, 426.   11 *London Gaz.* 20 July 1841, p. 1894.
12 TNA, HO 129/4, 1/1/4 (f. 6).
13 *Crockford* (1926 edn).
14 Harris and Bryant, *Chs and London*, 426; *PO Dir.* (1927 edn).   15 *PO Dir.* (passim).

60. *The district church of St Stephen, Rochester Row, and its schools, c.1850, a picturesque Gothic group paid for by Baroness Burdett-Coutts and designed by Benjamin Ferrey. The setting was altered when school and vicarage were demolished in the 1890s and a new school was built to the north east.*

St Matthew, Great Peter Street

District chapelry having been formed in 1851 from St John's,[1] the rector hired Old Pye Street schoolroom for services in anticipation of a permanent church. Served by curates of St John's, the room seated 150 and had an average attendance of 115 (a.m.), 165 (p.m.).[2] The large new Middle Pointed style church in this bad slum area, designed in 1849 by Sir G.G. Scott, was paid for by private subscriptions and grants including one from the Church Building Commissioners. An income of £200 p.a. was paid by the rector of St John's,[3] patron from 1871, when the value of the benefice was £500.[4] By 1970 the patronage had passed to the dean and chapter of Westminster.[5]

The church, which had a nave with one N and two S aisles, seated 1,200 (900 free), but had not been completed in 1866. The entrance tower was never given its spire, and in 1869 the gallery was removed. A High Church tradition had developed by 1884 when the church was embellished under Revd W.B. Trevelyan with handsome fittings (which survive and have been added to). In 1891 Comper added a vestry south of chancel with Lady chapel over, and in 1894 a chapel for daily worship was formed by screening an aisle, and in 1903 Lee added a detached mortuary chapel dedicated to All Souls'.[6] In 1886, however, attendance was only

367 (a.m.), 364 (p.m.), and in 1903 575 (a.m.), 334 (p.m.).

After a fire in 1977 Donald Buttress designed a smaller church built in 1982–4 with reversed orientation and retaining the Lady chapel, tower and chancel; the clergy house by J.O. Scott, 1891, was linked to form a courtyard building. A boys' club occupied the site of the nave, and offices lay north of the chancel.[7] The church retained its High Church tradition in 2008.

Good Shepherd, Victoria St St Matthew's mission chapel seated 100, served by the All Saints' Sisters in 1894, with Sunday morning communion and evening mission service.[8] Attendance in 1903 was 109 (a.m.), 131 (p.m.).

St Stephen, Rochester Row

A district chapelry formed 1847 from St John's,[9] it was united with St Mary, Tothill fields, by 1926, and with St John, Smith Sq., by 1952. The church was built and endowed in a slum area by Baroness Angela Burdett-Coutts as a memorial to her father, Sir Francis Burdett (d. 1844), MP for Westminster 1807–37; with vicarage and schools she spent more than £90,000. She also created a new and complete parochial organization, including guilds, working and friendly societies, temperance societies, Bible classes, soup kitchens, and self-help

1 *London Gaz.* 8 Aug. 1851, p. 2034.
2 TNA, HO 129/4, 1/1/2 (f. 3).
3 TNA, HO 129/4, 1/1/2 (f. 3).
4 *Mackeson's Guide* (1871).
5 *London Diocese Bk* (1970 edn).

6 Pevsner, *London I* (1973 edn), 496; Clarke, *London Chs*, 187–8; *Mackeson's Guide* (1894).
7 Pevsner, *London 6: Westm.* 681–2.
8 *Mackeson's Guide* (1894).
9 *London Gaz.* 28 May 1847, p. 1963.

associations, aiming to create a city community similar to rural ones she had known from her childhood.[1] In 1851 there was a permanent endowment of £300 a year. The patron was Lady Burdett-Coutts during her lifetime, by 1970 the Crown.

Benjamin Ferrey designed the group of buildings in a scholarly medieval manner in 1847. The elegant Decorated-style ragstone church with richly decorated interior, consecrated in 1850, has a NW tower with fine spire

(partially removed 1968, restored 1994), long chancel, nave with tall aisles and clerestory, and well-designed furnishings (which survive). Though one of the most costly (£25,000) of its time in London, it was not one of the largest, and in 1851 it seated only 800 of which 650 were free.[2] It was well attended in 1851 (858 a.m., 558 aft., 935 evg.) but less so later (494 a.m., 411 p.m. in 1886; 440 a.m., 327 p.m., plus mission, 58 in 1903). It was still in use in 2008.

ST MARY LE STRAND

MEDIEVAL PARISH CHURCH OF ST MARY OF STRAND

The medieval church of St Mary of Strand, which is not to be confused with Holy Innocents, lay on the south side of the Strand just west of the later Strand Lane.[3] Its early history is uncertain, but it may well go back to at least c.1100, when it may probably be identified as the church of St Mary of London, restored to Worcester cathedral priory by the chaplain Fritheric, who had received it on the death of a previous bishop of Worcester.[4] Although it has been suggested that the church in question was St Mary Somerset, in the City near Queenhithe, where the bishops of Worcester had been given property by Alfred in the late 9th, there seems no evidence that this church was ever connected with the bishop of Worcester, and almost certainly it lay on land assigned by Alfred to the archbishop of Canterbury.[5] At all events, it may confidently be identified as the church of St Mary at the Strand of London which Simon, bishop of Worcester, restored to the monks of the cathedral priory, shortly before he died in 1150, having formerly taken it away from them by granting it to Hugh brother of Bertram the clerk.[6] The site of the church, within the area formerly covered by *Lundenwic*, may well be within land granted to the bishop of Worcester in 857.[7]

By the 12th century, the church and parish had developed strong associations with the honor of Leicester which held property adjoining the church; in the late 12th century a charter was attested at St Mary of Strand, and it may have been the setting for the honor's court.[8] In 1204, Richard, reeve of the honor, was described as

the son of Edward of St Mary of Strand.[9] The church, which was served by a chaplain in the early 13th century, was certainly parochial by the 1230s, and was often referred to simply as St Mary de or at Strand, or simply the church of Strand, as in the 1240s visitation by the dean of St Paul's.[10] Thereafter the parish of Strand was well documented, though its extent is in some doubt, particularly on the north side of the Strand.[11] The usage 'St Mary le Strand' only emerged in the 17th century.

Although the church had been restored by the bishop of Worcester to his cathedral priory in 1150, the bishop was again patron in the 1240s.[12] Except when the see was vacant, he continued to present until 1547, when he was forced to grant his Strand property and the advowson of St Mary's to Henry VIII.[13] Shortly afterwards the king granted the advowson to Sir Ralph Sadler, gentleman of the Privy Chamber,[14] who immediately sold it to the Lord Protector, Edward Seymour, duke of Somerset.[15] By the time the chantry certificate was drawn up in 1548 the church had been dissolved by Somerset, and the building demolished as part of the site for Somerset Place.[16]

The benefice was valued at 10 marks (£6 13s. 4d.) in the 1240s and 1254.[17] In 1535 the rectory was valued at £13 8s. 4d. net.[18] There was no vicarage.

The earliest incumbents were termed chaplains. The church of St Mary *Littoream* said to have been granted to Thomas Becket by John, bishop of Worcester (presumably John of Pagham, bishop from 1151) has been identified as St Mary of Strand,[19] but the grant to Becket of such a minor benefice at that date seems unlikely. William the chaplain was recorded 1200x1219,[20] while the first recorded rector was Nicholas in 1239.[21] Others

1 *Oxford DNB* sv. Burdett-Coutts.
2 Pevsner, *London 6: Westm.* 682–3; Clarke, *London Chs*, 186–7.
3 For identity and boundaries see above, Gen. Intro.: Boundaries, Parishes (Strand); Parish Churches: Holy Innocents.
4 *Cartulary of Worcester Cathedral Priory* (PRS LXXVI), no. 53.
5 Pers. comm. Derek Keene.
6 *Cart. of Worc. Cath. Priory*, pp. 41–2.
7 Above, Intro.: Parishes.
8 Above, Landownership: Manorial (Soke of Leic.).
9 *Cartae Antiquae*, II, p. 113.
10 TNA, E 40/1665; CP 25/1/146/12, no. 176; Guildhall MS 25509, f. 85d.

11 Above, Gen. Intro.: Boundaries, Parishes.
12 Guildhall MS 25509, f. 85d.
13 TNA, E 328/43.
14 *Cal. Pat.* 1547–48, 258, 260.
15 TNA, E 326/12005.
16 Above, Landownership: Episcopal Inns (Chester).
17 Guildhall MS 25509, f. 85d.; *Val. of Norwich*, ed. Lunt, 360. Ch not mentioned 1291: *Tax. Eccl.* (Rec. Com.).
18 *Valor Eccl.* I. 433.
19 Wm Fitzstephen, *Materials for Hist. of Thos Becket*, ed. J. Robertson, III (1877), 17; if granted by Bishop John, it was not in 1143 as stated in *DNB*.
20 Above; TNA, E 40/1665.
21 TNA, CP 25/1/146/12, no. 176.

were recorded in 1279,[1] 1289,[2] and 1300.[3] Thereafter, in 1324, 1329 and 1336 incumbents were presented to the benefice and to the chantry in St Mary for William Louth, bishop of Ely (d. 1298).[4] John de Branketre, king's clerk, was rector by 1353 when he petitioned the pope for a canonry in Winchester diocese, which he had still not received in 1359 when the king of France petitioned on his behalf for a canonry in London; his only other living was Greenford, while the Strand was said to be of little value.[5] In 1375 the king presented Master William Wymondham, the king's physician, who died in 1377.[6] The cure was served by the rector with some assistance from curates and chantry priests. In 1381 there was a celebrant called Richard,[7] and in 1548 a morrow mass priest called Anthony Torky.[8]

Henry III gave 100 lbs of wax for candles in St Mary's to burn on the feast of the Eleven Thousand Virgins (21 Oct.) in 1236, 150 tapers for the feast of the Annunciation in 1240, and 1,500 tapers for the nativity of the Virgin in 1241.[9] The court of chancery was held in the church on several occasions 1349–51,[10] and the Middlesex coroner sat in the church on two killings in 1402–3.[11]

In 1354 the Pope gave dispensations from penance to any who visited the church on the feasts of Christmas, Easter, Whitsun, the Annunciation, St John Baptist and the Eleven Thousand Virgins, or who helped to repair the church, to hold good for ten years.[12] In 1355 Henry, duke of Lancaster, received a licence to grant to the church a plot 70 feet by 30 to enlarge the cemetery, probably on the south side.[13] William Blythe (d. 1445), rector, left goods for repair of the chancel, and 10 marks for the improvement of the church.[14] Anne Stafford, duchess of Buckingham, gave gifts of £6 2s. to the rector in 1465 and 6s. 8d. to the parish of Strand for the feast of Purification in 1466.[15] The church had a chapel of St Michael the Archangel by 1468.[16]

Rectory Houses and Property

Bishop Godfrey of Worcester granted a messuage in the parish to Richard the parson before 1279,[17] and in 1348 Philip the marshal and his wife Isabel quitclaimed in a messuage to the rector, Richard of Canterbury;[18] both grants may have been personal, however, as there is no indication of a permanent parsonage house. In 1356

Henry, duke of Lancaster, received licence to grant a plot 7 perches square, which lay between the church and the Thames, with a gateway and chamber built on it, to the rector, John de Branketre, to reside in for life, and to remain to his successors as rectors.[19] Despite that remainder, on the institution of William Wymondham to the rectory in 1375, John of Gaunt, duke of Lancaster, granted the plot to William with the houses that Branketre had built on it, with the proviso that it would revert to Lancaster when William ceased to be rector.[20] In 1401 the king as duke of Lancaster let to the rector for 50 years a messuage and garden in the Strand opposite the Savoy for 13s. 4d. a year,[21] and William Blythe, rector 1433–45, left goods to his successor for repair of the parsonage, as he was legally required to do.[22]

The chantry for William Louth, mentioned between 1324 and 1336, may be that for which Master Peter de Ascharn, clerk, gave land to the church in 1311 to maintain a chaplain to celebrate daily: the grant consisted of property in Holborn and a plot of land and tenement in St Mary of Strand, held of various lords and valued at £4 8s. 4d.[23] In 1398 it was found that for the past 60 years the rectors had been holding the property in mortmain without licence, described then as a cottage in Holborn and four cottages on the north side of the Strand in St Mary at Strand, and it escheated to the king, as the chaplains had long since ceased performing the services, and Peter, to whom the property would have reverted, had died without heirs.[24]

James Atkinson gave to the church the lease he had of the Flower de Luce (Fleur de Lis) brewhouse, held of the duchy of Lancaster for a term of years, from the profits of which £3 were to be paid towards the wages of the chantry priest for Atkinson's soul; by 1513 the wardens of the brotherhood and morrow mass of St Ursula in that church were letting the property.[25] In 1523 the rector and churchwardens issued a sub-lease for 46 years, presumably to the end of Atkinson's lease.[26]

THE PARISH 1548 TO 1724

By 1548 the church had been demolished by the duke of Somerset. A century later it was said that he had promised to build another church with a minister's house on a new site, but was executed before he could do so.[27] The laity recorded at the visitation in 1554 that there was no

1 TNA, CP 40/31, rot. 67d.
2 *Reg. of Bp Godfrey Giffard* (Worcs. Hist. Soc. 1902), II. 329; *Cal. Inq Misc.* I. 619.   3 *Reg. Bp Godfrey Giffard*, II. 541.
4 *Reg. Baldock* (Cant. & York Soc.), 273, 290, 308; TNA, CP 25/1/150/62, no. 243.
5 *Cal. Papal Pet.* I. 255, 341.
6 *Cal. Pat.* 1374–77, 166; *John of Gaunt's Register 1371–5*, I (Camden Soc. 3rd ser., 20), no. 726, p. 263.
7 *Ch in London*, 1375–92, 36.
8 *Chantry Cert.* 70 (no. 159).
9 *Cal. Lib. R.* 1267–72, 288; 1226–40, 462; 1240–45, 66.
10 *Cal. Close*, 1349–54, 89, 208, 247, 358.
11 *Cal. Pat.* 1401–5, 31, 221.   12 *Cal. Papal Reg.* III. 536.
13 TNA, C 143/318, no. 27; *Cal. Pat.* 1354–8, 178.

14 TNA, C 1/16/335.
15 BL, Add. MS 34213, ff. 93, 106 (from Prof. M. Erler).
16 Guildhall MS 9171/6, ff. 35v., 88.
17 TNA, CP 40/31, rot. 6d.; /33, rot. 56; /41, rot. 77.
18 TNA, CP 25/1/150/62, no. 243.
19 TNA, C 143/322, no. 17; *Cal. Pat.* 1354–8, 488.
20 *John of Gaunt's Reg.* p. 263; TNA, DL 42/13, f. 98d.
21 TNA, DL 29/287/4708; DL 41/437.
22 TNA, C 1/16/335.
23 TNA, C 143/210, no. 10; *Cal. Pat.* 1307–13, 333.
24 *Cal. Inq. Misc.* VI. 230–1; *Cal. Pat.* 1396–9, 422, 466.
25 *Chantry Cert.* 70 (no. 159); Cal. Burghley Ho. MSS, Cecil 5/2.   26 Cal. Burghley Ho. MSS, Cecil 5/3.
27 *Chantry Cert.* 70; *Home Counties Mag.* I. 117.

61. *The parish church of St Mary le Strand, shown from the south-west two years after its completion in 1717. Built on the Crown's land in the middle of the Strand, formerly the site of the maypole, to a design by James Gibbs intended to be seen from all sides.*

church in the parish.[1] In 1564 Bishop Grindal of London wrote to the master of the Savoy about the long delay in uniting the parishioners of Strand to suitable parishes, which had led to complaints. Grindall ordered that those who were not allotted to the neighbouring parish of St Clement Danes, which lay in the same precinct as the Strand (presumably referring to the duchy), must be united to St Martin's unless they were able to procure by legal means the right to be allotted to the Savoy, which had to be done by agreement between the bishop, Sir William Cecil, patron of St Clement's of which parish the Savoy was considered part, and the master of the Savoy, and also with the consent of the parson of St Clement's. The bishop had allowed many Strand parishioners to attend services in the Savoy, but now requested that the minister there should announce that after a month the parishioners of Strand would not be admitted to the Savoy, until the situation had been legally resolved.[2] What transpired is not clear, but obviously the

parishioners continued to use the Savoy chapel.[3] In 1574 the parish of Strand had a curate, Thomas Chambers, and from about that date was usually known as the Strand alias Savoy, or St Mary Savoy alias le Strand.[4] By 1650 the parishioners of St Mary's claimed to have used the Savoy chapel for the last hundred years, and contributed to its upkeep, and they appealed, unsuccessfully, for this chapel to be made into their parish church.[5] The use of the name St Mary le Strand seems to have been first recorded in 1669, when the church was referred to as St Mary le Strand alias Savoy. In 1676 the parish had 210 communicants.[6]

PARISH CHURCH OF ST MARY LE STRAND

When the commissioners for building fifty new churches in and around London approached all local incumbents and parish officers in 1711 regarding the need for new churches, the inhabitants of St Mary le Strand were given leave to petition for their parish to receive one of the churches, and within a month it was decided that the area around the maypole in the middle of the Strand would make a suitable site.[7] A petition to the queen was necessary as the site belonged to the Crown; she gave permission for a bill for the site to be introduced in 1713, passed that year. The church, built 1714–17, seated 394, of which 86 were free, in 1851;[8] all 399 were free in 1871.[9] It was consecrated in 1724, when the parish was formed, and served the whole of its small parish, which later also contained the chapel of King's College London.[10]

The patron of the new rectory was the Crown, on whose behalf patronage was exercised by the lord chancellor in the 19th and 20th centuries. The benefice was united with St Clement Danes c.1953, after which presentations were made alternately by the lord chancellor and the marquess of Exeter (Burleigh House Preservation Trust).[11] In 1780 the rectory of Strand alias St Mary le Strand was valued at £270.[12] In 1837 the rector valued it at only about £300 a year gross including all fees and rent from the parsonage house.[13] In 1851 the gross annual income of £300 included a house let for £55, and other endowments of £219; the rector lived at no. 1 New Inn, Wych St.[14] In 1871 the weekly offertory produced £250 p.a.; the benefice was valued at £266 from endowments and the rector's rate.[15]

James Robinson Hayward, presented to the living in 1786, was non resident, living in Kent. James Edward Gambier, presented to the rectory in 1813, was also rector of Langley (Kent), where he resided by the 1830s, and his duties in St Mary were discharged by his curate,

1 Guildhall MS 9537/1, f. 67A.
2 TNA, SP 12/35, f. 40 (no. 16).
3 Below, Royal Chapels (Savoy).
4 Guildhall MS 9537/3, f. 31; /6, f. 128.
5 *Home Counties Mag.* I. 117; below, Royal Chapels (Savoy).
6 Guildhall MS 9537/19, f. 57v.; *Compton Census of 1676*, ed. Whiteman, 57.   7 *Fifty New Chs*, 1, 4–5, 7.
8 TNA, HO 129/13, 2/4 [?3] (f.13).

9 *Mackeson's Guide* (1871).
10 Reserved for treatment with King's College in a future volume.
11 *London Diocese Bk* (1970, 1980, 1995 edns).
12 Guildhall MS 9557, f. 25.
13 Guildhall MS 19224/440.
14 TNA, HO 129/13, 2/4 [?3] (f. 13).
15 *Mackeson's Guide* (1871).

Joshua F. Derham. Curates in the 18th century received £40 a year, but only £20 in the early 19th century with fees of £70–80. J.J. Ellis, licensed as curate in 1810, was also licensed as evening lecturer in 1811.[1]

In the 1780s the parish had 237 houses, and 15–20 communicants at communion held monthly and on the three great festivals. Other services were held twice on Sundays, and on Wednesdays and Fridays. The charity children were catechised in Lent.[2] In 1829 the rector and parishioners sought the bishop's permission to hold Sunday services at the infant school, no. 90 Drury Lane, in the poorest part of the parish: there were 1,500 to 1,600 poor in the parish for whom there was no church accommodation; about 400 of those stayed away from church because they did not have proper clothes, but would attend services expressly for them. The church committee had leased a room at the school for 10 years, which would hold 300 adults, and the curate, J. Derham, had offered to hold divine service and preach there every Sunday afternoon.[3]

In 1851 attendance was 344 (a.m.), 165 (evg), reduced because of the weather from an average put at 420 (a.m.), 220 (evg).[4] An organ by Hunter & Webb was added in 1862, and in 1871 there was a rector, curate, and precentor; eucharistic vestments were worn.[5] In 1886 attendance had fallen to 84 (a.m.), 84 (p.m.), and in 1903 to 43 (a.m.), 81 (evg). In 1995 the church had a Reader, and there was a church day school in the parish.[6]

In 2008 the church served the united parish of St Mary le Strand and St Clement Danes, and continued the Anglo-Catholic tradition introduced in the 19th century.

Church Fabric

Thomas Archer was originally commissioned as architect but James Gibbs took over after the foundations had been laid. The church, freestanding in a 'fair cemetery', was designed to be seen from all sides, its lively facades incorporating motifs from St Paul's cathedral, such as the semi-circular west porch, and inspiration from contemporary Roman architecture. A tower, which forms part of the architectural composition of the west front, replaced an earlier proposal for a giant statue of Queen Anne. The interior is a single simple space with decoration focussed on the complex geometrical pattern of the ceiling by the plasterers John and Chrysostom Wilkins after a Roman model. The pulpit is original.[7] The interior was drastically altered and Anglo-Catholic fittings introduced in 1869–70 under the incumbency of the Tractarian, Revd Alfred Bowen Evans (1861–78).[8]

Churchyard   Most of the cemetery was taken to widen the Strand in late 18th century. The remainder, *c.*200 sq. yards at the west end of the church, was closed and not well kept in 1895; it formed a small railed garden and entrance in 2008. The parish had an additional ground in Russell Court, off Drury Lane (St Martin), closed in 1853.[9]

ST PAUL, COVENT GARDEN

Francis Russell, 4th earl of Bedford, arranged for the construction of a church to serve his Covent Garden estate, which was being built on from the 1630s. A church and churchyard had been planned by May 1631 and work began that year, though it was probably not completed until sometime in 1633.[10] The earl paid for most of the building work; the residents of Covent Garden had to pay for the steeple and bells and reimburse the earl for the interior fittings, such as altar, pews, wainscotting, pulpit and font, and reimburse the vicar for ornaments for the chapel and altar.[11] The earl obtained a building licence from the Crown in 1635, which included retrospective permission for a church, on the grounds it would relieve the pressure on accommodation in St Martin's, the parish in which Covent Garden then stood, but disputes with the vicar and vestry of St Martin's delayed its opening.[12] The earl apparently intended that the area should become a new parish, but the vicar objected and his claim that an Act of Parliament was required was upheld by the Privy

Council in 1638. The Council ordered that when a Parliament was next held (which at that time did not seem likely to be soon), the church should be made parochial and the patronage vested in the earl; meanwhile it was to be a chapel of ease to St Martin's with the vicar appointing and paying the curate. St Paul's was consecrated in 1638 after an agreement was signed between the earl and residents of Covent Garden on the one hand, and the vicar, churchwardens, and parishioners of St Martin's on the other, concerning the boundary of the chapelry. This was set as 40 feet outside the brick wall of Covent Garden and also included Bedford House in the Strand, but the rationale is unclear since the boundary of both parish and chapelry did not always adhere to this line. The earl planned to give £100 a year and a house for the minister, which gave him the right to nominate a preacher, subject to the approval of the bishop of London. Arrangements for chapelwardens and overseers of the poor were also made; tithes to St Martin's remained payable as before, and arrangements

1 Guildhall MSS 9557, f. 25; 19224/440.
2 Ibid. MS 9557, f. 25.
3 Ibid. MS 19224/440.
4 TNA, HO 129/13, 2/4 [?3] (f. 13).
5 *Mackeson's Guide* (1871).
6 *London Diocese Bk* (1995 edn).

7 Pevsner, *London 6: Westm.* 294–5.
8 Inf. from ch website (www.stmarylestrand.org).
9 LCC, *Burial Grounds*, 5.
10 *Survey of London*, XXXVI. 98.
11 *Cal. SP Dom.* 1639–9, 132–3; 1639, 217–18.
12 *Survey of London*, XXXVI. 98.

62. *The parish church of St Paul, Covent Garden, as the east front looked before the fire of 1795. Built in 1631–3 as the first new Anglican church in London since the mid 16th century to designs by Inigo Jones. The deep Tuscan portico was intended to be the entrance, but the orientation was changed during construction.*

were made for mutual exchange of worshippers to endorse St Martin's rights over the chapelry.[1]

CREATION OF THE PARISH AND BENEFICE

Following attempts by the earl and inhabitants of Covent Garden to obtain the necessary Act, an ordinance to make the chapelry a parish was finally approved early in 1646.[2] The new parish of St Paul had the same boundary as in 1638, the earl of Bedford being patron; the rector received a stipend of £100 a year charged on three houses in the Piazza. A parochial rate was to raise £400 a year for salaries, from which the rector and an assistant minister, to be chosen by the 'governors' of the parish or close vestry, were to have £150 each. The ordinance was confirmed by an Act in 1660, when the curate's stipend was reduced to £50.[3] The earl of Bedford was confirmed as patron in 1660, and successive earls and dukes retained the right until 1938, when at the request of Herbrand Russell, 11th duke of Bedford, the advowson was vested in the bishop of London by an Order in Council.[4] The church served whole parish alone and continued to do so in 2007. The district of St Michael's, Burleigh Street (St Martin's), was united to St Paul's when the former closed in 1905.[5]

INCOME AND RECTORY HOUSES

In the mid 18th century the living was valued at £350.[6] By 1851 the church had endowments of £500, and the clergy received £85 in fees;[7] in 1871 the value was £500

with a house.[8] The rectory house designated in 1637, later no. 27 James Street, was occupied by the minister in the mid 1640s and possibly earlier; a house at no. 42 King Street was used from 1646 to 1671. In 1665 the house in James Street was conveyed to the 5th earl in trust for use as a rectory house, though it was occasionally occupied by others.[9] In the 1780s the rector resided in Conduit Street (St George's parish), and one of his curates in the City of London.[10] By the early 19th century it was found desirable to move away from the market area, and in 1833 the duke formally gave no. 7 Henrietta Street in exchange for the James Street house. The new rectory house remained in use until c.1934. In 1905 St Michael's former vicarage house, no 14 Burleigh Street, was taken over as St Paul's clergy house, when St Michael's district was united with St Paul's; it became the rectory house c.1934.[11]

CLERGY AND CHURCH LIFE

The first curate was Samuel Porter from 1638; later incumbents included Thomas Manton (1656–ejected 1662) and Dr Simon Patrick (1662–89). Local residents including Lord Bedford and the Verney family contributed voluntary subscriptions amounting to £560 a year to pay James Ussher, archbishop of Armagh, to preach at St Paul's 1641–2.[12] Mr Price was minister in 1643 when called to attend an assembly of divines to settle the government of the Church.[13] In 1685 the parish trustees bought land in Nazeing (Essex) and Hoddesdon

1 Ibid. 53.
2 *Acts and Ordinances of the Interregnum, 1642–60*, I. 814–17, 827–8.
3 *Survey of London*, XXXVI. 54; HMC, *7th Rep.* 137b.
4 Guildhall MS 19224/549.
5 *Survey of London*, XXXVI. 224.
6 Guildhall MSS 9556, p. 42; 9557, f. 29.
7 TNA, HO 129/13, 2/1/1 (f. 8)

8 *Mackeson's Guide* (1871).
9 *Survey of London*, XXXVI. 127–8.
10 Guildhall MS 9557, f. 29.
11 *Survey of London*, XXXVI. 127–8; Guildhall MS 19224/549.
12 HMC, *7th Rep.* App. pp. 435b, 443b; *Survey of London*, XXXVI. 103.
13 *Acts and Ordinances of the Interregnum, 1642–60*, I. 182.

(Herts.), at a cost of £931 taken from offertory money and other parish funds. From the income thus generated, £20 paid a curate, appointed by the rector, to read morning and evening prayers twice daily in the church, the residue being used for the parish poor.

Piecemeal alterations to the church reflecting the religious life of the parish began in the 1640s with the insertion of a south gallery and dormer windows.[1] A north gallery was added in 1655, and in that decade the chancel was destroyed. By 1675 east and west galleries had been built, with outside staircases on the north and south sides. In 1685 the church had a substantial collection of plate – two great gilt flagons and two smaller ones, two gilt bowls, a large gilt basin and four gilt patens.[2] The church was embellished inside and out throughout the late 17th and 18th century, funded by public subscription with support from the earl. Between 1704–8 part of the east gallery was removed to make way for a great altarpiece, and in 1720 the vestry bought an organ. The church also underwent frequent repair, most notably in 1727 by Lord Burlington as an admirer of Jones.[3]

In 1714 the rector, the Hon. Robert Lumley Lloyd, of Cheam, was assisted by Henry Topping, lecturer, and John Harris, curate. Prayers were held four times a day, and communion on the 1st and 3rd Sundays of the month and solemn occasions. A lecture, maintained by parishioners' subscriptions, was preached on the last Sunday of the month by the curate.[4] The vestry polled for a lecturer in 1784.[5] In 1723–48 there were two services on Sundays and communion on the first and third Sundays of the month.[6] In 1780 services were twice a day, communion monthly, and children catechised in Lent.[7]

In 1830 the land consisted of 40 acres at Roydon (Essex), and the £20 was regularly paid to the curate, but by the 1830s, though the curate attended daily at the vestry room each morning, no congregation ever assembled so the service was not performed. In 1899, however, the new rector, E.H. Mosse, started holding a service twice daily.[8] John Yarwell in 1711 had left a sum to be invested, and from the income 40s. a year to be used for a sermon on 29 May, but by 1836 the sermon was no longer preached unless the date fell on a Sunday.[9] In 1851 the church seated 1100 (350 for adults being free),[10] but the removal of the galleries by Wm Butterfield in 1871–2 reduced capacity from 832 to 538.[11] Attendance was quite high in 1851 (874 a.m., 945 evg.),[12] but thereafter dropped dramatically (125 a.m.,

194 p.m. in 1886; 74 a.m., 112 evg. in 1903).[13] In the 20th century, in addition to remaining the parish church for Covent Garden and Lincolns' Inn Fields, St Paul's also found a new role as the Actors' Church because of the many theatrical venues in the vicinity, becoming the focus for memorials and services for actors and others involved in the performing arts.[14]

CHURCH FABRIC

Designed by the court architect, Inigo Jones, St Paul's was the first completely new Anglican church to be built in London since the mid 16th century and, because of Jones's interest in recovering the elements of classical architecture and the need to be appropriate for Protestant worship, was strikingly novel in its design.[15] It formed a set piece in the earl of Bedford's new development. The church, a plain undivided oblong, had on the east towards the piazza a deep Tuscan portico of stone on the east facing the piazza, inspired by Palladio and Scamozzi; it had wide overhanging eaves and low arches in the flank walls and was intended to be the entrance, but during construction the orientation was apparently changed, the altar was placed on the east wall, and a west entrance was made. The most dramatic internal feature was the flat ceiling painted in false perspective. The external walls were originally of brick, rendered and stone coloured; the present red brick facing dates from 1886–7, replacing stone facing added by Thomas Hardwick in 1788. It was Hardwick who reconstructed the church and returned it a building closer to Jones's intentions after fire reduced the church to a shell in 1795. Victorian architects made minor changes, Henry Clutton particularly to the exterior in 1878–82, enlarging the arches in the portico to ease market traffic and reducing the original screen walls to the churchyard in height. William Butterfield blocked two of the originally three east doors, and removed two galleries. In 2008 much of the interior and many fittings were still Hardwick's but the plaster ceiling was of 1887–8.

Churchyard By 1714 the churchyard was paved with stone:[16] its wrought-iron gates are 18th-century. It covered about three-quarters of an acre around the church and was used for burials until it closed in 1853; the ground was laid out in 1878–82 by Clutton. A burial-ground at the parish workhouse in St Pancras was consecrated in 1790.[17] Parish registers date from 1653.[18]

1 For a full acct see *Survey of London*, XXXVI. 98–128.
2 Guildhall MS 9537/20, p. 140.
3 *Survey of London*, XXXVI. 56.
4 Paterson, *Pietas Lond.* 226–8.
5 *Survey of London*, XXXVI. 56.
6 Guildhall MS 9550.
7 Ibid. MS 9557, f. 29.
8 *Endowed Chars London*, V (1900), 509–10, 519.
9 Ibid. 511, 519.
10 TNA, HO 129/13, 2/1/1 (f. 8).

11 *Survey of London*, XXXVI. 118.
12 TNA, HO 129/13, 2/1/1 (f.8).
13 *Brit. Weekly*, 5 Nov. 1886, p. 3; Mudie-Smith, *Rel. Life*, 105.
14 Inf. from ch website (www.actorschurch.org.uk).
15 *Survey of London*, XXXVI. 98–128, for a detailed account which this para. summarizes.
16 Paterson, *Pietas Lond.* 226–8.
17 *Survey of London*, XXXVI. 125; TNA, C 54/6847, no. 3; Mrs B. Holmes, *London Burial Grounds* (1896), 286.
18 In WCA.

ROYAL CHAPELS

A royal chapel at Westminster was first mentioned in 1184, but the dedication to St Stephen is not known until the reign of King John (1199–1216).[1] St Stephen's was the most important of the palace chapels, attaining exceptional architectural grandeur and significance following its reconstruction begun by Edward I in 1292 and only completed by Edward III in 1348, when a grand college with a dean, 12 canons, and 13 vicars was established to serve it.[2] Treatment of this chapel and that of St Mary in its undercroft, which never had a public function, apart from serving the royal family and household and latterly MPs, is reserved for a future volume dealing with the Palace of Westminster. Other chapels within the precincts of the medieval palace include those of St John (first mentioned 1186–7), Our Lady of the Pew (associated with Edward III's royal pew in St Stephen's), and, perhaps, the church of St Beatus.[3] Elsewhere in Westminster, chapels associated with royal property included the hermitage at Charing, dedicated to St Katharine by 1268, where Henry III appointed a chaplain to celebrate for his daughter Katherine (d. 1257), and the Mews chapel at Charing, recorded in 1306.[4]

A body of priests and men and boy singers had long accompanied the monarch on his or her journeys around the kingdom.[5] This body formed an institution known as the Chapel Royal and by the 15th century had become one of the largest and most important of its kind in Europe, staffed by 30 or more chaplains, clerks and boys, and headed by a dean (after the Reformation usually a bishop). Its plate, ornaments and vestments were kept in a vestry staffed by a small group of officials, headed by a serjeant. The Chapel Royal enjoyed a period of especial grandeur under the music-loving Tudors and early Stuarts, by which time the establishment included three organists.

As Westminster grew in importance as a royal residence, the Chapel Royal's sophisticated services were increasingly performed there, and indeed by the early 17th century the institution was more or less permanently established in the city. The building of St James's palace in the 1530s and the acquisition of Whitehall in 1529 provided the two main venues. After the destruction of Whitehall Palace in January 1697/8, the Chapel Royal was based exclusively at St James's Palace,

although housed in two buildings, one within the palace itself and the other just outside on Marlborough Road.

The services performed by the Chapel Royal were, of course, designed primarily for the monarch and the Court, but with their relatively permanent establishment at Westminster they appear to have attracted a wider audience, at least among persons of a certain status. By then the Chapel Royal's affairs were administered in chapter meetings in the vestry, presided over by the dean. The ordinances of this body clearly envisaged a congregation of some number and wide social standing, not all from the royal household.[6] After the Restoration, Pepys was a regular attender at the Whitehall chapel, and much enjoyed the musical quality of the services re-established by Charles II.[7] In recent times the general public as a whole has been welcome to attend the Chapel Royal's services at both chapels.

From time to time, monarchs provided for services, not of the Established Church, for their foreign queens. In the 17th century, a catholic Chapel Royal was set up for royal consorts and housed in a new building near St James's Palace. From 1702, this and other royal venues housed Protestant congregations, originally associated with foreign queens but later acquiring a life of their own.

Westminster also contained other extra-parochial chapels of royal foundation. The chapel of the Savoy, founded for the hospital established on the site of John of Gaunt's palace by Henry VIII, was regarded as a royal chapel from the 18th century. That in Somerset House was established for Charles I's queen, Henrietta Maria. Although of rather different status from the Chapels Royal, they are also treated in this section.

ST JAMES'S PALACE

Chapel Royal

This chapel is located within the precincts of Henry VIII's palace, and its architectural history is therefore reserved for treatment in a future volume. Although the Chapel Royal from time to time performed there from the mid 16th century, in the 17th century musical services were generally in the Whitehall chapel. After the latter's destruction in 1698 and Queen Anne's move to St James's Palace in 1702, the Chapel Royal found a

1 Hist. King's Works, I. 493.
2 Ibid. 510–27; above, Landownership: Other Eccles. Ests (Coll. of St Mary and St Stephen).
3 Hist. King's Works, I. 493, 517; Cal. Lib. R. 1245–51, 123.
4 TNA, C 143/61, no. 11. For hermitage: Cal. Lib. R. 1267–72, 18; Cal. Pat. 1266–72, 187.
5 For what follows on the Chapel Royal, see The New Grove

Dictionary of Music and Musicians, ed. S. Sadie (2001), s.v. London II; David Baldwin, The Chapel Royal, Ancient and Modern (1990).
6 The Old Cheque-Book or Book of Remembrance of the Chapel Royal from 1561 to 1744, ed. E.F. Rimbault (Camden Soc., New series III, 1872), 62–90.
7 Baldwin, Chapel Royal, 102, 103, 110, 189.

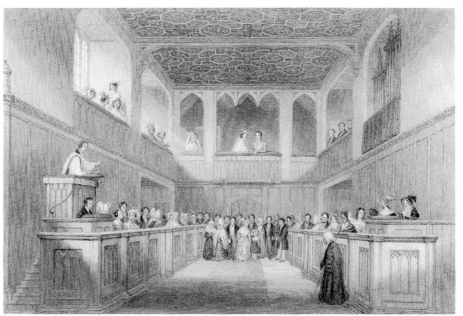

63. *The Chapel Royal, St James's Palace, in the 1840s, interior showing Queen Victoria and Prince Albert in the royal pew which, with the side galleries, were added to the mid 16th-century chapel in 1836.*

permanent home in the chapel at St James's.[1] Although the additional post of composer was then created, under the Hanoverians it occupied a less pre-eminent role in English church music than hitherto, and the number of organists was reduced to two.

The setting of several Stuart baptisms and the marriage of Queen Victoria, the chapel at St James's also came to be regarded as a place of worship for a wider public (see above). Side galleries were added in 1836, and in 1851, when Charles Wesley was chaplain, the chapel was attended chiefly by the peers and by members of the House of Commons, all of whom had a right of admission; attendances were then 13 (at 8 a.m.), c.100 (noon), c.30 (5.30 p.m.).[2] By the early 20th century, the general public could attend the evening service, but attendance at the midday service required an order from the Lord Chamberlain. The admittance of the general public may have started earlier, particularly after the chapel in Buckingham Palace was formed in 1843 for the queen and her household.[3]

In 1714 the staff of the Chapel Royal in 1714 amounted to 113 persons, headed by the dean, usually by then the bishop of London and invariably so from 1748. There was also a subdean, drawn from the singing men (the 'gentlemen of the chapel'), who had charge of music and minor matters of discipline. The staff included 48 chaplains in ordinary who served, four at a time, in a monthly rotation, 32 gentlemen of the chapel, who included 12 priests, 8 clerks, 3 organists, a composer, a master of music, and an organ-builder, 12 children for the choir, and the serjeant and yeomen of

the vestry. The whole institution cost c.£7,000 a year in salaries. Prayers were said 3 times daily, with communion twice each Sunday, when the queen was in residence, otherwise twice daily, and communion once.[4]

In the mid 19th century the personnel of the Chapel Royal were reduced. In 1860 the number of chaplains in ordinary was set at 36 and that of the gentlemen of the chapel was halved to 16. By 1866, besides the dean and sub-dean, the staff included 30 chaplains in ordinary, 8 priests in ordinary, and 3 organists/composers. Sunday services were then at 3, with communion twice a month.[5] Since the opening of the Queen's Chapel in 1938, the chapel in St James's has been used primarily for winter services, between October and Easter. The dean remains the head of the Chapel Royal which continues to be staffed by a subdean assisted by a small number of priests in ordinary, by a choirmaster, organist and composer, and by a choir comprising 6 gentlemen in ordinary and 10 children (all boys) of the chapel. Services between October and Easter, at which the general public is welcomed, are communion at 8.30 and choral matins or eucharist at 11.15.

The Queen's Chapel, Marlborough Road

The queen's chapel at St James's Palace was designed by Inigo Jones and built 1623–7, eventually for Queen Henrietta Maria's use. It continued to be used by the Catholic queen consorts until c.1700.[6] The design by Inigo Jones, for the first purely classical ecclesiastical building in England and still one of the most beautiful and elegant, fulfilled the brief by providing a deep gallery

1 Unless indicated otherwise, information in this section is drawn from *New Grove* and Baldwin, *Chapel Royal*.
2 TNA, HO 129/5, 1/1/1 (f. 1).
3 T.F. Bumpus, *Ancient London Chs* [ea. 20th cent.], 196–8.
4 Paterson, *Pietas Lond.* 106–10.

5 *Mackeson's Guide* (1866).
6 Acct of building follows Pevsner, *London 6: Westm.* 587–8. More detailed architectural history reserved for treatment under Royal Palaces.

(the Royal Closet) lit by three long windows and double-cube congregational space with coffered barrel vault to the east. How the chapel looked in the 1620s is not known, as the first illustrations are post-Restoration, but many of the fittings, including the reredos date from the 1660s. Beyond the east wall, the upper part filled with a Serlian window, was until the early 18th century a low choir for the use of friars.

In 1700 use of the Friary chapel in the palace, formerly the Roman Catholic queen's chapel, was granted to French and Dutch Protestants attached to Court, their ministers being appointed as royal chaplains. In 1702–3 a new altar-table, altar-rail, and reading-desk were provided at Queen Anne's expense, of which the altar rails appear to remain.[1] Services were at first French Reformed, but in 1710 conformed to the Anglican liturgy in French. The chapel continued to be used by French Protestants until 1781, when the reduced congregation exchanged chapels with German Lutherans who had a room on the south side of Great (Colour) Court, which they used as a chapel (below). After the destruction of the latter in 1809 the French then shared the Queen's Chapel with the German Lutherans until 1810, after which the French congregation seems to have disbanded. In 1830 the chaplaincies, by then sinecures, were suppressed.[2] The German Lutherans, however, continued to use the Queen's Chapel and were there in 1851, describing it as the Royal German Chapel.[3] They registered it in 1873, when Dr Adolphus Walbaum was minister.[4] Attendance in 1886 was 101 (a.m.). A chaplaincy was supported by the Crown and accommodation provided in the palace, but the arrangement was ended by Edward VII in 1901, probably to reduce the number of sinecures connected with the Chapel Royal. The congregation was given 3 weeks to vacate the chapel and chaplain's accommodation, which gave rise to complaints, especially as the Danish congregation were allowed to continue to use the chapel.[5]

Danish Lutherans, associated with Edward VII's Danish queen, Alexandra, registered the Queen's Chapel for their worship in 1902.[6] In 1913, when they included members of Alexandra's household as Queen Dowager at Marlborough House, they held a Sunday afternoon service.[7] Those arrangements ended in 1952 when the congregation moved to St Katharine's precinct, Regent's Park (St Pancras parish).[8]

The Queen's Chapel became a Chapel Royal again in 1938 and Anglican services were resumed. Its present appearance owes much to the restoration by the Ministry of Works in 1949–51.[9] Choral services, at which the public are welcome, are still held there between Easter and July.

Great (Colour Court) Chapel

By 1781, German Lutherans worshipped in a room on the south side of the Great (Colour) Court in St James's Palace, but they then exchanged chapels with the French congregation who had been using the Queen's or Friary chapel. In 1809 the chapel in Great Court was burnt in the fire that consumed the south-east part of the palace, and was not rebuilt.[10]

WHITEHALL PALACE
Chapel Royal

The chapel built at York Place by Cardinal Wolsey 1528–9, and seized by Henry VIII in 1529, continued in use as the Chapel Royal until it was burnt down with Whitehall Palace in 1698. It lay north to south between the great hall and the Thames. Built of brick with stone dressings, it had crenellations of flint chequerwork and the body of the building was painted in black-and-white squares. It had two towers and a gallery along its south front, with vestries to east and west. During the Commonwealth the interior was plastered, the organ removed, and the altar replaced by a communion table. After the Restoration, alterations included new organs in 1660 and 1662 and an organ loft designed by Wren in 1663. The King's closet or pew, which overlooked the chapel, was refurbished in 1675, and in 1676 Wren refitted the east end, giving it a new altarpiece.[11]

James II, who built a Catholic chapel at Whitehall,[12] permitted his daughter Princess Anne, who had remained a Protestant, to use the Chapel Royal. After the fire in 1698, Wren converted the Banqueting House into a chapel for William III, which in 1714 was also used by nobility, gentry, and other inhabitants in vicinity. Prayers were held daily and public communion on the first Sunday of the month. Lectures were given in Lent by preachers appointed by Lord Chamberlain and published in annual list. The bishop of London was dean, with six preaching chaplains and two readers.[13] In 1851 the chapel seated 600, half of them free; attendance was 500 (a.m.) and 100 (aft.).[14] The chapel was closed in 1890.[15]

Queen's Chapel Royal (Roman Catholic)

The queen's Chapel Royal was built at Whitehall Palace for James II and his wife, Mary of Modena, created by Sir Christopher Wren by closing off 85 feet at the west end

1 *Hist. King's Works*, V. 253.
2 *Hist. King's Works*, V. 253–5; VI. 366; Beeman, 'French Chs in London', 46–7.
3 TNA, HO 129/5, 1/1/8 (f. 8).
4 ONS, Worship Reg. nos 21256.
5 *Survey of London*, XLV, 125–6.
6 ONS, Worship Reg. no. 38921.
7 Harris and Bryant, *Chs and London*, 306.
8 ONS, Worship Reg. no. 63367.

9 Pevsner, *London 6: Westm.* 587–8.
10 *Hist. King's Works*, V. 253–4.
11 S. Thurley, *Whitehall Palace: an Architectural History of the Royal Apartments, 1240–1698* (1999), 30–1, 36, 76, 98, 116–17, 135.
12 Below, Rom. Cathm.
13 Paterson, *Pietas Lond.* 281–3.
14 TNA, HO 129/4, 2/1/1 (f. 13).
15 S. Thurley, *The Lost Palace of Whitehall* (1998), 61.

of the privy gallery, abutting on King Street and the Holbein Gate on the west, and the privy garden on the south. It was begun in 1685 and first used at Christmas 1686, but seems to have been too 'Anglican' in its layout for the Italian queen, so alterations were immediately made by extending into the garden, possibly incorporating a Lady chapel and deeper chancel for liturgical reasons, and allowing a processional route from the royal pew, in a gallery, to the chancel for communion. It ceased to be used after the Revolution in 1688, and William and Mary had most of the fittings removed; the magnificent altarpiece designed by Wren and carved by Grinling Gibbons and Arnold Quellin was dismantled and most of it was given in 1706 to Westminster Abbey, where it remained until it went to the church of Burnham-on-Sea (Som.) in 1820. Four of its statues were placed in the garden of Westminster School. The organ built by Renatus Harris and its case carved by Gibbons were given by Mary II to St James's church, Piccadilly, in 1691. The chapel was destroyed in the fire at Whitehall in 1698.[1]

THE SAVOY CHAPEL

The hospital of the Savoy, built 1510–16 under the will of Henry VII, included a chapel to serve the inmates, situated at the north-west end of the hospital buildings behind the houses fronting the Strand. It was not orientated: a plan of 1736 shows the altar at the north-west end, a small vestry room on the east near the altar, and a belfry on the same side at the south-east end. On the east side lay a burial ground.[2] By the early 18th century there was confusion over the early dedication and history of the Savoy chapel; it was thought that it had originally been known as St John in the Strand and been a chapel royal for the king and other personages dwelling there.[3]

By 1564, after the demolition c.1548 of the nearby parish church of St Mary of Strand, many parishioners of Strand were using the Savoy chapel for worship, rather than St Martin-in-the-Fields or St Clement Danes. By 1574 the parishioners of St Mary's had a curate at the chapel to minister to them, and they were said to repaired the chapel in 1600, and had a new gallery built in 1618.[4] In 1650 the parishioners petitioned unsuccessfully for the chapel to become their parish church. They continued to use the Savoy chapel until the new church of St Mary was opened in the Strand in 1724.[5] Because of this the chapel, whose original dedication is unknown, was often called St Mary, as in 1736, and the burial ground was used for parishioners of St Mary's.[6]

The hospital also used the chapel, and paid for preaching and the reading of prayers. Dr Samuel Pratt was appointed as preacher of the hospital in 1698 by the master of the Savoy on the death of Dr Anthony Horneal, and preached regularly in the chapel on Sunday mornings or provided a substitute, receiving £20 a year out of the hospital's revenues. There was also a reader who assisted the preacher and received 20s. a year payable to Dr Pratt from the hospital for reading prayers, and another 20s. from Dr Pratt for assisting in preaching. Neither man resided within the hospital in 1700.[7] At the visitation in 1700 articles were presented against the hospital's clerk, Edmund Taylor, apparently by the parishioners of St Mary, on the grounds, amongst other failings, that for the last 4–8 years he had neglected to attend public preaching and services or lectures on Wednesdays and Fridays, had failed to notify the minister of burials and christenings, and had permitted others than the minister and curate of St Mary to celebrate marriages.[8] In 1703 Taylor brought a case against the churchwardens of St Mary, who had intruded a clerk of their own on the grounds that as the Savoy lay in their parish, they had the right to appoint the clerk.[9]

After the hospital was suppressed in 1702, the chapel continued to be used as the parish church of St Mary le Savoy, as the parish was then sometimes called, and was commonly called the Savoy church in 1714, when it was described as a strong and ancient building of stone, covered with lead, but somewhat dark and low. The altar was at the north end; it had a fine chancel, portraits of the 12 apostles, some painting on the glass windows, and several ancient monuments. Prayers were held twice a day, with extra on Wednesdays, Fridays and holy days. Communion was held twice on the first Sunday of the month and solemn feasts. There was a preparation sermon before the sacrament on the last Sunday in the month, maintained by a society of the vestry who provided a preacher in their several turns. There was a minister and a lecturer/curate.[10] In 1724 George I gave the German Reformed Congregation in the Savoy part of the former Master's house as a dwelling for their minister, while the rest of house was occupied by the Anglican minister of the Savoy chapel.[11]

In 1851 the incumbent commented that the chapel was consecrated to the Saviour, St Mary and St John Baptist, but was commonly known as the Royal Chapel of the Savoy. He also believed that it had formerly been the household chapel of the Savoy palace, belonging to the dukes of Lancaster, who had allowed its use by the parishioners of the Savoy and that it so continued although the property of sovereign as duchess [sic] of Lancaster. By then its income included endowment by warrant of the duchy (£100), pew rents (c.£50), and fees (c.£20). It seating for 80 (free), plus 100 (other), and average attendance was over 178 (a.m.) and c.68 (aft.).[12]

1 Thurley, *Whitehall Palace* (1999), 51–2.
2 *Hist. King's Works*, V, plate 49.
3 Paterson, *Pietas Lond.* 177–80.
4 Ibid.
5 Above, St Mary of Strand.

6 *Hist. King's Works*, V, plate 49.
7 Bodl., MS Rawl. B 377, ff. 29–30.   8 Ibid., ff. 67v.–73.
9 Ibid., ff. 7–18.   10 Paterson, *Pietas Lond.* 177–80.
11 *Hist. King's Works*, V. 361–2.
12 TNA, HO 129/13, 2/2 (f. 12).

In 1864 fire destroyed all the chapel except its walls, and it was rebuilt at the sole cost of the queen, with a window given in memory of Prince Albert. In 1866 it was known as the Chapel Royal, Savoy, with one service on Sundays. Although the benefice was by then a royal peculiar, the building was unconsecrated, and the clergy unlicensed. The queen paid all the expenses of the chapel and services.[1] In 1886 no attendance figures were recorded and the chapel was listed as closed, perhaps in error. In 1903, when it was recorded as the Chapel Royal, Savoy, attendance was 105 (a.m.), 36 (evg).

By the late 20th century little of the 16th-century building remained. The rebuilding to designs by Sir Robert Smirke in 1820–1 seems to have been more-or-less accurate, except for the south wall and bell turret. The chapel was aisleless, of five unbuttressed bays, and had three-light windows with cusped lights. Smirke's work replaced an ante-chapel that was part of the hospital's west range. Restored and refitted 1864–5 by Sydney Smirke after a fire which destroyed all but the walls, it was adapted by Malcolm Matts for the Royal Victorian Order in 1939–40. In 1957–8 low offices and a robing room designed by A.B. Knapp-Fisher were built round a vestry of 1877 by J.T. Perry.[2] In 1970 it was known as the Queen's Chapel of the Savoy, Chapel of the Royal Victorian Order, Savoy Hill, with the Queen as patron.[3]

Churchyard Formerly much used for the interment of soldiers, by 1895 it covered a quarter-acre and had been laid out as a public garden at the cost of Queen Victoria and others, and was well maintained by the parish of St Mary le Strand.[4]

SOMERSET HOUSE CHAPEL

In the 17th century Somerset House formed part of the queen consort's jointure, and in 1625 was granted for life to Queen Henrietta Maria. Until a chapel was built, a room there was fitted up for use by the queen. The foundation stone of the chapel was laid by the queen in 1632 on the site of the former tennis court and other buildings on the west side of the main house. It included a vestry and other rooms, and had a stair from the queen's chambers. A house for the Capuchin friars and other priests was provided by the queen on the south side of the chapel. The first high mass took place in 1636. In 1643 the friars were expelled and the chapel stripped of its fittings; it was used by French Protestants until 1660.[5] The Capuchins returned with Queen Henrietta Maria in 1660, and were there when she died in 1669. Possession of the house passed to Charles II's wife, Catherine of Braganza, who often resided there from the early 1670s, and the chapel was maintained as a Roman Catholic chapel for her use; she continued in possession of the house and chapel until her death in 1705.[6]

After Queen Catherine of Braganza died in 1705 it was unoccupied until Queen Anne granted it to the bishop of London. In 1714 it was an Anglican extra-parochial chapel for the use of the royal family and other inhabitants of Somerset House. Prayers were said twice daily, communion held on the 3rd Sunday of each month, and sermons every Sunday morning and on public feasts; the chapel was served by two of the bishop's chaplains. It lay on the west side of the house in the stableyard, built of brick covered with lead, and described in 1714 as very beautiful and spacious, curiously painted, and paved with free stone. It had three galleries, and an altar-piece of Moses and Aaron in marble, life size and set in niches, but without the Commandments on it as in other churches.[7] It was closed and demolished in 1775 when Somerset House was rebuilt.

ROMAN CATHOLICISM

Roman Catholics continued to practise their faith in Westminster during the reign of Elizabeth, despite proximity to the Protestant Court and national government. In Westminster presentments for non-attendance at the parish church in the 16th century were generally more numerous than elsewhere in Middlesex, often including clerks, and mainly Catholics rather than separatists. They were increasing by 1577, except among members of Chancery Inns where there were only three non-attenders, all at New Inn.[8] Mass was said at the house of John Pynchin in 1576;[9] the wife of a Westminster resident was indicted for housing a priest; and Ralph Collyer, clerk, was convicted several times for non-attendance and also for celebrating mass in St Clement Danes.[10] In 1581, and again in 1582, 22 residents were presented from Westminster, St Martin-in-the-Fields, St Clement Danes, and Knightsbridge, most designated as gentleman or esquire. Further presentments were made in the 1590s,[11] but the impression is of a controlled situation that did not cause much worry and was limited in number.

In the early 17th century the problem of recusancy

1 *Mackeson's Guide* (1866)
2 Pevsner, *London 6: Westm.* 297–8.
3 *London Diocese Bk* (1970).   4 LCC, *Burial Grounds*, 6.
5 Needham and Webster, *Somerset Ho.* 107, 109–10, 114, 123, 125; below, Foreign Chs (French Prot.).
6 Paterson, *Pietas Lond.* 260–1.   7 Ibid.

8 *Misc. XII* (Cath. Rec. Soc. 22), 107.
9 P. Hine, 'Cath. Worship in London', *London Recusant*, VI (1976), 67.
10 *Middx County Rec.* I. 127, 181; *Recusants in the Exchequer Pipe Rolls 1581–1592* (Cath. Rec. Soc. 71, 1986), 39.
11 *Middx County Rec.* I. 128–9, 250, 254.

grew as greater numbers of gentry came to Westminster to be near the court and there was more building to accommodate them. In 1610 the Crown and Privy Council responded by banning convicted recusants from entering Whitehall and St James's palaces when the king or the prince of Wales were in residence, unless they were commanded to attend.[1] In 1625 the king ordered the bishop of Durham to prevent English Catholics from attending mass at Durham House, where the French ambassador was staying, but without interfering with the French;[2] royal messengers were ordered to watch the entrance to the chapel and arrest English attenders as they left, but the result was a pitched battle in which the French became embroiled.[3] The situation worsened with the arrival from France in 1625 of the new queen, Henrietta Maria. Her household included many priests, accused of converting the Anglicans who often out of curiosity thronged the queen's oratory in Somerset House. The king expelled about 450 of the queen's retainers in 1626, but under an agreement negotiated by the French ambassador, she was permitted a household of *c.*50, including a bishop and 10 priests, who were Capuchin friars, a confessor, and 10 musicians for her chapel. The chapel at St James's, designed by Inigo Jones, was to be finished, and another built at Somerset House, both for her use.[4]

The friars at Somerset House remained the cause of much suspicion and distrust. After they had sheltered a priest, who escaped after being apprehended at Lady Shrewsbury's house, Piccadilly Hall, in 1631,[5] the sub-curate of St Margaret's complained to Archbishop Laud that two priests, under pretence of distributing alms from the friars in houses stricken by plague, were converting the inhabitants, who then attended mass in the friars' chapel.[6] The presence of foreign Catholics eventually created so much difficulty for Charles I that he had to send his mother-in-law, Marie de Medicis, and her train of 600 back to France in 1641.[7]

Justices sent to the Privy Council lists of recusants which included several knights and lawyers as well as servants of the king and queen.[8] Investigations into the number of recusants living in Westminster revealed many landowners from elsewhere lodging there, suspected of evading subsidy assessments in their own parish.[9] The situation was not helped by a number of highly-placed lay Catholics, principally the Talbots at Piccadilly Hall, and the earl and countess of Arundel. Although the earl publicly distanced himself from

Catholicism by taking the Anglican communion, his wife, Aletheia Talbot, attended mass with the queen at Somerset House. The establishment in 1633 of her own house at Tart Hall on the west side of St James's park seems to have been partly to enable her to entertain Catholic friends and priests and possibly to hold mass in a less ostentatious place; one of her most trusted servants was a priest.[10] Efforts to pin down Catholics increased. Parish officers were ordered to make lists, and to return to get the full names of all those of rank, including their wives, children, and servants, or send the stewards of such families to the justices if names were not forthcoming: *c.*73 in St Martin and *c.*46 in Covent Garden were listed.[11]

Under the Commonwealth the Capuchin friars were expelled, but Catholicism was by then less of a problem to the government as many of the leading aristocratic Catholics were Royalists and not in Westminster. At a mass held in a house in Long Acre the attenders arrested were mainly craftsmen plus Henry Parker, Lord Morley, and a couple of gentlemen.[12] With the Restoration, however, the difficulties that Catholicism presented at the heart of government returned. The dowager queen, Henrietta Maria settled at Somerset House with her Catholic household, and the new queen, Catherine of Braganza, wife of Charles II was also a Catholic. In 1662 the king ordered English Catholics not to attend the queens' chapels, though with doubtful effect.

From 1670 presentments for not attending the parish church increased in the climate of hysterical anti-Catholicism, which culminated in Titus Oates's plot in 1678 and the Exclusion Crisis. In 1676 the Privy Council found that English Catholics continued to attend the queen's chapel and the houses of ambassadors, who were allowing English-speaking priests to hold services. It enjoined messengers to arrest any English attenders at the masses. The order was repeated in 1678,[13] when recusants were ordered to leave the palace and London and Westminster. Established householders who took an oath and the queen's male servants could remain, but royal officials were expected to dismiss Catholic servants.[14] From 1678 large numbers of recusants were presented in all the Westminster parishes: in December the numbers in different presentments (possibly duplicating names) for not attending church for one month totalled 594 in St Martin, 184 in St Margaret, 128 in St Paul, 115 in St Clement Danes, and 39 in St Mary Savoy.[15]

1 *Middx County Rec.* II. 59.
2 *Acts of PC*, 1625–6, 347; above, Rel. Hist. Intro.: Influence of Central Govt.
3 Wheatley, 'Durham Ho.', 151–5.
4 Needham and Webster, *Somerset. Ho.* 99, 104.
5 *Cal. SP Dom.* 1631–3, 89.
6 Ibid. 1636–7, 109.
7 Howarth, *Lord Arundel*, 207.
8 *Cal. SP Dom.* 1628–9, 414.
9 *Acts of PC*, 1628–9, 369.
10 E.V. Chew, 'Female Art Patronage and Collecting in Seventeenth-Century Britain' (Univ. of N. Carolina Ph.D. thesis, 2000), chap. 3.
11 BL, Add. MS 38856, f. 38.
12 *Middx County Rec.* III. 199–200.
13 *Cal. SP Dom.* 1676–7, 349, 510; 1678 & Add., 556.
14 Ibid. 1678 & Add., 494, 507.
15 *Middx County Rec.* IV. 97–100.

With the accession of the openly Catholic James II, official toleration of the presence of priests increased, putting the government at odds with popular feeling. In 1687 the Jesuits were allowed to take up residence in part of the hospital buildings in the Savoy, and started a large school for boys there; Benedictines were allowed to occupy two small houses nearby. All were expelled in 1689 after the accession of William and Mary.[1]

In 1689 various proclamations tried to limit the perceived Catholic threat, with all non-resident Catholics lodging in London and Westminster being ordered to return to their homes.[2] Catherine of Braganza, now queen dowager, still, however, had possession of Somerset House, and priests were suspected of taking refuge there.[3] In 1706 some 148 Catholics were listed in St Clement Danes, 51 in Covent Garden, and 29 in Strand.[4]

During the 18th century, although popular antagonism still had to be considered, the government's anxiety over the political dangers of Catholicism decreased. Consequently, although the number of foreign Catholic envoys with well-established chapels in Westminster increased, English Catholics seem to have been able to attend without official molestation, and the chapels formed the nucleus of Catholic congregations, which, when penal laws against Catholics were modified, were able to establish English Catholic churches with parochial responsibilities by the end of the century. In Westminster in 1780 the parishes of St George and St James were said to have large numbers of Catholics as well as chapels and priests.[5] Some chapels were attacked during the Gordon Riots in 1780, but a change in public attitude was greatly helped by sympathy felt for the hundreds of French Catholics, especially priests and religious, who came to London to escape the Terror in France in the 1790s. At any one time in that decade there were thought to be c.1,500 French clergy in London, who stayed at first in 'emigrant' hotels around Leicester Square and Soho. Chapels were established to cater for the priests (who each had to say mass daily) and relieve pressure on embassy chapels: c.300 French priests crowded into the Bavarian chapel in Warwick Street. The first of the French chapels to open was *La Sainte Croix* in Dudley Court, Crown Street, Soho, in 1795. Though the exiles largely kept themselves apart, the clergy had some influence on the local Catholic residents; French chapels soon included a wider congregation, and Charles Adrien Langreney was among the first to minister to Catholics of an area later served by Westminster Cathedral. French priests also assisted in the existing English chapels in the 1790s, such as St Patrick, Soho Square, and at the Spanish and Bavarian chapels.[6]

In 1814 there were 49,000 Catholics in the area comprising the City of London, Westminster, Southwark, and the inner suburbs, of whom 8,000 were in Soho.[7] There were five foreign embassy or foreign-supported chapels in Westminster (Bavarian, Portuguese, Spanish, German, French) serving 9,300 Catholics, two English Catholic chapels (St Patrick, and St Mary, Romney Terrace) serving 8,500, and the earl of Shrewsbury's private chapel. The Sardinian chapel, Lincoln's Inn Fields, which lay in Duke Street just inside St Giles-in-the-Fields, served 7,000 Catholics who included those living in the eastern part of Westminster.[8]

After the restoration of the Roman Catholic hierarchy in 1850, Westminster was part of the archdiocese of Westminster under Cardinal Wiseman. Attendance at all masses on a Sunday in 1851 was estimated at over 9,000 at five churches, in Soho (2), Covent Garden, Mayfair, and Westminster.[9] Two more churches opened before the end of the 19th century, one at Victoria, the other in Soho for French Catholics. Attendances in 1886 totalled 5,025 (excluding Maiden Lane for which figures were not recorded), and 7,705 in 1903 including services held in the cathedral chapter house before the cathedral was in use. The long-awaited Westminster Cathedral was finally opened later in 1903: the site had been purchased as early as 1867 by Cardinal Manning. St Mary, Horseferry Road (Romney Terr.), closed when the cathedral opened, but two chapels of ease to the cathedral were added later, in Orchard Street and Horseferry Road, and a church to serve Pimlico opened in 1916. Some closures occurred by the end of the 20th century as population changed: St Ann c.1972, St Peter and St Edward in 1975. Although the resident English Catholic population had fallen by the end of the 20th century, the remaining churches also provided masses and support for the many foreign Catholics working or studying in Westminster and, particularly on holydays, were attended by English Catholics working in Westminster.

EMBASSY CHAPELS

Only some are noted here: ambassadors moved frequently, and had chapels fitted up wherever they lived; at least 5 addresses are known for the Spanish embassy, and 3 each for Portuguese, Neapolitan, and

1 Somerville, *Savoy*, 78–9; T.G. Holt, 'Sch. in the Savoy 1687–8', *TLMAS*, 41 (1990), 21–7.
2 HMC 29, *Portland*, II, 54.
3 *Cal. SP Dom.* 1689–90, 424.
4 Guildhall MS 9800/2, ff. 86, 98, 102.
5 Ibid. MS 9557, ff. 20, 25–6, 28–9, 33.
6 D.A. Bellenger, *The French Exiled Clergy* (1986), 67, 69, 72–3.　　　　7 *VCH Middx*, I. 142–3.
8 *London Recusant*, III(1), Jan. 1973, 14–15.
9 Below, accts of individual chs.

French embassies. Those that became Catholic parish churches are covered in that section.

Portuguese Embassy   In 1740 a house and back buildings no. 74 South Audley Street[1] were conveyed to Francis Salvador, merchant, acting for the kingdom of Portugal, to form the Portuguese embassy chapel. The ambassador paid rates there from 1747. Most of the back buildings were converted to form the chapel, replacing the embassy's previous one in Warwick Street behind Golden Square.[2] The square building over the basement fronted South Street, but was probably entered from a passage along the west side and connected to no. 74 by a narrow corridor from its south-east corner. The inventory of the chapel in 1757 suggests that there was a full set of fittings. It was in use by the Portuguese from 1747 to 1829; in 1814 it served 1,000 Catholics.[3] The new lessee pulled down the chapel in 1831 and replaced it with stables.

Venetian Embassy   The Venetian Resident in 1728 took a house in Suffolk Street (St James), where a Roman

Catholic chapel was fitted up;[4] registers for this chapel or its successors exist for 1744–96.[5]

The Venetian chapel, fronting the east side of Dean Street in 1746, was presumably the chapel of the Venetian ambassador who c.1744–7 lived at no. 31 Soho Square, which backed westwards onto Dean Street.[6]

Spanish Embassy   The chapel was built in 1749 behind no. 7 Soho Square (north side), which was occupied by the Spanish ambassador until 1761. It was later used successively by Baptists and French Protestants.[7]

Neapolitan Embassy   Located at Carlisle House, Soho Square, was occupied by an envoy of the King of Naples 1754–8, and buildings in Sutton Street (on the site of the present St Patrick's) were fitted up as a Roman Catholic chapel for the use of envoy and staff.[8]

Imperial Legation of Austria   The Austrians had a chapel in Charles Street (St James), from 1764 until they moved to Twickenham in 1784.[9]

WESTMINSTER CATHEDRAL

The metropolitan cathedral church of the Most Precious Blood of Jesus Christ, Ashley Place, Victoria Street, is one of the most significant landmarks in Westminster's skyline. The site for the cathedral in Carlisle Place was bought by Cardinal Manning in 1867–72, but exchanged by him in 1883 for part of the neighbouring site of the Middlesex House of Correction (Westminster Bridewell). The church was begun in 1895, the Chapter house, Ashley Place, being used for services until the fabric had been completed and the church opened and registered for worship in 1903.[10] Attendance in 1903 (at the chapter house) was 165 in the morning. The cathedral was consecrated in 1910, and was still in use in 2008.

John Francis Bentley was the architect chosen by Manning's successor.[11] Cardinal Vaughan favoured the Early Christian style, rejecting the Gothic of earlier unrealised schemes by H. Clutton and Baron Von Ferstel,[12] in order to escape comparison with Westminster Abbey, but Bentley persuaded him to adopt the Byzantine style, based mainly on published illustrations of Santa Sophia, Constantinople, and his visit to St Vitale at Ravenna and St Mark's Venice. Bentley was not reliant on those sources alone but fused the models they provided with Italian Renaissance ones; for

example the Byzantine plan form is elongated and given side chapels in the manner of church of the Gesu in Rome. It is a cross within a rectangle, its centre articulated by four huge domed bays flanked by vaulted passage aisles and side chapels, which combined space for a large congregation with areas for private devotion and excellent circulation (cf. Immaculate Conception, Farm St). The domes are of mass concrete in the Roman manner. The style was thought amenable to being finished over a long period and many of the elements, for example the single 285-ft high Italianate campanile and the west portal were not designed until after Bentley's death in 1902; the latter was designed by J.A. Marshall, but possibly to Bentley's designs. The bold banding of the red brick and Portland stone exterior is delicately modelled and enlivened by a variety of openings and domed towers. The interior was left unfinished longer and only the lower part is covered by marble as Bentley intended, with the rough brick higher up, left bare because of financial constraints, unintentionally contributing towards an impression of religious mystery: the chapels of Holy Souls, of St Gregory, and of St Augustine show what Bentley intended. The other side chapels, transepts and east end were decorated with

1 Para. based on *Survey of London*, XL. 309, 340.
2 Below, Our Lady of Assumption.
3 *London Recusant*, III(1), Jan. 1973, 14–15.
4 *Survey of London*, XX. 90.
5 In WCA.   6 *Survey of London*, XXXIII. 117, 131.
7 Ibid. 60; below, Prot Nonconf.; Foreign Chs.
8 *Survey of London*, XXXIII. 73–4.
9 WCA, cal. to regs.
10 ONS, Worship Reg. no. 39581.
11 Archit. acct follows Pevsner, *London 6: Westm.* 673–9; Rottmann, *London Cath. Chs*, 1–13.
12 *Architectural Hist.* 20 (1977), 63–4, plates 36–8.

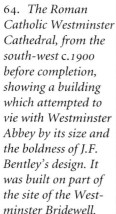

64. *The Roman Catholic Westminster Cathedral, from the south-west c.1900 before completion, showing a building which attempted to vie with Westminster Abbey by its size and the boldness of J.F. Bentley's design. It was built on part of the site of the Westminster Bridewell.*

65. *The Roman Catholic Westminster Cathedral. It was intended to cover the whole interior with marble and mosaic, Byzantine-style work still not completed in 2009, leaving some bare concrete vaults which have their own drama.*

murals, mosaic and carving by various hands, one of the most notable being Eric Gill, and work was continuing in 2008.

In 1979 the cathedral premises included the College of Cathedral Chaplains, Clergy House, 42 Francis Street; the Catholic Choir School, Ambrosden Avenue; the Catholic Central Library and Information Centre, St Francis Friary, 47 Francis Street; and attached were the Franciscan Friars of the Atonement; Franciscan Sisters of Our Lady of Victories, serving the Cathedral Clergy House; and the Sisters of Mercy, serving the Archbishop's house. The cathedral clergy also served the mass centre for Swiss at John Southworth Centre, no. 48 Great Peter Street.[1]

St Ann, (Abbey) Orchard Street, Victoria Street, opened in a former Catholic Apostolic church in 1923, as a chapel of ease to Westminster Cathedral; it also served as a chapel for Swiss Catholics in the 1960s.[2] It was a tiny stock brick chapel of the 1860s in Gothic style, on an

1 *Cath. Dir. 1979*, 32.   2 *Westm. Year Bk 1966*, 111.

irregular site and carefully planned with nave, one aisle, apsidal sanctuary.[1] It closed *c.*1972,[2] and was demolished.

Church of the Sacred Heart, no. 112a Horseferry Road (St John) A chapel of ease to Westminster Cathedral, probably using a former Methodist church, was regis- tered as Sacred Heart chapel in 1929.[3] Bombed in 1944, it was replaced by a building in Gothic style designed by Harry G. Clacy, in 1962, and registered in 1965 as the Church of the Sacred Heart and crypt chapel.[4] It remained a chapel of ease to the cathedral in 2008; the attached block on the NE side was the Institute and Convent of Perpetual Adoration, Arneway Street, in 1966, which held public masses under the direction of the convent chaplain, the Very Revd Mgr Bruce Kent;[5] in 1979, as the Corpus Domini convent, it housed the order of Religious of the Eucharist, and was still so called in 2003.[6]

PARISH CHURCHES AND CHAPELS

CORPUS CHRISTI, MAIDEN LANE, COVENT GARDEN

The church originated in a mission by Oratorians, who started schools in Charles Street, Drury Lane (St Giles-in-the-Fields), and in March 1849 opened their first church, the Oratory, in King William Street, Strand.[7] It seated 500–600, all free in 1851. Attendance was full at the 3 main services in the morning, afternoon, and evening. There were also five low masses in the morning, where attendance averaged 100–150 each.[8]

Corpus Christi's temporary chapel was registered in Charles Street in October 1874,[9] but was replaced a fortnight later by the newly-built Corpus Christi church, Maiden Lane,[10] designed by F.H. Pownall, who had to overcome difficulties caused by the restricted site, and sunken floor nearly 3 ft below street level. The yellow brick building in early French Gothic style was built in 1873–4, with a north (ritual west) tower with pyramid spire and adjoining presbytery. The dim interior was originally finished in red brick and the Caen stone altar was carved by Thomas Earp.[11] Attendance in 1903 was 496 in the morning and 69 in the afternoon. In 1926 workers at a neighbouring market formed a large part of the congregation, which was swelled by Catholic visitors from hotels in Strand and Aldwych. The freehold of the site, formerly part of the Bedford estate, was bought by Catholic diocesan authorities shortly before 1926,[12] and the church was consecrated In 1956.[13] It was still in use in 2008, as a parish church for the area from Covent Garden to St Giles.

HOLY APOSTLES, WINCHESTER STREET, PIMLICO

The church opened in 1917 in a former Wesleyan chapel, at no. 25 Claverton Street, Pimlico, as a chapel of ease to Westminster Cathedral serving the Pimlico area, and in 1926 had a large parish hall beneath the church, which was flanked by the presbytery, and convent of Franciscan Missionaries of Mary.[14] All was destroyed by enemy action in 1941; the congregation used temporary accommodation at the Catholic chapel at 33 Warwick Square in 1942,[15] and between 1945 and 1957 a prefabricated building on the site of the bombed church.[16] A new site in Winchester Street was obtained in 1948 by Fr (later Canon) Edmund Hadfield, parish priest of Pimlico until his death in 1982. A new brick-faced church was built in 1956–7, designed by his family firm of Hadfield, Cawkwell & Davidson in a modern idiom but with a conventional plan of nave, aisles and chancel, and campanile over the entrance. There was a large hall below the church.[17] In addition to being the parish church for Pimlico, the church also served the Maltese Catholic Centre, and the convent and hostel of the Maltese Franciscan Sisters in St George's Drive in 1979 and 2008. It was still in use in 2008.[18]

IMMACULATE CONCEPTION, FARM STREET, MAYFAIR

The Society of Jesus, who had a house in York Place by the 1840s, appealed to Rome for permission to form a mission in London and to build a church, which became the church of the Immaculate Conception.[19] The large

1 Pevsner, *London I* (1973 edn), 485; Rottmann, *London Cath. Chs*, 14.

2 ONS, Worship Reg. no. 49503.

3 Ibid. no. 51031.

4 Ibid. no. 69939.

5 *Westm. Yr Bk 1966*, 111.

6 *Cath. Dir. 1979*, 54; Pevsner, *London 6: Westm.* 683.

7 Rottmann, *London Cath. Chs*, 136–8.

8 TNA, HO 129/5, 1/1/9 (f. 9).

9 ONS, Worship Reg. no. 21985.   10 Ibid. no. 22001.

11 Pevsner, *London 6: Westm.* 298; Rottmann, *London Cath. Chs*, 136–8.

12 Rottmann, *London Cath. Chs*, 136.

13 *Cath. Dir. 1979*, 50.

14 Rottmann, *London Cath. Chs*, 13; ONS, Worship Reg. no. 46956.

15 ONS, Worship Reg. no. 60266.

16 Ibid. no. 61218.

17 Evinson, *Cath. Chs of London*, 54–5; ONS, Worship Reg. no. 66400; Pevsner, *London 6: Westm.* 768.

18 *Cath. Dir. 1979*, 53; inf. from church's website, www.holyapostlespimlico.org.

19 Evinson, *Cath. Chs of London*, 41.

66. *Immaculate Conception R.C. church, Farm Street, designed for the Jesuits by J.J. Scoles, opened in 1846, and enlarged several times subsequently. Shown here the richly decorated nave looking east towards the high altar by A.W.N. Pugin.*

and unorientated church, with an eight-bayed aisled nave, was designed by J.J. Scoles in a rich mixture of Decorated and Flamboyant styles, and provided by A.W.N. Pugin with an elaborate high altar dedicated to Monica Tempest, who paid for it and helped fund the building.[1] The church was first used in 1846, but had its formal opening in 1849. In 1851 it seated c.500, of which 100 were free, with c.50 standing,[2] but attendance was c.600 in the morning, though only c.200 in the afternoon. In 1858–9 Henry Clutton designed the 13th-century style Sacred Heart chapel to replace one destroyed by fire. The church was enlarged later with series of side chapels, sumptuously furnished and decorated by a number of prominent architects: Clutton added an outer aisle on the east side, divided into side chapels in 1878–9, and in 1898–1903 W.H. Romaine-Walker designed a western aisle of polygonal chapels divided by traceried internal buttresses.[3] Attendance in 1886 was 323 in the morning; in 1903 it was 1,048 in the

morning and 493 in the afternoon. From 1966 it was a parish church serving Mayfair. The church continued to be staffed by Jesuits in 2008.

In 1984 Jesuits also registered for worship at the Sodality chapel at no. 114 Mount Street, the headquarters and residence of the Jesuits' English Provincial in 2008.[4]

NOTRE DAME DE FRANCE (THE FRENCH CHURCH), LEICESTER PLACE

When Marist Fathers from France were asked to found a church for French Catholics in Westminster, Fr Charles Fauré raised funds in France and acquired the lease of Burford's panorama, built 1792–3, with entrance at no. 16 Leicester Square, and an adjoining house at no. 5 Leicester Place. A temporary chapel opened in 1865, and a school and orphanage in 1866. The building was registered in 1866,[5] blessed in 1868 and registered in 1875.[6] It had been converted by Louis-Auguste Boileau, a French architect expert in cast-iron construction, who built a cruciform church of that material within the circular shell of the panorama, using the remaining quadrants to accommodate galleries.[7] The work was supervised by the local A. Sauvée who designed the entrance porch in Leicester Place with living quarters, and the porch was enlarged when Nos 4 and 6 Leicester Place were acquired in 1903. Attendance in 1886 was 280 (a.m.) and 360 (p.m.), but by 1903 had risen to 842 (a.m.) and 284 (p.m.). The church was severely damaged in 1940, and rebuilt 1953–5 to designs by Hector Corfiato, which inside recalled French neoclassical architecture. He added an impressive front to Leicester Place, with fine narrow bricks sparingly dressed with stone, a relief of the Virgin by Georges Saupique, whose students at École de Beaux-Arts in Paris executed the sculptural decoration on the portals. The circular plan was retained for the interior, with twelve columns forming a narrow ambulatory, and plain square windows like coffers in the flat ceiling. Fine fittings, some given by the French government, included a modern Aubusson tapestry, wall paintings by Jean Cocteau, and a powerful organ by Cavaillé-Coll of Paris.[8] No. 16 Leicester Square and crypt were used as a club for young French men and women in London.[9] It was still run by Marist Fathers in 2008, when services were held on a Sundays and weekdays in French, with an Engish mass on holydays.

OUR LADY OF THE ASSUMPTION AND ST GREGORY

This church in Warwick Street (St James) originated as the Catholic chapel of the Portuguese envoy living at nos 23–4 Golden Square, from 1724; the earliest registers of

1 Eastlake, *Gothic Revival*, App. p. 73.
2 TNA, HO 129/3, 2/1/7 (f. 102).
3 Pevsner, *London 6: Westm.* 483–4; Rottmann, *London Cath. Chs*, 68–8.
4 ONS, Worship Reg. no. 76530; ch's website, www.farmstreet.org.uk.

5 ONS, Worship Reg. no. 22576.
6 Ibid. no. 17197.
7 Acct of building follows *Survey of London*, XXXIV. 482, 484–6; Pevsner, *London 6: Westm.* 392.
8 Rottmann, *London Cath. Chs*, 134–6.
9 *Cath. Dir. 1979*, p. 40.

mission date from 1735.[1] It stood behind houses in Golden Square and was entered from the house, but there was a public entry through a passage from Warwick Street. English Catholics apparently worshipped there unmolested, and continued under the Bavarian envoys, who occupied the house and chapel 1747–88. Though technically the priests serving the chapel were the envoy's chaplains, in practice they mainly ministered to neighbouring English Catholics, of whom in 1780 there were nearly 1,000 in St James's parish and many more in St Anne's: of 44 priests who served the chapel, only 3 had foreign names. The chapel was plundered by the Gordon rioters in 1780: the altarpiece, possibly by Andrea Casali, the organ, and pews were broken up, but the chapel was saved from burning by the arrival of the army. After the Bavarian envoys left, English Catholics obtained the 800-year lease: after an appeal for funds a new church was built 1789–90, designed by Joseph Bonomi, and dedicated to St Gregory the Great, but the chapel continued to be known as the Bavarian chapel for many years, and Electors of Bavaria paid annually towards its support until 1871; it was registered in 1858 as the Royal Bavarian chapel.[2]

The building was deliberately unobtrusive with a plain neo-classical front to Warwick Street; a cross, stars and angels were added in 1952 and 1957 when the brick was stained red.[3] The interior was originally a simple rectangle with a deep sloping gallery along both sides. In 1851 it seated 860, of which 120 were free (all were free for the evening), with 80 standing. Attendance was 800 in the morning (at 5 services) and 600 in the evening. Alterations to add considerable free space were considered in 1851,[4] and carried out in 1853 under the architect John Erlam. At that time the seats were rearranged, a new ceiling was constructed, and a new altarpiece in Italian Baroque style made, with a bas-relief of the Assumption carved by John Edward Carew over the altar. The relief was placed over the sacristy door when J.F. Bentley remodelled the east end. Plans to remodel the whole church in Byzantine style were drawn up in 1874–5 and, although J.F. Bentley made lavish plans, for structural reasons only the east apse was built, and decorated in Veneto-Byzantine style. Bentley's scheme included a Lady chapel on the south side of the chancel, and shortening the side galleries, probably because attendance was dropping (in 1886 120 in the morning and 458 in the afternoon; in 1903 it was 665 in the morning and 141 in the afternoon). In 1900 Bentley produced a new decorative scheme, which was carried out after his death in 1902; the apse mosaic of 1910 by

Geo. Bridge and Geo. Daniels was based on Bentley's designs. Internal embellishments have continued until *c.*1960, with an early 19th-century altar brought from Foxcote House, Ilmington (Warw.) in 1958, and new furnishings designed by Douglas Purnell. The organ in the west gallery was built in the 1790s, and subsequently rebuilt several times.

The church was re-registered in 1919 as the Church of Our Lady of the Assumption, and as Church of Our Lady of the Assumption and St Gregory in 1928,[5] the year of consecration.[6] In 1979 the chapel included a chaplaincy to hotel workers at no. 24 Golden Square.[7] It was still in use as a parish church in 2008.

ST PATRICK, SOHO SQUARE

In 1791 Catholics established a chapel in the neighbourhood of St Giles-in-the-Fields to serve the large population of poor Irish: using subscriptions they purchased the lease of the two-storeyed assembly rooms behind Carlisle House, removing the upper floor and consecrating the rest as a Roman Catholic chapel dedicated to St Patrick.[8] In 1851 it seated 960, of which 460 were free, with 50 standing; attendance was 3,000 in the morning (with 3 services), 500 in the afternoon, and 1,000 in the evening. A senior priest estimated its parish at *c.*10,000, with baptisms averaging over 300 a year.[9] In 1866 church trustees bought the freehold of the two houses which had been built in 1791–3 to replace Carlisle House: one was used as a presbytery in 1868–91. The chapel and presbytery were demolished in 1891, and St Patrick's schools, Great Chapel Street, Soho, were used for services 1890–3.[10] A new church opened in 1893,[11] and was consecrated in 1900.[12] It was designed by John Kelly of Leeds in Italianate style, faced with red brick with Portland stone dressings, and has a campanile to the square.[13] The impressive Italianate interior, with clerestory, shallow side chapels instead of aisles, a broad barrel vault, apse and domed side chapel, is approached through the tower and ante-chapel. Attendance in 1886 was 732 (a.m.) and 1092 (p.m.), and in 1903 was 1,129 (a.m.) and 322 (p.m.). The church was still in use as a parish church in 2008, and contained furnishings which were rare survivals of 18th-century Roman Catholic worship in Westminster.

OTHER ROMAN CATHOLIC CHAPELS

St Edward's Chapel, no. 1 Earl Street, Westminster It was registered in 1906 but had closed by 1925.[14] In 1913 St Edward's convent, no. 6 Earl Street, was served from Westminster Cathedral.

1 Rottmann, *London Cath. Chs*, 65–6.
2 ONS, Worship Reg. no. 8524.
3 Architectural acct follows *Survey of London*, XXXIII, 79–80; Pevsner, *London 6: Westm.* 393–4.
4 TNA, HO 129/6, 3/1/4 (f. 13).
5 ONS, Worship Reg. nos 47581, 51409.
6 *Cath. Dir.* 1979, 56.   7 Ibid. 60.

8 *Survey of London*, XXXIII. 79–80.
9 TNA, HO 129/13, 1/1/7 (f. 14).
10 ONS, Worship Reg. no. 32368.
11 Ibid. no. 33721.
12 *Cath. Dir.* 1979, 56.
13 Pevsner, *London 6: Westm.* 393–4.
14 ONS, Worship Reg. no. 42179.

St Mary's, Romney Terrace, Horseferry Road Masses were said at this chapel in Horseferry Road (St John's) by 1813. The chapel served a congregation of 500 in 1814,[1] although the date of the building was later given as 1815.[2] It was formally registered for worship in 1856.[3] Attendance in 1851 was 500 (a.m.), 50 (aft.), 400 (p.m.); in 1886 it was 377 (a.m.) and 651 (p.m.); and in 1903 it was 848 (a.m.) and 252 (p.m.). It served as the parish church for the Westminster area, served by Jesuits, until it closed in 1903 and was replaced by the Lady chapel of Westminster Cathedral as a temporary parish church; the altar from St Mary's was used in the cathedral crypt.[4] A new chapel of ease for the cathedral to serve the area was opened in Horseferry Road in 1929.[5]

St Peter and St Edward, no. 43 Palace Street, Victoria (St Margaret) A mission by Oblates of St Charles started in 1856 in a single-storeyed building fitted up as a chapel, built alongside William (later Wilfred) Street. The building was formerly the Albert hall, no. 99 York Street, Westminster, which was registered in 1857–8 for Roman Catholics,[6] and it may have been used by this mission while a new church was built above the mission chapel, which was then used as a school. St Edward's church (later St Peter and St Edward), on Palace Street, was registered in 1858.[7] The church was designed by W.W. Wardell, in a very plain round-arched style in yellow and red brick. It style and simple rectangular plan were dictated apparently by its location over the school. In contrast the fittings were quite rich, and included a high altar and side altar of 1867 and 1863 by Bentley,

and figures of St Peter and St Edward in canopied niches, thought to be by Phyffers. Palace Street was extended *c.*1879 through to Victoria Street close to the west end of the church, and a presbytery designed by J.F. Bentley was built in 1880–3 facing Palace Street, through which the church was entered thereafter.[8] Attendance in 1886 was 312 (a.m.) and 320 (p.m.), but had risen in 1903 to 717 (a.m.) and 234 (p.m.). Church was also known as the Guards' Catholic chapel: it was attended by soldiers from nearby barracks, and the staff included a Catholic chaplain to the Guards. Cardinal Henry Manning, archbishop of Westminster 1865–92, frequently said mass in this church, the nearest to his residence in Carlisle Place. The church ceased to be a parish church in 1913, when it was surrendered by the Oblates of St Charles to the Catholic authorities and became a chapel of ease to the cathedral.[9] It closed in 1975, and the building was converted to offices in 1990.[10]

UKRAINIAN GREEK CATHOLIC CHURCH

The Ukrainian Greek Catholic Church, which uses the Byzantine rite but acknowledges the spiritual and jurisdictional authority of the Pope of Rome, acquired the former Congregational chapel in Duke Street, Mayfair, in 1967, and opened it in 1968 as the Catholic Cathedral of the Holy Family in Exile. The ancillary buildings in Binney Street became the residence of the Apostolic Exarch for Ukrainian Catholics in Great Britain. Services for the congregation of about 1,000 were temporarily moved to Farm Street Roman Catholic church from August 2007, after the cathedral ceiling collapsed.[11]

PROTESTANT NONCONFORMITY

After the Act of Uniformity, in 1662, Westminster offered nonconformists the possibility of large congregations and the anonymity of a numerous and fluctuating population, but also the danger of proximity to the government, which required authorities to set an example in its neighbourhood. Several Presbyterians and Independents ejected from the universities came to London and preached in Westminster, and one in particular, Thomas Cawton, together with two ejected incumbents in Westminster, Gabriel Sangar, formerly vicar of St Martin-in-the-Fields, and Dr Thomas Manton, formerly rector of St Paul's, Covent Garden,

continued their Presbyterian ministries and formed the core of nonconformist teaching in Westminster.[12] In addition, the Society of Friends had been active from the 1650s despite harassment, meeting in New Palace Yard at the heart of Parliament, before moving to the quieter surroundings of Pall Mall.

Informers regularly told the government of meetings which may have been religious or seditious in character: 14 to 16 Fifth Monarchy men were said to meet two or three times a week at the Maiden Head tavern in Piccadilly in 1661, and Dr Holmes and George Cockaine held weekly meetings in an alehouse in Ivy Lane.[13] In

1 *London Recusant*, VI. 63–8; III. 14–15.
2 TNA, HO 129/4, 1/1/8 (f. 11).
3 ONS, Worship Reg. no. 7580.
4 J. Browne and T. Dean, *Building of Faith: Westm. Cathedral* (1995), 121; ONS, Worship Reg. no. 39681.
5 Above, Ch of Sacred Heart.
6 ONS, Worship Reg. no. 7912.
7 Ibid. no. 8431.

8 Pevsner, *London 6: Westm.* 712; Rottmann, *London Cath. Chs*, 15.
9 Rottmann, *London Cath. Chs*, 15.
10 Pevsner, *London 6: Westm.* 712.
11 Inf. from Independent Catholic News (accessed 17 Sep. 2007).
12 *Calamy Revised*, 35, 68, 106, 338, 427; below, Presbs.
13 *Cal. SP Dom.* 1660–1, 506; 1661–2, 128.

1664 Cockaine, by then a Fifth Monarchy man, preached at the house of a former justice in Covent Garden to a congregation said to number 200, including three countesses and others of rank.[1] The growth of building in Westminster also provided a variety of houses in which to meet, some becoming so regularly known that they acquired the name of the occupant: in the 1680s Mrs Meggs's house in Bridges Street, Covent Garden, became known as Meggs meeting house, and Stephen Lobb's house, in or near Swallow Street, was referred to as Lobb's meeting house.[2]

Before the introduction of licensing in 1672, Cawton, Manton, and Sangar were all presented at quarter sessions in 1669 for living in Westminster in contravention of the Five Mile Act,[3] and a conventicle held at the house of Richard Beach in St Margaret's was presented in 1670, attended by c.40 from a wide area: Southwark, Wapping, Shoreditch, and Kensington.[4] In the 1670s Richard Baxter was prevented from preaching in his chapels in Oxendon Street and Swallow Street, although substitute preachers had no such difficulty.

In 1682–3 the Tory campaign against dissenters led to an increasing number of convictions by the Westminster and Middlesex justices, with heavy fines (£20 for a first conviction, then £40) levied on those who allowed their houses to be used, as well as on the preachers. Between July 1682 and February 1683 £1,820 in fines were imposed at quarter sessions on the holders and preachers of conventicles in Westminster: of that, £340 was imposed on Mrs Meggs for the house with £180 on preachers there, and £320 on Gilbert Holles, earl of Clare, for allowing the Old Playhouse in Vere Street, St Clement Danes, to be used.[5]

Despite some harassment and heavy fines at certain periods, however, the persecution was far less severe in Westminster than east of London, in Tower Hamlets, where not only were meetings broken up with troops, but punishment for attenders at conventicles included transportation.[6] Undoubtedly the presence in Westminster of influential aristocrats living among the nonconformist meetings, and the necessity of not antagonising highly-placed individuals and justices who showed tolerance towards nonconformists, tempered the persecution, as did the need to avoid having running battles near their houses. The Society of Friends were able to have a meeting house on property of the dean and chapter of Westminster in Little Almonry from c.1666, and held the lease directly from the chapter from 1688; they had another meeting house actually on Crown property in the Savoy for many years. Proximity to government was later thought to have been important in

getting support for the cause of religious liberty amongst those in power: the Presbyterian chapel in Princes Street, St Margaret's, attracted a numerous and wealthy congregation including those with a high social position, and Dr Edmund Calamy, minister there 1703–32, became leader of the dissenting interest for many years.[7]

In the 1690s other sects joined the Presbyterians and Friends: Baptists in 1691, Philadelphians in 1697, Independents in 1709. Dissenters whose affiliation was unknown met in 1691 at the New chapel in Charles Street, Long Acre, with Dr Daniel Rolls as preacher; at the house of Robert Hopkins, their preacher, in Chandos Street, Covent Garden; at Hart Street, St Paul's, with John Reeson as preacher; and in St Clement Danes with Henry Slade, preacher.[8] English Presbyterian congregations virtually disappeared in the early 18th century, and their remnants either joined or were taken over by the emerging churches of Scottish Presbyterians, who were settling in Westminster. A number of foreign Protestant churches were also significant in Westminster, and are treated separately.[9]

In 1780 the local incumbents recorded Methodists in all parishes except St Martin and St Clement Danes, but only St Anne and St James had meeting houses, probably both for Primitive Methodists. In St Anne, St Mary le Strand, and St Paul, dissenters were said to be decreasing. St Anne had Methodist and Baptist meetings, St Martin had Independents, Baptists, and Friends; St James had two dissenting meetings and one Methodist, and St Paul had no meeting houses. The reliability of the incumbents was dubious however: St Clement's rector noted 'a notorious socinian conventicle' in Essex Street (Unitarians from 1774), but omitted mention of the Independents in New Court. The survey did not include St Margaret's parish, which did not come within the jurisdiction of the bishop of London.[10]

Though meetings of the New Dissent were being held in Westminster by the mid 18th century, the establishment of meeting houses occurred rather later. Unitarians built their own chapel in 1777; Primitive Methodists seem to have held meetings from c.1746 and in the 1770s, and though they were probably the group who had a meeting house in St Anne in 1780, the location is uncertain. Wesleyan Methodists met above a slaughter-house in St George in 1791, and moved to a chapel in 1801. Other sects registering meeting places included Swedenborgians in 1799; Arminian Bible Christians in 1823; Latter-Day Saints in 1849; Brethren in 1854; the Catholic Apostolic Church in 1855; Spiritualists in 1867; and the Salvation Army in 1882. The 19th century also saw an increase in the number of

---

1 *Cal. SP Dom.* 1663–4, 678.
2 *Middx County Rec.* IV. 166, 170, 173, 180, 194; *Cal. SP Dom.* 1682, 521.
3 *Middx County Rec.* IV. 15.
4 Ibid. 18.
5 Ibid., passim.

6 Beck and Ball, *London Friends' Meetings*, 241; *Middx County Rec.* III–IV, passim.
7 Wilson, *Dissenting Chs*, IV. 57–9.
8 *Middx County Rec. Sess. Bks 1689–1709*, 43.
9 Below.
10 Guildhall MS 9557.

congregations of the major sects, particularly in areas such as Pimlico settled by lower middle-class tradesmen.[1]

In 1903 protestant nonconformist attendance amounted to 24 per cent of all church attendance surveyed.[2] A few new sects appeared in the 20th century: Christian Scientists in 1910; Seventh-day Adventists in 1953; Bible-Pattern Church in 1976; Emmanuel Evangelical Church in 1997. Despite the new sects, however, the overall trend was one of decline as members moved out of the central area to the new suburbs. In 2008 only the following were still open: Society of Friends, St Martin's Lane; Westminster Chapel and Orange Street (Congregationalists); Methodist Central Hall, Westminster; Westminster Baptist

chapel, Horseferry Road; Salvation Army, no. 275 Oxford Street, and Rochester Row; Christian Scientists, Curzon Street; Emmanuel Evangelical Church, Marsham Street.

Accounts of the most long-lived or numerous individual sects are given below in alphabetical order, followed by other congregations, also listed alphabetically, and undenominational meetings. The sects with the greatest number of meetings listed – Baptists, Congregationalists, Methodists, and Presbyterians – are grouped in four geographic categories: Eastern Westminster (covering Covent Garden, Strand, St Clement Danes); Northern (Soho, St James, Mayfair); Southern (St Margaret and St John); and Western (Belgravia, Pimlico, Knightsbridge).

BAPTISTS

Eastern Westminster

Members of five General Baptist societies in the City of London, led by John Turner from White's Alley, formed a new society in 1691 in Covent Garden nearer their residences.[3] They met at the Two Golden Balls, in Hart Street at the upper end of Bow Street; the society was constituted in 1692. John Piggott was asked to be minister and was teaching in 1692 at a house called the Two Blue Balls, perhaps the same place.[4] The union with the City congregations dissolved in 1693 over doctrinal differences but in 1694 Piggott's congregation registered a newly-erected house in nearby St John's Court, off Great Hart Street. In 1699 it again registered the house formerly known as the Two Golden Balls, and in 1714 used a large back room there belonging to Edward Hewetson. Piggott may have left c.1700, but the congregation continued until 1738 when it broke up; most members joined White's Alley.[5] In 1828 Baptists registered a building in Hart Street opposite the rear of Covent Garden theatre.[6]

Independent Baptists registered the ground floor of the dwelling of James Trinder, a member of the congregation at no. 61 St Clement's Lane (St Clement Danes), in 1810.[7]

Particular Baptists registered a room at no. 8 Plum Court, Carey St (St Clement Danes), in 1818.[8] The same congregation registered a room in 1820 at no. 3 Ship Place by Temple Bar (St Clement Danes), belonging to

Thomas Oldfield, a member of the congregation, and a meeting house built by another member, William House, at the back of St Clement's Lane in Clare Market in 1822.[9] William House continued at Enon chapel, St Clement's Lane, until 1835.[10]

Baptists under the minister Henry Webb registered a building fitted up as a chapel in Helmet Court (St Mary le Strand), in 1827.[11]

Baptists from Little Wild Street chapel (St Giles-in-the-Fields) used the Olympic theatre, Wych Street (St Clement Danes) in 1902–6.[12]

Northern Westminster

Congregationalists and Baptists registered a large upper room over market house in Newport Market, St Anne, in 1713, with Joseph Harrington as minister.[13] It was used by various religious groups; those paying rates on the room and using it as a meeting house 1730–3 were probably Baptists, as were possibly Thomas Barnett 1734–6, and Mr Palmer 1737.[14]

Thomas Ely (or Eley) and Particular Baptists from Little Wild Street (St Giles-in-the-Fields) went to Glasshouse Yard or Street, Swallow Street, near Piccadilly in 1715.[15] They then moved in 1743 to a new chapel built by their minister William Anderson, in Grafton Street, backing onto the slaughter-house of Newport Market. Elizabeth Seward, by will proved 1754, left £100 of stock, the income from which was to be used for the relief of the poor of Anderson's congregation.[16] Anderson was

1 Based on accts of individual sects.
2 Mudie-Smith, *Rel. Life*, 108.
3 Acct based on Wilson, *Dissenting Chs*, IV. 11–13; W.T. Whitley, *Baptists of London* [1928], 121.
4 *Middx County Rec. Sess. Bks 1689–1709*, 82.
5 Guildhall MS 9579/2.
6 Ibid. MS 9580/6, p. 185.
7 Ibid. /3.
8 Ibid. /4.

9 Ibid. /5.   10 Whitley, *Baptists of London*, 150.
11 Guildhall MS 9580/6, pp. 169–70.
12 ONS, Worship Reg. no. 39282.
13 Guildhall MS 9579/2.
14 *Survey of London*, XXXIV. 370; Wilson, *Dissenting Chs*, IV. 23–4; Whitley, *Baptists of London*, 127.
15 Para. based on Wilson, *Dissenting Chs*, IV. 24–5, 39–40; *Survey of London*, XXXIV. 373–4.
16 *Endowed Chars London*, V. 13.

driven away by dissensions and went to Dudley Court, Hog Lane (q.v.),[1] and the congregation moved to a new chapel in Keppel St, Bloomsbury, *c.*1795. The Grafton Street chapel was leased to the congregation from Edward Street, Soho (q.v.) 1795–1813, and the congregation under William Williams in 1823–47. The chapel was used intermittently after 1849, but was bought and demolished by MBW between 1879 and 1883.

The Particular Baptists who left Grafton Street in 1774 over the new minister met for 2–3 yrs in an auction room in Berwick St, Soho, until they began building a chapel in James Street in the Adelphi (St Martin), *c.*1777. They chose John Sandys as minister in 1781–2; the congregation declined after his departure, and disbanded in 1789. The chapel was sold to Calvinist Methodists (below).[2]

There was a house occupied by Thomas Sanders at 6 Grafton Street that was registered for Baptists, mostly from the Seven Dials area, in 1814.[3]

Salem Chapel   Particular Baptists gathered by Richard Burnham (d. 1810) converted a large room in Edward Street, Soho, *c.*1785 and called it the Elim chapel. It was registered for Baptists in 1791 under Burnham.[4] Minister and congregation moved to the Grafton Street chapel in 1795; the church was very popular among poor inhabitants. The chapel was described in the early 19th century as being square with three galleries.[5] John Stevens (d. 1847) was the minister from 1811. The congregation moved to York Street, St James, in 1813. Reorganized in 1823, and Salem chapel, Meard's Court, built for Stevens in 1823 on a site leased from the Crown for 70 years at the rear of numbers 8 and 10 Meard St, Soho, was registered in 1824 for Particular Baptists.[6] The congregation purchased the lease and chapel from Stevens in 1834 for £3,950 and the chapel was conveyed to trustees for Baptists.[7] The chapel was said to seat 1000 in 1848, including galleries, but in 1851 seating was given as *c.*120 free and *c.*300 other, of which *c.*200 sittings were not let.[8] Attendance in 1851 was *c.*500. J.E. Bloomfield was the minister 1852–67, and also preached in the large room in Exeter Hall, Strand, from 1852.[9] The chapel was sold in 1878, but was later used as the Bloomsbury Baptist Chapel mission hall, registered in 1886; attendance in 1886 was 236 (a.m.) and 463 (p.m.); in 1903 it was 257 (p.m.). It closed in 1907 and the building became a garage.[10]

A former member of Burnham's congregation, John P. Bateman (d. 1806), formed new society of Particular Baptists at Edward Street in 1805, succeeded by William Willmott.[11] After a split the majority formed a congregation at Brewer Street in 1810–21, but disappeared in 1823, possibly joining the congregation at Meard's Court. Others remained in Edward Street, where T. Simmonds brought a group from Great Castle Street in 1811 (below, Soho chapel). The chapel was used by French Protestants in 1836.[12]

Piccadilly   A large auction room on the north side of Piccadilly was converted into a place of worship *c.*1783 by Baptists, said to be mostly Calvinists who left their own congregations because pastors were not sufficiently instructed for their point of view. They formed a society and Joseph Gwennap was invited to be pastor. He was very popular at first, but he was deserted by his congregation when he began putting into practice the theory of Martin Madan, and the church was dissolved *c.*1798.[13] A public hall built at the back of no. 22 Piccadilly may have been this chapel.[14]

Soho Baptist Chapel   Particular Baptists from Edward Street met in 1790 in Lincoln's Inn Fields, 1794 at Chapel Street, Soho, and by 1798 merged with a congregation from Great Castle Street (St Marylebone).[15] By 1811 they met in Edward Street under T. Simmonds. Reorganized 1818 at Soho chapel. In 1818 Particular Baptists registered a building formerly used as school rooms for the Soho Classical School. The building formed the back part of no. 8 Soho Square,[16] with an entrance at nos 406–7 Oxford Street, and is thought to have been the former chapel of the Spanish ambassador who occupied no. 7. In 1835 the congregation obtained an 80-year lease of the site and right of way through the passage from Oxford Street, and rebuilt the chapel.[17] In 1851 it seated 550, of which 70 were free seats.[18] Attendance in 1851 was 460 in the morning and 500 in the evening. The congregation moved to Shaftesbury Avenue (St Giles-in-the-Fields) in 1857.

Baptists registered an apartment in the possession of their minister William Foxwell, at no. 9 St Ann's Court, Soho, in 1803.[19] Members of this congregation were among those who registered a room in the possession of Richard Kidwell in Ham Yard, Great Windmill Street (St James), in 1798.[20] Kidwell was among those who registered 2 rooms belonging to James Padget in Green Street (St Geo.), in 1792, with William Ganise as minister.[21]

1 Wilson, *Dissenting Chs*, IV. 37.
2 Wilson, *Dissenting Chs*, IV, 16–17.
3 Guildhall MS 9580/4.
4 Ibid. /1, p. 6.
5 Wilson, *Dissenting Chs*, IV. 24–5.
6 Guildhall MS 9580/5.   7 TNA, C 54/11057, no. 7.
8 TNA, HO 129/13, 1/1/5 (f. 6).
9 Guildhall MS 9580/9, p. 124; ONS, Worship Reg. no. 6301.
10 ONS, Worship Reg. no. 29506; *Survey of London*, XXXIII. 241.   11 Wilson, *Dissenting Chs*, IV. 30.

12 *Survey of London*, XXXI. 223.
13 Wilson, *Dissenting Chs*, IV. 51; Whitley, *Baptists of London*, 135.   14 *Survey of London*, XXXI. 62.
15 Based on Whitley, *Baptists of London*, 134; *Survey of London*, XXXIII. 60.
16 Guildhall MS 9580/5.
17 TNA, C 54/11430, no. 2; ONS, Worship Reg. no. 6583.
18 TNA, HO 129/13, 1/1/6 (f. 3).
19 Guildhall MS 9580/2, p. 108.
20 Ibid., p. 14.   21 Ibid. /1, p. 32.

Premises in the possession of William Foxwell, no. 50 Rupert Street (St James), were registered in 1814, with Jonathan Cossington as minister.[1]

No. 40 Brewer Street (St James), was registered in 1808 by Baptists under the minister Joseph Lakin, and worshippers possibly included those who split from Edward Street in 1810. It continued until 1821.[2]

Baptists registered the house of Richard Unite, at no. 7 Lisle Street (St Anne), in 1821, and the same congregation registered the house of William Forster, at no. 41 Lisle Street, later the same year, and a room in the house of William Clark, Maiden Lane, Covent Garden, in 1822.[3]

Baptists registered no. 15 Queen Street, Oxford Street (St George) in 1844.[4]

Western Westminster

Baptists in Knightsbridge under their minister, John Chesney, registered a room in 1802.[5]

Carmel Chapel, Westbourne Street, Pimlico (St George) It was built in 1825 and registered in 1826 for Particular Baptists under the minister Robert Upton.[6] The chapel was enlarged and church rooms were built in 1844. It seated 440 in 1851 of which 70 were free and 60 were standing. John Stenson was minister.[7] Attendance in 1851 was 223 in the morning, 112 in the afternoon and 270 in the evening. In 1886 there were 71 in the congregation in the morning and 109 in the afternoon, while in 1903 there were 48 in the morning and 56 in the afternoon. It was registered again for Baptists in 1887,[8] and described as Strict Baptist in 1913.[9] It closed 1919, when

the proceeds were divided between various Strict Baptist societies.[10]

The Old Baptist Union had a mission room at no. 57 Winchester Street (Pimlico) from 1894, served by various pastors; attendance in 1903 was 6 (a.m.) and 12 (p.m.). It closed in 1913.[11]

Southern Westminster

Westminster Baptist Church, Horseferry Rd (St John) Seceders from the congregation using Grafton Street chapel formed a society at Panton Street in 1807, moving to Lewisham Street. Under Christopher Woollacott, Baptists purchased the site and built Romney Street chapel, near Marsham Street (St John), in 1828.[12] It closed in 1865, but was reopened in the same year by C.H. Spurgeon.[13] It seated 600 in 1928. Attendance in 1886 was 202 in the morning and 225 in the afternoon; in 1903 it was 138 in the morning and 148 in the afternoon. A new chapel designed by Spalding & Myers was built in 1934-5 on the north side of Horseferry Road, and was registered in 1936 as the Westminster Baptist church, Horseferry Road.[14] The chapel seated 350 in 1965,[15] and was still in use in 2008.

Rehoboth Chapel, Prince's Row, Buckingham Palace Road (St George).[16] A Strict Baptist congregation formed in Rochester Row in 1846 and moved to Great Smith Street in 1847. Rehoboth chapel, which was built c.1851, seating c.150,[17] was registered in 1851.[18] Attendance in 1851 was 66 in the morning, 19 in the afternoon and 90 in the evening. It closed c.1866, but was reconstituted in 1871. Attendance in 1886 was 80 in the morning and 103 in the afternoon. It was closed by 1894.

CONGREGATIONALISTS (INDEPENDENTS)

Eastern Westminster

Richard Stretton was fined in 1682 for preaching in St Clement Danes. His son, Richard junior, was a minister to the Independents at a meeting-house in York Buildings located on the Strand in 1688.[19] By 1727 John Bond was a minister there with 2 assistants. He died in 1740 but the church was probably already dissolved, as it was not mentioned in the list of congregations in 1738.[20]

Independents registered the house of Peter Cuff, Newcastle Court (St Clement Danes), in 1709.[21]

Independents, all with French names, registered the house of Peter Joubert, Rose Street, Long Acre, in 1717.[22]

New Court, Carey Street, Lincoln's Inn Fields (St Clement Danes) Presbyterians at New Court became Independents under Thomas Bradbury (minister 1728-59): the chapel's debts were paid off and a full congregation worshipped there during his time. In 1810 the chapel was described as a good square brick building of a moderate size with three galleries; its obscure situation, with access by a narrow passage from Carey Street,[23] was

1 Ibid. /4.
2 Ibid. /3; Whitley, *Baptists of London*, 142.
3 Guildhall MS 9580/5.
4 Ibid. /8, p. 205.
5 Ibid. /2, p. 84.
6 Ibid. /6, p. 84.
7 TNA, HO 129/3, 3/1/12 (f. 114).
8 ONS, Worship Reg. no. 29881.
9 Harris and Bryant, *Chs and London*, 426.
10 Whitley, *Baptists of London*, 154.
11 Ibid. 243.　12 TNA, C 54/11446, no. 1.
13 Whitley, *Baptists of London*, 146.
14 ONS, Reg. of marr. certs. no. 2967; Worship Reg. no. 56758; foundation tablet.
15 *Baptist Handbk 1966*, 159.
16 Based on Whitley, *Baptists of London*, 171.
17 TNA, HO 129/3, 3/1/11 (f. 113).
18 Guildhall MS 9580/9, p. 102.
19 *Calamy Revised*, 467.
20 Wilson, *Dissenting Chs*, IV. 18-19.
21 Guildhall MS 9579/2.
22 Ibid.　23 Guildhall MS 2012.

67. *Westminster Baptist Church, Horseferry Road, a plain building of 1935 for a fairly impoverished area.*

necessary when it was built because of the persecution the Independents faced, but had by then become a drawback.[1] It was registered in 1837 by 5 trustees, and there was a Sunday school at number 3 New Court, which was registered in 1838.[2] In 1851 the chapel seated 440 free and 440 other; the attendance consisted of 178 plus 91 scholars in the morning, 147 scholars in the afternoon and 234 in the evening, though many regulars were said to be absent.[3] The chapel and adjoining school closed in 1866,[4] and were demolished to make way for the Law Courts. The congregation met in Whitefield Chapel, Long Acre, and at the hall in Red Lion Square, before moving to a new chapel in Tollington Park (Islington) in 1871.[5]

Independents also registered a house in White Hart Court, Castle Street (St Martin) in 1802;[6] a house at no. 21 Maiden Lane, Covent Garden, in 1804;[7] Isaac

Tapper's house, no. 23 James Street, Covent Garden, 1808, with John Garrett as minister;[8] and no. 13 Castle Street in 1814.[9] A large room occupied by Joseph Baldree at no. 18 Wych Street (St Clement Danes) was also registered in 1819.[10]

William Clark Yonge registered a room in his occupancy in a house in Brockes Yard, Milford Lane (St Clement Danes) for Independents in 1822.[11]

Independents registered an infant school room at no. 6 Charles Court (St Martin), in 1832.[12]

A building at the junction of Charles and Wilson streets, Long Acre (St Martin), known as Whitefield chapel, was registered by Revd Charles Brake for Independents in 1841.[13] Said to have been built before 1800, in 1851 it had 100 free seats and 400 other; attendance was 200 in the morning and 300 in the evening.[14]

1 Wilson, *Dissenting Chs.* III. 492–4.
2 Guildhall MS 9580/7, pp. 273, 304.
3 TNA, HO 129/13, 3/1/(v. faint), (f. 18).
4 ONS, Worship Reg. nos 5268, 6614.
5 A. Mearns, *Guide to Cong. Chs of London* (1882), 40; *VCH Middx*, VIII. 105.
6 Guildhall MS 9580/2, p. 103.   7 Ibid. /2, p. 127.

8 Ibid. /3.
9 Ibid. /4.
10 Ibid. /5.
11 Ibid. /5.
12 Ibid. /7, p. 87.
13 Ibid. /8, p. 122.
14 TNA, HO 129/5, 2/1/4 (f. 13).

Northern Westminster

Orange Street Chapel (St Martin) A chapel on the east side of St Martin's Street was bought from French Protestants by Thomas Hawkes in 1787 and converted into a Congregationalist chapel by its first minister, Revd John Townsend, the founder of the London Asylum for the Deaf and Dumb.[1] A Sunday school was held at no. 36 St Martin's Street, registered for worship in 1816.[2] In 1851 the chapel seated 966, of which 154 were free, with 291 for children; attendance was 600 with 200 scholars in the morning and 750 with 60 scholars in the evening.[3] Attendance had fallen considerably by 1886 when it was 73 (a.m.) and 82 (p.m.), and in 1903 it was 34 (a.m.) and 66 (p.m.). It was registered again by Congregationalists in 1861.[4] The last service in the old chapel was held in 1917, a temporary structure was built on the site, and an architectural competition for a new building was held in the early 1920s. It resulted in a small chapel on a new site in Orange Street, designed with a simple pedimented front by Kieffer, Fleming and Keesey and built in 1927–9.[5] It was still in use in 2008; the chapel also provided services for the Chinese community.

Independents also registered the 1st floor of no. 19 Orange Street, the dwelling of Elizabeth Barr, a member of the congregation, in 1796, with Thomas Madden as minister.[6]

Independents, possibly the same group, registered a building on the east side of York Street (St James), formerly the chapel of a Spanish ambassador, in 1794, with James Tuffs as minister;[7] they also registered the Assembly Room on the south side of Brewer Street (St James), in 1796, again with James Tuffs.[8] Finally, they registered no. 4 Upper James Street, Golden Square (St James), occupied by Thomas Hillier, who was minister in 1798.[9]

Wardour Chapel, Little Chapel Street, Soho Part of the congregation of the Swallow Street Scottish church,[10] under assistant minister Thomas Stollery, formed the separate Independent Church in 1796, taking over the lease of the former French Protestant chapel in Little Chapel Street. It was said to have been over half the congregation, which by 1814 was considerable.[11] In 1824 the Crown leased to them the site with the chapel fronting Little Chapel Street for 70 years from 1822 in consideration of building the chapel, and it was conveyed to trustees for Independents.[12] The chapel was called Wardour chapel in 1851, when it was said to have been built in 1824. It seated 170 free and 700 other. Attendance in 1851 was 529 plus 150 scholars in the morning and 627 in the evening.[13] In 1886 the congregation was 63 in the morning and 81 in the evening.

Independents registered a room in the dwelling of William Balliston, in Porters Street (St Anne), in 1791, with John Cureton as pastor;[14] a room at no. 13 Princes Street, Leicester Fields (St James), occupied by William Spence in 1800;[15] no. 16 Brewer Street, Golden Square, occupied by William Pidduson, in 1804;[16] no. 19 East Row, Carnaby Market (St James), occupied by Mrs Margaret Browne, in 1804 for worship or Sunday school.[17]

A dwelling house occupied by John Mills at no. 11 Charles Street, Market Lane (St James), was registered in 1806 with Edward Edwards as minister.[18]

Independents registered a room in the dwelling of John Cunningham at no. 63 Poland Street (St James) in 1807, with C. Morrison as minister.[19]

Independents registered no. 53 Marshall Street, Golden Square, belonging to Henry Stibbs, in 1815, with Joseph Francis Burrell as minister.[20]

Independents under Edward Boddington, minister, registered unoccupied buildings at no. 40 Brewer Street (St James) in 1795,[21] and at no. 11 Shepherd Market, Mayfair, in 1796.[22]

Ebenezer Chapel, Market Street, Shepherd Market This was used by a small religious society formed *c.*1795 by a few young men, who were using rooms in a private house, but were soon turned out. They obtained a license to use other rooms and after 5 years were augmented by the remnants of Mr Gwennap's congregation (see Baptists).[23] In 1801 they opened the Market Street premises as Ebenezer chapel. It was registered in 1800 by Walter Hughes, butcher, and others,[24] and as numbers increased a Church was formed on a Congregationalist plan in 1802, recognised by the Congregationalist Union in 1803. They were supplied by various ministers until 1806 when Revd Samuel Hackett took over, having visited the congregation in 1805. Numbers greatly increased, and the chapel had twice been enlarged by 1814. In 1817 the lease of the chapel, which was built over a coachhouse and stretched between Market Street

1 R.W. Frere, *Hist. of Orange St Chapel*; *Survey of London*, XX. 110–11; below, Foreign Prot. Chs.

2 Guildhall MS 9580/4.

3 TNA, HO 129/5, 1/1/6 (f. 6).

4 ONS, Worship Reg. no. 14716.

5 *Survey of London*, XX. 109–11; Pevsner, *London 6: Westm.* 394.

6 Guildhall MS 9580/1, p. 106.

7 Ibid., p. 82.   8 Ibid., p. 104.

9 Ibid., p. 169.   10 Below, Ch of Scotland.

11 Wilson, *Dissenting Chs*, IV. 31; Guildhall MS 9580/1, p. 109; Mearns, *Guide to Cong. Chs of London* (1882 edn), 44.

12 TNA, C 54/10257, no. 15.

13 TNA, HO 129/13, 1/1/4 (f. 5).

14 Guildhall MS 9580/1, p. 4.

15 Ibid. /2, p. 52.

16 Ibid., p. 133.

17 Ibid., p. 134.

18 Ibid. MS 9580/3.

19 Ibid.

20 Ibid. MS 9580/4.

21 Ibid. /1, p. 92.

22 Ibid. /1, p. 107.   23 Wilson, *Dissenting Chs*, IV. 55–6.

24 Guildhall MS 9580/2, p. 71.

and Carrington Mews, was assigned to trustees for Congregational worship and registered. Registers exist for 1804–37.[1]

Independents registered the home of William Coleman, at 29 Grosvenor Market (St George), in 1791, with Joel Abraham Knight as minister.[2] They also registered no. 16 Woodstock Street (St George) in 1799.[3]

A room in the house of Richard Wormall, at no. 12 Alms Houses, Crown Street (Charing Cross Road), was registered for Independents in 1820.[4]

Greek Church   Trustees for the Calvinistic Independents in 1818 bought the site and buildings in Crown Street (Charing Cross Rd) known as the Greek Church and occupied by French Protestants.[5] The French congregation left in 1822, and Independents occupied the chapel, perhaps intermittently, until 1849: Revd John Rees was minister between 1823 and 1833; Revd Charles Brake, formerly at Whitefield chapel, was minister in 1848, and Revd Robert Hunt was minister in 1849. A schoolroom was built on the former burial ground north of the chapel between 1823 and 1846. In 1849 the chapel was sold to the Rector of St Anne's, and became St Mary's Anglican district church.[6]

Craven Chapel, Foubert's Place (St James)   was built and opened in 1822 on part of the site of the former Carnaby Market. Financed by Thomas Wilson, a retired merchant, who from 1799 devoted himself to the building and repair of Congregationalist Chapels, it was designed by Mr Abraham, possibly Robert Abraham, to accommodate a large congregation rather than for architectural effect. The brick building was oblong with a staircase in each corner leading to a gallery with ran all round the interior; the north entrance faced the pulpit at the south end, and the organ was in the gallery above.[7] The chapel seated 1,500–2,000 and cost *c.*£11,000, all apparently met initially by Wilson. A Church was formed in 1823, but for 8 years was served by visiting preachers. In 1831 Revd John Leifchild became minister. He attracted a large congregation, with many who travelled some distance to hear him.. In 1851 the chapel seated 470 free and 1230 other, with 100 standing, and attendance was 857 in the morning and 1160 in the evening, judged to be below average because of bad weather that day.[8] Leifchild retired in 1854, but the congregation continued to be large, and in 1874 the Craven schools and lecture hall, designed by R.H. Burden, opened on the north side of Foubert's Place, replacing the schoolrooms under the chapel. Attendance

in 1886 amounted to only 326 in the morning and 270 in the afternoon, and by 1894 the congregation felt unable to continue in that area, and the leases of the chapel and hall were assigned to the West London Methodist Mission.[9]

Independents living around Windmill Street, Soho, registered no. 6 Archer Street (St Anne), which was in the possession of Robert Wedderburn, in 1818.[10]

George P. Wigram registered his house, no. 33 Argyle Street (St James) for Congregationalists in 1834.[11]

Robert Street Chapel, Weighhouse Street, Mayfair[12]   The congregation is thought to have originated *c.*1814.[13] The chapel was built 1823–4 by Seth Smith, a prominent speculative builder and Congregationalist, on the north side of Robert (later Weighhouse) Street where a Methodist chapel formerly stood. It had a modest two-storeyed front of brick in Greek Doric style, the lower half of which was stuccoed, and seated up to 400. In 1851 it seated 240 free and 490 other; attendance then was 262 (a.m.) and 269 (p.m.),[14] but had dropped in 1886 to 92 (a.m.) and 80 (p.m.). When the lease expired, the duke of Westminster offered a larger site at peppercorn rent, but plans to rebuild were abandoned in 1887 when the congregation was unable to raise funds. The congregation then merged with that of King's Weigh House in new chapel (below). The Robert Street chapel closed in 1890 and was demolished.

When the Robert Street congregation were unable to rebuild their chapel, a merger was proposed with the congregation from King's Weigh House Chapel (City of London), displaced by the building of (Monument) underground railway station. Andrew Mearns and the London Congregationalist Union persuaded the duke of Westminster to grant a large site at the corner of Robert (later Weighhouse) and Duke streets for 99 years at peppercorn rent. This was described as 'the largest gift ever made to the Nonconformist cause'. The freehold of the site was granted by the duke in 1892. The chapel was built between 1889 and 1891 to seat 600–800 people, the total cost of over £30,000 was paid by Weigh House trustees. It was registered as King's Weigh House chapel, Duke Street, in 1891.[15] The chapel, designed by Alfred Waterhouse in French Romanesque style and built in brick with much terracotta, had an oval auditorium with a gallery, which could seat 900 people, within a rectangular building with a very tall south-west tower.[16] The chapel extended from Duke Street to Binney Street, and the site also provided space for an adjoining school room with a hall (no. 21) above it, and a minister's house (no.

1 Guildhall MS 9580/4; TNA, C 54/9604, no. 3; note in cal. in WCA.   2 Guildhall MS 9580/1, p. 20.

3 Ibid. /2, p. 25.

4 Ibid. /5.

5 Below, French Prots (*L'Eglise des Grecs*).

6 *Survey of London*, XXXIII. 282–4; above, Par. Chs (St Anne).   7 *Survey of London*, XXXI. 200–1.

8 TNA, HO 129/6, 3/1/3 (f. 12).

9 ONS, Worship Reg. no. 25826; below, Methodists.

10 Guildhall MS 9580/5.

11 Ibid. /7, p. 127.

12 Para. based on *Survey of London*, XL. 69, 93.

13 Mearns, *Guide to Cong. Chs of London* (1882 edn), 34.

14 TNA, HO 129/3, 1/1/4 (f. 95).

15 ONS, Worship Reg. no. 32786.

16 Pevsner, *London 6: Westm.* 484.

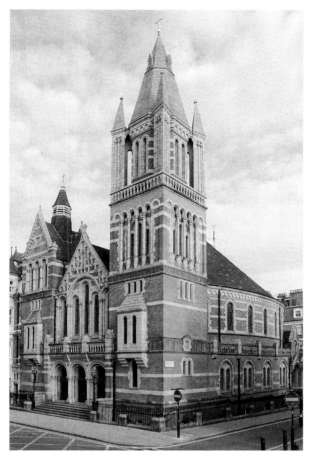

68. *The Congregational King's Weigh House Chapel, Duke Street, built 1889–91 for a displaced City of London congregation on a site provided by the Grosvenors to an ambitious design by Alfred Waterhouse; now the Ukrainian Catholic Cathedral.*

22) on Binney Street. Beneath the chapel an ample basement originally housed the Thomas Binney Institute, named after the Weigh House congregation's most famous minister. In 1903, under the successful ministry of John Hunter, J.J. Burnet created a chancel by removing the organ and building a new one to flank the ends of the gallery. Attendance in 1903 was 358 in the morning and 458 in the evening. The chapel declined after Hunter left in 1904, until William Edwin Orchard came in 1914. A Catholic sympathizer, he introduced incense, ritual, and reservation of sacrament, and converted to Rome in 1932; he added wooden reredos by A.E. Henderson in 1927. The chapel continued to decline. After bomb damage in 1940, the building was restored in 1953 and reopened, but in 1965 the congregation merged with that of Whitefield Memorial church

(St Pancras), and the chapel closed in 1966. The freehold of the chapel and the lease of adjoining premises were sold to the Ukrainian Catholic Church.[1]

Southern Westminster

Independents in St Margaret, under the ministry of William Mason Smith, successively registered a room in the house of Mr Potts, Great St Ann's Court, St Ann's Street, in 1800; a room belonging to Mrs Eleanor White, Union Place, Orchard Street, in 1801; and a building belonging to William Mason Smith in Dartmouth Row, in 1803.[2]

The School House, Vincent Square, built in 1818, was used by Congregationalists in 1851, when it had 200 free seats; attendance was 160 in the morning and 199 in the afternoon (school only); attendance in the evening was below average at 120.[3]

William Russel registered a room in the Broadway, York Street (St Margaret), formerly known as the Westminster theatre, for Congregationalists in 1841.[4]

Frederic Cane registered the British & Foreign school room in Horseferry Road for Congregationalists in 1841.[5]

Westminster Chapel, Buckingham Gate A Congregationalist chapel built on the site of the Westminster hospital in 1840–1 by the Metropolis Chapel Building Fund Association.[6] Schools and vestries were added in 1843 and almshouses in 1859. Revd Samuel Martin was minister in 1842 until at least 1865; he also registered a large room in Exeter Hall, Strand, for temporary worship in 1849.[7] In 1851 the chapel had 368 free seats, 1046 other and 214 standing; attendance was 990 in the morning and 1238 in the evening, but numbers in the congregation were below average because of bad weather. There were 290 Sunday scholars who worshipped in a separate building.[8] The building was too small and was demolished in 1864, but it was replaced by a new chapel on the same site in 1864–5, designed by W.F. Poulton in dark red, red, and yellow brick. The auditorium was nearly oval, with 2 tiers of galleries and a large roof span.[9] It opened and was registered in 1865.[10] Attendance in 1886 was 535 (a.m.) and 394 (p.m.); in 1903 it was 226 (a.m.) and 231 (p.m.). It was still in use in 2008. In 1898 the congregation ran a mission in Bessborough Hall, Grosvenor Road;[11] attendance in 1903 was 86 in the evening.

Western Westminster

Buckingham Chapel, Palace Street, Pimlico A substantial building, formerly occupied by Primitive Methodists (below), and taken over in 1801 by Independents. Revd E.A. Dunn was minister for 40 years from c.1814.[12] In

1 *Survey of London*, XL. 87–8; above, Rom. Cathm.
2 Guildhall MS 9580/2, pp. 63, 77, 110.
3 TNS, HO 129/4, 1/1/6 (f. 9).
4 Guildhall MS 9580/8, p. 100.
5 Ibid., p. 102.   6 Foundation stone.
7 Guildhall MS 9580/9, p. 22.
8 TNA, HO 129/4, 2/1/19 (f. 33).
9 Pevsner, *London 6: Westm.* 684.
10 ONS, Worship Reg. no. 16825.
11 *Cong. Yr Bk 1898.*   12 Wilson, *Dissenting Chs*, IV. 56–7.

1818 the congregation leased ground on the west side of the chapel for use as a burial ground, and a school room was built on part of it *c.*1820. It was used for British day school pupils and Pimlico Sunday school.[1] In 1851 the chapel seated 200 free, 600 other and 500 standing; attendance in 1851 was 180 scholars in the morning and 299 in the evening, but the congregation was reduced because of wet weather. The group formed daughter chapels at Westminster and Eccleston, which greatly reduced their own congregation.[2] Buckingham chapel was renovated in 1883 and opened as a Congregationalist hall under the care of Westminster chapel, with services on Sundays and Thursdays.[3] It closed in 1886.[4]

Eccleston Square Chapel, Belgrave Rd, Victoria   In 1836 Seth Smith registered for Independents 2 rooms formerly occupied by him as warehouse on his wharf in Gillingham Street, near Belgrave Road, south of Grosvenor Basin.[5] In 1848 he built and registered Eccleston Square chapel, which was conveyed in trust for Congregationalists.[6] It seated 1,000 in 1851, none free. Attendance in 1851 was *c.*600 in the morning and *c.*600 in the evening. There was no settled minister.[7] In 1878 the interior was altered and the galleries reduced; the building included a school room in 1881.[8] It was renamed in 1880 as the Eccleston Square Congregationalist Church.[9] Attendance in 1886 was 448 in the morning and 427 in the afternoon; in 1903 it was 247 in the morning and 310 in the afternoon. It had closed by 1927.[10]

St Leonard's Street Chapel, Upper Tachbrook Street, Vauxhall Bridge Road   Formed by a mission from Craven chapel *c.*1837. The first services there were taken by students from Coward College, but after the college amalgamated with New College, preaching was undertaken by members of the congregation, and there continued to be an annually elected lay unpaid ministry in 1882. The chapel was built in 1854 costing £2,000 and seating 350.[11] Attendance in 1886 was 60 in the morning and 56 in the afternoon; in 1903 it was 22 in the morning and 128 in the afternoon. It closed in 1906.[12]

Trevor Chapel, Trevor Square (formerly Arthur Street), Knightsbridge[13]   Independents led by Dr John Morison, who resigned as minister of Union Chapel, Sloane Street (Chelsea), following differences, met in Smith & Baber's floorcloth factory in 1816 until the newly-built chapel opened in December 1816 at the corner of Arthur Street and Lancelot Place. It was built by John Souter, a member of congregation, who took the lease of the site for the chapel and houses in Trevor Square. The chapel was greatly enlarged during the 1830s, and schoolrooms were added at the top of the building in 1840. In 1851 it seated 200 free and 200 other; there was a room above for day and Sunday schools with a separate entrance. Attendance in 1851 was 700 in the morning and 1200 in the evening; many had to stand in the aisles and the vestry.[14] A gallery was added later, perhaps during alterations in 1865. It was renamed the Trevor Congregationalist chapel in 1880.[15] There were 2 services on Sunday and one on Wednesday in 1882, but no permanent minister. Attendance in 1886 was 389 in the morning and 337 in the afternoon.[16] It closed *c.*1902 and was taken over by Harrods as a showroom and garage. It was demolished in the early 1950s.

METHODISTS

Methodist Churches are grouped below under the denomination with which each began. Some regrouping took place in the 20th century, with the union of New Connexion and others to form the United Methodist Church in 1907, and the major union of the Wesleyans, the United Methodist Church, and the Primitive Methodists in 1932 to form the United Methodists; these changes are often reflected in changes of name and re-registration. The more numerous meetings of the Weslyans are also subdivided into four geographic groupings.

Southern Westminster

Horseferry Road (Romney Terrace Chapel)   Although Wesleyans had been meeting elsewhere in Westminster since the 1780s,[17] they established their most enduring presence in St Margaret and St John. In 1814 they built a chapel in Romney Terrace, Horseferry Road, originally known as Romney Terrace chapel.[18] The freehold of the site, which backed onto Medway Street,[19] was bought from the earl of Romney and conveyed to trustees 1839.

1   TNA, C 54/11059, no. 3.
2   TNA, HO 129/4, 2/1/18 (f. 32).
3   Mearns, *Guide to Cong. Chs of London* (1884 edn), 61.
4   ONS, Worship Reg. no. 11566.
5   Guildhall MS 9580/7, p. 217.
6   Ibid. /8, p. 309; Mearns, *Guide to Cong. Chs of London* (1882 edn), 33.   7   TNA, HO 129/3, 3/1/9 (f. 111).
8   Mearns, *Guide to Cong. Chs of London* (1884 edn), 61.
9   ONS, Worship Reg. no. 24890.   10   *PO Dir.* (1927).
11   Mearns, *Guide to Cong. Chs of London* (1882 edn), 33.

12   ONS, Worship Reg. no. 24880.
13   Para. based on *Survey of London*, XLV. 100.
14   TNA, HO 129/4, 2/1/20 (f. 34).
15   ONS, Worship Reg. no. 24931.
16   Mearns, *Guide to Cong. Chs of London* (1882 edn), 7; *Trans. Cong. Hist. Soc.* XX. 32.
17   Below, Northern Westm.
18   Except where noted, acct based on *Endowed Chars London*, V. 380–3.
19   TNA, C 54/9506, no. 5.

69. *Methodist Central Hall, Storey's Gate, 1905–11, looking south towards the Houses of Parliament. The magnificent multi-purpose hall was designed by masters of neo-baroque design, Lanchester and Rickards, for a site at the heart of national life.*

In 1851 the chapel seated 600, of which 150 were free, with 100 standing; attendance was 406 in the morning and 360 in the evening.[1] In 1861 it was registered as a Wesleyan Methodist chapel.[2] It was demolished in c.1866 and a larger chapel was built on the site, enlarged with the acquisition of no. 16 Romney Terrace. The Charity Commission Scheme of 1872 allowed up to 350 seats to be set aside rent-free for staff and students of the Wesleyan Training College, Horseferry Road; half the chapel's trustees were to be local and half appointed by the Wesleyan Methodist Conference; surplus income was to go towards the support of ministers of the circuit, or towards funds of any other Wesleyan chapel. The freehold abutting Medway and Allington (later Arneway) streets was also acquired in 1866, and rents of £169 p.a. from 12 houses there and in Horseferry Rd were used for the upkeep of the chapel. Attendance in 1886 was 430 in the morning and 671 in the evening. By 1899 seats were still being provided for the college, which paid an annual sum for the rent of the seats because of the chapel's worsening financial position. The Sunday school used rooms underneath the chapel, paying £20 p.a. Attendance in 1903 was 145 in the morning and 190 in the evening. It was closed by November 1927,[3] but the building was possibly used by the Roman Catholic chapel of the Sacred Heart (above).

The Wesleyan Methodist Temperance chapel in Arneway Street was registered briefly in 1919.[4]

Elswhere in the parish a large former carpenter's shop in Princes Place, Princes Street, was registered for Wesleyans in 1840,[5] possibly the same building as the Temperance Hall, no. 6 Princes Place, which was used in 1851: it seated 100 (all free), with 50 standing; attendance was 6 plus 42 scholars in the morning, and 9 plus 28 scholars in the evening. The chapelkeeper reported that the congregation was so small because of prejudice and intolerance, but 269 boys and girls belonged to the Juvenile Band of Hope.[6]

Westminster Central Hall, Storey's Gate (formerly Princes Street) With the construction of Westminster Hall between 1905 and 1911 the Wesleyans greatly enhanced their presence at the very heart of Westminster, opposite the abbey and the Houses of Parliament. Built out of contributions to the 'one million guineas' fund and designed by Lanchester & Rickards, this was the most impressive of the multi-purpose central halls built by Methodists in major cities.[7] Registered and opened in 1912,[8] it seated 3,000. In 1970 the school seated 599 in 9 classrooms.[9] The building also housed a Methodist Conference office, and was constantly in demand for public meetings and exhibitions: the first meeting of the

1 TNA, HO 129/4, 1/1/5 (f. 8).
2 ONS, Worship Reg. no. 11323.
3 Ibid.
4 Ibid. no. 47484.
5 Guildhall MS 9580/8, p. 93.

6 TNA, HO 129/4, 2/1/17 (f. 31).
7 Pevsner, *London 6: Westm.* 211.
8 ONS, Worship Reg. no. 45392.
9 Methodist Ch Dept for Chapel Affairs, *Statistical Returns*, 20.

UN General Assembly was held there in 1946. It was still in use in 2008. The Westminster Pastoral Foundation was established there to provide training in pastoral counselling and a counselling service concentrating on personal and family problems.[1]

Eastern Westminster

A group of Wesleyans in St Martin's parish registered several addresses: a Sunday school in George Yard, Drury Lane in 1804;[2] the house of George Furby at no. 6 Rose St, Long Acre, in 1814; the house of Daniel Roberts at no. 9 Charles Court, Strand, in 1814;[3] the house of John Furby at no. 5 Rose St, in 1818; and the house of John Wade at no. 1 Hungerford Market, in 1820.[4]

Other premises in the vicinity registered for Wesleyans included the dwelling of Jonathan Wacey or Wacer, at no. 5 Drury Court (St Mary le Strand), in 1818,[5] and the house of Samuel Harrison, at no. 6 Vere St (St Clement Danes), in 1832.[6] Wesleyans also registered no. 28 St Clement's Lane (St Clement Danes), as a chapel in 1836, and the same group registered no. 43 St Clement's Lane, in 1837.[7]

Northern Westminster

In St George's parish, meetings were held from an early period in a room above a slaughter-house in Grosvenor Market, Davies Street, by 1791. The slaughter-house had been leased in 1785 to John Jenkins, a member of the congregation and possibly a member of the family of Methodist preachers and chapel architects of that name.[8] In 1800 the congregation, including Jenkins, was registered at no. 26 Grosvenor Market, which was occupied by a member, John Middleton.[9] In 1801 Jenkins and others registered the house of Christopher Scott on the north side of Chandler (later Weighhouse) Street,[10] which was adapted or rebuilt as a chapel. They had left by 1823 when an Independent chapel was built on the site.[11]

In 1823 Wesleyans registered the house occupied by William Joice at no. 21 Shepherd Market, Mayfair.[12] In 1847 the 2 lower rooms at no. 7 Shepherd Market, occupied by Mr Clerger, were registered by Robert Insley for Wesleyans.[13]

Wesleyans were said to have taken over a Scottish Presbyterian chapel in Peter Street (near Poland Street), c.1816. In 1851 it had 303 seats, and attendances were 82 in the morning and 110 in the evening;[14] it was apparently closed in 1858 when the fittings were sold.[15]

Elsewhere in Soho, J.W. Williams registered no. 41 Brewer Street, Golden Square, for the Wesleyans in 1823.[16]

By 1896 Wesleyans had also taken over the Craven Chapel, a former Independent chapel in Foubert's Place, east of Regent Street. Craven Hall opposite was also registered in 1897 by Wesleyans of the West London mission. Although in 1903 attendances there were given as 27 in the morning and 243 in the evening, the chapel was closed in 1906 and the hall in 1907.[17] Better attended were the Wesleyan services in St James's Hall, Piccadilly, where 927 worshipped in the morning and 2,406 in the evening in 1903, perhaps because of special mission services.

Western Westminster

In Pimlico Francis Herbert registered no. 14 Lower Belgrave Place (St Georges) for Wesleyans in 1843;[18] Edward Riggs registered no. 4 Lower St Leonard's Street for Wesleyans in 1843.[19]

Ranelagh Chapel, Belgrave district   George Scott, minister of Horseferry Road chapel, reported on this chapel in 1851: it was built in 1827 and seated 54 free, 84 other and 30 standing. The attendance was 23 + 48 Sunday School scholars in the morning, and 32 in the evening.[20]

Belgrave Place Rooms   These were used by Wesleyans (Reformers) in 1851; they were built in 1843 and seated 120 free and 120 other. Attendance for 1851 was 130 plus 82 scholars in the morning, 100 in the afternoon, and 160 in the evening.[21]

Claverton Street Wesleyan Methodist Chapel, Pimlico
Registered in 1864,[22] and 1865 with Francis John Sharr as minister.[23] Attendance in 1886 was 258 in the morning and 332 in the evening. In 1903 it was 122 in the morning and 174 in the evening. The street frontage was of classical design with large round-headed windows and there was a gallery on 2 sides. It closed at the end of 1916, but was reopened in 1917 by Roman Catholics.[24]

In 1903 Wesleyans held services at Conference hall, Pimlico, with 89 attending in the morning. Services were also held at Gothic hall, Thomas Street, where there was an attendance of 23 in the morning and 75 in the evening.

Divine Service hall on ground floor of the Duke of

1 J. Vickers and B. Young, *Methodist Guide to London and SE* (1980), 19.
2 Guildhall MS 9580/2, p. 126.
3 Ibid. /4.
4 Ibid. /5.
5 Ibid. /4.
6 Ibid. /7, pp. 69, 261.
7 Ibid. /7, p. 228.
8 *Survey of London*, XL. 69.
9 Guildhall MS 9580/2, p. 57.
10 Ibid., p. 73.   11 Above, Congs (Robert St).
12 Guildhall MS 9580/5.   13 Ibid. /8, p. 280.

14 TNA, HO 129/6, 1/1/2 (f. 2).
15 *Survey of London*, XXXI. 228–9.
16 Guildhall MS 9580/5.
17 ONS, Worship Reg. nos 35796, 35918.
18 Guildhall MS 9580/8, p. 153.
19 Ibid. /8, p. 182.
20 TNA, HO 129/3, 3/1/7 (f. 109).
21 Ibid., 3/1/8 (f. 110).
22 ONS, Worship Reg. no. 16226.
23 Ibid. no. 16782.
24 Ibid. no. 16782; Rottmann, *London Cath. Chs*, 13; above, Rom. Cathm (Ch of Holy Apostles).

Connaught's Soldiers' and Sailors' Home, no. 6 Eccleston St, registered for Wesleyans 1913; renamed 1936 Regnal House Hall for Methodist Ch. Closed by 1964.[1]

Welsh Wesleyans

The chapel in Portland (later D'Arblay) Street, off Poland St (St James), was registered for Welsh Wesleyans in 1873, although it was gone by 1896.[2] Attendance in 1886 was 33 in the morning and 60 in the evening.

PRIMITIVE METHODISTS

Calvinistic Methodists under Howell Harris considered taking a playhouse in Haymarket for services in 1746,[3] and Methodists used the former French Protestant chapel in Little Chapel St, Soho, for a period between 1784 and 1796.[4]

Primitive Methodists registered the house of Richard Shepherd at no. 7 Gilbert Street, Clare Market (St Clement Danes) in 1823; the house of Dr John Gardener at no. 74 Long Acre (St Martin), in 1824; and the house of George Cobb, at no. 21 Kings Road, Pimlico (St George), in 1824.[5]

Thomas Duffett registered no. 3 Ship Place (St Clement Danes) for teaching and preaching for Methodists in 1827, possibly Primitive Methodists.[6]

Primitive Methodists opened a Preaching Room at no. 11 St Margaret's Terrace, Westminster, in 1849. All sittings were free in 1851; attendance was 20 in the morning with 16 scholars in the afternoon, and 42 in the evening.[7]

There was also a Primitive Methodist Preaching Room in Artillery Row, Victoria Street, which was registered in 1861, but it was gone by 1866.[8]

Buckingham Chapel, Palace St, Pimlico This was a substantial building, occupied by Methodists for many years, and said to have been built in 1794.[9] Obadiah Bennett preached there until 1800. It was taken over by Independents in 1801.[10]

Adelphi Chapel, James St (St Martin) The chapel, which was built by Particular Baptists, was sold c.1789 to Calvinistic Methodists, who were still there in 1814. The chapel was fitted up with an organ and a reading-desk, and from 1791 was regulated like Tottenham Court chapel by an alternate change of ministers.[11] This or another Trinitarian congregation at the Adelphi chapel shared school premises in Hart Street, Covent Garden, with St Paul's parish, and held a British day school and the Adelphi chapel Sunday school there c.1839.[12]

Methodists registered no. 3 North Audley St (St Geo.), occupied by John Shegog, in 1811.[13]

METHODIST NEW CONNEXION

No. 7 Great Windmill Street (St James) was registered in 1819 by members of the Methodist New Connexion. The same congregation registered Princes Street chapel, at no. 12 Leicester Street (St Anne), in 1820, with ministers William Haslam and Thomas Yearsley.[14]

UNITED METHODIST FREE CHURCH

Victoria and Chelsea (formerly Ebury Bridge) Methodist Church, Westmoreland Terrace, Pimlico This Methodist Free Church was registered as Pimlico chapel, Westmoreland St (later Terrace), in 1856. Attendance in 1886 as 119 in the morning and 110 in the afternoon. In 1903 it was 162 in the morning and 257 in the afternoon. It became the Pimlico United Methodist Church in 1907.[15] In 1913 it shared ministers with Victoria chapel, Vauxhall Bridge Road.[16] A new chapel on the same site was built 1960–2, and dedicated September 1962 as Ebury Bridge Methodist church, incorporating Victoria Methodist church, Willow Place.[17] In 1970 Ebury Bridge church seated 150, with a school seating 208.[18] Its name was later altered to Victoria Methodist church, and then Victoria and Chelsea Methodist church. It closed c.1996, and the building was empty in 2000.

Victoria Chapel no. 192 Vauxhall Bridge Rd, Westminster Registered in 1877 for the United Methodist Free Church. It became the Victoria United Methodist church in 1907 but was closed by 1940.[19] Attendance in 1886 was 131 (morning) and 168 (evening), and in 1903 was 32 (morning) and 74 (evening).

Victoria Methodist Church, Willow Place, Westminster Built 1949–50, and opened in June 1950. It was put up for sale in 1960, and closed by 1962 when the congregation joined Ebury Bridge Methodist church.[20]

A building in Lewisham Street, near Storey's Gate (St Margt), was registered for the United Methodist Free Church in 1861; it was no longer in use by 1876.[21]

1 ONS, Worship Reg. nos 45755, 56452.
2 Ibid. no. 21519.
3 *Two Calvinistic Methodist Chapels, 1743–1811*, ed. E. Welch (London Rec. Soc. XI, 1975), 25.
4 *Survey of London*, XXXIII. 294–5.
5 Guildhall MS 9580/5.
6 Ibid. /6, p. 160.
7 TNA, HO 129/4, 2/1/21 (f. 35).
8 ONS, Worship Reg. no. 13605.
9 TNA, HO 129/4, 2/1/18 (f. 32).
10 Wilson, *Dissenting Chs*, IV. 56–7; above, Congs.
11 Wilson, *Dissenting Chs*, IV. 16–17.
12 TNA, C 54/12066, no. 6.
13 Guildhall MS 9580/3.
14 Ibid. /5.
15 ONS, Worship Reg. no. 7588.
16 Harris and Bryant, *Chs and London*, 427.
17 ONS, Worship Reg. no. 68742; WCA, CMC/2339/23.
18 Methodist Ch Dept for Chapel Affairs, *Statistical Returns*, 20.
19 ONS, Worship Reg. no. 23655.
20 WCA, CMC/2339/9, 35–6; ONS, Worship Reg. no. 62703.
21 ONS, Worship Reg. no. 11815.

PRESBYTERIANS

Southern Westminster

Princes Street, St Margaret   Thomas Cawton received a licence for Presbyterian meetings at his house in St Anne's Lane, Westminster, and for himself as teacher in 1672, and a few months later a licence for a newly-built meeting-house in nearby New Way, Westminster.[1] Cawton's congregation later dated their Church to 1666, and their first chapel, in Tothill Street, opened before 1677, may refer to the one in the New Way, which led south from Great Almonry, near Tothill Street. Cawton was minister until 1677, when he was succeeded by Vincent Alsop, who held the post until 1703. Dr Edmund Calamy was minister from 1703 to 1732. Alsop claimed he had been required to divide his congregation into two because of its size, administering communion to each group alternately.[2] The congregation moved to chapel in Princes Street, Westminster, *c.*1703, and to another in Princes Street address in 1799. That closed 1818, and the congregation joined St Thomas's Street chapel, Southwark (Surrey).[3]

Eastern Westminster

Gabriel Sangar or Sanger, the former minister of St Martin-in-the-Fields, was preaching in 1669 to congregations of 200 in the house of Richard Newby, in the Strand.[4] He was granted a licence in 1672 to preach and to hold Presbyterian services in his own lodgings and in the home of Catherine Lloyd (Floyd), a widow, in the Strand, supported by a petition of 12 inhabitants of St Martin's.[5] The remains of his congregation, which met in Peter's Court and dissolved *c.*1710, may have formed the nucleus of the Scottish Presbyterian church there.[6]

Licences were granted in 1672 to John Dan of St Martin's as the Presbyterian preacher[7] for meetings at the house of Thomas Soper in Westminster,[8] and to a Presbyterian, William Farrington, to teach and for the Old Theatre, Vere Street (St Clement Danes).[9]

New Court   Dr Thomas Manton was preaching at his own home in Covent Garden in 1669 to a congregation of 100,[10] and was granted a licence in 1672 to continue to preach there until a more convenient place could be found.[11] Manton's congregation afterwards met in Brydges Street, and may have been the congregation of

which John Quick from Plymouth was minister from the 1670s until 1681.[12] The remains of Manton's congregation were said to have gathered around well-known preacher Daniel Burgess *c.*1687, forming a regular society in Brydges Street which included many distinguished people. They later moved to a newly-built chapel in nearby Russell Court (St Martin), which was registered in 1692 by Independents under Burgess.[13] It was a substantial brick building with 3 deep galleries seating a numerous congregation.[14] When the lease expired the congregation was forced to leave, and they built a chapel in New Court, Carey Street, Little Lincoln's Inn Fields (St Clement Danes), and registered it in 1704.[15] A large part of the congregation left soon afterwards over differences with Burgess, and joined Dr Earle at Hanover Street (q.v.), leaving the remaining members with building debts of £700–800. In 1709 Dr Sacheverell's mob broke all the windows, tore down the pulpit and pews, and burned them in Lincoln's Inn Fields. The cost of the damage was £300 which the congregation were unable to meet, and they were without place of worship for some time. Other Presbyterians helped them to recover the chapel and repair it, but the main debt remained and congregation did not flourish under Burgess (d. *c.*1713) or his successor James Wood. When the latter moved in 1727, the congregation nearly broke up, but were revitalised by Thomas Bradbury (minister 1728–59) with a splinter group from Fetter Lane. Originally strictly Presbyterian, with the ministry contributing to the Presbyterian fund, Bradbury insisted they become Independents and contribute to the Independent fund: thereafter they remained an Independent congregation.[16]

Hanover Street, Long Acre (St Martin)   English Presbyterians worshipped in a meeting house in Drury Lane, where Abraham Hume, former chaplain to the duke of Lauderdale and ordained by English Presbyterians in 1647, was minister from 1687 till he died in 1707.[17] He was succeeded by Dr Jabez Earle, who was minister in 1728.[18] A new chapel was built on the east side of Hanover Street, and registered in 1718.[19] John Lee, afterwards Principal of Edinburgh University, was ordained as minister to Hanover Street in 1804 by the Presbyterians of Edinburgh.[20] The chapel had gone by 1873, and Wilson Street laid out across the site.

1 *Cal. SP Dom.* 1671–2, 273; 1672–3, 178; *Orig. recs of Early Nonconf.* ed. Turner, I. 206, 576.

2 *Calamy Revised*, 8; *Middx County Rec. Sess. Bks 1689–1709*, 26.

3 G.E. Evans, *Vestiges of Protestant Dissent* (1897), 141–2; Wilson, *Dissenting Chs*, IV. 57–9.

4 *Orig. recs. of Early Nonconf.* ed. Turner, I. 85.

5 Ibid. 267; *Cal. SP Dom.* 1671–2, 387, 586; 1672–3, 94.

6 Below, Ch of Scotland (Crown Ct).

7 *Cal. SP Dom.* 1671–2, 517, 550.   8 Ibid. 1672–3, 94.

9 Ibid. 1671–2, 304.

10 *Orig. recs of Early Nonconf.* ed. Turner, I. 85.

11 *Cal. SP Dom.* 1671–2, 273–4.   12 *Calamy Revised*, 402.

13 Guildhall MS 9579/2; Paterson, *Pietas Lond.* 251. Chapel and ct not on Morgan's map 1687.

14 Wilson, *Dissenting Chs*, III. 568–72.

15 Guildhall MS 9579/2.

16 Above, Congs, for later hist.   17 *Calamy Revised*, 283–4.

18 Dr Williams's Libr., Evans MS 34.4, f. 76.

19 Guildhall MS 9579/2.   20 Cameron, *Scots Kirk*, 42–3.

Whitefield Church, Wilson Street, Drury Lane (St Martin) was registered for the Presbyterian Church of England in 1877; it was cancelled in 1985 on notice of disuse.[1] Attendance in 1886 was 46 in the morning and 67 in the evening.

St Martin's Hall, Long Acre (St Martin), was registered in 1857 for Scottish Reformed Presbyterians; it was cancelled 1866.[2]

Northern Westminster

Oxendon Chapel, Oxendon Street (St Martin)   Built in 1676 by Mrs Margaret Baxter for the use of her husband Richard: through a friend she leased ground on which the chapel was built with 2 houses in front to screen it. Baxter preached there once, but Henry Coventry, Secretary of State, whose house was behind the chapel, used local justices to prevent him preaching again, and the chapel was therefore offered to St Martin's parish as a chapel of ease. When the parish ceased to use it c.1807 a lease was taken by Scotch Presbyterians under Revd George Jerment. The Congregation was described in 1814 as Seceders from the Church of Scotland, of the Anti-Burgher class, and oldest society of Seceders in London. The chapel was a square building with 3 galleries, and was well fitted.[3] In 1819 Presbyterians under the General Associate Synod of Scotland registered the chapel, after they had been using it for over 10 yrs.[4] In 1851 it was used by the United Presbyterian Church. It seated 600, of which 100 were free, with 200 standing. Attendance in 1851 was 450 in the morning.[5] It was still extant in 1870, but the site had apparently been rebuilt by 1894, and was part of the Civil Service Stores by 1914.[6]

Presbyterians registered the Musick Room in York Buildings (St Martin's) in 1701.[7]

Swallow Street Chapel (St James)   When Richard Baxter was unable to preach in Oxendon chapel (above),

Margaret Baxter hired the chapel built to let in Swallow Street in 1676. When it was clear that Baxter would never be allowed to preach there either, she found another preacher to occupy the pulpit, and in 1681 Baxter wrote that the minister there, not named, had done much good work. Later ministers included Joseph Hill, Mr Carlisle until 1699, and Mr Stort, and the congregation probably dissolved on the latter's death c.1710; most of the congregation joined Dr Anderson's Scottish church in the same street.[8] The site of the chapel is not known but was possibly on the east side.[9]

Western Westminster

Belgrave Presbyterian Chapel, Halkin Street West, Belgrave Square (St George)   This chapel originated as a mission to Jews by the Church of Scotland's Presbytery of London in 1846, with Henry Douglas as missioner and minister of the congregation. It was established that year in Halkin Street West. Work continued successfully for 20 years, but on dismissal of minister Lawrence McBeth, in 1866, the congregation merged with the Presbyterian Church of England. The congregation from Ranelagh Gardens (Chelsea) using the Halkin Street premises, renamed it the Belgrave Presbyterian Chapel and registered it in 1866.[10] Attendance in 1886 was 264 in the morning and 137 in the afternoon. In 1903 it was 179 in the morning and 141 in the afternoon. There were two services on Sundays in 1913.[11] The chapel had moved to Emperor's Gate, Kensington, by 1923, and the Halkin Street building was later occupied as a private residence.[12]

Free Presbyterians worshipped at conference hall, Eccleston Street, Victoria, in 1913, with a Gaelic service in the afternoon.[13] This is possibly the same as Trent Hall, Eccleston Street, where two floors were registered in 1938 for the Free Presbyterian Church of Scotland, cancelled in 1957.[14]

SOCIETY OF FRIENDS

Westminster Meeting, St Martin's Lane (St Martin)[15] In the 1650s public meetings were held by Friends in Westminster in a large room near the abbey, said to hold a thousand people, with private meetings in people's homes. The first of the latter was recorded in Westminster and held in the home of Stephen Hart in New Palace Yard from c.1655, where attenders were harassed by

General Monk's soldiers in 1660. Meetings moved to the house of convert Elizabeth Trott, who lived on the south side of Pall Mall, but the local justice was pressured into preventing any conventicle so near St James's Palace, and from 1662 worshippers often had to assemble in the street. After Elizabeth Trott's death in 1666 the meeting purchased the lease of a house and garden plot at the end

1 ONS, Worship reg. no. 23255.
2 Ibid. no. 7789.
3 Wilson, *Dissenting Chs*, IV. 52–4.
4 Guildhall MS 9580/5.
5 TNA, HO 129/5, 1/1/7 (f. 7).
6 *Old OS Map*, sheet 61 (1870, 1894, 1914).
7 Guildhall MS 9579/2.
8 Below, Ch of Scotland.

9 *Survey of London*, XXXI. 64; Wilson, *Dissenting Chs*, IV. 43–5.   10 ONS, Worship reg. no. 17381.
11 Harris and Bryant, *Chs and London*, 426.
12 Cameron, *Scots Kirk*, 115–16.
13 Harris and Bryant, *Chs and London*, 426.
14 ONS, Worship reg. no. 58166.
15 Acct based on W. Beck and T.F. Ball, *London Friends' Meetings* (1869), 36, 240–4.

of Little Almonry; it obtained the head lease from the dean and chapter of Westminster in 1688 and renewed it in 1717 and 1751. Extensive repairs were made several times, involving its closure for 2 to 3 months: by 1772 rebuilding was required, and a bigger site was sought to allow room for Friends from the Savoy meeting and elsewhere to join them. In 1776 it obtained a 99-year lease of land in Peter's Court, off St Martin's Lane, part of the Salisbury estate. The meeting-house and other premises were built there at a cost of £2,684, and the rest of the land was sub-let for housing, which reverted to the Friends c.1845. The new meeting house opened in 1779, by which time the Little Almonry premises were unusable and the lease was sold back to the dean and chapter. In 1851 the main floor of the chapel was 52 ft by 35 ft, with seating for 300, with galleries on each side with double rows, seating 100 each;[1] it was described in the 1860s as one of the most commodious and well-fitted of the London meeting houses, with a Sunday school held in the basement. Attendance in 1851 was 106 in the morning and 49 in the evening. The building was registered for Friends from 1854 to 1883.[2] A visitor in c.1876 describing the meeting-house said that it was approached through a passage which led between nos 110 and 111 St Martin's Lane into a small quadrangle, and was a little, unpretentious building was painted from ceiling to basement, with seats around four walls and the centre fitted with benches running laterally, and two rows on the dais facing the entrance: the congregation of c.150 included several children, all of whom maintained the silence.[3] The lease was not renewed as the site was required for the Duke of York's theatre in 1880, so the congregation moved to a new meeting-house on the opposite side of St Martin's Lane, at no. 52, which was registered in 1883.[4] Attendance in 1903 was 198 in the morning and 70 in the afternoon. The building was destroyed by enemy action in 1941, and rebuilt within

the shell, to designs by Hubert Lidbetter, in 1956.[5] It was still in use in 2008.

Savoy Meeting Meetings were held in the 1650s at the homes of Nicholas Bond at Worcester House and William Woodcock in the Savoy. Woodcock was granted lease of the tower over the main gateway and 5 adjoining houses, and Friends met in one until it was gutted by fire in 1670. Woodcock's widow Jane successfully petitioned for the grant of reversionary lease of her houses and additional land so that she could rebuild;[6] she obtained a 40-year lease from 1691. The houses were rebuilt to include entry to the meeting-house at the rear, with vaults and a kitchen under and chambers over the meeting-house; all leases were later assigned to the Friends. One house was let to Gilbert Latey, a leading member of the congregation, who was convicted for holding conventicles in his house, probably the meeting-house, in 1683.[7] Later that year George Foxe was convicted of preaching to a congregation of c.200 in a house in the Savoy, and Joshua Vaughton was convicted of preaching in the house of Martha Fisher.[8] The Westminster Monthly Meeting was held there alternatively with Little Almonry. After the dissolution of the Savoy hospital in 1702 the meeting-house was held at pleasure from the Crown and the tenancy was renewed until 1781, when redevelopment of the precinct was planned; the meeting-house was demolished in 1782. The Savoy Meeting amalgamated with Westminster in St Martin's Lane.[9]

Long Acre A meeting-house and burial ground opened in the space bounded by Long Acre and Hanover, Castle, and King streets, and was approached through a court from Long Acre. It was in use between 1675 and 1716. The burial ground was recovered in 1717, but passed out of Friends' hands by 1757 and was eventually built over.[10]

OTHER CONGREGATIONS

BIBLE CHRISTIANS

Henry Freeman, minister of Gospel, registered the house of the labourer John Peckman, at no. 1 Great Scotland Yard (St Martin), in 1823 for Arminian Bible Christians. On the same day Freeman was associated with the registering of the house of James Brown on Thames Bank (St George). Later in 1823 he registered a room in no. 3 Browns Court, off Green Street (St George), and a room

at no. 27 Swan Yard (St Mary le Strand), belonging to John Peckman, as well as a large room over Exeter Exchange, Strand, occupied by Freeman himself.[11]

Francis Martin registered the dwelling occupied by John Menton at no. 5 Robert Street, Commercial Road, Pimlico (St George), for Bible Christians in 1842.[12]

BRETHREN

Brethren registered a building occupied by Chas Benjamin

1 TNA, HO 129/5, 2/1/6 (f. 15).
2 ONS, Worship Reg. no. 4749.
3 C.M. Davies, *Unorthodox London* (1876 edn), 115.
4 ONS, Worship Reg. no. 27258.
5 Pevsner, *London 6: Westm.* 361.
6 *Cal. SP Dom.* 1670, 324.
7 *Middx County Rec.* IV. 207; Beck and Ball, *London Friends' Meetings*, 250.

8 *Middx County Rec.* IV. 226, 229–30.
9 Beck and Ball, *London Friends' Meetings*, 36, 244–6; Somerville, *Savoy*, 83.
10 Beck and Ball, *London Friends' Meetings*, 247; Mrs B Holmes, *London Burial Grounds* (1896), 140.
11 Guildhall MS 9580/5.
12 Ibid. /8, p. 140.

Caldwell, at no. 16 Great Smith Street, Westminster, in 1854; it was cancelled in 1861.[1]

In 1855 they registered school rooms at no. 67a Ebury Street, Pimlico, cancelled in 1876.[2] Services held in the Ebury Rooms at no. 184a Ebury Street in 1903 had an attendance of 51 (a.m.) and 42 (p.m.). Those rooms were registered for Christians in 1907, who were still there in 1913, but had gone by 1955.[3]

Brethren also held services in Pimlico Rooms, Winchester Street, where the attendance in 1903 was 29 in the morning.

CATHOLIC APOSTOLIC CHURCH

Irvingites were worshipping at their chapel in Rochester Row, where baptisms took place in 1835–40.[4] In 1855 a building belonging to W.L. Blanche, no. 21 Warwick St, Belgrave Rd, Pimlico, was registered by Irvingites for the Catholic Apostolic Church, but they had left by 1866.[5]

A Catholic Apostolic church, on the corner of Old and New Pye streets, was registered in 1857;[6] later called Orchard Street, attendance in 1886 was 39 (a.m.) and 27 (p.m.), which had risen to 52 (a.m.) and 50 (p.m.) in 1903. The church was still there in 1913,[7] but had gone by 1924 when the building was registered by Roman Catholics.[8]

Rooms in a building belonging to Charlotte A. Forbes, at no. 13 Abingdon Street, were registered in 1867 for the Catholic Apostolic Church. The church had gone by 1876.[9]

CHRISTIAN SCIENTISTS

The Third Church of Christ, Scientist in England was located in London's Curzon Street, Piccadilly, and was registered by Christian Scientists in 1910.[10] The building, designed 1910–12 by Lanchester and Rickards, echoed the American style and grandeur of the mother church in Boston (USA), but borrowed elements from Wren's churches: the tower was added in 1930–1. The imposing auditorium was mostly demolished in 1980 and replaced by a small church and remodelled reading room flanking the entrance, now the route to a court-yard of offices.[11] Part of the building was still in use by the Church in 2008.

The Ninth Church of Christ, Scientist was registered to the basement of Australia House on the Strand, by Christian Scientists in 1921; it was replaced in 1926 by the Christian Science social hall, in cinema hall, Australia House. It closed in 1955.[12] The Ninth Church also registered the front room in Broadway Buildings, Westminster, in 1926; which was replaced in 1929 by a Sunday school in the same building and closed in 1955;[13] and nos 9 to 23 Marsham Street in 1928 and 1930.[14] For Marsham Street a impressive church was designed in 1926 by Sir Herbert Baker & Scott in the brick Early Christian style favoured by Christian Scientists at the date, with a plan tailored to Christian Science use, including a lobby for socializing, a domed circular meeting hall, which seated 1,000, and a barrel-vaulted basilica for use as a Sunday school.[15] It closed in 1997, and the building was used by the Emmanuel Evangelical Church (below).

LATTER-DAY SAINTS

Charles Roberts registered a room at no. 48 Grosvenor Place, Pimlico, for the Latter-Day Saints in 1849.[16]

Temperance Hall, Broadway, was registered in 1852 for the Latter-Day Saints; they had left by 1866.[17]

A branch chapel of the Church of Jesus Christ of Latter-Day Saints, was registered at a room in no. 50 Princes Gate in 1957, but it closed in 1978.[18]

PHILADELPHIANS

A school house in Hungerford Market, Charing Cross, occupied by John Booth, was registered in 1697 for Philadelphians.[19]

SALVATION ARMY

Regent's Hall, at no. 275 Oxford Street (St George), was registered in 1882 by the Salvation Army.[20] Attendance in 1903 was 253 in the morning and 1,467 in the evening. The premises had been converted from a former ice rink building, and it was remodelled again in 1957–9.[21] It was still in use in 2008; services were also held there by other denominations.

Salvation Army Barracks at no. 7 Blackmoor Street, Drury Lane (St Clement Danes), were registered in 1889; they had closed by 1896.[22]

Portcullis Hall, Regency Street (St George), formerly registered for the Church Army in 1883,[23] was registered for the Salvation Army in 1891; it was replaced in 1894 by the Salvation Army Barracks at no. 93 Regency Street. Attendance in 1903 was 85 in the morning and 165 in the evening. It closed c.1907.[24]

Salvation Army Barracks at nos 12 and 14 Horseferry Road were registered in 1892, and closed by 1896.[25]

1 ONS, Worship Reg. no. 3443.
2 Ibid. no. 6485.
3 Ibid. no. 42813; Harris and Bryant, *Chs and London*, 426.
4 Reg. in WCA.
5 ONS, Worship Reg. no. 6442.
6 Ibid. no. 8190.
7 Harris and Bryant, *Chs and London*, 427.
8 Above, Rom. Cathm.
9 ONS, Worship Reg. no. 18262.
10 Ibid. no. 44592.
11 Pevsner, *London 6: Westm.* 485.
12 ONS, Worship Reg. nos 48224, 50324.
13 Ibid. nos 50344, 51673.
14 Ibid. nos 51633, 52450.
15 Pevsner, *London 6: Westm.* 684.
16 Guildhall MS 9580/9, p. 19.
17 ONS, Worship Reg. no. 8.
18 Ibid. no. 66039.
19 Guildhall MS 9579/2.
20 ONS, Worship Reg. no. 26133.
21 Pevsner, *London 6: Westm.* 465.
22 ONS, Worship Reg. no. 31942.
23 Ibid. no. 26779.
24 Ibid. nos 32591, 34273.
25 Ibid. no. 33383.

The Rose and Crown, at no. 11 Clare Court, Drury Lane (St Clement Danes), was registered for the Salvation Army in 1894; it was cancelled in 1902.[1]

Congress or Strand hall at the junction of Strand and Aldwych, was used by the Salvation Army in 1904 and 1914.[2]

The Salvation Army Hall at Rochester Row, near Horseferry Road opened in a single-storeyed building by 1908, and was registered for worship in 1909.[3] It was in use in 2008 as a Salvation Army Outreach and Drop-in Centre for the Homeless, with services still being held there.

The Salvation Army Hall at no. 10 Churton Street, Westminster, was registered in 1909 and closed in 1912.[4]

SEVENTH-DAY ADVENTISTS

The New Gallery (Auditorium) at no. 123 Regent Street was registered for Seventh-day Adventists in 1953; they also registered a first floor room in New Gallery House at no. 1 Heddon Street in the same block in 1954. Both closed in 1992 and were replaced by the Advent Centre at no. 39 Brendon St (St Marylebone).[5]

SPIRITUALISTS

Polygraphic Hall in King William Street, Strand (St Martin), was registered in 1867 for the Spiritual Church. It was cancelled in 1904.[6]

Spiritualists registered rooms at no. 93 Jermyn Street for their church in 1951; it had closed by 1964.[7]

The Victoria Christian Spiritualist Church registered a room at nos 90–2 Rochester Row, Westminster in 1963.[8] It had gone by 2000.

The Spiritualist Association of Great Britain registered their headquarters, no. 33 Belgrave Square, for worship in 1995.[9] It was still in use in 2008.

SWEDENBORGIANS

York Street, St James's Square A Swedenborgian congregation, formerly based in Cross St, Hatton Garden, built a large building as the principal place of their sect in London,[10] on premises belonging to Messrs Wedgwood & Byerley. It was registered in 1799 by the minister, Dr Joseph Proud, and others.[11] The congregation left in 1813 and moved to the Swedenborgian Meeting-Room in Lisle Street. Dr Proud retired to Birmingham in 1814 and the Lisle Street congregation dwindled.[12]

Protestants, presumably Swedenborgians, registered a large room in Saville House, Leicester Square in 1824; in 1828 the same group registered New Jerusalem chapel in nearby Lisle Street, belonging to John Broom.[13]

THEISTIC CHURCH

In 1885 the congregation of the Theistic Church, led by Revd Charles Voysey, bought the lease of the former Scottish Presbyterian chapel, Swallow Street, Piccadilly,[14] used by the 4th Middlesex Rifles since 1880, and registered it for worship.[15] It was altered and refitted by Voysey's son, the architect C.F.A. Voysey, who removed the upper gallery, redecorated in colour with paint and wallpaper, and added a north entrance.[16] A new Crown lease was obtained in 1898 and the building was again repaired by Voysey; the spire was removed in or shortly after 1901. Undenominational services saw attendances in 1903 of 132 (a.m.) and 92 (p.m.). The church closed and was demolished in 1915.

UNITARIANS

Essex Street Chapel[17] The Essex Street chapel was founded by Revd Theophilus Lindsey, who resigned from an Anglican benefice in 1773 over doctrinal differences. He leased former auction rooms, later nos 2–5 Essex Street (St Clement Danes) in 1774, converting one large room into the chapel, seating 300. The first service at the chapel was attended by *c*.200 people. He bought the freehold in 1777 and rebuilt the building with the minister's house on the ground floor and the chapel above. The chapel included a gallery and was crowned by a circular lantern and dome; it opened in 1778. The site and the chapel were conveyed in 1783 to trustees for public worship, allowing the minister to occupy the house without rent; a trust also included provisions for the appointment and removal of ministers, who were to receive the pew rents and rents of the vaults. Lindsey resigned because of age 1793, but continued to live there until he died in 1808; he was succeeded in 1793 by Dr John Disney, who had joined him in 1782. Disney left in 1804, and was succeeded in 1805 by Revd Thomas Belsham, from Hackney, who was minister in 1814 when the congregation was described as respectable and numerous.[18] The chapel and congregation received several charitable gifts, including £440 in annuities from Lindsey and £200 in stock from Thomas Scott in 1812. The income was to be given to the minister for his own use. The congregation also received

---

1 ONS, Worship Reg. no. 34486.
2 Ibid. nos 40439, 46190.
3 Ibid. no. 43577.
4 Ibid. no. 43578.
5 Ibid. nos 64108, 64377, 78617.
6 Ibid. no. 18203.
7 Ibid. no. 62974.
8 Ibid. no. 68950.
8 Ibid. no. 79384.   10 Wilson, *Dissenting Chs*, IV. 54–5.

11 Guildhall MS 9580/2, p. 44.
12 *Survey of London*, XXXIV. 476.
13 Guildhall MSS 9580/5; /6, p. 173.
14 Below, Church of Scotland.
15 ONS, Worship Reg. no. 28557.
16 *Survey of London*, XXXI. 64.
17 Acct based on M. Rowe, *Story of Essex Hall* (1959); G.E. Evans, *Vestiges of Protestant Dissent* (1897), 150.
18 Wilson, *Dissenting Chs*, III. 479–81.

£100 from Percival North in 1822; £500 from Mrs M.L. Whyte in 1846 to be invested to pay income to the minister; and £300 from Harriett Pearson in 1866.

By the 1880s the congregation had declined as the population moved away: the congregation wished to use the premises for the British and Foreign Unitarian Association and the Sunday School Association, but under its trust deed the property had to be sold and the proceeds used for a new chapel elsewhere. The congregation joined another at Notting Hill Gate, and a new chapel was built in the Mall, Kensington. The Association purchased the Essex Street premises in 1885 at a valuation of £15,000, and appealed for funds to buy and rebuild.[1] The Essex Street chapel was remodelled by T. Chatfeild Clarke as Essex Hall, with reading room, bookshop, offices for the two associations, a large hall on the first floor, and a smaller hall below. The front of the chapel, which was on Essex Street, was built in classical style with Ionic pilasters and a central pediment, and finished in Portland cement. Essex Hall was used for many outside meetings, hosting the Fabian Society and other left-wing movements. The building, which was completely destroyed by enemy action in 1944, was rebuilt after an appeal in 1955. Designed by Kenneth S. Tayler, it opened in 1958, including the ground-floor Martineau Hall for meetings and services, and was registered for worship, being used for occasional services.[2] The Association and other similar Congregations formed the General Assembly of Unitarian and Free Christian Churches in 1928, and Essex Hall remained its headquarters and bookshop in 2008.[3]

Unitarians also registered a building in Hopkins Street (St James) for worship in 1819.[4]

WELSH CALVINISTIC METHODISTS

Welsh Calvinistic Methodists leased a building in Grafton Street (St Anne), for a chapel c.1849; it seated 500 in 1851 of which 150 were let. Attendance in 1851 was 80 in the morning and 130 in the evening.[5] It later presumably moved to Nassau Street.

Nassau Street Chapel, Nassau Street (later Gerrard Place), Soho In 1853 a house on the west side of Nassau Street with ground in the mews behind was purchased for Welsh Calvinistic Methodists. A chapel for 200 was built at the rear in 1855–6 to the designs of R.H. Moore, and the house in front let.[6] The chapel was registered in 1856.[7] Attendance in 1886 was 180 (a.m.) and 260 (p.m.). The chapel was bought by the MBW for the

formation of Shaftesbury Avenue, and was closed in 1888, to be replaced by the Welsh Chapel in Charing Cross Road.[8]

Welsh Chapel or Welsh Presbyterian Church, no. 82 Charing Cross Road[9] Built by Welsh Calvinistic Methodists it replaced the Nassau Street chapel, on a site on the west side of the road leased from the MBW. The freehold was acquired from the LCC in 1889. The Welsh Presbyterian church was registered for Welsh Calvinistic Methodists in 1888.[10] The chapel, built in 1886–7, was designed by James Cubitt with a strongly-modelled late Norman style façade, and an interesting plan with a large central space under an umbrella dome, with galleries on three sides. Adjoining on the north side was the minister's house, at no. 136 Shaftesbury Avenue, also by Cubitt. Attendance in 1903 was 137 (a.m.) and 486 (p.m.). The chapel's registration was cancelled in 1985.[11] The building was standing empty in 2000, but had been converted to a bar and other uses by 2003.

In 1851 Welsh Calvinistic Methodists also worshipped in the Workingmen's Institute, near Rochester Row, built in 1848. It seated c.200, all free; attendance was c.20 in the morning and 120 at the Sunday school.[12]

OTHER

The Bible-Pattern Church Registered at St Andrew's church hall, Carlisle Place, Victoria, in 1976,[13] it had gone by 2000.

Catholics (not Roman) Registered Duke Street chapel, at the south-east corner of St James's Park, Westminster, in 1855. It had gone by 1866.[14]

The Church of Humanity Located in Chapel Street, it held services between 1861 and 1901.[15]

The Commonwealth Church, North Audley Street (St George) Registered in 1995,[16] using the former St Mark's CE church, which was leased to the Commonwealth Christian Fellowship. Services were there Sunday mornings and Wednesday evenings, to a congregation said to number 200 in 2008. The Fellowship surrendered their lease in 2000 as they were unable to fund repairs, but were allowed to continue in the building until 2008, when the diocese of London sought planning permission for the building to be used for commercial purposes.[17]

1 *Endowed Chars London*, V. 76.
2 ONS, Worship Reg. no. 66906.
3 Inf. from General Assembly via website (www.unitarian.org.uk).
4 Guildhall MS 9580/5.
5 TNA, HO 129/13, 1/1/3 (f. 7).
6 *Survey of London*, XXXIII. 411.
7 ONS, Worship Reg. no. 7497.
8 *Survey of London*, XXXIII. 411.

9 Para. based on *Survey of London*, XXXIII. 307–9; Pevsner, *London 6: Westm.* 394–5.   10 ONS, Worship Reg. no. 31281.
11 Ibid. no. 31281.   12 TNA, HO 129/4, 1/1/7 (f. 10).
13 ONS, Worship Reg. no. 74365.   14 Ibid. no. 6369.
15 BL, Add. MS 43844 (Reg. of Sacraments).
16 ONS, Worship Reg. no. 79291.
17 West End Extra news item, 24 Oct. 2008 (www.thecnj.co.uk/westend/2008/102408/wnews102408_03.html)

Emmanuel Evangelical Church Registered the Emmanuel Centre, in the former Christian Scientist church, nos 9–23 Marsham Street, Westminster, in 1997.[1] It was still in use in 2008.

Positivists They worshipped at Essex Hall, Essex Street (St Clement Danes), in 1913.[2]

Reasoners Under Henry Roberts they registered a room he occupied at no. 59 Poland Street (St James), in 1835.[3]

Recreative Religionists Registered at St Martin's great hall, Long Acre (St Martin), in 1866. It was cancelled in 1904.[4]

The Revivalist Community Registered a meeting-house at the home of Valentine Harrison, no. 9 New Ranelagh Road, Pimlico, in 1824.[5]

MISSIONS AND OTHER MEETINGS

Archdeacon Dunbar's Congregation Located at the Imperial Theatre, corner of Tothill and Dartmouth streets (St Margaret), 1885–91.[6]

London City Mission Undenominational services were held in 1903 at Chadwick Street (attendance 34 p.m.) and Ebury Street (attendance 99 p.m.). Located at Bridewell Hall, Eccleston Place, Victoria, from 1948, it closed between 1972 and 2000.[7]

London Evangelistic Council registered the Great Hall, Strand, in 1905; it was cancelled 1906.[8]

Wingate M'Cheyne (McCheyne) Memorial Mission House, no. 12 Bateman Street, Soho Registered in 1908 for the British Society for the Propagation of the Gospel among the Jews, with minister Isaac Levinson.[9] It had gone by 1964.[10]

Shaftesbury Society Wyndham Ashley Mission was registered in 1947 but ceased by 1964, at the Society's premises, no. 112 Regency Street, Westminster.[11]

Sutcliffe School of Radiant Living Registered at Trafalgar House, no. 9 Great Newport Street, Westminster, in 1934, it moved to Ealing in 1940.[12]

UNDESIGNATED MEETINGS

In addition to the denominations and missions above, meetings for religious worship were registered from the end of the 18th century by groups who either did not specify their affiliation or refused to be designated. The 27 registrations up to 1851 were made to the diocesan authorities, and generally give several names of the congregation, perhaps all those in the group, and nearly half of the addresses registered were houses or rooms occupied by a member of the group. Ten were in or near Soho, 5 in St Margaret and Tothill, 3 in Pimlico/Millbank, 4 in Strand/Long Acre, 3 in Mayfair. Some occupations were also given, and include ironmonger, salesman, painter/glazier, medical doctor, musician, merchant, and a paper-hanging manufacturer who registered a room in his factory. Three school rooms were registered. Two registrations were specifically for the inhabitants of that street or neighbourhood.[13]

Registrations after 1851, to a national authority, give only one signatory, and most were registered public or commercial buildings.[14] Several registrations were obviously short-term use of a building for temporary services or a special mission. Such registrations include the following buildings: Royal Albert Hall, Kensington Gore (St Margaret det.), 1891–1913;[15] St George's Volunteer Drill Hall, Davies Street, Berkeley Square, 1892–6;[16] International Hall, Café Monaco, no. 46 Regent Street, 1896–1906;[17] Alhambra Theatre, Leicester Square, 1898 and 1899–1913;[18] Royal Opera House, Covent Garden, 1899–1913;[19] Guild House, Belgrave Road, 1929–55.[20]

Undenominational services were held at the Conference Hall, Eccleston Street, Victoria, where 25 (p.m.) attended in 1903, and the hall was registered 1906–38.[21] Other undenominational services were held in 1903 at the Pimlico Rooms, Ebury Street (used by Brethren in the morning), attendance 88 (p.m.); at Exeter Hall, YMCA, Strand, attendance 31 (p.m.); at Pear Street, Strutton Ground, attendance 61 (a.m.) and 115 (p.m.); and at the One Tun, Old Pye Street, attendance 83 (p.m.).

1 ONS, Worship Reg. no. 79657.
2 Harris and Bryant, *Chs and London*, 427.
3 Guildhall MS 9580/7, p. 179.
4 ONS, Worship Reg. no. 17670.
5 Guildhall MS 9580/5.
6 ONS, Worship Reg. no. 28508.
7 ONS, Worship Reg. no. 61866; *PO Dir.* (1972).
8 ONS, Worship Reg. no. 41125.
9 Ibid. no. 43154.
10 *PO Dir.* (1964).
11 ONS, Worship Reg. no. 61835.
12 Ibid. nos 55533, 59221.

13 Guildhall MS 9580/2, pp. 29, 104; /4; /5; /6, pp. 59, 146–7, 149, 274; /7, pp. 8, 40, 60, 112, 291; /8, pp. 186, 255, 258; /9, pp. 9, 37, 88–9, 107.
14 ONS, Worship Reg. nos 1803, 23678, and those below.
15 Ibid. no. 33010.
16 Ibid. no. 33091.
17 Ibid. no. 35291.
18 Ibid. nos 36763, 37040.
19 Ibid. no. 37379.
20 Ibid. no. 51800.
21 Ibid. no. 41942; *PO Dir.* (1902); Mudie-Smith, *Rel. Life*, 108.

CHURCH OF SCOTLAND

CROWN COURT (SCOTTISH NATIONAL CHURCH)

The Scottish National Church, meeting at Crown Court, Russell Street, near Covent Garden, originated in meetings in the early 18th century.[1] Remains of Gabriel Sangar's congregation, said to have been joined by Scottish Presbyterians settled in London,[2] were meeting in Peter's Court, St Martin's Lane, by 1711, with Revd George Gordon (d. 1715) and Revd Patrick Russell (d. 1746) as ministers. Their constitution was defined by the 1711 lease and designated a Scots Presbyterian congregation, which at that date meant it belonged to the Church of Scotland. They registered a large room in a 2-storeyed building at the upper end of Peter's Court in 1712.[3] The building was in poor repair 1714, and the congregation were unable to rebuild, but bought pews, pulpit, and other fittings in 1715 with a loan from Gordon. In 1718 the church elders took a 61-year lease of the site in a small court next to the Crown Inn on the north side of Russell Street, near Drury Lane, with the requirement to build a brick chapel within 2 years costing £400 or more. Funds for the new church were raised from outside the congregation, and c.£620 was spent. It was rebuilt in 1777 under the ministry of William Cruden. The chapel was registered in 1791, presumably when debts had been paid off.[4] James Steven, minister 1787–1803, was a founder of the London Missionary Society 1795. By 1814 Crown Court been extended; the chapel, at the south end, was a substantial square structure with 3 irregular galleries, and a vestry taking one corner. The minister in 1814 was an Independent; in addition to services on Sun., lectures were given on Sunday and Wednesday evenings by variety of ministers, chiefly Independent or Baptist.[5] The chapel seated 1,200 in 1834, when minister was nominated by the elders and elected by seat-holders; his income came from seat rents of at least c.£200. Church also had a reversion on £250 p.a. and other endowments of £15 p.a. for the poor.[6]

Revd Dr John Cumming, minister 1832–79, was one of London's most popular preachers: he attracted huge congregations, from the aristocracy as well as from the labourers and poor of the area, and carriages blocked the neighbourhood on Sundays. The congregation were able to engage in extensive philanthropic work among the poor. At the Secession in 1843, Crown Court was one of only four congregations remaining in the London Presbytery of the Church of Scotland, and continued to extend its influence in the metropolis. Charles Henry Purday was appointed conductor of psalmody by 1854, and published much well-known church music. Largely through Cumming's leadership, the Presbytery of London was re-established, a new Scottish congregation formed, and he inspired care for London's children. The Sunday school restarted 1836 in a former stable in Kingshead Yard adjoining the church; it opened with 10 teachers and 23 children. A library for children was also built up. A lease was obtained from the Bedford Estate in 1838, and the site extended 1842 and 1848. Two adjacent buildings were bought, the church enlarged, and a new school built. A day school existed from 1845. A large room in Exeter Hall was used for worship during the building work in 1847,[7] when the congregation there was often c.4,000. In 1851, known as the Scottish National Church, it seated 1,450, of which 250 were free, with 300 standing. Attendance was c.1700 both morning and evening, and the church was overcrowded all year; the morning congregation was different from the evening, and many sittings were let twice.[8] The church was enlarged again under Cumming. An assistantship was established to run the Sunday school, visit poor Scots, and share in the Brewers' Court mission and ragged school. In 1876 Crown Court chapel was described as 'the shrine of Dr Cumming of Millennial notoriety', with a queue of visitors for the service.[9] Eventually, however, Cumming's tendency towards prophesying undermined his ministry, and the congregation and church membership dropped, until the attendance was only c.50 by the time he retired.

By 1880s Covent Garden was no longer the focal point of Scottish life in London, and a site for a church further west was sought. Land was leased in Pont Street (Chelsea) and a new church opened in 1884 as St Columba's.[10] Crown Court reopened 1884 as a mission station with a Sunday morning service and a special evening mission service. Its success led to the appointment of a minister and Crown Court became a separate

1 Acct below based on Cameron, *Scots Kirk*, 56, 60–2, 93–4, 132, 134, 138–40, 144–5, 150, 155–6, 158, 166, 168; *London Jour.* XVII (1992), 54–70. 2 Wilson, *Dissenting Chs*, IV. 3–4.
3 Guildhall MS 9579/2.
4 Guildhall MS 9580/1, p. 3.
5 Wilson, *Dissenting Chs*, IV. 3–4.
6 Cameron, *Scots Kirk*, endpapers, Chs of Scottish Presb. of London 1834, no. 4.
7 Guildhall MS 9580/8, p. 282.
8 TNA, HO 129/5, 2/1/5 (f. 14).
9 C.M. Davies, *Unorthodox London* (1876 edn), 120.
10 *VCH Middx*, XII. 272.

church again in 1885, with an annual grant from Pont Street. Attendance in 1886 was 155 a.m.; 135 p.m. Work continued among poor children with the ragged school, clubs and societies, and a Sunday school. The congregation had a big turnover from Scots newly arrived in London, and Scottish visitors from hotels and boarding houses. Saturday and night schools were well attended; clubs provided social life for mainly young Scots, and a Gaelic service was held quarterly, later monthly, drawing 500–600 Highlanders. Attendance in 1903 was 113 (a.m.) and 166 (p.m.).

The ruinous state of the building led to fund-raising efforts from 1905 under Lady Frances Balfour, emphasizing the role of the church amongst visiting Scots and new arrivals. Part of the school site was sold for widening Russell Street, and the remainder surrendered to the Bedford Estate in return for a 99-year lease of the church site. The old church closed in 1908, replaced in 1909 by the new one, designed by Eustace Balfour in neo-Elizabethan style, with galleries, tie-beams, and strapwork decoration:[1] the church was situated on the upper floor, while below it screens divided classrooms from a hall. As it was lit only from the east side, a clerestory was constructed. A gallery above the main sanctuary seated 213; the main floor seated 275. The organ and case were paid for by Andrew Carnegie. Rebuilding led to an increased congregation and income from seat rents: membership rose from 309 c.1905, to c.450 in 1912. The church was still open in 2008.

SWALLOW STREET, PICCADILLY

A Scottish Presbyterian Church was gathered in early 18th century by Dr James Anderson from Scots living in the West End:[2] Anderson's house in Glasshouse Street (St James), was registered as a meeting house in 1708.[3] They moved in 1710 to the former French Protestant chapel in Swallow Street, Piccadilly. Anderson's congregation bought the lease, and were augmented by most of the congregation from Baxter's Swallow Street chapel.[4] The chapel was described as a slight building out of repair in 1729, and may have been rebuilt before the Crown lease was renewed in 1734. It stood back from the street, approached by a passage through the house standing in front of the south end of the chapel, while the north was masked by a stable and coach-house. Anderson was a forceful character, soon acknowledged as leader of the Presbyterian cause in London, but left in 1734 with some of his flock after disagreement with the elders, and formed a new congregation in Lisle Street (Ryder's Court, below). He was succeeded at Swallow Street by William Crookshank, ordained 1735, who had

a distinguished ministry before leaving under a cloud 33 years later. He was succeeded by Dr John Trotter, 1768–d.1808, assisted by William Nicol from 1796, sole minister from 1808 until his death in 1821. In 1796 the congregation split again, part following Thomas Stollery, the assistant minister, to the former French church in Chapel Street, Soho, as Independents (q.v.). In 1798 Trotter sought a 99-year lease from the Crown, granted from 1801, in order to rebuild the chapel, 'only kept from falling by the galleries'. The congregation acquired the leases of the house and stables in front, and a larger chapel was built 1801–4, in line with the street frontage, an oblong building with 3 galleries, and a 3-stage tower and spire. It was described in 1814 as always a considerable place of resort for Scots and very flourishing. In 1834 the chapel seated 600 with an extra gallery for Sunday scholars, and had endowments of £100, the income from which was used for poor among the congregation. The minister was nominated by the elders with the right of approval for the communicants. The minister's income, at least £300 p.a., came from seat rents. The Church was bound to the worship and discipline of the Church of Scotland, under the Presbytery of London. The Secession movement in 1843 affected Swallow Street badly: most of the congregation left, and in 1845 the minister issued an appeal to Scottish nobility and gentry in England for financial support, evidently with some success as the church continued for another 40 years. Described 1851 as St James's Scotch church, with schools attached, it seated 784 of which 64 were free; attendance in 1851 was 400 (a.m.) and 250 (evg).[5] Soon afterwards, the shift of population to the suburbs caused the congregation to fall sharply, and the London Presbytery recommended that the church close and the site be sold. Despite protests from members still living in the area, the 35 members were joined to Crown Court in 1879, and the chapel was converted into a drill hall for the 4th Middlesex Rifles.[6]

OTHER

Ryder's Court Chapel and Peter Street A French Protestant chapel of c.1700 on the east side of Leicester House, later Lisle Street, Leicester Fields, was used from 1734 by Scottish Presbyterians from Swallow Street under Dr James Anderson. Anderson (d. 1739) was succeeded by Dr John Patrick. The lease expired in 1755, and when the owner refused to renew, Patrick and the congregation moved to Peter Street, Soho, where they built a chapel on the site of two houses, described as a small neat building with 3 galleries and fitted with pews. The congregation was never large, and was quite small in

1 Pevsner, *London I* (1973 edn), 317.
2 Acct based on Wilson, *Dissenting Chs*, IV. 45–6; *Survey of London*, XXXI. 63–4, 225; Cameron, *Scots Kirk*, 43–5, 134, 148, endpapers, Chs of Scottish Presb. of London 1834, no. 3.
3 Guildhall MS 9579/2.
4 Above, Prot. Nonconf. (Presbs).
5 TNA, HO 129/6, 2/1/5 (f. 8).
6 Above, Prot. Nonconf., Other Congs (Theistic Ch), for later hist. of chapel..

1814 when it apparently dissolved.[1] The chapel was subsequently used by Independents and Methodists, and later became St Luke's National school.[2]

Hanover Square Hanover Square rooms, Hanover Square (St Geo.), were registered in 1856 for the Presbyterian Church of Scotland, but they had gone by 1876.[3]

FOREIGN CHURCHES

Foreign nationals in Westminster established Protestant churches in their own language, of which the earliest and largest were the French, both conformist and reformed. The former originated in meetings in the 1640s; the latter first appeared *c.*1687. In 1668 Charles II permitted Dutch living in Westminster to hold their own meetings locally, on condition they used a translation of the English Prayer Book and were subject to the Dutch Church in London.[4] German Lutherans established a chapel in 1692, and German Calvinists *c.*1700. The Savoy was a particularly popular location for foreign chapels: a commentator in 1714 noted that the many old large buildings within the ancient palace housed French, Dutch, High German, Quakers, and other nations and professions.[5] Congregations of German and Danish Lutherans as well as one of French Protestants also used the royal chapels in St James's Palace.[6] More recently, the Italian Reformed Church appeared in 1850.

Non-English speaking Roman Catholics were generally catered for through the existing Catholic church network; the few foreign-language churches are covered under Roman Catholicism.[7] Russian Orthodox Catholics also established a church in Westminster after the Russian Revolution (below).

FRENCH PROTESTANT CHURCHES

French Protestant Churches were established by refugees from persecution in France, which was particularly heavy following the Revocation of the Edict of Nantes in 1685. They settled in two main areas of London, Spitalfields and Soho, and several chapels sprang up in the city of Westminster to serve this population.[8]

The French churches fell into two main groups: those which retained the form of worship and church government in accord with the discipline of the Reformed Church of France, commonly called Nonconformist Churches, and those which adopted a French translation of the English liturgy, known as Conformist or French Episcopal. Individual congregations occasionally drifted from one group to the other, but Conformists were more numerous in the western parts of London than in the east.[9] In Westminster the earliest congregations were Conformist.

The Crown paid a £60 annuity to the dean and chapter of Westminster in the later 17th century for the French ministers of the Savoy.[10] Possibly that included the grant of £40 in perpetuity made by Charles II from Crown revenues in 1675 to the French church in the Savoy, which passed to *Les Grecs* after amalgamation, and which included payment by the Treasury from interest on £200,000 collected in 1687 for the relief of French refugees. The government in 1831 decided not to continue to support French churches with 'grants' beyond the lives of the current incumbents, but proposed to submit an estimate to Parliament of support for one French Protestant church, in Crown Street, Soho. They decided on a grant of £250 to include the £40 granted by Charles II.[11]

By letters patent in 1688 James II authorized ten French ministers to incorporate, with a licence to establish nonconforming churches for Huguenot refugees in the City of London and suburbs. One of the churches, La Patente, was established in Westminster, and other reformist congregations in Westminster were united with City congregations such as Jewin Street to share the protection that the patent gave.

The accounts of the individual churches below are in chronological order within the two liturgical groups of Conformist (Episcopal) and Reformed, with some unidentified meetings at the end. An account of the French Chapel Royal in St James's Palace will be found under the Royal Chapels (above).

1 *Survey of London*, XXXIV. 351; Wilson, *Dissenting Chs*, IV. 32–3.
2 *Survey of London*, XXXI. 228–9.
3 ONS, Worship reg. no. 7174.
4 *Cal. SP Dom.* 1667–8, 315.
5 Paterson, *Pietas Lond.* 180.
6 Above, Royal Chapels.
7 Above, Rom. Cathm.
8 J.W. De Grave, 'French Prot. Chs of Glasshouse St, Leicester Fields, Le Tabernacle, and Ryder's Court', *Procs Hug. Soc. London*, III (1888–91), 386–417.
9 Beeman, 'French Chs in London', 17.
10 *Cal. Treas. Bks*, V. 578; 1679–80, 561; *Cal. SP Dom.* 1690–1, 100.
11 W.M. Beaufort, 'The last of the Huguenot Chs', *Procs Hug. Soc. London*, II, 1887–8), 491–518.

FRENCH EPISCOPAL OR CONFORMIST

L'Eglise de la Savoie

Jean d'Espagne, formerly chaplain in England to the duc de Soubise, established a French Church meeting at Durham House in 1643 with support of the owner, the earl of Pembroke. The wealth and standing of the congregation led to resentment from the existing French church in Threadneedle Street (City), and the congregation were excluded from the City church from 1646. They enjoyed considerable support from those in power during the Interregnum and were allowed to use the chapel in Somerset House from 1653.[1] D'Espagne died in 1659, but his congregation refused reconciliation with Threadneedle Street. They had to leave Somerset House when the Crown resumed possession in 1660. After a petition, Charles II granted them permission to use the eastern end of the Savoy hospital building in 1661, but to protect the rights of the City church made it a condition that they used a French translation of the Anglican Prayer Book, accepted the ministers he appointed, and had them instituted by the bishop of London.[2] The king granted an annuity to the Savoy church which was paid as a stipend to their minister. In addition to appointing the minister, the king also instructed the congregation to allow other refugee ministers to preach there.[3] Daughter churches were established in Soho and Spring Gardens, but the chapel in the Savoy still had to be enlarged to accommodate the growing numbers. In 1684 they petitioned for a licence to enlarge their chapel, which was granted in 1686 after a plan and report in favour was drawn up by Christopher Wren as Surveyor of the King's Works;[4] it seems to have been enlarged by extending it the whole length on the south side.[5] In 1689 the congregation complained to king about problems for enlargement caused by disorderly assemblies of destitute French refugees.[6] The chapel closed c.1731 because of the ruinous state of the roof, which the congregation could not afford to repair, and members joined *L'Eglise des Grecs*, Soho, and Spring Gardens, both of which had been served by the Savoy.[7] The chapel was finally given up in 1740, and was later used by German Calvinists.[8]

La Chapelle de Spring Gardens (la Petite Savoie or la chapelle du Parc), La Savoie With the advice of the bishop of London, the Conformists built a chapel in Spring Gardens in the 1680s for French near St James's

Park, said to have been on a plot granted by the Crown. The exact date is unknown, but a drawing of Horse Guards Parade c.1685 shows a chapel among the trees of Spring Gardens called the French chapel. It was also said to have burnt down early on and rebuilt. It was referred to in the Savoy registers in 1700. The chapel stood on the north verge of the park (later nos 10, 12 and 14 Spring Gardens) facing the west end of Spring Gardens. In 1753 the Crown lessee of the surrounding property, Gerrard Smith, ejected the French,[9] and the chapel closed in 1755, with the congregation probably joining *Les Grecs*.[10] On appeal to the Treasury they obtained a reversionary lease of the building in 1757, but sold it, and it went into secular use as the Great Rooms.

L'Eglise des Grecs

La Savoie opened a daughter church in Hog Lane (Charing Cross Road) for French living in or near Soho, taking a 31-year lease in 1682 of a church built for Greek Christians but found unsuitable for the Greek community.[11] Services may have started by 1681, when one of its ministers was attacked by a mob in Newport Market, but riots in support of Greeks led to suspension of services until 1684. By 1686 a house had been built adjoining the chapel on the east side for the minister. In 1700 the congregation leased an additional strip of land on the north for enlargement of the church. Generally known as *L'Eglise des Grecs*, it gave its name to the neighbourhood, called by the French the 'quartier des Grecs'. In the late 17th and early 18th centuries the chapel was also used for English worship under an Anglican minister in connexion with the almshouses. From c.1691 to c.1714 a French Protestant school of high reputation was held nearby in Greek Street, with passage connecting it to the church site. In the 18th century the congregation were of good standing: Hogarth's *Noon* (1738) is said to portray the church and its smartly-dressed congregation. Reduction in the number of French families in neighbourhood meant that by 1730 pew rents no longer supported two ministers, a reader, and a sexton: leading aristocratic members of the church applied for part of the royal bounty for relief of poor French ministers, and £150 a year was settled on Les Grecs.[12] The church was joined by most of the Savoy congregation (q.v.) when that chapel closed c.1731, and by the congregation from Spring Gardens in 1755 (q.v.). The freehold of the chapel was sold by St Martin's parish to Calvinist Independents in 1818, and in 1822 the French moved out to a building

1 *Cal. SP Dom.* 1652–3, 138, 343.
2 C.L. Hamilton, 'Jean d'Espagne and 2nd Earl of Bridgewater (1622–1686)', *Procs Hug. Soc. London*, XXIV, 1983–8), 232–9; *Cal. SP Dom.* 1660–1, 277, 529; *Hist. King's Works*, V. 361.
3 *Cal. SP Dom.* 1678 & Add. 1674–9, 133; 1679–80, 430.
4 *Cal. SP Dom.* 1684–5, 82, 115; TNA, C 66/3282, no. 12; *Hist. King's Works*, V. 361.
5 *Hist. King's Works*, V, plate 49.
6 *Cal. SP Dom.* 1689–90, 227.

7 Beeman, 'French Chs in London', 19–21.
8 *Hist. King's Works*, V. 361; below, Foreign Prot. Chs (German Prot.).
9 *Survey of London*, XX. 67.
10 Beeman, 'French Chs in London', 22–3.
11 Acct based on W.H. Manchee, 'First and Last Chapters of the Ch of 'Les Grecs', Charing Cross Rd', *Procs Hug. Soc. London*, XVI, 1937–41), 143; Beeman, 'French Chs in London', 21–2; *Survey of London*, XXXIII. 282.
12 Beaufort, 'Last of the Huguenot Chs', 491–518.

on the north side of Edward (Broadwick) Street, between Berwick and Wardour streets. In 1845 they moved again to Bloomsbury Street (later upper Shaftesbury Avenue) in the parish of St Giles-in-the-Fields as St Jean de Savoie. It closed in 1924, when the congregation said to consist of strangers attending merely to improve their French.

Newport Market Churches

A church worshipping in the chapel of Weld House, Great Wild Street (St Giles-in-the-Fields) *c.*1690 under the authority of the bishop of London, moved 3 years later to a room over Newport Market house, often called *L'Eglise de la Boucherie*, then to a building erected in West Street (St Giles) opened 1700 as *L'Eglise de la Piramide* or *La Tremblade*. Between 1695 and 1700 they adopted the Anglican liturgy, and were entitled to share in the Royal Bounty Fund. The church closed *c.*1742 after numbers declined, and its members probably joined *Le Quarré*.[1] Part of the congregation had remained at Newport Market in 1700, forming a new church, but united with another congregation and moved to the chapel in Ryder's Court (q.v.) later in 1700. A third congregation under its own minister used same room from 1701, called *L'Eglise du Petit Charenton*, and was joined by the minister and congregation from Wapping (Stepney). Both ministers left in 1702, and the congregation dwindled, until absorbed by *La Piramide* at West Street in 1705.[2]

FRENCH REFORMED

L'Eglise de Glasshouse Street

Opened by French nonconformists in Glasshouse Street, Piccadilly,[3] near the corner of Savile Row, probably in 1687, though registers only start in May 1688; it was often called *L'Eglise de Piccadilly*. The building was probably shared with English Presbyterians. Because of increased numbers, a new chapel was built in 1692 at the corner of Long's Court and Orange Street, known as *Leicester Fields* or *Orange Street* chapel, opened 1693. it was well attended for 30 years, not only by Huguenots but by fashionable London society attracted by the fame of eloquent French pastors. It had an annexe at *Le Tabernacle*, Milk Alley (q.v.) 1696–1720, and was in union with Spitalfields church until 1701. The consistory of Ryder's Court merged with Leicester Fields *c.*1722. By 1787 dwindling congregation could no longer maintain a minister, so they joined *Le Quarré*. The chapel was sold and became a Congregationalist chapel 1787.[4]

L'Eglise de Hungerford Market

After much opposition, four ministers opened a room for worship over Hungerford market house at Charing Cross early in 1688, having obtained a lease from Sir Stephen Fox for £36 p.a. The church was in union 1691 with Jewin Street and *Le Quarré*. In 1700–1 the church moved to new premises in Castle Street, St Martin's Lane, known as *L'Eglise de Castle Street* or *La Rondolette*, the building afterwards used as the Court of Requests. When numbers declined, they moved in 1760 to a smaller building on the south side of Moor Street, Soho, but it closed *c.*1762 and the congregation joined *Le Quarré*.[5]

L'Eglise de la Place de St James

The Jewin Street (Aldersgate) congregation established a new church in 1689 under the letters patent of 1688, first meeting 1689–94 in a chapel in York Street attached to the French ambassador's house, St James's Square, owned by Lord Jermyn who leased it to them for £45 p.a. They entered a union in 1691 with the Jewin Street, *Le Quarré*, and Hungerford Market congregations. In 1694 they built a new church in *Swallow Street*, just north of Piccadilly, costing *c.*£350, financed initially by the ministers, to be repaid from collections and pew rents; the buildings included a chapel and house. It was known as *L'Eglise de Piccadilly* from 1694, the name formerly used by the Glasshouse Street church. By 1707 the membership had declined, the union was abolished, and the consistory united to that of *Le Quarré*: worship continued in Swallow Street until 1709, when they moved to *Le Quarré*. The lease was sold to Scottish Presbyterians from Glasshouse Street.[6]

L'Eglise de la Patente (L'Ancienne Patente), Berwick Street[7]

A church was established in Berwick Street under letters patent of 1688, possibly opened 1689, and certainly extant b*y 1691, when* they complained of overassessment for poor rates. In 1694 part of the congregation moved to Little Chapel Street and became known as La Petite Patente; three ministers remained with the rest of congregation in Berwick Street, thereafter known as *L'Ancienne* or *La Vieille Patente*. They were still there in 1702, but had dispersed by 1707 when the rector of St James proposed buying the building for a chapel of ease.[8] The congregation may have joined *Le Quarré* in the same street.

1 Beeman, 'French Chs in London', 43–4.
2 Ibid. 48; *Survey of London*, XXXIV. 368–9.
3 Acct based on *Survey of London*, XX. 110–11; Beeman, 'French Chs in London', 25–7; De Grave, 'French Prot. Chs', 386–417.
4 Above Prot. Nonconf. (Congs).
5 Beeman, 'French Chs in London', 34–5.
6 Ibid. 33–4; *Survey of London*, XXIX. 117; ibid. XXXI. 63; above Ch of Scotland (Swallow St).
7 *Survey of London*, XXXI. 225–6; Beeman, 'French Chs in London', 42–3.
8 Above, Par. Chs, St James (St Luke).

L'Eglise du Quarré, Soho[1]

Church first met in Monmouth House, on the south side of Soho Square, in a room granted by King William and Queen Mary in 1689 for use of Huguenot refugees settling in Soho. In union with Jewin St and local congregations 1691. A gallery was built in 1691 to accommodate the increasing congregation. In 1694 they moved to a chapel on the west side of Berwick Street, probably 'Mr Kemps Chappell', a little north of *La Patente*, taking with them the pulpit, pews, and gallery. In 1709 they were joined by the congregation from Swallow Street, and formed a joint vestry with Castle Street c.1726; in 1762 the congregations amalgamated and Castle Street closed. *L'E. de la Piramide*, West Street (St Giles-in-the-Fields) probably joined *Le Quarré* 1742. The declining congregation moved from Berwick Street between 1767 and 1769 and built a small church on the south side of Milk Alley (later Bourchier Street). It closed c.1850 and the congregation merged with *St Jean de Savoie*, Shaftesbury Avenue (St Giles).

La Petite Patente (La Nouvelle Patente), Little Chapel (later Sheraton) Street[2]

Part of the congregation of *La Patente* under Samuel Mettayer moved to Little Chapel Street where they built new chapel on the north side in 1694, known as *La Petite* or *La Nouvelle Patente*. Lady Eleanor Holles gave £300 towards building costs; a further sum was raised by ministers and congregation for building galleries, pews, and vestry behind. In 1784 the congregation joined *Les Grecs*; the chapel was later used by Methodists.[3]

L'Eglise de Ryder's Court, Leicester Fields

A chapel at the north-west corner of Ryder's Court, later Lisle Street, was opened in 1700 by merged congregations from St Martin's Lane, possibly those meeting in Peter's Court,[4] and Newport Market house. It had no ministers in 1701, and entered a union with Leicester Fields. Never a large congregation, it was described as practically an annexe of Leicester Fields. Evidently it had ceased by 1734 when Scottish Presbyterians from Swallow Street moved there;[5] the congregation probably continued at Leicester Fields.[6]

Le Tabernacle, Milk Alley, Soho.[7] French chapel existed there 1692–5 with an unknown congregation. Leicester Fields acquired it as a chapel of ease from 1696 until 1710 (or 1720), and galleries were built in 1699. Public worship ceased c.1720. *Le Quarré* built new church there c.1769.

70. *The French Protestant Church, Soho Square, the sole remaining representative of once numerous French congregations in Westminster, built for a congregation from Threadneedle Street (City of London), 1891–3. Though much larger than earlier chapels, with library and living quarters, it stands not far from the sites of former French chapels in Soho Square and Little Chapel Street.*

French Protestant Church, Soho Square

A congregation originally from Threadneedle Street moved to Athenaeum, Tottenham Court Road, in 1887, when their church in St Martin le Grand was demolished. They eventually found a site for a new church, purchasing the freehold of nos 8–9 Soho Square in 1891. They used the former Baptist chapel behind no. 7 Soho Square until their new church opened in 1893,[8] registered as *L'Eglise Française Protestante de Londres*.[9] It had associated schools in Noel Street (St James). Attendance in 1903 was 66 (a.m.), 63 (p.m.).[10] The church, designed

1 Acct based on *Survey of London*, XXXI. 225; ibid. XXXIII. 108; Beeman, 'French Chs in London', 36–8.

2 Acct based on *Survey of London*, XXXIII. 294–5; Beeman, 'French Chs in London', 39.

3 Above Prot. Nonconf. (Meths).

4 De Grave, 'French Prot. Chs', 386–417; Beeman, 'French Chs in London', 49.

5 Beeman, 'French Chs in London', 28; *Survey of London*, XXXIV. 351.   6 De Grave, 'French Prot. Chs', 386–417.

7 Acct based on *Survey of London*, XXXIII. 141–2; De Grave, 'French Prot. Chs', 386–417; Beeman, 'French Chs in London', 27–8.   8 *Survey of London*, XXXIII. 62–3.

9 ONS, Worship Reg. no. 33777.

10 Mudie-Smith, *Rel. Life*, 107.

by Aston Webb 1891–3 and said to be his favourite work, derived in part from late Franco-Flemish Gothic, with late Romanesque overtones. Built of plum-coloured brick and light red terracotta, with a steeply pitched roof of greenish slates, the frontage to the square was a 4-storeyed block like an office building, with living accommodation over the entrance lobby flanked by library and ante-room, leading to the aisled church

behind, of four bays with a curved apse between a pair of vestries. The tympanum by J. Prangnelli was inserted over the central doorway in 1950.[1] It was still open in 2008.

Other French Protestant services were held in 1903 at *Maison des Etrangers*, Frith Street, with attendance of 57 (p.m.), and *Mission Française*, Soho, attendance 51 (p.m.).[2]

GERMAN PROTESTANT CHURCHES

GERMAN LUTHERANS

St Mary's German Lutheran Church, precinct of the Savoy German Lutherans, who seceded from Hamburg Church in London in 1692, moved into part of the Savoy hospital and consecrated a chapel in the former sisters' hall in 1694. the congregation grew, especially after George I's accession, and Princess Caroline, later wife of George II, paid for building a school.[3] The congregation raised subscriptions to enlarge the church and open up a coach-way from the Strand: in 1721 they obtained a licence from the Crown to make a passageway through the hospital, then used as barracks, to the east side of their church to allow coaches and chairs to reach the chapel from the Middle Savoy gate; it also confirmed their use of the chapel, minister's house, vestry room, and burial ground on the west side of the chapel,[4] consecrated by the archbishop of Canterbury. In 1766 they rebuilt the church, securing a royal warrant to hold the premises at £8 a year, and obtaining the services of the Surveyor-General of the King's Works, Sir William Chambers, to design a new church, holding c.1,000. The exterior was plain, possibly incorporating some old walls, but the interior was elegant, in the style of St Martin-in-the-Fields.[5] In 1780 the rector of St Paul, Covent Garden, reported he had 30 German Lutheran families in his parish,[6] who presumably worshipped in the Savoy.

Clearance of the Savoy hospital buildings in 1816 for rebuilding also swept away the Lutherans' school, vestry, and minister's house. To replace them the Crown (the Duchy of Lancaster) erected a new building west of the chapel c.1817;[7] the school had 60–80 boys and girls c.1817.[8] St Mary's German Lutheran church in the Savoy, vested by the Crown grant in minister and churchwardens of the congregation, was registered in 1838.[9] In 1851 the church seated 120 free and 480 other,

with 200–300 standing; attendance was 200 (a.m.), 60 (aft.).[10] The church and minister's house were demolished as part of the redevelopment of the Savoy in 1870s. The Crown built a new church and house at the corner of Howland and Cleveland streets (St Pancras) for the congregation, which received a licence from Queen Victoria in continuation of that of 1766, permitting them to occupy the new premises for £8 a year; the new church opened in 1877. The burial ground was also cleared and remains re-interred at Colney Hatch in 1880.[11] Registers exist for baptisms 1694–1877, and marriages to 1907–19.[12]

Edward Street A German Lutheran Church was worshipping in 1851 in part of a building in Edward Street (St James) under Augustun Rimpler, minister, with an attendance of 50 (a.m.).[13]

Christuskirche, Montpelier Place, Knightsbridge German Lutherans removed from St James's Palace in 1901,[14] continued to meet using Eccleston Hall, Eccleston Street, Victoria, where attendance in 1903 was 33 (a.m.). A new church was built in 1904 at the expense of Baron Sir John Hen. Wm Schroder in memory of his wife, on the site of nos 18–20 Montpelier Place (Knightsbridge) and nos 1–3 Alfred Cottages behind. Designed by Edward Boehmer and Charles G.F. Rees in Decorated style, it was built of orange brick with stone dressings, with a large meeting-room beneath the church.[15] It was registered in 1905 as Christchurch (*Christuskirche*), Montpelier Place, for German Evangelical Lutherans.[16] In 1913 one service was held on Sundays.[17] It was still in use in 2008.

German Chapel Royal See Royal Chapels

1 *Survey of London*, XXXIII. 62–3; Pevsner, *London 6: Westm.* 394.   2 Mudie-Smith, *Rel. Life*, 107.
3 Somerville, *Savoy*, 80–1.
4 TNA, DL 41/1194, no. 1; *Hist. King's Works*, V. 361, plate 49.
5 Somerville, *Savoy*, 81; *Hist. King's Works*, V. 361.
6 Guildhall MS 9557, f. 29.
7 Somerville, *Savoy*, 112.
8 Ibid. 217, n. 27 (DL 41/45).
9 Guildhall MS 9850/8, p. 1.
10 TNA, HO 129/13, 2/4 (f. 14).
11 Somerville, *Savoy*, 117–18.
12 Held at WCA.
13 TNA, HO 129/6, 1/1/3? (f. 3).
14 Above, Royal Chapels.
15 *Survey of London*, XLV. 125–6.
16 ONS, Worship Reg. no. 41003.
17 Harris and Bryant, *Chs and London*, 427.

GERMAN REFORMED PROTESTANT (CALVINIST)

Thomas Liveings surrendered his house in the Savoy *c.*1700 for officers of the German Calvinistic Church, who were permitted to use it for worship,[1] perhaps the building they occupied in 1736 in the range along the river front, south of the German Lutheran chapel.[2] In 1724 George I gave them part of the former Master's house as a dwelling for their minister.[3] The received a bounty from Frederick William I of Prussia to maintain a minister. The floor below the church was used by a mill, and the house was threatened by proposed Thames embanking: this and difficulties with the Anglican minister who shared the Master's house, led congregation in 1769 to purchase the derelict French Protestant chapel in the Savoy and rebuild it, receiving a gift of £500 from the king. The new church was consecrated in October 1771.[4] The church was demolished *c.*1817 to make way for the approach road to Waterloo bridge, and the congregation received £800 from the Crown and £5,000 from the proprietors of the bridge company in compensation.[5]

OTHERS

ITALIAN REFORMED CHURCH

In 1850 Lewis Hippolytus Joseph Sonna or Fonna, secretary of the London committee for the Religious Improvement of Italy and the Italians, registered for worship part of a warehouse and workrooms at rear of no. 21 Broad Street, Golden Square, with an entrance in Dufours Place.[6] Called the Italian Church in 1851, it seated 150, all free, with space for *c.*100 standing; attendance at the Sunday afternoon service was 20; it was described as a temporary building, very small and chiefly resorted to by a few foreigners.[7] It may not have continued long, as the church was not listed by 1855.[8]

By 1902 an Italian mission had opened at no. 2 Frith Street,[9] and attendance at the Italian Protestant church there in 1903 was 16 (p.m.).[10]

RUSSIAN ORTHODOX CHURCH

The Russian Orthodox Church had a parish in London based at the chapel in the Russian Embassy, Welbeck Street, until the revolution of 1917.[11] From 1923 to 1956 the congregation used St Philip's Anglican church, Buckingham Palace Road. They leased All Saints Anglican church, Ennismore Gardens (St Margaret detached) after it became redundant for Anglican worship, moving there in 1956, subsequently purchasing the freehold in 1979 with help from many supporters. Known as the Russian Orthodox Cathedral of the Dormition of the Mother of God and All Saints, it became the Patriarchal church of the diocese of Sourozh, the Russian Orthodox diocese for Great Britain and Ireland, and the cathedral celebrated its 50th anniversary in October 2006.[12]

The interior of the church was adapted for Orthodox worship in 1956: the pews were removed, and an icon screen was installed at the eastern end. The Royal Gates in the centre of this screen were rescued from the former Czarist embassy chapel in Welbeck Street after the 1917 revolution. The icons on the screen were painted at various times by three students of the celebrated Russian iconographer Leonid Ouspensky. Many of the other icons around the cathedral were the gifts of families. A major restoration of the cathedral was undertaken in 2005.[13] In the early 1990s a parish hall and other buildings were erected along the south side of the church, entailing the demolition of some structures including the south-east vestry.

OTHER FAITHS

JUDAISM

Jewish merchants and craftsmen began moving into the West End from the City of London in the later 18th century, and opened their first synagogue (which later became the Western) in the 1760s just south of Covent Garden.[14] By the early 19th century another had opened in Soho, re-forming in Maiden Lane: its members were engaged in the fruit trade, in the manufacture of watches, cigars, and umbrellas, or were jewellers and

1 *Cal. Treas. Papers*, 1697–1702, 363.
2 *Hist. King's Works*, V, plate 49.
3 Ibid. 361.
4 Ibid. 362; Somerville, *Savoy*, 82–3.
5 Somerville, *Savoy*, 111–12.
6 Guildhall MS 9580/9, p. 51.
7 TNA, HO 129/6, 3/1/5 (f. 14).
8 *PO Dir. London* (1855).

9 Ibid. (1902).
10 Mudie-Smith, *Rel. Life*, 107.
11 Acct based on Pevsner, *London 3: NW.* 465; *Survey of London*, XLV. 189–90.
12 Inf. from Cathedral's web site, www.sourozh.org (viewed 4 Dec. 2006).
13 Ibid.
14 Intro. based on accts of individual synagogues below.

engravers, amongst other trades.[1] The Jewish community also opened a free day school for boys in 1811,
supported by voluntary subscriptions, which taught
secular subjects as well as Hebrew and religion to 5 to 13
year-olds, who were also clothed by a benevolent society.
A girls' school was opened in 1846 and the two were
amalgamated in 1853 as the Westminster Jews' Free
school: it was housed at no. 59 Greek Street by 1850 and
bought the adjoining no. 60 in 1853, where it remained
until it moved to Hanway Place (St Pancras) in 1884,
having c.360 pupils in 1880.[2]

By the 1820s the Jewish population of Westminster
included not just tradesmen but more affluent residents,
and the Western, fashionable and successful for a time,
built its own synagogue just off the Haymarket. There
was some decline in the Jewish population by the 1880s
as the residents moved away and new synagogues were
opened elsewhere, but by the end of the 19th century
there was a dramatic increase in the number of Jews in
the Soho area with migration there of Polish and Russian
Jews, many engaged in tailoring trades, from White-
chapel; by 1903 40 per cent of the population of Soho
were Polish Jews.[3] Hebrew classes for children were
started, followed by new synagogues such as the West
End and the Shibath Zion. Some English-born Jews,
however, found these congregations too 'foreign' and
preferred to join the Central synagogue in St
Marylebone, and in the course of the 20th century all
congregations were affected by the steady movement of
the population to the suburbs. The synagogues in Westminster gradually amalgamated and closed, so that by
2000 the nearest Jewish services were held just outside
Westminster in St Marylebone. In Knightsbridge,
however, the Westminster synagogue opened in 1963,
and also housed a library and centre for Jewish studies.

Maiden Lane Synagogue, Covent Garden
A secession group from Denmark Court met in Soho,
first in Dean Street then in Brewer Street, but dwindled
in 1827. Restarted 1829 in Maiden Lane,[4] and by 1844
occupied no. 21,[5] where in 1851 part of the building was
used for worship, seating 160, of which 20 free, with 30
standing; attendance was 30 (a.m.), 30 (aft.), 30 (evg),
with 80 given as the average for each service.[6] Attendance in 1886 was 31 (a.m.), 24 (p.m.),[7] and in 1903 was
69.[8] The synagogue closed in 1907, and its congregation
joined Western synagogue.[9]

Shibath Zion Synagogue (later Beth Hasepher and Federation Synagogue)
Shibath Zion, which registered no. 82 Berwick Street,
Soho, in 1917,[10] was amalgamated in 1919 with the West
Central Jewish National Hebrew Religious Class Rooms,
no. 26a Soho Square, registered in 1918,[11] in the latter's
premises to form Shibath Zion Synagogue and Religious
Class Rooms.[12] It closed in 1926,[13] and was replaced by
Beth Hasepher and Federation Synagogue at the same
address, registered in 1928.[14] The latter closed in 1948,
when the congregation joined the West End to form
West End Great Synagogue (below).

West End Great Synagogue
The synagogue[15] originated in West End Talmud Torah,
established 1880 at no. 10 Green's Court, off Brewer
Street, Soho, where Hebrew classes were given to c.100
children of small tradesmen and artisans living or
working nearby. Attendance in 1903 was 254.[16] In 1910
it amalgamated with Bikkur Cholim Synagogue and
moved to no. 41 Brewer Street, and then in 1916 moved
to a larger building, the former St Anne's parish workhouse at no. 14 Manette Street, registered in 1919, where
it remained until c.1941.[17] The congregation grew after
the First World War, and in 1926 the Scala theatre was
used for big holyday services. The congregation acquired
no. 21 Dean Street, formerly St Anne's National schools,
in 1941,[18] but bomb damage prevented it being used
until after the war. It was re-registered in 1948 as West
End Great Synagogue after amalgamation with Beth
Hasepher.[19] The 3-storeyed 19th-century building was
adapted for use with the synagogue on the ground floor,
and an office and top-lit hall above. In 1961 it was demolished and replaced by a buildings designed by Joseph
Fiszpan, of red brick on a black granite plinth, with a
recessed vertical feature at the north end and recessed
entrance, and 2 tiers of 6 windows framed with artificial
stone to light the synagogue. Completed 1963 it brought
together Jewish social, cultural, and political activities,
with a youth-club hall in the basement, a synagogue
seating 306 on the ground floor and 196 in a 3-sided
gallery on the 1st, a hall with stage and kitchen on the 2nd
floor, Ben Uri Art Society gallery on the 3rd floor, and
residential quarters at the top.[20] It closed in 1999,[21] and
the congregation moved to the Western Marble Arch
synagogue, Crawford Place (St Marylebone), where they

1 P. Renton, *Lost Synagogues of London* (2000), 51.
2 *Endowed Chars London*, III. 759; Renton, *Lost Synagogues*, 52–3; *Survey of London*, XXXIII. 189; G. Black, *JFS: hist. of Jews' Free Sch., London, since 1732* (1998), 11, 28–9, 122.
3 *Survey of London*, XXXIII. 11.
4 P. Lindsay, *Synagogues of London* (1993) 66; Renton, *Lost Synagogues*, 51.
5 *Survey of London*, XXXVI. 241; ONS, Worship Reg. no. 30823.   6 TNA, HO 129/13, 2/1 (f. 11).
7 *British Weekly*, 5 Nov. 1886, p. 3.
8 Mudie-Smith, *Rel. Life*, 265.
9 Renton, *Lost Synagogues*, 51.

10 ONS, Worship Reg. no. 47115.
11 Ibid. no. 47346.
12 Ibid. no. 47515.
13 Ibid. no. 47515.
14 Ibid. no. 51325.
15 Acct based on Lindsay, *Synagogues of London*, 81–2.
16 Mudie-Smith, *Rel. Life*, 265.
17 *Survey of London*, XXXIII. 191; ONS, Worship Reg. no. 46946.
18 ONS, Worship Reg. no. 59618.
19 Ibid. no. 62074.   20 *Survey of London*, XXXIII. 132–3.
21 ONS, Worship Reg. no. 62074.

held separate services from 2000. The Dean Street building reopened in 2000 as Soho theatre with a new frontage on the lower floors, and a Mizrath on the 2nd-floor landing commemorating the synagogue.[1]

Western Synagogue

A small group of Jewish merchants, shopkeepers, and artisans met 1761 in Great Pulteney Street, Soho, at the home of Wolf Liepman of St Petersburg, who maintained a group for prayers. This evolved into a congregation which formed the Westminster Synagogue in Denmark Court, Strand, from c.1765.[2] In 1797 the congregation took a lease of the Sans Souci theatre in Denmark Court, where they remained until 1826.[3] They then moved to St Alban's Place, where a synagogue by Robert Abraham was built 1827–8 behind no. 12 St Alban's Place and the houses on the north side of Charles Street: it apparently occupied the 1st floor of a stable block, while no. 12 was occupied by the rabbi.[4] For a while it was one of the great synagogues of London, and many of the wealthiest London Jews left synagogues in the City to join it. Rebuilding or refurbishing continued until 1832, when the name was changed to Western Synagogue, and a building seating 462, with an interior of white marble richly decorated with gold, was consecrated in 1836. By 1850 the congregation was in financial difficulties, and the building again in disrepair. Attendance in 1851 was only c.50 because of repairs, and services were held in small room adjoining; the average attendance was said to be 100.[5] The synagogue was re-consecrated in 1851, and again in 1857. It was apparently rebuilt in 1865, and in 1870 repaired and redecorated from designs by J.D. Hayton.[6] The opening of

Central synagogue in Great Portland Street (St Marylebone), and migration away from the Haymarket area to the suburbs, reduced the congregation and its financial viability,[7] though Jewish immigration seems to have increased numbers c.1900. Attendance in 1886 was 88 (a.m.), 9 (aft.);[8] and in 1903 was 376.[9] In 1907 the congregation was joined by that from Maiden Lane Synagogue (q.v.). As the lease of St Alban's Place had nearly expired, a scheme to rebuild on the same site was abandoned in favour of a new building in Alfred Place, Tottenham Court Road.[10] The St Alban's building was demolished in 1914,[11] with the congregation moving temporarily to Albert Rooms, no. 40 Whitfield Street (St Pancras).[12]

Westminster Synagogue, Rutland Gardens, Knightsbridge

A group from the New London Jewish Congregation broke away in 1957 over the enforced retirement of Rabbi Harold Reinhardt and worshipped in Caxton Hall, Westminster, before buying the five-storeyed Kent House, Rutland Gardens, in 1960 to form an independent Synagogue under Dr Reinhardt. The congregation restored the neglected building and adapted the large first-floor music room as a synagogue, consecrated in 1963.[13] In 1993 it was an independent synagogue within the Reform tradition, and a centre of Jewish prayer and study, housing since 1964 over 1,500 Scrolls of Scripture saved from Czech synagogues destroyed by Nazis, an extensive library, and collections of synagogue vestments and objects.[14] Still in use in 2008.

OTHERS

MUSLIMS

The Islamic Centre at number 10 Berwick Street was registered for Muslim worship in 1979.[15]

In 2006 Muslims had three centres of worship in Westminster: the IQRA Trust at number 24 Culross Street (St George), Mayfair Islamic Centre at number 19 Hertford Street (St George), and the Greta Mosque at number 31 Schomberg House, Page Street (St John).

BAHA'IS

The Baha'i Centre at number 1 Victoria Street, Westminster, was registered in 1944 and closed by 1964.[16]

The Baha'i Centre on the first floor of number 27 Rutland Gate, Knightsbridge, was registered in 1955.[17] It was still in use in 2008, when it was the Spiritual Assembly and headquarters of the Baha'is of the UK.

BUDDHISTS

In 2008 the Buddhist Society had a centre at number 58 Eccleston Square, Westminster.

1 Renton, *Lost Synagogues*, 57.
2 Lindsay, *Synagogues of London*, 66.
3 Renton, *Lost Synagogues*, 50, 54.
4 *Survey of London*, XXIX. 221.
5 TNA, HO 129/6, 2/1/6 (f. 9).
6 *Survey of London*, XXIX. 221.
7 Renton, *Lost Synagogues*, 54.
8 *British Weekly*, 5 Nov. 1886, p. 3.
9 Mudie-Smith, *Rel. Life*, 265.
10 Lindsay, *Synagogues of London*, 68.
11 *Survey of London*, XXIX. 221.
12 ONS, Worship Reg. no. 46184; Renton, *Lost Synagogues*, 54.   13 ONS, Worship Reg. no. 71868.
14 Lindsay, *Synagogues of London*, 81; *Survey of London*, XLV. 138–9.
15 ONS, Worship Reg. no. 75302.
16 Ibid. no. 60687.
17 Ibid. no. 65066.

INDEX

NOTE. Page numbers in bold denote the main entry for that item. An italic number refers to the figure no. of a map or illustration. Buildings, streets and localities are in Westminster except where otherwise stated.